UNDERSTANDING ARGUMENTS
An Introduction to Informal Logic

FIFTH EDITION

UNDERSTANDING ARGUMENTS
An Introduction to Informal Logic

Robert J. Fogelin
Dartmouth College

Walter Sinnott-Armstrong
Dartmouth College

Harcourt Brace College Publishers

Fort Worth   Philadelphia   San Diego   New York   Orlando   Austin   San Antonio
Toronto   Montreal   London   Sydney   Tokyo

Publisher	Christopher P. Klein
Senior Acquisitions Editor	David Tatom
Developmental Editor	J. Claire Brantley
Project Editor	Jeff Beckham
Production Manager	Jane Tyndall Ponceti
Art Director	Carol Kincaid

Cover Image: © 1995 *Horizons #6,* oil stick on canvas by Neal Parks

Address for Editorial Correspondence: Harcourt Brace College Publishers, 301 Commerce Street, Suite 3700, Fort Worth, TX 76102.

Address for Orders: Harcourt Brace & Company, 6277 Sea Harbor Drive, Orlando, FL 32887-6777. 1-800-782-4479, or 1-800-433-0001 (in Florida).

Attn: Returns Department
Troy Warehouse
465 South Lincoln Drive
Troy, MO 63379

ISBN: 0-15-502098-6

Library of Congress Catalog Card Number: 95-82360

Printed in the United States of America

6 7 8 9 0 1 2 3 4 5   090   10 9 8 7 6 5 4 3 2 1

*To Eric, John, Lars, Miranda, and Nicholas
and the colleges of their choice*

PREFACE

Traditionally, logic has been considered the most general science dealing with arguments. The task of logic is to discover the fundamental principles for distinguishing good arguments from bad ones. For certain purposes, arguments are best studied as abstract patterns of reasoning. Logic is not concerned with particular arguments—for example, your attempt to prove to the bank that they, not you, made a mistake. The study of those general principles that make certain patterns of argument reasonable (or valid) and other patterns of argument unreasonable (or invalid) is called *formal logic*. Three chapters of this work are dedicated to formal logic.

A different, but complementary, way of viewing an argument is to treat it as a particular use of language: Presenting arguments is one of the important things we do with words. This approach stresses that arguing is a linguistic activity. Instead of studying arguments as abstract patterns, it examines them as they occur in concrete settings. It raises questions of the following kind: What is the place of argument within language as a whole? What words or phrases are characteristic of arguments, and how do these words function? What task or tasks are arguments supposed to perform? When an approach to argument has this emphasis, the study is called *informal logic.* Though it contains a substantial treatment of formal logic, *Understanding Arguments,* as its subtitle indicates, is primarily a textbook in informal logic.

This fifth edition of *Understanding Arguments* differs from the fourth edition in a number of significant ways. The order of chapters has been changed so that topics in formal logic are introduced earlier than they were in the previous edition. It has been our experience—and the experience of others who have used the text—that a rudimentary knowledge of the central notions of formal logic sharpens students' understanding of such fundamental notions as validity and logical form. We have, however, been careful not to make the intelligibility of later chapters depend upon studying them. The text can still be used without assigning these chapters on formal logic. The fifth edition contains a great number of other changes beyond the reordering of chapters. Chapter Seven is entirely new. It presents a rudimentary version of modern quantificational logic. This chapter introduces the reader to the basic ideas of quantificational logic including its fundamental concepts and methods of translation. By limiting the range of application, it also lays down a system of rules that is much simpler than those found in standard treatments of quantifiers.

There have also been significant changes in many of the chapters. In Chapter Six the discussion of categorical propositions has been made more complete. An appendix to Chapter Six also presents a new method for keeping track of existential commitment in Venn Diagrams when the classical interpretation of existential commitment is adopted.

Chapter Eight, which concerns inductive arguments, has been expanded in significant ways. Most importantly, it now contains discussions of inferences to the best explanation and of arguments from analogy.

There are also a number of important changes in the specimen arguments used in Part Two. *Peevyhouse v. Garland Coal and Mining Co.* is presented to give the feel of a standard law-school case. The cases on discrimination law have been supplemented in the Discussion Questions. Chapter Thirteen, which considers moral arguments, now contains a forceful statement of the pro-life position, "Why Abortion is Immoral," by Don Marquis. Chapter Fourteen, which concerns scientific reasoning, includes essays concerning conflicting theories of the extinction of the dinosaurs. Because of numerous requests, we have reinstated part of Turing's classic piece, "Computing Machinery and Intelligence" in Chapter Fifteen, which considers the philosophical question of whether computers can think.

Finally, we added many exercises and discussion questions to almost every chapter, including new passages for close analysis in Chapter Three and actual examples of the fallacies discussed in Chapter Ten. This material should provide the basis for class discussion or written assignments.

This new edition has been influenced by our teaching this material with various colleagues, including visitors, at Dartmouth College. In this regard, we wish to thank Joel Blum, David Denby, Stephen Jacobson, and Jim Moor of Dartmouth College. We are also indebted to the following reviewers: Sven Arvidson, College of Mount St. Joseph; Martha Bolton, Rutgers University; Bridgette Newell, University of Utah; and Jim Page, University of Kansas.

At Harcourt Brace, we also received expert advice from Claire Brantley, Jeff Beckham, David Tatom, Jane Ponceti, and Carol Kincaid.

Finally, we owe a great debt of thanks to Jane Taylor, our copy editor; Bill Fontaine, librarian; Lynda Cowin, research assistant; and Florence Fogelin, proofreader extraordinaire. Without all of these people this book would contain many more mistakes than it undoubtedly does.

CONTENTS

PART TWO   Areas of Argumentation 389

PART ONE

THE ANALYSIS OF ARGUMENT

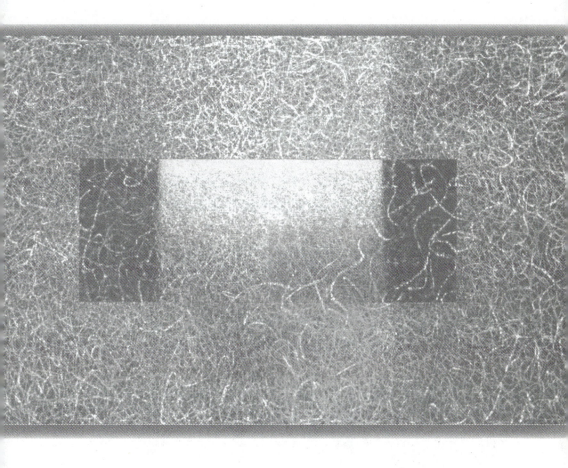

Chapter One

THE WEB OF LANGUAGE

Because presenting an argument is something that we do using language, this chapter will examine some of the basic features of language. In doing so, it will stress three main ideas. First, language is *conventional*. Words acquire meaning within a rich system of linguistic conventions or rules. Second, the uses of language are *diverse*. We use language to communicate information, but we also use it to ask questions, issue orders, write poetry, keep score, formulate arguments, and perform an almost endless number of other tasks. Third, meaning is often conveyed *indirectly*. In order to understand the significance of many utterances, we must go beyond what is literally said to examine what is conversationally implied by saying it.

LANGUAGE AND ARGUMENT

Logic is the general science of argument: its goal is to lay down principles for distinguishing good arguments from bad arguments. The word "argument" may suggest quarrels or squabbles, but here it is used in the broader, logician's sense of *giving reasons* for or against some claim. Viewing arguments this way, we see that they are a common feature of daily life. We are often involved in the business of giving reasons for things we believe or evaluating reasons given by others for things they want us to believe. Trying to decide which way to vote in an election, what play to use on third down and long, where to go to college, whether to support or oppose capital punishment—all involve weighing and evaluating reasons.

Arguing is also an activity—in particular, a *linguistic* activity. Arguing is one of the many things we can do with words. In fact, unlike things that we can accomplish both with words and without words (like making people happy, angry, and so forth), arguing is something we can *only* do with words. To understand how arguments work, it is thus important to understand how language works. Unfortunately, our understanding of human languages is far from complete, and linguistics is a young science in which disagreement exists on many important issues. Still, there are certain facts about language that are beyond dispute, and recognizing them will provide a background for understanding how arguments work.

LANGUAGE AND CONVENTION

As everyone who has bothered to think about it knows, language is conventional. There seems to be no reason why we, as English speakers, use the word "dog" to refer to a dog rather than to a cat, a tree, or anything else. It seems that any word might have been used to stand for anything. Beyond this, there seems to be no reason why we put words together in the way we do. In English, we put adjectives before the nouns they modify. We thus speak of a *green salad*. In French, adjectives usually follow the noun, and so instead of saying *verte salade* the French say *salade verte*. The conventions of our own language are so much with us that it strikes us as odd when we discover that other languages have different conventions. A French diplomat once praised his own language because, as he said, it followed the natural order of thought. This strikes English speakers as silly, but in seeing why it is silly, we see that the word order in our own language is conventional as well.

Although it is important to realize that our language is conventional, it is also important not to misunderstand this fact and draw false conclusions from it. From the idea that language is conventional, it is easy to conclude that language is *totally arbitrary*. If language is totally arbitrary, then it might seem that it really does not matter which words we use or how we put them together, since these are all simply matters of convention. It takes only a little thought to see that this view, however daring it might seem, misrepresents the role of conventions in language. If we wish to communicate with others we must follow the system of conventions that others use. Communication can only take place from *within a shared* system of conventions. Conventions do not destroy meaning by making it arbitrary; conventions bring meaning into existence.

A misunderstanding of the conventional nature of language can lead to pointless disputes. Sometimes, in the middle of a discussion, someone will declare that "the whole thing is just a matter of definition" or "what you say is true by your definition, false by mine." There are times when definitions are important and the truth of what is said turns upon them, but usually this is not true. Suppose someone has fallen off a cliff and is heading toward certain death on the rocks below. Of course, it is a matter of convention that we use the word "death" to describe the result of the sudden sharp stop at the end of the fall. We might have used some other word—perhaps "birth"—instead. But it certainly will not help a person who is falling to his certain death to shout out "By birth I mean death." It will not help even if *everyone* agrees to use these words in this new way. If we all decided to adopt this new convention, we would then say "He is falling from the cliff to his certain birth" instead of "He is falling from the cliff to his certain death." But speaking in this way will not change the facts. It will not save him from perishing. It will not make those who care for him feel better.

The upshot of this simple example is that the truth of what we say is rarely just a matter of definition. Whether what we have said is true or not will depend, for the most part, on how things stand in the world. For example, if Germans wish to say that snow is black, they will use the words "Der Schnee ist schwartz." Other Germans will *understand* these words, but unless snow is different in Germany than everywhere else, they will also think that what is being said is false. In general, then, though the *meaning* of what we say is dependent on convention, the *truth* of what we say is not.

In the last sentence we used the qualifying phrase "in general." To say that a claim holds *in general* indicates that there may be exceptions. This qualification is needed because sometimes the truth of what we say *is* simply a matter of definition. Take a simple example. The claim that a triangle has three sides is true by definition, because a triangle is defined as "a closed figure having three sides." Again, if someone says that sin is wrong, he or she has said something that is true by definition, for a sin is defined as, among other things, "something that is wrong."

In sum, people are able to communicate with each other because they share certain linguistic conventions. These conventions could have been different, and in this sense they are arbitrary. But it does not follow from this that the truth of what we say is always just a matter of convention. Sometimes things are true just as a matter of convention; however, in general, the truth of what we say is settled not by definition, but by looking at the facts.

LEVELS OF LANGUAGE

LINGUISTIC ACTS

In the previous section we saw that a language is a system of shared conventions that allows us to communicate with one another. If we examine language, we will see that it contains many different kinds of conventions. We have seen that words have meanings conventionally attached to them. The word "dog" is used conventionally to talk about a dog, though it might have been used to talk about a cat. Proper names are also conventionally assigned, for Harry Jones could have been named Wilbur Jones. Other conventions concern the ways in which words can be put together to form sentences. These are often called grammatical rules. Using the three words "John," "hit," and "Harry," we can formulate sentences with quite different meanings; for example, "John hit Harry" and "Harry hit John." We recognize that these sentences have different meanings because we understand the grammar of our language. This grammatical understanding also allows us to see that the sentence "Hit John Harry" does not mean anything at all—even though the individual words possess meaning. (Notice that "Hit John, Harry!" does mean something: it is a way of telling Harry to hit John.) Grammatical rules are important because they play an essential role in giving meaning to combinations of words— for example, sentences.

There are, then, at least two kinds of conventions that give meaning to what we say. The ones that assign meanings to individual words are commonly called *semantic* conventions. The conventions that lay down rules for combining words into meaningful wholes are called *grammatical* or *syntactical* conventions. When these conventions are satisfied, we will say that we have performed a *linguistic act*: we have said something meaningful in a language.[1] Later we will look more closely at semantic and syntactical conventions, for at times they are a source of fallacies and other confusions. In particular, we shall see how these conventions can generate fallacies of ambiguity and fallacies of vagueness. But before examining the defects of our language, we should first appreciate that language is a powerful and subtle tool that allows us to perform a wide variety of jobs important for living in the world.

SPEECH ACTS

When we are asked about the function of language, it is natural to reply that we use language to communicate ideas. But this is only one way in which we use language. This becomes obvious as soon as we look at the ways in which our language actually works. Adding up a column of figures is a linguistic activity— though it is rarely looked at in this way—but it does not communicate any ideas to others. When I add the figures I am not even communicating anything to myself: I am trying to figure something out.

A look at our everyday conversations produces a host of other examples of language being used for different purposes. Grammarians, for example, have divided sentences into various moods, among which are:

---

[1] J. L. Austin used the phrase "locutionary act" to refer to a level of language closely related to what we refer to as a "linguistic act." See J. L. Austin, *How to Do Things with Words*, 2d ed. (Cambridge: Harvard University Press, 1975), 94–109.

(1) Indicative

(2) Interrogative

(3) Imperative

(4) Expressive

For example:

(1) He is in England now that spring is here.

(2) Is he in England now that spring is here?

(3) Go to England now that spring is here!

(4) Oh to be in England, now that spring is here!

The first sentence states a fact; we can use it to communicate information about a person's location. If we use it in this way, what we say will be either true or false. Notice that none of the other sentences can be called either true or false.

PERFORMATIVES

The different types of sentences recognized by traditional grammarians indicate that we use language to do more than convey information. But this traditional classification of sentences gives only a small idea of the wide variety of things that we can accomplish using language. Sometimes, for example, in using language, we actually *do* things in the strong sense of bringing something about. In one familiar setting, if one person says "I do" and another person says "I do," and finally a third person says "I now pronounce you husband and wife," the relationship between the first two people changes in a fundamental way: they are thereby married. With luck, they begin a life of wedded bliss, but they also alter their legal relationship. For example, they may now file joint income tax returns and may not legally marry other people without first getting divorced.

Sentences of this kind, those that can be used *to bring something about* rather than merely *to state something,* were labeled *performatives* by the philosopher J. L. Austin.[2] He called them performatives in order to bring out the contrast between performing an action and simply describing one. For example, if an umpire shouts "You're out!" then the batter is out. The umpire is not merely describing the situation, but *declaring* the batter out. By way of contrast, if someone says "I am the best tennis player in Tennessee," that person is not *thereby* the best tennis player in Tennessee. Becoming the best tennis player in Tennessee is something you do with a tennis racket, not simply with words. In this case, saying does not make it so.

Performatives come in a variety of forms, but to avoid complications, we shall examine a simplified version of what Austin called explicit performatives. An utterance expresses an explicit performative if it is in the first person singular

---

[2] See, for example, J. L. Austin, "Performative Utterances," in *Philosophical Papers,* ed. J. O. Urmson and G. J. Warnock, 2d ed. (Oxford: Clarendon Press, 1970), 233–52. See also his *How to Do Things with Words,* where Austin expresses some dissatisfaction with his notion of a performative.

indicative present and yields a true statement when it is plugged into the follow-ing pattern:

In saying "I–––," I thereby–––.

We will call this the *thereby test* for explicit performatives. With an important qualification to be noted shortly, the thereby test provides a convenient way of identifying explicit performatives. Thus, "I congratulate you" expresses an explicit performative, because it is true that in saying "I congratulate you," I thereby congratulate you. Here a quoted expression occurs on the left side of the word "thereby," but not on the right side. This reflects that the *saying,* which is referred to on the left side of the pattern, amounts to the *doing* referred to on the right side of the word "thereby."

The thereby test has to be qualified in an important way: *the context of the utterance must be appropriate.* You have not congratulated anyone if you say "I congratulate you" when no one is around, unless, that is, you are congratulating yourself. Congratulations said by an actor in a play are not real congratulations. And so on. Later in this chapter we will try to get clearer concerning what makes a context appropriate.

Assuming an appropriate context, all of the following utterances meet the thereby test:

I promise to meet you tomorrow.

I bid sixty-six dollars.

I resign from this club.

I apologize for being late.

There are also explicit performatives that play important roles in constructing arguments. These include sentences of the following kind:

I conclude that this bill should be voted down.

I grant that there is much to be said on both sides of this issue.

We will call this kind of performative an *argumentative performative.* These performa-tives will be examined more closely in the next chapter.

In contrast to the above sentences, which pass the thereby test, none of the following sentences does:

I'll meet you tomorrow. (This may simply be a prediction that can turn out to be false.)

Yesterday I bid sixty dollars. (This is a statement about a past activity and may be false.)

I am sorry for being late. (This is a common way of apologizing, but it is not an explicit performative. If someone says "I apologize" (at least in a nonsarcastic way), he thereby apologizes. If someone says "I am sorry," he is not thereby sorry. Whether he is sorry or not depends on his state of mind.)

Finally, questions, imperatives, and exclamations are not explicit performatives since they cannot sensibly be plugged into the pattern at all.

EXERCISE I

Using the thereby test, as described above, indicate which of the following sentences express explicit performatives (EP) and which do not express explicit performatives (N):

(1) I resign from this rotten club.

(2) Pierre is the capital of South Dakota.

(3) I order you to leave.

(4) I own the World Trade Towers.

(5) I claim this land for Queen Victoria. (Said by an explorer.)

(6) I'm out of gas.

(7) Get lost!

(8) I bring you official greetings from the Socialist Party of Finland.

(9) Ask not what your country can do for you, but what you can do for your country.

(10) I feel devastated.

EXERCISE II

Follow the same instructions for the following dialogue:

(1) Lefty: I assure you that George caught only one fish.

(2) Righty: I already conceded that George caught only one fish.

(3) Righty: My only claim is that George can fish with style.

(4) Lefty: I deny that he can fish with style.

(5) Lefty: I wonder why you think that.

(6) Righty: My sources told me so.

(7) Righty: Then I saw how he wields a fishing rod.

(8) Righty: And you told me so yourself.

(9) Lefty: I lied.

(10) Lefty: In fact, I am lying right now.

KINDS OF SPEECH ACTS

Studying explicit performatives not only helps break the spell of the idea that language functions only to transmit information, it also introduces us to a level of language distinct from *linguistic acts*. We will call these acts *speech acts,* and the rules that govern them *speech-act rules*.

It is difficult to give a precise definition of a speech act, but we can begin by contrasting speech acts with linguistic acts. A linguistic act, we said, is the act of saying something meaningful in a language. It is important to see that the same linguistic act can play different roles as it occurs in different contexts. This is shown by the following brief conversations.

(1) A: Is there any pizza left?

   B: Yes.

(2) A: Do you promise to pay me back by Friday?

   B: Yes.

(3) A: Do you swear to tell the truth?

   B: Yes.

(4) Do you refuse to leave?

   B: Yes.

Here the same linguistic act, uttering the word "yes," is used to do four different things: to state something, to make a promise, to take an oath, and to refuse to do something. We will call such acts as stating, promising, swearing, and refusing *speech acts*. A speech act is the *conventional move* that a remark makes in a language exchange. It is what is done *in* saying something.[3]

We can make this idea clear using the notion of explicit performatives. Explicit performatives are important because they provide a systematic way of identifying different kinds of speech acts. The basic idea is this: different speech acts are named by the different verbs that occur in explicit performatives. For this reason, we can use the thereby test to search for different kinds of speech acts. For example:

If I say "I promise," I thereby promise.
   So *promising* is a kind of speech act.

If I say "I resign," I thereby resign.
   So *resigning* is a kind of speech act.

If I say "I apologize," I thereby apologize.
   So *apologizing* is a kind of speech act.

If I say "I question his honesty," I thereby question his honesty.
   So *questioning* is a kind of speech act.

If I say "I conclude that she is guilty," I thereby conclude that she is guilty.
   So *concluding* is a kind of speech act.

---

[3] Austin calls this an "illocutionary act." See *How to Do Things with Words,* 98–132.

We will call the main verbs that appear in such explicit performatives *performative verbs*. *Performative verbs* name kinds of *speech acts*.[4]

MAKING STATEMENTS

Thus far, we have emphasized that we do a great deal more with language than make statements, assert facts, and describe things. That is, we do more with language than put forward claims that are either true or false. But we also use language to do these things, so stating, asserting, and describing are themselves kinds of speech acts. This can be shown by using the thereby test:

> If I say "I state that I am a U.S. citizen," I thereby state that I am a U.S. citizen.
>
> If I say "I assert that the defendant was in Detroit at the time of the crime," I thereby assert that the defendant was in Detroit at that time.
>
> If I say "I describe him as being dark haired and just over six feet tall," I thereby describe him as being dark haired and just over six feet tall.

We now have a more accurate conception of the way in which language functions than the common one that the function of language is to convey ideas. Making claims that are either true or false is one important kind of speech act, but we perform a great many other kinds of speech acts that are also important. In this brief survey we have identified the following kinds of speech acts:

promising	resigning	swearing
apologizing	refusing	stating
asserting	describing	questioning
concluding		

EXERCISE III

Using a college dictionary, add to the list above by finding ten verbs that can be used to construct explicit performatives—that is, utterances in the first-person singular indicative present—that pass the thereby test.

---

[4] Although performative verbs name kinds of speech acts, not every kind of speech act has a corresponding performative verb. For example, *insulting* seems to be a kind of speech act, but "insult" is not a performative verb since you cannot insult someone simply by saying "I insult you." We might have had a convention that enabled us to insult people just by saying "I insult you." In English, however, we do not.

DISCUSSION QUESTION

The importance of deciding what kind of speech act has been performed is illustrated by a classic case from the law of contracts: *Hawkins v. McGee.*[5] McGee performed an operation on Hawkins that proved unsuccessful, and Hawkins sued for damages. He did not sue on the basis of malpractice, however, but on the basis of breach of contract. His attorney argued that the doctor initiated a contractual relationship in that he tried to persuade Hawkins to have the operation by saying such things as "I will guarantee to make the hand a hundred percent perfect hand." He made statements of this kind a number of times, and finally Hawkins agreed to undergo the operation on the basis of these remarks. Hawkins's attorney maintained that these exchanges, which took place in the doctor's office on a number of occasions, constituted an offer of a contract that Hawkins explicitly accepted. The attorney for the surgeon replied that these words, even if uttered, would not constitute an offer of a contract, but merely expressed a *strong belief.*

It is important to remember that contracts do not have to be written and signed in order to be binding. A proper verbal offer and acceptance is usually sufficient to constitute a contract.[6] The case, then, turned on two questions: (i) Did McGee utter the words attributed to him? In other words, did McGee perform the *linguistic act* attributed to him? The jury decided that he did. (ii) The second, more interesting, question was whether these words, when uttered in this particular context, amounted to an offer of a contract, as Hawkins's attorney maintained, or merely were an expression of strong belief, as McGee's attorney held. In other words, the fundamental question in this case was what kind of *speech act* McGee performed when trying to convince Hawkins to have the operation.

Explain how you would settle this case. (The court actually ruled in favor of Hawkins, but you are free to disagree.)

SPEECH-ACT RULES

The distinctive feature of a performative utterance is that, in a sense we have tried to make clear, the saying constitutes a doing of something. In saying "I pronounce you husband and wife," a minister is not simply describing a marriage ceremony,

---

[5] Supreme Court of New Hampshire, 1929, 84 N.H. 114, A. 641.

[6] In general, verbal contracts are binding if it can be shown that the verbal agreement did take place. More technically, a signed document is not a contract but evidence of one. A verbal agreement, though sometimes harder to prove, can also be evidence of a contract.

she is performing it. Here, however, an objection might arise. Suppose someone who is a supporter of family values goes about the streets pronouncing random couples husband and wife. First of all, unless this person is a member of the clergy, a justice of the peace, a ship's captain, or the like, that person will have no right to make such pronouncements. Furthermore, even if this person is, say, a crazed member of the clergy, the pronouncement will still not come off. The parties addressed have to say "I do," they must have a proper license, and so on. This example shows that a speech act will *not come off* or will be void unless certain rules or conventions are satisfied. These rules or conventions that must be satisfied for a speech act to come off and not be void we will call *speech-act rules*. We will look briefly at some of the main types of speech-act rules by considering the following questions:

(1) Must the person have a *special position* in order to perform the speech act?

Sometimes a speech act will come off only if it is performed by someone with an *official position*. We have already seen that for someone to make two people husband and wife by pronouncing them husband and wife, that person must have a certain *official* position. In the same way, although a shortstop can perform the linguistic act of *shouting* "You're out," she cannot perform the speech act of *calling* someone out. Only an umpire can do that. A janitor cannot pronounce a body dead on arrival, even if the body is plainly dead when it arrives at the hospital. That is the job of a doctor or a coroner.

(2) Are there any *special words or formulas* associated with the speech act?

Sometimes a speech act will come off only if certain *words or formulas* are used. In baseball the umpire must say "strike two," or something very close to this, in order to call a second strike. In a pickup game it might be all right to say instead "Hey, that's two bad ones on you, baby!" but that way of calling strikes is not permitted in serious play. Certain legal documents are not valid if they are not properly signed, endorsed, notarized, and so forth.

(3) What *facts are presupposed* in the use of the speech act?

Most speech acts also involve assumptions or presuppositions that certain *facts* obtain. A father cannot bequeath an antique car to his son if he does not own one. You cannot resign from the American Civil Liberties Union or the Veterans of Foreign Wars if you are not a member.

(4) Is any *response or uptake* needed to complete the speech act?

Sometimes a speech act will come off only if there is an *uptake* by another person. A person can *offer* a bet by saying "I bet you ten dollars that the Angels will win today," but this person will have *made* a bet only if the other person says "Done," or "You're on," shakes hands, or in some other way accepts the bet. A marriage ceremony is completely flawed if one of the parties does not say "I do," but instead says "Well, maybe I should think about this for a while."

(5) What *feelings and beliefs* is the person performing the speech act expected to have?

Thus far, we have considered conventions that must be satisfied in order for the speech act to come off (in order for it not to be void). Speech acts can, however, be flawed in another way: they can be *insincere*. If we apologize for something, we are expected to feel sorry for what we have done. Of course, the person who says "I apologize" has apologized even if he or she does not feel sorry, but the apology will not be sincere. If we congratulate someone, we are usually supposed to be pleased with that person's success. If we state something, we are expected to believe what we say. In all these cases—in apologizing, congratulating, and stating—we do succeed in performing a speech act, but are subject to criticism when our feelings or beliefs were not appropriate for the kind of speech act we performed.

EXERCISE IV

In Exercise III, you were asked to find ten verbs that can be used to construct sentences that pass the thereby test. These verbs, as we have seen, provide names for particular kinds of speech acts. We have also seen that for these speech acts to come off, certain rules must be satisfied. Specifying what these rules are for a particular kind of speech act is called giving a *speech-act analysis*. Give a speech-act analysis of the five verbs given in (1)–(5) below. That is, for these five speech acts, answer the five questions given above.

For example, here is a speech-act analysis of "to appoint," as in "I appoint you to the judiciary committee":

(a) Normally, someone who appoints a person to something must have the *power* to make such appointments. For example, Queen Elizabeth does not have the power to appoint the commissioner of baseball.

(b) Appointments are usually made by using the word "appoint," but other words can be used as well; for example, "name" and "designate" can also be used to do this job.

(c) A wide variety of facts is presupposed in this speech act; for example, that a position exists, that the person appointed to it is eligible for this appointment, and so on.

(d) Sometimes further actions by others are necessary for an appointment to come off. Perhaps ratification is needed. Before ratification, the word "nominate" is often used. In such cases, only after the nomination is ratified has the appointment been made. Usually the appointment does not come off if the person declines the appointment.

(e) Appointments are often made with the belief that the person appointed will do a good job. This is not always the case, however, since appointments are made for all sorts of different reasons—rewarding an important supporter, for example.

(1) to thank

(2) to deny

(3) to promise

(4) to vote

(5) to give up (in a fight)

Do the same for five of the ten verbs that you found as answers to Exercise III.

CONVERSATIONAL ACTS

In first examining linguistic acts (saying something meaningful in a language) and then examining speech acts (doing something in using words), we have largely ignored one of the central features of language: it is primarily an activity that takes place among people.[7] It is usually a social activity. We use language in order to inform people of things, get them to do things, amuse them, calm them down, and so on. We can capture this aspect of language by introducing the notion of a conversational *exchange*–that is, a situation in which one person, the speaker, uses language in order to bring about some effect in another person, the listener, or, more generally, in which a number of speakers use language to bring about various effects in each other. We will call this act of causing an effect in another a *conversational act*.

   Suppose, for example, *A* says to *B* "Radon is seeping into your basement." In this case, *A* has performed a linguistic act; that is, *A* has uttered a meaningful sentence in the English language. At the same time, *A* has performed a speech act; that is, *A* has made a statement. Beyond this, if the communication has been

---

[7] With some variations, this discussion of conversational rules and conversational implication is based on Paul Grice's important essay "Logic and Conversation." It appears as the second chapter of his collected works, entitled *Studies in the Way of Words* (Cambridge: Harvard University Press, 1989). To avoid British references that an American reader might find perplexing, we have sometimes altered Grice's exact wording. The topics discussed occur between pages 22 and 40 of this work in the same order in which they are examined here.

successful, *A* has also performed a conversational act; that is, she has *made B aware* that radon is seeping into his basement.

Although we have a rich vocabulary of verbs indicating speech acts, the number of verbs indicating conversational acts is really quite small. The following contrasts may help bring out the difference between speech acts and conversational acts:

(1) We often *urge* people to do things in order to *persuade* them to do these things.

   Here, urging is the speech act, and persuading is the conversational act.

(2) We often *tell* people something in order to *get them to believe* something.

   Here, telling is the speech act, and getting them to believe something is the conversational act.

(3) We sometimes *warn* people in order to *put them on guard*.

   Here, warning is the speech act, and putting them on guard is the conversational act.

The contrast between a speech act and a conversational act is clear in the first example. If I say "I urge you to go," I thereby urge you to go. This shows that urging is a kind of speech act. In contrast, it makes no sense to say "I persuade you to go." Persuading someone involves getting that person to believe something. This is an *effect* we are trying to produce in another; it is not something that can be conventionally achieved using a performative utterance. The contrast is a bit less obvious in the second two cases, but still, telling and warning are both kinds of speech acts; getting people to believe something and putting them on guard are not.

EXERCISE V

Indicate whether each of the following verbs primarily names a linguistic act, a speech act, a conversational act, or none of these kinds of act. Assume a standard context. Explain your answers.

(1) to inform

(2) to deny

(3) to hum

(4) to mispronounce

(5) to alert

(6) to fire (from employment)

(7) to praise

(8) to convince

(9) to exhale

(10) to whisper

(11) to pledge

(12) to frighten

(13) to advise

(14) to blame

(15) to enlighten

(16) to conclude

(17) to challenge

(18) to amuse

(19) to abbreviate

(20) to condemn

CONVERSATIONAL RULES

Just as there are rules that govern linguistic acts and rules that govern speech acts, there are also rules that govern conversational acts. This is not surprising, because conversational exchanges can be complicated interpersonal activities in need of rules to make them effective in attaining their goals. These underlying rules are implicitly understood by users of the language, but the philosopher Paul Grice was the first person to examine them in careful detail.

We can start by examining standard or normal conversational exchanges in which conversation is a cooperative venture–that is, the people involved in the conversation have some common goal they are trying to achieve in talking with one another. (A prisoner being interrogated is *not* in such a cooperative situation.) According to Grice, such exchanges are governed by what he calls the Cooperative Principle (CP). This principle states that the parties involved should use language in a way that contributes toward achieving their common goal. It tells them to cooperate.[8]

This general principle gets more content when we examine more-specific principles that aid speakers in cooperating with one another. Grice discusses four such principles. The first he calls the rule of *Quantity*. It tells us to give the right amount of information. More specifically:

(1) Make your contribution as informative as is required (for the current purposes of the exchange),

and possibly

(2) Do not make your contribution more informative than is required.

---

[8] Grice states the Cooperative Principle in these words: "Make your conversational contribution such as is required, at the stage at which it occurs, by the accepted purpose or direction of the talk exchange in which you are engaged" (p. 26).

Here is an application of this rule: A person comes rushing up to you and asks "Where is a fire extinguisher?" You know that there is a fire extinguisher five floors away in the basement, and you also know that there is a fire extinguisher just down the hall. Suppose you say that there is a fire extinguisher in the basement. Here you have said something true, but you have violated the rule of Quantity. You have failed to reveal an important piece of information that, under the rule of Quantity, you should have produced. A violation of the second version of the rule would look like this: As smoke billows down the hall, you start with the basement, and say where a fire extinguisher is located on each floor. Eventually you will get around to saying that there is a fire extinguisher just down the hall, but you bury the point in a mass of unnecessary information.

Another of Grice's rules is called the rule of *Quality*. In general:

Try to make your contribution one that is true.

More specifically:

(1) Do not say what you believe to be false.

(2) Do not say that for which you lack adequate evidence.

In a cooperative activity, you are not supposed to tell lies. Beyond this, you are expected not to talk off the top of your head either. When we make a statement, we can be challenged in the following ways:

Do you really believe that?

Why do you believe that?

That a person has the right to ask such questions shows that statement making is governed by the rule of *Quality*. In a court of law, witnesses promise to tell the whole truth and nothing but the truth. The demand for *nothing but the truth* reflects the rule of Quality; the demand for *the whole truth* roughly reflects the rule of Quantity.

The next rule is called the rule of *Relevance*. Simply stated, it says: Be relevant! Though easy to state, the rule is not easy to explain, because relevance itself is a difficult notion. It is, however, easy to illustrate. If someone asks me where he can find a doctor, I might reply that there is a hospital in the next block. Though not a direct answer to his question, it does not violate the rule of Relevance since it provides him with a piece of useful information. If, however, in response I tell the person that I like his haircut, then I have violated the rule of Relevance. Clear-cut violations of this principle usually involve *changing the subject*. Interruptions are typically violations of the rule of Relevance.

Another rule concerns the *Manner* of our conversation. We are expected to be clear in what we say. Under this general rule come various special rules:

(1) Avoid obscurity of expression.

(2) Avoid ambiguity.

(3) Be brief.

(4) Be orderly.

As an example of the fourth part of this rule, in describing a series of events, it is usually important to state them in the order in which they occurred. It would certainly be misleading to say that two people had a child and got married when, in fact, they had a child after they were married.

There are probably many other rules that govern our conversations. *Be polite!* might be one of them. *Be charitable!* is another. That is, we should put the best interpretation on what others say and our replies should reflect this. We should avoid quibbling and being picky. For the most part, however, we will not worry about these other rules.

If we look at basic conversational rules, we notice that these rules sometimes clash, or at least push us in different directions. The rule of Quantity encourages us to give as much information as possible, but this is constrained by the rule of Quality, which restricts our claims to things we believe to be true and can back up with good reasons. The demands of the rule of Quantity can also conflict with the demand for brevity. In order to be brief, we must sometimes simplify and even falsify, and this can come into conflict with the rule of Quality, which demands that we say only what we believe to be true. Sometimes it is not important to get things *exactly* right; sometimes it is. An ongoing conversation is a constant series of adjustments to this background system of rules.

CONVERSATIONAL IMPLICATION

We have seen that conversational exchanges are governed by a system of rules that help those involved in the exchange in achieving their goals. Of course, when people make statements they do not always follow these rules. People withhold information, they lie, they say the first thing that pops into their heads, they wander off the subject, they talk vaguely and obscurely. Yet in a normal setting where people are cooperating toward reaching a shared goal, they often conform quite closely to these rules. If, on the whole, people did not do this, we could not have the linguistic practices we do. If we thought, for example, that people very often lied (even about the most trivial matters), the business of exchanging information would be badly damaged.

But not only do we follow these conventions, we also (1) implicitly realize that we are following them, and (2) expect others to assume that we are following them. This mutual understanding of the commitments involved in a conversational act has the following important consequence: *People are able to convey a great deal of information without actually saying it.*

A simple example will illustrate this. Again suppose that *A*, with smoke billowing behind him, comes running up to you and asks:

Where is a fire extinguisher?

And you reply:

There is one in the lobby.

As already noted, this commits you to the claim that this is the closest, or at least the most accessible, fire extinguisher. Furthermore, the person you are speaking to assumes that you are committed to this. Of course, you have not actually *said* that it is the closest fire extinguisher, but you have, we might say, *implied* this. When we do not actually say something, but do imply it by virtue of a mutually understood conversational rule, the implication is called a *conversational implication*.

Conversational implications have a feature that will be important to us later on: If saying something conversationally implies something that is false, this does not show that what has been said is itself false. Saying that Jay has his bags packed conversationally implies (by the rule of Relevance) that he is about to leave. Yet it might be true that Jay has his bags packed and he is not about to leave. This marks the difference between conversational implication and logical implication. Although saying that Jay has his bags packed may conversationally imply that he is leaving, the statement "Jay has his bags packed" does not logically imply this. We will begin our discussion of logical implication in the next chapter.

THE PERVASIVENESS OF CONVERSATIONAL IMPLICATION

It is important to realize that conversational implication is a pervasive feature of human communication. It is not something we employ only occasionally for special effect. In fact, virtually every conversation relies on these implications, and most conversations would fall apart if people refused to go beyond literal meanings to take into account the implications of saying things. In the following conversation *B* is literal-minded in just this way:

A: Do you know what time it is?

B: Not without looking at my watch.

B has answered *A*'s question, but it is hard to imagine that *A* has received the information she was looking for. Presumably she wanted to know what time it was, not merely whether *B*, at that very moment, knew the time. Finding *B* rather obtuse, *A* tries again:

A: Can you tell me what time it is?

B: Oh yes, all I have to do is look at my watch.

Undaunted, *A* gives it another try:

A: Will you tell me what time it is?

B: I suppose I will as soon as you ask me.

Finally:

A: What time is it?

B: Two o'clock.

Notice that in each of these exchanges *B* gives a direct and accurate answer to *A*'s question, yet, in all but the last answer, he does not provide *A* with what she wants. Here we might say that *B* is taking *A*'s questions too literally, but we might better say that the problem is that *B* does nothing *more* than take *A*'s remarks literally. In a conversational exchange, we expect others to take our remarks in the light of the obvious purpose we have in making them. We expect them to share our commonsense understanding of why people ask questions. In his replies, *B* is totally oblivious to the point of *A*'s questions and, like a computer in a science-fiction movie, gives nothing more than the literally correct answer to each question explicitly asked.

EXERCISE VI

People often say things so that they can conversationally imply something else. Assuming a natural conversational setting, what might a person intend to conversationally imply by making the following remarks? Briefly explain why each of these conversational implications holds; that is, explain the relationship between what the speaker *literally* says and what he or she intends to convey.

(1) It's getting a little chilly in here.

(2) The crowd didn't actually throw bottles at him. (Said of a rock singer.)

(3) You can trust him if you want to.

(4) I got here before he did. (Said at a lunch counter.)

(5) Well, he hasn't been sent to jail yet.

(6) There are planes leaving every day for China. (Said to a student radical.)

(7) These sweet potatoes are very filling.

(8) The West wasn't won with a registered gun.

VIOLATING CONVERSATIONAL RULES

Next, we will look at a set of conversational implications that particularly attracted Grice's attention. Sometimes our speech acts *seem* to violate certain conversational rules. On the assumption that the conversation is goodwilled and cooperative, the listener will then attempt to make sense of this in a way that will explain why the speaker is violating such a rule. Here is one of Grice's examples. Suppose *A* tells *B* that he wants to visit a friend, *C*, and the following conversation takes place:

A: I'm planning to visit *C;* where does he live?

B: Somewhere in the south of France.

If *A* is interested in visiting *C*, then *B*'s reply really does not give her the information she needs, and thus seems to violate the first part of the rule of Quantity. We can explain this departure on the assumption that *B* does not know *exactly* where *C* lives and would thus violate the rule of Quality if he said anything more specific.

In this case, *B*'s reply conversationally implies that he does not know exactly where *C* lives.

In a more extreme case, a person may even flout one of these conventions—that is, she may obviously violate it. Here is an adaptation of one of Grice's examples and his explanation of it:

> *A* is writing a letter of recommendation about one of his students who is applying to law school, and the letter reads as follows: "Dear Sir: Mr. *X*'s command of English is excellent, and his attendance in class has been regular. Yours, etc." (Gloss: *A* cannot be opting out, since if he wished to be uncooperative, why write at all? He cannot be unable, through ignorance, to say more, since the person is his student; moreover, he knows that more information is wanted. He must, therefore, be wishing to impart information he is reluctant to write down. This supposition is only tenable on the assumption that he thinks that Mr. *X* is not a good student. This, then, is what he is implicating.)

This is a case of damning with faint praise. Faint praise can be damning because, under the first part of the rule of Quantity, it conversationally implies that no stronger praise is warranted.

We can intentionally violate the rule of Relevance by pointedly changing the subject. Here is variation on another one of Grice's examples:

> Standing outside a classroom, *A* says "Professor *X* is a moron." There is a moment of shocked silence; then *B* says "Nice day, isn't it?"

A would have to be fairly dim not to realize that Professor *X*, whom he has just called a moron, may be somewhere nearby. Why else would *B* reply in such an irrelevant manner? So in saying "Nice day, isn't it?" *B* conversationally implies that Professor *X* is nearby.

EXERCISE VII

Indicate which, if any, of Grice's conversational rules are violated by the italicized sentence of each of the following conversations. Assume a standard context. More than one rule might be violated.

(1) "What did you get on the last test?" *"A grade."*

(2) "Did you like her singing?" *"Her costume was beautiful."*

(3) *"The governor has the brains of a three-year-old."*

(4) *"The Lone Ranger rode into the sunset and jumped on his horse."*

(5) *"Without her help, we'd be up a creek without a paddle."*

(6) "Where is Palo Alto?" *"On or near the surface of the Earth."*

(7) *"It will rain tomorrow."* "How do you know?" "I just guessed."

(8) *"Does the dog need to go out for a W-A-L-K [spelled out]?"*

(9) "Why did the chicken cross the road?" *"To get to the other side."*

(10) Psychiatrist: "You're crazy."
       Patient: "I want a second opinion."
       Psychiatrist: "Okay. *You're ugly,* too."

EXERCISE VIII

Each of the following remarks, if taken quite literally, is either false or otherwise plainly defective. First, explain why each remark is either false or defective on a literal reading. Second, state what you take to be the conversational implication of each remark. Third, explain the source of this conversational implication by making reference to Grice's conversational rules.

(1) "Ain't got nothin' but love, babe, eight days a week." (Beatles lyric)

(2) "An army marches on its stomach." (attributed to Napoleon)

(3) "The way to a man's heart is through his stomach." (Traditional saying)

(4) "Ich bin ein Berliner." ("I am a Berliner"; President John F. Kennedy, in a speech before the Berlin Wall)

(5) "It isn't a car, it's a Volkswagen." (Advertisement)

(6) "The only thing we have to fear is fear itself." (President Franklin D. Roosevelt)

(7) "Beauty is truth, truth beauty;—that is all
      Ye know on earth, and all ye need to know."
      (John Keats, "Ode on a Grecian Urn")

CONVERSATIONAL IMPLICATION AND RHETORICAL DEVICES

Conversational implication is so much a part of our everyday use of language that we hardly notice when we are employing it. Many rhetorical devices depend on conversational implication. Consider how *rhetorical questions* work. Normally when we ask a question we are requesting information, but not always. If you ask someone "Could you hurry up?" you certainly know that this person *can* hurry up. It is not likely that you are asking this question in order to find out whether the person is suffering from some physical disability such as a leg cramp. The point of the question is to force the person to *admit* that he can hurry up, and that in turn conversationally implies (by the rule of Relevance) that he should hurry up. For this reason a rhetorical question can have the force of an assertion or an order. To take another example, if you say to someone "Do you really expect me to believe that?" you are indicating that the person should answer this question "No," and thus your question has the force of the assertion "*I don't* believe that."

It is important to see that the same question can be rhetorical in one context and not in another. If you hear (or think you hear) someone in the basement, you might ask "Do you want me to call the police?" Here you are genuinely interested in someone's opinion, for calling the police might be unnecessary or even dangerous. On the other hand, if you are trying to get someone to move her car from your driveway, these same words will have the force of a rhetorical question. Your question "Do you want me to call the police?" has the expected answer "No," and because of this it conversationally implies the threat "If you don't move your car, I will call the police." Rhetorical questions are used (and often abused) in everyday arguments. They are, as we shall see, often a sign of weakness in an argument.

EXERCISE IX

For each of the following questions, describe one context in which the question is rhetorical and one context in which it is not:

    (1) Is that the last piece of pizza?

    (2) How can you say that to me?

    (3) Are you looking for trouble?

    (4) Could you just wait a minute?

    (5) Did I hear you correctly?

    (6) Do you know who I am?

    (7) Can I say what I think?

    (8) Didn't I tell you?

With a rhetorical question, we are asking a question even though the question itself is not used in the standard (information-seeking) way. We do not expect people to take our *questioning* at face value. At other times, we do not expect our listeners to take even our *words* at face value. For example, we tend to exaggerate. When people claim to be hungry enough to eat a bear, that usually indicates that they are very hungry. In most cases, it does not dawn on us to take an assertion of this kind at face value, for to do so would be to attribute a wildly false belief to people concerning how much they can eat. Exaggeration of this kind, in which the person does not expect to be taken literally, is called *overstatement* or *hyperbole*. We sometimes use the opposite ploy and attempt to achieve rhetorical effect by *understating* things. We describe something as pretty good when, as all can see, it is terrific.

Sometimes, then, we do not intend to have our words taken at face value. But even beyond this, we sometimes expect our listeners to interpret us as claiming just the *opposite* of what we assert. This occurs, for example, with *irony* and *sarcasm*. For example, at a crucial point in a game, the second baseman fires the ball ten feet over the first baseman's head, and someone shouts "Great throw." Literally, it was not a great throw; it was the opposite of a great throw, and this is just what the person who says "Great throw" is indicating. How do the listeners know they are supposed to interpret it in this way? Sometimes this is indicated by tone of voice. A sarcastic tone of voice usually indicates that the person means the opposite of what he or she is saying. But even without the tone of sarcasm, the remark "Great throw" is not likely to be taken literally. The person who says this knows, after all, that it was not a great throw. He is thus knowingly saying something false, so his utterance violates the first part of Grice's rule of Quality: "Do not say what you believe to be false." Furthermore, the person is not trying to lie or mislead anyone, since everyone knows that the remark is false and the speaker knows they know this. This forces us to the conclusion, which we draw immediately, that the person does not wish to be taken literally. By saying something outrageously inappropriate, the person draws attention to the true state of affairs—that is, to just how bad the throw really was.

Metaphors and similes are perhaps the most common form of figurative language. With a metaphor, we speak of something by using a vocabulary that, at a literal level, is not appropriate to it. George Washington was not literally the father of his country. Taken literally, it hardly makes sense to speak of someone fathering a country. Countries do not have fathers, even though inhabitants of countries do. But the metaphor is so natural (or so familiar) that it does not cross our minds to treat the remark literally, asking, perhaps, who the mother was. With similes, we draw a comparison, but in a way that, taken literally, is inappropriate. To say that the home team fought like tigers does not mean that they clawed the opposing team and took large bites out of them. Taken literally, metaphors are usually obviously false, and thus violate Grice's rule of Quality. Again, as with irony, when someone says something obviously false, we have to decide what to make of that person's utterance. Perhaps the person is very stupid or a very bad liar, but often neither suggestion is plausible. In such a situation sometimes the best supposition is that the person is speaking metaphorically rather than literally.

Not all metaphors, however, are literally false. For example, "No man is an island" is literally true. We treat this remark as a metaphor because, taken literally, it is so obviously and boringly true that we cannot imagine why anyone would want to say it. Taken literally, it would make no greater contribution to the conversation than any other irrelevant, obvious truth—for example, that no man is a socket wrench. As a metaphor it is an apt, if somewhat overworked, way of indicating that no one is isolated and self-contained.

A metaphor can die of overuse. Slang metaphors usually have a short shelf life. Think of the various metaphorical ways of describing drunkenness and how quickly they are replaced by others. Other metaphorical expressions continue to be used but lose their metaphorical meaning. Most people who use the expression "He has something up his sleeve" are not thinking about magicians or cardsharps who literally fool people by hiding things up their sleeves. It has simply become a way of saying that someone is about to do something sneaky and unexpected.

Poets make a living using metaphors, but so do politicians. It is, in fact, remarkable how dense political talk is with metaphorical expressions. Politicians in favor of welfare benefits will speak of a safety net. The metaphor is fairly obvious: A safety net is something that protects aerialists from being injured if they fall. Welfare programs protect workers when they become unemployed. Those who think that welfare benefits encourage loafing have produced a metaphor of their own: "We need a safety net, not a hammock." Politicians are constantly speaking about level playing fields, being caught between a rock and a hard place, opening cans of worms, not moving the goalposts, looking at the bottom line, and so on.

How do metaphors work? This is a difficult and disputed question, but many metaphors have the force of an implicit analogy. A metaphor leads us to view something in terms of striking or salient features of something else. The underlying structure has the following form:

A is to *B* as *C* is to *D.*

A safety net is a good thing to have when an aerialist falls. Analogically, welfare benefits are a good thing to have when people lose their jobs. In contrast, hammocks are places to loaf, so by comparing welfare benefits to a hammock, the suggestion is made that welfare benefits support loafing. Thus, by using these metaphors, people are being induced to look at welfare programs in ways that will shape their attitudes toward them. In this way, metaphors often function as vivid, highly condensed arguments.

The problem with metaphors is that they can be clever, vivid, and entertaining but still be deeply unfair, biased, or misleading. Since metaphors very often appear in arguments—especially in political arguments—we will have to develop ways of evaluating their argumentative force. This matter will be examined in the next chapter.

EXERCISE X

Identify each of the following sentences as overstatement, understatement, metaphor, or simile. For each sentence, write another expressing its literal meaning.

(1) He missed the ball by a mile.

(2) A midair collision can ruin your whole day.

(3) "Religion is the opiate of the masses." (Karl Marx)

(4) Joe Montana was the heart of the 49er offense.

(5) He had to eat his words.

(6) The concert was totally awesome.

(7) This is a case of the tail wagging the dog.

(8) They are throwing the baby out with the bathwater.

(9) He acted like a bull in a china shop.

(10) The exam blew me away.

DECEPTION

In the examples we have examined thus far, a speaker intentionally violates a conversational rule in order to achieve some special effect—for example, to make a metaphorical comparison. It is important in these cases that the listeners *recognize* that a rule is being intentionally broken, for otherwise they may simply be misled. At other times, however, speakers intentionally break conversational rules because they are trying to mislead their listeners. A speaker may violate the first part of Grice's rule of Quality by uttering something she knows to be false with the intention of producing a false belief in her listeners. That is called lying. Notice that lying depends on the general acceptance of the Cooperative Principle. Because audiences generally assume that speakers are telling the truth, successful lying is possible.

Flat-out lying is not the only way (and often not the most effective way) of intentionally misleading people. We can say something literally true that, at the same time, conversationally implies something false. This is sometimes called making a *false suggestion*. If a son tells his parents that he "has had some trouble with the car," that could be true, but deeply misleading, if, in fact, he had totaled it. It would be misleading because it would violate the rule of Quantity. In saying only that he has had some trouble with the car, he conversationally implies that nothing very serious happened. He conversationally implies this because, in this context, he is expected to come clean and reveal *all* that actually happened. Notice that saying that he has had *some* trouble with the car is not, in this context, a case of understatement. The function of understatement is not to conceal something, but rather to stress it. Standing in front of the totaled car, the son might say to his parents "I guess I banged it up a bit." That would be a case of understatement, not false suggestion.

A more complex example of false suggestion arose in a lawsuit that went all the way to the Supreme Court.

■ BRONSTON V. UNITED STATES
(409 U.S. 352, 1973)

MR. CHIEF JUSTICE BURGER delivered the opinion of the Court.

Petititioner's perjury conviction was founded on the answers given by him as a witness at that bankruptcy hearing, and in particular on the following colloquy with a lawyer for a creditor of Bronston Productions:

> "Q. Do you have any bank accounts in Swiss banks, Mr. Bronston?
> "A. No, sir.
> "Q. Have you ever?
> "A. The company had an account there for about six months, in Zurich.
> "Q. Have you any nominees who have bank accounts in Swiss banks?
> "A. No, sir.
> "Q. Have you ever?
> "A. No, sir."

It is undisputed that for a period of nearly five years, between October 1959 and June 1964, petitioner had a personal bank account at the International Credit Bank in Geneva, Switzerland, into which he made deposits and upon which he drew checks totaling more than $180,000. It is likewise undisputed that petitioner's answers were literally truthful. (i) Petitioner did not at the time of questioning have a Swiss bank account. (ii) Bronston Productions, Inc., did have the account in Zurich described by petitioner. (iii) Neither at the time of questioning nor before did petitioner have nominees who had Swiss accounts. The government's prosecution for perjury went forward on the theory that in order to mislead his questioner, petitioner answered the second question with literal truthfulness but unresponsively addressed his answer to the company's assets and not to his own—thereby implying that he had no personal Swiss bank account at the relevant time.

It is hard to read the witness's response to the second question in any other way than as a deliberate attempt to mislead the Court, for his response plainly implies that he did not have a personal account in a Swiss bank, when, in fact, he did. But the issue before the Court was not whether he intentionally misled the Court, but whether in doing so he committed perjury. The relevant statute reads as follows:

> Whoever, having taken an oath before a competent tribunal . . . that he will testify . . . truly, . . . willfully and contrary to such oath states or subscribes to any material matter which he does not believe to be true, is guilty of perjury. (18 U.S.C. 1621)

The lower courts ruled that Bronston violated this statute and thus had committed perjury. The Supreme Court reversed this decision, in part for the following reasons:

> It should come as no surprise that a participant in a bankruptcy proceeding may have something to conceal and consciously tried to do so, or that a debtor may be embarrassed at his plight and yield information reluctantly. It is the responsibility of the lawyer to probe; testimonial interrogation, and cross-examination in particular, is a probing, prying, pressing form of inquiry. If a witness evades, it is the lawyer's responsibility to recognize the evasion and to bring the witness back to the mark, to flush out the whole truth with the tools of adversary examination. (409 U.S. 352 at 358–359 [1973])

In other words, in a courtroom, where the relationship is typically adversarial rather than cooperative, not all the standard conversational rules are in force, or fully in force. In particular, it would be unrealistic to assume that the rule of Quantity will be consistently honored in a courtroom clash; therefore it becomes the task of the cross-examiner to force the witness to produce all the relevant facts.

DISCUSSION QUESTION

Refer back to the dialogue quoted in *Bronston v. United States*. Because it is difficult to read the witness's second response as anything but a willful attempt to deceive, why should this case be treated differently from lying? Alternatively, why not even drop the demand that witnesses tell the truth, and make it the responsibility of the lawyers to get at the truth itself (rather than just the whole truth), through *probing, prying, pressing inquiry?*

AN OVERVIEW

In this chapter we have developed a rather complex picture of the way our language functions. In the process we have distinguished three kinds or levels of acts that are performed when we employ language. We have also examined the rules associated with each kind or level of act. The following table summarizes this discussion:

Three Levels of Language

Kinds of Acts	Governing Rules
A LINGUISTIC ACT is an act of saying something meaningful in a language. It is the basic act that is needed to make anything part of language.	Semantic rules (such as definitions) and syntactical rules (as in grammar).
A SPEECH ACT concerns the move a person makes in saying something. Different kinds of speech acts are indicated by the various verbs found in explicit performatives.	Speech-act rules about special agents, formulas, circumstances, facts, and feelings appropriate to different kinds of speech acts.
A CONVERSATIONAL ACT is a speaker's act of causing a standard kind of effect in the listener. It is what I do by saying something—for example, I persuade.	Conversational rules (the Cooperative Principle; Quantity, Quality, Relevance, and Manner).

EXERCISE XI

It is late and *A* is very hungry. *A* asks *B* "When will dinner be ready?" Describe the linguistic act, the speech act, and some of the possible conversational acts this person may be performing in this context.

Chapter Two

THE LANGUAGE OF ARGUMENT

Using the techniques developed in Chapter 1, this chapter will examine the use of language to formulate arguments and will provide methods to analyze genuine arguments in their richness and complexity. The first stage in analyzing an argument is the discovery of its basic *structure*. To do this, we will examine the words, phrases, and special constructions that indicate the premises and conclusions of an argument. The second stage is the study of techniques used to *strengthen* an argument. These include *guarding* premises so that they are less subject to criticism, offering *assurances* concerning debatable claims, and *discounting* possible criticisms in advance. Finally, we will examine the role of *evaluative* and *figurative* language in arguments.

THE BASIC STRUCTURE OF ARGUMENTS

In the previous chapter, we saw that language is used for a great many different purposes. One important thing that we do with language is construct arguments. Arguments are constructed out of statements, but arguments are not just lists of statements. Here is a simple list of statements:

> Socrates is mortal.
> All men are mortal.
> Socrates is a man.

It is not an argument, because none of these statements is presented as a reason for any other statement.

It is, however, simple to turn this list into an argument. All we have to do is to add the single word "therefore":

> Socrates is mortal.
> All men are mortal.
> Therefore, Socrates is a man.

Now we have an argument. The word "therefore" converts these sentences into an argument by signaling that the statement following it is a *conclusion*, and that the statement or statements that come before it are offered as *reasons* in behalf of this conclusion. The argument we have produced in this way is a bad one, since the conclusion does not follow from the reasons stated in its behalf, but it is an argument nonetheless.

There are other ways to turn this same list into an argument. Here is one:

> Socrates is mortal,
> since all men are mortal,
> and Socrates is a man.

This is a new argument, and this time a good argument in the sense that the conclusion does follow from the premises offered in its behalf.

Notice that the word "since" works in roughly the opposite way to the way "therefore" works. The word "therefore" is a *conclusion marker*, because it indicates that the statement that follows it is a conclusion. In contrast, the word "since" is a *reason marker*, because it indicates that the statement or statements that follow it are reasons. In our example, the conclusion comes before the word "since," but there is a variation on this. Sometimes the conclusion is tacked onto the end of the argument:

Since all men are mortal and Socrates is a man, Socrates is mortal.

"Since" flags reasons; the remaining connected statement is then taken to be the conclusion, whether it appears at the beginning or at the end of the sentence.

Many other terms are used to introduce an argumentative structure into language by marking either reasons or conclusions. Here is a partial list:

Reason Markers	Conclusion Markers
since	therefore
because	then
for	thus
	so
	hence
	accordingly

We shall call such terms *warranting connectives*, because each presents one or more statements as the *warrant* or backing for some other statement.

It is important to realize that these words are not always used as warranting connectives. The words "since" and "then" are often used as indicators of time, as in "He's been an American citizen since 1973" and "He ate a hot dog, then a hamburger." The word "for" is often used as a preposition; for example, "John works for IBM." Since some of these terms have a variety of meanings, it is not possible to identify warranting connectives in a mechanical way just by looking at words. It is necessary to examine the function of words in the context in which they occur. One test of whether a word is functioning as a warranting connective in a particular sentence is whether you can substitute another warranting connective without changing the meaning of the sentence. In the last example, it makes no sense to say "John works since IBM."

In fact, there are many phrases available to signal that an argument is being presented. Here is just a small sample:

from which it follows that . . .

from which we may conclude that . . .

from which we see that . . .

which goes to show that . . .

which establishes that . . .

We can also indicate conclusions and reasons by using *argumentative performatives*, which we examined briefly in the previous chapter. If someone says "I conclude that . . . ," the words that follow are given the status of a conclusion. More pretentiously, if someone says "I here base my argument on the claim that . . . ," what comes next has the status of a reason.

Examination of actual arguments will show that we have a great many ways of introducing an argumentative structure into our language by using the two forms of warranting connectives: reason markers and conclusion markers. The first, and in many ways the most important, step in analyzing an argument is to identify the conclusion and the reasons given in its behalf. We do this by paying close attention to these warranting connectives.

IF . . . THEN . . .

If-then sentences are called *conditional* sentences. Though they often occur in arguments, they do not present arguments. To see this, consider the following indicative conditional:

> If the Dodgers get better hitting, then they will win the Western Division.

The sentence that occurs between the "if" and the "then" is called the *antecedent* of the conditional. The sentence that occurs after the "then" is called its *consequent.* In using an indicative conditional, we are not asserting the truth of its antecedent, and we are not asserting the truth of the consequent either. Thus, the person who makes the above remark is not claiming that the Dodgers will win the Western Division. All she is saying is that *if* they get better hitting, they will win. Furthermore, she is not saying that they will get better hitting. The word "if" cancels this suggestion. Because the speaker is not committing herself to either of these claims, she is not presenting an argument. This becomes clear when we contrast this indicative conditional with a statement that does formulate an argument:

> INDICATIVE CONDITIONAL: *If* the Dodgers get better hitting, *then* they will win the Western Division.
>
> ARGUMENT: *Since* the Dodgers will get better hitting, they will win the Western Division.

Even though indicative conditionals do not formulate arguments, there is obviously a close connection between indicative conditionals and arguments. Although indicative conditionals do not present arguments, they provide a *pattern* that can be converted into an argument whenever the antecedent is taken to be true.[1] Thus, we often hear people argue in the following way:

> If international terrorism continues to grow, there will be a worldwide crisis. But international terrorism will certainly continue to grow, so a world crisis is on the way.

The first sentence is an indicative conditional, and it makes no positive claims about terrorism or a coming world crisis. The next sentence indicates that the antecedent of this conditional is true and then proceeds immediately to draw a conclusion signaled by the warranting connective "so." We might say that when the antecedent of an indicative conditional is found to be true, the indicative conditional can be *cashed in* for an argument.

It is easy to see why indicative conditionals are a useful feature of our language.

---

[1] We also get an argument when the consequent is shown to be false. This will be discussed in Chapter 5.

By providing patterns for arguments, they prepare us to draw conclusions when the circumstances are right. Much of our knowledge of the world about us is contained in indicative conditionals. Here is an example:

If your computer does not start, the plug might be loose.

This is a useful piece of practical information, for when your computer does not start, you can immediately infer that the plug might be loose, and then check it out.

ARGUMENTS IN STANDARD FORM

Since arguments come in all shapes and forms, it will help to have a standard way of presenting arguments. For centuries, logicians have used a format of the following kind:

> All men are mortal.
> <u>Socrates is a man.</u>
> ∴ Socrates is mortal.

The reasons (or premises) are listed above the line, the conclusion is listed below the line, and the symbol "∴" is read "therefore." Arguments presented in this way are said to be in *standard form.*

The notion of a standard form is useful because it helps us see that the same argument can be expressed in different ways. For example, the following two sentences formulate the argument stated in standard form above.

Socrates is mortal, since all men are mortal, and Socrates is a man.

All men are mortal, so Socrates is mortal, because he is a man.

More importantly, by putting arguments into standard form, we perform the most obvious, and in some ways most important, step in the analysis of an argument: the identification of premises and conclusion.

EXERCISE 1

   (a) Identify which of the following sentences expresses an argument.

   (b) For each that does,
      (i) circle the warranting connective (or connectives), and
     (ii) restate the argument in standard form.

   (1) Since Chicago is north of Boston, and Boston is north of Charleston, Chicago is north of Charleston.

   (2) Toward evening, clouds formed and the sky grew darker; then the storm broke.

(3) Texas has a greater area than Topeka, and Topeka has a greater area than the Bronx Zoo, so Texas has a greater area than the Bronx Zoo.

(4) Both houses of Congress may pass a bill, but the president may still veto it.

(5) Other airlines will carry more passengers because United Airlines is on strike.

(6) Since Jesse James left town, taking his gang with him, things have been a lot quieter.

(7) Things are a lot quieter because Jesse James left town, taking his gang with him.

(8) Witches float, because witches are made of wood, and wood floats.

(9) The hour is up, so you must hand in your exams.

(10) Joe quit because his boss was giving him so much grief.

VALIDITY, TRUTH, AND SOUNDNESS

Not all arguments are good arguments, so, having identified an argument, the next task is to *evaluate* it. Evaluating arguments is a complex business, and, in fact, this entire book is aimed primarily at developing procedures for doing so. There are, however, certain fundamental terms used in evaluating arguments that should be introduced from the start. They are validity, truth, and soundness. Here they will be introduced informally; later (in Chapters 5–7) they will be examined with more rigor.

VALIDITY

Validity is a technical notion, but it closely matches the commonsense idea of a conclusion *following from* its premises. To say that a conclusion follows from its premises means that the conclusion must be true if the premises are true. We will take this to be our definition of validity: *an argument is valid if and only if it is not possible for all of the premises to be true and the conclusion false.* The following argument passes this test for validity:

> All senators are paid.
> Sam Nunn is a senator.
> ∴ Sam Nunn is paid.

If the two premises are true, then the conclusion has to be true as well. Contrast this with a different argument:

> All senators are paid.
> Sam Nunn is paid.
> ∴ Sam Nunn is a senator.

Here the premises and the conclusion are all in fact true, but that is not enough to make the argument valid, because validity concerns what is possible. This conclusion *could* be false even when these premises are true, since Sam Nunn *could* leave the Senate but still be paid for some other job. That possibility is enough to make this argument invalid.

Given our definition of validity, it should be clear why validity is valuable: there can be no valid arguments that lead us from true premises to a false conclusion. This should square with your commonsense ideas about reasoning: if you reason well, you should not be led from truth into error. This makes validity one criterion for a good *deductive* argument, since deductive arguments are put forward as meeting this standard. Other arguments—*inductive* arguments—are not intended to meet this rigorous standard. Roughly, an inductive argument is intended to provide strong support for its conclusion. The criteria for evaluating inductive arguments will be examined in Chapter 8. For now we will concentrate solely on deductive arguments.

TRUTH

Although a deductive argument must be valid in order to be a good argument, validity is not enough. One reason is that an argument can be valid even when some (or all) of the statements it contains are false. For example:

> All clowns are from Tennessee.
> Sam Nunn is a clown.
> ∴ Sam Nunn is from Tennessee.

This is a bad argument, because both of its premises are false. Nonetheless, this argument does satisfy our definition of validity: if all of the premises were true, then the conclusion could not be false. This makes it obvious that validity is not the same as truth. It also makes it obvious that another requirement of a good argument is that *all of its premises must be true.*

SOUNDNESS

We thus make at least two demands of a deductive argument that we will accept as proving its conclusion:

(1) The argument must be valid.

(2) The premises must be true.

When an argument meets both these standards, it is said to be *sound.* If it fails to meet either one, it is *unsound.* Thus, an argument is unsound if it is invalid, and it is also unsound if at least one of its premises is false.

	All Premises True	At Least One False Premise
Valid	Sound	Unsound
Invalid	Unsound	Unsound

Soundness has one great benefit: a sound argument must have a true conclusion. We know this because its premises are true, and because it is valid, it is not possible that its premises are true and its conclusion is false. This is why people who seek truth want sound arguments.

EXERCISE II

Indicate whether each of the following statements is an argument and, if so, whether it is valid and whether it is sound. Explain your answers where necessary.

(1) Charles Holmes went bald, and most men go bald.

(2) Charles Holmes went bald because most men go bald.

(3) Most professors agree that they are paid too little, so they are.

(4) Republicans agree that the Contract with America will work, and it will.

(5) If this school were at the South Pole, I'd be at the South Pole. But I'm not at the South Pole. Therefore, this school is not at the South Pole.

(6) There can't be a largest six-digit number, because six-digit numbers are numbers, and there is no largest number.

(7) Lee can't run a company right, since he can't do anything right.

(8) David Letterman is over five feet tall, so he is over two feet tall.

(9) Since Clinton is president, he must have won the election.

EXERCISE III

Assume that the truth-value assignments given to the right of each statement are correct.

(1) All dogs are animals. (T)

(2) All animals have hearts. (T)

(3) All animals are dogs. (F)

(4) All dogs have hearts. (T)

Using these assigned values, label each of the following arguments as (i) either valid or invalid and (ii) either sound or unsound.

(a) All dogs are animals.
   All animals have hearts.
∴ All dogs have hearts.

(b) All dogs have hearts.
   All animals have hearts.
∴ All dogs are animals.

(c) All animals are dogs.
   All dogs have hearts.
∴ All animals have hearts.

(d) All animals have hearts.
   All dogs have hearts.
∴ All dogs have hearts.

EXERCISE IV

Using this set of statements and assigned truth values,

(1) All talented people are insightful. (T)

(2) All talented people are ugly. (F)

(3) All seniors are ugly. (F)

(4) All seniors are talented. (F)

(5) All ugly people are insightful. (T)

(6) All seniors are insightful. (F)

(7) All ugly people are seniors. (F)

construct arguments with two premises and a conclusion such that:

(a) The argument is valid, but all the premises are false, and the conclusion is false as well.

(b) The argument is valid, both premises are false, and the conclusion is true.

(c) The argument is valid, one premise is true, one premise is false, and the conclusion is true.

(d) The argument is valid, one premise is true, one premise is false, and the conclusion is false.

EXERCISE V

Indicate whether each of the following sentences is true. For those that are true, explain why they are true. For those that are false, show why they are false by giving an example.

(1) Every argument with a false conclusion is invalid.

(2) Every argument with a false premise is invalid.

(3) Every argument with a false premise and a false conclusion is invalid.

(4) Every argument with a false premise and a true conclusion is invalid.

(5) Every argument with true premises and a false conclusion is invalid.

(6) Every argument with a true conclusion is sound.

(7) Every argument with a false conclusion is unsound.

A PROBLEM AND SOME SOLUTIONS

Although soundness guarantees a true conclusion, we usually expect even more from an argument than soundness. In the first place, an argument can be sound, but trivially uninteresting:

> Nigeria is in Africa.
> ∴ Nigeria is in Africa.

Here the premise is true. The argument is also valid, because the premise cannot be true without the conclusion (which repeats it) being true as well. Yet the argument is completely worthless as a proof that Nigeria is in Africa. The reason is that this argument is *circular*. We will examine circular arguments in detail in Chapter 10, but it is obvious why such arguments are useless. If *A* is trying to prove something to *B* that *B* has doubts about, then citing the very matter in question will not do any good. In general, for *A* to convince *B*, *A* must marshal facts that *B* accepts and then show that they justify the claim at issue. In circular arguments, the doubt about the conclusion immediately turns into a doubt about the premise as well.

Now, however, *A* seems to run into a problem. *A* cannot cite a proposition as a reason for *itself*, for that would be circular reasoning. If, however, *A* cites some *other* propositions as premises leading to the conclusion he is trying to establish, the question naturally arises why these premises should be accepted. Does *A* not have to present arguments for them as well? Yet if *A* does that, *A* will introduce further premises that are also in need of proof, and so on indefinitely. It now looks as if every argument, to be successful, will have to be infinitely long.

The answer to this ancient problem depends on the activity of arguing or presenting reasons relying on a shared set of beliefs, and on a certain amount of trust. When we present reasons, we try to cite these shared beliefs—things that will not *in fact* be challenged. Beyond this, we expect people to believe us when we cite information that only we possess. But there are limits to this, for people do believe things that are false and sometimes lie about what they know to be true. This presents a practical problem: how can we present our reasons in a way that does not produce just another demand for an argument—a demand for more reasons? Here we use three main strategies:

(1) *Assuring*: Indicating that there are backup reasons even though we are not giving them right now.

(2) *Guarding*: Weakening our claims so that they are less subject to attack.

(3) *Discounting*: Anticipating criticisms and dismissing them.

In these ways we build a defensive perimeter around our premises. Each of these defenses is useful, but each can also be abused.

ASSURING

When will we want to give assurances about some statement we have made? If we state something that we know everyone believes, assurances are not necessary. For that matter, if everyone believes something, we may not even state it at all; we let others "fill in" this step in the argument. We offer assurances when we think that someone might doubt or challenge what we say.

There are many ways to give assurances. Sometimes we cite authorities:

Doctors agree . . .

Recent studies have shown . . .

An unimpeachable source close to the White House says . . .

It has been established that . . .

Here we do not actually give reasons. We merely indicate that good reasons do exist, even if we ourselves do not produce them. When the authority cited can be trusted, this is often sufficient, but authorities often can and should be questioned. This topic will be discussed more fully in Chapter 10. Another way to give assurances is to comment on the strength of our own belief:

I'm certain that . . .

I'm sure that . . .

I can assure you that . . .

Over the years, I have become more and more convinced that . . .

Again, when we use these expressions, we do not actually present reasons, but we conversationally imply that there are reasons that back our assertions. A third kind of assurance abuses the audience:

Everyone with any sense agrees that . . .

Of course, no one will deny that . . .

It is just common sense that . . .

There is no question that . . .

Nobody but a fool would deny that . . .

These assurances not only do not give any reason, they also suggest that there is something wrong with you if you ask for a reason. We call this the *trick of abusive assurances.*

Just as we can give assurances that something is true, we can also give assurances that something is false. For example:

It is no longer held that . . .

It is wholly implausible to suppose that . . .

No one seriously maintains that . . .

You would have to be pretty dumb to think that . . .

The last two examples clearly involve abusive assurances.

Although many assurances are legitimate, we as critics should always view assurances with some suspicion. Following the conversational rule of Quality, we should expect people to give assurances only when they have good reasons to do so. Yet assuring remarks often mark the weakest parts of the argument, not the strongest parts. If someone says "I hardly need argue that . . . ," it is often useful to ask why she has gone to the trouble of saying it. In particular, when we distrust an argument—as we sometimes do—this is precisely the place to look for weakness. If assurances are used, they are used for some reason. Sometimes the reason is a good one. Sometimes, however, it is a bad one. In honest argumentation, assurances save time and simplify discussion. In a dishonest argument, they are used to paper over cracks.

GUARDING

Guarding represents a different strategy for protecting premises from attack. We reduce our claim to something less strong. Thus, instead of saying "all," we say "many." Instead of saying something straight out, we use a qualifying phrase such as "it is likely that . . . " or "it is very possible that. . . ." Law school professors like the phrase "it is arguable that. . . ." This is wonderfully noncommittal, for it does not indicate how strong the argument is, yet it does get the statement into the argument.

Broadly speaking, there are three ways of guarding what we say:

(1) Weakening the *extent* of what has been said: retreating from "all" to "most" to "a few" to "some," and so on.

(2) Using *probability* phrases such as "it is virtually certain that . . . ," "it is likely that . . . ," and so on.

(3) Describing our *cognitive* state: moving from "I know that . . . " to "I believe that . . . " to "I tend to believe that . . . ," and so on.

These guarding phrases are often legitimate and useful. If you want to argue that a friend needs fire insurance for her house, you do not need to claim that her house *will* burn down. All you need to claim is that there is a significant *chance* that her house will burn down. Your argument is better if you start with this weaker premise, because it is easier to defend, and it is enough to support your conclusion.

If we weaken a claim sufficiently, we can make it completely immune to criticism. What can be said against a remark of the following kind: "There is some small chance that perhaps a few politicians are honest on at least some occasions"? You would have to have a *very* low opinion of politicians to deny this statement. On the other hand, if we weaken a premise too much, we pay a price. The premise no longer gives strong support to the conclusion.

The goal in using guarding terms is to find a *middle way*: We should weaken our premises sufficiently to avoid criticism, but not weaken them so much that they no longer provide strong enough evidence for the conclusion. Balancing these factors is one of the most important strategies in making and criticizing arguments.

Just as it was useful to zero in on assuring terms, it is useful to keep track of guarding terms. Guarding terms are easily corrupted. One common trick is to use guarding terms to *insinuate* things that cannot be stated explicitly in a conversation.

Consider the effect of the following remark: "Perhaps the secretary of state has not been candid with the Congress." This does not actually say that the secretary of state has been less than candid with the Congress, but, by the rule of Relevance, clearly suggests it. Furthermore, it suggests it in a way that is hard to combat.

A more subtle device for corrupting guarding terms is to introduce a statement in a guarded form and then go on to speak as if it were not guarded at all.

> Perhaps the secretary of state has not been candid with the Congress. Of course, he has a right to his own views, but this is a democracy where officials are accountable to Congress. So even the secretary of state cannot escape justice.

The force of the guarding term "perhaps" that begins this passage disappears at the end.

What is commonly called *hedging* is a sly device that operates in the opposite direction from our last example. With hedging, one shifts ground from a strong commitment to something weaker. Things, as they say, get "watered down" or "taken back." Strong statements made at one stage of an argument are later weakened without any acknowledgement that the position has thereby been changed in a significant way. A promise to *pass* a piece of legislation is later whittled down to a promise to *bring it to a vote*.

DISCOUNTING

The general pattern of discounting is to cite a possible criticism in order to reject it or counter it. Notice how different the following statements sound:

> The ring is beautiful, but expensive.

> The ring is expensive, but beautiful.

Both statements assert the same facts—that the ring is beautiful and that the ring is expensive. Both statements also suggest that there is some opposition between these facts. Yet these statements operate in different ways. We might use the first as a reason for *not* buying the ring; we can use the second as a reason *for* buying it. The first sentence acknowledges that the ring is beautiful, but overrides this by pointing out that it is expensive. In reverse fashion, the second statement acknowledges that the ring is expensive, but overrides this by pointing out that it is beautiful. Such assertions of the form "*A* but *B*" thus have four components:

(1) The assertion of *A*

(2) The assertion of *B*

(3) The suggestion of some opposition between *A* and *B*

(4) The indication that the truth of *B* is more important than the truth of *A*

The word "but" thus discounts the statement that comes before it in favor of the statement that follows it.

"Although" is also a discounting connective, but it operates in reverse fashion from the word "but." We can see this using the same example:

Although the ring is beautiful, it is expensive.

Although the ring is expensive, it is beautiful.

Here the statement following the word "although" is discounted in favor of the connected statement. A partial list of terms that function as discounting connectives includes the following conjunctions:

although	but
though	however
even if	nonetheless
still	nevertheless
	yet

The clearest cases of discounting occur when we are dealing with facts that point in different directions. We discount the facts that go against the position we wish to take. Discounting is, however, often more subtle than this. We sometimes use discounting to block certain conversational implications of what we have said. This comes out in examples of the following kind:

Jones is an aggressive player, but he is not dirty.

The situation is difficult, but not hopeless.

The Republicans have the upper hand in Congress, but only for the time being.

A truce has been declared, but who knows for how long?

Take the first example. There is no opposition between Jones being aggressive and his not being dirty. Both would be reasons to pick Jones for our team. However, the assertion that Jones is aggressive might *suggest* that he is dirty. The "but" clause discounts this suggestion without, of course, denying that Jones is aggressive.

The nuances of discounting terms can be subtle, and a correct analysis is not always easy. All the same, the role of discounting terms is often important. It can be effective in an argument to beat your opponents to the punch by anticipating and discounting criticisms before your opponents can raise them. The proper use of discounting can also help you avoid side issues and tangents.

But discounting terms, like the other argumentative terms we have examined, can be abused. People often spend time discounting weak objections to their views in order to avoid other objections that they know are harder to counter. Another common trick is *discounting straw men*. Consider the following remark: "A new building would be great, but it won't be free." This does not actually say that the speaker's opponents think we can build a new building for free, but it does conversationally imply that they think this, since otherwise it would be irrelevant to discount that objection. The speaker is thus trying to make the opponents look bad by putting words into their mouths—words they would never say themselves. In order to counter tricks like this, we need to ask whether a discounted criticism is one that really would be raised, and whether there are stronger criticisms that should be raised.

ARGUMENTATIVE PERFORMATIVES

We have looked at many acts that are performed in arguments. Speakers can draw conclusions, give reasons, assure, guard, and discount. Since these are speech acts, it should come as no surprise that many of these acts can also be done by explicit performatives that pass the thereby test:

> If I say "I conclude that such and such," I thereby conclude that such and such.
>
> If I say "I base my argument on the claim that such and such," I thereby base my argument on that claim.
>
> If I say "I assure you that he will meet you," I thereby assure you that he will meet you.[2]
>
> If I say "I give my qualified support to this measure," I thereby give my qualified support to this measure.

There are, in fact, a great many examples of performatives used for argumentative purposes. Here are a few more:

> If I say "I deny such and such," I thereby deny such and such.
>
> If I say "I reply that such and such," I thereby reply that such and such.
>
> If I say "I concede the point," I thereby concede the point.
>
> If I say "I stipulate that such and such," I thereby stipulate that such and such.

When a performative is used to make a move in an argument, we call it an *argumentative performative*. As with other performatives, it is inappropriate to deny such utterances. If a lawyer finishes his speech to the jury by saying "I conclude that the evidence merits acquittal," it would be ridiculous for someone to say "No you don't!" We may disagree that the evidence merits acquittal, but we cannot disagree that the lawyer has drawn this conclusion.

We can also make these argumentative moves in other ways. Instead of saying "I deny that," we can say "That's not so," "No way," or "Oh, yeah?" Since there are so many ways to make each move, why do we have argumentative performatives at all? Part of the answer is that argumentative performatives make our argumentative moves explicit. If I want to make it perfectly clear *that* I am disagreeing and also exactly what *part* of my opponent's argument I am disagreeing with, I can do this by saying "I deny that. . . ." We usually reserve argumentative performatives for the *important* parts of opposing arguments.

Performatives also allow *subtle* moves to be made in the course of an argument. Sometimes an arguer will say "I grant the point for the sake of argument" (thereby granting the point for the sake of argument). This is a powerful move if it can be carried off, for nothing is better than refuting an opponent on his own grounds. This device also contains an escape hatch, for if our efforts go badly, we can still

---

[2] This is a tricky case, because, even though I assured you, you still might not *feel* assured.

challenge the statement previously granted just for the sake of argument. Somewhat differently, we can say "I reserve comment" (thereby reserving comment). Here we neither reject nor accept a claim (even for the sake of argument). We let it pass until we see what is made of it. This is a useful tactical device. By reserving comment we can avoid being drawn into irrelevant discussions that will cloud the issue. At other times we do not know what we want to say in response to a particular point or we are not quite sure what the person is going to make of it. Reserving comment is a way of not sticking our necks out prematurely. Argumentative performatives are, then, powerful and subtle tools for making different kinds of moves in an argument.

EXERCISE VI

For each of the numbered words or expressions in the following sentences, indicate whether it is a warranting connective, an assuring term, a guarding term, a discounting term, an argumentative performative, or none of these. For each warranting connective, specify what the conclusion and the reasons are, and for each discounting term, specify what criticism is being discounted and what the response to this criticism is.

(1) *Although* [1] no mechanism has been discovered, *most* [2] *researchers in the field agree* [3] that smoking *greatly increases the chances* [4] of heart disease.

(2) *Since* [5] *historically* [6] public debt leads to inflation, *I maintain* [7] that, *despite* [8] recent trends, inflation will return.

(3) *Take it from me* [9], there hasn't been a decent center fielder *since* [10] Joe DiMaggio.

(4) *Whatever anyone tells you* [11], there is *little* [12] to the rumor that Queen Elizabeth will step down *for* [13] her son Prince Charles.

(5) The early deaths of Janis Joplin and Jimi Hendrix *show* [14] how *really* [15] dangerous drugs are.

(6) I *think* [16] he is out back somewhere.

(7) I *think* [17], *therefore* [18] I am.

(8) I *concede that* [19] the evidence is *hopelessly* [20] weak, *but* [21] I still think he is guilty.

(9) I *deny* [22] that I had *anything* [23] to do with it.

(10) The wind has shifted to the northeast, *which means* [24] that snow is *likely* [25].

EXERCISE VII

(1) Construct three new and interesting examples of statements containing assuring terms.

(2) Do the same for guarding terms.

(3) Do the same for argumentative performatives.

(4) Do the same for discounting terms, and indicate which statement is being discounted in favor of the other.

(5) Do the same for warranting connectives, and indicate what is presented as a reason for what.

EVALUATIVE LANGUAGE

Although many words in our language are neutral, others have a positive or negative force. They are used not just to describe but to *evaluate* things positively or negatively. The clearest cases of evaluative language occur when we say something is *good* or *bad*, that some course of action is *right* or *wrong*, or that it *should* or *should not* (or *ought* or *ought not to*) be done. The meaning of such evaluative terms as "good" and "bad" is controversial, but one theory is that to evaluate something as good is to say that it meets relevant standards. This is fairly empty until the standards are specified, but that is because the word "good" is applied to many different subjects, and the context determines which standards are relevant. When we say that Hondas are good cars, we are probably applying standards that involve reliability, efficiency, comfort, and so on. To call someone a good firefighter means that that person is skilled at the tasks of a firefighter, is motivated to perform the tasks, works well with other firefighters, and so on.

As the above examples show, different kinds of standards govern different areas. We speak of aesthetic values, economic values, personal values, religious values, and, of course, moral values. All these kinds of values have associated with them standards for evaluation. These different standards of evaluation relate to one another in complex ways: they sometimes support each other; they sometimes conflict. Religious values and moral values often support each other. To cite an extreme example of a possible conflict: given the huge amount of pollution that human beings produce, it might, from an ecological standpoint, be a good thing to wipe out half the world's human population. Yet virtually everyone would agree that from a moral perspective this would be a profoundly wrong thing to do.

Because they invoke standards, evaluative statements stand in contrast to utterances that *merely express* personal feelings. If I say that I like a particular singer, then I am expressing a personal taste, one that I might realize others do not share. Unless I were being accused of lying or being self-deceived, it would normally be odd for someone to reply "Oh no you don't." Generally, people have a good idea about what they like or dislike. On the other hand, if I call someone a good singer (or a great singer or the best singer in years), then I am going beyond expressing my personal tastes. I am saying something that others may accept or reject. Of course, the standards for judging singers may be imprecise, and they may shift from culture to culture. Still, to call someone a good singer is to evaluate that person as a singer. This involves invoking standards and indicating that the person in question meets them.

The words "good" and "bad" are perfectly general evaluative terms in the sense that they can be applied to all sorts of things for all sorts of reasons. Other evaluative terms are more restrictive in their range of application. The word "delicious" is usually used for evaluating the taste of foods. It means "good tasting." A sin is a kind of wrong action, but, more specifically, it is an action that is wrong according to religious standards. A sin is something religiously wrong. An illegal action is one that is legally wrong. Words of this kind indicate that things are good or bad, right or wrong, and so forth, in certain specific ways. In fact, our language contains a great many such specific terms of evaluation. Here are some other examples:

beautiful	careful	cute
wasteful	sneaky	murderous
deceitful	prudent	snoopy
sloppy	honest	scuzzy

Each of these words expresses either a positive or a negative evaluation of a quite specific kind.

Positive and negative evaluations can be subtle. Consider a word such as "clever." It presents a positive evaluation in terms of quick mental ability. In contrast, "cunning" often presents a negative evaluation of someone for misusing mental abilities. It thus makes a difference which one of these words we choose. It also makes a difference where we apply them. When something is supposed to be profound and serious, it is insulting to call it merely clever. Prayers, for example, should not be clever.

Sometimes seemingly innocuous words can shift evaluative force. The word "too" is the perfect example of this. This word introduces a negative evaluation, sometimes turning a positive quality into a negative one. Compare the following sentences:

John is smart.	John is too smart.
John is honest.	John is too honest.
John is ambitious.	John is too ambitious.
John is nice.	John is too nice.
John is friendly.	John is too friendly.

The word "too" indicates an excess, and thereby contains a criticism. If you look at the items in the second column, you will see that the criticism is sometimes rather brutal—for example, calling someone "too friendly."

In analyzing arguments it is important to identify evaluative terms, for the strength of an argument often depends on whether these terms are used legitimately. This, however, can be a subtle task because the difference between an evaluative term and a descriptive term is not always obvious. To see this, consider the terms "homicide" and "murder." The words are closely related, but do not mean the same thing. "Homicide" is a descriptive term meaning "the killing of a human being." "Murder" is an evaluative term meaning, in part at least, "the *wrongful* killing of a human being." It takes more to show that something is a murder than it does to show that something is a homicide. The test for an evaluative term is this: does the word mean that something is good or bad (right or wrong) in a particular way?

Just as it is easy to miss evaluative terms because we fail to recognize the evaluative component built into their meanings, it is also possible to take a word as evaluative that is not because of positive or negative associations that the term might evoke. The word "nuclear," for example, has bad connotations surrounding it because of its association with bombs and wars, but the word itself is purely descriptive. To call someone a nuclear scientist is not to say that she is bad in a certain way. Similarly, although most people think that biological warfare would be a very bad thing, this does not mean that the term "biological" is an evaluative term.

Words such as "good," "bad," "right," and "wrong" commonly occur in *moral* or *ethical* judgments. Not all uses of these words are moral, for we can speak about a good pipe wrench or a wrong turn, and in such cases we are not making moral judgments. Moral judgments are, however, a centrally important kind of evaluative judgment. They are used often in daily life and a great many arguments concern them. In fact, arguments over moral questions may be both the most common and the most important kind of argument that human beings engage in. What then makes a judgment a moral judgment? Moral judgments are judgments that invoke moral standards. Saying this does not take us very far, for we now want to know what moral standards are and what determines which moral standards are correct. These are all difficult issues. We will return to them in Chapter 13, where we examine specifically moral arguments. The general point being made here is that in making an evaluative judgment of any kind, we are invoking standards. Thus, in general, if a person makes an evaluative claim (a value judgment), we have a right to ask him to specify the relevant standards and show that they apply.

EXERCISE VIII

Indicate whether the following italicized terms are positively evaluative (E+), negatively evaluative (E−), or simply descriptive (D). Remember, the evaluations need not be moral evaluations.

(1) Janet is an *excellent* golfer.

(2) The group was playing very *loudly*.

(3) The group was playing *too* loudly.

(4) William was *rude* to his parents.

(5) William *shouted* at his parents.

(6) They mistakenly turned *right* at the intersection.

(7) *Fascists* ruled Italy for almost twenty years.

(8) That's a *no-no*.

(9) Today is a day that will live in *infamy*.

(10) Debbie *lied*.

(11) Debbie *said something false*.

(12) Joe *copped out*.

(13) Jake is a *bully*.

(14) Mary Lou was a *gold medalist*.

(15) The course was a *gut*.

(16) They are pursuing a program of *genocide*.

(17) Debbie *bogeyed* the first hole.

(18) Nothing succeeds like *success*.

(19) He suffered from a hormonal *imbalance*.

(20) Enough is *enough*.

EXERCISE IX

For each of the following sentences, construct two others—one that reverses the evaluative force and one that is as neutral as possible. The symbol "0" stands for neutral, "+" for positive evaluative force, and "−" for negative evaluative force.

Example: − Professor Conrad is rude.

+ Professor Conrad is uncompromisingly honest in his criticisms.

0 Professor Conrad often upsets people with his criticisms.

(1) − Martin is a lazy lout.

(2) + Brenda is vivacious.

(3) + John is a natural leader.

(4) + Selby is a methodical worker.

(5) − Marsha is a snob.

(6) + Clara is imaginative.

(7) − Bartlett is a buffoon.

(8) − Wayne is a goody-goody

(9) − Sidney talks incessantly.

(10) − Dudley is a weenie.

(11) ? Floyd is a hot dog. (Decide whether this is + or −.)

(12) + Martha is liberated.

(13) + Ralph is sensitive.

(14) + Betty is a fierce competitor.

(15) – Psychology is a trendy department.

(16) – This is a Mickey Mouse exercise.

PERSUASIVE DEFINITIONS

Slanting involves the improper use of language to place something in a good or bad light without adequate justification. Slanting can take place in a variety of ways. Facts can be suppressed or distorted. As we have noted, evaluative terms can be used without adequate justification.

A particularly subtle form of slanting involves the use of a definition to gain an argumentative advantage. Charles L. Stevenson calls such definitions "persuasive definitions."[3] The pattern looks like this:

Something to be criticized	Definitional link	Something considered bad

Here is an example that uses this pattern:

> Admissions quotas that favor minorities are nothing more than reverse discrimination.

Since discrimination is usually thought to be something bad, a person will have a hard time making a case for minority quotas if he is trapped into accepting "reverse discrimination" as a defining characteristic of a system of minority quotas. On the other side, defenders of admissions quotas tend to call them "affirmative action." This is a persuasive definition in the other direction: it associates something to be praised with something good. Sometimes these definitions are crude and heavy-handed; for example:

> Capital punishment is institutionalized murder.

Since murder is, by definition, a wrongful act of killing, this definition assumes the very point at issue: that capital punishment is wrong. At other times the argumentative move can be quite subtle; for example:

> Abortion is the killing of an unborn baby.

At first sight, this definition may seem neutral. It does not contain any obviously evaluative word like "murder." All the same, one of the central issues in the debate over abortion is whether a human fetus is already a person. Since most people agree that a baby is a person, calling a fetus a baby involves putting forward a controversial thesis. (See Chapter 13.) This, however, is a matter to be established

---

[3] Charles L. Stevenson, "Persuasive Definitions," *Mind* 47, 187 (July 1938), 331–350.

by argument, not by definition. In general we have a right to be suspicious of any-one who tries to gain an argumentative advantage through an appeal to definitions. Confronted with a definition in the midst of an argument, we should always ask whether the definition clarifies the issues or merely slants them.

EXERCISE X

For each of the following persuasive definitions, indicate who would use it and why:

(1) Stinginess is charity at home.

(2) Communism is true democracy.

(3) Communism is fascism without property.

(4) "The better part of valor is discretion." (Falstaff in Shakespeare, *Henry IV, Part I*, 5.4.119.)

(5) A liberal is someone who raises taxes.

(6) A conservative is someone who does not care about the poor.

EUPHEMISM AND SPIN DOCTORING

There are many other ways in which language can be used to gain argumentative advantage through either associating something with or disassociating something from other things that are viewed either positively or negatively. With euphemism, for example, we attempt to substitute a delicate, inoffensive, or even positive term for one that in some way carries negative connotations. The standard example is the use of such words as "bathroom," "restroom," "lavatory," and "Gents" as euphemisms for the word "toilet"; "toilet" itself was at one time an elegant, French-sounding euphemism. Euphemisms tend to get replaced by other euphemisms. Countries that were at one time called *primitive* or *backward* were then called *underdeveloped*, then *developing*, then *newly emerging* nations. People who at one time were called *crippled* were referred to as *handicapped*, then as *physically challenged*.

Euphemisms are often used simply to be polite or considerate. Saying that someone *has passed away* or *is no longer with us* is certainly gentler than the alternative of bluntly saying the person *has died* or, worse yet, *croaked*. Euphemism can, however, also be used to cover things up—such as, for example, when *concealment* and *evasion* are referred to as *damage control*. Here are some other examples:

Being *ruthless* is referred to as *playing hardball* (the old national pastime).

A *death in a hospital* is called a *negative patient-care outcome*.

New taxes are called *revenue enhancements*.

Chickens that are *frozen solid* are labeled *hard chilled*.

Genocide is called *ethnic cleansing*.

We should always be suspicious of euphemisms that serve the speaker's own purposes.

The expression "spin doctor" seems to combine two metaphors. The first concerns putting the right spin on things—that is, presenting things in ways that make them look good or bad, depending on what you are up to. A spin doctor is one who doctors things up in order to accomplish this. Spin doctoring often involves trying to find the right way of describing or labeling something. To take a fictitious example, suppose Congress was considering sharp cuts in Social Security benefits for the elderly. Supporters of such a measure might refer to it as the "Senior Citizen's Self-Reliance Act." To cite an actual example, when discussing a measure that would repeal a large number of environmental regulations, President Clinton sarcastically referred to it as the "Polluter's Bill of Rights"—not exactly a generous way of describing a bill based on the belief that environmental regulations had gone too far. The Republican "Contract with America" has entries entitled "The American Dream Restoration Act" and "The Common Sense Legal Reforms Act." These are things it is hard to be against, but it is also hard to tell from these titles what the acts are all about. The first entry concerns, among other things, giving a five-hundred-dollar-per-child tax credit; the second act is primarily intended "to place reasonable limits on punitive damages, and reform product liability laws." The dream that is going to be restored is fairly modest, and just about any legal reform can be called a *common sense* legal reform.

Slogans often come in pairs, reflecting opposing sides of an issue. Here are four contrasting pairs that have gotten considerable play in the contemporary scene:

Pro-Choice versus Pro-Life

Progressive Education versus Back to Fundamentals

Liberal versus Conservative

Alternative Lifestyles versus Family Values

The task of critical analysis is to see through such sloganeering to the important issues that lie behind it.

EXERCISE XI

Be a spin doctor yourself by writing upbeat, good-sounding titles or descriptions for the following proposals. Remember, as a professional spin doctor you should be able to make things you personally despise sound good.

(1) Imposing a thousand-dollar fee on graduating seniors.

(2) Requiring all students to participate in a twenty-one-meal-per-week food plan.

(3) Abolishing coed dormitories.

(4) Abolishing fraternities.

(5) Requiring women students to return to their dormitories by midnight. (Such rules were once quite common.)

(6) Abolishing failing grades.

(7) Restoring failing grades.

(8) Requiring four years of physical education.

(9) Abolishing intercollegiate football.

(10) Introducing a core curriculum in Western civilization.

(11) Abolishing such a curriculum.

(12) Abolishing faculty tenure.

EXERCISE XII

Listen to a talk show and collect at least five examples of people using rhetorical devices in either an utterly unfair or a just plain stupid way. (This will take less time than you think.)

DISCUSSION QUESTION

It is sometimes not clear whether certain terms are evaluative or have any negative connotations. One controversial area is the language used in talking about women. To take just one example, Robin Lakoff discusses the term "lady":[4]

> If, in a particular sentence, both *woman* and *lady* might be used, the use of the latter tends to trivialize the subject matter under discussion, often subtly ridiculing the woman involved. Thus, for example, a mention in the *San Francisco Chronicle* of January 31, 1972, of Madalyn Murray O'Hair as the "lady atheist" reduces her position to that of a scatterbrained eccentric, or at any rate, one who need not be taken seriously. Even *woman atheist* is scarcely defensible: first, because her sex is irrelevant to her philosophical position, and second, because her name makes it clear in any event. But *lady* makes matters still worse. Similarly a reference to a *woman sculptor* is only mildly annoying (since there is no term **male sculptor*, the discrepancy suggests that such activity is normal for a man but not for a woman), but still it could be used with reference to a serious artist. *Lady sculptor*, on the other hand, strikes me as a slur against the artist, deliberate or not, implying that the woman's art is frivolous,

---

[4] Robin Lakoff, *Language and Woman's Place* (New York: Harper & Row, 1975), 23–25. Lakoff follows a common practice in linguistics of putting an asterisk before any expression that is linguistically anomalous.

something she does to fend off the boredom of suburban housewifery, or at any rate, nothing of moment in the art world. Serious artists have shows, not *dilettantes*. So we hear of *one-woman shows*, but never *one-lady shows*.

Another realm of usage in which *lady* contrasts with *woman* is in titles of organizations. It seems that organizations of women who have a serious purpose (not merely that of spending time with one another) cannot use the word *lady* in their titles, but less serious ones may. Compare the *Ladies' Auxiliary* of a men's group, or the *Thursday Evening Ladies Browning and Garden Society*, with **Ladies' Lib* or **Ladies Strike for Peace*. . . .

Besides or possibly because of being explicitly devoid of sexual connotation, *lady* carries with it overtones recalling the age of chivalry: the exalted stature of the person so referred to, her existence above the common sphere. This makes the term seem polite at first, but we must also remember that these implications are perilous: they suggest that a "lady" is helpless, and cannot do things for herself. In this respect the use of a word like *lady* is parallel to the act of opening doors for women— or ladies. At first blush it is flattering: the object of the flattery feels honored, cherished and so forth; but by the same token, she is also considered helpless and not in control of her own destiny. Women who protest that they *like* receiving these little courtesies, and object to being liberated from them, should reflect a bit on their deeper meaning and see how much they like *that*.

Do you agree with Lakoff's claims about the connotations of the term "lady"? Why or why not? In your opinion, which other terms that are used to refer to women reflect a sexist bias in our society? Lakoff also discusses "mistress," "girl," "widow," "spinster," and, of course, "Mrs." (as opposed to "Ms."). You should also consider terms like "broad" and "chick."

Finally, you might want to collect a series of articles concerning women and see whether they reveal a sexist bias. One way to bring this matter into sharper focus is to compare the language used about a woman with the language used about a man in a similar context—for example, in a description of the individual's appointment to some high position. Pay attention not only to what is mentioned but also to what is left out, such as when a woman's spouse is mentioned but a man's spouse is not. ∎

FIGURATIVE LANGUAGE

People often use language in ways that violate conversational rules. Sometimes they do this with the intention to deceive—for example, when they lie or attempt to convey a false impression. In these cases, the speaker attempts to conceal her violation of a conversational rule. We saw in the previous chapter that someone who uses figurative language also violates conversational rules, but in a different way. In using figurative language, speakers want it to be mutually recognized that a conversational rule is being violated. The person who speaks ironically or metaphorically does not want to be taken for a liar or a fool.

When we examine arguments that occur in everyday life, we discover that they often contain language being used figuratively. Indeed, sometimes the whole force of an argument is carried by figurative language. Just as there is nothing inherently wrong with using evaluative language in arguments, there is nothing inherently wrong with employing figurative language in arguments. In both cases this way of speaking is legitimate, provided that a basis has been established for doing so.

When metaphors appear in poetry it is, perhaps, a mistake to attempt to replace them with more-literal statements. When metaphors appear in arguments, however, this is often precisely what we should do. If a metaphor draws an implicit comparison, we should try to make the comparison explicit. We can then ask a number of straightforward questions: How close is the comparison? Is the comparison, even if close, relevant to the present discussion? Does the comparison obscure other, more-relevant considerations? By asking such questions, we can analyze the metaphor (or unpack it) in order to assess its argumentative force.

Our general attitude to the occurrence of figurative language in argumentative contexts should be one of caution, not simply rejection. Figurative language can be a way of presenting an argument in a clear and forceful way. Figurative language cannot be a substitute for argument.

EXERCISE XIII

Unpack the following political metaphors by giving their literal content.

(1) Don't change horses in the middle of the stream.

(2) It's time for people on the welfare wagon to get off and help pull.

(3) If you can't stand the heat, get out of the kitchen.

(4) The clowns are running the circus.

(5) We need to restore a level playing field.

Chapter Three

THE ART OF CLOSE ANALYSIS

This chapter will be largely dedicated to a single purpose: the close and careful analysis of a speech drawn from the *Congressional Record*, using the argumentative devices introduced in Chapter 2. The point of this study is to show in detail how these methods of analysis can be applied to an actual argument of some richness and complexity.

It is now time to apply all of these notions to a genuine argument. Our example will be a debate that occurred in the House of Representatives on the question of whether there should be an increase in the allowance given to members of the House for clerical help—the so-called "clerk hire allowance." The argument against the increase presented by Representative Kyl (Republican, Iowa) will be examined in detail. We will put it under an analytic microscope.

The choice of this example may seem odd, for the question of clerk hire allowance is not one of the burning issues of our time. This, in fact, is one reason for choosing it. It will be useful to begin with an example about which feelings do not run high to learn the habit of objective analysis. Later on we shall examine arguments about which almost everyone has strong feelings and try to maintain an objective standpoint even there. The example is a good one for two other reasons: (1) it contains most of the argumentative devices we have listed, and (2) relatively speaking, it is quite a strong argument. This last remark may seem ironic after we seemingly tear the argument to shreds, but in comparison to other arguments we shall examine, it stands up well.

We can begin by reading through a section of the *Congressional Record*[1] without comment:

■ CLERK HIRE ALLOWANCE, HOUSE OF REPRESENTATIVES

Mr. FRIEDEL. Mr. Speaker, by direction of the Committee on House Administration, I call up the resolution (H. Res. 219) to increase the basic clerk hire allowance of each Member of the House, and for other purposes, and ask for its immediate consideration.

The Clerk read the resolution as follows:

Resolved, That effective April 1, 1961, there shall be paid out of the contingent fund of the House, until otherwise provided by law, such sums as may be necessary to increase the basic clerk hire allowance of each Member and the Resident Commissioner from Puerto Rico by an additional $3,000 per annum, and each such Member and Resident Commissioner shall be entitled to one clerk in addition to those to which he is otherwise entitled by law.

Mr. FRIEDEL. Mr. Speaker, this resolution allows an additional $3,000 per annum for clerk hire and an additional clerk for each Member of the House and the Resident Commissioner from Puerto Rico. Our subcommittee heard the testimony, and we were convinced of the need for this provision to be made. A few Members are paying out of their own pockets for additional clerk hire. This

---

[1] *Congressional Record*, vol. 107, part 3 (March 15, 1961), 4059–60.

$3,000 is the minimum amount we felt was necessary to help Members pay the expenses of running their offices. Of course, we know that the mail is not as heavy in some of the districts as it is in others, and, of course, if the Member does not use the money, it remains in the contingent fund.

Mr. KYL. Mr. Speaker, will the gentleman yield?

Mr. FRIEDEL. I yield to the gentleman from Iowa [Mr. KYL] for a statement.

Mr. KYL. Mr. Speaker, I oppose this measure. I oppose it first because it is expensive. I further oppose it because it is untimely.

I do not intend to belabor this first contention. We have been presented a budget of about $82 billion. We have had recommended to us a whole series of additional programs or extensions of programs for priming the pump, for depressed areas, for the needy, for unemployed, for river pollution projects, and recreation projects, aid to education, and many more. All are listed as "must" activities. These extensions are not within the budget. Furthermore, if business conditions are as deplorable as the newspapers indicate, the Government's income will not be as high as anticipated. It is not enough to say we are spending so much now, a little more will not hurt. What we spend, we will either have to recover in taxes, or add to the staggering national debt.

The amount of increase does not appear large. I trust, however, there is no one among us who would suggest that the addition of a clerk would not entail allowances for another desk, another typewriter, more materials, and it is not beyond the realm of possibility that the next step would then be a request for additional office space, and ultimately new buildings. Some will say, "All the Members will not use their maximum, so the cost will not be great." And this is true. If the exceptions are sufficient in number to constitute a valid argument, then there is no broad general need for this measure. Furthermore, some Members will use these additional funds to raise salaries. Competition will force all salaries upward in all offices and then on committee staffs, and so on. We may even find ourselves in a position of paying more money for fewer clerks and in a tighter bind on per person workload.

This measure proposes to increase the allowance from $17,500 base clerical allowance to $20,500 base salary allowance. No member of this House can tell us what this means in gross salary. That computation is almost impossible. Such a completely absurd system has developed through the years on salary computations for clerical hire that we have under discussion a mathematical monstrosity. We are usually told that the gross allowed is approximately $35,000. This is inaccurate. In one office the total might be less than $35,000 and in another, in complete compliance with the law and without any conscious padding, the amount may be in excess of $42,000. This is possible because of a weird set of formulae which determines that three clerks at $5,000 cost less than five clerks at $3,000. Five times three might total the same as three times five everywhere else in the world—but not in figuring clerk hire in the House.

This is an application of an absurdity. It is a violation of bookkeeping principles, accounting principles, business principles and a violation of commonsense. Listen to the formula:

First, 20 percent increase of first $1,200; 10 percent additional from $1,200 to $4,600; 5 percent further additional from $4,600 to $7,000.

Second, after applying the increases provided in paragraph 1, add an additional 14 percent or a flat $250 whichever is the greater, but this increase must not exceed 25 percent.

Third, after applying the increases provided in both paragraphs 1 and 2, add an additional increase of 10 percent in lieu of overtime.

Fourth, after applying the increases provided in paragraphs 1, 2, and 3, add an additional increase of $330.

Fifth, after applying the increases provided in paragraphs 1, 2, 3, and 4, add an additional increase of 5 percent.

Sixth, after applying the increases provided in paragraphs 1, 2, 3, 4, and 5, add an additional increase of 10 percent but not more than $800 nor less than $300 a year.

Seventh, after applying the increases provided in paragraphs, 1, 2, 3, 4, 5, and 6, add an additional increase of 7½ percent.

Eighth, after applying the increases provided in paragraphs, 1, 2, 3, 4, 5, 6, and 7, add an additional increase of 10 percent.

Ninth, after applying the increases provided in paragraphs 1, 2, 3, 4, 5, 6, 7, and 8, add an additional increase of 7½ percent.

The Disbursing Office has a set of tables to figure house salaries for office staffs and for about 900 other employees. It contains 45 sheets with 40 entries per sheet. In the Senate, at least, they have simplified the process some by figuring their base in multiples of 60, thus eliminating 11 categories. Committee staffers, incidentally, have an $8,880 base in comparison to the House $7,000 base limitation.

Now, Mr. Speaker, I have planned to introduce an amendment or a substitute which would grant additional clerk hire where there is a demonstrable need based on heavier than average population or "election at large" and possible other factors. But after becoming involved in this mathematical maze, I realize the folly of proceeding one step until we have corrected this situation. We can offer all kinds of excuses for avoiding a solution. We cannot offer reasonable arguments that it should not be done or that it cannot be done.

Someone has suggested that the Members of this great body prefer to keep the present program because someone back in the home district might object to the gross figures. I know this is not so. When a Representative is busy on minimum wage, or aid to education, or civil rights, such matters of housekeeping seem too picayune to merit attention. The Member simply checks the table and hires what he can hire under the provisions and then forgets the whole business. But I know the Members also want the people back home to realize that what we do here is open and frank and accurate, and that we set an example in businesslike procedures. The more we can demonstrate responsibility the greater will be the faith in Congress.

May I summarize. It is obvious that some Members need more clerical help because of large population and large land area. I have been working for some time with the best help we can get, on a measure which would take these items into consideration. Those Members who are really in need of assistance should realize that this temporary, hastily conceived proposition we debate today will probably obviate their getting a satisfactory total solution.

First, we should await redistricting of the Nation.

Second, we should consider appropriate allowance for oversize districts considering both population and total geographic area.

Finally, I hope we can develop a sound and sensible formula for computing salaries of office clerks and other statutory employees in the same category.

Before going any further, it will be useful to record your general reactions to this speech. Perhaps you think that on the whole Kyl gives a well-reasoned argument in behalf of his position. Alternatively, you might think that he is making a big fuss over nothing, trying to confuse people with numbers, and just generally being obnoxious. When you are finished examining this argument in detail, you can look back and ask yourself why you formed this original impression and how, if at all, you have changed your mind.

The first step in the close analysis of an argument is to go through the text, labeling the various argumentative devices we have examined. Here some abbreviations will be useful:

warranting connective	W
assuring term	A
guarding term	G
discounting term	D
argumentative performative	AP
evaluative term	E $(+ \ or \ -)$
rhetorical device	R

The last label is a catchall for the various rhetorical devices discussed in Chapter 1, such as rhetorical questions, irony, metaphor, and so on. There is no label for slanting, because the decision whether or not the use of evaluative terms amounts to slanting depends on the justification the writer provides for employing them. Often this decision can only be made after the entire argument is examined.

Even this simple process of labeling brings out features of an argument that could pass by unnoticed. It also directs us to ask sharp critical questions. To see this, we can look at each part of the argument in detail.

W ——— Mr. KYL. Mr. Speaker, I oppose this measure. I oppose it — AP
first because it is expensive. I further oppose it because it is — AP
untimely. — W

This is a model of clarity. By the use of a performative utterance in the opening sentence, Kyl makes it clear that he opposes the measure. Then by twice using the warranting connective "because," he gives his two main reasons for opposing it: *it is expensive* and *it is untimely*. We must now see if he makes good on each of these claims. This paragraph begins the argument for the claim that the measure is expensive:

> (I do not intend to belabor this first contention.) We have been — *A*
> presented a budget of about $82 billion. We have had recom-
> mended to us a whole series of additional programs or exten-
> sions of programs for priming the pump, for depressed areas,
> for the needy, for unemployed, for river pollution projects, and
> recreation projects, aid to education, and many more. All are — *R*
> listed as "must" activities. These extensions are not within the
> budget. (Furthermore), if business conditions are as deplorable — *W*
> as the newspapers indicate, the Government's income will not
> be as high as anticipated. (It is not enough to say) we are spend- — *D*
> ing so much now, a little more will not hurt. What we spend,
> we will either have to recover in taxes, or add to the stagger-
> ing national debt.

(a) "I do not intend to belabor this first contention. . . ." This is an example of *assuring*. The conversational implication is that the point is so obvious that little has to be said in its support. Yet there is something strange going on here. Having said that he will *not* belabor the claim that the bill is expensive, Kyl actually goes on to say quite a bit on the subject. It is a good idea to look closely when someone says that he or she is not going to do something, for often just the opposite is happening. For example, saying "I am not suggesting that Smith is dishonest" is one way of suggesting that Smith *is* dishonest. If no such suggestion is being made, why raise the issue at all?

(b) Kyl now proceeds in a rather flat way, stating that the proposed budget comes to $82 billion and that it contains many new programs and extensions of former programs. Since these are matters of public record and nobody is likely to deny them, there is no need for guarding or assuring. Kyl also claims, without qualification, that these extensions are not within the budget. This recital of facts does, however, carry an important conversational implication: Since the budget is already out of balance, any further extensions should be viewed with suspicion.

(c) Putting the word "must" in quotation marks, or saying it in a sarcastic tone of voice, is a common device for denying something. The plain suggestion is that some of these measures are *not* must activities at all. We see the same device in a more dramatic fashion when Marc Antony ironically repeats "Brutus is an honorable man." Anyway, Kyl here suggests that some of the items already in the budget are not necessary. He does this, of course, without defending this suggestion.

(d) "Furthermore, if business conditions are as deplorable as the newspapers indicate, the Government's income will not be as high as anticipated." The word "furthermore" suggests that an argument is about to come. However, the following sentence as a whole is an *indicative conditional* (with the word "then" dropped out). As such, the sentence does not produce an argument, but instead provides a pattern for an argument. To get an argument from this pattern, one would have to assert the antecedent of the conditional. The argument would then come to this:

(1) If business conditions are as deplorable as the newspapers indicate, then the Government's income will not be as high as anticipated.

(2) Business conditions are as deplorable as the newspapers indicate.

(3) Therefore, the Government's income will not be as high as anticipated.

The first premise seems like a perfectly reasonable conditional, so, if Kyl could establish the second premise, he would have moved the argument along in an important way. Yet he does not explicitly state that business conditions are so deplorable; all he says is that "the newspapers *indicate*" this. Still, he never questions what the newspapers claim, and it would be misleading to bring up these newspaper reports without questioning them if he thought they were way off the mark. So Kyl does seem to have in mind something like the argument (1)-(3).[2]

(e) "It is not enough to say we are spending so much now, a little more will not hurt." The opening phrase is, of course, used to deny what follows it. Kyl is plainly rejecting the argument that we are spending so much now, a little more will not hurt. Yet his argument has a peculiar twist, for who would come right out and make such an argument? If you stop to think for a minute, it should be clear that nobody would want to put it that way. An opponent, for example, would use quite different phrasing. He might say something like this: "Considering the large benefits that will flow from this measure, it is more than worth the small costs." What Kyl has done is to attribute a bad argument to his opponents and then reject it in an indignant tone. This is a common device, and when it is used, it is often useful to ask whether anyone would actually argue or speak in the way suggested. When the answer to this question is no, as it often is, we have what was called "the trick of discounting straw men" in Chapter 2. In such cases, it is useful to ask what the speaker's opponent would have said instead. This leads to a further question: Has the arguer even addressed himself to the *real* arguments of his opponents?

So far, Kyl has not addressed himself to the first main point of his argument: that the measure is *expensive*. This is not a criticism, because he is really making the preliminary point that the matter of expense is significant. Here he has stated some incontestable facts—for example, that the budget is already out of balance. Beyond this he has indicated, with varying degrees of strength, that the financial situation is grave. It is against this background that the detailed argument concerning the cost of the measure is actually presented in the next paragraph.

---

[2] This passage also contains a vague *appeal to authority*, since no specific newspaper is cited. We will discuss appeals to authority in Chapter 10.

D

The amount of increase does not appear large. (I trust,) — A

(however,)(there is no one among us who would suggest that)

the addition of a clerk would not entail allowances for anoth- — G

er desk, another typewriter, more materials, (and it is not

beyond the realm of possibility that)the next step would then

be a request for additional office space, and ultimately new

D

buildings.(Some will say), "All the Members will not use their

maximum, so the cost will not be great." And this is true. If

the exceptions are sufficient in number to constitute a valid

argument, then there is no broad general need for this mea-

W

sure.(Furthermore,)some Members will use these additional

funds to raise salaries. Competition will force all salaries

upward in all offices and then on committee staffs, and so on.

G

We (may even) find ourselves in a position of paying more

money for fewer clerks and in a tighter bind on per person

workload.

(a) "The amount of increase does not appear large." Words like "appear" and "seem" are sometimes used for guarding, but we must be careful not to apply labels in an unthinking way. The above sentence is the beginning of a *discounting* argument. As soon as you hear this sentence, you can feel that a word like "but" or "however" is about to appear. Sure enough, it does.

(b) "I trust, however, there is no one among us who would suggest that the addition of a clerk would not entail allowances for another desk, another typewriter, more materials. . . ." This is the beginning of Kyl's argument that is intended to rebut the argument that the increase in expenses will not be large. Appearances to the contrary, he is saying, the increase *will* be large. He then ticks off some additional expenses that are entailed by hiring new clerks. Notice that the whole sentence is covered by the assuring phrase: "I trust . . . there is no one among us who would suggest. . . ." This implies that anyone who would make such a suggestion is merely stupid. But the trouble with Kyl's argument so far is this: He has pointed out genuine additional expenses, but they are not, after all, very large. It is important for him to get some genuinely large sums of money into his argument. This is the point of his next remark.

(c) "And it is not beyond the realm of possibility that the next step would then be a request for additional office space, and ultimately new buildings." Here, at last, we have some genuinely large sums of money in the picture, but the difficulty is that the entire claim is totally guarded by the phrase "it is not beyond the realm of possibility." There are very few things that *are* beyond the realm of possibility. Kyl's problem, then, is this: There are certain additional expenses that he can point to without qualification, but these tend to be small. On the other hand, when he points out genuinely large expenses, he can only do so in a guarded way. So we are still waiting for a proof that the expense will be large. (Parenthetically, it should be pointed out that Kyl's prediction of new buildings actually came true.)

(d) "Some will say, 'All the Members will not use their maximum, so the cost will not be great.' And this is true. If the exceptions are sufficient in number to constitute a valid argument, then there is no broad general need for this measure." This looks like a "tricky" argument, and for this reason alone it demands close attention. The phrase "some will say" is a standard way of beginning a discounting argument. This *is*, in fact, a discounting argument, but its form is rather subtle. Kyl cites what some will say, and then adds, somewhat surprisingly: "And this is true." To understand what is going on here, we must have a good feel for conversational implication. Kyl imagines someone reasoning in the following way:

> All the Members will not use their maximum.
> So the cost will not be great.
> Therefore, since the measure will not be expensive, let's adopt it.

Given the same starting point, Kyl tries to derive just the *opposite* conclusion along the following lines:

> All the Members will not use their maximum.
> If very few use their maximum, then the cost will not be great.
> But if very few use their maximum, then there is no broad general need for this measure.
> Therefore, whether it is expensive or not, we should reject this measure.

In order to get clear about this argument, we can put it into schematic form:

Kyl's argument
If (1) expensive, then   → Reject
If (2) inexpensive, then, because that demonstrates no general need, → Reject

The opposite argument
If (1) inexpensive, then   → Accept
If (2) expensive, then, because that demonstrates a general need,   → Accept

When the arguments are spread out in this fashion, it should be clear that they have equal strength. Both are no good. The question that must be settled is this: Does a genuine need exist that can be met in an economically sound manner? If there is no need for the measure, then it should be rejected, however inexpensive. Again, if there is a need, then some expense is worth paying. The real problem is to balance need against expense and then to decide on this basis whether the measure as a whole is worth adopting. Kyl's argument is a *sophistry* because it has no tendency to answer the real question at hand. By "a sophistry" we mean a clever but fallacious argument intended to establish a point through trickery. Incidentally, it is one of the marks of a sophistical argument that, though it may baffle, it almost never convinces. I think that few readers will have found this argument persuasive even if they cannot say exactly what is wrong with it. The appearance of a sophistical argument (or even a complex and tangled argument) is a sign that the argument is weak. Remember, when a case is strong, people usually argue in a straightforward way.

(e) "Furthermore, some Members will use these additional funds to raise salaries. Competition will force all salaries upward in all offices and then on committee staffs, and so on." The word "furthermore" signals that further *reasons* are forthcoming. Here Kyl returns to the argument that the measure is more expensive than it might at first sight appear. Notice that he speaks here in an unqualified way: no guarding appears. Yet the critic is bound to ask whether Kyl has any right to make these projections. Beyond this, Kyl here projects a *parade of horrors*. He pictures this measure leading by gradual steps to quite disastrous consequences. Here the little phrase "and so on" carries a great burden in the argument. Once more, we must simply ask ourselves whether these projections seem reasonable.

(f) "We may even find ourselves in a position of paying more money for fewer clerks and in a tighter bind on per person workload." Once more, the use of a strong guarding expression takes back most of the force of the argument. Notice that if Kyl could have said straight out that the measure *will* put us in a position of paying more money for fewer clerks and in a tighter bind on per-person workload, that would have counted as a very strong objection. You can hardly do better in criticizing a position than showing that it will have just the opposite result from what is intended. In fact, however, Kyl has not established this; he has only said that this is something that we "may even find."

Before we turn to the second half of Kyl's argument, which we shall see in a moment is much stronger, we should point out that our analysis has not been entirely fair. Speaking before the House of Representatives, Kyl is in an *adversarial* situation. He is not trying to prove things for all time; rather, he is responding to a position held by others. Part of what he is doing is *raising objections*, and a sensitive evaluation of the argument demands a detailed understanding of the nuances of the debate. But even granting this, it should be remembered that objections themselves must be made for good reasons. The problem so far in Kyl's argument is that the major reasons behind his objections have constantly been guarded in a very strong way.

Turning now to the second part of Kyl's argument—that the measure is untimely—we see that he moves along in a clear and direct way with little guarding.

> This measure proposes to increase the allowance from $17,500 base clerical allowance to $20,500 base salary allowance. No member of this House can tell us what this means in gross salary. That computation is (almost) impossi- ―G ble. Such (a completely absurd system) has developed through ―E― the years on salary computations for clerical hire that we have under discussion a (mathematical monstrosity.) We are ―E―

usually told that the gross allowed is approximately $35,000. This is inaccurate. In one office the total might be less than $35,000 and in another, in complete compliance with the law and without any conscious padding, the amount may be in excess of $42,000. This is possible because of a weird set of formulae which determines that three clerks at $5,000 cost less than five clerks at $3,000. Five times three might total the same as three times five everywhere else in the world—but not in figuring clerk hire in the House.

    This is an application of an absurdity. It is a violation of bookkeeping principles, accounting principles, business principles and a violation of commonsense. Listen to the formula.

The main point of the argument is clear enough: Kyl is saying that the present system of clerk salary allowance is utterly confusing, and this matter should be straightened out before *any* other measures in this area are adopted. There is a great deal of negative evaluation in this passage. Notice the words and phrases that Kyl uses:

    a completely absurd system
    weird set of formulae
    violation of commonsense
    mathematical monstrosity
    an absurdity

There is also a dash of irony in the remark that five times three might total the same as three times five everywhere else in the world, but not in figuring clerk hire in the House. Remember, there is nothing wrong with using negative evaluative and expressive terms if they are deserved. We would only describe the use of such terms as *slanting* if they were used without adequate justification. Looking at the nine-step formula in Kyl's speech, you can decide for yourself whether Kyl is on strong grounds in using this negative language.

    Now, Mr. Speaker, I have planned to introduce an amendment or a substitute which would grant additional clerk hire where there is a demonstrable need based on heavier than average population or "election at large" and possible other factors.

    (a) This passage rejects any suggestion that Kyl is unaware that a genuine problem does exist in some districts. It also indicates that he is willing to do something about it.

    (b) The phrase "and possible other factors" is not very important, but it seems to be included to anticipate other reasons for clerk hire that should at least be considered.

D ——————————— (But) after becoming involved in this (mathematical maze,) I   E–

A ——————————— (realize) the (folly) of proceeding one step until we have corrected   E–

this situation.

(a) Here Kyl clearly states his reason for saying that the measure is untimely. Notice that the reason offered has been well documented and is not hedged in by qualifications.

(b) The phrases "mathematical maze" and "folly" are again negatively evaluative.

We can offer all kinds of (excuses) for avoiding a solution.   E–

(We cannot offer reasonable arguments that) it should not be   A

done or that it cannot be done.

(a) Notice that the first sentence ridicules the opponents' arguments by calling them *excuses*, a term with negative connotations. The second sentence gives assurances that such a solution can be found.

Someone has suggested that the Members of this great body

prefer to keep the present program because someone back in

the home district might object to the gross figures. (I know) this   A

is not so. When a Representative is busy on minimum wage,

or aid to education, or civil rights, such matters of housekeep-

ing seem too picayune to merit attention. The Member simply

checks the table and hires what he can hire under the provi-

D ——————— sions and then forgets the whole business. (But) (I know) the   A

Members also want the people back home to realize that what

we do here is (open and frank and accurate,) and that we set an   E+

example in businesslike procedures. The more we can demon-

strate responsibility the greater will be the faith in Congress.

(a) Once more the seas of rhetoric run high. Someone (though not Kyl himself) has suggested that the Members of the House wish to conceal information. He disavows the very thought that he would make such a suggestion by the sentence "I know this is not so." All the same, he has gotten this suggestion into the argument.

(b) Kyl then suggests another reason why the Members of the House will not be concerned with this measure: It is "too picayune." The last two sentences rebut the suggestion that it is too small to merit close attention. Even on small matters, the more the House is "open and frank and accurate," the more it will "set an example in businesslike procedures" and thus "demonstrate responsibility" that will increase "the faith in Congress." This is actually an important part of Kyl's argument, for presumably his main problem is to get the other Members of the House to take the matter seriously.

W ——
A ——
A ——
A ——

> May I summarize. (It is obvious that) some Members need ——— *A*
> more clerical help (because) of large population and large land
> area. (I have been working for some time with the best help)
> (we can get,) on a measure which would take these items into
> consideration. Those Members who are really in need of assis- ——— *E—*
> tance should (realize) that this (temporary, hastily conceived)
> proposition we debate today will (probably) obviate their get- ——— *G*
> ting a satisfactory total solution.

(a) This is a concise summary. Kyl once more assures the House that he is aware that a genuine problem exists. He also indicates that he is working on it.

(b) The phrase "temporary, hastily conceived proposition we debate today" refers back to his arguments concerning untimeliness.

(c) The claim that "it will probably obviate their getting a satisfactory total solution" refers back to the economic argument. Notice, however, that, as before, the economic claim is guarded by the word "probably."

E+ ——
E+ ——

> First, we (should) await redistricting of the Nation.
> Second, we (should) consider appropriate allowance for over-
> size districts considering both population and total geographic
> area.
> Finally, I hope we can develop a (sound and sensible) formula ——— *E+*
> for computing salaries of office clerks and other statutory
> employees in the same category.

This is straightforward except that a new factor is introduced: we should await re-districting of the nation. This was not mentioned earlier in the argument, and so seems a bit out of place in a summary. Perhaps the point is so obvious that it did not need any argument to support it. On the other hand, it is often useful to keep track of things that are smuggled into the argument at the very end. If redistricting was about to occur in the *near* future, this would give a strong reason for delaying action on the measure. Because the point is potentially so strong, we might wonder why Kyl has made so little of it. Here, perhaps, we are getting too subtle.

EXERCISE I

The following two passages are letters to the editor that argue for opposing positions on single-sex fraternities. In each case, read the whole passage first. Then, for each of the numbered expressions, either answer the corresponding question or label the main argumentative move, if any, using these abbreviations:

W = warranting term

A = assuring term

G = guarding term

D = discounting term

E– = negative evaluative term

E+ = positive evaluative term

N = none of the above

PASSAGE 1

The following letter to the editor appeared in the *New York Times* on June 16, 1985. The writer was the bishop's vicar for corporate affairs of the Episcopal Diocese of New York. The letter begins with a reference to an earlier article on fraternities by Fred M. Hechinger, but knowledge of that article is not necessary for understanding the Reverend Mr. Stemper's argument.

Fraternities, Where Men May Come to Terms with Other Men

To the Editor:

"The Fraternities Show Signs of New Strength," Fred M. Hechinger's analysis of the nature of college fraternities (*Science Times,* May 21) and the reason for their present growth, is *superficial* [1]. Apart from its *condescending* [2] tone, it *misses the point* [3].

College fraternities are growing today *because* [4] college curriculums are increasingly technical, preprofessional, competitive, and in *most* [5] instances *remote from the principal challenge of finding meaning in life* [6]. Their growth is *not unrelated to* [7] the rapid rise in teen age suicide: a pervasive sense that no one—*certainly* [8] no institution—*really* [9] cares for the nation's youth.

Local college fraternity chapters provide the only segment of the undergraduate's life he controls. *Thus* [10], it is *one of the few* [11] arenas open to creative expression in self-government, same-sex relationships, and forensic abilities apart from some *evaluatory scrutiny by thesis-grading, recommendation-writing members of college faculties and administrations* [12].

Within a fraternity, a student can live without *looking over his shoulder* [13]—*if, in fact, this is still possible in our society* [14]. If there is *occasional* [15] violence associated with initiations and *reprehensible* [16] treatment of women, the cause is much more deeply rooted in the materialism of our culture, which reduces "life" to "career."

In borrowing from older fraternal and classical *traditions* [17], modern college fraternities have provided in the 1980s symbolic structures within which men might come to terms with other men. *Far from "a return to a macho kind of adolescence tinged with elitist exclusivity,"* [18] nurturing, compassion and empathy are commonplace in the college fraternity—*sometimes* [19] for the first and last time in a man's life with other male friends.

Such vulnerabilities come hard for *most* [20] young men. A collegiate brotherhood provides the same shelter, in social terms, as a room of one's own provides, or a first automobile in adolescence. It is a symbol of self.

A *disturbing* [21] aspect of the article is the equation of college fraternities with antifeminism. Women have taught men in recent years the meaning of solidarity. A *genuine* [22] *tragedy* [23] of our times is that men's liberation movements were a casualty of the post-1960s era.

A man—and a male institution—*may* [24] affirm a feminist critique of society and still seek to *enrich* [25] male bonding. One *could* [26] argue that an objective of feminism is that men should get on with other men in more *constructive* [27] ways. Fraternities and fraternal orders are the only institutions in our society that have this objective as a primary and lasting goal. *For this reason alone* [28], *cynical superficiality* [29] should give way to *honest respect* [30].

(Rev.) William H. Stemper, Jr.
New York, May 24, 1985

Questions:

[1]–[8]: Write labels.

[9]: What is the force of "really" here?

[10]–[11]: Write labels.

[12]: Why does the author add this qualification?

[13]: What kind of rhetorical device is this?

[14]: What does this qualification conversationally imply?

[15]–[17]: Write labels.

[18]: What is the point of quoting Hechinger here?

[19]–[30]: Write labels.

PASSAGE 2

This letter to the editor appeared in the *Dartmouth* on September 23, 1992, although references to a specific college have been removed. The author was president of the student assembly and a member of a single-sex fraternity at the time.

Greeks Should Be Co-ed
by Andrew Beebe

For some time now, people have been asking the question "Why should the Greek [fraternity and sorority] system go co-ed?" To them, *I pose an answer* [1] in a question, "Why not?" [2]

Learning in college extends beyond the classrooms, onto the athletic fields, into the art studios, and into our social environs. [3] *In fact* [4], *some* [5] say that *most* [6] of what we learn at college comes from interaction with people and ideas during time spent outside of the lecture halls. The concept of segregating students in their social and residential environments by gender directly contradicts the *ideals of a college experience* [7]. This is *exactly* [8] what the fraternity and sorority system does.

With all the *benefits* [9] of a small, closely-bonded group, the potential for strong social education would seem *obvious* [10]. *But* [11] is it *fair* [12] for us to remove the other half of our community from that education? [13] In many colleges, this voluntary segregation exists in fraternities and sororities.

From the planning of a party or involvement in student activities to the sharing of living and recreational space, the fraternity and sorority system is a social environment *ripe* [14] with *educational potential* [15]. The idea that women and men would receive as complete an experience from these environments while *virtually* [16] separated is *implausible* [17].

But [18] what do women and men learn from one another that they don't already know? [19] Problems in gender relations between all ages *prove that* [20] our society is *plagued by gender-based prejudice* [21]. *Since* [22] *prejudice is the ignorance of one group by another* [23], it will best be addressed by education. The question *then* [24] becomes: Which way is best to educate one another?

Sexism, homophobia, date rape, eating disorders, and other social *problems* [25] are *often* [26] connected to gender-relation issues. As campus experience *shows* [27], we have a long way to go in combating these problems. Defenders of fraternities and sororities *may* [28] argue that they do not, solely by nature of being single sex, promote sexism or other prejudices. *But* [29], if we can recognize that these problems exist in our society, it is not important to find the blame, *but* [30] rather to offer a solution. It is *clear* [31] that separating people by gender is not the *right* [32] way to promote *better* [33] understanding between the sexes. To the contrary, bringing different people together is the only way prejudice, *no matter what the cause (or result) may be* [34], can be overcome.

Acknowledging that breaking down walls of separation *may* [35] help foster better understanding, it is important to look at what *might* [36] change for the worse. There would be *some* [37] *obvious* [38] logistical changes in rush, pledging, relationships with national organization, and house leadership. *But* [39] where are the real consequences? [40] Men *could* [41] still cultivate strong bonds with other men. Women *could* [42] still bond with other women. The difference is that there would be a *well-defined* [43] environment where men and women *could* [44] create strong, lasting bonds and friendships between one another.

There are many more *benefits* [45] to a coed system than there are *sacrifices* [46]. Men and women could share the responsibilities of running what is now a *predominantly* [47] male-controlled social structure. First-year men and women could interact with older students in a social environment beyond the classroom or the dining halls. People in a coed system could find a strong support group that extends beyond their own sex. With these *advantages* [48] and more, it is *clear* [49] that the all-coed system offers everything found in a single-sex organization and more. *Although* [50] there are *some* [51] minor sacrifices to be made, they are insignificant in comparison to the *gain* [52] for all.

College is the last place we want to isolate ourselves. The entire idea of the "holistic education" is *based on* [53] expanding our knowledge, not separating ourselves from one another. Our fraternity and sorority system includes *many* [54] different types of students. *So* [55] why should some houses refuse women simply *because* [56] they are women? Why do some houses refuse men solely *because* [57] they are men? The only solution is desegregation of the fraternity and sorority system. *After all* [58], when it comes to challenging one another to learn, what are we afraid of? [59]

Questions:

[1]: Is this sentence an explicit performative?

[2]: Explain the difference between asking "why?" and asking "why not?" in this context.

[3]: Why does the author begin with this point?

[4]–[12]: Write labels.

[13]: What is the expected answer to this rhetorical question?

[14]: What kind of rhetorical device is this? What is its point?

[15]–[18]: Write labels.

[19]: Who is supposed to be asking this question?

[20]–[22]: Write labels.

[23]: What is the point of this persuasive definition?

[24]–[33]: Write labels.

[34]: Why does this author add this dependent clause?

[35]–[39]: Write labels.

[40]: What does this question imply in this context?

[41]–[58]: Write labels.

[59]: What is the expected answer to this rhetorical question?

EXERCISE II

The following passage is excerpted from the presidential debates during the 1992 campaign. These answers were spoken live and unrehearsed, so they lack some of the polish of written articles, but they do illustrate how the same argumentative devices are used in a different context. Begin by reading the whole passage.

The Presidential Debates in 1992

Sander Vanocur: Secretary of the Army Michael Stone said he had no plans to abide by a Congressional mandate to cut U.S. forces in Europe from 150,000 to

100,000 by the end of September 1996. Now, why, almost 50 years after the end of World War II, and with the collapse of the Soviet Union, should American taxpayers be taxed to support armies in Europe when the Europeans have plenty of money to do it for themselves?

Pres. Bush: Well, Sander, that's a *good* [1] question, and the answer is *for* [2] 40-some years we kept the peace. If you look at the cost of not keeping the peace in Europe, it would be *exorbitant* [3]. We have reduced the number of troops that are deployed, and going to be deployed. I have cut defense spending. And *the reason* [4] we could do that is because of our *fantastic success* [5] in winning the Cold War. We never would have got there *if* [6] we'd gone for the nuclear freeze crowd, never would have got there if we'd listened to those that wanted to cut defense spending. I think it is important that the United States stay in Europe and continue to guarantee the peace. We *simply cannot* [7] pull back. Now, when anybody has a spending program they want to spend money on at home, they say, "Well, let's cut money out of the Defense Department." I will accept—and have accepted—the recommendations of two *proven leaders* [8]—General Colin Powell and Secretary Dick Cheney. *They feel that* [9] the levels we're operating at, and the reductions that I have proposed, are *proper* [10]. And, *so* [11], I simply do not think we should go back to the isolation days and start blaming foreigners. We are the sole remaining superpower, and we *should* [12] be that. And we have a *certain* [13] disproportionate responsibility. *But* [14] I would ask the American people to understand that if we make *imprudent* [15] cuts, if we go *too* [16] far, we risk the peace, and I don't want to do that. I've seen what it is like to see the *burdens* [17] of a war, and I don't want to see us make *reckless* [18] cuts. *Because* [19] of our programs, we have been able to significantly cut defense spending. *But* [20], let's not cut into the muscle, and let's not cut down our insurance policy, which is participation of American forces in NATO, the *greatest* [21] peace-keeping organization ever made. Today you've got *problems* [22] in Europe. Still bubbling along, *even though* [23] Europe's going democracy's route. *But* [24], we are there, and I think this insurance policy is necessary. I think it goes with world leadership, and I think the levels we've come up with are *just about* [25] *right* [26].

Mr. Perot: If I am poor and you are rich, and I can get you to defend me, that's *good* [27]. *But* [28], when the tables get turned, I ought to do my share. Right now we spend *about* [29] $300 billion a year on defense, and the Japanese spend *around* [30] $30 billion in Asia, the Germans spend *about* [31] $30 billion in Europe. For example, Germany will spend $1 trillion building infrastructure over the next 10 years. It's *kind of* [32] easy to do *if* [33] you only have to pick up a $30 billion tab to defend your country. The European community is in a position to pay a lot more than they have in the past. I agree with the president—when they couldn't, we should have. Now that they can, they *should* [34]. We *sort of seem to* [35] have a desire to try to stay over there and control it. They don't want us to control it, very candidly, *so* [36] it, *I think* [37], is very important for us to let them assume more of the burden and for us to bring that money back here and rebuild our infrastructure, *because* [38] we can only be a superpower if we are an economic superpower. And we can only be an economic superpower if we have a growing expanding job base.

Gov. Clinton: I agree with the *general* [39] statement Mr. Bush made. I disagree that we need 150,000 troops to fulfill our role in Europe. We *certainly* [40] must maintain an engagement there. There are *certainly* [41] *dangers* [42] there. There are *certainly* [43] other trouble spots in the world which are closer to Europe than to the United States, *but* [44] *two former Defense Secretaries recently issued a report saying that* [45] 100,000 or slightly fewer troops would be enough, including President Reagan's former Defense Secretary Mr. Carlucci. *Many* [46] of the military experts whom I consulted on this agreed. We're going to have to spend more money in the future on military technology, and on greater mobility, greater airlift, greater sealift, the V-22 airplane. We're going to have to do some things that are *quite* [47] costly, and I simply don't believe we can afford, nor do we need, to keep 150,000 troops in Europe, *given* [48] how much the Red Army, now under the control of Russia, has been cut. The Arms Control Agreement concluded between Mr. Bush and Mr. Yeltsin [is] *something I have applauded* [49]. I don't think we need 150,000 troops. . . .

John Mashek, *Boston Globe:* Mr. Perot, you talked about *fairness* [50] just a minute ago, and sharing the pain. As part of your plan to reduce the *ballooning* [51] federal deficit you've suggested that we raise gasoline taxes 50 cents a gallon over five years. Why *punish* [52] the middle-class consumer to such a degree?

Mr. Perot: It's 10 cents a year. Cumulative, it finally gets to 50 cents at the end of the fifth year. I think "punish" is the *wrong* [53] word. Again, see, I didn't create this problem; we are trying to solve it. Now, if you study our international competitors, *some* [54] of our international competitors collect *up to* [55] $3.50 a gallon in taxes, and they use that money to build infrastructure and to create jobs. We collect 35 cents, and we don't have it to spend. I know it's not popular, and I understand the nature of your question, *but* [56] the people who will be *helped* [57] the most by it are the working people who will get the jobs created because of this tax. Why do we have to do it? *Because* [58] we have so *mismanaged* [59] our country over the years, and it is now time to pay the fiddler. If we don't, we will be spending our children's money. We have spent $4 trillion worth. An incredible number of young people are active in supporting my efforts, *because* [60] they're deeply concerned that we have taken the American Dream from them. I think it's *fitting* [61] that we are on the campus of a university tonight. These young people, *when* [62] they get out of this *wonderful* [63] university, will have difficulty finding a job. We have got to clean this *mess* [64] up, leave this country in good shape, and pass on the American Dream to them. We have got to collect the taxes to do it. If there's a *fairer* [65] way, I'm all ears. *But* [66], let me make it *very clear* [67]. If people don't have the stomach to fix these problems, I think it's a good time to fix it in November. *If* [68] they do, then they will have heard the harsh *reality* [69] of what we had to do. I'm not playing Lawrence Welk music tonight.

Gov. Clinton: I think Mr. Perot has confronted this deficit issue, *but* [70] I think it's important to point out that we *really* [71] have two deficits in America, not one. We have a budget deficit in the federal government, *but* [72] we also have an investment, a jobs, an income deficit. People are working harder for less money than they were making 10 years ago—two-thirds of our people. A $1,600 drop in average income in just the last two years. *The problem I have* [73] with the Perot prescription is that *almost* [74] *all the economists who have looked at it say* [75] that if you cut the deficit this much, this quick, it will increase unemployment, it will slow down the economy. *That's why* [76] I think we shouldn't do it that quickly. We have a disciplined reduction in the deficit of 50 percent over the next four years, *but* [77], first, get incentives to invest in this economy, put the American people back to work. We have got to invest in growth. And *our Nobel Prize–winning economist, and 500 others, including numerous Republican and Democratic business executives, have endorsed* [78] this approach *because* [79] it offers the *best* [80] hope to put Americans back to work and get our incomes rising, instead of falling.

Pres. Bush: The question was on fairness. I just disagree with Mr. Perot. I don't believe it is *fair* [81] to slap a 50-cent-a-gallon tax over whatever many years on the people that have to drive for a living, people that go long distances. I don't think we need to do it. You see, I have a fundamental difference. I agree with what he's talking about in trying to get this spending down, and the discipline, *although* [82] I think we ought to totally exempt Social Security, *but* [83] he's talking tough medicine and I think that's *good* [84]. I disagree with the tax-and-spend philosophy. You see, I don't think we need to tax more and spend more, and *then* [85] say, "That's going to make the problem better," and I'm afraid that's what I think I'm hearing from Governor Clinton. I believe what you need to do is *some* [86] of what Ross is talking about—control the growth of mandatory spending and get taxes down. He's mentioned some ways to do it, and I agree with those. I've been talking about getting a capital gains cut *forever* [87], and his friends in this Congress have been telling me that's a tax break for the rich. It would stimulate investment. I'm for an investment tax allowance. I am for a first-time tax break for first-time homebuyers, and *with* [88] this new Congress coming in, *gridlock* [89] will be gone, and I'll sit down with them and say, "Let's get this done." *But* [90] I do not want to go the tax-and-spend route.

Labeling:

Using these abbreviations:

W = warranting term

A = assuring term

G = guarding term

D = discounting term

E– = negative evaluative term

E+ = positive evaluative term

N = none of the above

indicate the primary function of each numbered expression by placing the appropriate letter in the corresponding box in this table:

[1]	[2]	[3]	[4]	[5]
[6]	[7]	[8]	[9]	[10]
[11]	[12]	[13]	[14]	[15]
[16]	[17]	[18]	[19]	[20]
[21]	[22]	[23]	[24]	[25]
[26]	[27]	[28]	[29]	[30]
[31]	[32]	[33]	[34]	[35]
[36]	[37]	[38]	[39]	[40]
[41]	[42]	[43]	[44]	[45]
[46]	[47]	[48]	[49]	[50]
[51]	[52]	[53]	[54]	[55]
[56]	[57]	[58]	[59]	[60]
[61]	[62]	[63]	[64]	[65]
[66]	[67]	[68]	[69]	[70]
[71]	[72]	[73]	[74]	[75]
[76]	[77]	[78]	[79]	[80]
[81]	[82]	[83]	[84]	[85]
[86]	[87]	[88]	[89]	[90]

Questions:

(1) Does any of the speakers use an unusual number of assuring terms? Guarding terms? Discounting terms? Evaluative terms? Warranting connectives? What, if anything, does this show you about their styles or positions?

(2) Toward the end of his answer to the first question, Bush defines "our insurance policy" as "participation of American forces in NATO." What kind of move is this? Explain how it works.

(3) In his answer to the first question, Clinton lists several things that "we're going to have to spend more money in the future on." Why does he talk about spending money at this point in the debate?

(4) In his answer to the second question, Perot says things like "pay the fiddler," "I'm all ears," "have the stomach," and "playing Lawrence Welk music." What kind of rhetorical devices are these? Discuss their role in Perot's argument.

EXERCISE III

The following passages argue for opposing views on the religious duties of elected officials. In each case, read the whole passage; then, for each of the numbered expressions, either answer the corresponding question or label the main argumentative move, if any, using the abbreviations listed in Exercises I and II.

PASSAGE I

The first passage is excerpted from a speech given by Mario Cuomo at the University of Notre Dame, a Catholic institution, in September 1984, while Cuomo was governor of New York.[3]

Religious Belief and Public Morality: A Catholic Governor's Perspective
by Mario Cuomo

In addition to all the *weaknesses, dilemmas, and temptations* [1] that impede every pilgrim's progress, the Catholic who holds political office in a pluralistic democracy—who is elected to serve Jews and Muslims, atheists and Protestants, as well as Catholics—bears special responsibility. He or she undertakes to help create conditions under which *all* can live with a maximum of *dignity* [2] and with a *reasonable* [3] degree of freedom; where everyone who chooses may hold beliefs different from specifically Catholic ones—*sometimes* [4] contradictory to them; where the laws protect people's right to divorce, to use birth control and even to choose abortion.

In fact [5], Catholic public officials take an oath to preserve the Constitution that guarantees this freedom. And they do so gladly. Not *because* [6] they love what others do with their freedom, *but* [7] *because* [8] they realize that in guaranteeing freedom for all, they guarantee our right to be Catholics: our right to pray, to use the sacraments, to refuse birth control devices, to reject abortion, not to divorce and remarry if we believe it to be wrong. . . .

But [9] insistence on freedom is easier to accept as a general proposition than in its applications to specific situations. There are other *valid* [10] general principles firmly embedded in our Constitution, which, operating at the same time, create

---

[3] Mario Cuomo, "Religious Belief and Public Morality: A Catholic Governor's Perspective," *Notre Dame Journal of Law, Ethics, and Public Policy* 1 (1984): 13–31.

interesting and *occasionally* [11] troubling problems. *Thus* [12], the same amendment of the Constitution that forbids the establishment of a State Church affirms my legal right to argue that my religious belief would serve *well* [13] as an article of our universal public morality. I *may* [14] use the prescribed processes of government—the legislative and executive and judicial processes—to convince my fellow citizens—Jews and Protestants and Buddhists and nonbelievers—that what I propose is as *beneficial* [15] for them as I believe it is for me: that it is not just parochial or narrowly sectarian *but* [16] fulfills a human desire for *order, peace, justice, kindness, love* [17], any of the values *most* [18] of us agree are desirable *even* [19] apart from their specific religious base or context.

I am free to argue for a governmental policy for a nuclear freeze not just to avoid sin *but* [20] *because* [21] I think my democracy should regard it as a *desirable* [22] goal.

I can, if I wish, argue that the State should not fund the use of contraceptive devices not *because* [23] the Pope demands it *but* [24] *because* [25] I think that the whole community—*for* [26] the *good* [27] of the whole community—should not sever sex from an openness to the creation of life.

And *surely* [28], I can, if so inclined, demand some kind of law against abortion not *because* [29] my Bishops say it is wrong *but* [30] *because* [31] I think that the whole community, regardless of its religious beliefs, should agree on the importance of protecting life—including life in the womb, which is *at the very least* [32] potentially human and should not be extinguished casually [33].

No law prevents us from advocating any of these things: I am free to do so. *So* [34] are the Bishops. And so is Reverend Falwell. *In fact* [35], the Constitution guarantees my right to try. And theirs. And his. *But* [36] *should* [37] I? Is it *helpful* [38]? Is it essential to human *dignity* [39]? Does it promote *harmony and understanding* [40]? Or does it divide us so fundamentally that it *threatens* [41] our ability to function as a pluralistic community? . . .

Today there are *a number* [42] of issues involving life and death that raise questions of public morality. . . . Abortion is one of these issues, and *while* [43] it is one issue among many, it is one of the most controversial and affects me in a special way as a Catholic public official. *So* [44] let me spend some time considering it.

I should start, I believe, by noting that the Catholic Church's actions with respect to the interplay of religious values and public policy make *clear* [45] that there is no inflexible moral principle which determines what our *political* conduct should be. For example, on divorce and birth control, *without changing its moral teaching* [46], the Church abides the civil law as it now stands, *thereby* [47] accepting—without making much of a point of it—that in our pluralistic society we are not required to insist that *all* our religious values be the law of the land.

Abortion is treated differently.

Of course [48] there are differences both in degree and quality between abortion and *some* [49] of the other religious positions the Church takes: abortion is a "matter of life and death," and degree counts. *But* [50] the differences in approach reveal a truth, *I think* [51], that is not well enough perceived by Catholics and *therefore* [52] still further complicates the process for us. That is, *while* [53] we always owe our Bishops' words respectful attention and careful consideration, the question whether to engage the political system in a struggle to have it adopt certain articles of our belief as part of public morality, is not a matter of doctrine: it is a matter of prudential political judgment. . . .

As [54] Catholics, my wife and I were enjoined never to use abortion to destroy the life we created, and we never have. We thought Church doctrine was *clear* [55] on this, and—more than that—both of us felt it in full agreement with what our hearts and our consciences told us. For me, life or fetal life in the womb *should* [56] be protected, *even if* [57] five of nine Justices of the Supreme Court and my neighbor disagree with me. A fetus is different from an appendix or a set of tonsils. *At the very least* [58], *even if* [59] the argument is made by *some* [60] scientists or some theologians that in the early stages of fetal development we can't discern human life, the full potential of human life is *indisputably* [61] there. That—to my less subtle mind—by itself *should demand respect, caution, indeed . . . reverence* [62].

But [63]*not everyone* [64] in our society agrees with me and Matilda. And those who don't—those who endorse legalized abortions—aren't a ruthless, callous alliance of anti-Christians determined to overthrow our moral standards [65]. In many cases, the proponents of legal abortion are the very people who have worked with Catholics to realize the goals of social justice set out in papal encyclicals: the American Lutheran Church, the Central Conference of American Rabbis, the Presbyterian Church in the United States, B'nai B'rith Women, the Women of the Episcopal Church [66]. These are just a few of the religious organizations that don't share the Church's position on abortion.

Certainly [67], we should not be forced to mold Catholic morality to conform to disagreement by non-Catholics *however* [68] sincere or severe their disagreement. Our bishops *should* [69] be teachers, not pollsters. They *should not* [70] change what we Catholics believe in order to ease our consciences or please our friends or protect the Church from criticism.

But [71] if the breadth, intensity, and sincerity of opposition to church teaching shouldn't be allowed to shape our Catholic morality, it *can't help but* [72] determine our ability—our realistic, political ability—to translate our Catholic morality into civil law, a law not for the believers who don't need it *but* [73] for the disbelievers who reject it.

And it is here, in our attempt to find a political answer to abortion—an answer beyond our private observance of Catholic morality—that we encounter controversy within and without the Church over how and in what degree to press *the case that our morality should be everybody else's* [74], and to what effect. . . .

Respectfully, and after careful consideration [75] of the position and arguments of the bishops, *I have concluded that* [76] the approach of a constitutional amendment is not the *best* [77] way for us to seek to deal with abortion.

I believe that legal interdicting of abortion by either the federal government or the individual states is not a *plausible* [78] possibility, and, *even* [79] if it could be obtained, it wouldn't work. *Given* [80] present attitudes, it would be "Prohibition" revisited, *legislating what couldn't be enforced and in the process creating a disrespect for law in general* [81]. And as much as I admire the bishops' hope that a constitutional amendment against abortion would be the basis for a full, new bill of rights for mothers and children, I disagree that this would be the result.

I believe that, *more likely* [82], a constitutional prohibition would allow people to ignore the causes of many abortions instead of addressing them, *much* [83] the way the death penalty is used to escape dealing more fundamentally and more *rationally* [84] with the problem of violent crime. Other legal options that have been proposed are, *in my view* [85], equally ineffective. . . .

I am not implying that we should stand by and pretend indifference to whether a woman takes a pregnancy to its conclusion or aborts it [86]. I believe we should in all cases try to teach a respect for life. And I believe with regard to abortion that, *despite* [87] *Roe v. Wade*, we can, in practical ways. Here, *in fact* [88], *it seems to me* [89] that *all of us can agree* [90].

Without lessening their insistence on a woman's right to an abortion [91], the people who call themselves "pro-choice" can support the development of government programs that present an impoverished mother with the full range of support she needs to bear and raise her children, to have a *real* [92] choice.

Without dropping their campaign to ban abortion [93], those who gather under the banner of "pro-life" can join in developing and enacting a legislative bill of rights for mothers and children, as the bishops have already proposed.

While [94] we argue over abortion, the United States' infant mortality rate places us sixteenth among the nations of the world. Thousands of infants die each year because of inadequate medical care. Some are born with birth defects that, *with proper treatment, could* [95] be prevented. Some are stunted in their physical and mental growth because of improper nutrition.

If [96] we want to prove our regard for life in the womb, for the helpless infant—if we care about women having real choices in their lives and not being driven to abortions by a sense of helplessness and despair about the future of their child—then there is work *enough* [97] for all of us. Lifetimes of it.

Questions:

[1]–[32]: Write labels.

    [33]: Explain the point of this paragraph.

[34]–[45]: Write labels.

    [46]: Why does Cuomo add this clause?

[47]–[64]: Write labels.

    [65]: Explain the point of this sentence.

    [66]: Why does Cuomo list these groups?

[67]–[73]: Write labels.

    [74]: Is this a fair description of the controversy? Who wants to press *this* case?

[75]–[80]: Write labels.

    [81]: Explain the point of this clause.

[82]–[85]: Write labels.

[86]: Explain the point of this sentence.

[87]–[89]: Write labels.

[90]: Why is it important to Cuomo that "all of us can agree"?

[91]: Explain the point of this clause.

[92]: Write a label.

[93]: Explain the point of this clause.

[94]–[96]: Write labels.

[97]: Explain the point of this word.

PASSAGE 2

The following response to Cuomo's speech is from the *New Republic*, May 6, 1991, pp. 16–18.

Dead End–Cuomo's Abortion Contortion
by Andrew Sullivan

Mario Cuomo's September 1984 speech on abortion at Notre Dame University is second only to his convention keynote address of the same year in the lore surrounding the philosophical *prowess* [1] of the governor of New York. *Some* [2] likened the Notre Dame speech to John F. Kennedy's 1960 address to Protestant ministers in Houston on the role of Catholics in American public life. *The New Republic* said it contained a "*seriousness and depth* [3] rarely seen in the American political arena." A *National Review* writer called it "*brilliant* [4]." *Although* [5] criticisms were made at the time, they failed to stick. The *tour de force* [6] *largely* [7] ended the abortion issue as a *major problem* [8] in Mario Cuomo's career.

It shouldn't have. *In fact* [9], the speech is a work of *evasion* [10], and so *muddled* [11] on *so* [12] pressing a moral matter that it *casts doubt* [13] on Cuomo's seriousness both as an intellectual and as a politician. It *glosses over* [14] its own central contradiction, finds a solution where there is only an impasse. Cuomo's singular *achievement* [15] *may* [16] *in fact* [17] have been to have staked out the only *truly* [18] *incoherent* [19] position imaginable for a Catholic politician on abortion.

Cuomo argues in his speech that, *though* [20] as a Catholic he accepts the Church's teaching that abortion is *wrong* [21], as a politician in a pluralist society he upholds the right of others to abort. He argues that, *although* [22] he is bound as a Catholic to believe the Church's teaching, he can differ from the Church on the practical response to such a teaching, which is a matter of prudential political judgment, and not of *ecclesiastical obedience* [23].

The problem with the position is *simple* [24]: its private-Catholic/public-pluralist position makes *some* [25] sense for *almost* [26] any other moral issue for Catholics *except* abortion. It's *possible* [27], for example, for a Catholic to hold that, say, divorce is *wrong* [28] *but* [29] not wish to make it illegal, out of a respect for the right of others to choose differently. The upshot of such a stance, *after all* [30], is not so *bad* [31]: at worst a *lowering of public morals* [32], at best an affirmation of the good of *free moral choice* [33].

With abortion, *however* [34], this balance between public and private *goes awry* [35]. To accept the Church's position on abortion is to believe that abortion is the taking of human life, a *somewhat* [36] more drastic event than the breakup of a *marriage* [37]. In his Notre Dame speech, Cuomo states that he accepts this position in the *clearest* [38] terms:

> *As* [39] Catholics, my wife and I were enjoined never to use abortion to destroy the life we created, and we never have. We thought Church doctrine was *clear* [40] on this, and—more than that—both of us felt it in full agreement with what our hearts and our consciences told us. For me, life or fetal life in the womb *should* [41] be protected. . . . *At the very least* [42] . . . the full potential of human life is there. That . . . by itself *should demand respect, caution, indeed . . . reverence* [43].

For a Catholic holding this belief, merely enforcing the public laws as a public servant, *while* [44] arguing for their reversal, is hard enough. *But* [45] actually favoring legal abortion, and the provision of public funds for it, *must mean* [46] consciously tolerating the taking of millions of human lives as a normal occurrence in American society. And this is Cuomo's position. *At times* [47] he has gone even further than this. He recently joined eight governors in an amicus brief to the Supreme Court that *implicitly* [48] asked the Court not to overturn *Roe v. Wade*. He *ducked* [49], in a recent interchange with the editors of the liberal Catholic journal *Commonweal*, an invitation to support a ban on third trimester abortions, preferring to say that the ethical and legal implications of medical data "be explored." And he has made statements, subsequently qualified, that, *as* [50] a man, he has no right to discuss abortion at all.

Cuomo recognizes that he is free to act otherwise, to argue democratically against abortion according to his own convictions. *But* [51] in the Notre Dame speech, he adds: "But should I? Is it *helpful* [52]? Is it *essential to human dignity* [53]? Does it promote *harmony and understanding* [54]? Or does it *divide us* [55] so fundamentally that it *threatens* [56] our ability to function as a pluralistic community?" There is a virtue, *to be sure* [57], in harmony—and a Catholic virtue at that. *But* [58] could it possibly outweigh what Cuomo himself *must* [59] believe is legal homicide? Cuomo, in short, says he'd never "destroy life" himself (his words) but actively supports the right of others to do so, *in order to* [60] avoid public *discord* [61]. Compare this with the clarity of his opposition to the death penalty, where he has vetoed, to public uproar, capital punishment laws passed by majorities in both houses of the New York legislature, and favored by a majority of New York voters.

None of this *contortion* [62], *of course* [63], is necessary. Cuomo could, for example, say he doesn't believe abortion *is* the taking of life. He could say he doesn't believe it's homicide; or that "life" is at stake, *but* [64] a "person" does not exist until a certain number of weeks of pregnancy. Or he could simply say he's so deeply troubled by the issue *that* [65] he's prepared to give others the benefit of the doubt. All of these views *might* [66] fit with his pro-choice position. *For this* [67], he would *doubtless* [68] receive sympathy from his fellow Catholics. Instead, he chooses to affirm the Church's view that abortion is life-taking and *yet* [69] be in favor of laws that permit it.

A college student raised this *problem* [70] in an interview in the Catholic Columbia undergraduate magazine, *Newman Journal*, in the spring of 1988. At one point in the dialogue, Cuomo claims the bishops don't mandate the same obedience to the teaching on birth control as they do on abortion, which prompts the reply:

NEWMAN JOURNAL: It's not the same.

MARIO CUOMO: Well, why is it not the same?

NJ: Well, one is murder.

MC: No, murder is a word that doesn't count. Murder is a civil word, and the Supreme Court says it's not murder. *So* [71] you can't do it with the word "murder."

NJ: Well, the Church teaches that it's a taking of a life and *therefore* [72] the *violation of the natural law* [73].

MC: Well, that's what you teach about birth control. You don't teach that there is a different order of seriousness. Then they get all upset on that point. Now, I *may* [74] have my theology wrong *but* [75] I don't think so. . . .

The truth is, *of course* [76], that Cuomo does have his theology wrong. The Church does teach that there is an order of seriousness in breaches of natural law, homicide being far *graver* [77] than the use of condoms.

How did the governor manage to avoid confronting this issue in his Notre Dame speech? By two *rhetorical sleights of hand* [78]. First, he plays down his belief in the public doctrine of the Church on abortion. *Rather than* [79] saying that he actually "believes" in the teaching of the Church on abortion, he uses the term "accept." His "belief" in the sin of abortion is reserved entirely for himself, in a firmly private context.

Second, Cuomo faces up to the *central dilemma* [80] of legal killing once—and rebuts it with an *irrelevance* [81]. He admits *at one point* [82] that "abortion is treated differently" by the Church than other social evils:

> Abortion is a "matter of life and death," and degree counts. *But* [83] the differences in approach reveal a truth, *I think* [84], that is not well enough perceived by Catholics and *therefore* [85] still further complicates the process for us. That is, *while* [86] we always owe our bishops' words respectful attention and careful consideration, the question whether to engage the political system in a struggle to have it adopt certain articles of our belief as public morality, is not a matter of doctrine: it is a matter of prudential political argument.

This is a *decent* [87] point. The Church defers to lay people in matters of prudential political judgment. *The trouble* [88] is, Cuomo's argument doesn't actually tackle the question raised. The issue is whether the fact that Catholics believe abortion is homicide short-circuits much political judgment on what to do about it. And *surely* [89] it does. There cannot be *much* [90] debate among Catholics over whether killing should be legal or not. There may be differences over tactics, *to be sure* [91]: making abortion illegal, for example, could be the last part of a broad social, educational, economic, and spiritual strategy to end it. *But* [92] the *goal* is *unmistakable* [93]. *Yet* [94] it is precisely on this goal—of ultimately banning abortion—that Cuomo is silent. And on making it illegal now, he's actively opposed.

No one's pretending, *of course* [95], that this is an easy problem for a Catholic politician to grapple with, and Cuomo *deserves respect* [96] for engaging with it in public. What he shouldn't *get away with* [97], *however* [98], is the impression of having made a *definitive contribution* [99] to the subject, when *in reality* [100] he hasn't confronted the central issue at all.

Labeling:

Using the abbreviations listed in Exercises I and II, indicate the primary function of each numbered expression by placing the appropriate letter in the corresponding box in this table:

[1]	[2]	[3]	[4]	[5]
[6]	[7]	[8]	[9]	[10]
[11]	[12]	[13]	[14]	[15]
[16]	[17]	[18]	[19]	[20]
[21]	[22]	[23]	[24]	[25]
[26]	[27]	[28]	[29]	[30]
[31]	[32]	[33]	[34]	[35]
[36]	[37]	[38]	[39]	[40]
[41]	[42]	[43]	[44]	[45]
[46]	[47]	[48]	[49]	[50]
[51]	[52]	[53]	[54]	[55]
[56]	[57]	[58]	[59]	[60]
[61]	[62]	[63]	[64]	[65]
[66]	[67]	[68]	[69]	[70]
[71]	[72]	[73]	[74]	[75]
[76]	[77]	[78]	[79]	[80]
[81]	[82]	[83]	[84]	[85]
[86]	[87]	[88]	[89]	[90]
[91]	[92]	[93]	[94]	[95]
[96]	[97]	[98]	[99]	[100]

EXERCISE IV

Advertisements also often contain arguments. Provide a close analysis of each of the following advertisements by circling and labeling each of the key argumentative terms. Then state what you take to be the central conclusions and premises. What criticisms, if any, do you have of each argument?

PASSAGE 1

This advertisement first appeared in the late 1960s or early 1970s in the *New York Times*. It was written by Walter Hoving, then chair of Tiffany and Co., New York, which placed the ad and mainly sells expensive goods to rich customers.

Are the Rich a Menace?

Some people think they are, so let's look at the record.

Suppose you inherit, win or otherwise acquire a million dollars after taxes. That would make you rich, wouldn't it? Now, what's the first thing you'd do? Invest it, wouldn't you?—in stocks, bonds or in a savings bank.

So, what does that mean? It means that you have furnished the capital required to put about 30 people to work.

How is that? National statistics show that for every person graduating from school or college, at least thirty thousand dollars of capital must be found for bricks, fixtures, machinery, inventory, etc. to put each one to work.

Now, on your million dollar investment you will receive an income of sixty thousand, eighty thousand, or more dollars a year. This you will spend for food, clothing, shelter, taxes, education, entertainment and other expenses. And this will help support people like policemen, firemen, store clerks, factory workers, doctors, teachers, and others. Even congressmen.

So, in other words, Mr. Rich Man, you would be supporting (wholly or partially) perhaps more than 100 people.

Now, are you a menace? No, you are not.

PASSAGE 2

This advertisement appeared in the *New York Times* on June 21, 1994.

Today It's Cigarettes.
Tomorrow?

The Government, through the FDA, the Department of Labor and some Congressmen, is attempting to prohibit smoking in America. They're proposing a tax increase of up to 800% that will make cigarettes too expensive for people to afford. They're introducing regulations that could lead to a total smoking ban in private as well as public places.

And regardless of their reasons, both their tactics and the end result they are seeking are threats to the freedom we enjoy in our society.

Let's understand exactly what they're trying to do. They're pursuing a new era of prohibition, and in the process are ignoring the individual rights of not just the 45 million Americans who smoke, but all other Americans as well.

But the most threatening aspect of their program is their intention to force their views on the whole country.

If they are successful in their bid to abolish cigarettes, will they then pursue other targets? Will alcohol be next? Will caffeine and cholesterol "addicts" need to be protected from themselves? Will books, movies and music get the treatment? Who knows where it will end?

Prohibition solves nothing. Never mind that Americans do not want to create another prohibition era. In fact 86% reject such a notion. (Gallup/CNN/USA Today Poll, March 1994) What we need is a policy of accommodation, where common courtesy between smokers and non-smokers can prevail.

This opinion is brought to you in the interests of an informed debate by the R. J. Reynolds Tobacco Company.

EXERCISE V

Provide a close analysis of the following passages by circling and labeling each of the key argumentative terms. Then state what you take to be the central conclusions and premises. What criticisms, if any, do you have of each argument?

PASSAGE 1

The following encomium was written by an art critic for the *New York Times*, in which this review appeared. (*New York Times* [June 6, 1992], p. 1 col. 5 and p. 31) If you are not familiar with Eakins's work, looking at some reproductions might help you appreciate this argument. You might also look up the rest of the essay, since only a small part is reproduced here.

Is Eakins Our Greatest Painter?
by John Russell

There never was a painter like Thomas Eakins, who was born in 1844, died in 1916, and is the subject of a great exhibition that has just opened in the Philadelphia Museum of Art. It is not simply that in his hands painting became an exact science, so that if he paints two men rowing on a river, we can tell the month, day, and the hour that they passed under a certain bridge. We admire Eakins for that, but we prize him above all for the new dimension of moral awareness that he brought to American painting.

The question that he asks is not "What do we look like?" It is "What have we done to one another?" And it is because he gives that question so full and so convincing an answer that we ask ourselves whether Thomas Eakins was not the greatest American painter who ever lived. Even if the question strikes us as meaningless, we find it difficult after an exhibition such as this to think of a convincing rival. . . .

PASSAGE 2

This editorial appeared in the *New York Times* on September 22, 1989. Barney Frank was then a member of the House of Representatives from Massachusetts.

Barney Frank's Right to Judgment

If Representative Barney Frank knew a male prostitute was selling sex from Mr. Frank's Washington apartment, he cannot remain in the House. If he was unaware of what went on while he was back in Massachusetts, he is guilty only of admitted abysmal judgment and misplaced trust in a man he had hired for household errands.

Who should decide? Mr. Frank has put the issue to the House Ethics Committee, and he rightly rejects the counsel of friends and admirers to resign now. Some Democrats want him to leave to avoid another ethics cloud over their party. Republicans call for his resignation, but probably wouldn't mind his staying around as a punching bag. But to press him to resign now would deprive the House of a chance to debate the issue of personal behavior and public ethics. Worse, it would deny him a just conclusion.

Only last spring the House used the resignation of Speaker Jim Wright as an excuse to avoid deciding when a favor from a legislator's friend becomes an impermissible gift. If Mr. Frank's account is correct, his case raises the issue of what kind of personal behavior disqualifies public officials—drinking, philandering, consorting with prostitutes, or what? These issues need evaluation. The public can't drive people out of office without some agreed standards.

Mr. Frank was indisputably stupid, whether or not he proves more blameworthy. But his defense is plausible on currently available evidence. The prostitute had the capacity to deceive the Congressman; he drove Mr. Frank to and from the airport and knew his schedule. It's pertinent that the Congressman, who later made his homosexuality known to the public, fired the prostitute even though doing so then risked disclosure.

The evidence could show Mr. Frank was highly culpable, or merely misguided, or that he took unacceptable risks to his own reputation and that of the House. But those judgments ought to be made on evidence, not the opinion and speculation that have preoccupied Washington for weeks. Mr. Frank deserves to be judged, after his trial.

PASSAGE 3

The following passage is an excerpt from an essay that appeared in the *Boston Review* vol. 7, no. 5 (October 1982), pp. 13–19, which is funded by the National Endowment for the Humanities, a government agency that supports scholarship and the arts. Its author is a professor of drama at Stanford University.

Beyond the Wasteland:
What American TV Can Learn from the BBC
by Martin Esslin

What are the advantages and disadvantages of a public TV service as compared to a completely commercial system? One of the dangers inherent in a public service system is paternalism: some authority decides what the viewers should see and hear simply on the basis of what it arbitrarily feels would be good for them. Yet in countries where a highly developed public system exists alongside a commercial one, that danger is minimized because of the market pressure on the commercial system to give its audience what it wants. Indeed, in a dual system the danger is often that the public service may be tempted to ignore its stated purpose to serve the public interest and instead pander to mass preferences because of a sense of competition with the commercial networks.

Another problem that plagues public TV service is that it may run short of money, which in turn can increase its dependence on the government. The extent of government dependence is intimately connected to how the public broadcasting service is financed. In West Germany and Italy, for example, the public broadcasting service takes advertising, but it is usually confined to a clearly delimited area of the network's programming. In Britain the BBC . . . relies entirely on its annual license fee, which guarantees it a steady income and allows long-term planning. In periods of severe inflation, the license-fee system leaves the BBC in a dangerous position vis-a-vis the government, and the network's income may decline in real terms. In countries where the public broadcasting service is financed by an annual allocation in the national budget, long-term planning becomes more difficult and the dependence on the government is far greater. Nevertheless, public TV services financed on that pattern, such as the ABC in Australia and the CBC in Canada, provide programs of high quality that are genuine alternatives to the fare on the numerous popular and prosperous commercial networks. In Canada, this includes programs from the three commercial American networks.

One of the most important positive features of services under public control is their ability to provide planned, high-quality viewing alternatives. The BBC, for example, has two television channels, BBC 1 and BBC 2. The program planning on these two networks is closely coordinated so that highly popular material on one channel is regularly paired with more specialized or demanding fare on the other. And though the percentage of the audience that tunes in to the challenging programming may be small, the scale of magnitude operative in the mass media is such that even a small percentage of the viewing audience represents a very large number of people indeed. A popular dramatic series on BBC 1, for instance, may reach an audience of 20 percent of the adult population of Britain—about ten million people. A play by Shakespeare on BBC 2 that may attract an audience of only 5 percent nonetheless reaches about two-and-a-half million people—a substantial audience for a work of art. It would take a theater with a seating capacity of 1,000 about seven years, or 2,500 performances, to reach an equivalent number of people! Nor should it be overlooked that this audience will include people whose influence may be greater in the long run than that of the ten million who watched the entertainment program. In this system, no segment of the viewing public is forced to compromise with any other. In our example, not only did BBC 1 provide a popular entertainment program as an alternative to the Shakespeare, but, in addition, the commercial network offered still another popular program. By careful–perhaps paternalistic–planning the general audience satisfaction was substantially increased.

One of the difficulties of the American situation is that the size of the United States favors decentralization and the fragmentation of initiatives for the more ambitious programming of the public service network. A revitalized PBS would need a strong central governing body that could allocate to local producing stations the substantial sums of money they require for ambitious projects–projects that could compete with the best offerings of the rich commercial competitors.

Using existing satellite technology, such a truly national network of public service television could be made available to the entire country. If a public service television organization was able to provide simultaneous, alternative programming along the lines of BBC 1 and BBC 2, the cultural role of television in the United States could be radically improved, and the most powerful communication medium in history could realize its positive potential to inform, educate, and provide exposure to diverse cultural ideas.

EXERCISE VI

Practice close analysis some more by doing close analyses of:

    (1) an editorial or advertisement from your local paper, or

    (2) one of the articles in Part 2 of this book, or

    (3) something that you read for another course, or

    (4) a lecture by your professor in another course, or

    (5) a paper by you or a friend in another course.

DISCUSSION QUESTIONS

    (1) If, as some social critics have maintained, the pervasive nature of television has created generation upon generation of intellectually passive automatons, why study close analysis?

    (2) Television commercials are often arguments in miniature. Recount several recent television commercials and identify the argumentative devices at work.

Chapter Four

DEEP ANALYSIS

Arguments in everyday life rarely occur in isolation. They usually come in the middle of much that is not essential to the argument itself. Everyday arguments are also rarely complete. Essential premises are often omitted. Many such omissions are tolerable because we are able to convey a great deal of information indirectly by conversational implication. However, to give a critical evaluation of an argument, it is necessary to isolate the argument from extraneous surroundings, to make explicit unstated parts of the argument, and to arrange them in a systematic order. This puts us in a better position to decide on the soundness or unsoundness of the argument in question. This chapter will develop methods for reconstructing arguments so that they may be understood and evaluated in a fair and systematic fashion. These methods will then be illustrated by applying them to a disagreement that depends on fundamental principles.

GETTING DOWN TO BASICS

To understand an argument, it is useful to put it into standard form. As we saw in Chapter 2, this is done by writing down the premises, then drawing a line, then adding the symbol "∴", and then writing down the conclusion. That is all we write down. But there is often a lot more in the passage that includes the argument. It is not uncommon for the stated argument to stretch over several pages, whereas the basic argument has only a few premises and a single conclusion.

One reason is that people often go off on *tangents*. They start to argue for one claim, but that reminds them of something else, so they talk about that for a while; then they finally return to their original topic. Such tangents can be completely irrelevant or just unnecessary, but they often make it hard to follow the argument. Some people even go off on tangents on purpose to confuse their opponents and hide gaping holes in their arguments. This might be called the trick of *excess verbiage*. It violates the rules of Relevance and of Manner. To focus on the argument itself, we need to look carefully at each sentence to determine whether that particular sentence affects the validity of the argument or the truth of its premises.[1] If we decide that a sentence is not necessary for the argument, we should not add it when we list the premises and conclusion in standard form. Of course, we have to be careful not to omit anything that would improve the argument, but including irrelevant material simply makes the task of analyzing the argument more difficult.

Another source of extra material is *repetition*. People often repeat their main points to remind their audience of what was said earlier. Repetition is more subtle when it is used to explain something. A point can often be clarified by restating it in a new way. Repetition can also function as a kind of assurance, as an expression of confidence, or as an indication of how important a point is. Some writers seem to think that if they say something often enough, people will come to believe it. Whether or not this trick works, when two sentences say equivalent things, there is no need to list both sentences when the argument is put into standard form. Listing the same premise twice will not make the argument any better from a logical point of view.

Sometimes *guarding* terms can also be dropped. If I say "I think Miranda is at home, so we can meet her there," this argument might be represented in standard form thus:

I think Miranda is at home.
_____

∴ We can meet her there.

But this is misleading. My *thoughts* are not what make us able to meet Miranda at home. It is the *fact* that Miranda is at home that provides a reason for the conclusion. Thus, it is clearer to drop the guarding phrase ("I think") when putting the argument

---

[1] Other factors are important in inductive arguments. We will discuss inductive arguments in Chapter 8. The present chapter will focus on deductive arguments.

into standard form. But you have to be careful. Not all guarding phrases can be dropped. If a friend says that you ought to buckle your seat belt because you could have an accident, it would distort her argument to drop the guarding term ("could"), since she is not claiming that you definitely will have an accident, or even that you probably will have one. The *chance* of an accident is significant enough to show that you ought to buckle your seat belt, so the guarding term should be kept when the argument is put into standard form.

It is also possible to drop *assuring* terms in some cases. Suppose someone says "You obviously cannot play golf in Alaska in January, so there's no point in bringing your clubs." There is no need to keep the assuring term ("obviously") in the premise. It might even be misleading, since the issue is whether the premise is true, not whether it is obvious. The argument cannot be refuted by showing that, even though you in fact cannot play golf in Alaska in January, this is not obvious, since there might be indoor golf courses. In other cases, assuring terms cannot be dropped without losing the whole argument. For example, if someone argues that "We know that poverty causes crime, because many studies have shown that it does," then the assuring term ("studies have shown that . . . ") cannot be dropped without turning the argument into an empty shell: "We know that poverty causes crime, because it does."

There is no mechanical method for determining when guarding or assuring terms and phrases can be dropped, or whether certain sentences are unnecessary tangents. We simply have to look closely at what is being said and think hard about what is needed to support the conclusion. It takes great skill, care, and insight to pare an argument down to its essential core without omitting anything that would make it better.

EXERCISE I

Put the following arguments into standard form and omit anything that does not affect the validity of the argument or the truth of its premises.

(1) Philadelphia is rich in history, but it is not now the capital of the United States, so the U.S. Congress must meet somewhere else.

(2) Not everybody whom you invited is going to come to your party. Some of them won't come. So this room should be big enough.

(3) I know that my wife is at home, since I just called her there and spoke to her. We talked about our dinner plans.

(4) I'm not sure, but Joseph is probably Jewish. Hence, he is a rabbi if he is a member of the clergy.

(5) Some students could not concentrate on the lecture because they did not eat lunch before class, although I did.

(6) The most surprising news of all is that Johnson dropped out of the race because he thought his opponent was better qualified than he was for the office.

(7) Clinton is likely to win, since experts agree that more women support him.

(8) It seems to me that married people are happier, so marriage must be a good thing, or at least I think so.

CLARIFYING CRUCIAL TERMS

After the essential premises and conclusion are isolated, we often need to clarify these claims before we can begin our logical analysis. The goal here is not perfect clarity, for there probably is no such thing. It is, however, often necessary to eliminate ambiguity and reduce vagueness before we can give an argument a fair assessment. In particular, it is often necessary to specify the referents of pronouns, since such references can depend on a context that is changed when the argument is put into standard form. Another common problem is exemplified when someone argues like this:

You should just say "No" to drugs, because drugs are dangerous.

Is the premise about some drugs, most drugs, all drugs, or drugs of a certain kind? What about alcohol, nicotine, or aspirin? It might seem obvious what was meant: illegal drugs. But we cannot begin to evaluate this argument if we do not know the extent of what is claimed. Of course, we should not try to clarify every term in the argument. Even if this were possible, it would make the argument extremely long and boring. Instead, our goal is to clarify anything that seems likely to produce confusion later if it is not cleared up now. As our analysis continues, we can always return and clarify more if the need arises, but it is better to get the most obvious problems out of the way at the start.

DISSECTING THE ARGUMENT

A single sentence often includes several different clauses that make separate claims. When this happens, it is usually useful to dissect the sentence into its smallest parts, so that we can investigate each part separately. Simpler steps are easier to follow than complex ones, so we can understand the argument better when it is broken down. Dissection makes us more likely to notice any flaws in the argument. It also enables us to pinpoint exactly where the argument fails, if it does.

The process of dissecting an argument is a skill that can be learned only by practice. Let us start with a simple example:

Joe won his bet, because all he had to do was eat five pounds of oysters, and he ate nine dozen, which weigh more than five pounds.

The simplest unpacking of this argument yields the following restatement in standard form:

>All Joe had to do was eat five pounds of oysters, and he
>ate nine dozen, which weigh more than five pounds.
>
>─────────────
>
>∴ Joe won his bet.

If we think about the premise of this argument, we see that it actually contains three claims. The argument will be clearer if we separate these claims into independent premises and add a few words for the sake of clarity. The following, then, is a better representation of this argument:

>All Joe had to do (to win his bet) was eat five pounds of oysters.
>Joe ate nine dozen (oysters).
>Nine dozen oysters weigh more than five pounds.
>
>─────────────
>
>∴ Joe won his bet.

With the premise split up in this way, it becomes obvious that there are three separate ways in which the argument could fail. One possibility is that Joe had to do more than just eat five pounds of oysters to win his bet. Maybe what he bet was that he could eat five pounds in one minute. Another possibility is that Joe did not really eat nine dozen oysters. Maybe he really ate one dozen oysters cut into nine dozen pieces. A final way in which the argument could fail is if nine dozen oysters do not weigh more than five pounds. Maybe the oysters that Joe ate were very small, or maybe nine dozen oysters weigh more than five pounds only when they are still in their shells, but Joe did not eat the shells. In any case, breaking down complex premises into simpler ones makes it is easier to see exactly where the argument goes wrong, if it does. Consequently, we can be more confident that an argument does not go wrong if we do not see any problem in it even after we have broken it down completely.

Although it is a good idea to break down the premises of an argument when this is possible, we have to be careful not to do this in a way that changes the logical structure of the argument. Suppose someone argues like this:

>Socialism is doomed to failure because it does not provide the incentives
>that are needed for a prosperous economy.

The simplest representation of this argument yields the following standard form:

>Socialism does not provide the incentives that are needed for a prosperous
>　economy.
>
>─────────────
>
>∴ Socialism is doomed to failure.

It is tempting to break up the first premise into two parts:

>Socialism does not provide incentives.
>Incentives are needed for a prosperous economy.
>
>─────────────
>
>∴ Socialism is doomed to failure.

In this form, the argument is open to a fatal objection: socialism *does* provide *some* incentives. Workers often get public recognition when they produce a great deal in socialist economies. But this does not refute the original argument. The point of the original argument was not that socialism does not provide any incentives at all, but only that socialism does not provide enough incentives or the right kind of incentives to create a prosperous economy. This point is lost if we break up the premise in the way suggested. A better attempt is this:

> Socialism does not provide adequate incentives.
> Adequate incentives are needed for a prosperous economy.
> _____
> ∴ Socialism is doomed to failure.

The problem now is to specify when incentives are *adequate*. What kinds of incentives are needed? How much of these incentives? The process of dissection has thus brought out a central issue in this argument, and we cannot evaluate the argument until we go back and clarify the premises further.

ARRANGING SUBARGUMENTS

When the premises of an argument are dissected, it often becomes clear that some of these premises are intended as reasons for others. The premises then form a chain of simpler arguments that culminate in the ultimate conclusion, but only after some intermediate steps. Consider this argument:

> There's no way I can finish my paper before the 9 o'clock show, since I have to do the reading first, so I won't even start writing until at least 9 o'clock.

It might seem tempting to put this argument into standard form as:

> I have to do the reading first.
> I won't even start writing until at least 9 o'clock.
> _____
> ∴ I can't finish my paper before the 9 o'clock show.

This reformulation does include all three parts of the original argument, but it does not indicate the correct role for each part. The two warranting connectives in the original argument indicate that there are really *two* conclusions. The word "since" indicates that what precedes it is a conclusion, and the word "so" indicates that what follows it is also a conclusion. We cannot represent this as a single argument in standard form, since each argument in standard form can have only one conclusion. Thus, the original sentence must have included two arguments. The relation between these arguments should be clear: the conclusion of the first argument functions as a premise or reason in the second argument. To represent this, we let the two arguments form a chain. This is the first argument:

> I have to do the reading first.
> _____
> ∴ I won't even start writing until at least 9 o'clock.

This is the second argument:

> I won't even start writing until at least 9 o'clock.
> _____
> ∴ I can't finish my paper before the 9 o'clock show.

If we want to, we can then write these two arguments in a chain like this:

> I have to do the reading first.
> _____
> ∴ I won't even start writing until at least 9 o'clock.
> _____
> ∴ I can't finish my paper before the 9 o'clock show.

Such chains of reasoning are very common. This is a simple example, but some argument chains can get so complex that you might need a flowchart to follow them.

Although it is often illuminating to break an argument into stages, this can be misleading if done incorrectly. For example, the first sentences of Kyl's speech cited in Chapter 3 read as follows:

> Mr. Speaker, I oppose this measure. I oppose it first because it is expensive. I further oppose it because it is untimely.

Here we have two separate reasons for the same conclusion. They cannot be put into a chain of arguments because the claim that the measure is expensive is not a reason to believe it is untimely, nor is the claim that it is untimely a reason to believe that it is expensive. We have to be careful not to confuse a chain of arguments leading to a conclusion with multiple or parallel arguments leading to the same conclusion.

EXERCISE II

Put the following arguments into standard form. Break up the premises and form chains of arguments wherever this can be done without distorting the argument.

(1) I know Pat can't be a father, because she is not a male. So she can't be a grandfather either.

(2) Either Jack is a fool or Mary is a crook, because she ended up with all of his money.

(3) Our team can't win this Saturday, both because they are not going to play, and because they are no good, so they wouldn't win even if they did play.

(4) Mercury is known to be the only metal that is liquid at room temperature, so a pound of mercury would be liquid in this room, which is at room

temperature, and it would also conduct electricity, since all metals do. Therefore, some liquids do conduct electricity.

(5) Since he won the lottery, he's rich and lucky, so he'll probably do well in the stock market, too, unless his luck runs out.

(6) Joe is not a freshman, since he lives in a fraternity, and freshmen are not allowed to live in fraternities. He also can't be a senior, since he has not declared a major, and every senior has declared a major. And he can't be a junior, because I never met him before today, and I would have met him before this if he were a junior. So Joe must be a sophomore.

(7) Since many newly emerging nations do not have the capital resources necessary for sustained growth, they will continue to need help from industrial nations to avoid mass starvation.

(8) A chemical weapons treaty cannot be safe, because the Iraqis are much too proud and paranoid to allow surprise inspections, and there is no way to verify treaty compliance without surprise inspections, since chemical weapons could be moved as soon as the inspections were announced.

SUPPRESSED PREMISES

SHARED FACTS

Arguments in everyday life are rarely completely explicit. They usually depend on unstated facts understood by those involved in the conversation. Thus, if we are told that Chester Arthur was a president of the United States, we have a right to conclude a great many things about him—for example, that at the time he was president, he was a live human being. Appeals to facts of this kind lie behind the following argument:

> Benjamin Franklin could not have been our second president, because he died before the second election was held.

This argument obviously turns on a question of fact: Did Franklin die before the second presidential election was held? (He did.) The argument would not be sound if this explicit premise were not true. But the argument also depends on a more general principle that ties the premise and conclusion together—namely, that the dead are not eligible for the presidency. This new premise is needed to make the argument valid (and thus sound).

Traditionally, logicians have called premises that are needed but are not stated *suppressed premises*. An argument depending on suppressed premises is called an *enthymeme* and is said to be *enthymematic*. If we look at arguments that occur in daily life, we discover that they are, almost without exception, enthymematic. Therefore, to trace the pathway between premises and conclusion, it is usually necessary to fill in these suppressed premises that serve as links between the stated premises and the conclusion.

Suppressed premises often concern rules or conventions that might have been otherwise. Our example assumed that the dead cannot be president, but we can imagine a society in which the deceased are elected to public office as an honor (something like posthumous induction into the Baseball Hall of Fame). However, our national government is not like that, and this is something that most Americans know. This makes it odd to come right out and say that the deceased cannot hold public office. In most settings, this would involve a violation of the conversational rule of Quantity.

But even if it would be odd to state it, this fact plays a central role in the argument. To assert the conclusion without believing the suppressed premise would involve a violation of the conversational rule of Quality, since the speaker would not have adequate reasons for her conclusion. Furthermore, if this suppressed premise were not believed to be true, then to give the explicit premise as a reason would violate the conversational rule of Relevance (just as it would be irrelevant to point out that Babe Ruth is dead when someone asks whether he is in the Baseball Hall of Fame). For these reasons, anyone who gives the original argument conversationally implies a commitment to the suppressed premise.

Suppressed premises are not always so obvious. A somewhat more complicated example is this:

> Henry Kissinger cannot become president of the United States, because he was born in Germany.

Why should being from Germany disqualify someone from being president? It seems odd that the Founding Fathers should have something against that particular part of the world. The answer is that the argument depends on a more general suppressed premise:

> Only a natural-born United States citizen may become president of the United States.

It is this provision of the United States Constitution that lies at the heart of the argument. Knowing this provision is, of course, a more special piece of knowledge than knowing that you have to be alive to be president. For this reason, more people will see the force of the first argument (about Franklin) than the second (about Kissinger). The second argument assumes an audience with more-specialized knowledge.

The argument still has to draw a connection between being born in Germany and being a natural-born United States citizen. So it turns out that the argument has three stages:

> Kissinger was born in Germany.
> Germany has never been part of the United States.
> _____
> ∴ Kissinger was born outside the United States.

Anyone who was born outside the United States is not a natural-born United States citizen.

∴ Kissinger is not a natural-born United States citizen.
Only a natural-born United States citizen may become president of the United States.

∴ Kissinger cannot become president of the United States.

Now the argument is valid.

The argument is still not sound, however, because some of the suppressed premises that were added are not true. In particular, there is an exception to the suppressed premise about who is a natural-born United States citizen. This exception is well known to United States citizens who live overseas. People who were born in Germany are still United States citizens if their parents were United States citizens. They also seem to count as natural-born citizens, since they are not naturalized. This is not completely settled, but it does not matter here, since Henry Kissinger's parents were not United States citizens when he was born. Thus, the second stage of the above argument can be reformulated as follows:

Kissinger was born outside the United States.
Kissinger's parents were not United States citizens when he was born.
Anyone who was born outside the United States and whose parents were not United States citizens at the time is not a natural-born United States citizen.

∴ Kissinger is not a natural-born United States citizen.

This much of the argument is now sound.

EXERCISE III

There is a less well known exception to the premise that only a natural-born citizen may become president of the United States. The Constitution does allow a person who is not a natural-born citizen to become president if he or she was "a citizen of the United States at the time of the adoption of this Constitution." This exception is said to have been added to allow Alexander Hamilton to run for president, but it obviously does not apply to Kissinger or to anyone else alive today. Nonetheless, this exception keeps the argument from being sound in its present form. Reformulate the final stage of the argument to make it sound.

An argument with a single premise has grown to include three stages with at least four suppressed premises. Some of the added premises are obvious, but others are less well known, so we cannot assume that the person who gave the original argument had the more complete argument in mind. And many people would be convinced by the original argument even without all these added complexities. Nonetheless, the many suppressed premises are necessary to make the argument sound. Seeing this brings out the assumptions that must be true for the conclusion to follow from the premises. This process of making everything explicit enables us to assess these background assumptions directly.

LINGUISTIC PRINCIPLES

Often an argument is valid, but it is not clear *why* it is valid. It is not clear *how* the conclusion follows from the premises. Arguments are like pathways between premises and conclusions, and some of these pathways are more complicated than others. Yet even the simplest arguments reveal hidden complexities when examined closely. For example, there is no question that the following argument is valid:

Harriet is in New York with her son.

∴ Harriet's son is in New York.

It is not possible for the premise to be true and the conclusion false. If asked why this conclusion follows from the premise, it would be natural to reply that you cannot be someplace with somebody unless that person is there too. This is not something we usually spell out, but, nonetheless, it is the principle that takes us from the premise to the conclusion.

One thing to notice about this principle is that it is quite general—that is, it does not depend on any special features of the people or places involved. It is also true that if Benjamin is in St. Louis with his daughter, then Benjamin's daughter is in St. Louis. Although the references have changed, the general pattern that lies behind this inference will seem obvious to anyone who understands the words used to formulate it. For this reason we shall say that principles of this kind are basically *linguistic* in character.

If we look at arguments as they occur in everyday life, we will discover that almost all of them turn on unstated linguistic principles. To cite just one more example, if a wife is taller than her husband, then there is at least one woman who is taller than at least one man. This inference relies on the principles that husbands are men and wives are women. We do not usually state these linguistic principles, for to do so will often violate the rule of Quantity, discussed in Chapter 1. (Try to imagine a context in which you would come right out and say "Husbands, you know, are men." Unless you were speaking to someone just learning the language, this would be a peculiar remark.) But even if in most cases it would be peculiar to come right out and state such linguistic principles, our arguments typically presuppose them. This observation reveals yet another way in which our daily use of language moves within a rich, though largely unnoticed, framework of rules.

OTHER KINDS OF SUPPRESSED PREMISES

We have examined two kinds of suppressed premises: those that are factual and those that are linguistic. Many arguments also contain unstated *moral* premises. Consider the following argument as a case in point:

> You shouldn't buy pornography, because it leads to violence toward women.

This argument clearly relies on the moral principle that you should not buy anything that leads to violence toward women. A different example comes from *religion*:

> You shouldn't take the name of the Lord in vain, because this shows disrespect.

The suppressed premise here is that you should not do anything that shows disrespect (to the Lord). More examples could be given, but the point should be clear. Most arguments depend on unstated assumptions, and these assumptions come in many different varieties.

THE USE OF SUPPRESSED PREMISES

Talk about *suppressed* premises may bring to mind suppressing a rebellion or an ugly thought, and using *hidden* premises may sound somewhat sneaky. But the way we are using them, these expressions do not carry such negative connotations. A suppressed or hidden premise is simply an *unstated* premise. It is often legitimate to leave premises unstated. It is legitimate if (i) those who are given the argument can easily supply these unstated premises for themselves, and (ii) the unstated premises are not themselves controversial. If done properly, the suppression of premises can add greatly to the efficiency of language. Indeed, without the judicious suppression of obvious premises, many arguments would become too cumbersome to be effective.

Suppressed premises can also be used improperly. People sometimes suppress questionable assumptions so that their opponents will not notice where an argument goes astray. For example, when election debates turn to the topic of crime, we often hear arguments like this:

> My opponent is opposed to the death penalty, so he must be soft on crime.

The response sometimes sounds like this:

> Since my opponent continues to support the death penalty, he must not have read the most recent studies, which show that the death penalty does not deter crime.

The first argument assumes that anyone who is opposed to the death penalty is soft on crime, and the second argument assumes that anyone who read the studies in question would be convinced by them and would turn against the death penalty. Both of these assumptions are questionable, and the questions they raise are central to the debate. If we want to understand these issues and address them directly, we have to bring out these suppressed premises explicitly.

EXERCISE IV

The following arguments depend for their validity on suppressed premises of various kinds. For each of them, list enough suppressed premises to make the argument valid and to show why it is valid. This might require several suppressed premises of various kinds.

> EXAMPLE: Carol has no sisters, because all her siblings are brothers.
>
> SUPPRESSED PREMISES: A sister would be a sibling.
> A brother is not a sister.

(1) Macaulay Culkin is under thirty-five. Therefore, he cannot run for president of the United States.

(2) Nixon couldn't have been president in 1950, since he was still in the Senate.

(3) Eighty-one is not a prime number, because eighty-one is divisible by three.

(4) There's no one named Rupert here; we have only female patients.

(5) Columbus did not discover the New World, because the Vikings explored Newfoundland centuries earlier.

(6) There must not be any survivors, since they would have been found by now.

(7) Lincoln could not have met Washington, because Washington was dead before Lincoln was born.

(8) Philadelphia cannot play Los Angeles in the World Series, since they are both in the National League.

(9) Mildred must be over forty-three, since she has a daughter who is thirty-six.

(10) He cannot be a grandfather, because he never had children.

(11) That's not acid rock; you can understand the lyrics.

(12) Harold can't play in the Super Bowl, because he broke his leg.

(13) Manute must be a basketball player, since he is so tall.

(14) Dan is either stupid or very cunning, so he must be stupid.

(15) Susan refuses to work on Sundays, which shows that she is lazy and inflexible.

(16) Jim told me that Bathsheba is a professor, so she can't be a student, since professors must already have degrees.

(17) This burglar alarm won't work unless we are lucky or the burglar uses the front door, so we can't count on it.

(18) His natural talents were not enough; he still lost the match because he had not practiced sufficiently.

THE METHOD OF RECONSTRUCTION

We can summarize the discussion so far by listing the steps to be taken in reconstructing an argument. The first two steps were discussed in Chapters 2 and 3.

(1) Do a *close analysis* of the passage containing the argument.

(2) List all explicit premises and the conclusion in *standard form*.

(3) *Clarify* the premises and the conclusion where necessary.

(4) *Break up* the premises and the conclusion into smaller parts where this is possible.

(5) *Arrange* the parts of the argument into a chain of subarguments where this is possible.

(6) Assess each argument and subargument for *validity*.[2]

(7) If any argument or subargument is not valid, or if it is not clear why it is valid, add *suppressed premises* that will show how to get from the premises to the conclusion.

(8) Assess the *truth* of the premises.

This method is not intended to be mechanical. Each step requires care and intelligence. As a result, a given argument can be reconstructed in various ways with varying degrees of illumination and insight. The goal of this method is to reveal as much of the structure of an argument as possible and to learn from it as much as you can. Different reconstructions approach this goal more or less closely.

The whole process is more complex than our discussion thus far has suggested. This is especially clear in the last three steps. They must be carried out together. In deciding whether an argument is acceptable, we try to find a set of true suppressed premises that, if added to the stated premises, yields a sound argument for the conclusion. Two problems typically arise when we make this effort:

(1) We find a set of premises strong enough to support the conclusion, but at least one of these premises is false.

---

[2] With inductive arguments we assess the argument for *strength* instead of validity. Inductive arguments will be examined in Chapter 8.

(2) We modify the premises to avoid falsehood, but the conclusion no longer follows from them.

The reconstruction of an argument typically involves shifting back and forth between the demand for a valid argument and the demand for true premises. Eventually, we either show the argument to be sound or we abandon the effort. In the latter case, we conclude that the argument in question has no sound reconstruction. It is still possible that *we* were at fault in not finding a reconstruction that showed the argument to be sound. Perhaps we did not show enough ingenuity in searching for a suppressed premise that would do the trick. There is, in fact, no purely formal or mechanical way of dealing with this problem. A person presenting an argument may reasonably leave out steps, provided that they can easily be filled in by those to whom the argument is addressed. So in analyzing an argument we should be charitable, but our charity has limits. After a reasonable search for those suppressed premises that would show the argument to be sound, we should not blame ourselves if we fail to find them. Rather, the blame shifts to the person who formulated the argument for not doing so clearly.

EXERCISE V

Practice the method of reconstruction on one or more of the following:

(1) One of the passages at the end of Chapter 3.

(2) An editorial from your local paper.

(3) Your last term paper or a friend's last term paper.

(4) Part of one of the articles in Part 2.

DIGGING DEEPER

After we have reconstructed an argument as well as we can, doubts still might arise about its premises. If we agree with its premises, others might deny them or ask why they are true. If we disagree with some premise, we may be able to understand the source of our disagreement better if we determine why it is believed by other people—including the person who gave the argument. Either way, it is useful to try to construct supporting arguments for the premises that might be questioned. These supporting arguments are not parts of the explicit argument or even of its reconstruction; they are arguments further back in a chain of arguments.

When we look for further arguments to support the premises in an argument, we might then wonder whether the premises of this new argument can be accepted without supporting arguments as well. We seem faced with the unpleasant task of producing endless chains of argument. (A similar problem was mentioned in Chapter 2.) When pressed in this way to give reasons for our reasons, and reasons for our reasons for our reasons, we eventually come upon fundamental principles— principles for which we cannot give any more-basic argument. These fundamental principles can concern morality, religion, politics, and our general views concerning the nature of the world. We often argue within a framework of such principles without actually stating them because we assume (sometimes incorrectly) that others accept them as well. When someone argues that environmental destruction should be stopped because it will lead to the annihilation of the human race, he or she will not feel called upon to say explicitly "And the annihilation of the human race would be a very bad thing." That, after all, is something that most people take for granted. Though fundamental principles are often obvious and generally accepted, at times it is not clear what principles are being assumed and just how acceptable they really are. Then we need to make our assumptions explicit and to look for deeper arguments, continuing the process as far as we can. There is a limit to how far we can go, but the deeper we go, the better we will understand our own views and, in addition, the views of our opponents.

EXERCISE VI

The following arguments depend for their validity on suppressed premises. First, state what these underlying principles might be. In some cases, there might be more than one. Second, indicate whether these principles are fundamental in the sense just described. If not, try to give supporting arguments for the premises in each argument until you arrive at principles that are fundamental. Remember, you do not have to accept an argument to detect its underlying principles and to understand the kind of argument that could be used to support it.

EXAMPLE: General Snork has no right to rule, because he came to power by a military coup.

SUPPRESSED PREMISE: Someone who came to power by a military coup has no right to rule.

SUPPORTING ARGUMENT: Someone has a right to rule only if he or she has been elected by the people.

Someone who comes to power by a military coup has not been elected by the people.

—————————

∴ Someone who came to power by a military coup has no right to rule.

(Further support for the first premise might be provided by some general theory of democracy, such as that all rights to use power come from the people, and the only legitimate way for the people to delegate these rights is in elections.)

(1) You shouldn't call Kirk guilty, because he has not even been tried yet.

(2) Cows cannot live in a desert, because they eat grass.

(3) The liquid in this glass must not be water, since the sugar I put in it isn't dissolving.

(4) People can vote and be drafted at eighteen, so they should also be allowed to drink at eighteen.

(5) We have no right to attack left-wing dictatorships if we support right-wing dictatorships. So we should not attack left-wing dictatorships.

(6) That chair won't hold you, since it almost broke a few minutes ago when your little sister sat in it.

(7) Bringing down our deficits should be a high priority, since, if high deficits continue, inflation will return.

(8) The thought of eating ostrich meat will seem strange to most people, so your ostrich farm is bound to go broke.

(9) Getting good grades must be hard, since, if getting good grades were easy, more people would do it.

(10) Morris does not deserve his wealth, for he merely inherited it.

(11) Frank should not be punished, since it is wrong to punish someone just to make an example of him.

(12) There can't be UFOs (unidentified flying objects), because there is no life on other planets.

(13) The sky is red tonight, so it isn't going to rain tomorrow.

(14) Parents take care of their children when they are young, so their children should take care of them when they get old.

ADVANCED SECTION: CAPITAL PUNISHMENT

We can illustrate these methods of deep analysis by examining the difficult question of the constitutionality of capital punishment. It has been argued before the Supreme Court that the death penalty should be declared unconstitutional because it is a cruel and unusual punishment. The explicitly stated argument has the following basic form:

> The death penalty is a cruel and unusual punishment.
> _____
> ∴ The death penalty should be ruled unconstitutional.

The argument plainly depends on two suppressed premises:

SP1: The Constitution prohibits cruel and unusual punishments.

SP2: Anything that the Constitution prohibits should be declared unconstitutional.

So the argument, more fully spelled out, looks like this:

> (1) The death penalty is a cruel and unusual punishment.
> (2) SP: The Constitution prohibits cruel and unusual punishments.
>
> ─────────
>
> ∴ (3) The Constitution prohibits the death penalty.
> (4) SP: Anything that the Constitution prohibits should be declared unconstitutional.
>
> ─────────
>
> ∴ (5) The death penalty should be declared unconstitutional.

This reconstruction seems to be a fair representation of the intent of the original argument.

We can now turn to an assessment of this argument. First, the argument is valid: given the premises, the conclusion does follow. So we can turn our attention to the plausibility of the premises themselves. The second premise is clearly true, for the Constitution does, in fact, prohibit cruel and unusual punishments. The Eighth Amendment reads, "Excessive bail shall not be required, nor excessive fines imposed, nor cruel and unusual punishments inflicted," and its amendments are part of the Constitution. It is not clear, however, just what this prohibition amounts to. In particular, does the punishment have to be *both* cruel *and* unusual to be prohibited, or is it sufficient for it to be *either* cruel *or* unusual? This would make a big difference if cruel punishments were usual, or if some unusual punishments were not cruel. For the moment, let us interpret the language as meaning "both cruel and unusual."

Premise 4 seems uncontroversial. Indeed, it might sound like a truism to say that anything that violates a constitutional provision should be declared unconstitutional. However, as a matter of fact, this notion was once controversial, for nothing in the Constitution explicitly gives the courts the right to declare acts of legislators unconstitutional and hence void. The courts have acquired and consolidated this right in the years since 1789, and it is still sometimes challenged by those who think that it gives the courts too much power. But even if the judiciary's power to declare laws unconstitutional is not itself a constitutionally stated power, it is so much an accepted part of our system that no one would challenge it in a courtroom procedure today.

Although premise 4 has a more complicated backing than most people realize, it is obviously the first premise—"The death penalty is a cruel and unusual punishment"—that forms the heart of the argument. What we would expect, then, is a good supporting argument to be put forward in its behalf. Consider the following argument by Supreme Court Justice Potter Stewart, intended to support this claim in particular cases in which the death penalty was imposed for rape and murder:

> In the first place, it is clear that these sentences are "cruel" in the sense that they excessively go beyond, not in degree but in kind, the punishments that the state legislatures have determined to be necessary. . . . In the second place, it is equally clear that these sentences are "unusual" in the sense that the penalty of death is infrequently imposed for murder, and that its imposition for rape is extraordinarily

rare. But I do not rest my conclusion upon these two propositions alone. These death sentences are cruel and unusual in the same way that being struck by lightning is cruel and unusual. For, of all the people convicted of rapes and murders in 1967 and 1968, many just as reprehensible as these, the petitioners are among a capriciously selected random handful upon whom the sentence of death has in fact been imposed. My concurring brothers have demonstrated that, if any basis can be discerned for the selection of these few to be sentenced to die, it is the constitutionally impermissible basis of race.[3]

The first sentence argues that the death penalty is *cruel*. The basic idea is that a punishment is cruel if it inflicts more harm than is necessary (for any legitimate and worthwhile purpose). Stewart then seems to accept the state legislatures' view that the death penalty inflicts more harm than is necessary. This makes it cruel.

Now let us concentrate on the part of this argument intended to show that the death penalty is an *unusual* punishment. Of course, in civilized nations the death penalty is reserved for a small range of crimes, but this is hardly the point at issue. The point of the argument is that the death penalty is unusual even for those crimes that are punishable by death, including first-degree murder. Moreover, Stewart claims that, among those convicted of crimes punishable by death, who actually receives a death sentence is determined either capriciously or on the basis of race. The point seems to be that whether a person who is convicted of a capital crime will be given the death penalty depends on the kind of legal aid he receives, the prosecutor's willingness to offer a plea bargain, the judge's personality, the beliefs and attitudes of the jury, and many other considerations. There are many points in the process where choices that affect the outcome could be based on mere whim or caprice, or even on the race of the defendant or the victim. Why are these factors mentioned? Because, as Stewart says, it is unconstitutional for sentencing to be based on caprice or race.

We can then restate the basic argument more carefully as follows:

> Among those found guilty of crimes punishable by death, who is given the death sentence depends on caprice or race.
> It is unconstitutional for sentencing to depend on caprice or race.
> A punishment is unusual in the relevant sense if who gets it depends on factors on which it is unconstitutional for sentencing to depend.

> ∴ The death penalty is an unusual punishment in the relevant sense.

Now we can spread the entire argument out before us:

> (1) An act is cruel if it inflicts more harm than is necessary (for any legitimate and worthwhile purpose).

---

[3] From Justice Stewart's concurring opinion in *Furman v. Georgia*, 408 U.S. 239 at 309–310 (1972). Stewart provided one of the crucial swing votes in this important case.

(2) The death penalty inflicts more harm than is necessary (for any legitimate and worthwhile purpose).

∴ (3) The death penalty is cruel.

(4) Among those found guilty of crimes punishable by death, who is given the death sentence depends on caprice or race.

(5) It is unconstitutional for sentencing to depend on caprice or race.

(6) A punishment is unusual in the relevant sense if who gets it depends on factors on which it is unconstitutional for sentencing to depend.

∴ (7) The death penalty is an unusual punishment in the relevant sense.

∴ (8) The death penalty is both cruel and unusual in the relevant sense.

(9) The Constitution prohibits cruel and unusual punishments.

∴ (10) The Constitution prohibits the death penalty.

(11) Anything that the Constitution prohibits should be declared unconstitutional.

∴ (12) The death penalty should be declared unconstitutional.

These propositions provide at least the skeleton of an argument with some force. The conclusion does seem to follow from the premises, and the premises themselves seem plausible. It seems, then, that we have produced a charitable reconstruction of the argument.

We can now see how an opponent might respond to it. One particularly probing objection goes like this:

> It is sadly true that caprice and race sometimes determine who, among those found guilty of crimes punishable by death, is given the death sentence. However, this fact reflects badly not on the law but on its administration. If judges and juries met their obligations, these factors would not affect who receives the death penalty, and this punishment would no longer be unusual in any relevant sense. What is needed, then, is judicial reform and not the removal of the death penalty on constitutional grounds.

This response is probing because it insists on a distinction between a law itself and the effects of its application—or, more pointedly, its misapplication. Since this distinction was not drawn in the argument above, it is not clear which premise is denied in this response. Probably the best interpretation is that this response denies premise 6 because it is not the death penalty itself that is unusual in the relevant sense when the conditions in premise 6 are met. Instead, it is the present administration of the death penalty that is problematic.

To meet this objection, the original argument could be strengthened in the following way:

A law should not be judged in isolation from the likely effects of implementing it. Because of the very nature of our system of criminal justice, for the foreseeable future, the death penalty will almost certainly continue to be applied in a capricious and racially discriminatory manner, and those who receive it will be determined partly by factors that the Constitution forbids as a basis for sentencing. The death penalty will therefore remain an unusual punishment, so it should be declared unconstitutional.

This argument suggests ways to avoid the above objection by strengthening premises 4 through 6 of the above argument. The new versions of these premises can be spelled out in the following way:

(4*) It is very likely in the foreseeable future that, among those found guilty of crimes punishable by death, who is given the death sentence will continue to depend on either caprice or race.

(5) It is unconstitutional for sentencing to depend on caprice or race.

(6*) A punishment is unusual in the relevant sense if it is very likely in the foreseeable future that who gets it will continue to depend on factors on which it is unconstitutional for sentencing to depend.

∴ (7) The death penalty is an unusual punishment in the relevant sense.

Of course, an opponent can still respond that these premises are false if he or she can show that there is some way to avoid the problems that are raised by premises 4* and 5. However, this will not be easy to show if the argument is right about "the very nature of our system of criminal justice."

Another kind of question is raised by premise 6*. Should a law be declared unconstitutional whenever there is a good chance that it will be abused in ways that infringe on constitutional rights? Of course, a great many laws have this potential—for example, all laws involving police power. This is why certain police powers have been limited by court rulings. Strict rules governing interrogations and wiretaps are two results. However, only an extremist would suggest that we should abolish all police powers because of the inevitable risk of unconstitutional abuse. Accordingly, those who argue in favor of the death penalty might try to show that the problems in the application of the death penalty are not sufficiently important to be constitutionally intolerable.

The supporter of the death penalty can go beyond this criticism in the following way:

Those who argue against the constitutionality of the death penalty on the grounds that it is a cruel and unusual punishment use the expression "cruel and unusual" in a way wholly different from that intended by the framers of the Eighth Amendment. By "cruel" they had in mind punishments that involved torture. By "unusual" they meant bizarre or ghoulish punishments of the kind that often formed part of public spectacles in barbaric times. Modern methods of execution are neither cruel nor unusual in the constitutionally relevant senses of these words. Therefore, laws demanding the death penalty cannot be declared unconstitutional on the grounds that they either directly or indirectly involve a punishment that is cruel and unusual.

The core of this counterargument can be expressed as follows:

(1) In appeals to the Constitution, its words should be taken as they were originally intended.
(2) Modern methods of carrying out a death penalty are neither "cruel" nor "unusual" if these words are interpreted as they were originally intended.

∴ (3) The death penalty should not be declared unconstitutional on the ground that it violates the prohibition against cruel and unusual punishments.

The second premise of this argument states a matter of historical fact that might not be altogether easy to verify. The chances are, however, that it comes close to the truth. Given this, the opponent of the death penalty must either attack the first premise or find some other grounds for holding that the death penalty should be declared unconstitutional.

The first premise may seem like a truism, for how can a document guide conduct if anyone can reinterpret its words regardless of what was intended? The literal meaning of the document is simply its meaning; everything else is interpretation. Of course, there are times when it is not easy to discover what its meaning is. (In the present case, for example, it is not clear whether the Eighth Amendment prohibits punishments that are either cruel or unusual or only those that are both cruel and unusual.) It seems unlikely, however, that those who drafted the Eighth Amendment used either the word "cruel" or the word "unusual" in the ways in which they are employed in the argument against the death penalty.

Does this last concession end the debate in favor of those who reject the anti–capital punishment argument that we have been examining? The argument certainly seems to be weakened, but there are those who would take a bold course by simply denying the first premise of the argument used to refute them. They would deny, that is, that we are bound to read the Constitution in the way intended by its framers. An argument in favor of this position might look something like this:

> The great bulk of the Constitution was written in an age almost wholly different from our own. To cite just two examples of this: Women were denied fundamental rights of full citizenship, and slavery was a constitutionally accepted feature of national life. The Constitution has remained a live and relevant document just because it has undergone constant reinterpretation. So, even if it is true that the expression "cruel and unusual" meant something quite special to those who framed the Eighth Amendment, plainly a humane desire to make punishment more civilized lay behind it. The present reading of this amendment is in the spirit of its original intention and simply makes it applicable to our own times.

The argument has now moved to an entirely new level: one concerning whether the Constitution should be read strictly in accord with the original intentions of those who wrote it or more freely to accommodate modern realities.

We shall not pursue the discussion further into these complex areas. Instead, we should consider how we were led into them. Recall that our original argument did not concern the general question of whether capital punishment is right or wrong. The argument turned on a much more specific point: Does the death penalty violate the prohibition against cruel and unusual punishments in the Eighth Amendment to the Constitution? The argument with which we began seemed to be a straightforward proof that it does. Yet, as we explored principles that lay in back of this deceptively simple argument, the issue became broader and more complex. We finally reached a point at which the force of the original argument was seen to depend on what we consider the proper way to interpret the Constitution—strictly or more freely. If we now go on to ask which method of interpretation is best, we will have to look at the role of the courts and, more generally, the purpose of government. Eventually we will come to fundamental principles for which we can give no further argument.

CONCLUSION

In examining the question of the constitutionality of capital punishment, we have had to compress a complicated discussion into a few pages. We have only begun to show how the issues involved in this complex debate can be sorted out and then addressed intelligently. There is, however, no guarantee that these procedures, however far they are carried out, will eventually settle this or any other fundamental dispute. It is entirely possible that the parties to a dispute may reach a point where they encounter a fundamental or rock-bottom disagreement that they cannot resolve. They simply disagree and cannot conceive of any deeper principles that could resolve their disagreement. But even if this happens, they will at least understand the source of their disagreement. They will not be arguing at cross-purposes, as so often happens in the discussion of important issues. Finally, even if they continue to disagree, they may come to appreciate that others may view things quite differently from the way they do. This may in turn help them deal with their basic disagreements in an intelligent, humane, and civilized way.

EXERCISE VII

What is the best argument Justice Stewart could give in support of the premise that the death penalty inflicts more harm than is necessary (for any legitimate and worthwhile purpose)? Is this argument adequate to justify this premise?

EXERCISE VIII

How could one best argue in support of premise 4*, that it is very likely in the foreseeable future that, among those found guilty of crimes punishable by death, who is given the death sentence will continue to depend on either caprice or race? How could defenders of the death penalty try to refute this argument?

EXERCISE IX

Formulate the best argument you can in support of the premise that in appeals to the Constitution, its words should be taken as they were originally intended? Is this argument adequate to justify this premise? Why or why not?

EXERCISE X

The final argument in our examination of whether or not the death penalty violates the Constitution attempts to show that the Constitution must be read in a free or liberal way that makes it relevant to present society. Filling in suppressed premises where necessary, restate this argument as a sequence of explicit steps. After you have given the argument the strongest restatement you can, evaluate it for its soundness.

DISCUSSION QUESTIONS

(1) How can you tell when you have reached a fundamental principle? Must every argument start with some basic claim for which no further argument can be given or for which you can give no argument?
(2) Does reconstructing an argument help you understand and evaluate it? If so, how? If not, why not?

Chapter Five

THE FORMAL ANALYSIS OF ARGUMENTS: PROPOSITIONAL LOGIC

This chapter will examine some more-technical procedures for analyzing and evaluating arguments. In particular, it will consider the notion of validity, for this is a central concept of logic. The first part of the chapter will show how the notion of validity introduced in Chapter 2 can be developed rigorously in one area—what is called propositional logic. This branch of logic deals with connectives such as "and" and "or," which allow us to build up compound propositions from simpler ones. Throughout most of the chapter, the focus will be theoretical rather than immediately practical. It is intended to provide insight into the concept of validity by examining it in an ideal setting. The chapter will close with a discussion of the relationship between the ideal language of symbolic logic and the language we ordinarily speak.

VALIDITY AND THE FORMAL ANALYSIS OF ARGUMENTS

When we carry out an informal analysis of an argument, we pay close attention to the key terms used to present the argument and then ask ourselves whether these key terms have been used properly. So far, we have no exact techniques for answering the question: Is such and such a term used correctly? We rely, instead, on logical instincts that, on the whole, are fairly good. In a great many cases, people can tell whether a warranting connective is used correctly in indicating that one claim follows from another. But if we ask the average intelligent person *why* one claim follows from the other, he or she will probably have little to say except, perhaps, that it is just obvious. That is, it is often easy to see *that* one claim follows from another, but to explain *why* can turn out to be difficult. The purpose of this chapter is to provide such an explanation for some arguments.

This quality of "following from" is called validity, as we saw in Chapter 2. The focus of our attention will be largely on the *concept* of validity. We are not, for the time being at least, interested in whether this or that argument is valid; we want to understand validity itself. To this end, the arguments we will examine are so simple that you will not be able to imagine anyone not understanding them at a glance. Who needs logic to deal with arguments of this kind? There is, however, good reason for dealing with simple–trivially simple–arguments at the start. The analytic approach to a complex issue is first to break it down into subissues, repeating the process until we reach problems simple enough to be solved. After these simpler problems are solved, we can reverse the process and construct solutions to larger and more-complex problems. When done correctly, the *result* of such an analytic process may seem dull and obvious–and it often is. The *discovery* of such a process, in contrast, often demands the insight of genius.

PROPOSITIONAL LOGIC

CONJUNCTION

The first system of arguments we will examine concerns propositional (or sentential) connectives. Propositional connectives are terms that allow us to build new propositions from old ones, usually combining two or more propositions into a single proposition. For example, given the propositions "John is tall" and "Harry is short," we can use the term "and" to *conjoin* them, forming a single compound proposition: "John is tall and Harry is short."

Let us look carefully at the simple word "and" and ask how it functions. "And," in fact, is a curious word, for it does not seem to stand for anything, at least in the way in which a proper name ("Churchill") and a common noun ("dog") seem to stand for things. Instead of asking what this word stands for, we can ask a different question: What *truth conditions* govern this connective? That is, under what conditions are propositions containing this connective true? To answer this question, we imagine every possible way in which the component propositions can be true or false. Then for each combination we decide what truth value to assign to the entire proposition. This may sound complicated, but an example will make it clear:

John is tall.	Harry is short.	John is tall and Harry is short.
T	T	T
T	F	F
F	T	F
F	F	F

Here the first two columns cover every possibility for the component propositions to be either true or false. The third column states the truth value of the whole proposition for each combination. Clearly, the conjunction of two propositions is true if both of the component propositions are true; otherwise, it is false. It should also be obvious that our reflections have not depended on the particular propositions we have selected. We could have been talking about dinosaurs instead of people, and we still would have come to the conclusion that the conjunction of two propositions is true if both propositions are true, but false otherwise. This neglect of the particular content of propositions is what makes our account *formal*. In order to reflect the generality of our concerns, we can drop the reference to particular sentences altogether and use variables instead. Just as the letters x, y, and z can be replaced by any numbers in mathematics, so we can use the letters p, q, r, s, ... as variables that can be replaced by any propositions in logic. We will also use the symbol "&" (called an "ampersand") for "and."

Consider the expression "p & q." Is it true or false? There is obviously no answer to this question. This is not because we do not know what "p" and "q" stand for, for in fact "p" and "q" do not stand for any proposition. Thus, "p & q" is not a proposition, but rather a pattern for a whole series of propositions. To reflect this, we will say that "p & q" is a *propositional form*. It is a pattern, or form, for a whole series of propositions, including "John is tall and Harry is short."

To repeat the central idea, we can pass from a proposition to a propositional form by replacing propositions with propositional variables.

Proposition	*Propositional form*
John is tall and Harry is short.	p & q

When we proceed in the opposite direction by uniformly substituting propositions for propositional variables, we get what we will call a *substitution instance* of that propositional form.

Propositional Form	*Substitution Instance*
p & q	Roses are red and violets are blue.

Thus, "John is tall and Harry is short" and "Roses are red and violets are blue" are both substitution instances of the propositional form "p & q."

These ideas are perfectly simple, but to be clear about them, it is important to notice that "p" is also a propositional form, with *every* proposition, including "Roses are red and violets are blue," as its substitution instances. There is no rule against substituting compound propositions for propositional variables. Perhaps a bit more surprisingly, our definitions allow "Roses are red and roses are red" to be a substitution instance of "p & q." We get a substitution instance of a propositional form by uniformly replacing the same variable with the same proposition throughout. We have not said that different variables must be replaced with different propositions throughout. The rule is this:

> Different variables may be replaced with the same proposition, but different propositions may not be replaced with the same variable.

To summarize the discussion thus far:

> "Roses are red and violets are blue" is a substitution instance of "p & q."
>
> "Roses are red and violets are blue" is also a substitution instance of "p."
>
> "Roses are red and roses are red" is a substitution instance of "p & q."
>
> "Roses are red and roses are red" is a substitution instance of "p & p."
>
> "Roses are red and violets are blue" is *not* a substitution instance of "p & p."
>
> "Roses are red" is *not* a substitution instance of "p & p."

We are in a position to give a perfectly general definition of conjunction, using propositional variables where previously we used specific propositions.

p	q	p & q
T	T	T
T	F	F
F	T	F
F	F	F

There is no limit to the number of propositions we can conjoin to form a new proposition. "Roses are red and violets are blue; sugar is sweet and so are you" is a substitution instance of "(p & q & r & s)." We can also use parentheses to group propositions. This last example could be treated as a substitution instance of "((p & q) & (r & s))"—that is, as a conjunction of two conjunctions. Later we will see that parentheses can make an important difference to the meaning of a total proposition.

One cautionary note. The word "and" is not always used to connect two distinct sentences. Sometimes a sentence has to be rewritten for us to see that it is equivalent to a sentence of this form. For example,

Steffi Graf and Monica Seles are tennis players

is simply a short way of saying

Steffi Graf is a tennis player and Monica Seles is a tennis player.

At other times, the word "and" is *not* used to produce a conjunction of propositions. For example,

Steffi Graf and Monica Seles are playing each other

does not mean that

Steffi Graf is playing each other, and Monica Seles is playing each other.

That does not even make sense. The original sentence does not express a conjunction of two propositions. Instead, it expresses a single proposition about two people taken as a group. At other times, it is unclear whether a sentence expresses a conjunction of propositions or a single proposition about a group. The sentence

Steffi and Monica are playing tennis

could be taken either way. When a sentence containing the word "and" expresses the conjunction of two propositions, we will say that it expresses a *propositional conjunction*. When a sentence containing "and" does not express the conjunction of two propositions, we will say that it expresses a *nonpropositional conjunction*. In this chapter we are concerned only with sentences that express propositional conjunctions. A sentence should be translated into the symbolic form "$p \ \& \ q$" only if it expresses a propositional conjunction. There is no mechanical procedure that can be followed to determine whether a certain sentence expresses a conjunction of two propositions. One must think carefully about what the sentence means and about the context in which that sentence is used. This takes practice.

EXERCISE I

The proposition "The night is young, and you're so beautiful" is a substitution instance of which of the following propositional forms?

(1) p

(2) q

(3) $p \ \& \ q$

(4) $p \ \& \ r$

(5) $p \ \& \ q \ \& \ r$

(6) $p \ \& \ p$

(7) p or q

EXERCISE II

Give three different propositional forms of which the following proposition is a substitution instance:

> The night is young, and you're so beautiful, and my flight leaves in thirty minutes.

EXERCISE III

Indicate whether each of the following sentences expresses a propositional conjunction or a nonpropositional conjunction—that is, whether or not it expresses a conjunction of two propositions. If the sentence could be either, then specify a context in which it would naturally be used to express a propositional conjunction and a different context in which it would naturally be used to express a nonpropositional conjunction.

(1) A Catholic priest married John and Mary.

(2) Fred had pie and ice cream for dessert.

(3) The presidential candidate who wins the election usually carries New York and California.

(4) Susan got married and had a child.

(5) Jane speaks both French and English.

(6) Someone who speaks both French and English is bilingual.

(7) Ken and Naomi are two of my best friends.

(8) Miranda and Nick cooked dinner.

(9) I doubt that John is poor and happy.

VALIDITY FOR CONJUNCTION

Now we can look at an argument involving conjunction. Here is one that is ridiculously simple:

> Harry is short and John is tall.
> _____
> ∴ Harry is short.

This argument is obviously valid. But why is the argument valid? Why does the conclusion follow from the premise? The answer in this case seems obvious, but we will spell it out in detail as a guide for more-difficult cases. Suppose we replace these particular propositions with propositional forms, using a different variable for each distinct proposition throughout the argument. This yields what we will call an *argument form*; for example:

$$p \ \& \ q$$

$$\therefore p$$

This is a pattern for endlessly many arguments, each of which is called a substitution instance of this argument form. Every argument that has this general form will also be valid. It really does not matter which propositions we put back into this schema; the resulting argument will be valid—so long as we are careful to substitute the same proposition for the same variable throughout.

   Let us pursue this matter further. If an argument has true premises and a false conclusion, then we know at once that it is invalid. But in saying that an argument is *valid*, we are not only saying that it does not have true premises and a false conclusion; we are saying that the argument *cannot* have a false conclusion when the premises are true. Sometimes this is true because the argument has a structure or form that rules out the very possibility of true premises and a false conclusion. We can appeal to the notion of an argument form to make sense of this idea. A somewhat more complicated truth table will make this clear:

		Premise	Conclusion
p	*q*	*p* & *q*	*p*
T	T	T	T
T	F	F	T
F	T	F	F
F	F	F	F

The first two columns give all the combinations for the truth values of the propositions that we might substitute for "*p*" and "*q*." The third column gives the truth value of the premise for each of these combinations. (This column is the same as the definition for "&" given above.) Finally, the fourth column gives the truth value for the conclusion for each combination. (Here, of course, this merely involves repeating the first column. Later on, things will become more complicated and interesting.) If we look at this truth table, we see that no matter how we make substitutions for the variables, we never have a case in which the premise is true and the conclusion is false. In the first line, the premise is true and the conclusion is also true. In the remaining three lines, the premise is not true, so the possibility of the premise being true and the conclusion false does not arise. Here it is important to remember that a valid argument can have false premises, for one proposition can follow from another proposition that is false. Of course, an argument that is sound cannot have a false premise, since a sound argument is defined as a valid argument with true premises. But our subject here is validity, not soundness.

   Let us summarize this discussion. In the case we have examined, validity depends on the form of an argument and not on its particular content. A first principle, then, is this:

   An *argument* is valid if it is an instance of a valid argument form.

So the argument "Harry is short and John is tall; therefore, Harry is short" is valid because it is an instance of the valid argument form "*p* & *q*; ∴ *p*."

Next we must ask what makes an argument form valid. The answer to this is given in this principle:

> An argument *form* is valid if and only if it has no substitution instances in which the premises are true and the conclusion is false.

We have just seen that the argument form "*p* & *q*; ∴ *p*" meets this test. The truth-table analysis showed that. Incidentally, we can use the same truth table to show that the following argument is valid:

John is tall.	*p*
Harry is short.	*q*
∴ John is tall and Harry is short.	∴ *p* & *q*

The argument on the left is a substitution instance of the argument form on the right, and a glance at the truth table will show that there can be no cases for which all the premises could be true and the conclusion false. This pretty well covers the logical properties of conjunction.

Notice that we have not said that *every* argument that is valid is so in virtue of its form. There may be arguments in which the conclusion follows from the premises but we cannot show that the argument's validity is a matter of logical form. There are, in fact, some obviously valid arguments that have yet to be shown to be valid in terms of their form. Explaining validity by means of logical form has been an ideal of logical theory, but there are arguments—many of them quite commonplace—where this ideal has yet to be adequately fulfilled. Many arguments in mathematics fall into this category. At present, however, we will only consider arguments in which the strategy we used for analyzing conjunction continues to work.

EXERCISE IV

Are the following arguments valid? Why or why not?

(1) Donald owns a tower in New York and a palace in Atlantic City. Therefore, Donald owns a palace in Atlantic City.

(2) Tom owns a house. Therefore, Tom owns a house and a piece of land.

(3) Ilsa is tall. Therefore, Ilsa is tall, and Ilsa is tall.

(4) Bernie has a son and a daughter. Bernie has a father and a mother. Therefore, Bernie has a son and a mother.

(5) Mary got married and had a child. Therefore, Mary had a child and got married.

(6) Bess and Katie tied for MVP. Therefore, Bess tied for MVP.

EXERCISE V

For each of the following claims, determine whether it is true or false. Defend your answers.

(1) An argument that is a substitution instance of a valid argument form is always valid.

(2) An argument that is a substitution instance of an invalid argument form is always invalid.

(3) An invalid argument is always a substitution instance of an invalid argument form.

DISJUNCTION

Just as we can form a conjunction of two propositions by using the connective "and," we can form a *disjunction* of two propositions by using the connective "or," as in the following compound sentence:

John will win or Harry will win.

Again, it is easy to see that the truth of this whole compound proposition depends on the truth of the component propositions. If they are both false, then the compound proposition is false. If just one of them is true, then the compound proposition is true. But suppose they are both true, what shall we say then? Sometimes when we say "either-or" we seem to rule out the possibility of both; if a waiter says "You may have chicken or steak," this probably means that you cannot have both. Sometimes, however, it is not true that both are ruled out—for example, when we say to someone, "If you want to see tall mountains, go to California or Colorado." So one way (in fact, the standard way) to deal with this problem is to say that "or" has two meanings: one *exclusive*, which rules out both, and one *inclusive*, which does not rule out both. We could thus give two truth-table definitions, one for each of these senses of the word "or":

	Exclusive			Inclusive	
p	q	p or q	p	q	p or q
T	T	F	T	T	T
T	F	T	T	F	T
F	T	T	F	T	T
F	F	F	F	F	F

For reasons that will become clear in a moment, we will adopt the inclusive sense of the word "or." Where necessary, we will define the exclusive sense using the inclusive sense as a starting point. Logicians symbolize *disjunctions* using the connective "∨" (called a "wedge"). The truth table for this connective has the following form:

p	q	$p \vee q$
T	T	T
T	F	T
F	T	T
F	F	F

We will look at some arguments involving this connective in a moment.

NEGATION

With conjunction and disjunction, we begin with two propositions and construct a new proposition from them. There is another way in which we can construct a new proposition from another one—by *negating* it. Given the proposition "John is clever," we can get a new proposition, "John is not clever," simply by inserting the word "not" in the correct place in the sentence. What, exactly, does the word "not" mean? This can be a difficult question to answer, especially if we begin with the assumption that all words stand for things. Does it stand for nothing or, maybe, nothingness? Although some respectable philosophers have sometimes spoken in this way, it is important to see that the word "not" does not stand for anything at all. It has an altogether different function in the language. To see this, think how conjunction and disjunction work. Given two propositions, the word "and" allows us to construct another proposition that is true only when both original propositions are true, and is false otherwise. With disjunction, given two propositions, the word "or" allows us to construct another proposition that is false only when both of the original propositions are false, and true otherwise. (Our truth-table definitions reflect these facts.) Using these definitions as models, how should we define *negation*? A parallel answer is that the negation of a proposition is true just in the cases in which the original proposition is false, and it is false just in the cases in which original proposition is true. Using the symbol " ~ " (called a "tilde") to stand for negation, this gives us the following truth-table definition:

p	$\sim p$
T	F
F	T

Negation might seem as simple as can be, but people quite often get confused by negations. If Diana says "I could not breathe for a whole minute," she might mean that something made her unable to breathe for a whole minute (maybe she was choking), or she might mean that she was able to hold her breath for a whole minute (if she had to, say, to win a bet). If "*A*" symbolizes "Diana could breathe some time during this minute," then " ~ *A*" symbolizes the former claim (that Diana was unable to breathe for this minute). Consequently, the latter claim (that Diana could hold her breath for this minute) should not also be symbolized by " ~ *A*." Indeed, this interpretation of the original sentence is not a negation, even though the original sentence did include the word "not." Moreover, some sentences are negations even though they do not include the word "not." For example, "Nobody owns Mars" is the negation of "Somebody owns Mars"; if the latter is symbolized as "*A*," the former can be symbolized as "*~A*," even though the former does not include the word "not." There is no mechanical procedure for determining whether an English sentence can be symbolized as a negation. All you can do is think carefully about the sentence's meaning and context. The best way to get good at this is to practice.

EXERCISE VI

Put each of the following sentences in symbolic form. Be sure to specify exactly which sentence is represented by each capital letter, and pay special attention to the placement of the negation. If the sentence could be interpreted in more than one way, symbolize each interpretation and describe a context in which it would be natural to interpret it in each way.

(1) It won't rain tomorrow.

(2) It might not rain tomorrow.

(3) There is no chance that it will rain tomorrow.

(4) I believe that it won't rain tomorrow.

(5) Joe is not too smart, or else he's very clever.

(6) Kristin is not smart or rich.

(7) Sometimes you feel like a nut; sometimes you don't.

HOW TRUTH-FUNCTIONAL CONNECTIVES WORK

We have now defined conjunction, disjunction, and negation. That, all by itself, is sufficient to complete the branch of modern logic called propositional logic. The definitions themselves may seem peculiar. They do not look like the definitions we find in a dictionary. But the form of these definitions is important, for it tells us something interesting about the character of such words as "and," "or," and "not." Two things are worth noting: (1) These expressions are used to construct a new proposition from old ones; (2) The newly constructed proposition is always a *truth function* of the original propositions—that is, the truth value of the new proposition is always determined by the truth value of the original propositions. For this reason these connectives are called *truth-functional connectives*. (Of course, with negation, we start with a *single* proposition.) For example, suppose that "*A*" and "*B*" are two true propositions and "*G*" and "*H*" are two false propositions. We can then determine the truth values of more-complex propositions built from them using conjunction, disjunction, and negation. Sometimes the correct assignment is obvious at a glance:

A & B	True
A & G	False
~A	False
~G	True
$A \vee H$	True
$G \vee H$	False
~A & G	False

As noted earlier, parentheses can be used to distinguish groupings. Sometimes the placement of parentheses can make an important difference, as in the following two expressions:

$$\sim A \ \& \ G \qquad \sim(A \ \& \ G)$$

Notice that in one expression the negation symbol applies only to the proposition "A," whereas in the other expression it applies to the entire proposition "$(A$ & $G)$." Thus, the first expression above is false, and the second expression is true. Only the second expression can be translated as "Not both A and G." Both these expressions are different from "~A & ~G," which means "Neither A nor G."

As expressions become more complex, we reach a point where it is no longer obvious how the truth values of the component propositions determine the truth value of the entire proposition. Here a regular procedure is helpful. The easiest method is to fill in the truth values of the basic propositions and then, step by step, make assignments progressively wider, going from the inside out. For example:

$$\sim((A \vee G) \ \& \sim(\sim H \ \& \ B))$$
$$\sim((T \vee F) \ \& \sim(\sim F \ \& \ T))$$
$$\sim((T \vee F) \ \& \sim(T \ \& \ T))$$
$$\sim(T \ \& \sim(T))$$
$$\sim(T \ \& \ F)$$
$$\sim(F)$$
$$T$$

With a little practice, you can master this technique in dealing with other highly complex examples.

EXERCISE VII

Given that "A," "B," and "C" are true propositions and "X," "Y," and "Z" are false propositions, determine the truth values of the following compound propositions:

(1) ~$X \vee Y$

(2) ~$(X \vee Y)$

(3) ~$(Z \vee Z)$

(4) ~$(Z \vee \sim Z)$

(5) $\sim\sim(A \lor B)$

(6) $(A \lor Z) \& B$

(7) $(A \lor X) \& (B \lor Z)$

(8) $(A \& Z) \lor (B \& Z)$

(9) $\sim(A \lor (Z \lor X))$

(10) $\sim(A \lor \sim(Z \lor X))$

(11) $\sim A \lor \sim(Z \lor X)$

(12) $\sim Z \lor (Z \& A)$

(13) $\sim(Z \lor (Z \& A))$

(14) $\sim((Z \lor Z) \& A)$

(15) $A \lor ((\sim B \& C) \lor \sim(\sim B \lor \sim(Z \lor B)))$

(16) $A \& ((\sim B \& C) \lor \sim(\sim B \lor \sim(Z \lor B)))$

TESTING FOR VALIDITY

But what is the point of all this? In everyday life we rarely run into an expression as complicated as the one given in our example. Our purpose here is to sharpen our sensitivity to how truth-functional connectives work, and then to express our insights in clear ways. This is important because the validity of many arguments depends on the logical features of these truth-functional connectives. We can now turn directly to this subject.

Earlier we saw that every argument with the form "$p \& q; \therefore p$" will be valid. This is obvious in itself, but we saw that this claim could be justified by an appeal to truth tables. A truth-table analysis shows us that an argument with this form can never have an instance in which the premise is true and the conclusion is false. We can now apply this same technique to arguments that are more complex. In the beginning, we will take arguments that are still easy to follow without the use of technical help. In the end, we will consider some arguments that most people cannot follow without guidance.

Consider the following argument:

> Valerie is either a doctor or a lawyer.
> Valerie is neither a doctor nor a stockbroker.
> _____
> ∴ Valerie is a lawyer.

We can use the following abbreviations:

D = Valerie is a doctor.

L = Valerie is a lawyer.

S = Valerie is a stockbroker.

Using these abbreviations, the argument and its counterpart argument form look like this:

$$D \lor L \qquad\qquad p \lor q$$
$$\sim(D \lor S) \qquad\qquad \sim(p \lor r)$$
$$\overline{} \qquad\qquad \overline{}$$
$$\therefore L \qquad\qquad \therefore q$$

The expression on the right gives the argument *form* of the argument presented on the left. To see whether the argument is valid, we ask if the argument form is valid. The procedure is cumbersome, but perfectly mechanical:

			Pr.	Pr.	Cn.	
p	q	r	$(p \lor q)$	$(p \lor r)$	$\sim(p \lor r)$	q
T	T	T	T	T	F	T
T	T	F	T	T	F	T
T	F	T	T	T	F	F
T	F	F	T	T	F	F
F	T	T	T	T	F	T
F	T	F	T	F	T	T	O.K.
F	F	T	F	T	F	F
F	F	F	F	F	T	F

Notice that there is only one combination of truth values for which both premises are true, and in that case the conclusion is true as well. So the original argument is valid since it is an instance of a valid argument form—that is, an argument form with no substitution instances for which true premises are combined with a false conclusion.

This last truth table may need some explaining. First, why do we get eight rows in this truth table where before we got only four? The answer to this is that we need to test the argument form for *every possible combination of truth values* for the component propositions. With two variables, there are four possible combinations: (TT), (TF), (FT), and (FF). With three variables, there are eight possible combinations: (TTT), (TTF), (TFT), (TFF), (FTT), (FTF), (FFT), and (FFF). The general rule is this: If an argument form has *n* variables, the truth table used in its analysis must have 2^n rows. For four variables there will be sixteen rows; for five variables, thirty-two rows; for six variables, sixty-four rows; and so on. You can be sure that you capture all possible combinations of truth values by using the following pattern in constructing the columns of your truth table:

First column	*Second column*	*Third column* . . .
First half Ts, second half Fs.	First quarter Ts, second quarter Fs, and so on.	First eighth Ts, second eighth Fs, and so on.

A glance at the earlier examples in this chapter will show that we have been using this pattern, and it is the standard way of listing the possibilities. Of course, as soon as an argument becomes at all complex, these truth tables become very large indeed. But there is no need to worry about this, since we will not consider arguments with many variables. Those who do so turn to a computer for help.

The style of the truth table above is also significant. The premises (Pr.) are plainly labeled and so is the conclusion (Cn.). A line is drawn under every row in which the premises are all true. (In this case, there is only one such row–row 4.) If the conclusion on this line is also true, it is marked "O.K." If every line in which the premises are all true is O.K., then the argument form is valid. Marking all this may seem rather childish, but it is worth doing. First, it helps guard against mistakes. More importantly, it draws one's attention to the purpose of the procedure being used. Cranking out truth tables without understanding what they are about–or even why they might be helpful–does not enlighten the mind or elevate the spirit.

For the sake of contrast, we can next consider an invalid argument:

> Valerie is either a doctor or a lawyer.
> Valerie is not both a lawyer and a stockbroker.
> _____
> ∴ Therefore, Valerie is a doctor.

Using the same abbreviations used earlier, this becomes:

$$D \vee L \qquad\qquad p \vee q$$
$$\sim(L \ \& \ S) \qquad\qquad \sim(q \ \& \ r)$$
$$\overline{} \qquad\qquad \overline{}$$
$$\therefore D \qquad\qquad\quad \therefore p$$

The truth table for this argument form looks like this:

			Pr.	Pr.	Cn.		
p	q	r	$(p \vee q)$	$(q \ \& \ r)$	$\sim(q \ \& \ r)$	p	
T	T	T	T	T	F	T	
T	T	F	T	F	T	T	O.K.
T	F	T	T	F	T	T	O.K.
T	F	F	T	F	T	T	O.K.
F	T	T	T	T	F	F	
F	T	F	T	F	T	F	Invalid
F	F	T	F	F	T	F	
F	F	F	F	F	T	F	

This time, we find four rows in which all the premises are true. In three cases the conclusion is true as well, but in one of these cases (row 6) the conclusion is false. This line is marked "Invalid." Notice that every line in which all of the premises are true is marked either as "O.K." or as "Invalid." If even one row is marked

"Invalid," then the argument form as a whole is invalid. The argument form under consideration is thus invalid, because it is possible for it to have a substitution instance in which all the premises are true and the conclusion is false.

The labeling not only shows *that* the argument form is invalid, it also shows *why* it is invalid. Each line that is marked "Invalid" shows a combination of truth values that makes the premises true and the conclusion false. Row 6 presents the combination in which Valerie is not a doctor, is a lawyer, and is not a stockbroker. With these assignments, it will be true that she is either a doctor or a lawyer (premise 1), and also true that she is not both a stockbroker and a doctor (premise 2), yet false that she is a doctor (the conclusion). It is this possibility that shows why the argument form is not valid.

EXERCISE VIII

Using the truth-table technique outlined above, test the following argument forms for validity:

(1) $p \lor q$
    $\sim p$
    _____
∴ q

(2) $p \lor q$
    p
    _____
∴ $\sim q$

(3) $\sim p \lor q$
    p
    _____
∴ $\sim q$

(4) $\sim (p \lor q)$
    _____
∴ $\sim q$

(5) $\sim (p \lor q)$
    p
    _____
∴ q

(6) $\sim (p \lor q)$
    p
    _____
∴ r

(7) $\sim (p \,\&\, q)$
    q
    _____
∴ $\sim p$

(8) $\sim(p \,\&\, q)$

    $\sim q$

_____

$\therefore p$

(9) $(p \,\&\, q) \vee (p \,\&\, r)$

_____

$\therefore p \,\&\, (q \vee r)$

(10) $(p \vee q) \,\&\, (p \vee r)$

_____

$\therefore p \,\&\, (q \vee r)$

(11) $p \,\&\, q$

_____

$\therefore (p \vee r) \,\&\, (q \vee r)$

(12) $p \vee q$

_____

$\therefore (p \,\&\, r) \vee (q \,\&\, r)$

SOME FURTHER CONNECTIVES

We have developed the logic of propositions using only three basic notions corresponding (perhaps roughly) to the English words "and," "or," and "not." Now let us go back to the question of the two possible senses of the word "or": one exclusive and the other inclusive. Sometimes "or" seems to rule out the possibility that both options are open; at other times "or" seems to allow this possibility. This is the difference between exclusive and inclusive disjunction.

Suppose we use the symbol "$\underline{\vee}$" to stand for exclusive disjunction. (After this discussion, we will not use it again.) We could then define this new connective in the following way:

$$(p \mathbin{\underline{\vee}} q) = \text{(by definition)} \; ((p \vee q) \,\&\, \sim(p \,\&\, q))$$

It is not hard to see that the expression on the right side of this definition captures the force of exclusive disjunction. Since we can always define exclusive disjunction when we want it, there is no need to introduce it into our system of basic notions.

EXERCISE IX

Construct a truth-table analysis of the expression on the right side of the preceding definition, and compare it with the truth-table definition of exclusive disjunction given earlier in this chapter.

Use truth tables to test the following argument forms for validity:

(1) p

———————

∴ $p \lor q$

(2) $p \lor q$

   p

———————

∴ $\sim q$

(3) $p \,\&\, q$

———————

∴ $\sim(p \lor q)$

(4) $\sim(p \,\&\, q)$

———————

∴ $p \lor q$

(5) $p \lor q$

———————

∴ $p \lor q$

(6) $p \lor q$

———————

∴ $p \lor q$

Actually, in analyzing arguments we have been defining new logical connectives without much thinking about it. For example, "not both p and q" was symbolized as "$\sim(p \,\&\, q)$." "Neither p nor q" was symbolized as "$\sim(p \lor q)$." Let us look more closely at the example "$\sim(p \lor q)$." Perhaps we should have symbolized it as "$\sim p \,\&\, \sim q$." As a matter of fact, we could have used this symbolization, because the two expressions amount to the same thing. Again, this may be obvious, but we can prove it by using a truth table in yet another way. Compare the truth-table analysis of these two expressions:

p	q	$\sim p$	$\sim q$	$\sim p \,\&\, \sim q$	$(p \lor q)$	$\sim(p \lor q)$
T	T	F	F	F	T	F
T	F	F	T	F	T	F
F	T	T	F	F	T	F
F	F	T	T	T	F	T

Under "$\sim p \,\&\, \sim q$" we find the column (FFFT), and we find the same sequence under "$\sim(p \lor q)$." This shows that, for every possible substitution we make, these two expressions will yield propositions with the same truth value. We will say that these propositional forms are *truth-functionally equivalent*. The above table also shows that the expressions "$\sim q$" and "$\sim p \,\&\, \sim q$" are *not* truth-functionally equivalent, because the columns underneath these two expressions differ in the second row, so some substitutions into these expressions will not yield propositions with the same truth value.

Given the notion of truth-functional equivalence, the problem of more than one translation can often be solved. If two translations are truth-functionally equivalent, then it does not matter which one we use in testing for validity. Of course, some translations will seem more natural than others. For example, "$p \vee q$" is truth-functionally equivalent to

$$\sim((\sim p \mathbin{\&} \sim p) \mathbin{\&} (\sim q \vee \sim q)).$$

Despite this equivalence, the first form of expression is obviously more natural than the second when translating sentences such as "It is either cloudy or sunny."

EXERCISE XI

Use truth tables to test which of the following propositional forms are truth-functionally equivalent to each other:

(1) $\sim(p \vee q)$

(2) $\sim(\sim p \vee \sim q)$

(3) $\sim p \mathbin{\&} \sim q$

(4) $p \mathbin{\&} q$

EXERCISE XII

Use truth tables to determine whether the expressions in each of the following pairs are truth-functionally equivalent:

(1) "p" and "$p \mathbin{\&} p$"

(2) "p" and "$p \vee p$"

(3) "$p \vee \sim p$" and "$\sim(p \mathbin{\&} \sim p)$"

(4) "p" and "$p \mathbin{\&} (q \vee \sim q)$"

(5) "p" and "$p \mathbin{\&} (q \mathbin{\&} \sim q)$"

(6) "p" and "$p \vee (q \mathbin{\&} \sim q)$"

(7) "$p \mathbin{\&} (q \vee r)$" and "$p \vee (q \mathbin{\&} r)$"

(8) "$p \mathbin{\&} (q \mathbin{\&} r)$" and "$(p \mathbin{\&} q) \mathbin{\&} r$"

SUMMARY

So far in this chapter we have seen that by using conjunction, disjunction, and negation, it is possible to construct compound propositions out of simple propositions. A distinctive feature of compound propositions constructed in these three ways is that the truth of the compound propositions is always a function of the truth of its component propositions. Thus, these three notions allow us to construct truth-functionally compound propositions. Some arguments depend for their validity simply on these truth-functional connectives. When this is so, it is possible to test for validity in a purely mechanical way. This can be done through the use of truth tables. Thus, in this area at least, we are able to give a clear account of validity and to specify exact procedures for testing for validity. Now we will go on to examine an area in which the application of this approach is more problematic. It concerns *conditionals*.

CONDITIONALS

Conditionals often occur in arguments. They have the form "If _____, then _____." What goes in the first blank of this pattern is called the *antecedent* of the conditional; what goes in the second blank is called its *consequent*. Sometimes conditionals appear in the indicative mood:

>   If it rains, then the crop will be saved.

Sometimes they occur in the subjunctive mood:

>   If it had rained, then the crop would have been saved.

There are also conditional imperatives:

>   If a fire breaks out, then call the fire department first!

There are conditional promises:

>   If you get into trouble, then I promise to help you.

Indeed, conditionals get a great deal of use in our language, often in arguments. It is important, therefore, to understand them.

Unfortunately, there is no general agreement among experts concerning the correct way to analyze conditionals. We will simplify matters, and avoid some of these controversies, by considering only indicative conditionals. We will not examine conditional imperatives, conditional promises, or subjunctive conditionals. Furthermore, at the start, we will examine only what we will call *propositional conditionals*. We get a propositional conditional by substituting indicative sentences that express propositions—something either true or false—into the schema "If _____, then _____." Or, to use technical language already introduced, a propositional conditional is a substitution instance of "If *p*, then *q*" in which "*p*" and "*q*" are propositional variables. Of the four conditional sentences listed above, only the first is clearly a propositional conditional.

Even if we restrict our attention to propositional conditionals, this will not avoid all controversy. Several competing theories exist concerning the correct analysis of propositional conditionals, and no consensus has been reached concerning which is right. It may seem surprising that disagreement should exist concerning such a simple and fundamental notion as the if-then construction, but it does. In what follows, we will first describe the most standard treatment of propositional conditionals, and then consider a number of alternatives to it.

TRUTH TABLES FOR CONDITIONALS

For conjunction, disjunction, and negation, the truth-table method provides an approach that is at once plausible and effective. A propositional conditional is also compounded from two simpler propositions, and this suggests that we might be able to offer a truth-table definition for these conditionals as well. What should the truth table look like? When we try to answer this question, we get stuck almost at once, for it is unclear how we should fill in the table in three out of four cases.

p	q	If p, then q
T	T	?
T	F	F
F	T	?
F	F	?

It seems obvious that a conditional cannot be true if the antecedent is true and the consequent is false. We record this by putting an F in the second row. But suppose "p" and "q" are replaced by two arbitrary true propositions—say "Two plus two equals four" and "Chile is in South America." Consider what we shall say about the conditional:

If two plus two equals four, then Chile is in South America.

The first thing to say is that this is a *very* strange statement, because the arithmetical remark in the antecedent does not seem to have anything to do with the geographical remark in the consequent. So this conditional is odd—indeed, extremely odd—but is it true or false? At this point, a reasonable response is bafflement.

Consider the following argument, which is intended to solve all these problems by providing reasons for assigning truth values in each row of the truth table. First, it seems obvious that, if "If p, then q" is true, then it is not the case that both "p" is true and "q" is false. That in turn means that "$\sim(p \ \& \ \sim q)$" must be true. The following, then, seems to be a valid argument form:

If p, then q.

$$\therefore \ \sim(p \ \& \ \sim q)$$

Second, we can also reason in the opposite direction. Suppose that we know that "$\sim(p \ \& \ \sim q)$" is true. For this to be true, "$p \ \& \ \sim q$" must be false. We know that from the truth-table definition of negation. Next let us suppose that "p" is true. Then "$\sim q$" must be false. We know that from the truth-table definition of conjunction. Finally, if "$\sim q$" is false, then "q" itself must be true. This line of reasoning is supposed to show that the following argument form is valid:

$$\sim(p \,\&\, \sim q)$$

$$\therefore \text{If } p, \text{ then } q.$$

The first step in the argument was intended to show that we can validly derive "$\sim(p \,\&\, \sim q)$" from "If p, then q." The second step was intended to show that the derivation can be run in the other direction as well. But if each of these expressions is derivable from the other, this suggests that they are equivalent. We use this background argument as a justification for the following definition:

> If p, then q = (by definition) not both p and not q.

We can put this into symbolic notation using a horseshoe to symbolize the conditional connective:

$$p \supset q = \text{(by definition)} \;\sim(p \,\&\, \sim q)$$

Given this definition, we can now construct the truth table for propositional conditionals. It is simply the truth table for "$\sim(p \,\&\, \sim q)$":

p	q	$\sim(p \,\&\, \sim q)$	$p \supset q$	$(\sim p \lor q)$
T	T	T	T	T
T	F	F	F	F
F	T	T	T	T
F	F	T	T	T

Notice that "$\sim(p \,\&\, \sim q)$" is also truth-functionally equivalent to the expression "$(\sim p \lor q)$." We have cited it here because "$(\sim p \lor q)$" has traditionally been used to define "$p \supset q$." For reasons that are now obscure, when a conditional is defined in this truth-functional way, it is called a *material conditional*.

Let us suppose, for the moment, that the notion of a material conditional corresponds exactly with our idea of a propositional conditional. What would follow from this? The answer is that we could treat conditionals in the same way in which we have treated conjunction, disjunction, and negation. A propositional conditional would be just one more kind of truth-functionally compound proposition capable of definition by truth tables. Furthermore, the validity of arguments that depend on this notion (together with conjunction, disjunction, and negation) could be settled by appeal to truth-table techniques. Let us pause for a moment to examine this.

One of the most common patterns of reasoning is called *modus ponens*. It looks like this:

If p, then q. $p \supset q$
p p

$$\therefore q \qquad\qquad \therefore q$$

The truth-table definition of material implication shows at once that this pattern of argument is valid:

Pr.		Pr.	Cn.	
p	q	$p \supset q$	q	
T	T	T	T	O.K.
T	F	F	F	
F	T	T	T	
F	F	T	F	

EXERCISE XIII

The argument form called *modus tollens* looks like this:

$$p \supset q$$
$$\sim q$$

$$\therefore \sim p$$

Use truth tables to show that this argument form is valid.

These same techniques allow us to show that one of the traditional fallacies is, indeed, a fallacy. It is called the fallacy of *denying the antecedent*, and it has this form:

$$p \supset q$$
$$\sim p$$

$$\therefore \sim q$$

The truth table showing the invalidity of this argument form looks like this:

		Pr.	Pr.	Cn.	
p	q	$p \supset q$	$\sim p$	$\sim q$	
T	T	T	F	F	
T	F	F	F	T	
F	T	T	T	F	Invalid
F	F	T	T	T	O.K.

EXERCISE XIV

A second standard fallacy is called *affirming the consequent*. It looks like this:

$$p \supset q$$
$$q$$

$$\therefore p$$

Use truth tables to show that this argument form is invalid.

We can examine one last argument form that has been historically significant. It is called a *hypothetical syllogism* and has the following form:

$$p \supset q$$
$$q \supset r$$

$$\therefore p \supset r$$

Since we are dealing with an argument form containing three variables, we must perform the boring task of constructing a truth table with eight rows:

			Pr.	Pr.	Cn.	
p	q	r	$p \supset q$	$q \supset r$	$p \supset r$	
T	T	T	T	T	T	O.K.
T	T	F	T	F	F	
T	F	T	F	T	T	
T	F	F	F	T	F	
F	T	T	T	T	T	O.K.
F	T	F	T	F	T	
F	F	T	T	T	T	O.K.
F	F	F	T	T	T	O.K.

This is fit work for a computer, not for a human being, but it is important to see that it actually works.

Why is it important to see that these techniques work? Most people, after all, could see that hypothetical syllogisms are valid without going through all of this tedious business. We seem only to be piling boredom on top of triviality. This protest deserves an answer. Suppose we ask someone *why* he or she thinks that the conclusion follows from the premises in a hypothetical syllogism. The person might answer that anyone can see that—which, by the way, is false. Beyond this, he or she might say that it all depends on the meanings of the words, or that it is all a matter of definition. But if we go on to ask *which words* and *what definitions*, most people will fall silent. We have discovered that the validity of some arguments depends on the meanings of such words as "and," "or," "not," and "if-then." We have then gone on to give explicit definitions of these terms—definitions, by the way, that help us see how these terms function in an argument. Finally, by getting all these *simple* things right, we have produced what is called a *decision procedure* for determining the validity of every argument depending only on conjunctions, disjunctions, negations, and propositional conditionals. Our truth-table techniques give us a mechanical procedure for settling questions of validity in this area. In fact, truth-table techniques have practical applications, for example, in computer programming. But the important point here is that through an understanding of how these techniques work, we can gain a deeper insight into the notion of validity.

EXERCISE XV

Using the truth-table techniques employed above, test the following argument forms for validity. (For your own entertainment, guess whether the argument form is valid or invalid before working it out.)

(1) $p \supset q$

$\therefore q \supset p$

(2) $p \supset q$

$\therefore \sim q \supset \sim p$

(3) $\sim q \supset \sim p$

$\therefore p \supset q$

(4) $p \supset q$
   $q \supset r$

$\therefore p \supset (q \mathrel{\&} r)$

(5) $p \supset q$
   $q \supset r$
   $\sim r$

$\therefore \sim p$

(6) $p \supset q$
   $q \supset r$

$\therefore \sim r \supset \sim p$

(7) $p \vee q$
   $p \supset r$
   $q \supset r$

$\therefore r$

(8) $p \supset (q \vee r)$
   $\sim q$
   $\sim r$

$\therefore \sim p$

(9) $(p \vee q) \supset r$

$\therefore p \supset r$

(10) $(p \mathrel{\&} q) \supset r$

$\therefore p \supset r$

(11) $p \supset (q \supset r)$

$\therefore (p \& q) \supset r$

(12) $(p \& q) \supset r$

$\therefore p \supset (q \supset r)$

(13) $p \supset (q \supset r)$
q
$\sim r$

$\therefore \sim p$

(14) $p \supset (q \supset r)$
$p \supset q$

$\therefore r$

(15) $(p \vee q) \& (p \vee r)$
$\sim r$

$\therefore \sim q$

(16) $(p \supset q) \& (p \supset \sim r)$
$q \& r$

$\therefore \sim p$

(17) $(p \vee q) \supset p$

$\therefore \sim q$

(18) $(p \vee q) \supset (p \& q)$

$\therefore (p \supset q) \& (q \supset p)$

(19) $(p \& q) \supset (p \vee q)$

$\therefore (p \supset q) \vee (q \supset p)$

(20) r

$\therefore (p \supset q) \vee (q \supset p)$

LOGICAL LANGUAGE AND EVERYDAY LANGUAGE

Early in this chapter we started out by talking about such common words as "and" and "or," and then we slipped over to talking about *conjunction* and *disjunction*. The transition was a bit sneaky, but intentional. To understand what is going on here, we can ask how closely these logical notions we have defined match their everyday counterparts. We will start with conjunction, and then come back to the more difficult question of conditionals.

At first sight, the match between conjunction as we have defined it and the everyday use of the word "and" may seem fairly bad. To begin with, in everyday discourse, we do not go about conjoining random bits of information. We do not say, for example, that two plus two equals four and Chile is in South America. We already know why we do not say such things, for unless the context is quite extraordinary, this is bound to violate the rule of Relevance. But if we are interested in validity, the rule of Relevance—like all other conversational (or pragmatic) rules— is simply beside the point. When dealing with validity, we are interested in only one question: if the premises of an argument are true, must the conclusion be true as well? Conversational rules, as we saw in Chapter 1, do not affect truth.

The truth-functional notion of conjunction is also insensitive to another import- ant feature of our everyday discourse: by reducing all conjunctions to their bare truth-functional content, the truth-functional notion often misses the argumentative point of a conjunction. We have already seen that each of the following remarks has a very different force in the context of an argument:

> The ring is beautiful, but expensive.
>
> The ring is expensive, but beautiful.

These two remarks point in opposite directions in the context of an actual argument, but from a purely truth-functional point of view we treat them as equivalent. We translate the first sentence as "$B \,\&\, E$" and the second as "$E \,\&\, B$." Their truth- functional equivalence is too obvious to need proof. Similar oddities arise for all discounting terms, such as "although," "whereas," and "however."

It might seem that if formal analysis cannot distinguish an "and" from a "but," then it can hardly be of any use at all. This is not true. A formal analysis of an argument will tell us just one thing: whether the argument is valid or not. If we expect the analysis to tell us more than this, we will be disappointed. It is important to remember two things: (1) We expect deductive arguments to be valid, and (2) usually we expect much more than this from an argument. To elaborate on the second point, we usually expect an argument to be sound as well as valid; we expect the premises to be true. Beyond this, we expect the argument to be informative, intelligible, convincing, and so forth. Validity, then, is an important aspect of an argument, and formal analysis helps us evaluate it. But validity is not the only aspect of an argument that concerns us. In many contexts, it is not even our chief concern.

We can now look at our analysis of conditionals, for here we find some striking differences between the logician's analysis and everyday use. The following argument forms are both valid:

$$(1) \quad p \qquad\qquad (2) \quad \sim p$$
$$\overline{} \qquad\qquad\qquad \overline{}$$
$$\therefore \quad q \supset p \qquad\qquad \therefore \quad p \supset q$$

EXERCISE XVI

Check the validity of the argument forms above using truth tables.

Yet, though valid, both argument forms seem odd—so odd that they have actually been called *paradoxical.* The first argument form seems to say this: If a proposition is true, then it is *implied by* any proposition whatsoever. Here is an example of an argument that satisfies this argument form and is therefore valid:

Lincoln was president.

∴ If the moon is made of cheese, Lincoln was president.

This is a peculiar argument to call valid. First, we want to know what the moon has to do with Lincoln's having been president. Beyond this, how can his having been president depend on a blatant falsehood? We can give these questions even more force by noticing that even the following argument is valid:

Lincoln was president.

∴ If Lincoln was not president, then Lincoln was president.

Both arguments are instances of the valid argument form "p; ∴ $q \supset p$."

The other argument form is also paradoxical. It seems to say that a false proposition implies any proposition whatsoever. The following is an instance of this argument form:

Columbus was not president.

∴ If Columbus was president, then the moon is made of cheese.

Here it is hard to see what the falsehood that Columbus was president has to do with the composition of the moon.

At this point, nonphilosophers become impatient, whereas philosophers become worried. We started out with principles that seemed to be both obvious and simple. Now, quite suddenly, we are being overwhelmed with a whole series of peculiar results. What in the world has happened, and what should be done about it? Philosophers remain divided in the answers they give to these questions. The responses fall into two main categories: (1) Simply give up the idea that conditionals can be defined by truth-functional techniques and search for a different and better analysis of conditionals that avoids the difficulties involved in truth-functional analysis, or (2) take the difficult line and argue that there is nothing wrong with calling the aforementioned argument forms valid.

The first approach is highly technical and cannot be pursued in detail in this book. The general idea is this: Instead of identifying "If p, then q" with "Not both *p* and not *q*," identify it with "Not *possibly* both *p* and not *q*." This provides a stronger notion of a conditional and avoids some—though not all—of the problems concerning conditionals. This theory is given a systematic development by offering a logical analysis of the notion of possibility. This branch of logic is called *modal logic*, and it has shown remarkable development in recent decades.

The second line has been taken by Paul Grice, whose theories played a prominent part in Chapter 1. He acknowledges—as anyone must—that the two argument forms above are decidedly odd. He denies, however, that this oddness has anything to do with *validity*. Validity concerns one thing and one thing only: a relationship between premises and conclusion. An argument is valid if the premises cannot be true without the conclusion being true as well. The above arguments are valid by this definition of "validity."

Of course, arguments can be defective in all sorts of other ways. Look at the first argument form: (1) *p*; ∴ *q* ⊃ *p*. Because "*q*" can be replaced by any proposition (true or false), the rule of Relevance will often be violated. It is worth pointing out violations of the rule of Relevance, but, according to Grice, this issue has nothing to do with validity. Beyond this, arguments having this form can also involve violations of the rule of Quantity. A conditional will be true whenever the consequent is true. Given this, it does not matter to the truth of the whole conditional whether the antecedent is true or false. Yet it can be misleading to *use* a conditional on the basis of this logical feature. For example, it would be misleading for a museum guard to say "If you give me five dollars, then I will let you into the exhibition," when, in fact, he will admit you in any case. For Grice, this is misleading because it violates the rule of Quantity. Yet, strictly speaking, it is not false. Strictly speaking, it is true.

The Grice line is attractive, for, among other things, it allows us to accept the truth-functional account of conditionals, with all its simplicity. Yet sometimes it is difficult to swallow. Consider the following remark:

> If God exists, then there is evil in the world.

If Grice's analysis is correct, even the most pious will have to admit that this conditional is true provided only that she is willing to admit that there is evil in the world. Yet this conditional plainly suggests that there is some connection between God's existence and the evil in the world—presumably, that is the point of connecting them in a conditional. The pious will wish to deny this suggestion. All the same, this connection is something that is conversationally implied, not asserted. So, once more, this conditional could be misleading—and therefore is in need of criticism and correction—but it is still, strictly speaking, true.

Philosophers and logicians have had various responses to Grice's position. No consensus has emerged on this issue. The authors of this book find it adequate, at least in most normal cases, and therefore have adopted it. This has two advantages: (1) The appeal to conversational rules fits in well with our previous discussions, and (2) it provides a way of keeping the logic simple and within the range of a beginning student. Other philosophers and logicians continue to work toward a definition superior to the truth-table definition for indicative conditionals.

OTHER CONDITIONALS IN ORDINARY LANGUAGE

So far we have considered only one form in which propositional conditionals appear in everyday language: the conditional "If p, then q." But propositional conditionals come in a variety of forms, and some of them demand careful treatment.

We can first consider the contrast between constructions using "if" and those using "only if":

(1) I'll clean the barn if Hazel will help me.

(2) I'll clean the barn only if Hazel will help me.

Adopting the following abbreviations:

$B =$ I'll clean the barn, and

$H =$ Hazel will help me,

the first sentence is translated as follows:

$H \supset B$

Notice that in the prose version of (1), the antecedent and consequent appear in reverse order; "q if p" means the same thing as "If p, then q."

How shall we translate the second sentence? Here we should move slowly and first notice what seems incontestable: If Hazel does not help me, then I will not clean the barn. This is translated in the following way:

$\sim H \supset \sim B$

And that is equivalent to:

$B \supset H$

If this equivalence is not obvious, it can quickly be established using a truth table.

A more difficult question arises when we ask whether an implication runs the other way. When I say that I will clean the barn only if Hazel will help me, am I committing myself to cleaning the barn if she does help me? There is a strong temptation to answer the question "Yes" and then give a fuller translation of (2) in the following way:

$(B \supset H) \mathrel{\&} (H \supset B)$

Logicians call such two-way implications *biconditionals*, and we will discuss them in a moment. But adding this second conjunct is almost surely a mistake, for we can think of parallel cases where we would not be tempted to include it. A government regulation might read as follows:

> A student may receive a New York State Scholarship only if the student attends a New York State school.

From this it does not follow that anyone who attends a New York State school may receive a New York State Scholarship. There may be other requirements as well—for example, being a New York State resident.

Why were we tempted to use a biconditional in translating sentences containing the connective "only if"? Why, that is, are we tempted to think that the statement "I'll clean the barn only if Hazel will help me" implies "If Hazel helps me, then I will clean the barn"? The answer turns upon the notion of conversational implication first discussed in Chapter 1. If I am *not* going to clean the barn whether Hazel helps me or not, then it will be misleading—a violation of the rule of Quantity—to say that I will clean the barn only if Hazel helps me. For this reason, in many contexts, the *use* of a sentence of the form "*p* only if *q*" will conversationally imply a commitment to "*p* if and only if *q*."

We can next look at sentences of the form "*p* if and only if *q*"—so-called biconditionals. If I say that I will clean the barn if and only if Hazel will help me, then I am saying that I will clean it if she helps and I will not clean it if she does not. Translated, this becomes:

$$(H \supset B) \ \& \ (\sim H \supset \sim B)$$

This is equivalent to:

$$(H \supset B) \ \& \ (B \supset H)$$

We thus have an implication going both ways—the characteristic form of a biconditional. In fact, constructions containing the expression "if and only if" do not often appear in everyday speech. They appear almost exclusively in technical or legal writing. In ordinary conversation, we capture the force of a biconditional by saying something like this:

I will clean the barn, but only if Hazel helps me.

The decision whether to translate a remark of everyday conversation into a conditional or a biconditional is often subtle and difficult. We have already noticed that the use of sentences of the form "*p* only if *q*" will often conversationally imply a commitment to the biconditional "*p* if and only if *q*." In the same way, the *use* of the conditional "*p* if *q*" will carry this same implication. If I plan to clean the barn whether Hazel helps me or not, it will certainly be misleading—again, a violation of the rule of Quantity—to say that I will clean the barn *if* Hazel helps me.

We can close this discussion by considering one further, rather difficult case. What is the force of saying "*p unless q*"? Is this a biconditional, or just a conditional? If it is just a conditional, which way does the implication go? There is a strong temptation to treat this as a biconditional, but the following example shows this to be wrong:

Clinton will lose the election unless he carries the Northeast.

This sentence clearly indicates that Clinton will lose the election if he does not carry the Northeast. Using abbreviations, we get the following:

N = Clinton will carry the Northeast.

L = Clinton will lose the election.

$\sim N \supset L$

The original statement does not imply—even conversationally—that Clinton will win the election if he does carry the Northeast. Thus,

p unless $q = {\sim}q \supset p$

In short, "unless" means "if not." We can also note that "${\sim}p$ unless q" means the same thing as "p only if q," and they both are translated thus:

$p \supset q$

So far, then, we have the following results:

	Translates As	Often Conversationally Implies
p if q	$q \supset p$	$(p \supset q)$ & $(q \supset p)$
p only if q	$p \supset q$	$(p \supset q)$ & $(q \supset p)$
p unless q	${\sim}q \supset p$	$(p \supset {\sim}q)$ & $({\sim}q \supset p)$

EXERCISE XVII

Translate each of the following sentences into symbolic notation, using the suggested symbols as abbreviations.

(1) The Reds will win only if the Dodgers collapse. (*R, D*)

(2) The Steelers will win if their defense holds up. (*S, D*)

(3) If it rains or snows, the game will be called off. (*R, S, O*)

(4) If she came home with a trophy and a prize, she must have won the tournament. (*T, P, W*)

(5) If you order the dinner special, you get dessert and coffee. (*S, D, C*)

(6) If you order the dinner special, you get dessert; but you can have coffee whether or not you order the dinner special. (*S, D, C*)

(7) If the house comes up for sale, and if I have the money in hand, I will bid on it. (*S, M, B*)

(8) If you come to dinner, I will cook you a lobster, if you want me to. (*D, L, W*)

(9) You can be a success if only you try. (*S, T*)

(10) You can be a success only if you try. (*S, T*)

(11) Only if you try can you be a success. (*S, T*)

(12) You can be a success if you are the only one who tries. (*S, O*)

(13) Unless there is a panic, stock prices will continue to rise. (*P, R*)

(14) I won't scratch your back unless you scratch mine. (*I, Y*)

(15) You will get a good bargain provided you get there early. (*B, E*)

(16) You cannot lead a happy life without friends. (Let *H* = You can lead a happy life, and let *F* = You have friends.)

(17) The only way that horse will win the race is if every other horse drops out. (Let W = That horse will win the race, and let D = Every other horse drops out.)

(18) You should take prescription drugs if, but only if, they are prescribed for you. (T, P)

(19) The grass will die without rain. (D, R = It rains.)

(20) Given rain, the grass won't die. (R, D = The grass will die.)

(21) Unless it doesn't rain, the grass won't die. (R, D = The grass will die.)

EXERCISE XVIII

(a) Translate each of the following arguments into symbolic notation. Then (b) test each argument for validity using truth-table techniques, and (c) comment on any violations of conversational rules.

> EXAMPLE: Harold is clever; so, if Harold isn't clever, then Anna isn't clever either. (H, A)

(a) H p

    ――――――   ――――――

    $\therefore \sim H \supset \sim A$ $\therefore \sim p \supset \sim q$

(b)   Pr.   Cn.

p	q	$\sim p$	$\sim q$	$\sim p \supset \sim q$	
T	T	F	F	T	O.K.
T	F	F	T	T	O.K.
F	T	T	F	F	
F	F	T	T	T	

(c) The argument violates the rule of Relevance, because Anna's cleverness is irrelevant to Harold's cleverness.

(1) Jones is brave, so Jones is brave or Jones is brave. (J)

(2) The Republicans will carry either New Mexico or Arizona; but, since they will carry Arizona, they will not carry New Mexico. (A, N)

(3) Clinton will win the election whether he wins Idaho or not. Therefore, Clinton will win the election. (C, I)

(4) Clinton will win the election. Therefore, Clinton will win the election whether he wins Idaho or not. (C, I)

(5) Clinton will win the election. Therefore, Clinton will win the election whether he wins a majority or not. (C, M)

(6) If Bobby moves his queen there, he will lose her. Bobby will not lose his queen. Therefore, Bobby will not move his queen there. (M, L)

(7) John will play only if the situation is hopeless. But the situation is hopeless. So John will play. (*P, H*)

(8) Although Brown will pitch, the Rams will lose. If the Rams lose, their manager will get fired. So their manager will get fired. (*B, L, F*)

(9) America will win the Olympics unless Russia does. Russia will win the Olympics unless East Germany does. So America will win the Olympics unless East Germany does. (*A, R, E*)

(10) If you dial 0, you will get the operator. So, if you dial 0 and do not get the operator, then there is something wrong with the telephone. (*D, O, W*)

(11) The Democrats will run either Jones or Borg. If Borg runs, they will lose the South. If Jones runs, they will lose the North. So the Democrats will lose either the North or the South. (*J, B, S, N*)

(12) I am going to order either the fish special or the meat special. Either way, I will get soup. So I'll get soup. (*F, M, S*)

(13) The grass will die if it rains too much or it does not rain enough. If it does not rain enough, it won't rain too much. If it rains too much, then it won't not rain enough. So the grass will die. (*D* = The grass will die, *M* = It rains too much, *E* = It rains enough.)

(14) If you flip the switch, then the light will go on. But if the light goes on, then the generator is working. So if you flip the switch, then the generator is working. (*F, L, G*) (This example is due to Charles L. Stevenson.)

NECESSARY AND SUFFICIENT CONDITIONS

Our discussion of conditionals can help us understand two important notions used in the analysis of many forms of argumentation: that of a *sufficient condition* and that of a *necessary condition*. Later we will introduce a more general definition of both these notions, but we will begin here by defining when the truth of one proposition is necessary or sufficient for the truth of another proposition.

The definitions are simple. First,

A is a *sufficient condition* for *B* just in cases in which, if *A* is true, then *B* is true as well.

Thus, the antecedent of a propositional conditional always lays down a sufficient condition for its consequent:

Sufficient condition
$$\Downarrow$$
$$A \supset B$$

For example, if we say "If Joan is a mother, then Joan is female," we are indicating that Joan's being a mother is sufficient for her being female.

As an initial definition of a necessary condition, we will say that

B is a *necessary condition* for *A* just in case *A* is true *only if B* is true.

We know that this is equivalent to "$A \supset B$." Thus, the consequent of any propositional conditional lays down a necessary condition for its antecedent:

$$A \supset B$$
$$\Uparrow$$

Necessary condition

For example, if we say "If Joan is a mother, then Joan is female," we are indicating that Joan's being female is a necessary condition for her being a mother.

It is important not to confuse sufficient conditions and necessary conditions. Something can be a sufficient condition without being a necessary condition. For example, Joan's being a mother is a sufficient condition for Joan's being female, but it is not a necessary condition for her being female. Furthermore, something can be a necessary condition without being a sufficient condition. Although Joan's being a female is a necessary condition for Joan's being a mother, it is not a sufficient condition for her being a mother. Of course, some necessary conditions are also sufficient conditions. Joan's being a female parent is both necessary and sufficient for her being a mother. Nonetheless, because many necessary conditions are not sufficient conditions, and many sufficient conditions are not necessary conditions, we need to distinguish the two kinds of conditions.

Despite their distinctness, necessary conditions and sufficient conditions are related in interesting ways. The above definitions clearly imply the following:

Principle I. *A* is a sufficient condition for *B* if and only if *B* is a necessary condition for *A*.

More principles can be formulated by introducing negative conditions. For example, we can say that a car's being out of gas is *sufficient* to guarantee that it will *not* be able to run. Alternatively, we can say that a car's having gasoline is *necessary* for its being able to run. We can express these ideas symbolically in the following way:

Let *G* = The car has gas.

Let *R* = The car can run.

We can then state that not having gas is a sufficient condition for a car's not being able to run as follows:

(1) $\sim G \supset \sim R$

This means that, if a car does not have gas, the car cannot run. The claim that having gas is a necessary condition for a car's running can be stated this way:

(2) $R \supset G$

This means that a car can run only if it has gas. But we know from the earlier discussion of conditionals that (1) and (2) are logically equivalent. This allows us to introduce two further principles relating necessary conditions and sufficient conditions:

> **Principle II.** If *A* is a sufficient condition for *B*, then ~*A* is a necessary condition for ~*B*.

> **Principle III.** If *A* is a necessary condition for *B*, then ~*A* is a sufficient condition for ~*B*.

These principles are guaranteed by the equivalence of "*A* ⊃ *B*" and "~*B* ⊃ ~*A*."

PROBLEMS IN DISTINGUISHING SUFFICIENT CONDITIONS FROM NECESSARY CONDITIONS

Although the original definitions of necessary conditions and sufficient conditions are simple, the picture gets complicated by the introduction of negative conditions and of principles relating necessary conditions to sufficient conditions. These complications might explain part of the widespread tendency to confuse necessary conditions with sufficient conditions. We have also seen another reason for this common confusion: Conditionals often conversationally imply biconditionals. For example, recall the following statement:

(1) I'll clean the barn only if Hazel will help me.

Does this commit the speaker to cleaning the barn if Hazel will help? As we saw, the answer to this question is "No." The statement says that Hazel's helping is a necessary condition for the speaker's cleaning the barn, but it does not explicitly state that Hazel's helping is a sufficient condition of anything. Yet in many contexts a person who says (1) conversationally implies that he will clean the barn if Hazel will help and, thereby, that Hazel's helping is a sufficient condition for his cleaning the barn.

Confusing sufficient conditions and necessary conditions is especially easy when conditionals lay down complex conditions that include conjunctions or disjunctions. Suppose, for example, that you are caught speeding while under the influence of alcohol, and your insurance agent tells you:

(2) If you get one more ticket for speeding and one more ticket for DWI (driving while intoxicated), then you will lose your automobile insurance.

This conditional has a conjunction for an antecedent and, thus, lays down a conjunctive sufficient condition for losing one's insurance. Now suppose that in fact getting one more speeding ticket is *alone* sufficient for the loss of one's insurance, and so is getting one more ticket for DWI. Then what will we say about (2)? One temptation is to say that it is false, but that is wrong. To see this, suppose that you did get one more ticket for speeding *and* one more ticket for DWI. This will certainly be sufficient—we might want to say, more than sufficient—for you to lose your insurance. So, strictly speaking, (2) is true.

Yet in this context (2) seems misleading. We can explain why it is misleading by appealing to the rule of Quantity discussed in Chapter 1. Generally, people are interested in sufficient conditions because they are interested in what is needed in order to guarantee that something will happen. Given these practical concerns, what they want is a *minimal* sufficient condition. Statement 2 is then misleading because it does not state the minimum conditions that are sufficient for you to lose your insurance. In order for it to do so, (2) would have to be replaced by the following statement:

> (2*) If you get one more ticket for speeding *or* one more ticket for DWI, then you will lose your automobile insurance.

This statement, like (2), is true, but unlike (2), it is not misleading, since (2*) does state a minimal sufficient condition.

Misunderstandings can run in the other direction as well. We are sometimes inclined to treat necessary conditions as sufficient conditions. Suppose a student wants to take an advanced seminar, but she lacks the prerequisites, so she asks the professor what she needs to do in order to get into the seminar. The professor looks over the student's record and says,

> (3) I will let you into my seminar only if you read this book and write a five-page paper about it before next Monday.

The student reads the book and writes the paper before Monday, but the professor then says, "You must also read this second book and write a paper about it." The student would feel cheated. Why? It might be true that the professor would not have let this student into the seminar if she had not read the first book and written the first paper in time. If so, (3) is literally true: It specifies conditions that are necessary for getting into the seminar. Nonetheless, it was misleading for the professor to say what he did. The reason is that he violated the rule of Quantity as it concerns statements of necessary conditions. In stating necessary conditions, we are expected to specify *all* of the necessary conditions that are relevant in the given context, except, perhaps, those that are so obvious that they can be taken for granted. The professor failed to satisfy this expectation.

In addition, we often, though perhaps not always, assume that doing *everything necessary* to accomplish something is *sufficient* to accomplish it. If two parties do everything necessary to enter into a contract, then that is sufficient for them to have entered into a contract. If someone mixes all the ingredients necessary to make brownies, then that person has mixed ingredients sufficient to make brownies. And so on. We usually assume that in doing everything necessary, we have done enough. Stated more carefully, we often assume that the total set of necessary conditions is also a sufficient condition.[1]

---

[1] This principle might seem obviously true, but it might be false if there are genuinely indeterministic events at the subatomic level or genuinely spontaneous acts of free will at the human level. In both cases, it seems that everything necessary for an event to take place is present, yet the event need not take place.

If we grant these points, then it is easy to see how we can naturally treat a statement of necessary conditions as a statement of sufficient conditions:

(i) A statement that certain conditions are necessary often conversationally implies that these are all of the necessary conditions (except perhaps those that can be taken for granted).

(ii) In many contexts, we assume that all necessary conditions taken together will be a sufficient condition.

(iii) Therefore, in many contexts the statement of necessary conditions will often be taken as the statement of a sufficient condition.

Seeing how it is natural for us to confuse sufficient conditions and necessary conditions can help us guard against doing so. It is important to keep these concepts straight, for, as we have seen, the rules concerning them are fundamentally different.

EXERCISE XIX

Using the above definitions, state whether the underlined words express a necessary condition or a sufficient condition of the italicized words.

EXAMPLE:　If you work hard, *you will succeed.*

SOLUTION:　Your working hard is a sufficient condition for your success.

(1) *This piece of litmus paper will turn red* if it is put in acid.

(2) *This piece of litmus paper will turn red* only if it is put in acid.

(3) *This piece of litmus paper will not turn red* unless it is put in acid.

(4) *This piece of litmus paper will not turn red* provided that it is not put in acid.

(5) This piece of litmus paper will turn red if *it is put in acid.*

(6) This piece of litmus paper will not turn red if *it is not put in acid.*

(7) You have to rewrite your paper in order to *pass the course.*

(8) Rewriting your paper is all you have to do in order to *pass the course.*

(9) If you don't rewrite your paper, you can't *pass the course.*

(10) If you rewrite your paper, you can't fail to *pass the course.*

(11) You can't *pass this course* unless you rewrite your paper.

(12) You can't pass this course unless you *rewrite your paper.*

(13) If *you watch one episode of "Ellen" or one episode of "Roseanne,"* you will have wasted a half hour.

(14) If you watch one episode of "Ellen" or one episode of "Roseanne," *you will have wasted a half hour.*

(15) If *you watch one episode of "Ellen," and you also watch one episode of "Roseanne,"* then you will have watched an hour of television.

(16) If you want to *watch an hour of decent television tonight,* your only option is to <u>watch one episode of "Ellen" and one episode of "Roseanne."</u>

Indicate whether each of the following sentences is true or false.

(1) If ~A is a sufficient condition of X, then A is a necessary condition of ~X.

(2) If $A \vee B$ is a sufficient condition of X, then A is a sufficient condition of X.

(3) If $A \,\&\, B$ is a sufficient condition of X, then A is a sufficient condition of X.

(4) If $A \,\&\, B$ is a sufficient condition of X, then A is a necessary condition of X.

(5) If $A \vee B$ is a sufficient condition of X, then A is a necessary condition of X.

(6) If ~$(A \,\&\, B)$ is a sufficient condition of X, then ~A is a sufficient condition of X.

(7) If ~A is a necessary condition of X, then ~$(A \vee B)$ is a necessary condition of X.

(8) If $A \vee B$ is a sufficient condition of X, then ~A is a necessary condition of ~X.

Discussion Questions

(1) If "~p unless q" is translated as "$p \supset q$," then "p unless q" can be translated as "$p \vee q$." Why?

(2) Is a valid argument always a substitution instance of a valid argument form? Why or why not?

(3) Whatever its conclusion, any argument with inconsistent premises will always be valid. First of all, why is this true? Second, why does this not allow us to prove anything we please?

(4) Are arguments of the form "p; ∴ p" valid? Are they ever sound? Does this show that they are good and useful arguments? Why or why not?

(5) Symbolize the following argument and give its form. Does this example show that *modus ponens* is not always valid? Why or why not?

Opinion polls taken just before the 1980 election showed the Republican Ronald Reagan decisively ahead of the Democrat Jimmy Carter, with the other Republican in the race, John Anderson, a distant third. Those apprised of the poll results believed, with good reason:

Continued on next page

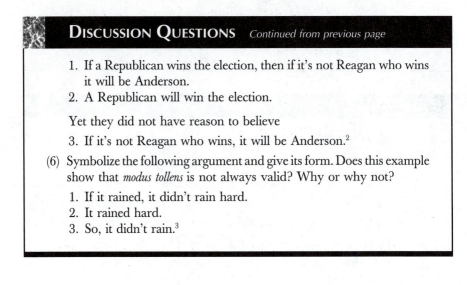

DISCUSSION QUESTIONS   *Continued from previous page*

1. If a Republican wins the election, then if it's not Reagan who wins it will be Anderson.
2. A Republican will win the election.

Yet they did not have reason to believe

3. If it's not Reagan who wins, it will be Anderson.[2]

(6) Symbolize the following argument and give its form. Does this example show that *modus tollens* is not always valid? Why or why not?

1. If it rained, it didn't rain hard.
2. It rained hard.
3. So, it didn't rain.[3]

---

[2] Vann McGee, "A Counterexample to Modus Ponens," *Journal of Philosophy* 82, no. 9 (September 1985): 462. See also Walter Sinnott-Armstrong, James Moor, and Robert Fogelin, "A Defense of Modus Ponens," *Journal of Philosophy* 83, no. 5 (May 1986): 296–300.

[3] Ernest Adams, "*Modus Tollens* Revisited," *Analysis* 48, no. 3 (1988): 122–28. See also Walter Sinnott-Armstrong, James Moor, and Robert Fogelin, "A Defense of Modus Tollens," *Analysis* 50, no. 1 (1990): 9–16.

Chapter Six

THE FORMAL ANALYSIS OF ARGUMENTS:
CATEGORICAL LOGIC

In Chapter 5, we saw how validity can depend on the external connections among propositions. This chapter will demonstrate how validity can depend on the internal structure of propositions. In particular, we will examine two types of categorical arguments—*immediate inferences* and *syllogisms*—whose validity or invalidity depends on relations among terms in their premises and conclusions. Our interest in these kinds of arguments is mostly theoretical. Understanding the theory of the syllogism deepens our understanding of validity, even if this theory is, in some cases, difficult to apply directly to complex arguments in daily life.

BEYOND PROPOSITIONAL LOGIC

Armed with the techniques developed in Chapter 5, let us look at the following argument:

> All squares are rectangles.
> All rectangles have parallel sides.
> _____
> ∴ All squares have parallel sides.

It is obvious at a glance that the conclusion follows from the premises, so this argument is valid. Furthermore, it seems to be valid in virtue of its form. But it is not yet clear what the form of this argument is. In order to show the form of this argument, we might try something of the following kind:

$$p \supset q$$
$$q \supset r$$
$$\overline{}$$
$$\therefore p \supset r$$

But this is a mistake, and a bad mistake. We have been using the letters "p," "q," and "r" as *propositional variables*–they stand for arbitrary propositions. But the proposition "All squares are rectangles" is not itself composed of two propositions. Nor does it contain "if _____, then _____," or any other propositional connective. In fact, if we attempt to translate the above argument into the language of propositional logic, we get the following result:

$$p$$
$$q$$
$$\overline{}$$
$$\therefore r$$

This, of course, is *not* a valid argument form. But if we look back at the original argument, we see that it is obviously valid. This shows that propositional logic–however adequate it is in its own area–is not capable of explaining the validity of all valid arguments. There is more to logic than propositional logic.

CATEGORICAL PROPOSITIONS

To broaden our understanding of the notion of validity, we will examine a modern version of a branch of logic first developed in ancient times–categorical logic. Categorical logic concerns immediate inferences and syllogisms that are composed of categorical propositions, so we need to begin by explaining what a categorical proposition is.

In the argument above, the first premise asserts some kind of relationship between squares and rectangles; the second premise asserts some kind of relationship between rectangles and things with parallel sides; finally, in virtue of these asserted relationships, the conclusion asserts a relationship between squares and things having parallel sides. Our task is to understand these relationships as clearly as possible so that we can discover the *basis* for the validity of this argument. Again, we shall adopt the strategy of starting from simple cases and then use the insights gained there for dealing with more-complicated cases.

A natural way to represent the relationships expressed by the propositions in an argument is through diagrams. Suppose we draw one circle standing for all things that are squares and another circle standing for all things that are rectangles. The claim that all squares are rectangles may be represented by placing the circle representing squares completely inside the circle representing rectangles.

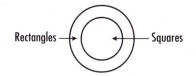

Another way of representing this relationship is to begin with overlapping circles.

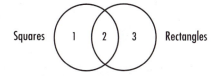

We then shade out the portions of the circles in which nothing exists, according to the proposition we are diagramming. If all squares are rectangles, there is nothing that is a square that is not a rectangle—that is, there is nothing in region 1. So our diagram looks like this:

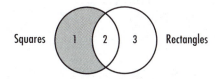

Either method of representation seems plausible. Perhaps the first seems more natural. We shall, however, use the system of overlapping circles, because they will work better when we get to more-complex arguments. They are called Venn diagrams, after their inventor, John Venn, a nineteenth-century English logician.

Having examined one relationship that can exist between two classes, it is natural to wonder what other relationships might exist. Going to the opposite extreme from our first example, two classes may have *nothing* in common. This relationship could be expressed by saying "All triangles are not squares," but it is more common and natural to say "No triangles are squares." We diagram this claim by indicating that there is nothing in the overlapping region of things that is both triangles and squares:

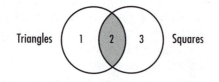

This is one of the relationships that could not be diagrammed by putting one circle inside another. (Just try it!)

In these first two extreme cases we have indicated that one class is either completely included in another ("All squares are rectangles") or completely excluded from another ("No triangles are squares"). Sometimes, however, we claim only that two classes have at least *some* things in common. We might say, for example, "Some aliens are spies." How shall we indicate this relationship in the following diagram?

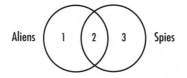

In this case, we do not want to cross out any whole region. We do not want to cross out region 1 because we are not saying that *all* aliens are spies. Plainly, we do not want to cross out region 2, for we are actually saying that some persons *are* both aliens and spies. Finally, we do not want to cross out region 3, for we are not saying that all spies are aliens. Saying that some aliens are spies does not rule out the possibility that some spies are homegrown. So we need some new device to represent claims that two classes have at least *some* members in common. We shall do this in the following way:

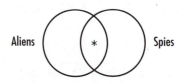

Here the asterisk indicates that there is at least one person who is both an alien and a spy. Notice, by the way, that we are departing a bit from an everyday way of speaking. "Some" is usually taken to mean *more than one*; here we let it mean *at least one*. This makes things simpler and will cause no trouble, so long as we remember that this is what we are using "some" to mean.

Given this new method of diagramming class relationships, we can immediately think of other possibilities. The following diagram indicates that there is someone who is an alien but not a spy. In more-natural language, it represents the claim that *some aliens are not spies.*

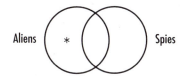

Next we can indicate that there is someone who is a spy but not an alien. More simply, the claim is that *some spies are not aliens,* and it is represented like this:

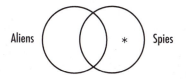

These last three claims are, of course, compatible, since there might be some aliens who are spies, some aliens who are not spies, and some spies who are not aliens.

THE FOUR BASIC CATEGORICAL FORMS

Although two classes can be related in a great many different ways, it is possible to examine many of these relationships in terms of four basic propositional forms:

A: All *S* is *P.*   E: No *S* is *P.*

I: Some *S* is *P.*   O: Some *S* is not *P.*

These forms are called *categorical forms,* and propositions with these forms are called *categorical propositions.*

As with the propositional forms discussed in the previous chapter, the A, E, I, and O forms for categorical propositions are not themselves propositions, so they are neither true nor false. Instead, they are patterns for whole groups of propositions. We get propositions from these forms by uniformly replacing the variables *S* and *P* with terms that refer to classes of things. For example, "Some spies are not aliens" is a substitution instance of the O propositional form. Nonetheless, we will refer to propositions with the A, E, I, or O form simply as A, E, I, or O propositions, except where this might cause confusion.

A and E propositions are said to be *universal* propositions (because they are about *all S*), and I and O propositions are called *particular* propositions (because they are about *some S*). A and I propositions are described as *affirmative* propositions (because they say what *is P*), and E and O propositions are referred to as *negative* propositions (because they say what is *not P*). Thus, these four basic propositional forms can be described this way:

A: Universal Affirmative

E: Universal Negative

I: Particular Affirmative

O: Particular Negative

These four forms fit into the following table:

	Affirmative	Negative
Universal	A: All S is P.	E: No S is P.
Particular	I: Some S is P.	O: Some S is not P.

Here are the Venn diagrams for the four basic categorical forms:

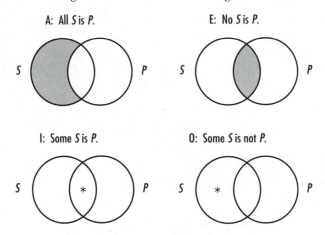

These basic categorical forms, together with their labels, classifications, and diagrams, should be memorized, because they will be referred to often in the rest of this chapter.

EXERCISE I

Using just the four basic categorical forms, indicate what information is given in each of the following diagrams:

Example:

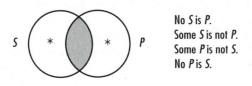

No S is P.
Some S is not P.
Some P is not S.
No P is S.

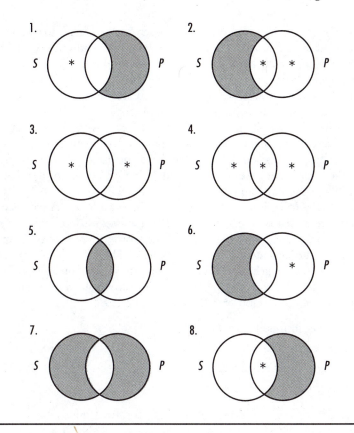

TRANSLATION INTO THE BASIC CATEGORICAL FORMS

Propositions with the specific A, E, I, and O forms do not appear often in everyday conversations. Normal people rarely say things like "All whales are mammals. All mammals breathe air. Therefore, all whales breathe air." Most people talk more like this: "Whales breathe air, since they're mammals." Thus, if our logical apparatus could be applied only to propositions with the explicit forms of A, E, I, and O, then it would apply to few arguments in everyday life.

Fortunately, however, many common statements that are not explicitly in a categorical form can be translated into a categorical form. For example, when someone says "Whales are mammals," the speaker presumably means to refer to *all* whales, so this statement can be translated into "All whales are mammals," which is an A proposition. We need to be careful, however. If someone says "Whales are found in the North Atlantic," the speaker probably does *not* mean to refer to *all* whales, since there are many whales in the Pacific as well. Similarly, if someone says, "A whale is a mammal," this can usually be translated as "All whales are mammals," which is an A proposition, but this translation would be inappropriate for "A whale is stranded on the beach," which seems to mean "One whale is stranded on the beach." Thus, we can be misled badly if we look only at the surface structure of what people say. We also need to pay attention to the context when we translate everyday talk into the basic categorical forms.

Despite these complications, it is possible to give some rough-and-ready guides that will provide help in translating many common forms of expression into propositions with the A, E, I, and O forms. Let us begin with one problem that arises for all these categorical forms. They all require a class of things as a predicate. Thus, "All whales are big" and "No whales live on land" should strictly be reformulated as "All whales are big things" and "No whales are things that live on land" or "No whales are land dwellers." This much is easy.

Things get more complicated when we look at the word "all" in A propositions. We have already seen that the word "all" is sometimes dropped in everyday conversation, as in "Whales are mammals." The word "all" can also be moved away from the start of a sentence. "Democrats are all liberal" usually means "All Democrats are liberal," which is an A proposition. Moreover, other words can be used in place of "all." Each of the following claims can, in standard contexts, be translated into an A proposition with the form "All *S* is *P*":

Every Republican is conservative.

Any investment is risky.

Anyone who is human is mortal.

Each ant is precious to its mother.

To translate such claims, we sometimes need to construct noun phrases out of adjectives and verbs. These transformations are often straightforward, but sometimes they require ingenuity, and even then they can seem somewhat contorted. For example, "Nobody but a fool would do that" can usually be translated into "All people who do that are fools." This translation might not seem so natural as the original, but, since it has the A form, it explicitly shows that this claim has the logical properties shared by other A propositions.

With some stretching, it is also possible to translate statements about individuals into categorical form. The standard method is to translate "Socrates is a man" as the A proposition "All things that are Socrates are men." Similarly, "The cannon is about to go off" in a typical context must not be translated as the I proposition "Some cannon is about to go off," since the original statement is about a particular cannon. Instead, the original statement should be translated as the A proposition "All things that are that cannon are about to go off." These translations might seem stilted, but they are necessary in order to apply syllogistic logic to everyday forms of expression.

Similar difficulties arise with the other basic propositional forms. If a woman says "I am looking for a man who is not attached," and a friend responds "All of the men in my church are not attached," then this response should probably be translated as "No men in my church are attached," which is an E proposition. In contrast, "All ocean dwellers are not fish" should usually be translated not as the

E proposition "No ocean dwellers are fish" but rather as "Not all ocean dwellers are fish." This means "Some ocean dwellers are not fish," which is an O proposition. Thus, some statements with the form "All *S* are not *P*" should be translated as E propositions, but others should be translated as O propositions. (This ambiguity in the form "All *S* are not *P*" explains why it is standard to give E propositions in the less ambiguous form "No *S* is *P*.") Other sentences should also be translated as E propositions even though they do not explicitly contain the word "No." "Underground cables are not easy to repair" and "If a cable is underground, it is not easy to repair" and "There aren't any underground cables that are easy to repair" can all be translated as the E proposition "No underground cables are easy to repair."

Similar complications also arise for I and O propositions. We already saw that "Whales are found in the North Atlantic" should be translated as the I proposition "*Some* whales are found in the North Atlantic." In addition, some common forms of expression can be translated as O propositions even though they do not contain either the word "not" or the word "some." For example, "There are desserts without chocolate" can be translated as "Some desserts are not chocolate," which is an O proposition.

Because of such complications, there is no mechanical procedure for translating common English sentences into A, E, I, and O propositions. To find the correct translation, you need to think carefully about the sentence and its context.

EXERCISE II

Translate each of the following sentences into an A, E, I, or O proposition. Be sure that the subjects and predicates in your translations use nouns that refer to classes of things (rather than adjectives or verbs). If the sentence can be translated into different forms in different contexts, give each translation and specify a context in which it seems natural.

(1) Real men eat ants.

(2) Everything that is cheap is no good.

(3) Some things that are expensive are no good.

(4) My friends are the only people who understand me.

(5) Somebody loves you.

(6) Not all crabs live in water.

(7) The hippo is a noble beast.

(8) The hippo is charging.

(9) Bats are not birds.

(10) Only seniors may take this course.

CONTRADICTORIES

Once we understand A, E, I, and O propositions by themselves, the next step is to ask how they are related to each other. From their diagrams, some relationships are immediately evident. Consider the Venn diagrams for the E and I propositional forms:

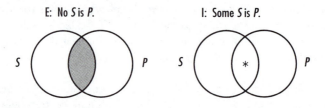

The first diagram has shading in the very same region that contains an asterisk in the second diagram. This makes it obvious that an E proposition and the corresponding I proposition (that is, the I proposition that has the same subject and predicate terms as the E proposition) cannot both be true. In order for an E proposition to be true, there must be *nothing* in the central region. But in order for the corresponding I proposition to be true, there must be *something* in the central region. Thus, they cannot both be true. They also cannot both be false. The only way for an E proposition to be false is for there to be something in the central region, but then the corresponding I proposition is not false but true. The only way for the I proposition to be false is if there is nothing in the central region, and then the E proposition is not false but true. Thus, they cannot both be true, and they cannot both be false. In other words, they always have opposite truth values. This relation is described by saying that these propositions are *contradictories*.

More generally, we can produce a diagram for the denial of a proposition by a simple procedure. The only information given in a Venn diagram is represented either by *shading out* some region, thereby indicating that nothing exists in it, or by *putting an asterisk in* a region, thereby indicating that something does exist in it. We are given no information about regions that are unmarked. To represent the denial of a proposition, we simply reverse the information in the diagram. That is, where there is an asterisk, we put in shading; where there is shading, we put in an asterisk. Everything else is left unchanged. Thus, we can see at once that corresponding E and I propositions are denials of one another, so they must always have opposite truth values. This makes them contradictories.

The same relation exists between an A proposition and its corresponding O proposition. Consider their forms:

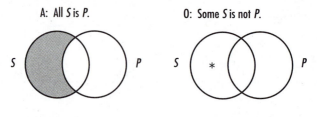

The diagram for an A proposition has shading exactly where the corresponding O proposition has an asterisk, and they contain no other information. Consequently, corresponding A and O propositions cannot both be false and cannot both be true, so they are contradictories.

EXERCISE III

(1) Is an A proposition a contradictory of its corresponding E proposition? Why or why not?

(2) Is an I proposition a contradictory of its corresponding O proposition? Why or why not?

EXISTENTIAL COMMITMENT

It might also seem that an A proposition (with the form "All *S* is *P*") implies the corresponding I proposition (with the form "Some *S* is *P*"). This, however, raises a difficult problem that logicians have not fully settled. Usually when we make a statement, we are talking about certain specific things. If someone claims that all whales are mammals, that person is talking about whales and mammals and stating a relationship between them. In making this statement, the person seems to be taking the *existence* of whales and mammals for granted. The remark seems to involve what logicians call *existential commitment* to the things referred to in the subject and predicate terms. In the same way, stating an E proposition often seems to commit the speaker to the existence of things in the subject and predicate classes and, thus, to imply an O proposition. For example, someone who says "No whales are fish" seems committed to "Some whales are not fish."

In other contexts, however, we seem to use universal (A and E) propositions without committing ourselves to the existence of the things referred to in the subject and predicate terms. For example, if we say "All trespassers will be fined," we are not committing ourselves to the existence of any trespassers or to any actual fines for trespassing; we are only saying "*If* there are trespassers, then they will be fined." Similarly, if we tell a sleepy child "No ghosts are under your bed," we are not committing ourselves to the existence of ghosts or anything under the bed. Given these examples of A and E propositions that carry no commitment to the things referred to, it is easy to think of many others. The question then arises whether we should include existential commitment in our treatment of universal propositions or not.

Once more, we must make a decision. (Remember that we had to make decisions concerning the truth-table definitions of both disjunction and conditionals in Chapter 5.) Classical logic was developed on the assumption that universal (A and E) propositions carry existential commitment. Modern logic makes the opposite decision, treating the claim "All men are mortal" as equivalent to "If someone is a man, then that person is mortal," and the claim "No men are islands" as equivalent to "If someone is a man, then that person is not an island." This way of speaking carries no commitment to the existence of any men.

Which approach should we adopt? The modern approach is simpler and has proved more powerful in the long run. For these reasons, we will adopt the modern approach and *not* assign existential commitment to universal (A and E) propositions, so these propositions do not imply particular (I and O) propositions. All the same, there is something beautiful about the classical approach, and it does seem appropriate in some contexts to some people, so it is worth exploring in its own right. Appendix A will show how to develop the classical theory by adding existential commitment to the modern theory.

EXERCISE IV

Give other examples of contexts in which:

    (1) stating an A proposition does not seem to commit the speaker to the existence of the things to which the subject term refers;

    (2) stating an A proposition does not seem to commit the speaker to the existence of the things to which the predicate term refers;

    (3) stating an E proposition does not seem to commit the speaker to the existence of the things to which the subject term refers;

    (4) stating an E proposition does not seem to commit the speaker to the existence of the things to which the predicate term refers.

VALIDITY FOR ARGUMENTS CONTAINING CATEGORICAL PROPOSITIONS

We have introduced Venn diagrams because they provide an efficient and illuminating way to test the validity of arguments made up of categorical (A, E, I, and O) propositions. The basic idea is simple enough. An argument made up of categorical propositions is valid if all the information contained in the Venn diagram for the conclusion is already contained in the Venn diagram for the premises. There are only two ways to put information into a Venn diagram: We can either shade out an area or put an asterisk in an area. So, to test the validity of an argument made up of categorical propositions, we need only examine the diagram of the conclusion for its information (its shading or asterisks) and then check to see if the diagram for the premises contains this information (the same shading or asterisks).

The following simple example will give a general idea of how this works:

Argument   Diagrams

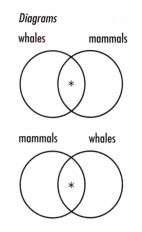

Some whales are mammals.

∴ Some mammals are whales.

Notice that the only information contained in the diagram for the conclusion is the asterisk in the overlap between the two circles, and that information is already included in the diagram for the premise. Thus, the argument is valid.

The same method can be used to test argument *forms* for validity. The form of the previous argument and the corresponding diagrams look like this:

Argument Form   Diagrams

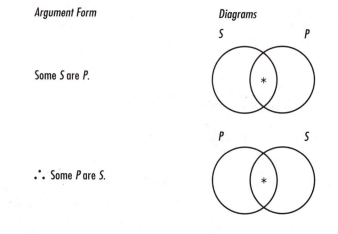

Some *S* are *P*.

∴ Some *P* are *S*.

This argument form is valid, because all the information contained in the Venn diagram for the conclusion is contained in the Venn diagram for the premise. And any argument that is a substitution instance of a valid argument form is valid.

Notice that we did not say that an argument is *invalid* if it fails these tests—that is, if some of the information in the Venn diagram for the conclusion (or its form) is not contained in the Venn diagram for the premises (or their forms). As with truth tables in propositional logic (see Chapter 5), Venn diagrams test whether arguments are valid by virtue of a certain form, but some arguments will be valid on a different basis, even though they are not valid by virtue of their categorical form. Here is one example:

Argument

Diagrams

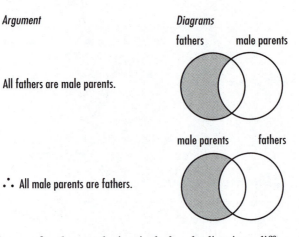

All fathers are male parents.

∴ All male parents are fathers.

The Venn diagram for the conclusion includes shading in a different circle than does the Venn diagram for the premise, so this *form* of argument is *not* valid, and some arguments of this form are not valid. Nonetheless, this particular argument *is* clearly valid, since it is not possible for the premise to be true when the conclusion is false. Because of such cases, Venn diagrams can show us that an argument is valid, but they cannot prove that an argument is invalid.

Despite this limitation, the method of Venn diagrams can be used to test many different kinds of arguments and argument forms for validity. We will show how this method works for two main kinds of argument: immediate inferences and syllogisms.

IMMEDIATE INFERENCES

An immediate inference is an argument with the following features:

(1) It has a single premise. (That is why the inference is called immediate.)

(2) It is constructed from A, E, I, and O propositions.

Of course, there are all sorts of other arguments involving just one premise, but those involving categorical propositions have been singled out for special attention. These arguments deserve such attention because they occur quite often in everyday reasoning.

We will focus on the simplest kind of immediate inference, which is *conversion*. We *convert* a proposition (and produce its *converse*) simply by reversing the subject term and the predicate term. By the *subject term*, we mean the term that occurs as the grammatical subject; by the *predicate term*, we mean the term that occurs as the grammatical predicate. In the A proposition "All spies are aliens," "spies" is the subject term and "aliens" is the predicate term; the converse is "All aliens are spies."

In this case, identifying the predicate term is straightforward, since the grammatical predicate is a noun—a predicate nominative. Often, however, we have to change the grammatical predicate from an adjective to a noun phrase in order to get a noun that refers to a class of things. "All spies are dangerous" becomes "All spies are dangerous things." Here "spies" is the subject term and "dangerous things" is the predicate term. Although this change is a bit artificial, it is necessary because, when we convert a proposition (that is, reverse its subject and predicate terms), we need a noun phrase to take the place of the grammatical subject. In English we cannot say "All dangerous are spies," but we can say "All dangerous things are spies."

Having explained what conversion is, we now want to know when this operation yields a *valid* immediate inference. To answer this question, we use Venn diagrams to examine the relationship between each of the four basic categorical propositional forms and its converse. The immediate inference is valid if the information contained in the conclusion is also contained in the premise—that is, if any region that is shaded in the conclusion is shaded in the premise, and if any region that contains an asterisk in the conclusion contains an asterisk in the premise.

Two cases are obvious at first sight. Both I and E propositions validly convert. From an I proposition with the form "Some S is P," we may validly infer its converse, which has the form "Some P is S."

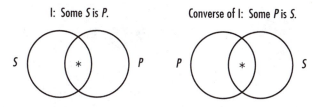

From an E proposition with the form "No S is P," we may validly infer its converse, which has the form "No P is S."

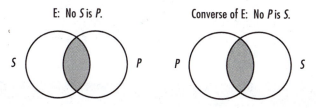

Notice that in both these cases, the information is in the center of the original diagram, and the diagram for the converse flips the original diagram. Thus, the two diagrams contain the same information, since the diagram for the converse has exactly the same markings in the same areas as does the diagram for the original propositional form. This shows that E and I propositions not only logically *imply* their converses, but are also logically *implied by* them. Since the implication runs both ways, these propositions are said to be *logically equivalent* to their converses, and they always have the same truth values as their converses.

The use of a Venn diagram also shows that an O proposition cannot always be converted validly. From a proposition with the form "Some S is not P," we may not always infer its converse, which has the form "Some P is not S."

O: Some *S* is not *P*.   Converse of O: Some *P* is not *S*.

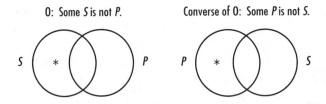

Notice that in this case the information is not in the center but is instead off to one side. As a result, the information changes when the diagram is flipped. The asterisk is in a different circle—it is in the circle for *S* in the diagram for an O proposition, but it is in the circle for *P* in the diagram for the converse of the O proposition. That shows that an argument from an O proposition to its converse is not always valid.[1]

Finally, we can see that A propositions also do not always validly convert. From a proposition with the form "All *S* is *P*," we may not always infer its converse, which has the form "All *P* is *S*."

A: All *S* is *P*.   Converse of A: All *P* is *S*.

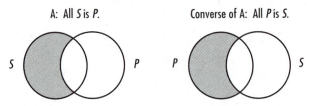

Since the diagram is not symmetrical, the information changes when the diagram is flipped; the shading ends up in a different circle. That shows why this form of argument is not always valid.

Traditionally, other immediate inferences have also been studied, but we will not run through them all here. (For those who are interested, a more complete theory of immediate inferences is presented in Appendix B.) The single example of conversion is enough to illustrate how Venn diagrams can be used to test some arguments for validity.

EXERCISE V

Use Venn diagrams to determine whether the following immediate inferences are valid:

(1) All dinosaurs are animals. Therefore, all animals are dinosaurs.

(2) Some pterodactyls can fly. Therefore, some flying things are pterodactyls.

---

[1] We say "not always" rather than simply "not," because there are some strange cases—logicians call them "degenerate cases"—for which inferences of this pattern are valid. For example, from "Some men are not men," we may validly infer "Some men are not men." Here, by making the subject term and the predicate term the same, we trivialize conversion. Keeping cases of this kind in mind, we must say that the inference from an O proposition to its converse is usually, but not always, invalid. In contrast, the set of valid arguments holds in all cases, including degenerate cases.

(3) Some eryopses are not meat eaters. Therefore, some things that eat meat are not eryopses.

(4) No tyrannosaurus is a king. Therefore, no king is a tyrannosaurus.

(5) Some dinosaurs are reptiles. Therefore, all dinosaurs are reptiles.

(6) Some dinosaurs are not alive today. Therefore, no dinosaurs are alive today.

(7) All dimetrodons eat meat. Therefore, some dimetrodons eat meat.

(8) No dinosaurs are warm-blooded. Therefore, some dinosaurs are not warm-blooded.

THE THEORY OF THE SYLLOGISM

In an immediate inference, we draw a conclusion directly from a single A, E, I, or O proposition. Moreover, when two categorical propositions are contradictories, the falsity of one can be validly inferred from the truth of the other, and the truth of one can be validly inferred from the falsity of the other. All these forms of argument contain only one premise. The next step in understanding categorical propositions is to consider arguments containing two premises rather than just one.

An important group of such arguments is called *categorical syllogisms*. The basic idea behind these arguments is commonsensical. Suppose you wish to prove that all squares have four sides. A proof should present some *link* or *connection* between squares and four-sided figures. This link can be provided by some intermediate class, such as rectangles. You can then argue that, because the set of squares is a subset of the set of rectangles and rectangles are a subset of four-sided figures, squares must also be a subset of four-sided figures.

Of course, there are many other ways to link two terms by means of a third term. All such arguments with categorical propositions are called categorical syllogisms. More precisely, a categorical syllogism is any argument such that:

(1) the argument has exactly two premises and one conclusion,

(2) the argument contains only basic A, E, I, and O propositions,

(3) exactly one premise contains the predicate term,

(4) exactly one premise contains the subject term, and

(5) each premise contains the middle term.

The *predicate term* is simply the term in the predicate of the conclusion. It is also called the *major term*, and the premise that contains the predicate term is called the *major premise*. The *subject term* is the term in the subject of the conclusion. It is called the *minor term*, and the premise that contains the subject term is called the *minor premise*. It is traditional to state the major premise first, the minor premise second.

Our first example of a categorical syllogism then looks like this:

> All rectangles are things with four sides.   (Major premise)
> All squares are rectangles.   (Minor premise)
> _____
> ∴ All squares are things with four sides.   (Conclusion)

> Subject term = "Squares"
> Predicate term = "Things with four sides"
> Middle term = "Rectangles"

To get the form of this syllogism, we replace the terms with variables:

> All M is P.
> All S is M.
> _____
> ∴ All S is P.

Of course, many other arguments fit the definition of a categorical syllogism. Here is one with a negative premise:

> No ellipses are things with sides.
> All circles are ellipses.
> _____
> ∴ No circles are things with sides.

The next categorical syllogism has a particular premise:

> All squares are things with equal sides.
> Some squares are rectangles.
> _____
> ∴ Some rectangles are things with equal sides.

EXERCISE VI

In each of the last two syllogisms, what is the subject term? The predicate term? The middle term? The major premise? The minor premise? The form of the syllogism (using S, P, and M)? Is the syllogism valid? Why or why not?

HONORS EXERCISE

Given the restrictions in the definition of a categorical syllogism, there are exactly two hundred fifty-six possible forms of categorical syllogism. Explain why.

VENN DIAGRAMS FOR SYLLOGISMS

In a previous section, we used Venn diagrams to test the validity of immediate inferences. Immediate inferences contain only two terms or classes, so the corresponding Venn diagrams need only two overlapping circles. Categorical syllogisms contain three terms or classes. To reflect this, we will use diagrams with three overlapping circles. If we use a bar over a letter to indicate that things in the area are not in the class (so that $\overline{S}$ indicates that something is not in S), then our diagram looks like this:

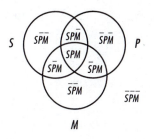

This diagram has eight different areas, which can be listed in an order that resembles a truth table:

S	P	M
S	P	$\overline{M}$
S	$\overline{P}$	M
S	$\overline{P}$	$\overline{M}$
$\overline{S}$	P	M
$\overline{S}$	P	$\overline{M}$
$\overline{S}$	$\overline{P}$	M
$\overline{S}$	$\overline{P}$	$\overline{M}$

Notice that, if something is neither an S nor a P nor an M, then it falls completely outside the system of overlapping circles. In every other case, a thing is assigned to one of the seven compartments within the system of overlapping circles.

THE VALIDITY OF SYLLOGISMS

To test the validity of a syllogism using a Venn diagram, we first fill in the diagram to indicate the information contained in the premises. Remember that the only information contained in a Venn diagram is indicated either by shading out an area or by putting an asterisk in it. The argument is valid if the information expressed by the conclusion is already contained in the diagram for the premises.[2] To see this, consider the diagrams for examples that we have already considered:

All rectangles have four sides.
All squares are rectangles.

∴ All squares have four sides.

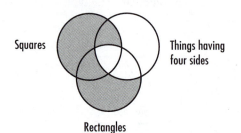

Notice that all the things that are squares are corralled into the region of things that have four sides. That shows that this syllogism is valid.

Next, let us try a syllogism with a negative premise:

No ellipses have sides.
All circles are ellipses.

∴ No circles have sides.

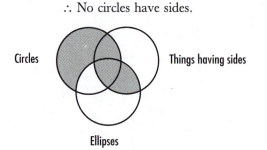

We diagram the conclusion "No circles have sides" as follows:

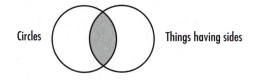

---

[2] We cannot say "only if" here because of degenerate cases of categorical syllogisms that are valid, but not by virtue of their syllogistic form. Here is one example: "All numbers divisible by two are even. No prime number other than two is divisible by two. Therefore, no prime number other than two is even." This syllogism is valid because it is not possible that its premises are true and its conclusion is false, but other syllogisms with this same form are not valid.

That information is already contained in the Venn diagram for the premises, so this syllogism is also valid.

Let us try a syllogism with a particular premise:

> All squares have equal sides.
> Some squares are rectangles.
> ───────────────
> ∴ Some rectangles have equal sides.

It is a good strategy to diagram a universal premise *before* diagramming a particular premise. The diagram for the above argument then looks like this:

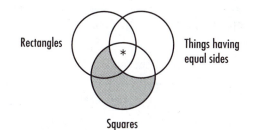

The conclusion—that there is something that is a rectangle that has equal sides—already appears in the diagram for the premises.

So far we have looked only at valid syllogisms. Let us see how this method applies to invalid syllogisms. Here is one:

> All pediatricians are doctors.
> All pediatricians like children.
> ───────────────
> ∴ All doctors like children.

We can diagram the premises at the left and the conclusion at the right:

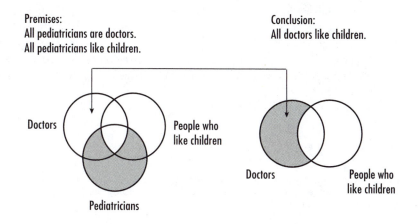

Premises:
All pediatricians are doctors.
All pediatricians like children.

Conclusion:
All doctors like children.

It is evident that the information in the diagram for the conclusion is *not* already contained in the diagram for the premises. The arrow shows differences in informational content. Thus, this form of syllogism is not valid.

Notice that the difference between these diagrams not only tells us *that* this form of syllogism is invalid; it also tells us *why* it is invalid. In the diagram for the premises, there is no shading in the upper left-hand area, which includes people who are doctors but are not pediatricians and do not like children. This shows that the premises do not rule out the possibility that some people are doctors without being pediatricians or liking children. But if anyone is a doctor and not a person who likes children, then it is not true that all doctors like children. Since this is the conclusion of the syllogism, the premises do not rule out all of the ways in which the conclusion might be false. As a result, this conclusion does not follow.[3]

Here is an example of an invalid syllogism with particular premises:

Some doctors are golfers.
Some fathers are doctors.

———————

∴ Some fathers are golfers.

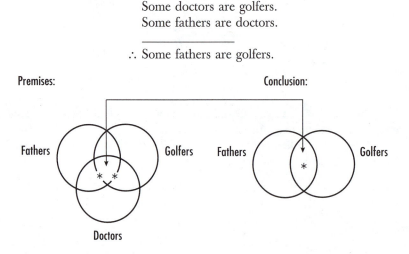

Examine this diagram closely. Notice that in diagramming "Some doctors are golfers" we had to put an asterisk *on the boundary* of the circle for fathers, since we were not given information saying whether anything falls into the category of fathers or not. For the same reason, we had to put an asterisk on the boundary of the circle for golfers when diagraming "Some fathers are doctors." The upshot was that we did not indicate that anything exists in the region of overlap between fathers and golfers. But this is what the conclusion demands, so the form of this syllogism is not valid.

Here is an invalid syllogism with negative premises:

---

[3] Actually, all the diagram proves is that the syllogism is not valid *by virtue of its categorical form.* As we saw above, it still might be valid on some other basis. In this particular example, however, nothing else makes this argument valid.

No babies are golfers.
No fathers are babies.

∴ No fathers are golfers.

Premises: Conclusion:

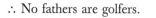

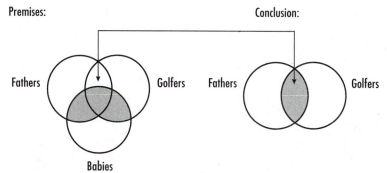

Fathers   Golfers   Fathers   Golfers

Babies

Again, we see that the form of this syllogism is not valid.

The method of Venn diagrams is adequate for deciding the validity or invalidity of all possible forms of categorical syllogism.

EXERCISE VII

Using Venn diagrams, test the following syllogistic forms for validity:

(1)   All *M* is *P.*
      All *M* is *S.*
      _____
      ∴ All *S* is *P.*

(2)   All *P* is *M.*
      All *M* is *S.*
      _____
      ∴ All *S* is *P.*

(3)   All *M* is *P.*
      Some *M* is *S.*
      _____
      ∴ Some *S* is *P.*

(4)   All *P* is *M.*
      Some *M* is *S.*
      _____
      ∴ Some *S* is *P.*

(5)   All *P* is *M.*
      Some *S* is *M.*
      _____
      ∴ Some *S* is *P.*

(6)   All *P* is *M.*
      Some *S* is not *M.*
      _____
      ∴ Some *S* is not *P.*

(7)   All *M* is *P.*
      Some *S* is not *M.*
      _____
      ∴ Some *S* is not *P.*

(8)   All *M* is *P.*
      Some *M* is not *S.*
      _____
      ∴ Some *S* is not *P.*

(9)   No *M* is *P.*
      Some *S* is *M.*
      _____
      ∴ Some *S* is not *P.*

(10) No *P* is *M.*
      Some *S* is *M.*
      _____
      ∴ Some *S* is not *P.*

(11) No *P* is *M*.
      Some *S* is not *M*.
      _____
      ∴ Some *S* is not *P*.

(12) No *M* is *P*.
      Some *S* is not *M*.
      _____
      ∴ Some *S* is not *P*.

(13) No *P* is *M*.
      Some *M* is not *S*.
      _____
      ∴ Some *S* is not *P*.

(14) No *P* is *M*.
      No *M* is *S*.
      _____
      ∴ No *S* is *P*.

(15) No *P* is *M*.
      All *M* is *S*.
      _____
      ∴ No *S* is *P*.

(16) No *P* is *M*.
      All *S* is *M*.
      _____
      ∴ No *S* is *P*.

(17) All *P* is *M*.
      No *S* is *M*.
      _____
      ∴ No *S* is *P*.

(18) All *M* is *P*.
      No *S* is *M*.
      _____
      ∴ No *S* is *P*.

(19) Some *M* is *P*.
      Some *M* is not *S*.
      _____
      ∴ Some *S* is not *P*.

(20) Some *P* is *M*.
      Some *S* is not *M*.
      _____
      ∴ Some *S* is *P*.

EXERCISE VIII

Explain why it is a good strategy to diagram a universal premise before diagramming a particular premise.

PROBLEMS IN APPLYING THE THEORY OF THE SYLLOGISM

After mastering the techniques for evaluating syllogisms, students naturally turn to arguments that arise in daily life and attempt to use these newly acquired skills. They are often disappointed with the results. The formal theory of the syllogism seems to bear little relationship to everyday arguments, and there does not seem to be any easy way to bridge the gap.

This gap between formal theory and its application occurs for a number of reasons. First, as we saw in Chapters 1 and 4, our everyday discourse leaves much unstated. Many things are conversationally implied rather than explicitly asserted. We do not feel called on to say many things that are matters of common agreement. Before we can apply the theory of the syllogism to everyday arguments, these things that are simply understood must be made explicit. This is often illuminating, and sometimes boring, but it usually involves a great deal of work. Second, the theory of the syllogism applies to statements only in a highly stylized form. Before we apply the theory of the syllogism to an argument, we must cast its premises and conclusion into the basic A, E, I, and O forms. As we saw earlier in this chapter, the needed translation is not always simple or obvious. It may not always be possible. For these and related reasons, modern logicians have largely abandoned the project of reducing all reasoning to syllogisms.

Why study the theory of the syllogism at all, if it is hard to apply in some circumstances and perhaps impossible to apply in others? The answer to this question was given at the beginning of Chapter 5. The study of formal logic is important because it deepens our insight into a central notion of logic: *validity*. Furthermore, the argument forms we have studied do underlie much of our everyday reasoning, but so much else is going on in a normal conversational setting that this dimension is often hidden. By examining arguments in idealized forms, we can study their validity in isolation from all the other factors at work in a rich conversational setting.

There is a difference, then, between the techniques developed in Chapters 1 through 4 and the techniques developed in Chapters 5 through 7. The first four chapters presented methods of informal analysis that may be applied directly to the rich and complex arguments that arise in everyday life. These methods of analysis are not wholly rigorous, but they do provide practical guides for the analysis and evaluation of actual arguments. These chapters concerning formal logic have the opposite tendency. In comparison with the first four chapters, the level of rigor is very high, but the range of application is correspondingly smaller. In general, the more rigor and precision you insist on, the less you can talk about.

DISCUSSION QUESTIONS

(1) What are the chief differences between the logical procedures developed in this chapter and those developed in the chapter on propositional logic?

(2) If we evaluate arguments as they occur in everyday life by using the exact standards developed in Chapters 5 and 6, we discover that our everyday arguments rarely satisfy these standards, at least explicitly. Does this show that most of our ordinary arguments are illogical? What else might it show?

APPENDIX A: THE CLASSICAL THEORY

The difference between classical and modern logic is simply that the classical approach adds one more assumption—namely, that every categorical proposition is about something. More technically, the assumption is that A, E, I, and O propositions all carry commitment to the existence of something in the subject class and something in the predicate class. To draw Venn diagrams for categorical propositions on the classical interpretation, then, all we need to do is add existential commitment to the diagrams for their modern interpretations, which were discussed above.

But how should we add existential commitment to Venn diagrams? The answer might seem easy: Just put an asterisk wherever there is existential commitment. However, the story cannot be quite so simple, for the following reason. The Venn diagram for the E propositional form on the modern interpretation is this:

Modern E: No *S* is *P.*

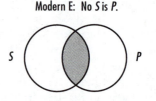

The classical interpretation adds existential commitment in both the subject and the predicate, so if we represent existential commitment with an asterisk, we get this diagram:

Classical E: No *S* is *P.* (???)

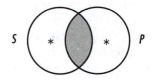

Although this diagram might seem to work, it breaks down when we perform operations on it. We are supposed to be able to diagram the contradictory of a proposition simply by substituting shading for asterisks and asterisks for shading. If we perform this operation on the previous diagram, we get this:

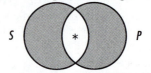

This diagram is very different from the Venn diagram for the I propositional form, which is the same on both classical and modern interpretations:

I: Some *S* is *P.*

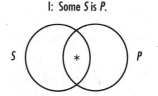

However, an I proposition is supposed to be the contradictory of the corresponding E proposition even on the classical interpretation, so something has gone wrong.

This problem shows that existential commitment cannot be treated exactly like explicit existential assertion, as in I and O propositions. As a result, we cannot use the same asterisk to represent existential commitment in Venn diagrams. Instead, we will use a plus sign: "+." With this new symbol, we can diagram the E propositional form on the classical interpretation this way:

Classical E: No *S* is *P*.

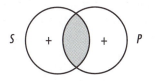

The plus sign indicates that an E proposition carries commitment to the existence of something in each class, even though it does not explicitly assert that something exists in either class.

From this new diagram, we can get the contradictory of a proposition by substituting shading for asterisks and asterisks for shading, as long as we also add plus signs to ensure that no class is empty, and drop plus signs that are no longer needed to indicate this existential commitment. When this procedure is applied to the previous diagram, the shading becomes an asterisk in the central area, and we can then drop the plus signs in the side areas, because the central asterisk already assures us that something exists in both circles. Thus, we get the (modern and classical) diagram for the I propositional form. Moreover, when this procedure is applied to the diagram for the I propositional form, it yields the above diagram for the E propositional form on the classical interpretation.

It might not be so clear, however, that E and I propositions are contradictories on their classical interpretations; let us see why this is so. Two propositions are contradictories if and only if they cannot both be true and also cannot both be false. The diagram for an E proposition has shading in the same area in which the diagram for its corresponding I proposition has an asterisk, so they cannot both be true. It is harder to see why these propositions cannot both be false on the classical interpretation, but this can be shown by the following argument. Suppose that an I proposition is false. Then there is nothing in the central area, so that area should be shaded. The classical interpretation insists that the subject and predicate classes are not empty, so if there is nothing in the central area, there must be something in each side area, which is indicated by a plus sign in each side area. That gives us the diagram for the corresponding E proposition, so that proposition is true. Thus, if an I proposition is false, its corresponding E proposition is true. That means that they cannot both be false. We already saw that they cannot both be true. So they are contradictories.

The same procedure yields a classical O proposition when it is applied to a classical A proposition, and a classical A proposition when it is applied to a classical O proposition:

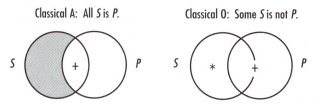

Classical A: All *S* is *P*.   Classical O: Some *S* is not *P*.

(The plus sign on the line indicates that the commitment is to something in the right-hand circle, but not to anything in either specific part of that circle.) Propositions of these forms on their classical interpretations cannot both be true and cannot both be false, so they are contradictories. Thus, this method of diagraming seems to capture the classical interpretation of the basic propositions.

EXERCISE IX

Explain why an A proposition and its corresponding O proposition are contradictories on their classical interpretations, using the diagrams above.

THE CLASSICAL SQUARE OF OPPOSITION

In addition to the contradictories, there is a more extensive and elegant set of logical relationships among categorical propositions on the classical interpretation. This system of relationships produces what has been called the *square of opposition*.

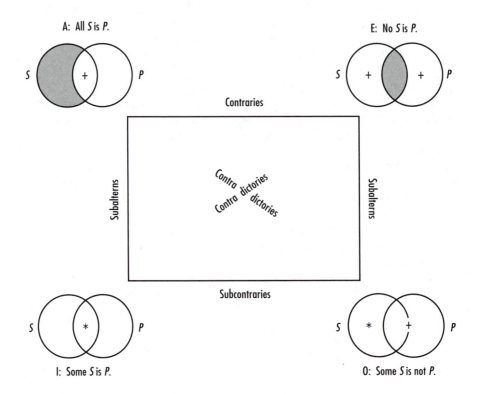

The lines in this diagram show the logical relationships each proposition has to the other three. These relationships are explained below. Throughout the discussion, it is important to remember that all of the basic propositions are interpreted as carrying existential commitment in both their subjects and their predicates.

CONTRADICTORIES

Two propositions are *contradictories* of each other (and they contradict each other) when they are so related that

(1) they cannot both be true, and

(2) they cannot both be false.

More simply, contradictory pairs of propositions always have opposite truth values. We have already seen that the E and I propositions are contradictories of one another, as are the A and O propositions. This relationship holds on both the modern interpretation and the classical interpretation.

CONTRARIES

Two propositions are said to be *contraries* of one another if they are so related that

(1) they cannot both be true, but

(2) they can both be false.

On the classical interpretation (but not the modern interpretation), A and E propositions with the same subject and predicate are contraries of one another.

In common life, the relationship between such corresponding A and E propositions is captured by the notion that one claim is the *complete opposite* of another. The complete opposite of "Everyone is here" is "No one is here." Clearly, such complete opposites cannot both be true at once. We see this readily if we look at the diagrams for A and E propositions on the classical interpretation. The middle region of the diagram for an A proposition shows the existence of something that is both *S* and *P*, whereas the middle region of the diagram for the corresponding E proposition is shaded, showing that nothing is both *S* and *P*. It should also be clear that these A and E propositions can both be false. Suppose that there is some *S* that is *P* and also some *S* that is not *P*.

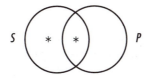

Going from left to right, the first asterisk shows that the A proposition of the form "All *S* is *P*" is false; the second asterisk shows that the corresponding E proposition of the form "No *S* is *P*" is also false. Thus, these propositions can both be false, but they cannot both be true. This makes them contraries.

SUBCONTRARIES

Propositions are *subcontraries* of one another when

    (1) they can both be true, and

    (2) they cannot both be false.

On the classical approach (but not the modern approach), corresponding I and O propositions are subcontraries. To see how this works, compare the diagrams for I and O propositions:

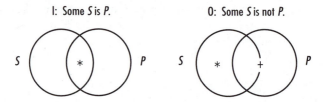

It should be clear that corresponding propositions with these forms can both be true, since there can be some *S* that is *P* and another *S* that is not *P*. But why can they not both be false? Consider the left-hand side of the following diagram:

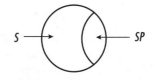

We know that, on the classical approach, there must be something in this circle somewhere. If there is something in the overlapping region *SP*, then the I proposition is true. And if there is something in the nonoverlapping region of *S*, then there must be something else in the circle for *P*, since *P* cannot be empty on the classical approach; therefore the O proposition is true. Thus, either the I proposition or the corresponding O proposition must be true, so they cannot both be false. We already saw that they can both be true. Consequently, corresponding I and O propositions are subcontraries.

SUBALTERNS

Subalternation is the relationship that holds down the sides of the classical square of opposition. Quite simply, an A proposition implies the corresponding I proposition, and an E proposition implies the corresponding O proposition. This relationship depends on the existential commitment found on the classical approach and does not hold on the modern approach.

The validity of subalternation is illustrated by the following diagrams:

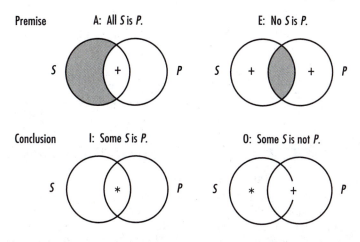

Premise A: All *S* is *P*.   E: No *S* is *P*.

Conclusion I: Some *S* is *P*.   O: Some *S* is not *P*.

An A proposition includes a plus sign where the corresponding I proposition includes an asterisk, but both these symbols indicate that something lies in the middle area. Thus, the information for the I proposition is already included in the diagram for the A proposition, which means that the A proposition implies the I proposition.

The same point applies to the implication on the right-hand side, since the diagram for an E proposition includes a plus sign in the same area as the asterisk in the diagram for the corresponding O proposition. The diagram for the E proposition also has a plus sign in the rightmost area. If something exists in that area, then something exists in either that area or the middle area, which is what is meant by the plus sign on the line in the diagram for the O proposition. Thus, an E proposition implies its corresponding O proposition.

The information given by the classical square of opposition can now be summarized in two charts. We shall ask two questions. First, for each propositional form, if we assume that a proposition with that form is *true*, what consequences follow for the truth or falsity of a corresponding proposition with a different form?

	A	**E**	**I**	**O**
A	T	F	T	F
E	F	T	F	T
I	?	F	T	?
O	F	?	?	T

Assumed true

"T" indicates that the corresponding proposition in that column is true, "F" indicates that it is false, and "?" indicates that it might have either truth value, because neither consequence follows.

Second, for each propositional form, if we assume that a proposition with that form is *false*, what consequences follow for the truth or falsity of a corresponding proposition with a different form?

$$
\begin{array}{c c c c c}
 & \mathbf{A} & \mathbf{E} & \mathbf{I} & \mathbf{O} \\
\mathbf{A} & F & ? & ? & T \\
\mathbf{E} & ? & F & T & ? \\
\mathbf{I} & F & T & F & T \\
\mathbf{O} & T & F & T & F \\
\end{array}
$$

Assumed false (label to the left of the **E** row)

THE CLASSICAL THEORY OF IMMEDIATE INFERENCE

The difference between the modern and classical approaches is simply that the classical approach assigns more information—specifically, existential commitment—to the basic propositions than the modern interpretation does. Because of this additional information, certain immediate inferences hold on the classical approach that do not hold on the modern approach. In particular, though conversion of an A proposition fails on both approaches, what is known as *conversion by limitation* holds on the classical approach but not on the modern approach. That is, from a proposition with the form "All *S* is *P*" we may not validly infer the proposition with the form "All *P* is *S*," but on the classical approach, we may validly infer "*Some P* is *S*." The reason is simple: From a proposition with the form "All *S* is *P*" on the classical interpretation we may infer a proposition with the form "*Some S* is *P*," and then we may convert this to get a proposition with the form "*Some P* is *S*."

EXERCISE X

Using the Venn diagrams for the classical interpretation of the A propositional form given above, show that conversion by limitation is classically valid for an A proposition.

THE CLASSICAL THEORY OF SYLLOGISMS

As in the case of immediate inferences, the premises of syllogisms will contain more information—specifically, existential commitment—on the classical interpretation than they do on the modern interpretation. This will make some syllogisms valid on the classical approach that were not valid on the modern approach.

We begin our study of this matter with an example that has had a curious history:

All rectangles are four-sided.
All squares are rectangles.

∴ *Some* squares are four-sided.

The argument is peculiar because its conclusion is weaker than it needs to be. We could, after all, conclude that *all* squares are four-sided. The argument thus violates the conversational rule of Quantity. Perhaps for this reason, this syllogism was often not included in traditional lists of valid syllogisms. Yet the argument is valid on the classical interpretation of existential commitment, and our diagram should show this.

Step I: Diagram the first premise

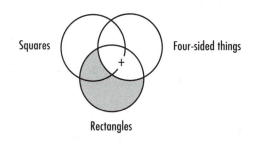

Notice that the plus sign is placed on the outer edge of the circle for squares, because we are not in a position to put it either inside or outside that circle. We now add the information for the second premise:

Step II: Add the second premise

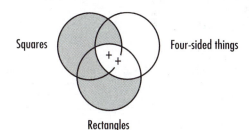

As expected, the conclusion that some squares are four-sided is already diagrammed, so the argument is valid—provided that we take A propositions to have existential commitment.

Because classical logicians tended to ignore the previous argument, their writings did not bring out the importance of existential commitment in evaluating it. There is, however, an argument that did appear on the classical lists that makes clear the demand for existential commitment. These are syllogisms with the following form:

All *M* is *P.*
All *M* is *S.*

∴ Some *S* is *P.*

This form of syllogism is diagrammed as follows:

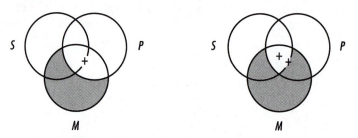

Step I: Diagram the first premise   Step II: Add the second premise

Again, we see that the conclusion follows, but only if we diagram A propositions to indicate existential commitment. This, then, is an argument that was declared valid on the classical approach, but invalid on the modern approach.

EXERCISE XI

Use Venn diagrams to test the following syllogism forms for validity on the classical approach:

(1) All *M* is *P.*
    No *M* is *S.*

∴ Some *S* is not *P.*

(2) No *M* is *P.*
    All *M* is *S.*

∴ Some *S* is not *P.*

(3) No *M* is *P.*
    All *S* is *M.*

∴ Some *S* is not *P.*

(4) No *M* is *P.*
    No *M* is *S.*

∴ Some *S* is not *P.*

EXERCISE XII

Are the following claims true or false? Explain your answers.

(1) Every syllogism that is valid on the modern approach is also valid on the classical approach.

(2) Every syllogism that is valid on the classical approach but not on the modern approach has a particular conclusion that starts with "Some."

APPENDIX B: IMMEDIATE INFERENCES WITH COMPLEMENTARY CLASSES

The standard theory of immediate inference includes not only conversion but also obversion and contraposition. These other inferences are more complicated than conversion, because they employ complements of classes.

The complement of a class is simple enough to define. Given any class *C*, its *complement* or *complementary class* is the class that includes all those things that are not in *C*. A *complementary term* is a term that refers to the complement of the class in question. One standard way of referring to the complementary class is to use the prefix "non." Here are some examples:

Class	Complementary Class
Residents	Nonresidents
Combatants	Noncombatants
Republicans	Non-Republicans
Squares	Nonsquares

A bar over a letter indicates a complementary class. If R is the class of Republicans, then $\overline{R}$ is the class of non-Republicans.

If we look at the class of non-Republicans, we see that it is a mixed bag, for we have defined it as everything that is not a Republican. This includes coyotes, subatomic particles, prime numbers, and the British royal family. In everyday life, we do not wish to include all these things in our notion of a non-Republican. When we speak about non-Republicans, the context will usually make it clear that we are referring to people, and even to a limited group of people, such as American voters. In other words, talk about non-Republicans normally *presupposes* that we are considering only persons or voting Americans.

We can capture this idea by using the notion of a *domain of discourse*. We might say that the domain of discourse here includes all Americans who can vote. A non-Republican is then someone in this domain of discourse who is not a Republican. To reflect this domain of discourse, we need to make our diagrams a bit more elaborate.

We will enclose the intersecting circles with a box that indicates the *domain of discourse* (DD):

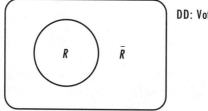

DD: Voting Americans

When two or more circles are used, we will assume that they share a domain of discourse, so we will enclose them all in the same box.

Deciding on a domain of discourse is somewhat arbitrary. It depends on good sense and present interests. In our example, we might have taken the domain of discourse to include only members of political parties, or perhaps only American politicians. Actually, it is not always useful to specify the domain of discourse precisely, although sometimes it is. In this discussion, we will be quite casual about specifying a domain of discourse, and will only do so when it serves some useful purpose.

OBVERSION

We can now define the immediate inference called *obversion*. To pass from a basic proposition to its obverse, we do the following:

(1) Reverse the quality of the proposition (that is, change it from affirmative to negative or negative to affirmative, as the case may be).

(2) Replace the predicate term with its complementary term.

Starting with "All men are mortal," this two-step process works as follows:

(1) Reversing the quality yields: No men are mortal.

(2) Replacing the predicate term with its complement yields: No men are non-mortal.

This final proposition is the obverse of "All men are mortal."

We now want to know when this operation of obversion is legitimate—that is, when obversion yields an immediate inference that is valid. The answer to this is that a proposition is always logically equivalent to its obverse.[4] To show this,

---

[4] This equivalence also holds in the classical system, because the standard classical theory assumes that not only the subject and predicate classes, but also the complements of these classes, are not empty; they have something in them.

we will run through the four basic propositional forms. Since all these equivalences hold between a proposition and its obverse, there is no need to draw a diagram twice. The reader should, however, check to see whether the diagram is accurate for both propositions.

A: A proposition with the form "All *S* is *P*" is logically equivalent to its obverse, which has the form "No *S* is non-*P*."

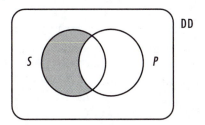

In this diagram, the class of things that are non-*P* includes all those things in the domain of discourse that are not in *P*. We can see that there is nothing in the class of things that are *S* that is also in the complementary class of *P*, because all the things in *S* are in the class *P*. This might sound a bit complicated, but with a little thought the validity of inferences through obversion becomes obvious.

E: A proposition with the form "No *S* is *P*" is logically equivalent to its obverse, which has the form "All *S* is non-*P*."

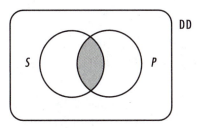

I: A proposition with the form "Some *S* is *P*" is logically equivalent to its obverse, which has the form "Some *S* is not non-*P*."

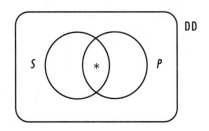

O: A proposition with the form "Some *S* is not *P*" is logically equivalent to its obverse, which has the form "Some *S* is non-*P*."

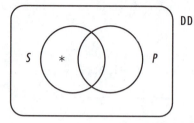

It is important to see that the final equivalence is a genuine equivalence and not a mere repetition. A proposition with the form "Some *S* is not *P*" is an O proposition, whereas a proposition with the form "Some *S* is non-*P*" is an I proposition. That is, the first proposition is negative, for it indicates that there is at least one thing that is *not* in a certain class. The second proposition is affirmative, for it indicates that something *is* in a given class—a complementary class.

CONTRAPOSITION

Contraposition is the final relationship we shall examine. We get the contrapositive of a proposition by using the following two-step process:

(1) We convert the proposition.

(2) We replace both terms with their complementary terms.

For example, starting with "All men are mortal," this two-step process works as follows:

(1) We convert "All men are mortal" to get "All mortal things are men."

(2) We replace each term with its complement to get "All nonmortal things are nonmen."

The final proposition is the contrapositive of "All men are mortal."

We must now ask when the contrapositive can be validly inferred from a given proposition. Here the situation is generally the reverse of what we discovered for conversion:

A: A proposition with the form "All *S* is *P*" is logically equivalent to its contrapositive, which has the form "All non-*P* is non-*S*."

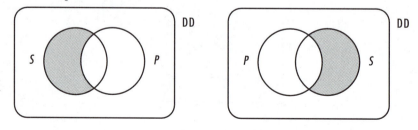

E: From a proposition with the form "No S is P" we may not always validly infer its contrapositive,[5] which has the form "No non-P is non-S."

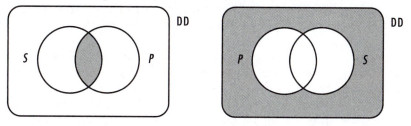

I: From a proposition with the form "Some S is P," we may not always validly infer its contrapositive, which has the form "Some non-P is non-S."

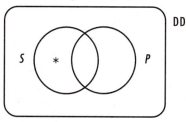
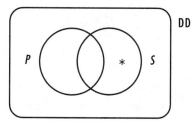

O: A proposition with the form "Some S is not P" is logically equivalent to its contrapositive, which has the form "Some non-P is not non-S."

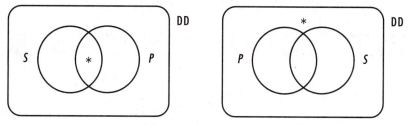

The following table summarizes all these equivalence relationships:

Propositional Form	Obverse	Converse	Contrapositive
A: All S is P.	No S is non-P. (Equivalent)	All P is S. (does NOT follow)	All non-P is non-S. (Equivalent)
E: No S is P.	All S is non-P. (Equivalent)	No P is S. (Equivalent)	No non-P is non-S. (does NOT follow)
I: Some S is P.	Some S is not non-P. (Equivalent)	Some P is S. (Equivalent)	Some non-P is non-S. (does NOT follow)
O: Some S is not P.	Some S is non-P. (Equivalent)	Some P is not S. (does NOT follow)	Some non-P is not non-S. (Equivalent)

---

[5] The qualification is needed here and in the next case because of degenerate cases of immediate inferences with this form that are valid, but not by virtue of their categorical form.

If we compare the propositions we have been studying with remarks that we make in everyday life, some of them, at least, will seem artificial. It is hard to imagine a case in which we would actually say "Some nonspies are not nonaliens." It would certainly be easier to say "Some aliens are not spies," which is its equivalent by contraposition.

In fact, we do use these complicated sentences in some contexts. Discussing the voting patterns of nonresidents, we might find ourselves saying that some nonresidents are not nonvoters. Given the context, this remark loses much of its oddness. Usually, however, we choose simple, clear formulations. The ability to do this depends on an implicit understanding of the logical relationships within this system of propositions. Here we are trying to bring this implicit understanding to the surface so that we can understand it better. That is, we are trying to give clear rules for inferences that we make routinely in everyday life.

EXERCISE XIII

For each of the following propositions, use Venn diagrams to determine which of the above immediate inferences are valid.

Example: All ministers are noncombatants.

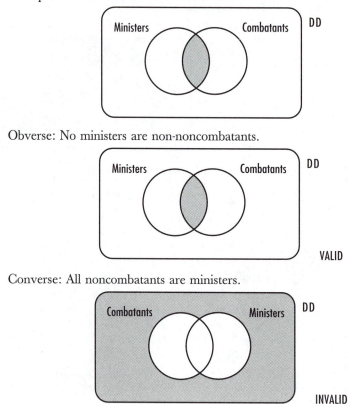

Obverse: No ministers are non-noncombatants.

Converse: All noncombatants are ministers.

Contrapositive: All non-noncombatants are nonministers. (Or, more simply: All combatants are non-ministers.)

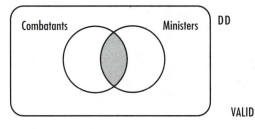

(1) Some dudes are not cowards.

(2) All nonresidents are taxpayers.

(3) Some nonaligned nations are wealthy (nations).

(4) No daughters are sons.

(5) No nonnegotiable stocks are safe (stocks).

(6) All that glitters is not gold.

(7) Some people cannot be bought.

(8) There is no such thing as a bad boy.

EXERCISE XIV

Put the following sentences into plain, respectable English. Indicate the immediate inference or immediate inferences you have used to do so. (Be careful!)

(1) No noncombatant is a minister.

(2) Some nonresident is not a non-nonvoter.

(3) Not all snakes are not dangerous (things).

(4) No all-time losers are non-nonpersons.

APPENDIX C: A SYSTEM OF RULES FOR EVALUATING SYLLOGISMS

The method of Venn diagrams that we have used in this chapter is probably the most natural technique for analyzing and evaluating syllogisms, because the relationship between overlapping figures is a clear analogy for the relationship between classes. Another method for evaluating syllogisms employs a system of rules. Although this system has less intuitive appeal than Venn diagrams do, it is easier to apply. The procedure is to lay down a set of rules such that any form of syllogism that satisfies all of the rules is valid, and any form of syllogism that fails to satisfy any one of them is invalid.

QUALITY

The system of rules that we will present here starts with the idea of the *quality* of a proposition—whether it is affirmative or negative. Recall that A and I propositions are said to be *affirmative* propositions, and E and O propositions are said to be *negative* propositions.

QUANTITY

The next idea used in this system of rules concerns the *quantity* of a proposition—whether it is universal or particular. Recall that A and E propositions are said to be *universal* propositions, and I and O propositions are said to be *particular* propositions.

DISTRIBUTION

The final idea used in these rules is new. It is the notion of the *distribution* or *extension* of a term. The basic idea is that a term is used distributively in a proposition if it is used to refer to the whole of a class or to all the members in it. We shall first simply state the distributional properties for A, E, I, and O propositions and then try to make sense out of the notion.

Proposition	Subject	Predicate
A	Distributed	Undistributed
E	Distributed	Distributed
I	Undistributed	Undistributed
O	Undistributed	Distributed

The subject term is distributed in universal (A and E) propositions, since they refer to *all S*. In contrast, particular (I and O) propositions are about *some S*, so the subject term is undistributed in these propositions.

The reasoning thus runs smoothly for the subject term, but the predicate term is not so easy to deal with. Notice that there is no word like "some" or "all" governing the predicate term. The reasoning for the predicate term usually proceeds along the following lines: Suppose we assert that no squares are circles.

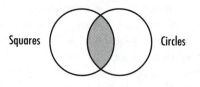

For this to be true, there can be no square that is identical with *any* circle. The appearance of the word "any" shows that the predicate term is distributed in this E proposition. Consider next the corresponding O proposition: some square is not a circle. For this to be true, there must be some square that is not identical with *any* circle. Again, the appearance of the word "any" shows that the predicate term is distributed in this O proposition. In contrast, consider the I proposition that some closed figures are circles. This means that some closed figures are identical with some circles. The word "any" does not appear, so the predicate term is not distributed in this I proposition. Our test for the distribution of terms is then to compare the basic A, E, I, or O proposition with a counterpart statement involving identity as follows:

A: All *S* is *P*.   For *any S*, there is *some P* that is identical with it.

E: No *S* is *P*.   For *any S*, there is not *any P* that is identical with it.

I: Some *S* is *P*.   For *some S*, there is *some P* that is identical with it.

O: Some *S* is not *P*.   For *some S*, there is not *any P* that is identical with it.

This comparison gives the pattern for the distribution of terms noticed earlier.

THE RULES

Now, using the ideas of quality, quantity, and distribution, we can formulate a set of rules that are adequate for testing the validity of all categorical syllogisms on the modern approach.

Rules of Quality:

(1) Nothing follows from two negative premises.

(2) If one premise is negative, then the conclusion must also be negative.

Rules of Distribution:

(3) The middle term must be distributed at least once.

(4) The subject term may not be distributed in the conclusion if it is not distributed in the premises.

(5) The predicate term may not be distributed in the conclusion if it is not distributed in the premises.

Rule of Quantity:

(6) A particular conclusion cannot be derived from two universal premises.[6]

The fallacies that result from violating these rules are called by the following names:

---

[6] The classical theory of the syllogism does not contain a rule of quantity of this kind. It does, however, contain an additional quality rule: (2′) If the conclusion is negative, then one premise must be negative. The fallacy that results from violating rule (2′) can be called the fallacy of *deriving a negative conclusion from two affirmative premises*.

(1) The fallacy of *two negative premises*

(2) The fallacy of *deriving an affirmative conclusion from a negative premise*

(3) The fallacy of *undistributed middle*

(4) The fallacy of *illicitly distributed subject*

(5) The fallacy of *illicitly distributed predicate*

(6) The fallacy of *deriving a particular conclusion from two universal premises*

The following devices facilitate the application of these rules. Mark each proposition in the syllogism with "+" or "−" to indicate its quality. Circle all terms that are distributed, leaving all undistributed terms uncircled. This makes it easy to see if the first five rules of the syllogism have been satisfied, and so whether the syllogism is valid or invalid. No special devices are necessary to check the sixth rule.

The following examples illustrate these methods:

(1)   + All Ⓜ is P.   Valid
      + All Ⓢ is M.

∴ + All Ⓢ is P.

(2)   − No Ⓜ is Ⓟ.   Valid
      + Some M is S.

∴ − Some S is not Ⓟ.

(3)   + All Ⓜ is P.   Invalid−[7]
      + All Ⓜ is S.   Particular conclusion from universal premises

∴ + Some S is P.

(4)   + All Ⓜ is P.   Invalid−
      + All Ⓜ is S.   Illicitly distributed subject

∴ + All Ⓢ is P.

(5)   + All Ⓟ is M.   Invalid−
      + All Ⓢ is M.   Undistributed middle

∴ + All Ⓢ is P.

(6)   − No Ⓟ is Ⓜ.   Invalid−
      − No Ⓢ is Ⓜ.   Two negatives premises

∴ − No Ⓢ is Ⓟ.

---

[7] This form of syllogism is valid in the classical approach.

EXERCISE XV

Using the rules in this appendix, test the syllogisms given in Exercise VII for validity. Where a fallacy occurs, give the name of that fallacy.

EXERCISE XVI

Using the rules in this appendix, test the syllogisms given in Exercise XI for validity. Where a fallacy occurs, give the name of that fallacy.

HONORS EXERCISE

To a person familiar with computer programming, this system of rules immediately suggests that a program can be written for the evaluation of syllogisms. In fact, such a program can be written and is only moderately difficult. The first problem is to find some method for encoding all possible syllogisms. After this, the notions of distribution and quality must be given mathematical analogues. In writing such a program, there is a good chance that the programmer will rediscover large portions of medieval logic. Try it.

Chapter Seven

THE FORMAL ANALYSIS OF ARGUMENTS:

QUANTIFICATIONAL LOGIC

Modern quantificational logic makes fundamental and far-reaching advances over previous
logical theories. It not only introduces mathematical rigor into the study of logic, but presents
a theory with a much wider range of application
than any previous logical theory. It encompasses propositional logic, categorical logic, and
much more that could not be dealt with in either
of these two logical systems. Since quantificational theory, when fully developed, becomes
very complicated, it is not possible to give a
complete account of it here. This chapter is
intended to do three things: explain the basic
concepts of quantificational logic, show how
sentences of everyday language can be translated into the notation of quantificational logic,
and show how validity can be determined in
one restricted area of quantificational logic.

COMBINING TWO BRANCHES OF LOGIC

In Chapter 5 we examined propositional logic, the logic concerned with truth-functional connections between propositions. In Chapter 6 we examined categorical logic, including the theory of immediate inference and the theory of the categorical syllogism, roughly, the logic concerned with relationships between classes of things.[1] We have presented these two branches of logic independently of one another. In fact, for centuries these two branches of logic were treated separately, and there was some debate concerning which was more important or more fundamental. A central achievement of modern symbolic logic was to combine these previously separate areas of logic into a single coherent system.[2] In this chapter we will examine some of the fundamental ideas involved in this important synthesis. Although we cannot present a fully developed system of quantificational logic, we can examine some of its basic ideas and show how they help us understand arguments in daily life that cannot be dealt with using the methods developed in the previous two chapters.

We will begin by presenting a new way of interpreting the four basic propositional forms discussed in Chapter 6—the A, E, I, and O categorical propositional forms:

A: All *S* is *P*.

E: No *S* is *P*.

I: Some *S* is *P*.

O: Some *S* is not *P*.

We will first show how these propositional forms are handled using modern logical techniques. We will then show how these modern techniques can be extended to deal with a vast number of other propositional forms (and hence argument forms) not addressed in traditional logic.

THE INTRODUCTION OF QUANTIFIERS

The following is an example of an A proposition:

(1) All sisters are female.

There are various ways we might paraphrase this proposition to bring out its logical structure. The following sounds like a reasonable paraphrase:

---

[1] Although this chapter contains a number of references to Chapter 6, it is not necessary to have read that chapter to follow the present discussion, since the material referred to in Chapter 6 is explained again here. However, this chapter cannot be understood without a thorough grasp of the material discussed in Chapter 5.

[2] The pioneering work in this area was done by Gottlob Frege (1848–1925) and Bertrand Russell (1872–1970).

(2) Anyone who is a sister is also female.

That seems to say:

(3) Take anything at all, if it is a sister, then it is female.

Thus, (3) suggests that (1) has an underlying conditional form. Modern logicians capture the meaning of (3) more formally by using the following translation:

(4) For all *x*, if *x* is a sister, then *x* is female.

If we examine this formula, we see that it begins with the expression "For all *x*." Logicians call expressions of this kind *quantifiers* because they indicate the quantity or range of things being referred to. The expression "for all *x*" indicates that we are referring to *all* instances of *x* rather than, say, to *some* or *most* of them. The symbol "(*x*)" is used to express "for all *x*." Since this expression refers to *all* instances of *x*, it is called the *universal* quantifier. Propositions that begin with this quantifier are called *universally quantified propositions*. So we can begin our translation of (4) in the following way:

(5) (*x*)(if *x* is a sister, then *x* is female).

In (5), the quantifier "For all *x*" is followed by the clause "if *x* is a sister, then *x* is female." This expression has a conditional form, but it is clearly not a propositional conditional, since neither "*x* is a sister" nor "*x* is female" expresses a proposition. Neither, that is, says anything either true or false. Here the letter "*x*" functions as a variable, which means that it can be replaced by names, but "*x* is a sister" does not express a proposition *until* "*x*" is replaced by a name. Logicians symbolize expressions of the form "*x* is a sister" as "*Sx*," where "*S*" refers to the property of being a sister. Adopting this convention, we can symbolize "*x* is female" as "*Fx*," where "*F*" refers to the property of being female. Here, by tradition, properties are represented by capital letters; lowercase letters from the end of the alphabet are used to stand for variables. We can now symbolize the universally quantified proposition "For all *x*, if *x* is a sister, then *x* is female" as follows:

(6) (*x*)(*Sx* ⊃ *Fx*)

Having translated an affirmative A proposition, we turn next to a negative E proposition. Just as we can say that *all* sisters are female, we can, in contrast, say that *no* brothers are female. We can express this second claim as follows:

(7) For all *x*, if *x* is a brother, then it is not the case that *x* is female.

Symbolically:

(8) (*x*)(*Bx* ⊃ ~*Fx*)[3]

---

[3] Where the context makes it clear, we will usually not offer an explicit interpretation of the symbols we use. In this example, it would be a waste of time to point out that "*Bx*" means "*x* is a brother."

This, then, is the way to translate a traditional E proposition into quantificational notation.

Having translated A and E propositions into the notation of modern quantificational theory, is there a way of doing the same thing for I and O propositions? In fact, these translations can be made using the universal quantifier already introduced, but this produces cumbersome translations that are hard to understand. For this reason a second quantifier, called the *existential quantifier,* is normally added to the notation. The intuitive idea is to analyze a proposition such as "Some ferns are green" as saying:

(9) There is at least one thing that is a fern and is green.

If we employ variables, (9) becomes:

(10) There is at least one x such that x is F and x is G.

Here the leading phrase "There exists at least one x" expresses the existential quantifier. We will represent it using the symbol "$(\exists x)$." Since the remainder of (10) is a conjunction, it gets translated thus:

(11) $(Fx \ \& \ Gx)$

And (10) is fully translated thus:

(12) $(\exists x)(Fx \ \& \ Gx)$

All propositions with the form "Some Fs are Gs" can be translated in this way. Similarly, propositions of the form "Some Fs are not Gs" (such as "Some ferns are not green") can be translated thus:

(13) $(\exists x)(Fx \ \& \ {\sim}Gx)$

There is something a bit odd about these translations, since "some" is usually taken to mean *more* than one rather than *at least* one. (It would be odd to say "Some women are the queen of England" when only one is.) As it turns out, however, this shift from ordinary language is a great simplification. One reason is that "There is at least one thing that is F" means the same as "It is not the case that everything is not F." Symbolically, "$(\exists x)Fx$" can be defined as "$\sim(x){\sim}Fx$." In any case, a fully developed theory provides ways of saying *more than one* if that needs to be said, so nothing is lost by interpreting the existential quantifier to mean "at least one."[4]

To summarize, the traditional A, E, I, and O propositions are translated into the notation of quantification theory as follows:

---

[4] The decision here in some ways parallels our earlier decision to take inclusive disjunction as primary and define exclusive disjunction when the need arises.

A:	All Fs are Gs.	$(x)(Fx \supset Gx)$
E:	No Fs are Gs.	$(x)(Fx \supset {\sim}Gx)$
I:	Some Fs are Gs.	$(\exists x)(Fx \ \& \ Gx)$
O:	Some Fs are not Gs.	$(\exists x)(Fx \ \& \ {\sim}Gx)$

EXERCISE I

Using the suggested symbols to the right of each sentence, translate it into the language of quantification theory, first in prose, then symbolically.

Example: No swans are green. (S, G)
   For any x, if x is a swan, then x is not green.
   $(x)(Sx \supset {\sim}Gx)$

Example: Some pigs eat turnips. ($P, T =$ "is a turnip eater")
   There is at least one x such that x is a pig and x is a turnip eater.
   $(\exists x)(Px \ \& \ Tx)$

(1) All whales are mammals. (W, M)

(2) Every story has two sides. (S, T)

(3) Some courses are not boring. (C, B)

(4) Some students are boring. (S, B)

(5) Elephants are mammals. (E, M)

(6) Cobras are never good pets. (C, P)

(7) Anyone who smokes is a fool. (S, F)

(8) There aren't any Civil War veterans alive today. (V, A)

(9) Some questions are hard to answer. (Q, H)

(10) Some questions are not hard to answer. (Q, H)

LIMITED DOMAINS

If we let "Hx" mean "x is happy," then "$(x)Hx$" says that everything is happy. This is clearly false, since at least some people are not happy. But since the claim is literally about *everything*, it is also false because there are trees that are not happy, waves in the middle of the ocean that are not happy, numbers that are not happy, and so on. Generally, when we use words such as "everything," "all," or "some," we have in mind a more restricted domain than literally everything. Sometimes we use language that explicitly makes this clear. For example, when we use words such as "everybody," "somebody," "everyone," or "someone," we are indicating that we are referring to people. At other times we rely on context to fix the domain of things under consideration. Seeing an empty place at the dinner table, a person might remark: "Someone isn't here." To this the reply "Of course someone isn't here; billions of people are not here" would clearly be out of order. As the context makes clear, in saying "Someone isn't here," the speaker does not have in mind all human beings, just those who were expected to attend the dinner. This example shows that a domain is assumed even when we use an existential quantifier.

It is, in fact, always possible to make clear what domain of things we are concerned with, and many logic texts insist that this always be done. This strikes us as excessively fussy. Except for cases in which confusion might arise, we will rely on context to determine the domain of things under consideration. There is, however, one restriction you need to remember in order to avoid confusion. If one sentence in an argument is about people, but another sentence in the same argument is about animals, then you should not limit the domain to people when translating the first sentence, since then you will need a different domain to translate the sentence about animals. The domain that you assume should always be big enough to be used consistently throughout the whole argument that you are translating.

MORE-ELABORATE A, E, I, AND O PROPOSITIONS

Since we have the resources of Chapter 5 at our command, we can easily construct complex propositions not normally considered in categorical logic. For example, the proposition "All males over eighteen are eligible for the draft" is translated thus:

$$(x)((Mx \mathbin{\&} Ox) \supset Ex)$$

Here "Ox" symbolizes "x is over eighteen." The interpretation of the other symbols is obvious. Here is another example: "All major-league teams are either in the National League or in the American League" is translated thus:

$$(x)(Mx \supset (Nx \lor Ax))$$

Existential generalizations can have complex contents as well. For example, the proposition "Someone here is either stupid or wicked" is translated thus:

$$(\exists x)(Hx \mathbin{\&} (Sx \lor Wx))$$

Thus, quantificational theory combines the resources of propositional logic with the resources of categorical logic in a way that allows us to symbolize many different kinds of propositions.

The examples we have given thus far are straightforward and present no special problems for translation. Sometimes, however, it is easy to go wrong. Consider the claim that both men and women may attend West Point. If you did not stop to think about it, you might be tempted to translate this as follows:

$$(x)((Mx \mathbin{\&} Wx) \supset Ax)$$

(Here, "Ax" means that x may attend West Point.) What that says is that anyone who is both a man and a woman may attend West Point—certainly not the point of the original statement. The correct translation is:

$$(x)((Mx \lor Wx) \supset Ax)$$

which means "Anyone who is either a man or a woman may attend West Point."

There is, in fact, no purely mechanical way of translating sentences from English into the symbolism of quantification theory. One problem, already mentioned in Chapter 6, is that the words used in a sentence do not always indicate whether *all* or only *some* things of a certain kind are being referred to. The following sentences illustrate this:

Dogs have fleas.

Dogs have a good sense of smell.

The first sentence is most naturally interpreted as "Some dogs have fleas." The second is most naturally interpreted as "All dogs, or at least all *normal* dogs, have a good sense of smell." The correct way to interpret a sentence often depends on its context.

Problems can also arise from the complexity of the sentence we are attempting to translate. Here, two rules of thumb for translating quantified propositions will prove helpful.

Universally quantified statements very often take the following form:
$(x)(\quad \supset \quad)$

This is the pattern for both A propositions and E propositions, and many propositions are simple or complex versions of A or E propositions.

Existentially quantified statements very often take the following form:
$(\exists x)(\quad \& \quad)$

This is the pattern for both I propositions and O propositions, and many propositions are simple or complex versions of I or O propositions.

Although a great many sentences can be translated into one of these two forms—including all the examples given in this section—other patterns of translation are possible. That is why we speak of a *rule of thumb* for translating quantified propositions. A simple example of a proposition that does not fit either pattern is "Everything is interesting," which is translated thus:

$$(x)Ix$$

EXERCISE II

Using the suggested letters, translate the following propositions into the language of quantification theory:

(1) Nothing lasts forever. (L = lasts forever)

(2) Everything is either good or bad. (G, B)

(3) Some person either stole the book or took it by mistake. (P, S, M)

(4) Oysters and clams are delicious. (O, C, D)

(5) Anyone who is sick or injured will be evacuated first. (S, I, F)

(6) No varsity football players are both slow and tiny. (*V, S, T*)

(7) No decent human being will attend. (*D, H, A*)

(8) Croats, Muslims, and Serbs are all human beings. (*C, M, S, H*)

(9) The thing in the box is animal, vegetable, or mineral. (*B, A, V, M*)

(10) Old soldiers never die; they just fade away. (*O, S, D, F*)

RELATIONS AND MULTIPLE QUANTIFIERS

Consider the following proposition:

(1) Some cats are bigger than some dogs.

This proposition differs from propositions we have already discussed in two ways: (i) it contains the *relational* term "bigger than," and (ii) it contains two occurrences of the quantifier "some." Both involve significant departures from what we have seen before. We will consider these new developments one at a time.

Until now, we have dealt only with *properties* that individual things possess. We have symbolized this using expressions of the form "*Fx*." But using a relational term such as "bigger than" involves a reference to two things. To capture this aspect of a relational claim, we need to employ two variables. It would seem natural, then, to symbolize "*x* is bigger than *y*" as "*xBy*." There is nothing wrong with this symbolization and, in fact, it has been used at times. It does have this inconvenience: sometimes relations involve more than two things being related to one another. Here are two examples:

(2) *x* is between *y* and *z*.

(3) *u, v, w,* and *x* play cards together.

The first relation is a three-term relation; the second is a four-term relation. A relation such as "marched off to war together" can be a million-term relation. It proves convenient to have a uniform way of representing relations, no matter how many terms they involve. This is done by starting with the relational term and then putting the variables after it. Thus, (2) and (3) can be symbolized as follows:

(2′) *Bxyz*

(3′) *Puvwx*

Notice that the order of the variables makes a difference in (2′), but not in (3′).

The second feature of "Some cats are bigger than some dogs" worth noting is that it contains two occurrences of a quantifier—in particular, two occurrences of the quantifier "some." This forces us to do something we have not done before: to introduce more than one quantifier into our translation of a single proposition. To see why we must do this, notice what happens if we try to translate (1) using only one existential quantifier. We would have to write something like this:

$$(\exists x)(Cx \mathbin{\&} Dx \mathbin{\&} Bxx)$$

What that says is that there is something that is both a cat and a dog and bigger than itself—certainly not what we were looking for. Furthermore, it will not be sufficient to use the same quantifier, "$(\exists x)$," twice in this translation. This becomes clear as soon as we try to decide where to place these two quantifiers. No placement will result in what we want. Since we cannot do what we want with a single variable, what we need is something we have not needed before—quantifiers containing *different* variables. Given two quantifiers containing different variables, the translation of "Some cats are bigger than some dogs" is actually quite simple:

$$(\exists x)(\exists y)(Cx \ \& \ Dy \ \& \ Bxy)$$

That says what we want: "There is at least one thing x and at least one thing y such that x is a cat, y is a dog, and x is bigger than y."

Propositions containing more than one quantifier are called *multiply quantified propositions*. The interaction between these quantifiers sometimes raises problems for translation. For example, it is true that every integer has an integer that is its immediate successor: one is followed by two, two by three, and so on. How can this claim be symbolized? We first notice that the remark is made about *every* integer. It is clearly a universal proposition. Using the first rule of thumb given above, we can begin our translation using the following general pattern:

$$(x)(\qquad \supset \qquad)$$

Since the proposition is plainly about all *integers,* we have no trouble filling in the antecedent of this conditional:

$$(x)(Ix \supset \qquad)$$

This leaves only the expression "an integer that is its immediate successor" to deal with. What the sentence as a whole seems to be saying is this: For any integer, there is *some* integer that is its immediate successor. The term "some" indicates that we are dealing with an existential, rather than a universal, quantifier. Using the second rule of thumb, which tells us that existentially quantified statements with more than one predicate usually involve conjunction, we continue the translation as follows:

$$(x)(Ix \supset (\exists y)(\qquad \& \qquad))$$

The completed translation, then, looks like this:

$$(x)(Ix \supset (\exists y)(Iy \ \& \ Syx))$$

In words: "For any x, if x is an integer, then there exists a y such that y is an integer and y is the immediate successor of x." A little thought will show that this is precisely what we were saying when we said that every integer has an immediate successor.

Two cautions: Because parentheses determine the scope of a quantifier, it is important when translating quantified propositions to be careful in using them. One sure sign that something has gone wrong is that the translation does not have the same number of right-hand and left-hand parentheses. That, however, is not enough. It is also important that no variable fall outside the scope of an appropriate quantifier, as in the following case:

$$(x)Ix \supset (\exists y)(Iy \ \& \ Syx)$$

Here the last x is not in the scope of any quantifier. What this sentence says is this:

> If everything is an integer, then there exists an integer that is the immediate successor of x.

This hardly makes sense. To avoid such nonsense, it is important to make sure that every variable lies inside the scope of a quantifier.

Another pitfall to avoid is using two quantifiers that range over the same variable. If "Bxy" means "x is bigger than y," then it makes sense to say "$(x)(\exists y)Bxy$" (which means "Everything is bigger than something") and "$(y)(\exists x)Bxy$" (which means "For everything, there is something that is bigger than it"). However, it does not make sense to say "$(x)(\exists x)Bxx$," since this formula does not tell us which quantifier refers to which place in the relation—the thing that is bigger or the thing it is bigger than. To avoid such confusions, each quantifier should use a different variable.

EXERCISE III

Translate the following propositions into quantificational notation. Let $Hx = x$ is a human being, and $Lxy = x$ loves y.

(1) Every human being loves some human being.

(2) Every human being loves himself.

(3) There is a human being whom every human being loves.

(4) Some human being loves every human being.

(5) Every human being who loves a human being also loves himself.

(6) No human being who does not love himself loves any human being.

EXERCISE IV

Translate the following propositions into quantificational notation. Let $Fx = x$ is a freshman, $Jx = x$ is a junior, $Sx = x$ is a senior, and $Oxy = x$ is older than y.

(1) Every senior is older than some freshman.

(2) Every senior is older than every freshman.

(3) Some senior is older than every junior.

(4) Some freshman is older than some junior.

(5) All seniors and juniors are older than any freshman.

(6) All seniors are older than any junior or freshman.

(7) Not every senior is older than every junior.

(8) Not every senior or junior is older than some freshman.

SCOPE FALLACIES

Propositions involving multiple quantifiers are complicated and hence easy to misunderstand. One problem is that it is easy to get confused about the scope of quantifiers since natural languages often fail to make this important logical feature of propositions clear. The standard example of such an ambiguity is the proposition

Everything has a cause.

This can be read in two distinct ways, depending on how one orders the quantifiers.

$$(y)(\exists x)(Cxy)$$
$$(\exists x)(y)(Cxy)$$

The first proposition tells us that for any y there exists some x that is its cause. That, roughly, is the thesis of determinism. The second proposition says something much stronger: that there exists something that is the cause of everything. This claim is often used in proofs for the existence of God. Logic alone cannot determine whether either of these propositions is true or false. It can, however, show that the inference from the first proposition to the second is a fallacy—in particular, a *scope* fallacy. The argument depends on ignoring the difference that the order of the quantifiers makes. We can see this at once by considering a parallel case. From the fact that every human being has a mother, it does not follow that there is someone who is the mother of all human beings. Or again, from the fact that every automobile has a steering wheel, it does not follow that there is a single steering wheel that every automobile has.

DISCUSSION QUESTIONS

(1) Is it fallacious to reason as follows: If something is the cause of everything $(\exists x)(y)(Cxy)$, then everything has a cause $(y)(\exists x)(Cxy)$? Why or why not?

(2) Above we said that it is a fallacy to argue from the claim that everything has some cause $(y)(\exists x)(Cxy)$ to the conclusion that there must be something that is the cause of everything $(\exists x)(y)(Cxy)$. Suppose someone replied in the following way: "When I speak of everything having a cause, I mean everything including the entire chain of causes itself. It is the cause of the entire chain of causes that I associate with God." Does this way of stating the argument avoid the fallacy? Is it a good argument?

VALIDITY FOR ARGUMENTS WITH QUANTIFIERS

In Chapters 5 and 6 we first gave a clear specification of two kinds of argument and then laid down principles for determining their validity. In each case we found a procedure for deciding whether or not arguments of the kind under consideration were valid: truth tables in one case, Venn diagrams in the other. It is not possible to proceed in the same way with quantificational theory, since it has been shown that no such procedure exists for a fully developed quantificational logic. In other words, there is no purely mechanical procedure for deciding for every argument employing quantified propositions whether it is valid or not. Even though no general decision procedure exists for quantification theory, such procedures do exist for large and important segments of it. But even where such procedures do exist, they are often complicated and often not particularly illuminating.

RUDIMENTARY QUANTIFICATIONAL LOGIC

Our goal in this section is to provide insight into validity as it is treated in quantificational logic without getting deeply involved in technical details. To do this, we will place the following simplifying restrictions on the arguments we will consider:

(1) They contain at most two premises.

(2) They contain no relational terms.

(3) The propositions that make up these arguments come in only three forms:

     (i) $(x)(\ldots x \ldots)$

     (ii) $(\exists x)(\ldots x \ldots)$

     (iii) $(\ldots a \ldots)$

The material within the scope of the two quantifiers in (i) and (ii) is made up only of expressions such as "Fx" and "Gx," and truth-functional combinations of them. The material contained in propositions of the third kind is made up of expressions such as "Fa" and "Ga," and truth-functional combinations of them.[5] This third kind of proposition is explained below.

Here are some examples of the kinds of propositions we will allow into the arguments we consider:

     (i') $(x)(Fx \lor (Gx \ \& \ Hx))$

     (ii') $(\exists x)(Fx \ \& \ (Gx \lor Hx))$

     (iii') $Fa \supset (Ga \lor Ha)$

---

[5] These restrictions exclude propositions that contain more than one quantifier, more than one individual constant, or a quantifier in addition to an individual constant.

We will call the theory that operates under these restrictions Rudimentary Quantificational Logic (RQL).

The motivation behind developing RQL is to present a system of quantificational logic rich enough to show how the basic rules of quantificational logic work, but not so rich that the methods for testing the validity of arguments become overly time-consuming and obscure. These restrictions do place severe limits on the range of arguments we can consider. Even with these restrictions in force, however, we still will be able to give a systematic account of a wide variety of arguments, including categorical syllogisms and many arguments that cannot be dealt with using syllogistic methods. RQL, though limited, is surprisingly powerful.

INSTANTIATIONS OF QUANTIFIED PROPOSITIONS

Our discussion thus far has peculiar limitations. In particular, we are not in a position to symbolize the following famous argument:

> All humans are mortal.
> Socrates is human.
>
> _____
>
> ∴ Socrates is mortal.

We have a way of saying that *all* humans are mortal and a way of saying that *some* humans are mortal, but not yet any way of naming a particular person (for example, Socrates) and saying of him that *he* is mortal. The situation is easily remedied. The standard way of doing this is to use lowercase letters from "a" through "t" as names for individual persons or things.[6] Logicians call such names *singular terms* or *individual constants*.[7] We will use the latter expression. If we assign to Socrates the individual constant "s," then we can symbolize "Socrates is human" thus:

$$Hs$$

The above argument can now be translated as follows:

> $(x)(Hx \supset Mx)$
> Hs
>
> _____
>
> ∴ Ms

This, however, still does not show us how "Socrates is mortal" follows from the stated premises.

One way to solve this problem is to look at the universal proposition

$$(x)(Hx \supset Mx)$$

_____

[6] Lowercase letters from the very end of the alphabet are usually reserved for variables.

[7] They are called "constants" because their reference is fixed, in contrast with variables that do not have a fixed reference.

as providing a pattern—or a recipe—for the propositional conditional

$$Hs \supset Ms$$

It also provides the pattern for indefinitely many other propositional conditionals, depending on which individual constant we substitute for the variable "*x*." For example:

$$Hb \supset Mb$$
$$Hc \supset Mc$$
$$Hd \supset Md$$

We will say that all these propositions are *instantiations* of the universal proposition "$(x)(Hx \supset Mx)$." We get an instantiation of a universal proposition by dropping the universal quantifier and replacing each of its variables with the same individual constant. In what follows, the notion of an instantiation will play a fundamental role in the analysis of arguments employing quantifiers.

UNIVERSAL INSTANTIATION

It should be clear that if a universal conditional is true, then all of its instantiations are also true. In fact, this is a feature of all universal propositions, whether they are conditionals or not. If something is true of everything, then it is true of each thing taken individually. (For example, what is true of all people is also true of Tom, Dick, and Hilary.) These thoughts are captured in the following principle:

If a universal proposition is true, then all of its instantiations are true.

Corresponding to this, we may introduce the following rule, called *universal instantiation* (UI).

UI: You may instantiate a universally quantified premise with any individual constant.[8]

Universal instantiation is one of the fundamental principles of modern quantification theory. Once you understand it, it should strike you as obviously true.

We are now in a position to see why

$$(1) \quad (x)(Hx \supset Mx)$$
$$Hs$$
$$\overline{}$$
$$\therefore Ms$$

is valid. If the first premise is true, then so are all of its instantiations. By instantiating the first premise with respect to Socrates, (1) becomes:

---

[8] We will see later why this rule is limited to premises and does not apply to conclusions.

(2) $Hs \supset Ms$ UI
    Hs

  ∴ Ms PL valid

The result of this instantiation is that we are now dealing with propositions related in a way already examined in our study of propositional logic in Chapter 5. Thus, this argument can be tested for validity simply by using the machinery of propositional logic. That its propositional form is, in fact, valid is indicated by putting "PL valid" to the right of the conclusion.[9]

At this point, the symbolism may be a bit confusing. In propositional logic, we symbolized specific propositions using capital letters such as *"A," "B,"* and *"C."* Propositional variables were symbolized using lowercase letters such as *"p," "q,"* and *"r."* The symbolism of quantification theory is more complex, because we are not simply dealing with whole propositions and the truth-functional connections among them; we are also interested in the inner structure of noncompound propositions. Thus, in propositional logic, we could have symbolized "Socrates is mortal" by the single letter *"M";* this letter gives no indication of the inner structure of "Socrates is mortal." In the notation of quantificational logic, we symbolize it as *"Ms,"* thus indicating that a particular individual (Socrates) has the specific property of being mortal. In this way, the notation of quantificational logic is more *fine-grained* than the notation of propositional logic.

But even so, the procedures of propositional logic apply to quantificational logic when we are dealing with truth-functional connections between whole propositions. Thus, (2) is a substitution instance of (3):

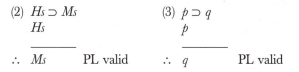

(2) $Hs \supset Ms$ (3) $p \supset q$
    Hs p

  ∴ Ms PL valid   ∴ q PL valid

Because (3) is a valid argument form in propositional logic, (2), its substitution instance, is a valid argument. It is for this reason that the conclusion is marked "PL valid."

This example gives us a model for constructing a test for the validity of arguments in RQL. The basic strategy will be to develop a system of rules that tell us how we may or may not instantiate the propositions in an argument. An instantiation that obeys these rules will be called a *proper instantiation.* An argument in RQL will then be valid if and only if it has a proper instantiation whose form is valid in propositional logic. Argument 1 satisfies this test.

One way to think about what is going on here is that the proper instantiation provides intermediate steps that enable us to argue from the premises to the conclusion of the original argument. First we move to the right and derive the

---

[9] This argument will be given a more rigorous analysis later in this chapter.

premises of the instantiation from the premises of the original argument. Next we move down and derive the conclusion of the instantiation from the premises of the instantiation, using propositional logic. Finally, we move back to the left and derive the conclusion of the original argument from the conclusion of the instantiation. In our example, the whole procedure looks like this:

$$(1)\ (x)(Hx \supset Mx) \qquad\qquad (2)\ Hs \supset Ms \quad \text{UI}$$
$$Hs \qquad\qquad\qquad\qquad\qquad Hs$$
$$\therefore\ Ms \qquad\qquad\qquad\qquad \therefore\ Ms \qquad \text{PL valid}$$

The original argument is then valid if both (i) the instantiation is valid in propositional logic and (ii) we can get to the instantiation and back by following the rules. To fill out this picture, what we now need is a set of rules that tell us when we can move to and from an instantiation properly.

EXERCISE V

Use rule UI to check the following arguments for validity in RQL:

(1) All humans are rational.
   Fido is not rational.

∴ Fido is not human.

(2) All rational beings are human.
   Fido is not human.

∴ Fido is not rational.

(3) No human is metallic.
   My clock is metallic.

∴ My clock is not human.

(4) No human is metallic.
   My brother is human.

∴ My brother is not metallic.

(5) No metallic object is human.
   My clock is metallic.

∴ My clock is not human.

(6) No metallic object is human.
   My brother is human.

∴ My brother is not metallic.

EXISTENTIAL GENERALIZATION

Turning now to existentially quantified propositions, we can speak of their instantiations as well. For example,

$$(\exists x)(Hx \ \& \ Mx) \text{ (that is, "Some humans are mortal")}$$

has an instantiation:

$$Hs \ \& \ Ms \text{ (that is, "Socrates is both human and mortal")}$$

There is, however, an important difference between this instantiation and the instantiation of "All humans are mortal." If *all* humans are mortal, then, if Socrates is human, he is mortal. In contrast, that *some* humans are mortal does not guarantee that Socrates is mortal, even though he is human.

In fact, the relationship between existential propositions and their instantiations is roughly the reverse of the relationship between universal propositions and their instantiations:

> If at least one of the instantiations of an existential proposition is true, then that existential proposition is true.

This allows us to introduce the following rule, called *existential generalization* (EG):

> EG: You may instantiate an existentially quantified conclusion with any individual constant.

For example, if Socrates is mortal, then at least one person is mortal. Symbolically:

Argument	**Instantiation**	
Ms	Ms	
———	———	
$\therefore \ (\exists x)(Mx)$	$\therefore \ Ms$	EG, PL valid

Because this instantiation obeys the rules, it is a proper instantiation. Its form $(p; \therefore \ p)$ is also valid in propositional logic. So the original argument is valid.

Rule EG allows us to derive a quantified or general conclusion (such as "$(\exists x)(Mx)$"), and that is why the rule is called existential *generalization*. Recall that what rule EG does is allow us to move left from the conclusion of the instantiation back to the conclusion of the original argument:

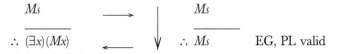

When you think of it that way, it should be obvious why we want to be able to move from something like *"Ms"* in the conclusion of the instantiation to something like "$(\exists x)(Mx)$" in the conclusion of the original argument. That is exactly what rule EG allows us to do.

EXERCISE VI

Use rule EG to check the following arguments for validity in RQL:

(1) My dog is not human.

───────────

∴ Something is not human.

(2) Spot is a dog that is frisky.

───────────

∴ Some dogs are frisky.

(3) Ariel is a cat that is not frisky.

───────────

∴ Some cats are not frisky.

(4) Everything is funny.

───────────

∴ Something is funny.

(5) All jokes are funny.

───────────

∴ Some jokes are funny.

UNIVERSAL GENERALIZATION

Universal instantiation and existential generalization are both easy rules. They are easy to understand and easy to apply. The next two rules are more difficult. The first is called *universal generalization*. Universal instantiation applies when a *premise* is universally quantified, but universal generalization applies when a *conclusion* is universally quantified.

To understand this rule, we can first note that the following generalization principle is clearly invalid:

If some particular thing has a property, then everything does.

From the fact that Albert is fifty years old, we clearly cannot conclude that everything or everyone is fifty years old. However, if we allowed a universally quantified conclusion to be instantiated with any individual constant, then the instantiation of this invalid argument would be PL valid. We will mark instantiations with the letter "i," so the symbolization of this argument and its instantiation look like this:

(1) *Fa*	(1i) *Fa*
───────	───────
∴ *(x)Fx*	∴ *Fa* UG ???

This seems to settle the issue concerning universal generalization: the rule is not valid in general.

As it turns out, however, a *restricted* version of this rule is useful. To see why, we can consider the following simple argument: Everything is funny, so everything is either funny or grave. Symbolically,

$$(2) \ (x)Fx$$

$$\therefore \ (x)(Fx \lor Gx)$$

That is, if everything has some property *F*, then everything has either the property *F* or the property *G*. This, of course, looks much like the following argument form, which is valid in propositional logic:

$$p$$

$$\therefore p \lor q$$

In fact, the argument involving quantifiers does rely on the validity of this argument form in propositional logic. Our problem, to put it crudely, is that we have to find some way of getting the quantifiers out of the way so that we can use this argument form from propositional logic to show the validity of the quantified argument.

This problem is solved by introducing a *controlled* version of universal generalization that does not lead to fallacious inferences. Returning to (2), suppose we instantiate the entire argument with respect to the letter *"a."* This yields:

(2) $(x)Fx$	(2i) Fa UI
$\therefore \ (x)(Fx \lor Gx)$	$\therefore \ Fa \lor Ga$ UG, PL valid

Of course, (2i) is valid in propositional logic. It is still not clear, however, how the validity of (2i) bears on the validity of (2). But we should notice that the premise of (2i) is itself an instantiation of a *universal* proposition. That shows that this premise could have been instantiated with respect to *any* individual constant whatsoever, so that, in this case, what holds for one individual holds for *all* individuals. That is what makes it all right to instantiate the conclusion with respect to the same individual.

To reflect this idea, we can formulate the rule of universal generalization (UG) as follows:

> UG: You may instantiate a universally quantified conclusion with an individual constant if, but only if, that individual constant does not appear anywhere else in the instantiation except where it was derived by UI.

This rule allows us to instantiate the conclusion of (2) as was done in (2i), because the premise in (2i) in which the individual constant "*a*" appears was derived by UI. However, UG does not allow us to instantiate the conclusion of (1) as was done in (1i), because the premise in (1i) includes "*a*" but was not derived by UI. To apply UG properly to the conclusion of (1), we would have to use some individual constant other than "*a*," but then this proper instantiation would not be valid in propositional logic. Rule UG thus explains why (2) is valid but (1) is not. The rule works because its restrictions force us to use a different constant when instantiating invalid arguments, and using a different constant makes the instantiation invalid in propositional logic.

The examples so far have been simple, but the same method also works for more-complex arguments with more than one premise. Consider the argument that all swimmers in the pool are members of the club, and all members of the club are politicians, so all swimmers in the pool are politicians. Here are its symbolization and an instantiation:

(3) $(x)(Sx \supset Mx)$	(3i) $Sa \supset Ma$	UI
$(x)(Mx \supset Px)$	$Ma \supset Pa$	UI
$\therefore$ $(x)(Sx \supset Px)$	$\therefore$ $Sa \supset Pa$	UG, PL valid

Because (3i) obeys our rules, it is a proper instantiation. Thus, because the form of (3i) is valid in propositional logic, (3) is valid.

We can next examine what happens when we apply this test to an invalid syllogism:

(4) $(x)(Sx \supset Mx)$	(4i) $Sa \supset Ma$	UI
$(x)(Px \supset Mx)$	$Pa \supset Ma$	UI
$\therefore$ $(x)(Sx \supset Px)$	$\therefore$ $Sa \supset Pa$	UG, PL invalid

The form of (4i) is invalid in propositional logic. Nonetheless, it is important to remember that the invalidity of this one proper instantiation does not show that the original argument is invalid, since there still might be a different proper instantiation that is valid in propositional logic, and all it takes to show that an argument is valid in RQL is *one* proper instantiation that is valid in propositional logic. In this case, however, it is clear that no other proper instantiation will turn out valid in propositional logic. Instantiating one or more of the premises of (4) with respect to an individual constant other than *"a,"* though legal, will not help here. It will only disconnect the premise from the conclusion, as the following example shows:

(4i*) $Sa \supset Ma$	UI
$Pb \supset Mb$	UI
$\therefore$ $Sa \supset Pa$	UG, PL invalid

It is also true that (4i*) is invalid in propositional logic. In fact, it is almost always obvious, just by looking, that instantiating universal premises with respect to an individual constant different from the individual constant used to instantiate the conclusion will weaken, not strengthen, the instantiated argument. Since there is no way to construct a proper instantiation of (4) that is valid in propositional logic, (4) is not valid in RQL, just as one would hope.

EXERCISE VII

Check the following arguments for validity in RQL:

(1) $(x)(Mx \supset Sx)$
$(x)(Px \supset Mx)$

$\therefore$ $(x)(Px \supset Sx)$

(2) $(x)(Mx \supset Sx)$
    $(x)(Mx \supset Px)$
    _____

∴ $(x)(Px \supset Sx)$

(3) $(x)(Sx \supset {\sim}Mx)$
    $(x)(Px \supset Mx)$
    _____

∴ $(x)(Px \supset {\sim}Sx)$

(4) $(x)(Sx \supset {\sim}Mx)$
    $(x)(Mx \supset {\sim}Px)$
    _____

∴ $(x)(Sx \supset {\sim}Px)$

(5) $(x)(Mx \supset Sx)$
    $(x)(Mx)$
    _____

∴ $(x)(Sx)$

(6) $(x)(Mx \supset Sx)$
    $(x)(Sx)$
    _____

∴ $(x)(Mx)$

(7) $(x)(Mx \supset Sx)$
    $(x)({\sim}Sx)$
    _____

∴ $(x)({\sim}Mx)$

(8) $(x)(Mx \supset Sx)$
    $(x)({\sim}Mx)$
    _____

∴ $(x)({\sim}Sx)$

EXISTENTIAL INSTANTIATION

We can now turn to our final quantification rule, *existential instantiation*. We already saw that the rule of existential *generalization* (EG) tells us what we may do when a *conclusion* is existentially quantified, but now we need an instantiation rule that applies when a *premise* is existentially quantified. Clearly, the following argument is invalid:

(5) $(\exists x)Fx$
    _____

∴ Fa

From the premise that something or someone is fat, we may not conclude that Alan is fat. However, if we allowed an existentially quantified premise to be instantiated with any individual constant, then the instantiation of this invalid argument would be PL valid:

$$(5i) \quad Fa$$

$$\therefore \quad Fa$$

Our rules should not allow such instantiations.

There are, however, other arguments with existential quantifiers in their premises that *are* valid, and we must find ways of dealing with them. The following is an example of such an argument:

$$(6) \quad (\exists x)(Fx \ \& \ Hx)$$

$$\therefore \quad (\exists x)(Hx)$$

From the premise that at least one thing is fat and happy, we may conclude that at least one thing is happy. Why is this argument valid? The reason is that it does not matter which thing is fat and happy. Whatever it is that is fat and happy, it will still be true that *something* is happy.

In contrast, it *does* matter that we used the constant *"a"* when we instantiated (5) to form (5i). If we had instantiated the premise with a different constant, say *"b,"* the resulting instantiation would not have been valid in propositional logic. Less formally, since the premise of (5) says only that *someone* is fat, it does matter *who* it is that is fat, since the conclusion that Alan is fat is true only if Alan is one of the people who make the premise true.

The general idea, then, is that you may instantiate an existentially quantified premise with respect to a particular individual constant provided that picking that individual constant rather than any other has no effect on the validity of the argument in question. To turn this vague idea into a precise rule, we need to determine when it matters which individual constant is used to instantiate an existentially quantified premise. We already saw that this does not matter in arguments like (6), in which the conclusion is existentially quantified, but it can matter in arguments like (5), in which the conclusion is not quantified. It also matters in arguments in which the conclusion is universally quantified, such as this:

$(7) \quad (\exists x)Fx$	$(7i) \quad Fa$	EI ???
$\therefore \quad (x)Fx$	$\therefore \quad Fa$	UG ???

From the premise that someone is fat, we cannot validly conclude that everyone is fat. Thus, the only case in which we can instantiate an existentially quantified premise with the same constant as in the conclusion is when the instantiation of the conclusion is derived by existential generalization, as in (6).

We also need to consider arguments with more than one premise. The following, for example, is clearly an invalid argument:

Some S is M.
Some M is P.

$\therefore$ Some S is P.

Even if some Swedes are marathoners, and some marathoners are from Poland, it does not follow that some Swedes are from Poland. Symbolically, this argument and an instantiation of it take the following form:

(8) $(\exists x)(Sx \,\&\, Mx)$ (8i) $(Sa \,\&\, Ma)$ EI ???
    $(\exists x)(Mx \,\&\, Px)$ $(Ma \,\&\, Pa)$ EI ???

$\therefore$ $(\exists x)(Sx \,\&\, Px)$ $\therefore$ $(Sa \,\&\, Pa)$ EG, PL valid

As it turns out, (8i) is a valid argument in propositional logic, so, if our rules did not declare this instantiation improper, our system would declare (8) valid when it is not. It should be clear what has gone wrong. By instantiating both premises with the same individual constant, we have introduced a relationship that was not found in the original argument. In the original, the M that is S need not be the same as the M that is P. To avoid mistakes of this kind, we need to prohibit the use of the same constant to instantiate two existentially quantified premises. If rule EI is restricted in this way, we can still construct a proper instantiation this way:

(8) $(\exists x)(Sx \,\&\, Mx)$ (8i′) $(Sa \,\&\, Ma)$ EI
    $(\exists x)(Mx \,\&\, Px)$ $(Mb \,\&\, Pb)$ EI

$\therefore$ $(\exists x)(Sx \,\&\, Px)$ $\therefore$ $(Sa \,\&\, Pa)$ EG, PL invalid

However, this proper instantiation is not valid in propositional logic. Moreover, it should be obvious that nothing would be gained by using a different pattern of instantiation. Using *"a"* in the second premise and *"b"* in the first would yield an argument that is invalid for the same reason. Instantiating one of the premises with some third individual constant would merely weaken the argument. This shows that argument (8) is not valid in RQL.

In contrast, consider an argument in which the other premise is universally quantified:

(9) $(\exists x)(Sx \,\&\, Mx)$ (9i) $(Sa \,\&\, Ma)$ EI
    $(x)(Mx \supset Rx)$ $(Ma \supset Ra)$ UI

$\therefore$ $(\exists x)(Sx \,\&\, Rx)$ $\therefore$ $(Sa \,\&\, Ra)$ UG, PL valid

Some Swedes are marathoners, and all marathoners are runners, so some Swedes are runners. This is valid, because the relationship between Swedish marathoners and runners is guaranteed if the second premise is true. Thus, we should allow existential instantiation in such cases.

Considering these and other cases, we can now formulate the rule of existential instantiation (EI) more precisely as follows:

EI: You may instantiate an existentially quantified premise with an individual constant if, but only if, that individual constant does not appear anywhere else in the instantiation except in a premise that was derived by UI or in a conclusion that was derived by EG.

This rule shows why (6) is valid, since the conclusion can be instantiated using EG, and why (5) and (7) are not valid, since their conclusions are not instantiated by applying EG. EI also explains why (9) is valid, but (8) is not, since UI is used to instantiate the other premise in (9), but not in (8).

APPLICATION TO IMMEDIATE INFERENCES AND SYLLOGISMS

Though RQL is restricted in its range of application, it still has a number of important applications. For example, both the theory of immediate inference and the theory of the syllogism examined in Chapter 6 can be handled elegantly in RQL with only the rules that we have learned so far (UI, UG, EI, and EG).

The only immediate inference examined in the body of Chapter 6 was conversion, which is the inference that results from reversing the subject and predicate terms. There are four cases: the conversions of A, E, I, and O propositions. We will consider two of them: those of A and I propositions.

	Categorical Form	Quantificational Form	Instantiation
A:	All S is P.	$(x)(Sx \supset Px)$	$Sa \supset Pa$ UI
	$\therefore$ All P is S.	$\therefore$ $(x)(Px \supset Sx)$	$\therefore$ $Pa \supset Sa$ UG, PL invalid

Since the instantiated argument is not valid in propositional logic, the conversion of an A proposition is not valid in RQL.[10]

I:	Some S is P.	$(\exists x)(Sx \,\&\, Px)$	$Sa \,\&\, Pa$ EI
	$\therefore$ Some P is S.	$\therefore$ $(\exists x)(Px \,\&\, Sx)$	$\therefore$ $Pa \,\&\, Sa$ EG, PL valid

Since the instantiation of this argument is valid in propositional logic, the conversion of an I proposition is valid in RQL.

Examples of applying these methods to categorical syllogisms have already been given in the process of explaining quantification rules. See (8) and (9) in the previous section, as well as (3) and (4) in the section before that.

EXERCISE VIII

Test to see if the conversions of E and O propositions are valid in RQL. In other words, test the validity of:

---

[10] When it is transparent that changing the pattern of instantiation will make no difference to the validity of the instantiated argument, we will not always bother to say so.

(1) No *S* is *P*.

———

∴ No *P* is *S*.

(2) Some *S* is not *P*.

———

∴ Some *P* is not *S*.

Using the methods of RQL, determine the validity of the syllogisms in Exercise VII in Chapter 6. To do this, you must first translate these arguments into quantificational notation.

APPLICATION TO NONCATEGORICAL ARGUMENTS

Because of the limitations we have introduced, the methods developed cannot be applied to all arguments that can be formulated in the symbolism of quantificational logic. Nonetheless, these procedures still apply to many arguments that cannot be handled using only the methods of categorical logic. Here we will give some more examples of such arguments.

First: All sunsets are pretty, and there are some sunsets, so there are some pretty things. This argument can be symbolized and instantiated as follows:

(1) $(x)(Sx \supset Px)$ (1i) $Sa \supset Pa$ UI
     $(\exists x)(Sx)$ Sa EI

———

∴ $(\exists x)(Px)$ ∴ Pa EG, PL valid

Because (1i) follows the rules, and its form is valid in propositional logic, (1) is valid.

Consider this argument: Since oysters and clams are delicious, clams are delicious. This gets translated thus:

(2) $(x)((Ox \lor Cx) \supset Dx)$ (2i) $(Oa \lor Ca) \supset Da$ UI

———

∴ $(x)(Cx \supset Dx)$ ∴ $Ca \supset Da$ UG, PL valid

Again, because (2i) follows the rules and is valid in propositional logic, (2) is valid.

In the next example, a restriction in a rule blocks an invalid argument from being declared valid. Here is the argument and its symbolization:

Everything is either alive or dead.   (3) $(x)(Ax \lor Dx)$
Some things are not alive. $(\exists x)(\sim Ax)$

———

∴ Everything is dead.   ∴ $(x)(Dx)$

One might instantiate this argument this way:

$$Aa \lor Da \qquad \text{UI}$$
$$\sim Aa \qquad \text{EI ???}$$

$$\therefore Da \qquad \text{UG ???}$$

This instantiation is valid in propositional logic. However, this is not a proper instantiation; it violates the restrictions in EI and UG, because the same constant appears in both the second premise and the conclusion. To avoid violating these restrictions, we must use a different individual constant in these two locations in the instantiation. Suppose, then, we use the constant *"a"* to instantiate the conclusion as *"Da,"* but we use the constant *"b"* to instantiate the second premise as *"~Ab."* Now there are two ways to instantiate the first premise. Because it is universally quantified, the rules allow us to instantiate it with respect to either *"a"* or *"b,"* but neither instantiation yields an argument that is valid in propositional logic:

$$(3\text{i}) \quad Aa \lor Da \qquad\qquad (3\text{i*}) \quad Ab \lor Db$$
$$\sim Ab \qquad\qquad\qquad\qquad\qquad \sim Ab$$

$$\therefore \quad Da \qquad\qquad\qquad\qquad \therefore \quad Da$$

It would not help to instantiate the conclusion with respect to *b,* since then the restrictions in EI and UG would require us to instantiate the second premise with a different individual constant, and the same problems would arise again. Thus, there is no way to construct a proper instantiation that is valid in propositional logic, so (3) is not valid in RQL.

Finally, we can look at a tricky example in which the order of instantiation makes a difference. The following is, in fact, a valid argument:

$$(4) \quad (\exists x)(Fx \,\&\, Gx)$$
$$(\exists x)(Hx \,\&\, Ix)$$

$$\therefore \quad (\exists x)(Hx)$$

(Since some things are both flat and gray, and some things are both heavy and made of iron, some things are heavy.) Proceeding in a natural way leads us into trouble. Suppose, as we are allowed to, we instantiate both the conclusion and the first premise with respect to the letter *"a,"* so that our instantiation has *"Fa & Ga"* as its first premise and *"Ha"* as its conclusion. Because of the restrictions in rule EI, we cannot now instantiate the second existential premise with respect to *"a,"* so we have to shift to a new letter, yielding this result:

$$(4\text{i}) \quad Fa \,\&\, Ga \qquad \text{EI}$$
$$Hb \,\&\, Ib \qquad \text{EI}$$

$$\therefore \quad Ha \qquad\qquad \text{EG, PL invalid}$$

This is a proper instantiation, but it is not valid in propositional logic. However, the invalidity of this one instantiation does not show that the original argument is invalid, because the original argument is still valid if it has another proper instantiation that is valid in propositional logic. In this case, it does have such an instantiation. If we had started out instead by instantiating the second premise with respect to *"a,"* the result would have been different:

$$(4i) \quad Fb \ \& \ Gb \qquad \text{EI}$$
$$Ha \ \& \ Ia \qquad \text{EI}$$
$$\therefore \quad Ha \qquad\qquad \text{EG, PL valid}$$

This argument is a proper instantiation, and it is also valid in propositional logic. Of course, it is odd because the first premise plays no role in supporting the conclusion. That, however, does not affect its validity. We have presented this argument because it shows that the order in which we instantiate premises can sometimes make a difference. That is why we must check *all* possible patterns of instantiation before we can conclude that an argument is invalid, since it is valid if *any* proper instantiation is valid in propositional logic.[11]

EXERCISE X

Test the following arguments for validity in RQL:

(1) $(x)(Sx \supset Px)$
      $(\exists x)(Sx)$

∴ $(\exists x)(Px)$

(2) $(x)(Sx \supset Px)$
      $(\exists x)(Sx)$

∴ $(\exists x)(Px \lor Mx)$

(3) $(x)(Sx \supset Px)$
      $(\exists x)(Px)$

∴ $(\exists x)(Sx)$

(4) $(x)(Sx \supset Px)$
      $(\exists x)(\sim Px)$

∴ $(\exists x)(\sim Sx)$

---

[11] One reason why we have limited RQL to arguments containing no more than two premises is that the number of ways in which the premises of an argument can be instantiated grows exponentially as the number of premises increases.

(5) $(x)(Sx \supset Px)$
$(\exists x)(Sx \vee \sim Px)$

∴ $(\exists x)(\sim Sx \vee Px)$

(6) $(x)(Sx \supset Px)$
$(\exists x)(Sx \supset \sim Px)$

∴ $(\exists x)(\sim Sx)$

(7) $(x)(Sx \ \& \ Px)$
$(\exists x)(\sim Px)$

∴ $(\exists x)(\sim Sx)$

(8) $(\exists x)(Sx \ \& \ \sim Px)$

∴ $(\exists x)\sim(Sx \supset Px)$

(9) $(x)\sim(Sx \supset Px)$

∴ $(x)(Sx \ \& \ \sim Px)$

(10) $(x)((Jx \supset Sx) \supset Ex)$

∴ $(x)(Sx \supset Ex)$

(11) $(x)(Jx \supset (Sx \supset Ex))$

∴ $(x)(Jx \supset Ex)$

(12) $(x)(Jx \supset (Sx \supset Ex))$
$(\exists x)(Sx)$

∴ $(\exists x)(Jx \supset Ex)$

(13) $(x)(Jx \supset (Sx \ \& \ Ex))$

∴ $(\exists x)(Jx \supset Sx)$

(14) $(x)(Jx \supset (Sx \vee Ex))$
$(\exists x)(Jx \ \& \ \sim Sx)$

∴ $(\exists x)(Ex)$

ARGUMENTS CONTAINING INDIVIDUAL CONSTANTS

Throughout this chapter we have used *individual constants* in evaluating arguments for validity. We have not, however, laid down general rules for evaluating arguments that themselves contain individual constants. Thus, we still have no rigorous way of exhibiting the validity of this argument:

All humans are mortal.
Socrates is human.

$\therefore$ Socrates is mortal.

As we said early on, the solution is to symbolize and instantiate this argument as follows:

(1) $(x)(Hx \supset Mx)$ (1i) $Hs \supset Ms$ UI
$\quad\ Hs$ $\quad\ Hs$

$\therefore\ Ms$ $\therefore\ Ms$ PL valid

However, we do not yet have any explicit rule that allows us to repeat the second premise of the argument on the second line of its instantiation. We simply took that for granted because it seemed obvious that this move cannot make the instantiation valid in propositional logic unless the argument was already valid in RQL. Even so, we now need to state that rule more formally:

REIT: You may reiterate any premise or conclusion with an individual constant.

In other words, the instantiation may contain the same premises or conclusion as the ones in the argument that contain an individual constant.

This simple rule might not seem so obvious in light of the restrictions that were needed in some other rules, but the rule REIT can be kept simple just because the restrictions in the other rules prevent problems from arising. To see how this works, let us apply REIT to some different kinds of examples.

We want this argument to turn out valid in RQL:

(2) $(x)Wx$ (2i) Wa UI

$\therefore\ Wa$ $\therefore\ Wa$ REIT, PL valid

Because (2i) follows the rules, and its form is valid in propositional logic, (2) is valid, just as we wanted. If we could not use REIT in the conclusion, we could not have shown how this argument is valid.

In contrast, we want this argument to turn out invalid in RQL:

(3) Wa (3i) Wa REIT

$\therefore\ (x)(Wx)$ $\therefore\ Wa$ UG ???

This instantiation is, of course, valid in propositional logic, but it is not a proper instantiation, because it violates one of the restrictions in UG: UG cannot be used to instantiate a universal conclusion with an individual constant if that individual constant appears anywhere else in the instantiation where it was not derived by UI. Here the constant *"a"* is used in UG, and *"a"* appears in the premise, where it was derived by REIT rather than by UI. Thus, this instantiation is not proper.

There is clearly no other way to construct a proper instantiation that will be valid in propositional logic. Therefore, this argument is not valid in RQL, again as we expected.

We get similar results when we test arguments with existential quantifiers. The following argument should be valid, and its instantiation is both proper and valid in propositional logic:

(4) *Wa*	(4i) *Wa*	REIT
∴ (∃x)(*Wx*)	∴ *Wa*	EG, PL valid

The following argument is not valid:

(5) (∃x)(*Wx*)	(5i) *Wa*	EI ???
∴ *Wa*	∴ *Wa*	REIT, PL valid

In propositional logic, (5i) is valid. However, it is not a proper instantiation of (5); (5i) violates the restriction in EI against instantiating with an individual constant that appears in the conclusion of the instantiation without being derived by EG, because the conclusion of (5i) was derived by REIT rather than by EG.

Finally, let us consider arguments with two premises. We already saw in (1) that reiterating a premise maintains validity when the other premise is universal, so we can turn to an example in which the other premise is existential:

(6) (∃x)(*Wx* ∨ *Hx*)	(6i) *Wa* ∨ *Ha*	EI ???
~*Wa*	~*Wa*	REIT
∴ (∃x)(*Hx*)	∴ *Ha*	EG, PL valid

This argument is clearly invalid, but its instantiation is valid in propositional logic. However, this instantiation is not a proper instantiation, because it violates the restriction in EI against using an individual constant that appears in another premise without being derived there by UI. Thus, REIT achieves the right results in all these cases. The reason why this simple rule works, as we said, is that the restrictions on UG and EI prevent any invalid arguments from being declared valid.

One tricky case might seem to create a problem. Consider the following valid argument: Albert is wise, so everyone who is wise is wise. This argument gets symbolized as follows:

(7) *Wa*
∴ (x)(*Wx* ⊃ *Wx*)

Admittedly, this is a peculiar argument. Because the conclusion cannot be false, there is obviously no way for the premise to be true and the conclusion false. But even if the argument is peculiar, we want to declare it valid. We seem to run into a problem, however, if we begin by instantiating the conclusion with the letter *"a:"*

....

$$\overline{}$$
$$\therefore \ Wa \supset Wa \quad \text{UG}$$

Now we are stuck, because we cannot use REIT to instantiate the first premise without violating the restrictions in UG.

The solution to this problem is actually quite simple. We begin by instantiating the premise using REIT, and then we have to instantiate the conclusion with a different constant in order to avoid violating the restrictions in UG. We end up with this:

(7) Wa (7i) Wa REIT

$$\therefore \ (x)(Wx \supset Wx) \qquad \therefore \ Wb \supset Wb \quad \text{UG, PL valid}$$

In propositional logic, (7i) is valid, and it is also a proper instantiation, because it violates none of the rules. Thus, (7) is valid. Things have worked out just exactly as we wanted them to.

EXERCISE XI

Test the following arguments for validity in RQL.

(1) $(x)(Sx \supset Px)$
     $\sim Pa$

$\therefore \ \sim Sa$

(2) $(x)(Sx \supset Px)$
     Sa

$\therefore \ (\exists x)(Px)$

(3) $(x)(Sx \supset Px)$

$\therefore \ \sim Sa \vee Pa$

(4) $(x)(Sx \supset Px)$
     $(Sa \supset \sim Pa)$

$\therefore \ \sim Sa$

(5) $(x)(Sx \supset (Px \vee Qx))$
     $Sa \ \& \ \sim Qa$

$\therefore \ (\exists x)(Px)$

(6) Fa
     $(\exists x)(\sim Fx \vee Gx)$

$\therefore \ Ga$

(7) $(\exists x)(Fx \mathbin{\&} Gx)$
     Fa

$\therefore$ Ga

(8) $(\exists x)(Fx \supset Gx)$
     $\sim Ga$

$\therefore$ $\sim Fa$

A GENERAL RULE FOR RQL

We are now in a position to state a general rule for the validity of arguments in RQL. As we have developed RQL, we have introduced five rules governing instantiation:

UI: You may instantiate a universally quantified premise with any individual constant.

EG: You may instantiate an existentially quantified conclusion with any individual constant.

UG: You may instantiate a universally quantified conclusion with an individual constant if, but only if, that individual constant does not appear anywhere else in the instantiation except where it was derived by UI.

EI: You may instantiate an existentially quantified premise with an individual constant if, but only if, that individual constant does not appear anywhere else in the instantiation except in a premise that was derived by UI or in a conclusion that was derived by EG.

REIT: You may reiterate any premise or conclusion with an individual constant.

These rules follow a pattern:

	Universal Quantifier	Existential Quantifier	Individual Constant
Premise	UI	EI	REIT
Conclusion	UG	EG	REIT

Thus, our rules allow instantiations for all of the propositions in arguments that meet the restrictions of RQL.

Any instantiation that obeys these rules is then called a *proper instantiation*. The notion of a proper instantiation allows us to lay down the following general rule for validity in RQL:

VALIDITY IN RQL: An argument is valid in RQL if and only if it has a proper instantiation whose form is valid in propositional logic.

This sounds quite simple, but, of course, a great deal of complexity is packed into the notion of a proper instantiation.

Given this account, it is fairly easy to show that an argument is valid. Just give a proper instantiation whose form is valid in propositional logic. It is not so easy, however, to show that an argument is *not* valid in RQL. To show invalidity, you have to show that there does not exist *any* proper instantiation that is PL valid. But even if one proper instantiation is not PL valid, that does not show that no other proper instantiation is PL valid. To show that, you need a procedure that will always produce a proper instantiation that is PL valid whenever there is one. Luckily, because of the restrictions on arguments in RQL, there is such a procedure:[12]

STEP 1: Reiterate all sentences that have individual constants (but no quantifiers).

STEP 2: Instantiate each existential premise and universal conclusion. In each case, use a constant that does not yet appear in the instantiation you are constructing.

STEP 3: Instantiate each universal premise and existential conclusion with each constant occurring in the instantiation after step 1 and step 2. (If no constant occurs, use a new constant. If two constants occur, construct one proper instantiation for each constant.)

If this procedure yields a proper instantiation whose form is valid in propositional logic, then the original argument is valid in RQL. Otherwise the original argument is invalid in RQL. Thus, we have a mechanical procedure that will tell us, for any argument that meets the restrictions of RQL, whether or not it is valid.

THE LIMITS OF RQL

In developing RQL we have placed strong limitations on its range of application. We have done this because our primary aim has been to explain the concepts and the basic rules of quantificational logic. Some of these restrictions are intended merely to keep matters clear and simple, and they could have been removed without having to alter RQL in fundamental ways. Limiting the number of premises to no more than two falls into this category. This just avoids complications. In contrast, extending RQL to include propositions with more than one quantifier would demand deep revisions. But even if our procedures are not adequate for dealing with all arguments employing quantifiers, they are still applicable to a wide variety of important types of arguments—including syllogisms and many others. Seeing how RQL works in its area of application provides a good understanding of the basic notions of quantificational logic. In particular, it shows how developing a single system that encompasses both categorical logic and propositional logic sheds light on the basic structure of many arguments.

---

[12] We are indebted to Jim Moor for suggesting this procedure.

Chapter Eight

INDUCTIVE REASONING

This chapter begins by explaining the difference between *deductive* and *inductive* arguments. The difference depends on the claimed relationship between the premises and the conclusion of each type of argument. An argument is deductive if the person who puts forward the argument intends for it to be valid. Validity is not claimed for inductive arguments, even when they place the conclusion beyond reasonable doubt.

Four kinds of inductive reasoning will be examined in detail. First, the chapter describes *inductive generalizations,* in which a statistical claim is made about a population on the basis of features of a sample of that population. Second, the chapter examines *statistical syllogisms.* Here a statistical claim is made about members of a population on the basis of features of the population. Third, the chapter examines inductive *inferences to the best explanation,* where explanatory power is said to provide evidence for the truth of some propositions. Fourth, the chapter examines the role of *analogies* in inductive reasoning. Here, two things having certain features in common is taken as evidence that they have further features in common.

INDUCTION VERSUS DEDUCTION

Since Chapter 2 we have been concerned almost exclusively with *deductive* arguments, but many arguments (perhaps most arguments) encountered in daily life are not intended to be deductive. In particular, many arguments are said to be *inductive* in character. In this chapter we shall examine some of the chief forms that inductive arguments take.

The distinction between deductive arguments and inductive arguments can be drawn in a variety of ways, but the fundamental difference concerns the relationship that is claimed to hold between the premises and the conclusion for each type of argument. As we know, in a valid deductive argument, if the premises are true, then it is impossible for the conclusion to be false. For example, the following is a valid deductive argument:

> All ravens are black.
> _____
>
> ∴ If there is a raven on top of Pikes Peak, then it is black.

Since the premise lays down a universal principle governing all ravens, if it is true, then it *must* be true of all ravens (if any) on top of Pikes Peak. Of course, this same relationship does not hold for an *invalid* deductive argument. Still, if someone puts forward an argument as deductive, that person is committed to the claim that this relationship holds—that is, that the argument is valid—and can be criticized if it does not.

This same relationship between premises and conclusion is not claimed to hold for inductive arguments. The following is an example of an inductive argument:

> All ravens we have observed are black.
> _____
>
> ∴ All ravens are black.

Here we have drawn an inductive inference from the characteristics of ravens we have observed (the sample) to the characteristics of all ravens, most of which we have not observed. We realize that the premise of this argument *could be* true yet the conclusion turn out to be false. A raven somewhere might be an albino. We put forth the premise as offering strong support for the conclusion; we do not put it forth as necessitating it.

The fundamental difference between an inductive argument and a deductive argument can be brought out in another way. Suppose we have a valid deductive argument of the following form:

$$P_1, \ldots, P_n; \text{ therefore } Q.$$

A fundamental feature of a valid deductive argument is that its validity cannot be changed through the addition of further premises. The definition of a valid deductive argument guarantees this: If an argument is valid, then the premises cannot be true without the conclusion being true as well, and that relationship between premises and conclusion cannot be canceled out or overridden by the introduction of further premises. Furthermore, if an argument is not only valid but sound, this property cannot be removed by adding further premises as long as they are true. Additional information might, of course, lead us to question the truth of one of the premises that we previously accepted, and we might then reconsider whether the argument that we previously considered sound really is sound—but that is another matter.

The situation is strikingly different with inductive arguments. First, since the notion of validity was introduced for the assessment of deductive arguments, we will not use the term when dealing with inductive arguments, which, after all, are not put forward as being deductively valid. We will, instead, speak of inductive arguments as being *strong* or *weak*. Suppose we have an inductive argument that gives very strong support to its conclusion.

$$P_1, \ldots, P_n; \text{ therefore } Q \text{ is very likely to be true.}$$

To cite a famous example, before the time of Captain Cook's voyage to Australia, Europeans had observed a great many swans, and every one of them was white. Thus, up to that time, Europeans had very strong inductive evidence to support the claim that all swans are white. Then Captain Cook discovered black swans in Australia. What happens if we add this new piece of information to the premises of the original inductive argument? Provided that we accept Captain Cook's report, we now produce a sound *deductive* argument in behalf of the claim that *not* all swans are white, for if some swans are black, then not all of them are white. This, then, is a feature of every inductive argument: No matter how strong an inductive argument is, the possibility remains open that further information can undercut the support that the premises give to the conclusion—perhaps *completely* undercut it. A valid deductive argument does not face a similar peril.

In much recent literature on the subject, this difference between deductive arguments and inductive arguments is sometimes described by saying that deductive inferences are *monotonic* whereas inductive inferences are *nonmonotonic*. These words are used on an analogy with mathematical curves. A (positive) monotonic curve rises, perhaps flattens out, but never changes direction. A nonmonotonic curve can change direction—for example, rise, then fall. Thus, in the white-swan example, before Captain Cook's voyages, the evidence in behalf of the claim that all swans are white had become very strong. After his discovery of black swans, the evidential support collapsed.

Because of the strong relationship between the premises and the conclusion of a valid deductive argument, it is sometimes said that the premises of valid deductive arguments (if true) provide *conclusive* support for their conclusions, whereas true premises in inductive arguments provide only *partial* support for their conclusions. This is obviously correct. Because the premises of a valid deductive argument (if true) necessitate the truth of the conclusion, they supply conclusive support for the conclusion. The same cannot be said for inductive arguments. But it would be altogether misleading to conclude from this that inductive arguments are inherently inferior to deductive arguments in supplying a justification or ground for a conclusion. In the first place, inductive arguments often place matters beyond doubt. It is possible that the next pot of water will not boil at any temperature, however high, but this is not something we worry about—we do not take precautions against it.

Second, and more importantly, deductive arguments often enjoy no advantages over their inductive counterparts. We can see this by examining the two following arguments:

Deductive	*Inductive*
All ravens are black.	All observed ravens have been black.
∴ If there is a raven on top of Pikes Peak, it is black.	∴ If there is a raven on top of Pikes Peak, it is black.

Of course, it is true for the deductive argument, and not true for the inductive argument, that if the premise is true, then the conclusion must be true, and this may seem to give an advantage to the deductive argument over the inductive argument. But before we can decide how much support a deductive argument gives its conclusion, we must ask if its premises are, after all, true. That is not something we can take for granted. If we examine the premises of these two arguments, we see that it is easier to establish the truth of the premise of the inductive argument than it is to establish the truth of the premise of the deductive argument. If we have observed carefully and kept good records, then we might be fully confident that all *observed* ravens have been black. On the other hand, how can we show that *all* ravens (observed and unobserved—past, present, and future) are black? The most obvious way, though there may be other ways, would be to observe ravens to see if they are black or not. But this, of course, involves producing an inductive argument (called an inductive generalization) for the premise of the deductive argument. Here our confidence in the truth of the premise of the deductive argument should be no greater than our confidence in the strength of the inference in the inductive generalization. In this case—and it is not unusual—the deductive argument provides no stronger grounds in support of its conclusion than does its inductive counterpart, because any reservations we might have about the *strength* of the inductive inference will be paralleled by doubts concerning the *truth* of the premise of the deductive argument.

In passing, we will also avoid the common mistake of saying that deductive arguments always move from the general to the particular, whereas inductive arguments always move from the particular to the general. In fact, both sorts of arguments can move in either way. There are inductive arguments intended to establish particular matters of fact, and there are deductive arguments that involve generalizations from particulars.

For example, scientists are currently debating whether or not the extinction of the dinosaurs was caused by the impact of an asteroid. (See Chapter 14.) Their discussions are models of inductive reasoning because they are assembling empirical evidence to confirm or disconfirm this hypothesis. Yet they are not trying to establish a generalization or a scientific law; instead they are trying to determine whether a particular event occurred some sixty million years ago. Inductive reasoning concerning particular matters of fact occurs constantly in everyday life as well—for example, when we check to see whether someone using a computer is messing up our television reception. Deductive arguments from the particular to the general also exist, though they tend to be trivial, and thus boring. Here is one: Benjamin Franklin was the first postmaster general; therefore, anyone identical with Benjamin Franklin was the first postmaster general.

Of course, many inductive arguments do move from particular premises to a general conclusion, and many deductive arguments move from the general to the particular. Again, however, this is not the *definitive* difference between these two kinds of arguments, and to suppose that it is can lead to serious misunderstandings. To repeat, the difference between inductive and deductive arguments consists in the claimed relationship between the premises and the conclusion.

Because inductive arguments involve different commitments than deductive arguments, it is a mistake to judge them by the same standards. What, then, are the standards appropriate for assessing inductive arguments? This question can be answered at various levels. At an informal level, we can lay down some general rules—or rules of thumb—that will allow us to avoid many of the more common errors of inductive reasoning. In complicated situations, however, our common-sense principles are often inadequate and can let us down. When common sense gets out of its depth, we must turn to the procedures of mathematical statistics for help. Here we shall concern ourselves almost exclusively with informal procedures for the evaluation of inductive arguments, but we shall also examine cases in which they are inadequate.

EXERCISE I

Assuming a standard context, label each of the following arguments as deductive or inductive:

(1) The sun is coming out, so the rain should stop soon.

(2) It's going to rain tomorrow, so it is either going to rain or going to be clear tomorrow.

(3) Diet cola doesn't keep me awake at night; I drank it just last night without any problems.

(4) No one in Paris seems to understand me, so either my French is rotten or Parisians are unfriendly.

(5) If Harold is innocent, he would not go into hiding; but he is in hiding, so he is not innocent.

(6) The house is a mess, so Jeff must be home from college.

(7) No woman has ever been elected president of the United States; therefore, no woman will ever be elected president of the United States.

(8) There is no even number smaller than two, so one is not an even number.

INDUCTIVE GENERALIZATIONS

Inductive generalizations are a common form of inductive reasoning. Here we cite characteristics of a sample of a population in order to support a claim about the character of the population as a whole. Opinion polls work this way. Suppose a candidate wants to know how popular she is with voters. Since it would be practically impossible to survey all voters, she takes a sample of voting opinion and then infers that the opinions of those sampled indicate the overall opinion of voters. Thus, if 60 percent of the voters sampled say they will vote for her, she concludes that she will get approximately 60 percent of the vote in the actual election. As we shall see later, inferences of this kind often go wrong, even when made by experts, but the general pattern of this reasoning is quite clear: statistical features of a sample are used to make statistical claims about the population as a whole.

How do we assess such inferences? To begin to answer this question, we can consider a simple example of an inductive generalization. On various occasions Harold has tried to use Canadian quarters in American telephones and found that they have not worked. From this he draws the conclusion that Canadian quarters do not work in American telephones. Harold's inductive reasoning looks like this:

> In the past, when I tried to use Canadian quarters in American telephones, they have not worked.
>
> ---
>
> ∴ Canadian quarters do not work in American telephones.

The force of the conclusion is that Canadian quarters *never* work in American telephones.

In evaluating this argument, what questions should we ask? As we proceed through the first half of this chapter, we will loosely frame some questions that can be applied to all inductive generalizations, and when we are through we should be able to restate those questions with greater accuracy. To start with, then, one question we should ask of any argument is about its premises.

SHOULD WE ACCEPT THE PREMISES?

Perhaps Harold has a bad memory, or has kept bad records, or is a poor observer. For some obscure reason, he may even be lying. It is important to ask this question explicitly, because fairly often the premises, when challenged, will not stand up to scrutiny.

If we decide that the premises are acceptable, we can then shift our attention to the relationship between the premises and the conclusion and ask how much support the premises give to the conclusion. One commonsense question is this: "Just how many times has Harold tried to use Canadian quarters in American telephones?" If the answer is "Once," then our confidence in his argument should drop to almost nothing. So, for inductive generalizations, it is always appropriate to ask about the size of the sample.

IS THE SAMPLE LARGE ENOUGH?

One reason we should be suspicious of small samples is that they can be affected by runs of luck. Suppose Harold flips a Canadian quarter four times and it comes up heads each time. From this, he can hardly conclude that Canadian quarters always come up heads when flipped. He could not even reasonably conclude that *this* Canadian quarter would always come up heads when flipped. The reason for this is obvious enough; if you spend a lot of time flipping coins, runs of four heads in a row are not all that unlikely (the probability is actually one in sixteen), and therefore samples of this size can easily be distorted by chance. On the other hand, if Harold flipped the coin twenty times and it continued to come up heads, he would have strong grounds for saying that this coin, at least, will always come up heads. In fact, he would have strong grounds for thinking that he has a two-headed coin. Because an overly small sample can lead to erroneous conclusions, we can say that it is unfair or biased, simply on a statistical level.

How many is enough? On the assumption, for the moment, that our sampling has been fair in all other respects, how many samples do we need to provide the basis for a strong inductive argument? This is not always an easy question to answer, and sometimes answering it demands subtle mathematical techniques. Suppose your company is selling ten million computer chips to the Department of Defense, and you have guaranteed that no more than 0.2 percent of them will be defective. It would be prohibitively expensive to test all the chips, and testing only a dozen would hardly be enough to reasonably guarantee that the total shipment of chips meets the required specifications. Because testing chips is expensive, you want to test as few as possible, but because meeting the specifications is crucial, you want to test enough to guarantee that you have done so. Answering questions of this kind demands sophisticated statistical techniques beyond the scope of this text.

Sometimes, then, it is difficult to decide how many samples are needed to give reasonable support to inductive generalizations, yet many times it is obvious, without going into technical details, that the sample is too small. Drawing an inductive conclusion from a sample that is too small can lead to the fallacy of *hasty generalization*. It is surprising how common this fallacy is. We see a person two or three times and find him cheerful, and we immediately leap to the conclusion that he is a cheerful person. That is, from a few instances of cheerful behavior, we draw a general conclusion about his personality. When we meet him later and find him sad, morose, or grouchy, we then conclude that he has changed—thus swapping one hasty generalization for another.

This tendency toward hasty generalization was discussed more than two hundred years ago by the philosopher David Hume, who saw that we have a strong tendency to "follow general rules which we rashly form to ourselves, and which are the source of what we properly call prejudice."[1] This tendency toward hasty generalization has been the subject of extensive psychological investigation. The cognitive psychologists Amos Tversky and Daniel Kahneman put the matter this way:

> We submit that people view a sample randomly drawn from a population as highly representative, that is, similar to the population in all essential characteristics. Consequently, they expect any two samples drawn from a particular population to be more similar to one another and to the population than sampling theory predicts, at least for small samples.[2]

To return to a previous example, we make our judgments of someone's personality on the basis of a very small sample of his or her behavior and expect this person to behave in similar ways in the future when we encounter further samples of behavior. We are surprised, and sometimes indignant, when the future behavior does not match our expectations.

By making our samples sufficiently large, we can guard against distortions due to "runs of luck," but even very large samples can give us a poor basis for an inductive generalization. Suppose that Harold has tried hundreds of times to use a Canadian quarter in an American telephone, and it has never worked. This will increase our confidence in his inductive generalization, but size of sample alone is not a sufficient ground for a strong inductive argument. Suppose that Harold has tried the same coin in hundreds of different telephones, or tried a hundred different Canadian coins in the same telephone. In the first case, there might be something wrong with this particular coin; in the second case, there might be something wrong with this particular telephone. In neither case would he have good grounds for making the general claim that *no* Canadian quarters work in *any* American telephones. This leads us to the third question we should ask of any inductive generalization.

IS THE SAMPLE BIASED IN OTHER WAYS?

When the sample, however large, is not representative of the population, then it is said to be unfair or biased. Here we can speak of the fallacy of *biased sampling*. One of the most famous errors of biased sampling was committed by a magazine named the *Literary Digest*. Before the presidential election of 1936, this magazine sent out ten million questionnaires asking which candidate the recipient would vote for: Franklin Roosevelt or Alf Landon. It received two and a half million returns, and on the basis of the results confidently predicted that Landon would win by a landslide: 56 percent for Landon to only 44 percent for Roosevelt. When

---

[1] David Hume, *A Treatise of Human Nature,* 2nd ed. (Oxford: Oxford University Press, 1978), 146. This work was first published in 1739.

[2] Amos Tversky and Daniel Kahneman, "Belief in the Law of Small Numbers," *Psychological Bulletin* 76, no. 2 (1971): 105.

the election results came in, Roosevelt had won by an even larger landslide in the opposite direction: 62 percent for Roosevelt to a mere 38 percent for Landon. What went wrong? The sample was certainly large enough; in fact, by contemporary standards it was much larger than needed. It was the way the sample was selected, not its size, that caused the problem: the sample was randomly drawn from names in telephone books and from club membership lists. In 1936 there were only eleven million telephones in the United States and many of the poor—especially the rural poor—did not have telephones. During the Great Depression there were more than nine million unemployed in America; they were almost all poor and thus underrepresented on club membership lists. Finally, a large percentage of these underrepresented groups voted for Roosevelt, the Democratic candidate. As a result of these biases in its sampling, along with some others, the *Literary Digest* underestimated Roosevelt's percentage of the vote by a whopping 18 percent.

Looking back, it may be hard to believe that intelligent observers could have done such a ridiculously bad job of sampling opinion, but the story repeats itself, though rarely on the grand scale of the *Literary Digest* fiasco. In 1948, for example, the Gallup poll, which had correctly predicted Roosevelt's victory in 1936, predicted, as did other major polls, a clear victory for Thomas Dewey over Harry Truman. Confidence was so high in this prediction that the *Chicago Tribune* published a banner headline declaring that Dewey had won the election before the votes were actually counted. What went wrong this time? The answer here is more subtle. The Gallup pollsters (and others) went to great pains to make sure that their sample was representative of the voting population. The interviewers were told to poll a certain number of people from particular social groups—rural poor, suburban middle class, urban middle class, ethnic minorities, and so on—so that the proportions of those interviewed matched, as closely as possible, the proportions of those likely to vote. (The *Literary Digest* went bankrupt after its incorrect prediction, so the pollsters were taking no chances.) Yet somehow bias crept into the sampling; the question was, how? One speculation was that a large percentage of those sampled did not tell the truth when they were interviewed; another was that a large number of people changed their minds at the last minute. So perhaps the data collected were not reliable. The explanation generally accepted was more subtle. Although Gallup's workers were told to interview specific numbers of people from particular classes (so many from the suburbs, for example), they were not instructed to choose people randomly from within each group. Without seriously thinking about it, they tended to go to "nicer" neighborhoods and interview "nicer" people. Because of this, they biased the sample in the direction of their own (largely) middle-class preferences and, as a result, underrepresented constituencies that would give Truman his unexpected victory.

SOURCES OF BIAS

Because professionals using modern statistical analysis can make bad inductive generalizations through biased sampling, it is not surprising that our everyday, informal inductive generalizations are often inaccurate. It will be useful, then, to look at some of the main sources of bias. We have already examined two sources of bias: small samples and bad sampling. Here are some other sources of bias.

PREJUDICE AND STEREOTYPES

People who are prejudiced will find little good and a great deal bad in those they despise, no matter how these people actually behave. In fact, most people have a mixture of good and bad qualities, and by ignoring the former and dwelling on the latter, it is easy enough for the prejudiced person to confirm her negative opinions. Similarly, stereotypes, which can be either positive or negative, often persist in the face of overwhelming counterevidence. Speaking of the beliefs common in Britain in his own day, David Hume remarked:

> An Irishman cannot have wit, and a Frenchman cannot have solidity; for which reason, though the conversation of the former in any instance be very agreeable, and of the latter very judicious, we have entertained such a prejudice against them, that they must be dunces and fops in spite of sense and reason.[3]

SLANTED QUESTIONS

Another common source of bias in sampling is the phrasing of questions in ways that encourage certain answers while discouraging others. It is well known that the way a question is phrased can exert a significant influence on how people will answer it. Questions like the following are not intended to elicit information, but instead to push people's answers in one direction rather than another.

(1) Which do you favor: (a) preserving a citizen's constitutional right to bear arms or (b) leaving honest citizens defenseless against armed criminals?

(2) Which do you favor: (a) restricting the sale of assault weapons or (b) knuckling under to the demands of the well-financed gun lobby?

In each case one alternative is made to sound attractive, the other unattractive. When questions of this sort are used, it is not surprising that different pollsters can come up with wildly different results.

INFORMAL JUDGMENTAL HEURISTICS

In daily life, we have to make a great many decisions, some of them important, most of them not. Furthermore, because we have to make a great many decisions, they often have to be made quickly, without our pausing to weigh the evidence

---

[3] Hume, *A Treatise of Human Nature,* 146–47.

carefully. To deal with this overload of decisions, we commonly employ what cognitive psychologists call *judgmental heuristics*. Technically, a heuristic is a device that provides a general strategy for solving a problem or coming to a decision. (For example, a good heuristic for solving geometry problems is to start with the conclusion you are trying to reach and then work backward.) Recent research in cognitive psychology has shown, first, that human beings rely heavily on heuristics, and second, that we often have too much confidence in them. The result is that our inductive inferences often go badly wrong, and that sometimes our thinking gets utterly mixed up. In this regard, two heuristics are particularly interesting: the *representative heuristic* and the *availability heuristic*.

The representative heuristic. A simple example illustrates how errors can arise from the representative heuristic. You are randomly dealt five-card hands from a standard deck. Which of the following two hands is more likely to come up?

(1)	(2)
Three of clubs	Ace of spades
Seven of diamonds	Ace of hearts
Nine of diamonds	Ace of clubs
Queen of hearts	Ace of diamonds
King of spades	King of spades

A surprisingly large number of people will automatically say that the second hand is much less likely than the first. Actually, if you think about it for a bit, it should be obvious that any two specific hands have exactly the same likelihood of being dealt. Here people get confused because the first hand is an unimpressive hand, and because unimpressive hands come up all the time, it strikes us as a *representative* hand. In many card games, however, the second hand would be very impressive—something worth talking about—and thus looks unrepresentative. Here our reliance on representativeness blinds us to a simple and obvious point about probabilities: any specific hand is as likely to occur as any other.

Another set of experiments carried out by Tversky and Kahneman yielded an even more remarkable result.[4] Students were given the following description of a fictitious person named Linda:

> Linda is 31 years old, single, outspoken and very bright. She majored in philosophy. As a student, she was deeply concerned with issues of discrimination and social justice, and also participated in anti-nuclear demonstrations.

The students were then asked to rank the following statements with respect to the probability that they were also true of Linda:

> Linda is a teacher in elementary school.

> Linda works in a bookstore and takes Yoga classes.

---

[4] Amos Tversky and Daniel Kahneman, "Extensional versus Intuitive Reasoning: The Conjunction Fallacy in Probability Judgment," *Psychological Review* 90, no. 4 (October 1983): 297.

Linda is active in the feminist movement.

Linda is a psychiatric social worker.

Linda is a member of the League of Women Voters.

Linda is a bank teller.

Linda is an insurance salesperson.

Linda is a bank teller and is active in the feminist movement.

Not surprisingly, the students thought that it was most likely that Linda was a feminist, and least likely that she was a bank teller. What was surprising was that 89 percent of the subjects in one experiment thought that it was more likely that Linda was both a bank teller and a feminist than that she was simply a bank teller. If you think about that for a moment, you will see that it cannot be right: the probability that two things are true can never be higher than the probability that just one of them is true. Presumably what happens here is something like this: unreflectively, people think that the claim that Linda is both a bank teller and a feminist at least says something plausible about her, whereas the simple claim that she is a bank teller is not plausible at all. But that is bad reasoning, and here reliance on the representative heuristic does not merely give us an inaccurate estimate of a probability, it actually leads us into a logical blunder.

The availability heuristic. Because sampling and taking surveys is expensive, we often do it imaginatively—that is, in our heads. If you ask a baseball fan which team has the better batting average, Detroit or San Diego, that person might remember, might go look it up, or might think about each team and try to decide which one has the most good batters. The last strategy would be a risky business, but many baseball fans have a remarkable knowledge of the batting averages of top hitters. Even with this knowledge, however, it is easy to go wrong. The players that naturally come to mind are the stars of each team: they are more *available* to our memory, and we are likely to make our judgments on the basis of them alone. Yet such a sample can easily be biased because *all* the batters contribute to the team average, not just the stars. That the weak batters on one team are much better than the weak batters on the other can swing the balance.

Tversky and Kahneman conducted a further experiment that shows how the influence of the availability heuristic (like the influence of the representative heuristic) can lead to incoherent results. Subjects were asked the following question:

> In four pages of a novel (about 2,000 words), how many words would you expect to find that have the form _ _ _ _ ing (seven-letter words that end with *ing*)? Indicate your best estimate by circling one of the values below:
>
>   1–2   3–4   5–7   8–10   11–15   16+
>
> A second version of the question requested estimates for words of the form _ _ _ _ _ _n_. The median estimates were 13.4 for *ing* words ... and 4.7 for _ _ _ _ _ _n_ words.

The result is again logically incoherent; there must be *at least* as many "_ _ _ _ _ _n_" words in the text as "_ _ _ _ _*ing*" words, because every

"_ _ _ _ _*ing*" word is also an "_ _ _ _ _ _*n*_" word. Why did people not think about this? The answer is that we rely on the availability heuristic, and it is easy to think of "_ _ _ _*ing*" words: all sorts of verbs with "ing" endings pop into our minds at once. There is nothing similarly memorable about seven-letter words ending with "_n_." Thus, relying on what naturally pops into our heads will often produce biased samples that will lead us to draw false, and even incoherent, conclusions.

The point of examining these two judgmental heuristics and noting the logical errors they produce is *not* to suggest that we should cease relying on them. First, there is a good chance that this would not be psychologically possible because the use of such heuristics seems to be built into our psychological makeup. Second, over a wide range of standard cases, these heuristics give *quick* and largely *accurate* estimates. Difficulties typically arise in using these heuristics when the situation is *nonstandard*—that is, when the situation is complex or out of the normal run of things. This suggests another question we should routinely ask about inductive generalizations.

IS THE SITUATION SUFFICIENTLY STANDARD TO ALLOW THE USE OF INFORMAL JUDGMENTAL HEURISTICS?

Because this is a mouthful, we might ask "Is this really the sort of thing that people can figure out in their heads?" When the answer to that question is "No," as it often is, then we should turn to the formal procedures of statistical analysis for our answers.

SUMMARY

We should now be able to summarize and restate our questions with more accuracy. Confronted with inductive generalizations, there are five questions we should routinely ask:

(1) Are the premises acceptable?

(2) Is the sample likely to be biased because it is too small?

(3) Is the sample likely to be biased because the sampling was affected by prejudice and stereotypes?

(4) Is the sample likely to be biased because the sampling involved slanted questions?

(5) Is the sample likely to be biased because it relies on informal heuristics in complex situations where they often prove unreliable?

EXERCISE II

Ann Landers caused a stir when she announced the results of a mail poll that asked her women readers to respond to the following question:

Would you be content to be held and treated tenderly, and forget about "the act"?

Her readers were instructed to answer "Yes" or "No" and indicate whether they were over (or under) forty years of age.

The result was that 72 percent of the respondents answered "Yes," and of those who answered "Yes," 40 percent indicated that they were under forty years of age.

What are we to make of these results? Ann Landers expressed surprise that so many of those who answered "Yes" came from the under-forty group. But for her, "the greatest revelation" was "what the poll says about men as lovers. Clearly, there is trouble in paradise" (*Ask Ann Landers,* January 14 and 15, 1985).

The poll, of course, did not employ scientific methods of sampling (nor did Ann Landers claim that it did), so it is important to look for sources of bias before drawing any conclusions from this poll. Discuss at least three possible sources of bias that could make the Landers sample unrepresentative of the opinions of the population of adult women in America.

STATISTICAL SYLLOGISMS

In a statistical generalization we draw inferences concerning a population from information concerning a sample of that population. From the fact that 60 percent of the population sampled said that they would vote for candidate *X* we might draw the conclusion that roughly 60 percent of the population will vote for candidate *X*. With a *statistical syllogism* we reason in the reverse direction: from information concerning a population, we draw a conclusion concerning a member or subset of that population. Here is an example:

> Ninety-seven percent of the Republicans in California voted for Bush.
> Marvin is a Republican from California.

∴ Marvin voted for Bush.

Such arguments have the following general form:

> *X* percent of *F*s have the feature *G*.
> *a* is an *F*.

∴ *a* has the feature *G*.[5]

---

[5] We can also have a *probabilistic* version of the statistical syllogism:

Ninety-seven percent of the Republicans in California voted for Bush.
Marvin is a Republican from California.

∴ There is a 97 percent chance that Marvin voted for Bush.

We will discuss arguments concerning probability in the next chapter.

Obviously, when we evaluate the strength of a statistical syllogism, the percentage of *F*s that have the feature *G* will be important. As the figure approaches 100 percent, the statistical argument gains strength. Thus our original argument concerning Marvin is quite strong. We can also get strong statistical syllogisms when the figure approaches 0 percent. The following is also a strong inductive argument:

> Three percent of the socialists in California voted for Bush.
> Maureen is a socialist from California.
> _____
> ∴ Maureen did *not* vote for Bush.

Statistical syllogisms of the kind considered here will be strong only if the figures are close to 100 percent or 0 percent. When the percentages are in the middle of this range, statistical syllogisms are weak.

A more interesting problem in evaluating the strength of a statistical syllogism concerns the *relevance* of the premises to the conclusion. In the above schematic representation of a statistical syllogism, *F* stands for what is called the *reference class*. In our first example, being a Republican from California is the reference class; in our second example, being a socialist from California is the reference class. A striking feature of statistical syllogisms is that using different reference classes can yield incompatible results. To see this, consider the following statistical syllogism:

> Three percent of Clinton's relatives voted for Bush.
> Marvin is a relative of Clinton.
> _____
> ∴ Marvin did not vote for Bush.

We now have a statistical syllogism that gives us strong support for the claim that Marvin did not vote for Bush, and this is incompatible with our first statistical syllogism, which gave strong support to the claim that he did. To overlook this conflict between statistical syllogisms based on different reference classes would be a kind of fallacy. Which statistical syllogism, if either, should we trust? This will depend on which of the reference classes we take to be more relevant. Which counts more, political affiliation or family ties? That might be hard to say.

One way of dealing with competing statistical syllogisms is to combine the reference classes. We could ask, for example, what percentage of Republicans from California who are relatives of Clinton voted for Bush? The result might come out this way:

> Forty-two percent of Republicans from California who were relatives of
>   Clinton voted for Bush.
> Marvin is a Republican from California who is a relative of Clinton.
> _____
> ∴ Marvin voted for Bush.

This statistical syllogism provides very weak support for its conclusion. It supplies stronger, but still weak, support for the denial of the conclusion—that is, that Marvin did not vote for Bush.

This series of arguments illustrates in a clear way what we earlier called the nonmonotonicity of inductive inferences: a strong inductive argument can be made weak by adding further information to the premises. Given that Marvin is a Republican from California, we seemed to have good reason to think that he voted for Bush. But when we added to this the additional piece of information that he was a relative of Clinton, the original argument lost most of its force. And new information could produce another reversal. Suppose we discover that Marvin, though a relative of Clinton, actively campaigned for Bush. Just about everyone who actively campaigns for a candidate votes for that candidate, so it seems that we again have good reason for thinking that Marvin voted for Bush.

It is clear, then, that the way we select our reference classes will affect the strength of a statistical syllogism. The general idea is that we should define our reference classes in a way that brings all relevant evidence to bear on the subject. But this raises difficulties. It is not always obvious which factors are relevant and which factors are not. In our example, party affiliation is relevant to how people voted in the 1992 election; shoe size presumably is not. Whether gender is significant, and, if so, how significant, is a matter for further statistical research.

These difficulties concerning the proper way to fix reference classes reflect a feature of all inductive reasoning: to be successful, such reasoning must take place within a broader framework that helps determine which features are significant and which features are not. Without this framework, there would be no reason not to consider shoe size when trying to decide how someone will vote. As we shall see, this reliance on a framework is particularly important when dealing with causes.

EXERCISE III

Carry the story of Marvin two steps further, producing two more reversals in the strength of the statistical syllogism with the conclusion that Marvin voted for Bush.

EXERCISE IV

For each of the following statistical syllogisms, identify the reference class, and then evaluate the strength of the argument in terms of the percentages or proportions cited and the relevance of the reference class.

(1) Less than 1 percent of the people in the world voted for Bush.
Gale is a person in the world.

∴ Gale did not vote for Bush.

(2) Very few teams repeat as Super Bowl champions.
San Francisco was the last Super Bowl champion.

∴ San Francisco will not repeat as Super Bowl champion.

(3) A very high percentage of people in the Senate are men.
Nancy Katzenbaum is in the Senate.

∴ Nancy Katzenbaum is a man.

(4) Three percent of socialists with blue eyes voted for Bush.
Maureen is a socialist with blue eyes.

∴ Maureen did not vote for Bush.

(5) Ninety-eight percent of what John says is true.
John said that the Giants are going to win.

∴ The Giants are going to win.

(6) Half the time he doesn't know what he is doing.
He is eating lunch.

∴ He does not know he is eating lunch.

REASONING ABOUT CAUSES

We often wonder why certain things have happened; why, for example, our car has gone dead in the middle of rush-hour traffic just after its twenty-thousand-mile checkup. We think that there must be some reason for this happening—cars do not stop for no reason at all—and reasons of this kind we commonly call *causes*. We could just as well have asked "What caused the car to stop?" The answer might be that it has run out of gas. If we find, in fact, that it *has* run out of gas, then that will usually be the end of the matter; we will have discovered (or at least *think* we have discovered) why this particular car has stopped running. But even if our thinking is about a particular car on a particular occasion, our reasoning rests on certain *generalizations*. In particular, we are confident that *our* car stopped running when it ran out of gas because we believe that *all* cars stop running when they run out of gas. We probably did not think about this, but our causal reasoning in this particular case appealed to a commonly accepted *causal generalization*: cars will not run without gas. And what holds in this case holds quite generally: when we offer a causal explanation of a particular event, we appeal, though not always explicitly, to causal generalizations.

A second important reason that we are interested in causal judgments is that we use them to *predict* the consequences of particular actions or events. A race-car driver might wonder, for example, what would happen if he added just a bit of nitroglycerine to his fuel mixture: would it give him better acceleration, blow him up, do very little, or what? In fact, the driver might not be in a position to answer this question right away, but his thinking will be guided by the causal generalization that igniting nitroglycerine can cause a dangerous explosion.

So a similar pattern arises for both causal explanation and causal prediction. These inferences contain two essential elements:

(1) The facts in the particular case. (For example, the car has stopped and the gas gauge says empty, or I have just put a pint of nitroglycerine in the gas tank of my Maserati and I am about to turn the ignition key.)

(2) Certain causal generalizations. (For example, that cars do not run without gasoline or that nitroglycerine explodes when ignited.)

The key idea, though this will turn out to be more complicated than these simple examples suggest, is that in drawing a causal inference we bring particular facts under causal generalizations. What, then, are *causal generalizations* and how are they tested? We will take these questions up one at a time.

CAUSAL GENERALIZATIONS

Causal generalizations are obviously important, but what exactly are they? This remains a controversial issue. Here we will treat them as a kind of *general conditional*. A general conditional has the following form:

> For all *x*, if *x* has the feature *F,* then *x* has the feature *G.*

We will say that *x*'s having the feature *F* gives a *sufficient condition* for its having the feature *G,* and *x*'s having the feature *G* lays down a necessary condition for its having the feature *F.*[6]

Not every general conditional lays down *causal* conditions. For example, neither of these two general conditionals expresses a causal relationship:

> If something is a square, then it is a rectangle.

> If you are eighteen years old, you are eligible to vote.

The first tells us that being a square is sufficient for being a rectangle, but this is a mathematical (or a priori) relationship, not a causal relationship. The second statement tells us that being eighteen years old is a sufficient condition for being eligible to vote. The relationship here is legal, not causal.

Although there are complications (and disagreements) in this area, general causal conditionals usually lay down sufficient and necessary conditions between *events*. It is important to know, for example, that if you put your finger in a light socket when the power is on, you are likely to receive a severe shock. In this case we recognize that a certain combination of factors is *sufficient* to bring about some effect. At other times we are interested in which factors are *necessary* to bring about an effect. This concern often arises when some expected event does not occur, and you wonder why. You have dialed a telephone number, and nothing happens. Of course, all sorts of things might account for this: perhaps the telephone lines

---

[6] It might be useful to review the discussion of necessary and sufficient conditions in Chapter 5.

are down, or the phone is disconnected, or you forgot to dial 1 before a long-distance number. In reflecting on these matters, you are concerned with a set of conditions that are causally necessary for completing a telephone call. Our common knowledge of the world consists, to a large extent, in having generalizations specifying those causal conditions that are necessary and those causal conditions that are sufficient for certain kinds of events to occur.

Our position, then, is that causal conditionals are a kind of general conditional. The picture looks like this:

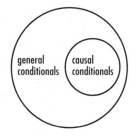

So if we are able to show that a general causal conditional is false just by virtue of its being a general conditional, we will have refuted it. This will serve our purposes well, for in what follows, we will be concerned almost exclusively with finding reasons for *rejecting* causal generalizations.

TESTING GENERAL CAUSAL CONDITIONALS

General causal conditionals are important for getting along in the world, but they will be helpful, of course, only if they are themselves correct and are applied correctly. What is needed, then, are principles for testing and applying such generalizations. It is one of the central tasks of inductive logic to supply these principles.

In the past, elaborate procedures have been developed for this purpose. The most famous set of such procedures was developed by John Stuart Mill and has come to be known as Mill's methods.[7] Though inspired by Mill's methods, the procedures introduced here involve a fundamental simplification: whereas Mill introduced five rules, or *methods* as he called them, here only two primary rules are introduced—one concerning sufficient conditions and the other concerning necessary conditions. Furthermore, the rules we will introduce for sufficient conditions and for necessary conditions are *negative* in the sense that they only provide ways of showing that something is *not* a sufficient condition or *not* a necessary condition. They are rules for *eliminating* suggested candidates for either a sufficient condition or a necessary condition. We will call these two rules the sufficient-condition test (SCT) and the necessary-condition test (NCT).

---

[7] Mill's "methods of experimental enquiry" are found in Book 3, Chapter 8, of *A System of Logic* (London: John W. Parker, 1843).

SUFFICIENT CONDITIONS AND NECESSARY CONDITIONS

Our ultimate concern in this discussion is with causal conditions. Causality, however, is a complicated subject about which significant disagreements still exist. We will therefore introduce the sufficient-condition test and the necessary-condition test first at an abstract level. Once it is clear how these rules work in general, we will apply them specifically to causal reasoning.

In order to keep our discussion as general as possible, we will adopt the following definitions of sufficient conditions and necessary conditions:

That *F* is a sufficient condition for *G* means that whenever *F* is present *G* is present.

That *F* is a necessary condition for *G* means that whenever *F* is absent *G* is absent.

Not everything that is a sufficient condition or a necessary condition in these senses will be a *causally* necessary or sufficient condition, but anything that fails to be a necessary or sufficient condition in these senses will also fail to provide a necessary or sufficient condition in any narrower sense of these terms. For this reason, these definitions will serve our purposes in formulating principles that *rule out* or *eliminate* proposed sufficient or necessary conditions of any kind, including those that are causal.[8]

THE SUFFICIENT-CONDITION TEST

It will simplify matters if we first state the sufficient-condition test abstractly, using letters.[9] We will also begin with a simple case in which we consider only four *candidates*—*A, B, C,* and *D*—for sufficient conditions for a *target* feature *G*. *A* will indicate that the feature is present; *~A* will indicate that the feature is absent. Using these conventions, suppose we are trying to decide whether any of the four features—*A, B, C,* or *D*—could be a sufficient condition for *G*. To this end we collect data of the following kind:

Table I:

Case 1.	*A*	*B*	*C*	*D*	*G*
Case 2.	*~A*	*B*	*C*	*~D*	*~G*
Case 3.	*A*	*~B*	*~C*	*~D*	*~G*

---

[8] Another advantage of introducing the notions of sufficient conditions and necessary conditions in this way is that it lays the foundation for discussing other kinds of sufficient and necessary conditions—for example, those that arise in legal and moral reasoning, the topics of Chapters 12 and 13.

[9] This procedure parallels, but is not identical to, Mill's Method of Difference.

We know by definition that for one thing to be a sufficient condition of another, when it is present, the other must be present as well. Thus, in applying the SCT, we only have to examine cases in which the target feature, G, is absent, and then check to see whether any of the candidate features are present.

SCT: Any candidate that is present when G is absent is eliminated as a possible sufficient condition of G.

The test applies to Table I as follows: Case 1 need not be examined because G is present, so there can be no violation of the SCT. Case 2 eliminates two of the candidates, B and C, for both are present in a situation in which G is absent. Finally, Case 3 eliminates A, and we are thus left with D as our only remaining candidate for a sufficient condition for G.

Let us consider D. Having survived the application of the sufficient-condition test, can we conclude that D *is* a sufficient condition for G? No—at least not on the basis of what we have been told thus far. It remains entirely possible that the discovery of a further case will reveal an instance in which D is present and G is absent, thus showing that D is not a sufficient condition for G either.

Case 4. A B $\sim C$ D $\sim G$

This reflects that inductive inferences, however well confirmed, are always subject to refutation. (Remember Captain Cook's discovery of black swans.) Suppose, however, that we have good reason to think that A through D contain *all* the possible candidates for a sufficient condition of G, and suppose further that we have good reason to think that *something* must be a sufficient condition for G. Given this additional *background information*, we could reasonably conclude that D is a sufficient condition for G, if we do not find any case (such as Case 4) where D and $\sim G$ are present. As we shall see, in the actual application of the sufficient-condition test, we can sometimes make a reasonable assignment of a sufficient condition in just this way.

THE NECESSARY-CONDITION TEST[10]

The necessary-condition test is like the SCT, but it works in the reverse fashion. With the SCT we eliminated a candidate F from being the sufficient condition for G if F was ever present when G was absent. With the NCT, we eliminate a candidate F from being a necessary condition for G if we can find a case in which G is present but F is not. This makes sense, because if G can be present when F is not, then F cannot be necessary for the occurrence of G. Thus, in applying the NCT, we only have to examine cases in which the target feature G is present, and then check to see whether any of the candidate features are absent.

NCT: Any candidate that is absent when G is present is eliminated as a possible necessary condition of G.

---

[10] The procedure parallels, but is not identical to, Mill's Method of Agreement.

The following table gives an example of an application of this test:

Table II:

Case 1.	A	B	C	D	$\sim G$
Case 2.	$\sim A$	B	C	D	G
Case 3.	A	$\sim B$	C	$\sim D$	G

Because Case 1 does not provide an instance in which G is present, it can be ignored. Case 2 eliminates A, because it shows that G can be present without A being present. Case 3 eliminates both B and D, leaving C as the only possible candidate for being a necessary condition for G. From this we cannot, of course, conclude that C *is* a necessary condition for G, for, as always, new cases might eliminate it as well. But if we have good reason to suppose that we have examined all the possible candidates for being a necessary condition for G and eliminated all of them but C, and, further, have good reason to think that something must be a necessary condition for G, then we may conclude that we have good reason to suppose that C is a necessary condition for G.

It is also possible to apply these rules simultaneously in the search for possible conditions that are both sufficient and necessary.[11] In Table I, for example, D is a possible sufficient condition for G, because D is never present when G is absent, but it may also be a necessary condition for G, because G is never present when D is absent. In Table II, C is the only possible necessary condition for G, but it is not also a possible sufficient condition, because in Case 1 it is present when G is absent.

EXERCISE V

For each of the following tables, decide:

(a) Which, if any, of the candidates—A, B, C, or D—is not eliminated by the sufficient-condition test?

(b) Which, if any, of the candidates—A, B, C, or D—is not eliminated by the necessary-condition test?

(c) Which, if any, of the candidates—A, B, C, or D—is not eliminated by either test?

Example:

Case 1.	A	B	$\sim C$	D	$\sim G$
Case 2.	$\sim A$	B	C	D	G
Case 3.	A	$\sim B$	C	D	G

(a) Only C passes the SCT.

(b) C and D both pass the NCT.

(c) Only C passes both.

---

[11] This procedure parallels, but is not identical to, Mill's Joint Method of Agreement and Difference.

1.	Case 1.	*A*	*B*	*C*	*D*	*G*
	Case 2.	~*A*	*B*	~*C*	*D*	~*G*
	Case 3.	*A*	~*B*	*C*	~*D*	*G*
2.	Case 1.	*A*	*B*	*C*	~*D*	*G*
	Case 2.	~*A*	*B*	*C*	*D*	*G*
	Case 3.	*A*	~*B*	*C*	~*D*	*G*
3.	Case 1.	*A*	*B*	*C*	*D*	~*G*
	Case 2.	~*A*	*B*	*C*	*D*	*G*
	Case 3.	*A*	~*B*	*C*	~*D*	*G*

RIGOROUS TESTING

Going back to Table I, it is easy to see that A, B, C, and D are not eliminated by the NCT, because G is only present in one case (Case 1) and they are present there as well. So far so good, but if we wanted to test these features more rigorously, it would be important to find more cases in which G is present and see if these candidates are also present and thus continue to survive the NCT.

The following table gives a more extreme example of nonrigorous testing:

Table III:

Case 1.	*A*	~*B*	*C*	*D*	*G*
Case 2.	*A*	~*B*	~*C*	~*D*	~*G*
Case 3.	*A*	~*B*	*C*	~*D*	~*G*
Case 4.	*A*	~*B*	~*C*	*D*	*G*

Here, A is eliminated by the SCT (in Cases 2 and 3), but is not eliminated by the NCT, so it is a possible necessary condition, but not a possible sufficient condition of G. B is not eliminated by the SCT, but is eliminated by the NCT (in Cases 1 and 4), so it is a possible sufficient condition, but not a possible necessary condition of G. C is eliminated by both rules (in Cases 3 and 4). Only D is not eliminated by either test, so it is the only candidate for being both a necessary and a sufficient condition for G.

The peculiarity of this example is that A is always present whether G is present or not, and B is always absent whether G is absent or not. If something is always present, as A is, it cannot possibly fail the NCT, for there cannot be a case in which the target is present and the candidate is absent if the candidate is *always* present. If we want to test A rigorously under the NCT, we should try to find cases in which A is absent and then check to see whether G is absent as well. In reverse fashion, if we want to test B rigorously under the SCT, we should try to find cases in which B is present and then check to see if G is present as well. Similarly, if we restrict our attention to cases in which G is always present, then no candidates can be eliminated by the SCT, and if we restrict our attention to cases in which G is always absent, then no candidates can be eliminated by the

NCT. For both rules, rigorous testing involves seeking out cases for which failing the test is a live possibility. Passing the tests without this is rather like a person bragging that she has never struck out when, in fact, she has never come to bat.

ADVANCED SECTION: SOME ELABORATIONS

Our discussion of necessary and sufficient conditions has been overly simple in two important respects: (i) We have limited the candidates to features that are present, and have not taken into account that the absence of a feature can be a necessary condition or a sufficient condition. (ii) We have limited our attention to simple features and have not considered the possibility of necessary or sufficient conditions that are complex. We will consider these matters one at a time.

NEGATIVE CONDITIONS

Sometimes the absence of a feature can serve as a sufficient condition for the presence or absence of something else. For example, if air is absent, then people will suffocate. Here the absence of air is a sufficient condition for suffocation. It is also true that wood will burn only if it is not wet. Here not having a trait—not being wet—is a necessary condition for wood's burning. Of course, it is often arbitrary whether we choose to describe things in positive or negative terms. In the last example we could just as well have said that being dry (rather than not being wet) is a necessary condition for wood burning. Even so, it is arbitrary to restrict the candidates for sufficient conditions and necessary conditions to features that are present.

To illustrate these points, we can look again at our first table:

Table I:
Case 1.	A	B	C	D	G
Case 2.	$\sim A$	B	C	$\sim D$	$\sim G$
Case 3.	A	$\sim B$	$\sim C$	$\sim D$	$\sim G$

Recall that in this setup only D was not eliminated as a possible sufficient condition. It is also easy to see that A, B, C, and D all remain candidates for being necessary conditions for G. But if we allow the absence of a feature to be a candidate, we see from the table that $\sim D$ is a possible necessary condition for $\sim G$, because it is not eliminated by the NCT. (There is no case in which $\sim G$ is present but $\sim D$ is absent.) $\sim D$ is also a possible sufficient condition for $\sim G$. (It gets by the SCT because there is no case in which $\sim D$ is present but $\sim G$ is absent.) In fact, $\sim A$, $\sim B$, and $\sim C$ are also possible sufficient conditions for $\sim G$. (They get by the SCT because they are only present in Cases 2 and 3, and in those cases $\sim G$ is present as well.)

DISCUSSION QUESTION

The new batch of possible sufficient conditions and possible necessary conditions that arises when we introduce negative conditions is fully determined by the following two principles:

(a) If the presence of property *F* is a necessary condition for the presence of property *G*, then the absence of property *F* is a sufficient condition for the absence of property *G*.

(b) If the presence of property *F* is a sufficient condition for the presence of property *G*, then the absence of property *F* is a necessary condition for the absence of property *G*.

Why do these principles hold?

COMPLEX CONDITIONS

Another way in which our discussion has been overly simple is that we have considered only simple conditions and have not taken into account the existence of complex conditions. Here are some examples of complex conditions:

If hydrogen and oxygen are combined and ignited, they will explode.

Here the conditional lays down a *conjunctive sufficient condition.*

If you eat mud or rocks, you will feel ill.

Here the conditional lays down a *disjunctive sufficient condition.*

A short circuit will cause a fire only if oxygen is present and combustible material is present.

Here the conditional lays down a *conjunctive necessary condition.*

EXERCISE VI

(1) Give an example of a conditional stating a true *disjunctive* necessary condition.

(2) Explain why if *A* is a sufficient condition for *B*, then *A* & *B* is a sufficient condition for *B*, for *any B.*

(3) Explain why if *A* is a necessary condition for *B*, then *A* ∨ *B* is a necessary condition for *B*, for *any B.*

APPLYING THESE METHODS

Our procedure thus far has been fairly mechanical; we have simply stated two rules and then showed how they can be applied to abstract patterns of conditions.

Applying these rules to actual concrete situations introduces a number of complicating factors.

NORMALITY

First, it is important to keep in mind that in our ordinary understanding of causal conditions, we usually take it for granted that the setting is normal. It is part of common knowledge that if you strike a match, then it will light. Thus, we consider striking a match sufficient to make it light. But if someone has filled the room with carbon dioxide, then the match will not light, no matter how it is struck. Here one may be inclined to say that, after all, striking a match is not sufficient to light it. We might try to be more careful and say that if a match is struck *and* the room is not filled with carbon dioxide, then it will light. But this new conditional overlooks other possibilities—for example, that the room has been filled with nitrogen, that the match has been fireproofed, that the wrong end of the match was struck, that the match has already been lit, and so forth. It now seems that the antecedent of our conditional will have to be endlessly long in order to specify a true or genuine sufficient condition. In fact, however, we usually feel quite happy with saying that if you strike a match, then it will light. We simply do not worry about the possibility that the room has been filled with carbon dioxide, the match has been fireproofed, and so on. Normally we think that things are normal, and give up this assumption only when some good reason appears for doing so.

These reflections suggest the following *contextualized* restatement of our original definitions of sufficient conditions and necessary conditions:

> That F is a sufficient condition for G means that whenever F is present in a normal context, G is present there as well.

> That F is a necessary condition for G means that whenever F is absent from a normal context, G is absent from it as well.

What will count as a normal context will vary with the type and the aim of an investigation, but all investigations into causally sufficient conditions and causally necessary conditions take place against the background of many factors that are taken as fixed.

BACKGROUND ASSUMPTIONS

If we are going to subject a causal hypothesis to rigorous testing employing the SCT and the NCT, we have to seek out a wide range of cases in which it might possibly be refuted. In general, the wider the range of possible refuters the better. But some limit must be put on this activity or else testing will get hopelessly bogged down. If we are testing a drug to see whether it will cure a disease, we should try it on a variety of people of various ages, medical histories, body types, and so on, but we will not check to see whether it works on people named Edmund or check to see whether it works on people who drive Volvos. Such factors, we want to say, are plainly irrelevant. But what makes them irrelevant? How do we distinguish relevant from irrelevant considerations?

The answer to this question is that our reasoning about causes occurs within a framework of beliefs that we consider already established as true. This framework contains a great deal of what is called *common knowledge*—knowledge we expect almost every sane adult to possess. We all know, for example, that human beings cannot breathe underwater, cannot walk through walls, cannot be in two places at once, and so on. The stock of these commonplace beliefs is almost endless. Since they are commonplace beliefs, they tend not to be mentioned, yet they play an important role in distinguishing relevant factors from irrelevant ones. Furthermore, *specialized* knowledge contains its own principles that are largely taken for granted by specialists. Doctors, for example, know a great deal about the detailed structure of the human body, and this background knowledge constantly guides their thought in dealing with specific illnesses. Thus, accepted beliefs establish a framework in which new ideas are judged. We can call the beliefs that give our system of beliefs its basic structure *framework beliefs*. In general, we do not question these framework beliefs, and things that do not fit in with them are not taken seriously. For example, if someone claimed to discover that blood does not circulate, no doctor would take the time to refute her. To take this suggestion seriously would be to challenge our whole way of viewing human beings and many other organisms.

Not all beliefs have this central status in our system of beliefs. They can be abandoned or modified without seriously harming our basic beliefs about the world. Someone might mistakenly believe that Portland is the capital of Oregon. Having discovered that the capital is really Salem, that person will drop one belief and replace it with another. Normally this change in belief will have little effect on many other beliefs and probably no effect on framework beliefs. In contrast, if scientists came to doubt that the sun is larger than the earth, most of their conception of the physical universe would have to change. This suggests the following picture of our system of beliefs: In it, some beliefs matter more or carry more weight than others, and they are given up only under great pressure. Other beliefs can be given up with hardly a thought. Discovering that Salem, not Portland, is the capital of Oregon can normally be taken in stride; discovering that half the world's population is made up of invading aliens from another planet would profoundly change our way of looking at things.

Given this picture, we see that beliefs are not tested in isolation from other beliefs. Testing takes place within a system of beliefs that shapes the form the testing will take. The Austrian philosopher Ludwig Wittgenstein put the matter this way:

> 105. All testing, all confirmation and disconfirmation of a hypothesis takes place already within a system. And this system is not a more or less arbitrary and doubtful point of departure for all our arguments: no, it belongs to the essence of what we call an argument. The system is not so much the point of departure, as the element in which arguments have their life.[12]

We can now see how our belief system develops and grows. Things that have been learned in the past guide the search for new knowledge. They do this in two

---

[12] Ludwig Wittgenstein, *On Certainty*, trans. G. E. M. Anscombe (Oxford; Basil Blackwell, 1969).

ways: we use the belief system to reject what we take to be false or irrelevant hypotheses, and we also use it to suggest interesting new hypotheses. New beliefs are added to old beliefs, and these, in turn, suggest further possible new beliefs. The more well-founded beliefs we have, the more we are able to discover further well-founded beliefs. Learning about the world is a bootstrap operation.

The situation, however, is more complicated than this. We not only increase our stock of beliefs but sometimes we discover that some of our previously held beliefs are false. For example, we might learn to our astonishment that a close friend is a member of a terrorist organization. Such a discovery almost certainly would lead us to reconsider a great many beliefs we have about him. Occasionally even framework beliefs are called into question and then rejected. The replacement of the earth-centered (geocentric) theory of the solar system of Ptolemy by the sun-centered (heliocentric) theory of Copernicus is one example of a revolutionary change;[13] the replacement of Newtonian physics by Einstein's relativistic physics is another. But such revolutions in thought are rare. Furthermore, such theories, as novel as they may be, leave most of the general framework beliefs untouched. If Einstein's theory (or any theory) entailed that human beings fly by flapping their ears, that would be enough reason for rejecting it. Even the most revolutionary changes in thought, when looked at from a distance, appear remarkably conservative of our *total* system of beliefs.

A Detailed Example

In order to get a clearer idea of the complex interplay between the rules we have been examining and the reliance on background information, it will be helpful to look in some detail at actual applications of these rules. For this purpose, we will examine an attempt to find the cause of a particular phenomenon, an outbreak of what came to be known as Legionnaires' disease. The example not only shows how causal reasoning relies on background assumptions, it has another interesting feature as well: in the process of discovering the cause of Legionnaires' disease the investigators were forced to *abandon* what was previously taken to be a well-established causal generalization. In fact, until it was discarded, this false background principle gave them no end of trouble.

The following account of the outbreak of Legionnaires' disease and the subsequent difficulties in finding out what caused it is drawn from an article in *Scientific American*.[14]

> The 58th convention of the American Legion's Pennsylvania Department was held at the Bellevue-Stratford Hotel in Philadelphia from July 21 through 24, 1976. ... Between July 22 and August 3, 149 of the conventioneers developed

---

[13] For the classic discussion of these two systems, see Galileo's *Dialogue Concerning the Two World Systems—Ptolemaic and Copernican,* which is excerpted in Chapter 14.

[14] These excerpts are drawn from David W. Fraser and Joseph E. McDade, "Legionellosis," *Scientific American,* October 1977, 82–99.

what appeared to be the same puzzling illness, characterized by fever, coughing and pneumonia. This, however, was an unusual, explosive outbreak of pneumonia with no apparent cause. . . . Legionnaires' disease, as the illness was quickly named by the press, was to prove a formidable challenge to epidemiologists and laboratory investigators alike.

Notice that at this stage the researchers begin with the assumption that they are dealing with a single illness and not a collection of similar but different illnesses. That assumption could turn out to be wrong, but if the symptoms of the various patients are sufficiently similar, this is a natural starting assumption. Another reasonable starting assumption is that this illness had a single causative agent. This assumption, too, could turn out to be false, though it did not. The assumption that they were dealing with a single disease with a single cause was at least a good simplifying assumption, one to be held onto until there was good reason to give it up. In any case, we now have a clear specification of our target feature *G:* the occurrence of a carefully described illness that came to be known as Legionnaires' disease. The situation concerning it was puzzling because people had contracted a disease with symptoms much like those of pneumonia, yet they had not tested positive for any of the known agents that cause such diseases.

The narrative continues as follows:

> The initial step in the investigation of any epidemic is to determine the character of the illness, who has become ill and just where and when. The next step is to find out what was unique about the people who became ill: where they were and what they did that was different from other people who stayed well. Knowing such things may indicate how the disease agent was spread and thereby suggest the identity of the agent and where it came from.

Part of this procedure involves a straightforward application of the NCT: was there any interesting feature that was always present in the history of people who came down with the illness? Progress was made almost at once on this front:

> We quickly learned that the illness was not confined to Legionnaires. An additional 72 cases were discovered among people who had not been directly associated with the convention. They had one thing in common with the sick conventioneers: for one reason or another they had been in or near the Bellevue-Stratford Hotel.

Strictly speaking, of course, all these people who had contracted the disease had more than one thing in common. They were, for example, all alive at the time they were in Philadelphia, and being alive is, in fact, a necessary condition for getting Legionnaires' disease. But the researchers were not interested in this necessary condition because it is a normal background condition for the contraction of any disease. Furthermore, it did not provide a condition that distinguished those who contracted the disease from those who did not. The overwhelming majority of people who were alive at the time did not contract Legionnaires' disease. Thus, the researchers were not interested in this necessary condition because it would fail so badly when tested as a sufficient condition. On the basis of common knowledge and specialized medical knowledge, a great many other conditions were also kept off the candidate list.

The application of the NCT to presence at the Bellevue-Stratford was straight-forward. Everyone who had contracted the disease had spent time in or near that hotel. The application of the SCT was more complicated, for not everyone who stayed at the Bellevue-Stratford contracted the disease. Other factors made a difference: "Older conventioneers had been affected at a higher rate than younger ones, men at three times the rate for women." It is, however, part of medical background knowledge that susceptibility to disease often varies with age and sex. Given these differences, some people who spent time at the Bellevue-Stratford were at higher risk of contracting the disease than others. The investigation so far suggested that, for some people, being at the Bellevue-Stratford was connected with a sufficient condition for contracting Legionnaires' disease.

As soon as spending time at the Bellevue-Stratford became the focus of atten-tion, other hypotheses naturally suggested themselves. Food poisoning was a reasonable suggestion, since it is part of medical knowledge that diseases are sometimes spread by food. It was put on the list of possible candidates, but failed.

> The obvious possibility that the disease might have been spread by food or drink was ruled out. Conventioneers who became ill were shown to be no more likely than those who remained well to have eaten at particular restaurants, to have attended particular functions where food and drink were served, or to have drunk water or used ice in the hotels.

Thus, the food/drink hypothesis was eliminated by the NCT.

Further investigation turned up another important clue to the cause of the illness.

> Certain observations suggested that the disease might have been spread through the air. Legionnaires who became ill had spent on the average about 60 percent more time in the lobby of the Bellevue-Stratford than those who remained well; the sick Legionnaires had also spent more time on the sidewalk in front of the hotel than their unaffected fellow conventioneers. . . . It appeared, therefore, that the most likely mode of transmission was airborne.

Again, appealing to background medical knowledge, there seemed to be three main candidates for the airborne agents that could have caused the illness: "heavy metals, toxic organic substances, and infectious organisms." However, examination of tissues taken from patients who had died from the disease revealed "no unusual levels of metallic or toxic organic substances that might be related to the epidemic," so this left an infectious organism as the remaining candidate. Once more we have an application of the NCT. If the disease had been caused by heavy metals or toxic organic substances, then there would have been unusually high levels of these substances in the tissues of those who had contracted the disease. Since this was not so, these candidates were eliminated.

Appealing to background knowledge once more, it seemed that a bacterium would be the most likely source of an airborne disease with the symptoms of Legionnaires' disease. But researchers had already made a routine check for bacteria that caused pneumonia-like diseases, and they had found none. For this reason, attention was directed to the possibility that some unknown organism had been responsible, but had somehow escaped detection.

It turned out that an undetected and previously unknown bacterium had caused the illness, but it took more than four months to find this out. The difficulties encountered in this effort show another important fact about the reliance on a background assumption: sometimes it turns out to be false. To simplify, the standard way to test for the presence of bacteria is to try to grow them in culture dishes—flat dishes containing nutrients that bacteria can live on. If, after a reasonable number of tries, a colony of a particular kind of bacterium does not appear, then it is concluded that the bacterium is not present. As it turned out, the bacterium that caused Legionnaires' disease would not grow in the cultures commonly used to detect the presence of bacteria. Thus, an important background assumption turned out to be false.

After a great deal of work, a suspicious bacterium was detected using a live-tissue culture rather than the standard synthetic culture. The task, then, was to show that this particular bacterium in fact caused the disease. Again to simplify, when people are infected by a particular organism, they often develop antibodies that are specifically aimed at this organism. In the case of Legionnaires' disease, these antibodies were easier to detect than the bacterium itself. They also remained in the patients' bodies after the infection had run its course. We thus have another chance to apply the NCT: if Legionnaires' disease was caused by this particular bacterium, then whenever the disease was present, this antibody should be present as well. The suspicious bacterium passed this test with flying colors and was named, appropriately enough, *Legionella pneumophila*.

The story of the search for the cause of Legionnaires' disease brings out two important features of the use of inductive methods in the sciences. First, it involves a complicated interplay between what is already established and what is being tested. Confronted with a new problem, established principles can be used to suggest theoretically significant hypotheses to be tested. The tests then eliminate some hypotheses and leave others. If at the end of the investigation a survivor remains that fits in well with our previously established principles, then the stock of established principles is increased. The second thing that this example shows is that the inductive method is fallible. Without the background of established principles, the application of inductive principles like the NCT and the SCT would be undirected, yet sometimes these established principles let us down, for they can turn out to be false. The discovery of the false background principle that hindered the search for the cause of Legionnaires' disease led to important revisions in laboratory techniques. The discovery that fundamental background principles are false can lead to revolutionary changes in science. This topic is discussed in Chapter 14, where the nature of scientific frameworks is examined.

CALLING THINGS CAUSES

After their research was finally completed, with the bacterium identified, described, and named, it was then said that *Legionella pneumophila* was the *cause* of Legionnaires' disease. What was meant by this? To simplify a bit, suppose *L. pneumophila* (as it is abbreviated) entered the bodies of *all* those who contracted the disease: whenever the disease was present, *L. pneumophila* was present. Thus, *L. pneumophila* passes the NCT. We will further suppose, as is common in bacterial infections, that some people's immune systems were successful in combating *L. pneumophila,* and they never actually developed the disease. Thus, the presence of *L. pneumophila* would not pass the SCT. This suggests that we sometimes call something a cause if it passes the NCT, even if it does not pass the SCT.

But even if we sometimes consider necessary conditions to be causes, we certainly do not consider *all* necessary conditions to be causes. We have already noted that to get Legionnaires' disease, one has to be alive, yet no one thinks that being alive is the cause of Legionnaires' disease. To cite another example, this time one that is not silly, it might be that another necessary condition for developing Legionnaires' disease is that the person be in a run-down condition—healthy people might always be able to resist *L. pneumophila.* Do we then want to say that being in a run-down condition is the cause of Legionnaires' disease? As we have described the situation, almost certainly not, but we might want to say that it is an important *causal factor* or *causally relevant factor.*

Although the matter is far from clear, what we call *the* cause rather than simply *a* causal factor or causally relevant factor seems to depend on a number of considerations. We tend to reserve the expression "the cause" for *changes* that occur prior to the effect, and describe *permanent* or *standing* features of the context as causal factors instead. That is how we speak about Legionnaires' disease. Being exposed to *L. pneumophila,* which was a specific event that occurred before the onset of the disease, *caused it.* Being in a run-down condition, which was a feature that patients possessed for some time before they contracted the disease, was not called the cause, but instead called a causal factor. It is not clear, however, that we always draw the distinction between what we call the cause and what we call a causal factor based on whether something is a prior event or a standing condition. For example, if we are trying to explain why certain people who came in contact with *L. pneumophila* contracted the disease whereas others did not, then we might say that the former group contracted the disease because they were in a run-down condition. Thus, by limiting our investigation only to those who came in contact with *L. pneumophila,* our perspective has changed. We want to know why some within that group contracted the disease and others did not. Citing the run-down condition of those who contracted the disease as the cause now seems entirely natural. These examples suggest that we call something *the* cause when it plays a particularly important role relative to the purposes of our investigation. Usually this will be an event or change taking place against the background of fixed necessary conditions; sometimes it will not.

Sometimes we call *sufficient* conditions causes. We say that short circuits cause fires because in many normal contexts a short circuit is sufficient to cause a fire. Of course, short circuits are not necessary to cause a fire, since, in the same normal contexts, fires can be caused by a great many other things. With sufficient conditions, as with necessary conditions, we often draw a distinction between what we call the cause as opposed to what we call a causal factor, and we seem to draw it along similar lines. Speaking loosely, we might say that we sometimes call the *key* components of sufficient conditions *causes*. Then, holding background conditions fixed, we can use the SCT to evaluate such causal claims.

In sum, we can use the NCT to eliminate proposed necessary causal conditions. We can use the SCT to eliminate proposed sufficient causal conditions. Those candidates that survive these tests may be called causal conditions or causal factors if they fit in well with our system of other causal generalizations. Finally, some of these causal conditions or causal factors will be called causes if they play a key role in our causal investigations. Typically, though not always, we call something the cause of an event if it is a prior event or change that stands out against the background of fixed conditions.

CONCOMITANT VARIATION

The use of the sufficient-condition test and the necessary-condition test depends on certain features of the world being sometimes present and sometimes absent. However, certain features of the world are always present to some degree. Because they are always present, the NCT will never eliminate them as possible necessary conditions of any event, and the SCT will never eliminate anything as a sufficient condition for them. Yet the *extent* or *degree* to which a feature exists in the world is often a significant phenomenon that demands causal explanation.

An example should make this clear. In recent years, a controversy has raged over the impact of acid rain on the environment of the northeastern United States and Canada. Part of the controversy involves the proper interpretation of the data that have been collected. The controversy has arisen for the following reason: the atmosphere always contains a certain amount of acid, much of it from natural sources. It is also known that an excess of acid in the environment can have severe effects on both plants and animals. Lakes are particularly vulnerable to the effects of acid rain. Finally, it is also acknowledged that industries, mostly in the Midwest, discharge large quantities of sulfur dioxide (SO_2) into the air, and this increases the acidity of water in the atmosphere. The question—and here the controversy begins—is whether the contribution of acid from these industries is the cause of the environmental damage downwind of them.

How can we settle such a dispute? The two rules we have introduced provide no immediate help, for, as we have seen, they provide a rigorous test of a causal hypothesis only when we can find contrasting cases with the presence or the absence of a given feature. The NCT provides a rigorous test for a necessary condition only if we can find cases in which the feature does not occur and then check to make sure that the target feature does not occur either. The SCT provides a rigorous test for a sufficient condition only when we can find cases in which the target phenomenon is absent and then check whether the candidate sufficient condition is absent as well. In this case, however, neither check applies, for there is always a certain amount of acid in the atmosphere, so it is not possible to check what happens when atmospheric acid is completely absent. Similarly, environmental damage, which is the target phenomenon under investigation, is so widespread in our modern industrial society that it is also hard to find a case in which it is completely absent.

So, if there is always acid in the atmosphere, and environmental damage always exists at least to some extent, how can we determine whether the SO_2 released into the atmosphere is *significantly* responsible for the environmental damage in the affected areas? Here we use what John Stuart Mill called the Method of Concomitant Variation. We ask whether the amount of environmental damage varies directly in proportion to the amount of SO_2 released into the environment. If environmental damage increases with the amount of SO_2 released into the environment and drops when the amount of SO_2 is lowered, this means that the level of SO_2 in the atmosphere is *positively correlated* with environmental damage. We would then have good reason to believe that lowering SO_2 emissions would lower the level of environmental damage, at least to some extent.

Arguments relying on the method of concomitant variation are difficult to evaluate, especially when there is no generally accepted background theory that makes sense of the concomitant variation. Some such variations are well understood. For example, everyone knows that the faster you drive, the more gasoline you consume. (Gasoline consumption varies *directly* with speed.) Why? There is a good theory here; it takes more energy to drive at a high speed than at a low speed, and this energy is derived from the gasoline consumed in the car's engine. Other correlations are less well understood. There seems to be a correlation between cholesterol level in the blood and the chances of heart attack. First, the correlation here is not nearly so good as the gasoline-consumption-to-speed correlation, for many people with high cholesterol levels do not suffer heart attacks, and many people with low cholesterol levels do. Furthermore, no generally accepted background theory has been found that explains the positive correlation that does seem to exist.

This reference to background theory is important, because two sets of phenomena can be correlated to a very high degree, even with no direct causal relationship between them. A favorite example that appears in many statistics texts is the discovered positive correlation in boys between foot size and quality of handwriting. It is hard to imagine a causal relation holding in either direction. Having big feet should not make you write better and, just as obviously, writing well should not give you big feet. The correct explanation is that both foot size and handwriting ability are positively correlated with age. Here a noncausal correlation between two phenomena (foot size and handwriting ability) is explained by a third common correlation (maturation) that *is* causal.

At times, it is possible to get causal correlations *backwards*. For example, a few years ago, sports statisticians discovered a negative correlation between forward passes thrown and winning. That is, the more forward passes a team threw, the less chance it had of winning. This suggests that passing is not a good strategy, since the more you do it, the more likely you are to lose. Closer examination showed, however, that the causal relationship, in fact, went in the other direction. Toward the end of a game, losing teams tend to throw a great many passes in an effort to catch up. In other words, teams throw a lot of passes because they are losing, rather than the other way around.

Finally, some correlations seem inexplicable. For example, a strong positive correlation holds between the birthrate in Holland and the number of storks nesting in chimneys. There is, of course, a background theory that would explain this—storks bring babies—but that theory is not favored by modern science. For the lack of any better background theory, the phenomenon just seems weird.

So, given a strong correlation between phenomena of types *A* and *B*, four possibilities exist:

(1) *A* is the cause of *B*.

(2) *B* is the cause of *A*.

(3) Some third thing is the cause of both.

(4) The correlation is simply accidental.

Before we accept any one of these possibilities, we must have good reasons for preferring it over the other three.

EXERCISE VII

In each of the following examples a strong correlation, either negative or positive, holds between two sets of phenomena, *A* and *B*. Try to decide whether *A* is the cause of *B*, *B* is the cause of *A*, both are caused by some third factor *C*, or the correlation is simply accidental. Explain your choice.

(1) At one time there was a strong negative correlation between the number of mules in a state (*A*) and the salaries paid to professors at the state university (*B*). In other words, the more mules, the lower professional salaries.[15]

(2) It has been claimed that there is a strong positive correlation between those students who take sex education courses (*A*) and those who contract venereal disease (*B*).

(3) LOCKED DOORS NO BAR TO CRIME, STUDY SAYS
"Washington (UPI)—Rural Americans with locked doors, watchdogs or guns may face as much risk of burglary as neighbors who leave doors unlocked, a federally financed study says.
"The study, financed in part by a three-year $170,000 grant from the Law Enforcement Assistance Administration, was based on a survey of nearly 900 families in rural Ohio.
"Sixty percent of the rural residents surveyed regularly locked doors [*A*], but were burglarized more often than residents who left doors unlocked [*B*]."[16]

(4) There is a high positive correlation between the number of fire engines

---

[15] From Gregory A. Kimble, *How to Use (and Misuse) Statistics* (Englewood Cliffs, N.J.: Prentice-Hall, 1978), 182.

[16] "Locked Doors No Bar to Crime, Study Says," *Santa Barbara* [California] *Newspress,* Wednesday, February 16, 1977.

in a particular borough in New York City (*A*) and the number of fires that occur there (*B*).[17]

(5) For a particular United States president, there is a negative correlation between the number of hairs on his head (*A*) and the population of China (*B*).

DISCUSSION QUESTIONS

(1) Many defenders of nuclear deterrence have relied on an inductive argument to the effect that World War III was avoided because of the balance of power between West and East. What evidence has been offered in support of this conclusion? How strong is the argument?

(2) Now that it seems beyond doubt that smoking is dangerous to people's health, a new debate has arisen concerning the possible health hazards of smoke on nonsmokers. Collect statements pro and con on this issue and evaluate the strength of the inductive arguments on each side.

(3) Although both in science and in daily life, we rely heavily on the methods of inductive reasoning, a number of perplexing problems exist concerning the legitimacy of this kind of reasoning. The most famous problem concerning induction was formulated by the eighteenth-century philosopher David Hume, first in his *Treatise of Human Nature* and then later in his *Enquiry Concerning Human Understanding*. A simplified version of Hume's skeptical argument goes as follows: Our inductive generalizations seem to rest on the assumption that *unobserved* cases will follow the patterns that we discovered in *observed* cases. That is, our inductive generalizations seem to presuppose that nature operates uniformly: the way things are observed to behave here and now are accurate indicators of how things behave anywhere and at any time. But by what right can we assume that nature is uniform? Because this claim itself asserts a contingent matter of fact, it could only be established by inductive reasoning. But because all inductive reasoning presupposes the principle that nature is uniform, any inductive justification of this principle would seem to be circular. It seems, then, that we have no ultimate justification for our inductive reasoning at all. Is this a good argument or a bad one?

(4) In mathematics, proofs are sometimes employed using the method of *mathematical induction*. If you are familiar with these procedures, decide whether these proofs are inductive or deductive in character.

---

[17] From Kimble, *How to Use (and Misuse) Statistics*, 182.

INFERENCES TO THE BEST EXPLANATION

In this section we will consider a form of inductive reasoning that has been discussed extensively in recent years. The basic idea is that a hypothesis gains inductive support if, when it is added to our stock of previously accepted beliefs, it increases our ability to make reliable predictions and illuminating explanations. Prediction is important because it tests our theories with new data and sometimes allows us to anticipate or even control future events. Explanation is important because it makes sense of things; it makes them more intelligible.[18] In fact, we sometimes accept a hypothesis as true, or as likely to be true, precisely because it enhances our previous ability to predict or explain. This style of reasoning is called, somewhat loosely, *inference to the best explanation*.[19] It is an important form of inductive reasoning both in science and in daily life, and it is worth examining in some detail.

To see how inferences to the best explanation work, suppose you return to where you live and discover that the lock on your front door is broken and several valuable objects are missing. In all likelihood you will immediately assume—or simply conclude—that you have been burglarized. Of course, other things *could* have happened. Perhaps there was a drug bust and the authorities had the wrong address. Perhaps your friends are playing a strange joke on you. Perhaps a meteorite struck the door and then vaporized your valuables. In fact, all these things *could* have happened (even the last), and further investigation could show that one of them did. Why, then, do we accept the burglary hypothesis without even considering these competing possibilities? The reason is that the assumption that your home was robbed is not itself highly improbable; and this assumption, taken together with other things we believe, provides the best—the strongest and the most natural—explanation of the phenomenon. The possibility that a meteorite struck your door is so wildly remote that it is not worth taking seriously. The possibility that your house was raided by mistake and the possibility that your friends are playing an obscure trick on you are not wildly remote, but neither fits the facts very well. If it was a police raid, you would expect to find a police officer there, or at least a note of some kind. If it is a joke, it is hard to see the point of it. In contrast, a burglary is not highly unlikely, and the assumption fits the facts extremely well. Logically, the situation looks like this:

> The hypothesis that your house has been burglarized, combined with previously accepted facts and principles, provides a suitably strong explanation of why your house is in the condition it is in.
>
> No other hypothesis provides an explanation nearly this good.
>
> From this we conclude that there is a very good chance (perhaps coming close to certainty) that your house was burglarized.[20]

---

[18] Explanations will be discussed more fully in Chapter 11.

[19] Gilbert Harman deserves much of the credit for calling attention to the importance of inferences to the best explanation. See, for example, his book *Thought* (Princeton: Princeton University Press, 1973).

[20] The American philosopher Charles Sanders Peirce discussed a form of argument, closely related to inferences to the best explanation, that he called *abduction*. He described this form of reasoning as follows:

Here it might help to compare inferences to the best explanation with other forms of argument. In a justificatory argument, we use true premises to establish the truth of the conclusion. In an explanatory argument, we try to make sense of something by deriving it (sometimes deductively) from premises that are themselves well understood. With an inference to the best explanation, we reason in the opposite direction from explanation: we cite the explanatory or predictive power of a premise to lend support to its truth. That a hypothesis provides an explanation of something whose truth is already known provides evidence for the truth of that hypothesis.

Here some clarifications are needed, particularly concerning the phrase "inference to the best explanation." Reference to the *best* explanation is not really right. It might turn out that the very best explanation is not much of an explanation at all. The best explanation in a group of weak explanations does not provide much evidence for saying that the explanatory hypothesis is true. For centuries people were baffled by the floods that occurred on the Nile each spring. The Nile, as far as anyone knew, flowed from an endless desert. Where, then, did the floodwater come from? Various wild explanations were suggested, mostly about deities of one kind or another, but none were any good. Looking for the best explanation among these weak explanations would be a waste of time. It was only after it was discovered that central Africa contains a high mountain range covered with snow in the winter that a reasonable explanation became possible. That, in fact, settled the matter. So the best explanation must also be a *strong* explanation.

It is also important to remember that inferences to the best explanation are typically inductive and thus nonmonotonic. However strong such an inference might be, it can always be overturned by future experience. This can happen in a number of ways. New facts may be discovered. To go back to the previous example: your friends might suddenly jump out, shouting "Surprise, Surprise!" A new explanatory hypothesis may suggest itself—the police had broken in because they had learned that terrorists had planted a bomb somewhere in your expensive electronic equipment. Of course, inferences to the best explanation being nonmonotonic does not show that they are all on a par, or are all equally no good. If you find a broken glass on the floor, it is a practical certainty that it broke as the result of falling, though it is at least possible that someone broke the glass with a hammer and then placed the pieces on the floor. This alternative is entirely possible, but it does not count as a strong explanation, because it is hard to think why anyone would do such a thing.

The surprising fact, C, is observed.
But if A were true, then C would be a matter of course.
Hence, there is reason to suspect that A is true.

Notice that Peirce says only that there is "reason to *suspect* that A is true." For him, abduction was a procedure for suggesting hypotheses that would be tested by other means. In contrast, with an inference to the best explanation, we conclude that there is reason to *believe* that A is true. An inference to the best explanation is thus an inductive form of reasoning.

The passage from Peirce comes from *Collected Papers of Charles Sanders Peirce* (Cambridge: Harvard University Press, 1934), 5:117.

Once we grasp the notion of an inference to the best explanation, we discover that it is a pattern of reasoning that we use constantly. Solutions to murder mysteries almost always have the form of an inference to the best explanation. The facts of the case are laid out and then the clever detective argues that, given these facts, only one person could possibly have committed the crime. In the story "Silver Blaze," Sherlock Holmes concludes that the trainer must have been the dastardly fellow who stole Silver Blaze, the horse favored to win the Wessex Cup, which was to be run the following day. Holmes's reasoning, as usual, was complex, but the key part of his argument was that the dog kept in the stable did not bark loudly when someone came and took away the horse.

> I had grasped the significance of the silence of the dog, for one true inference invariably suggests others. [I knew that] a dog was kept in the stables, and yet, though someone had been in and fetched out a horse, he had not barked enough to arouse the two lads in the loft. Obviously the midnight visitor was someone whom the dog knew well.[21]

This, together with other facts, was enough to identify the trainer, Straker, as the person who stole Silver Blaze. In this case, it is something *not* occurring that provides the basis for an inference to the best explanation. Of course, the inference is not *absolutely* airtight. Martians with hypnotic powers over dogs could have committed the crime, but that explanation is so far-fetched that it does not have to be considered at all.

We can now go back to an earlier question: under what conditions do we add a new causal claim to our previous stock? (1) Our negative test is that the generalization not be disconfirmed by counterexamples. (2) It should also fit in with other things we accept. (3) To this we can now add that a hypothesis will receive *positive* confirmation by enhancing the explanatory or predictive power of our system of beliefs.

In fact, the situation is sometimes more complicated than the previous paragraph suggests. Sometimes explanatory power will take precedence over evidential considerations; that is, if a principle has strong explanatory power, we may accept it even in the face of clear disconfirming evidence. We do not give up a powerful principle lightly—nor should we. To understand this, we must recall that we do not test propositions in isolation from other propositions in our system of beliefs. When faced with counterevidence to our beliefs, we often have a choice between what to give up and what to continue to hold onto. A simple example will illustrate this. Suppose we believe the following things:

(1) Either John or Joan committed the crime.

(2) Whoever committed the crime must have had a motive for doing so.

(3) Joan had no motive to commit the crime.

---

[21] "Silver Blaze" is found in many collections of the Sherlock Holmes mysteries written by Sir Arthur Conan Doyle.

From these three premises we can validly infer that John committed the crime. Suppose, however, that we discover that John could not have committed the crime. (Three bishops and a Boy Scout leader swear that he was somewhere else at the time.) Now, from the fact that John did not commit the murder, we could not immediately conclude that Joan committed it, for that would lead to an inconsistency. If she committed the crime, then according to (3) she would have committed a motiveless crime, but that conflicts with (2), which says that motiveless crimes do not occur. So the discovery that John did not commit the crime entails that at least one of the premises in the argument must be abandoned, but it does not tell us which one or which ones.

This same phenomenon occurs when we are dealing with counterevidence to a complex system of beliefs. Counterevidence shows that there must be something wrong somewhere in the system, but it does not determine exactly where. One possibility is that the *supposed* counterevidence is itself in error. Imagine that a student carries out an experiment and gets the result that one of the fundamental laws of physics is false. This will not shake the scientific community even a little, for the best explanation of the student's result is that she messed things up. Given well-established principles, she could not have gotten the result she did if she had run the experiment correctly. Of course, if a great many reputable scientists find difficulties with a supposed law, the situation is different. The hypothesis that all these scientists have, like the student, simply messed up is itself highly unlikely. But it is surprising how much contrary evidence will be tolerated when dealing with a strong explanatory theory. Scientists often continue to employ a theory when they know it is not quite right or even that it is seriously wrong in certain respects. This tolerance usually ceases only when the defects in the theory make serious trouble—that is, when they give bad results in areas that count.

In order to draw an inference to the best explanation, we need standards for deciding which explanation is best. There is, in fact, no simple rule for deciding this, but we can list some factors that go into the evaluation of the strength of an explanation:

First, the explanation should not contain claims that are themselves unlikely to be true—as in the meteorite example given above.

Second, the explanation should not itself be something in need of explanation. It does not help to explain something that is obscure by citing something at least as obscure.

Third, simplicity is a mark of excellence in an explanation because simple explanations are easier to understand, and explanations aim at understanding.

Fourth, the explanation should be powerful—that is, it is a mark of excellence in an explanation that the same kind of explanation can be used successfully over a wide range of cases.

Fifth, if the explanation forces us to give up other well-established beliefs, it should do this as little as possible. It should be conservative of past beliefs.

Sixth, the explanation should really explain. A good explanation makes sense out of the thing it is intended to explain.[22]

Of course, all these features of a good explanation are bound by context. As contexts shift, standards of rigor can change. In fact, even the ranking of these factors can vary with context. The desire for simplicity may have to be sacrificed to gain a more powerful explanation. Conservatism may have to give way in order to overcome some fundamental difficulty. And so on. Yet using standards of this kind often allows us to decide that a particular explanation is both strong and clearly better than any of its competitors. In such cases, an inference to the best explanation will have strong inductive support. At other times, no clear winner or even reasonable contender emerges. In such cases, an inference to the best explanation will be correspondingly weak.

EXERCISE VIII

Which hypotheses would best explain the following events? In each case, indicate how strong the explanation is. In the process of deciding this, consider a number of alternative explanations.

(1) Your house begins to shake so violently that pictures fall off your walls.

(2) Your key will not open the door.

(3) People start putting television cameras on your lawn, and a man with a big smile comes walking up your driveway.

(4) Virtually all of the food in markets has suddenly been sold out.

(5) Large mysterious patterns of flattened wheat appear in the fields of Britain.

(6) You put on a dress and notice that there are no pockets on the front.

(7) A cave is found containing the bones of both prehistoric men and now-extinct predators.

(8) You awaken to the sound of a choir of angels.

ARGUMENTS FROM ANALOGY

Another common kind of inductive argument is an *argument from analogy*. We often rely on such arguments in our everyday lives—when we buy shoes or a new novel or a meal or a car. Suppose, for example, that you need to buy a minivan for camping trips. You might decide to buy a Honda Odyssey minivan because you

---

[22] This discussion in many ways parallels and is indebted to the fifth chapter of W. V. Quine and J. S. Ullian, *The Web of Belief,* 2d ed. (New York: Random House, 1978).

bought a Honda Civic sedan ten years ago and it turned out to be reliable. These facts about a different car are supposed to support the prediction that the Odyssey will be reliable, because the Odyssey is similar to the Civic in many ways, such as its engine and transmission, as well as its manufacturer. Of course, no matter how great the Civic was, the Odyssey might be a lemon. Nonetheless, similarities between Odysseys and Civics can provide some reasons to believe that the Odyssey will be reliable. Indeed, you might not be able to find any better basis for your belief if the Odyssey is such a new model that there is no good statistical evidence for or against its reliability.

Arguments from analogy are not confined to everyday life; they are also common in science. Suppose archaeologists identify certain artifacts as sacrificial knives for religious ceremonies, and then they find another artifact that is similar to these sacrificial knives in the respects that the new artifact has a similar size and shape, is also made of gold and jewels, is carved with certain special patterns, and so on. On the basis of these similarities, archaeologists might conclude that this new artifact is probably also a ceremonial knife, or at least a knife, or at least something ceremonial. Of course, they could be wrong, but this pattern of reasoning is still common and forceful.

Such arguments from analogy have diverse contents, but they share a form that can be represented this way:

(1) Object A has properties P, Q, R, and so on.

(2) Objects B, C, D, and so on also have properties P, Q, R, and so on.

(3) Objects B, C, D, and so on have property X.

(4) Therefore, object A probably also has property X.

In the archaeological example, A is the newly discovered artifact, and B, C, D, and so on are the previously discovered knives. P, Q, R, and so on are the similar size, shape, materials, and carvings. X is the property of being used as a knife in religious sacrifices. Premise 3 says that the previously discovered artifacts have this property, and the conclusion, (4), says that the newly discovered artifact probably also has this property. Other arguments from analogy might refer to more or fewer properties and more or fewer objects, although at least two objects are needed for an analogy.[23]

Such arguments are called arguments from *analogy* because they are based on analogies between one thing (A) and some other things (B, C, D, . . .). When we draw an analogy, we often specify certain respects in which the two things are similar, but sometimes we say just that they are similar without specifying any particular respects. Such analogies are not used only in arguments. They are also pervasive in poetry, and they can be helpful in explanations to make a subject matter easier to understand. (See Chapter 1 on metaphors.) We get an *argument*

---

[23] Some analogical arguments refer to kinds or sets of objects, but we will simplify our discussion by focusing on analogical arguments about particular objects.

from analogy only when premises are supposed to support a conclusion because of a claimed analogy between the objects mentioned only in the premises and the object mentioned in the conclusion.

Arguments from analogy are usually not deductively valid. Even if the other knives were used in religious sacrifices, the newly discovered knife might turn out to have been used for some other purpose, such as shaving the king. Moreover, this form of reasoning is nonmonotonic, which is a mark of an inductive argument. The argument is destroyed if we add another premise that the newly discovered knife has a certain property that none of the other knives has, such as that its bottom is marked "Made in the U.S.A." Nonetheless, that they are neither deductively valid nor monotonic is not a criticism of arguments from analogy, since they are not claimed to be deductively valid. In short, they are not deductive, but inductive. Like other inductive arguments, arguments from analogy can still provide some reasons, and even strong reasons, for their conclusions.

How can we tell whether an argument from analogy is strong or weak? What kinds of standards should we apply? Of course, the premises must be *true*. If the previously discovered artifacts are not really ceremonial knives after all, or if they do not really have the same carvings on their handles as the newly discovered artifact, then the argument from analogy can be criticized and rejected on this basis.

Another obvious requirement is that the cited similarities must be *relevant and important*. Suppose someone argues that his old Civic sedan was red and had four doors and a sunroof, and his new Ford truck also has these properties, so his new Ford truck is probably as reliable as his old Civic. This argument is weak because the cited similarities are irrelevant to reliability. Even when similarities *are* relevant, some are more important than others. That two cars both have six-cylinder engines is relevant to reliability, but it is not so important to reliability as two different models using the same type of engine made on the same assembly line. To determine which properties are relevant and important, we need to apply background beliefs, such as that reliability depends on the drivetrain rather than on the body, and that six-cylinder engines vary a great deal in their reliability. Without relying on such background beliefs, it is difficult to evaluate arguments from analogy. Still, even if we do not know which respects are important, we could try to cite objects that are analogous in as many relevant respects as possible. By increasing the number of different respects for which the analogy holds, we can increase the likelihood that the important respects will be on our list.

Another factor that affects the strength of an argument from analogy is the presence of *relevant disanalogies*. Since arguments from analogy are nonmonotonic, as we saw, a strong argument from analogy can become weak if we add a premise that states an important disanalogy. For example, if the Honda Odyssey was made in a different country by a different designer than the Honda Civic, or if these models have totally different transmissions, then the Civic's reliability would not provide much support for the reliability of the Odyssey. Other disanalogies, such as different colors and seats, will not matter. And background knowledge will often be required in order for us to determine how important a disanalogy is. Still, an argument from analogy is stronger if there are fewer and less-important undermining disanalogies between the object (*A*) in the conclusion and the objects (*B, C, D, . . .*) mentioned in the premises.

Notice, however, that some disanalogies will not undermine an argument from analogy. If the Odyssey has a different transmission than the Civic, but the only differences were introduced by top engineers specifically to increase its reliability, then this disanalogy will not undermine the argument from analogy. Differences that point to more reliability rather than less might even strengthen the argument from analogy.

Other disanalogies can also increase the strength of an argument from analogy. Suppose I have owned or heard about many Hondas: *B, C, D,* and so on. If all these Hondas were 1992 Civics, then an argument from analogy to a conclusion about the Honda Odyssey might be affected by the many differences between 1992 Civics and Odysseys. However, if many Hondas of different models from different years all turned out to be reliable, the differences among these Hondas are probably not very important to their reliability, so an argument from analogy that cites all these Hondas (as *B, C, D,* and so on) would not be weakened if the Odyssey is different from some of the older Hondas in these respects. Thus, differences among the cases cited only in premises can strengthen an argument from analogy.

Finally, the strength of an argument from analogy also depends on its conclusion. Suppose the old Civic ran for ten years without needing any repairs. On the basis of important similarities between Civics and Odysseys, we might reach different conclusions:

(i) The Odyssey will run for ten years without any repairs.

(ii) The Odyssey will probably run for ten years without any repairs.

(iii) The Odyssey will probably run for at least five years without any repairs.

(iv) The Odyssey will probably be very reliable.

(v) The Odyssey will probably be reliable.

As we go down the line, these conclusions get weaker, in the sense that each conclusion implies but is not implied by the one above it (assuming that a car is very reliable if it runs even for three years without any repairs). And it should be clear that an analogy between Civics and Odysseys provides stronger support for conclusion (v) than for conclusion (i). More generally, an argument from analogy becomes stronger as its conclusion becomes weaker.

In sum, then, an argument from analogy is stronger when:

(a) It cites more and more-important similarities.

(b) There are fewer or less-important differences between the object in the conclusion and the other objects in the premises.

(c) The objects cited only in the premises are more diverse.

(d) The conclusion is weaker.

It will not always be easy to apply these criteria, because they often depend on background knowledge, but this list at least points us toward the main factors that need to be considered in evaluating an argument from analogy.[24]

EXERCISE IX

For each of the following arguments, state whether the indicated changes would make the argument weaker or stronger, and explain why. The strength of the argument might not be affected at all. If so, say why it is not affected.

(1) My friend and I have seen many movies together, and we have always agreed on whether they are good or bad. My friend liked the movie *Pulp Fiction*. So I probably will like *Pulp Fiction* as well.

Would this argument be weaker or stronger if:

   (a) The only movies that my friend and I have watched together are comedies, and *Pulp Fiction* is not a comedy.

   (b) My friend and I have seen very many, very different movies together.

   (c) My friend and I always watched movies together on Fridays, but my friend watched *Pulp Fiction* on a Saturday.

   (d) The conclusion claims that I definitely will like *Pulp Fiction*.

   (e) The conclusion claims that I probably won't think that *Pulp Fiction* is total trash.

(2) All the students from this high school with high grades and high board scores did well in college. Joe also had high grades and board scores. So he will probably do well in college.

Would this argument be weaker or stronger if:

   (a) Joe is lazy, but the other students worked hard.

   (b) Joe got good grades and board scores, but he did not go to the same high school as the students with whom he is being compared.

   (c) Joe also got good grades, but he did not get good board scores or go to the same high school as the students with whom he is being compared.

   (d) Joe is going to a different college than the students with whom he is being compared.

   (e) Joe is premed, but the other students are majoring in physical education.

---

[24] For more on arguments from analogy, see the section on legal precedents in Chapter 12 and the section on analogical reasoning in ethics in Chapter 13.

(f) Joe is majoring in physical education, but the other students are premed.

(g) The conclusion is that Joe will graduate first in his class.

(3) A new drug cures a serious disease in rats. Rats are similar to humans in many respects. Therefore, the drug will probably cure the same disease in humans.

Would this argument be weaker or stronger if:

(a) The disease affects the liver, and rat livers are very similar to human livers.

(b) The drug does not cure this disease in cats.

(c) The drug has to be injected into the rat's tail to be effective.

(d) No drug of this general type has been used on humans before.

EXERCISE X

Using the criteria mentioned above, evaluate each of the following arguments as strong or weak. Explain your answers. Be sure to specify the properties on which the analogy is based, as well as any background beliefs on which your evaluation depends.

(1) This landscape by Cézanne is beautiful. He did another painting of a similar scene around the same time. So it is probably beautiful too.

(2) My aunt had a Siamese cat that bit me, so this Siamese cat will probably bite me too.

(3) The students I know who took this course last year got grades of A. I am a lot like them, since I am also smart and hardworking; and the course this year covers very similar material. So I will probably get an A.

(4) This politician was convicted of cheating in his marriage, and he will have to face similarly strong temptations in his public duties, so he will probably cheat in political life as well.

(5) A very high minimum wage led to increased unemployment in one country. That country's economy is similar to the economy in a different country. So a very high minimum wage will probably lead to increased unemployment in the other country as well.

(6) Black rule will probably work smoothly in South Africa, because it has worked smoothly in Zimbabwe, which is similar in many ways to South Africa.

(7) I feel pain when someone hits me hard on the head with a baseball bat. Your body is a lot like mine. So you would probably feel pain if I hit

you hard on the head with a baseball bat. (This is related to the "Problem of Other Minds.")

(8) "We may observe a very great [similarity] between this earth which we inhabit, and the other planets, Saturn, Jupiter, Mars, Venus, and Mercury. They all revolve around the sun, as the earth does, although at different distances and in different periods. They borrow all their light from the sun, as the earth does. Several of them are known to revolve around their axis like the earth, and, by that means, must have a like succession of day and night. Some of them have moons that serve to give them light in the absence of the sun, as our moon does to us. They are all, in their motions, subject to the same law of gravitation, as the earth is. From all this [similarity], it is not unreasonable to think, that those planets may, like our earth, be the habitation of various orders of living creatures. There is some probability in this conclusion from analogy."[25]

(9) It is immoral for a doctor to lie to a patient about a test result, even if the doctor thinks that lying is in the patient's best interest. We know this because even doctors would agree that it would be morally wrong for a financial adviser to lie to them about a potential investment, even if the financial adviser thinks that this lie is in the doctor's best interests.

(10) Chrysler was held legally liable for damages due to defects in the suspension of its Corvair. The defects in the Pinto gas tank caused injuries that were just as serious. Thus, Ford should also be held legally liable for damages due to those defects.

EXERCISE XI

More-detailed examples of arguments from analogy can be found in Part 2.

(1) In Chapter 12, critics argue that preferential treatment is unconstitutional because of analogies to other forms of racial discrimination that were found unconstitutional in precedents.

(2) In Chapter 13, Thomson defends the morality of abortion by means of an analogy to a kidnapped violinist.

(3) In Chapter 14, Alvarez and Asaro argue that some material in the KT boundary clay probably came from outer space because it is similar in composition to materials found in meteors.

(4) In Chapter 15, Searle argues that computers cannot think just by virtue

---

[25] Thomas Reid, *Essays on the Intellectual Powers of Man* (Cambridge: M.I.T. Press, 1969), Essay 1, Section 4, p. 48.

of their formal structure, because of an analogy to a Chinese room with the same formal structure.

Evaluate each of these arguments by applying the criteria discussed above.

DISCUSSION QUESTION

Reconstruct and evaluate the following argument from analogy for the existence of God:

> In crossing a heath, suppose I pitched my foot against a *stone,* and were asked how the stone came to be there; I might possibly answer, that, for anything I knew to the contrary, it had lain there forever: nor would it, perhaps, be very easy to show the absurdity of this answer. But suppose I had found a *watch* upon the ground, and it should be inquired how the watch happened to be in that place. . . . When we come to inspect the watch, we perceive—what we could not discover in the stone—that its several parts are framed and put together for a purpose. . . . This mechanism being observed . . . the inference we think is inevitable, that the watch must have had a maker. . . . Every indication of contrivance, every manifestation of design, which existed in the watch, exists in the works of nature, with the difference on the side of nature of being greater and more. . . . Were there no example in the world of contrivance except that of the *eye,* it would be alone sufficient to support the conclusion which we draw from it, as to the necessity of an intelligent Creator. . . . Its coats and humors, constructed as the lenses of a telescope are constructed, for the refraction of rays of light to a point, which forms the proper action of the organ; the provision in its muscular tendons for turning its pupil to the object, similar to that which is given to the telescope by screws, and upon which power of direction in the eye the exercise of its office as an optical instrument depends; . . . these provisions compose altogether an apparatus, a system of parts, a preparation of means, so manifest in their design, so exquisite in their contrivance, so successful in their issue, so precious, and so infinitely beneficial in their use, as, in my opinion, to bear down all doubt that can be raised on the subject.[26]

---

[26] William Paley, *Natural Theology* (New York; Bobbs-Merrill, 1963), pp. 3, 4, 13, and 32.

Chapter Nine

TAKING CHANCES

This chapter offers an elementary discussion of reasoning about choices when outcomes involve risk. It shows how the related notions of *probability, expected monetary value,* and *relative value* bear on choices of this kind. The chapter concludes with an examination of two common mistakes in reasoning about probabilities: committing the so-called *gambler's fallacy,* and failing to understand the phenomenon of *regression to the mean.*

THE LANGUAGE OF PROBABILITY

In everyday life we express various degrees of certainty about the world around us. Looking out the window we might say that there is a fifty-fifty chance of rain. More vividly, someone might have remarked that the Dodgers did not have the chance of a pound of butter in hell of repeating the 1988 World Championship. In each case, the speaker is indicating the relative strength of the evidence for the occurrence or nonoccurrence of some event. To say that there is a fifty-fifty chance that it will rain indicates that we hold that the evidence is equally strong that it will rain rather than not rain. The events strike us as being equally likely. The metaphor in the second statement indicates that the person who uttered it believed that the probability of the Dodgers repeating as World Champions was essentially nonexistent.

Our common language provides various ways of expressing probabilities. The guarding terms discussed in Chapter 2 provide examples of informal ways of expressing probability commitments. Thus, someone might say that it is very unlikely that Colin Powell will seek the Republican presidential nomination without saying precisely *how* unlikely it is. We can make our probability claims more precise by using numbers. Sometimes we use percentages; for example, the weather bureau might say that there is a 75 percent chance of snow tomorrow. This can naturally be changed to a fraction: the probability is 3/4 that it will snow tomorrow. Finally, this fraction can be changed into a decimal expression: there is a .75 probability that it will snow tomorrow.

The probability scale has two endpoints: the absolute certainty that the event will occur and the absolute certainty that it will not occur. Because you cannot do better than absolute certainty, a probability can neither rise above 100 percent nor drop below 0 percent (neither above 1, nor below 0). (This should sound fairly obvious, but it is possible to become confused when combining percentages and fractions, as when Yogi Berra was supposed to have said that success is one-third talent and 75 percent hard work.) Of course, what we normally call *probability* claims usually fall between these two endpoints. For this reason it sounds somewhat peculiar to say that there is a 100 percent chance of rain and just plain weird to say the chance of rain is 1 out of 1. Even so, these peculiar ways of speaking cause no procedural difficulties and rarely come up in practice.

A PRIORI PROBABILITY

When people make probability claims, we have a right to ask why they assign the probability they do. In the previous chapter, we saw how statistical procedures

can be used for establishing probability claims. Here we will examine the so-called
a priori approach to probabilities. A simple example will bring out the differences
between these two approaches. We might wonder what the probability is of drawing
an ace from a standard deck of 52 cards. Using the procedure discussed in the
previous chapter, we could make a great many random draws from the deck
(replacing the card each time) and then form a statistical generalization concerning
the results. Using this approach we would discover that an ace *tends* to come up
roughly 1/13 of the time. From this we could draw the conclusion that the chance
of drawing an ace is 1 in 13.

But we do not have to go to all this trouble. We can assume that each of the
52 cards has an equal chance of being selected. Given this, an obvious a priori
line of reasoning runs as follows: there are 4 aces in a standard 52-card deck, so
the probability of selecting one randomly is 4 in 52. That reduces to 1 chance in
13. Here the set of favorable outcomes is a subset of the total number of
equally likely (equi-likely) outcomes, and to compute the probability that the
favorable outcome will occur, we merely divide the number of favorable
outcomes by the total number of possible outcomes. This fraction gives us the
probability that the event will occur on a random draw. Since all outcomes
here are equally likely:

$$\text{Probability of drawing an ace} = \frac{\text{number of aces}}{\text{total number of cards}} = \frac{4}{52} = \frac{1}{13}$$

Notice that in coming to our conclusion that there is 1 chance in 13 of
randomly drawing an ace from a 52-card deck, we simply used mathematical
reasoning. This illustrates the a priori approach to probabilities. It is called the
a priori approach because we arrive at the result simply by reasoning about
the circumstances.

In calculating the probability of drawing an ace from a 52-card deck, we took
the ratio of favorable equi-likely outcomes to total equi-likely outcomes. Generally,
then, the probability of a hypothesis *h,* symbolized "Pr(*h*)," when all outcomes are
equally likely, is expressed as follows:

$$\Pr(h) = \frac{\text{favorable outcomes}}{\text{total outcomes}}$$

We can illustrate this principle with a slightly more complicated example. What
is the probability of throwing an 8 on the cast of two dice? Here are all the equi-
likely ways in which two dice can turn up on a single cast:

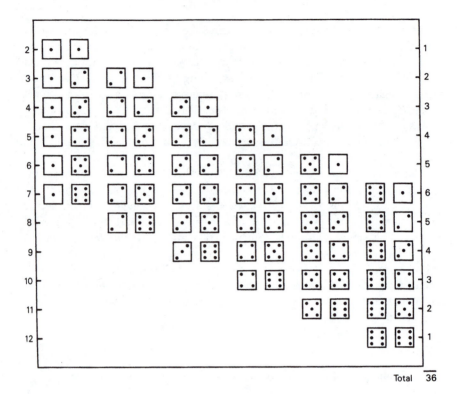

Total   36

As indicated, 5 of the 36 possible outcomes produce an 8, so the probability of throwing an 8 is 5/36.

EXERCISE 1

Using the above chart, answer the following questions:

(1) Which is more likely, throwing a 5 or an 8?

(2) What is the probability of throwing either a 5 or an 8?

(3) Which is more likely, to throw a 5 or an 8, or a 2 or a 7?

(4) What is the probability of throwing a 10 or above?

(5) What is the probability of throwing a value from 4 to 6?

SOME LAWS OF PROBABILITY

Suppose you have determined the probability that certain simple events will occur; how do you go about applying this to complicated combinations of events? This is a complex question, and one that can be touched on only lightly in this text.

There are, however, some simple rules of probability that are worth knowing because they can guide us in making choices when outcomes are uncertain.

By convention, events are assigned probabilities between 0 and 1 (inclusive). An event is either going to occur or not occur; that, at least, is certain (that is, it has a probability of 1). From this it is easy to see how to calculate the probability that the event will not occur given the probability that it will occur: we simply subtract the probability that it will occur from 1. This is our first rule:

RULE 1.   The probability that an event will not occur is 1 minus the probability that it will occur. Symbolically:

$$\Pr(\text{not } h) = 1 - \Pr(h)$$

For example, the probability of drawing an ace from a standard deck is 1 in 13, so the probability of *not* drawing an ace is 12 in 13. (This makes sense because there are 48 out of 52 ways of not drawing an ace, and this reduces to 12 chances in 13.)

RULE 2.   Given two independent events, the probability of their both occurring is the product of their individual probabilities. Symbolically (where h_1 and h_2 are independent):

$$\Pr(h_1 \ \& \ h_2) = \Pr(h_1) \times \Pr(h_2)$$

Here the word "independent" needs explanation. Suppose you randomly draw a card from the deck, then put it back (shuffle) and draw again. In this case the outcome of the first draw provides no information about the outcome of the second draw, so it is *independent* of it. What is the probability of drawing two aces in a row using this system? Using Rule 2, we see that the answer is $1/13 \times 1/13$, or 1 chance in 169.

The situation is different if we do not replace the card after the first draw. Rule 2 does not apply to this case because the two events are no longer independent. The chances of getting an ace on the first draw are still 1 in 13, but if an ace is drawn (and not returned to the pack) then there is one less ace in the deck, so the chances of drawing an ace on the next draw are reduced to 3 in 51. Thus the probability of drawing two consecutive aces (without returning the first draw to the deck) are $4/52 \times 3/51$, or 1 in 221, which is considerably lower than 1 in 169.

If we want to extend Rule 2 to cover cases in which the events are not independent, we will have to speak of the probability of one event occurring *given that another has occurred*. The probability that h_2 will occur given that h_1 has occurred is called the *conditional* probability of h_2 on h_1, and is usually symbolized thus: $\Pr(h_2/h_1)$. Rule 2 can be modified as follows to deal with cases where events need not be independent:

RULE 2G.   Given two events, the probability of their both occurring is the probability of the first occurring times the probability of the second occurring, given that the first has occurred.

$$\Pr(h_1 \ \& \ h_2) = \Pr(h_1) \times \Pr(h_2/h_1)$$

Notice that in the event that h_1 and h_2 are independent, the probability of h_2 is not related to the occurrence of h_1, so the probability of h_2 on h_1 is simply the probability of h_2. Thus, rule 2 is simply a special case of the more general Rule 2G.

We can extend these rules to cover more than two events. For example, with Rule 2, however many events we might consider, provided that they are independent of each other, the probability of all of them occurring is the product of each one of them occurring. For example, the chances of flipping a coin and having it come up heads is 1 chance in 2. What are the chances of flipping a coin 8 times and having it come up heads every time? The answer is:

$$1/2 \times 1/2 \times 1/2 \times 1/2 \times 1/2 \times 1/2 \times 1/2 \times 1/2$$

which equals 1 chance in 256.

Our next rule allows us to answer questions of the following kind: What are the chances of either an 8 or a 2 coming up on a single throw of the dice? Going back to the chart, we saw that we could answer this question by counting the number of ways in which a 2 can come up (which is 1) and adding this to the number of ways in which an 8 can come up (which is 5). We could then conclude that the chances of one or the other of them coming up is 6 chances in 36, or 1/6. The principle involved in this calculation can be stated as follows:

RULE 3.   The probability that at least one of two mutually exclusive events will occur is the sum of the probabilities that each of them will occur. Symbolically (where h_1 and h_2 are mutually exclusive):

$$\mathrm{Pr}(h_1 \text{ or } h_2) = \mathrm{Pr}(h_1) + \mathrm{Pr}(h_2)$$

To say that events are *mutually exclusive* means that they cannot both occur. You cannot, for example, get both a 10 and an 8 on the same cast of two dice. You might, however, throw neither one of them.

When events are not mutually exclusive, the rule for calculating disjunctive probabilities becomes more complicated. Suppose, for example, that exactly half the class is female and exactly half the class is over 19 and the age distribution is the same for females and males. What is the probability that a randomly selected student will be either a female or over 19? If we simply add the probabilities (1/2 + 1/2 = 1) we would get the result that we are certain to pick a female over 19. But that answer is wrong, since a quarter of the class is male and not over 19, and one of them might have been randomly selected. The correct answer is that the chances are 3/4 of randomly selecting someone who is either female or over 19.

We can see that this is the correct answer by examining the following table, which looks something like a truth table:

Female	Over 19	Percentage of Class
Yes	Yes	25
Yes	No	25
No	Yes	25
No	No	25

It is easy to see that in 75 percent of the cases a randomly selected student will be either female or over 19.

A general formulation for the rule governing the calculation of disjunctive probabilities is stated as follows:

RULE 3G.   The probability that at least one of two events will occur is the sum of the probabilities that each of them will occur, minus the probability that they both occur.

$$\Pr(h_1 \text{ or } h_2) = \Pr(h_1) + \Pr(h_2) - \Pr(h_1 \ \& \ h_2)$$

If h_1 and h_2 are mutually exclusive, then $\Pr(h_1 \ \& \ h_2) = 0$, and Rule 3G reduces to Rule 3.

Before stating Rule 4, we can think about a particular example. What is the probability of tossing heads at least once in 8 tosses of a coin? Here it is tempting to reason in the following way. There is a 50 percent chance of getting heads on the first toss and a 50 percent chance of getting heads on the second toss, so after 2 tosses it is already certain that we will toss heads at least once, and thus after 8 tosses there should be a 400 percent chance. In other words, you cannot miss. There are two good reasons for thinking that this argument is fishy. First, probability can never exceed 100 percent; and second, there must be some chance, however small, that we could toss a coin 8 times and not have it come up heads.

The best way to look at this question is to restate it so that the first two rules can be used. Instead of asking what the probability is that heads will come up at least once, we can ask what the probability is that it will *not* come up at least once. To say that heads will not come up even once is equivalent to saying that tails will come up 8 times in a row. By Rule 2 we know how to compute that probability: it is 1/2 multiplied by itself 8 times, and that, as we saw, is 1/256. Finally, by Rule 1 we know that the probability that this will not happen (that heads will come up at least once) is $1 - 1/256$. In other words, the probability of tossing heads at least once in 8 tosses is 255/256. That comes close to a certainty, but it is not quite a certainty.

We can generalize these results as follows:

RULE 4.   The probability that an event will occur at least once in a series of independent trials is simply 1 minus the probability that it will *not* occur in that number of trials. Symbolically (where n is the number of independent trials):

The probability that h will occur at least once in n trials =
$$1 - \Pr(\text{not } h)^n$$

Strictly speaking, Rule 4 is unnecessary since it can be derived from Rules 1 and 2, but it is important to know because it blocks a common misunderstanding about probabilities. *People often think that something is a sure thing when it is not.*

EXERCISE II

Compute the probability of making the following draws from a standard 52-card deck:

(1) Drawing either a 7 or a 5 on a single draw.

(2) Drawing neither a 7 nor a 5 on a single draw.

(3) Drawing a 7 and then, without returning the first card to the deck, drawing a 5 on the next draw.

(4) Same as (3), but the first card is returned to the deck and the deck is shuffled after the first draw.

(5) Drawing at least 1 spade in a series of 4 consecutive draws, when the card drawn is not returned to the deck.

(6) Same as (5), but the card is returned to the deck after each draw and the deck is reshuffled.

EXPECTED MONETARY VALUE

It is obvious that having some sense of probable outcomes is important for running our lives. If we hear that there is a 95 percent chance of rain, this usually provides a good enough reason for calling off a picnic. But the exact relationship between probabilities and decisions is complex and often misunderstood. The best way to illustrate these misunderstandings is looking at lotteries in which the numbers are fixed and clear.

A dollar bet in a lottery might make you as much as $10 million. That sounds good; why not take a shot at $10 million for only a dollar? Of course, there is not much chance of winning the lottery–only 1 chance in 20 million–and that sounds bad. Why throw $1 away on nothing? So we are pulled in two directions. What we want to know is just how good the bet is. Is it, for example, better or worse than a wager in some other lottery? To answer questions of this kind, we need to introduce the notion of *expected monetary value*.

The idea of expected monetary value takes into account three features that determine whether a bet is financially good or not: the probability of winning, the amount of money you gain if you win, and the amount you lose if you lose. Suppose that on a $1 ticket there is 1 chance in 20 million of winning the New York State Lottery, and you will get $10 million from the state if you do. First, it is important to remember that if the state pays you $10 million, what you have actually gained on your $1 ticket is $9,999,999. The state, after all, still has your original $1. So the amount gained equals the payoff minus the cost of betting. This is not something that those who win huge lotteries worry about, but taking into account the cost of betting can become important when this cost becomes high relative to the size of the payoff. There is nothing complicated about the amount you will lose when you lose on a $1 ticket: it is $1.

We compute the *expected monetary value* or *financial worth* of a bet in the following way: Expected monetary value equals

The probability of winning times the amount of money one gains by winning,

minus

the probability of losing times the amount of money one loses by losing.

In the example we are looking at, a person who buys a $1 ticket in the lottery has 1 chance in 20 million of gaining $9,999,999, and 19,999,999 chances in 20 million of losing a dollar. So the expected monetary value of this wager equals:

$(1/20,000,000 \times \$9,999,999)$

minus

$(19,999,999/20,000,000 \times \$1)$

That comes out to minus $.50.

What does this mean? One way of looking at it is as follows: If you could somehow buy up all the lottery tickets and thus ensure that you would win, your $20 million investment would net you $10 million, or $.50 on the dollar—certainly a bad investment. Another way of looking at the situation is as follows: If you invested a great deal of money in the lottery over many millions of years, you could expect to win eventually, but, in the long run, you would be losing fifty cents on every ticket you bought. One last way of looking at the situation is this: you go down to your local drugstore and buy a *blank* lottery ticket for $.50. Since it is blank, you have no chance of winning, with the result that you lose $.50 every time you bet. Although almost no one looks at the matter in this way, this is, in effect, what you are doing *over the long run* when you buy lottery tickets.

We are now in a position to draw a distinction between a favorable expected monetary value and an unfavorable expected monetary value. The expected monetary value is favorable when it is greater than zero. Changing our example, suppose the chances of hitting a $20 million payoff on a $1 bet are 1 in 10 million. In this case, the state still has the $1 you paid for the ticket, so your gain is actually $19,999,999. The expected monetary value is calculated as follows:

$(1/10 \text{ million} \times \$19,999,999)$

minus

$(9,999,999/10,000,000 \times \$1)$

That comes to $1. So financially this is a good bet. For *in the long run* you will gain $1 for every $1 you bet in such a lottery.

The rule, then, is this: If the expected monetary value of the bet is more than zero, then the expected monetary value is *favorable;* if the expected monetary value of the bet is less than zero, then the expected monetary value is *unfavorable.* If the expected monetary value of the bet is zero, then the bet is *neutral*—a waste of time as far as money is concerned.

EXERCISE III

Compute the probability and the expected monetary value for the following bets. Each time, you lay down $1 to bet that a certain kind of card will be drawn from a standard 52-card deck. If you win, you collect the amount indicated, so your gain is $1 less. If you lose, of course, you lose your $1.

> Example: Draw a seven of spades. Win: $26.
> Probability of winning = 1/52
> Expected value: $(1/52 \times \$25) - (51/52 \times \$1) = -\$.50$

(1) Draw a 7 of spades or a 7 of clubs. Win: $26.

(2) On two consecutive draws (without returning the first card to the deck), draw a 7 of spades, then a 7 of clubs. Win: $1,989.

(3) On two consecutive draws (without returning the first card to the deck), do not draw a club. Win: $1.78.

(4) Same as in (3), but this time the card is returned to the deck and the deck is shuffled before the second draw. Win: $1.78.

EXPECTED RELATIVE VALUE

Given that actual lotteries usually have an extremely unfavorable expected monetary value, why do millions of people invest billions of dollars in them each year? Part of the answer is that some people are stupid, superstitious, or both. People will sometimes reason, "Somebody has to win; why not me?" They can also convince themselves that their lucky day has come. But that is not the whole story, for most people who put down money on lottery tickets realize that the bet is a bad bet, but think that it is worth doing anyway. People fantasize about what they will do with the money if they win, and that is fun. Furthermore, if the bet is only $1, and the person making the bet is not desperately poor, losing is not going to hurt much. Even if the expected monetary value on the lottery ticket is the loss of fifty cents, this might strike someone as a reasonable price for the fun of thinking about winning. So a bet that is bad from a purely monetary point of view might be acceptable when other factors are considered.

The reverse situation can also arise: a bet may be unreasonable, even though it has a positive expected monetary value. Suppose, for example, that you are allowed to participate in a lottery in which a $1 ticket gives you one chance in 10 million of getting a payoff of $20 million. Here, as noted above, the expected monetary value of a $1 bet is a profit of $1, so from the point of view of expected monetary value it is a good bet. This makes it sound reasonable to bet in this lottery, and a small bet probably is reasonable. But under these circumstances, would it be reasonable for people to sell everything they owned to buy lottery tickets? The answer to this is almost certainly no, for even though the expected monetary value is positive, the odds of winning are still extremely low, and the loss of someone's total resources would be personally catastrophic.

When we examine the effects that success or failure will have on a *particular* person relative to his or her own needs, resources, preferences, and so on, we are then examining what we shall call the *expected relative value* or *utility* of a choice. Considerations of this kind often force us to make adjustments in weighing the significance of costs and payoffs. In the examples we have just examined, the immediate catastrophic consequences of a loss outweigh the long-term gains one can expect from participating in the lottery.

Another factor that *typically* affects the expected relative value of a bet is the phenomenon known as the *diminishing marginal value* or *diminishing marginal utility* of a payoff as it gets larger. Diminishing marginal value is illustrated by the following example. Suppose someone offers to pay a debt by buying you a hamburger. Provided that the debt matches the cost of a hamburger and you feel like having one, you might go along with this. But suppose this person offers to pay off a debt ten times larger by buying you ten hamburgers? The chances are that you will reject the offer, for even though ten hamburgers *cost* ten times as much as one hamburger, they are not *worth* ten times as much to you. At some point you will get stuffed and not want any more. The notion of marginal value applies to money as well. If you are starving, $10 will mean a lot to you. You might be willing to work hard to get it. If you are wealthy, $10 more or less makes little difference; losing $10 might only be an annoyance.

Because of this phenomenon of diminishing marginal value, betting on lotteries is even a worse bet than most people suppose. A lottery with a payoff of $20 million sounds attractive, but it does not seem to be 20 times more attractive than a payoff of $1 million. So even if the expected monetary value of your $1 bet in a lottery is the loss of $.50, the actual value to you is really something less than this, and so the bet is worse even than it seemed at first.

In general, then, when payoffs are large, the expected relative value of the payoff to someone is reduced because of the effects of diminishing marginal value. But not always. It is possible to think of exotic cases in which expected relative value increases with the size of the payoff. Suppose a witch told you that she would turn you into a toad if you did not give her $10 million by tomorrow. You believe her, because you know for a fact that she has turned others into toads. You have $1 to your name and you are given the opportunity to participate in the first lottery described above, where a $1 ticket gives you one chance in 20 million of hitting a $10 million payoff. We saw that the expected monetary value of that wager was an unfavorable minus $.50. But now consider the relative value or utility of $1 to you if you are turned into a toad. Toads have no use for money, so to you, as a toad, the value of the dollar would drop to nothing. Thus, unless some other, more-attractive alternatives are available, it would be reasonable to buy a lottery ticket, despite the unfavorable expected monetary value of the wager.

EXERCISE IV

(1) Though the situation is somewhat far-fetched, suppose you are going to the drugstore to buy medicine for a friend who will die without it. You

have only $10–exactly what the medicine costs. Outside the drugstore a young man is playing three-card monte, a simple game in which the dealer shows you three cards, turns them over, shifts them briefly from hand to hand, and then lays them out, face down, on the top of a box. You are supposed to identify a particular card (usually the ace of spades), and if you do, you are paid even money. You yourself are a magician and know the sleight-of-hand trick that fools most people, and you are sure that you can guess the card correctly 9 times out of 10. First, what is the expected monetary value of a bet of $10? In this context, would it be reasonable to make this bet? Why?

(2) Provide an example of your own where a bet can be reasonable even though the expected monetary value is unfavorable, and another example where the bet is unreasonable even though the expected monetary value is favorable.

THE GAMBLER'S FALLACY

In assessing probabilities, a little knowledge can be a dangerous thing. Ordinary people often refer to something called *the law of averages*. "In the long run," they say, "things will even out (or average out)." Interpreted one way, this amounts to what mathematicians call *the law of large numbers,* and it is perfectly correct. For example, when flipping a coin, we expect it to come up heads half the time, so with 10 flips, it should come up heads 5 times. But if we actually check this out, we discover that the number of times it comes up heads in 10 flips varies significantly from this predicted value, sometimes coming up heads more than 5 times, sometimes coming up less. What the law of large numbers tells us is that the actual percentage of heads will tend to come closer to the theoretically predicted percentage of heads the more trials we make. If you flipped a coin a million times, it would be very surprising if the percentage of heads were more than 1 percent away from the predicted 50 percent.

When interpreted as the law of large numbers, the so-called law of averages contains an important truth, but it is often interpreted in a way that involves a fundamental fallacy. People sometimes reason in the following way: If they have had a run of bad luck, they should increase their bets because they are due for a run of good luck to even things out. Gambling systems are sometimes based on this fallacious idea. People keep track of the numbers that come up on a roulette wheel, trying to discover a number that has not come up for a long time. They then pile their money on that number on the assumption that it is due.

To see that this is a fallacy, we can go back to flipping coins again. Toss a coin until it comes up heads 3 times in a row. (This will take less time than you might imagine.) What is the probability that it will come up heads a fourth time?

Put crudely, some people think that the probability of it coming up heads again must be very small because a string of tails is needed to *even things out*. Less crudely, but just as mistakenly, someone might use Rule 2 and argue that the chances of a coin coming up 4 times in a row equal $1/2 \times 1/2 \times 1/2 \times 1/2$, or 1 chance in 16, so the chance of it coming up heads again after 3 occurrences of heads is also 1 in 16. But that is wrong. Our assumption is that the chances of getting heads on any given toss is 1/2. This is true whatever happened on the preceding tosses. So the probability from the start of tossing heads 4 times in a row is 1 in 16, but the probability of tossing heads again after tossing heads 3 times in a row is just 1/2.

REGRESSION TO THE MEAN

The notion of *regression to the mean* is somewhat subtle, but an illustration should help make this notion clear. In a famous example, Israeli flight instructors claimed to notice the following phenomenon: when cadet pilots were praised for their good flying, they tended to do worse the next time up, whereas those cadets who were criticized for poor flying tended to do better. The explanation seemed obvious: the good pilots who were praised got cocky and overconfident and thus did not fly so well, while the bad pilots who were criticized knuckled down and did better. It seemed, then, that bad flying should be criticized, but good flying should not be praised.

It is possible that the explanation and the moral drawn from it are correct. Another possibility is that the observed phenomenon had nothing to do with praise and blame but was simply the result of statistical variation. The statistical explanation runs as follows: in early flight training, performance varies considerably from flight to flight. Sometimes the student pilot does well, sometimes not. Given this variation, a good many of those who did well on one flight will not do so well on the next. Of course, the reverse will also be true: as a matter of chance, a good many who flew badly one time will fly well the next. Consequently, statistical variation alone may explain why a good number of those who did well and were praised will do worse on their next flight, and a good number of those who did badly and were criticized will do better. It could well be that the praise and criticism had nothing to do with these results. The results might have been exactly the same if none of the student pilots was either praised or blamed.

Most people do not know about the phenomenon of regression to the mean, and when they hear about it, they are often not impressed. Here is a simple experiment that illustrates its significance. Suppose you decide that coming up heads is good for a coin, whereas coming up tails is bad. You now take a jug with 100 pennies in it and spill them out on the table. You "praise" the coins that come up heads by putting a red dot of paint on each of them. You "criticize" the coins that came up tails by putting a blue dot of paint on each of them. You put the coins back in the jug, shake them up, and pour them back on the table. When you examine the coins you find that they fall into four (roughly equal) groups:

(1) Heads with red dots on them

(2) Tails with blue dots on them

(3) Heads with no dots on them

(4) Tails with no dots on them

In the first group, we have coins that were "praised" without making them worse. In the second group we have coins that were "criticized" without making them better. But the last two groups are more interesting. If a coin shows heads with no dot, it must have a blue dot on its other side; that is, it is a coin that was previously criticized for being tails. Furthermore, if a coin shows tails with no dot, it must have a red dot on the other side; that is, it must have been previously praised for coming up heads. In other words, roughly half the coins exhibit the phenomenon attributed to the Israeli cadet pilots: they either got worse after praise or got better after blame. On the assumption that little dots of paint would not significantly affect the way a coin will come up, it is obvious that the so-called praise and blame had nothing to do with the matter: the distribution into these four groups can be explained on statistical grounds alone. It is entirely possible that the actual praise and blame bestowed on the student pilots had no more effect on their performance than the make-believe praise and blame had on the performance of these pennies.

There is a moral to be drawn from this: when trying to understand a phenomenon, we should always ask whether it can be explained simply on probabilistic grounds. To use commonsense language, we should always entertain the possibility that the phenomenon is just a matter of luck—good or bad. More carefully, we should always entertain the possibility that regression to the mean is a significant component in accounting for some phenomenon.

EXERCISE V

Illustrate the phenomenon of regression to the mean by having, say, ten people take two successive simple true-false exams—answering all the questions by flipping a coin.

STRANGE THINGS HAPPEN

What are the chances of tossing a fair coin and having it come up heads 19 times in a row? The answer is 1/2 multiplied by itself 19 times, which equals 1 chance in 524,288. Those chances are so remote that you might think it could never really happen. You would be wrong. Of course, if you sat flipping a single coin, you might spend a very long time before you hit a sequence of 19 consecutive heads, but there is a way of getting this result (with some help from friends) in a single afternoon. First of all, you start out with $5,242.88 worth of pennies and put them in a large truck. (Actually, the truck would not be very large.) Dump the coins out and then pick up all the coins that come up heads. Put them back in the truck and repeat the procedure. Do that over and over again, always returning those that come up heads to the truck. With tolerably good luck, on the nineteenth dump of the coins you will get at least one coin that comes up heads again. Any such coin will have come up heads 19 times in a row.[1]

What is the point of this example? Specifically, it is intended to show that we often attribute abilities or the lack of abilities to people when, in fact, their performances may be statistically insignificant. When people invest with stockbrokers, they tend to shift when they lose money. When they hit upon a broker who earns them money, they stay and praise this broker's abilities. In fact, some financial advisers seem to be better than others—they have a long history of sound financial advice—but the financial community is, in many ways, like the truckload of pennies we have just examined. There are a great many brokers giving all sorts of different advice and, by chance alone, some of them are bound to give good advice. Furthermore, some of them are bound to have runs of success, just as some of the pennies dumped from the truck will have long strings of coming up heads. Thus, in some cases, what appears to be brilliance in predicting stock prices may be nothing more than a run of statistically expected good luck.

The gambling casinos of the world are like the truck full of pennies as well. With roulette wheels spinning in a great many places over a great deal of time, startling long runs are bound to occur. For example, in 1918, black came up 26 consecutive times on a roulette wheel in Monte Carlo. The odds against this are staggering. But before we can decide what to make of this event, we would have to judge it in the context of the vast number of times that the game of roulette has been played.

HONORS EXERCISE

Students familiar with computer programming should not find it difficult to write a program that will simulate a Monte Carlo roulette wheel and keep track of long runs of black and long runs of red. On a Monte Carlo wheel, the odds of coming up black are 18/37. The same odds hold for coming up red. Write such a program; run it for a day; then report back the longest runs.

SOME PUZZLES CONCERNING PROBABILITY

We will conclude the chapter with several puzzles that will draw on your understanding of many of the concepts we have just discussed.

---

[1] According to our colleague J. Laurie Snell, starting with 524,288 pennies gives you a 63.2 percent chance of having at least one of the pennies come up heads 19 times in a row. If this seems too risky, you could get more pennies and find more friends to help you with the experiment.

(1) You are presented with two bags, one containing two ham sandwiches and the other containing a ham sandwich and a cheese sandwich. You reach in one bag and draw out a ham sandwich. What is the probability that the other sandwich in the bag is also a ham sandwich?

(2) You are presented with three bags: two contain a chicken-fat sandwich and one contains a cheese sandwich. You are asked to guess which bag contains the cheese sandwich. You do so, and the bag you have selected is set aside. (You obviously have one chance in three of guessing correctly.) From the two remaining bags, one containing a chicken-fat sandwich is then removed. You are now given the opportunity to switch your selection to the remaining bag. Will such a switch increase, decrease, or leave unaffected your chances of correctly selecting the bag with the cheese sandwich in it?

(3) Fogelin's Palace in Border, Nevada, offers the following unusual bet. If you win, then you make a 50 percent profit on your bet; if you lose, you take a 40 percent loss. That is, if you bet $1 and win, you get back $1.50; if you bet $1 and lose, you get back $.60. The chances of winning are fifty-fifty. This sounds like a marvelous opportunity, but there is one hitch: in order to play, you must let your bet ride with its winnings, or losses, for four plays. For example, starting with $100, a four-bet sequence might look like this:

	Win	Win	Lose	Win
Total	$150	$225	$135	$202.50

At the end of this sequence, you can pick up $202.50, and thus make a $102.50 profit.

It seems that Fogelin's Palace is a good place to gamble, but consider the following argument on the other side. Because the chances of winning are fifty-fifty, you will, on the average, win half the time. But notice what happens in such a case:

	Win	Lose	Lose	Win
Total	$150	$90	$54	$81

So, even though you have won half the time, you have come out $19 behind.

Surprisingly, it does not matter what order the wins and losses come in; if two are wins and two are losses, you come out behind. (You can check this.) So, because you are only going to win roughly half the time, and when you win half the time you actually lose money, it now seems to be a bad idea to gamble at Fogelin's Palace. What should you do, gamble at Fogelin's Palace or not?

Answers to these puzzles appear in the Appendix at the end of this chapter.

DISCUSSION QUESTIONS

(1) In a remarkable study, Thomas Gilovich, Robert Vallone, and Amos Tversky found a striking instance of people's tendency to treat things as statistically significant when they are not. In professional basketball certain players have the reputation of being *streak shooters*. Streak shooters seem to score points in batches, then go cold and are not able to buy a basket. Stated more precisely, in streak shooting "the performance of a player during a particular period is significantly better than expected on the basis of the player's overall record" (295–96).

To test whether streak shooting really exists, the authors made a detailed study of a year's shooting record for the players on the Philadelphia 76ers. This team included Andrew Toney, noted around the league as being a streak shooter. The authors found no evidence for streak shooting, not even for Andrew Toney. How would you go about deciding whether streak shooting exists or not? If, as Gilovich, Vallone, and Tversky have argued, belief in this phenomenon is a "cognitive illusion," why do so many people, including most professional athletes, believe that it does exist?[2]

(2) The idea discussed earlier—that in making decisions under conditions of uncertainty we should consider the prospective gains and losses together with relevant probabilities—was clearly stated in *The Port-Royal Logic*, an influential work on logic published by the French writers Arnauld and Nicole in 1662. Speaking of the majority of mankind, these writers tell us that they

> fall into an illusion which is more deceptive in proportion as it appears to them to be reasonable; it is, that they regard only the greatness or importance of the advantage which they hope for, or of the disadvantage which they fear, without considering at all the probability which there is of that advantageous or disadvantageous event befalling.
>
> Thus, when they apprehend any great evil, as the loss of their livelihood or their fortune, they think it the part of prudence to neglect no precaution for preserving these; and if it is some great good, as the gain of a hundred thousand crowns, they think that they act wisely in seeking to obtain it, if the hazard is a small amount, however little likelihood there may be of a success.

To correct this defect in reasoning, these authors suggest that "It is

Continued on next page

---

[2] For more on this, see Thomas Gilovich, Robert Vallone, and Amos Tversky, "The Hot Hand in Basketball: On the Misperception of Random Sequences," *Cognitive Psychology* 17 (1985): 295–314.

necessary to consider not only the good and evil in themselves, but also the probability of their happening and not happening." This is sound advice, for it will prevent us from taking excessive precautions against large evils that are hardly likely to occur and from squandering money (for example, in lotteries) seeking enormous gains that we have only a minute chance of obtaining.

These authors conclude their discussion with a striking remark concerning the reverse situation that obtains concerning *salvation*.

> It belongs to infinite things alone, as eternity and salvation, that they cannot be equalled by any temporal advantage; and thus we ought never to place them in the balance with any of the things of the world. This is why the smallest degree of facility for the attainment of salvation is of higher value than all the blessings of the world put together; and why the slightest peril of being lost is more serious than all temporal evils, considered simply as evils.[3]

The authors conclude that we ought to spend all our efforts, however great, in an attempt to attain salvation.

This is obviously an argument concerning what we have called *expected monetary value* and *expected relative value*. State it clearly and evaluate it.

(3) The following article raises another interesting problem in dealing with eternity.[4] How would you answer it?

■ PLAYING GAMES WITH ETERNITY: THE DEVIL'S OFFER
By Edward J. Gracely

Suppose Ms C dies and goes to hell, or to a place that seems like hell. The devil approaches and offers to play a game of chance. If she wins, she can go to heaven. If she loses, she will stay in hell forever; there is no second chance to play the game. If Ms C plays today, she has a 1/2 chance of winning. Tomorrow the probability will be 2/3. Then 3/4, 4/5, 5/6, etc., with no end to the series. Thus every passing day increases her chances of winning. At what point should she play the game?

The answer is not obvious: after any given number of days spent waiting, it will still be possible to improve her chances by waiting yet another day. And any increase in the probability of winning a game with

---

[3] This passage comes from the final chapter of *The Port-Royal Logic,* generally thought to be by Arnauld and Nicole, translated by Thomas Spencer Baynes (Edinburgh: Sutherland and Knox, 1851), 369.

[4] Edward J. Gracely, "Playing Games with Eternity: The Devil's Offer," *Analysis* 48, no. 3 (1988): 113.

infinite stakes has an infinite utility. For example, if she waits a year, her probability of winning the game would be approximately .997268; if she waits one more day, the probability would increase to .997275, a difference of only .000007. Yet even .000007 multiplied by infinity is infinite.

On the other hand, it seems reasonable to suppose the cost of delaying for a day to be finite—a day's more suffering in hell. So the infinite expected benefit from a delay will always exceed the cost.

This logic might suggest that Ms C should wait forever, but clearly such a strategy would be self-defeating: why should she stay forever in a place in order to increase her chances of leaving it? So the question remains: what should Ms C do?* ∎

APPENDIX: ANSWERS TO PROBABILITY PUZZLES

(1) Your first instinct may be to suppose that the chances must be 50/50 that the remaining sandwich is a ham sandwich, because that was the probability of picking the bag containing two ham sandwiches to begin with. But don't forget that drawing out a ham sandwich gives some evidence concerning which bag was selected. Because the chances are *twice* as good for drawing a ham sandwich out of the bag containing two ham sandwiches than it is for drawing it from the bag with only one ham sandwich, the chances are two in three that you are in the bag that started with two ham sandwiches. Thus, the probability that the remaining sandwich is a ham sandwich is actually 2/3.

(2) Again, the most common reaction to this puzzle is wrong. It seems obvious that the original probability of selecting the cheese sandwich (one in three) will not be affected by anything that happens after the selection is made. But don't forget that new information is provided after the initial choice, which makes a difference. In fact, the chances of getting the cheese sandwich are 2/3 if you switch.

To see this, first notice that it will be a *bad* idea to switch only if you have started by selecting the bag with the cheese sandwich in it. The probability of starting with the bag with the cheese sandwich in it is, of course, 1/3. On the other hand, 2/3 of the time you will have started with a bag with a chicken fat sandwich in it, and switching will get you the bag containing the cheese. So it is a *good* idea to switch after one of the bags containing a chicken fat sandwich is removed because two out of three times you will get the bag containing the cheese sandwich by doing so.

---

* I would like to thank Janet Fleetwood for her very helpful comments on the first version of this paper.

(3) To get a handle on the Fogelin's Palace puzzle, we can consider a simpler case where the bet only has to ride twice. Now, once more, if you win one and lose one (in whatever order), you come out behind:

	Win	Lose
Total	$150	$90

	Lose	Win
Total	$60	$90

So, again, it may seem a bad idea to gamble in Fogelin's Palace.

The flaw in this reasoning is that not all possible cases have been considered. The following chart shows the results of all possible combinations of wins and losses:

W	W	$225
W	L	$90
L	W	$90
L	L	$36

It is easy to see that the total winnings with two wins outweigh the losses in the other three cases. More exactly, the expected value can be calculated by dividing the sum of the figures on the right (the total payoffs) by four (the total number of equally likely outcomes):

$$\text{Expected value} = \$441/4 = \$110.25$$

The same line of reasoning will show that four-bet sequences have a favorable expected value as well. You will, in fact, have more losing sequences than winning sequences, but, as in the examples above, winning sequences pay off enough to outweigh the more frequent losing sequences.

WHAT IS A FALLACY?

Good arguments can accomplish a great deal, but bad arguments can do a lot of harm. They can confuse and mislead. They can contribute to bad theories, bad decisions, and bad governments. To avoid these problems, it is important to learn how to recognize, analyze, and respond to bad arguments.

When inferences are defective, they are called *fallacious*. Some defective styles of reasoning get repeated over and over, and then we have an argumentative *fallacy*. The number and variety of argumentative fallacies is limited only by the imagination. Arguers display amazing cunning, subtlety, and ingenuity in their attempts to trick other people by means of arguments. People also commit a multitude of mistakes on their own. Consequently, there is little point in trying to construct a complete list of fallacies. What is crucial is to get a feel for the main kinds of fallacy. Once one's critical faculties are trained to spot the most common fallacies, one should be able to recognize many other kinds of fallacy as well.

FALLACIES OF CLARITY

In a good argument, a person states a conclusion clearly and then, with equal clarity, gives reasons for this conclusion. The arguments of everyday life often fall short of this standard. Usually, unclear language is a sign of unclear thought. There are times, however, when people are intentionally unclear. They might use unclarity for poetic effect or in order to leave details to be decided later. But often their goal is to confuse others. This is called *obfuscation*.

Before we look at the various ways in which language can be unclear, a word of caution is needed. There is no such thing as absolute clarity. Whether something is clear or not depends on the context in which it occurs. A botanist does not use common vocabulary in describing and classifying plants. At the same time, it would usually be foolish for a person to use botanical terms in describing the appearance of her backyard. Thus, as Aristotle said, it is the mark of an educated person not to expect more rigor than the subject matter will allow. Because clarity and rigor depend on context, it takes judgment and good sense to pitch an argument at the right level.

VAGUENESS

Perhaps the most common form of unclarity is *vagueness*. It arises when a concept applies along a continuum or a series of very small changes. The standard example is baldness. A person with a full head of hair is not bald. A person without a hair on his head is bald. In between, however, there is a range of cases in which we cannot say definitely whether the person is bald or not. These are called *borderline cases*. Here we say something less definite, such as that this person is "going bald."

Chapter Ten

FALLACIES

In this chapter we shall examine some of the standard ways in which arguments can be fallacious or defective. Defects in arguments will be considered under three main headings: fallacies of *clarity*, fallacies of *relevance*, and fallacies of *vacuity*. Fallacies of clarity arise when language is not used precisely enough for the context. *Vagueness* and *ambiguity*, two common forms of unclarity, will be defined and discussed in detail. Fallacies of relevance arise when a premise, true or not, is not adequately related to the conclusion. Such irrelevance comes in endless varieties, but we will focus on two of the most common forms: *arguments ad hominem* and *appeals to authority*. Fallacies of vacuity arise when an argument does not get anywhere. Arguments that *beg the question* fall into this category. So do positions that make themselves immune to criticism by being *self-sealing*.

Notice that our inability to apply the concept of baldness in this borderline case is not due to ignorance. It will not help, for example, to count the number of hairs on the person's head. Even if we knew the exact number, we would still not be able to say whether the person was bald or not. The same is true of most adjectives that concern properties admitting of degrees—for example, "rich," "healthy," "tall," "wise," and "ruthless." We can also encounter borderline cases with common nouns. Consider the common noun "game." Baseball is a game and so is chess, but how about tossing a Frisbee? Is that a game? Is Russian roulette a game? Are prizefighting and bullfighting games? As we try to answer these questions, we feel an inclination to say "Yes" and an inclination to say "No." This uncertainty shows that the concept admits of borderline cases.

For the most part, this feature of our language—the lack of sharply defined limits—causes little difficulty. In fact, this is a useful feature of our language, for suppose we *did* have to count the number of grains of salt between our fingers in order to determine whether or not we hold a *pinch* of salt. It would take a long time to follow a simple recipe that calls for a pinch of salt.

Non Sequitur   **by Wiley**

Yet difficulties can arise when borderline cases themselves are at issue. Suppose that a state passes a law forbidding all actions that offend a large number of people. The law is backed up by stiff fines and imprisonment. There will be many cases that clearly fall under this law and many cases that clearly do not fall under it. But in many cases, it will not be clear whether they fall under this law or not. Laws are sometimes declared unconstitutional for this very reason. Here we shall say that the law is vague. In calling the law vague, we are criticizing it. We are not simply noticing the existence of borderline cases, for there will usually be borderline cases no matter how careful we are. Instead, we are saying that there are *too many* borderline cases for this context. More precisely, we shall say that an expression in a given context is *vague* or is used vaguely if it leaves open too wide a range of borderline cases for the successful and legitimate use of that expression in that context.

Vagueness thus depends on context. To further illustrate this context dependence, consider the expression "light football player." There are, of course, borderline cases between those football players who are light and those who are not light. But on these grounds alone we would not say that the expression is vague. It is usually a perfectly serviceable expression, and we can indicate borderline cases by saying such things as "Jones is a bit light for a football player." Suppose, however, that Ohio State and Cal Tech wish to have a game between their light football players. It is obvious that the previous understanding of what counts as being light is too vague for this new context. At Ohio State, anyone under 210 pounds is considered light. At Cal Tech, anyone over 150 pounds is considered heavy. What is needed then is a ruling—for example, that anyone under 175 pounds will be considered a lightweight. This example illustrates a common problem and its solution. A term that works perfectly well in one area becomes vague when applied in some other (usually more specialized) area. This vagueness can then be removed by adopting more-precise rules in the problematic area. Vagueness is resolved by definition.

EXERCISE I

For each of the following terms, give one case to which the term clearly applies, one case to which the term clearly does not apply, and one borderline case. Then try to explain why the borderline case is a borderline case.

Example: "Summer month" clearly applies to August, clearly does not apply to January, and June is a borderline case, because the summer solstice is June 21, and schools usually continue into June, but June, July, and August are, nonetheless, often described as the summer months.

(1) large animal

(2) populous state

(3) long book

(4) old professor

(5) popular singer

(6) powerful person

(7) red bird

(8) convoluted sentence

(9) difficult subject

(10) great president

(11) late meeting

(12) arriving late to a meeting

EXERCISE II

Each of the following sentences contains words or expressions that are potentially vague. Describe a context in which this vagueness might make a difference, and explain what difference it makes. Then reduce this vagueness by replacing the underlined expression with one that is more precise.

Example: Harold has <u>a bad reputation</u>.

Context: If Harold applies for a job as a bank security guard, then some but not all kinds of bad reputation are relevant. A reputation for doing bad construction work is irrelevant, but a reputation for dishonesty is relevant.

Replacement: Harold is a known thief.

(1) Ross has a <u>large</u> income.

(2) Cocaine is a <u>dangerous</u> drug.

(3) Ruth is a <u>clever</u> woman.

(4) Steffi is a <u>terrific</u> tennis player.

(5) Mark is not <u>doing too well</u> (after his operation).

(6) Shaq's a <u>big</u> fellow.

(7) Newt won <u>comfortably</u>.

(8) Pete worked <u>like a dog</u>.

(9) Bill played his sax <u>loudly</u>.

(10) Dan's grades are <u>low</u>.

(11) Walter can't see <u>well</u>.

(12) The earthquake was a <u>disaster</u>.

DISCUSSION QUESTIONS

(1) Is tossing a Frisbee a game? What about prizefighting? Russian roulette? Give the best reasons you can for your answers.

(2) When, if ever, is it acceptable or preferable for a criminal law to leave open borderline cases in which it is not clear which acts violate the law? Why then? Why not in other cases?

(3) Scientists usually try to formulate physical laws so as to avoid as many borderline cases as they can. Why?

HEAPS

The existence of borderline cases makes possible various styles of reasoning that have been identified and used since ancient times. One such argument was called the *argument from the heap*, for it was intended to show that it is impossible to produce a heap of sand by adding one grain at a time. As a variation on this, we will show that no one can become rich. The argument can be formulated as follows:

(1) If someone has one cent, he is not rich.
(2) If someone is not rich, then giving him one cent will not make him rich.

$\therefore$ (3) No matter how many times you give a person a cent, that person will not become rich.

Everyone will agree that there is something wrong with this argument, for, if we hand over a billion pennies to someone one at a time, that person will have ten million dollars. If he or she started out with nothing, that would certainly count as passing from not being rich to being rich.

We can see that this argument turns upon borderline cases in the following way: The argument would fail if we removed borderline cases by laying down a ruling (perhaps for tax purposes) that anyone with a million dollars or more is rich and anyone with less than this is not rich. A person with $999,999.99 would then pass from not being rich to being rich when given a single penny, so premise 2 would be false in this case. But this is not how we normally use the concept of being rich. We see some people as clearly rich, and others as clearly not rich; in between, there is a fuzzy area where we are not prepared to say that people either are or are not rich. In this fuzzy area, a penny one way or the other will make no difference to being rich.

But what exactly is wrong with the argument from the heap? This is not an easy question to answer and remains a subject of debate. Here is one way of viewing the problem. Consider a case in which we would all agree that a person would pass from being fat to being thin by losing more than 100 pounds. If he or she lost an ounce a day for five years, this would be *equivalent* to losing 114 pounds. Since the argument from the heap denies that this person would become thin, the argument seems to depend on the assumption that a series of insignificant changes cannot be equivalent to a significant change. Surely this is wrong. Here we might be met with the reply that every change must occur at some particular time and place, but there would be no particular day on which this person would pass from being fat to not being fat. The answer is that this merely shows a misunderstanding of concepts that admit of borderline cases. With concepts like this, changes can occur gradually over long stretches of time without occurring at any single moment.

CONCEPTUAL SLIPPERY-SLOPE ARGUMENTS

Near-cousins to arguments from the heap are *slippery-slope arguments*. Actually, several different kinds of arguments are called slippery-slope arguments. We will discuss three kinds, beginning with what can be called *conceptual* slippery-slope arguments, since they raise doubts about certain concepts.

Like arguments from the heap, conceptual slippery-slope arguments exploit borderline cases, but they reach different conclusions. Conceptual slippery-slope arguments inch their way through the borderline area in order to show that there is *no real difference* between things at opposite ends of a scale. Whereas the argument from the heap is used in an effort to show that nobody can really become or be bald, a slippery-slope argument could be trotted out to try to show that there is no real difference between being bald and not being bald.

As an example, consider the difference between living and nonliving things:

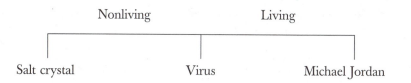

We will agree that a salt crystal is *not* alive. Yet a salt crystal is similar to other, more-complex crystals, and these crystals are similar to certain viruses. But a virus is on the borderline between living and nonliving things. It does not take nourishment and does not reproduce itself. Instead, a virus invades the reproductive mechanisms of cells, and these cells then produce the virus. As viruses become more complex, the differences between them and "higher" life forms become less obvious. Through a whole series of such small transitions, we finally reach a creature who is obviously alive: Michael Jordan. So far, we have merely described a series of gradual transitions along a *continuum*. We get a conceptual slippery-slope argument when we draw the following conclusion from these facts: There is no important difference between living and nonliving things.

In order to avoid this conclusion, we need to figure out where the argument goes wrong. Such arguments seem to depend on the following principles:

(1) We should not draw a distinction between things that are not significantly different.

(2) If A is not significantly different from B, and B is not significantly different from C, then A is not significantly different from C.

The first principle is interesting, complicated, and at least *generally* true. We shall examine it more closely in a moment. The second principle is obviously false. As already noted, a series of insignificant differences can add up to a significant difference. As Senator Everett Dirksen once said, "A billion dollars here and a billion dollars there can add up to some real money."

Since they depend on similar assumptions, conceptual slippery-slope arguments are no better than arguments from the heap, but, strangely, they are often taken quite seriously. Slippery-slope arguments have been used to deny the difference between sanity and insanity (some people are just a little weirder than others), between health and sickness (some people just feel a little better or die a little sooner than others), and between amateur and professional athletics (a professional athlete is just an athlete who gets paid more, or more directly, than other athletes who are called "amateurs"). When many small differences make a big difference, such conceptual slippery-slope arguments are fallacious.

EXERCISE III

Whenever we find one thing passing over into its opposite through a gradual series of borderline cases, we can construct (a) an argument from the heap and (b) a conceptual slippery-slope argument by using the following method: Find some increase that will not be large enough to carry us outside the borderline area. Then use the patterns of argument given above. Applying this method, formulate arguments for the following claims. Then explain what is wrong with these arguments.

   (1) (a) There are no heaps.

         (b) There is no difference between a heap and a single grain of sand.

   (2) (a) Nobody is tall.

         (b) There is no difference between being tall and being short.

   (3) (a) Books do not exist.

         (b) There is no difference between a book and a pamphlet.

   (4) (a) Heat is not real.

         (b) There is no difference between being hot and being cold.

   (5) (a) Taxes are never high.

         (b) There is no difference between high taxes and low taxes.

   (6) (a) Science is an illusion.

         (b) There is no difference between science and faith.

FAIRNESS SLIPPERY-SLOPE ARGUMENTS

When intermediate or borderline cases form a continuum, even if the endpoints are clearly different, it is still often difficult to draw a line between cases or to justify drawing a line at one point rather than at a different point. Then, if someone classifies a case at one end of the continuum, an opponent can offer a challenge by asking the question "Where do you draw the line?"

    Sometimes, even though a line is hard to draw, this challenge is out of place. If I say that Willie Mays was a superstar, I will not be refuted if I cannot draw a sharp dividing line between athletes who are superstars and those who are not. There are some difficult borderline cases, but Willie Mays is not one of them. Nor will we be impressed if someone tells us that the difference between Willie Mays and the thousands of players who never made it to the major leagues is "just a *matter of degree.*" What is usually wrong with this phrase is the emphasis on the word "just," which suggests that differences of degree do not count. Of course it is a matter of degree, but the difference in degree is so great that it should be marked by a special word.

    There are, however, occasions when a challenge to drawing a line is appropriate. For example, most schools and universities have grading systems that draw a fundamental distinction between passing grades and failing grades. Of course, a person who barely passes a course does not perform very differently from one who barely fails a course, yet they are treated very differently. Students who barely pass a course get credit for it; those who barely fail it do not. This, in turn, can lead to serious consequences in an academic career and even beyond. It is entirely reasonable to ask for a justification of a procedure that treats cases that are so similar in such strikingly different ways. We are not being tenderhearted; we are raising an issue of *fairness* or *justice*. It seems unfair to treat very similar cases in strikingly different ways.

The claim is not that there is no difference between passing and failing. That is why this argument is not a conceptual slippery-slope argument. The claim, instead, is that the differences that do exist (as little as one point out of a hundred on a test) do not make it fair to treat people so differently (credit versus no credit for the course). This unfairness does not follow merely from the scores forming a continuum, but the continuum does put pressure on us to show why small differences in scores do justify big differences in treatment.

Questions about the fairness of drawing a line often arise in the law. For example, given reasonable cause, the police generally do not have to obtain a warrant to search a motor vehicle, for the obvious reason that the vehicle might be driven away while the police go to a judge to obtain a warrant. On the other hand, with few exceptions, the police may not search a person's home without a search warrant. In the case of *California v. Carney*,[1] the United States Supreme Court had to rule on whether the police needed a warrant to search for marijuana in an "oversized van, fully mobile," parked in a downtown parking lot in San Diego. Because the van was a fully mobile vehicle, it seemed to fall under the first principle, but because it also served as its owner's home, it seemed to fall under the second. The difficulty, as the Court saw, was that there is a grey area between those things that clearly are motor vehicles and not homes (for example, motorcycles) and those things that clearly are homes and not motor vehicles (for example, apartments). Chief Justice Warren Burger wondered about a mobile home in a trailer park hooked up to utility lines with its wheels removed. Justice Sandra Day O'Connor asked whether a tent, because it is highly mobile, could also be searched without a warrant. As the discussion continued, houseboats (with or without motors or oars), covered wagons, and finally a house being moved from one place to another on a trailer truck came under examination. In the end, our highest court decided that the van in question was a vehicle and could be searched without first obtaining a warrant to do so. As for the other examples, the Court, as it often does, deferred action. It did not fully explain why it is fair to allow warrantless searches, and to send people to jail as a result, in cases of vans used as homes but not in other very similar cases.

---

[1] 471 U.S. 386 (1984). This case was reported by Linda Greenhouse in "Of Tents with Wheels and Houses with Oars," *New York Times*, May 15, 1985.

Questions about where to draw a line often have even more important implications than in the case just examined. Consider the death penalty. Most societies have reserved the death penalty for those crimes they consider the most serious. But where should we draw the line between crimes punishable by death and crimes not punishable by death? Should the death penalty be given to murderers of prison guards? To rapists? To drug dealers? To drunk drivers who cause death? Wherever we draw the line, it seems to be an unavoidable consequence of the death penalty that similar cases will be treated in radically different ways. A defender of the death penalty can argue that it is not unfair to draw a line because, once the line is drawn, the public will have fair warning about which crimes are subject to the death penalty and which are not. It will then be up to each person to decide whether to risk his or her life by crossing this line. It remains a matter of debate, however, whether the law can be administered in a way that makes this argument plausible. If the laws themselves are administered in an arbitrary way, arguments of this kind lose their force.

The finality of death raises a profoundly difficult problem in another area too: the legalization of abortion. There are some people who think abortion is never justified and ought to be declared totally illegal. There are others who think abortion does not need any justification at all and should be completely legalized. Between these extremes, there are many people who believe abortion is justified in certain circumstances but not in others (such as when abortion is the only way to save the life of the mother but not when it prevents only lesser harms to the mother, or when the fetus will suffer major birth defects but not when the fetus will suffer only minor problems). There are also those who think abortion should be allowed for a certain number of months of pregnancy, but not thereafter. People holding these middle positions face the problem of deciding where to draw a line, and this makes them subject to criticisms from holders of either extreme position.

This problem admits of no easy solution. Since every line we draw will seem arbitrary to some extent, a person who holds a middle position needs to argue that it is better to draw *some* line—even a somewhat arbitrary one—than to draw no line at all. The recognition that some line is needed, and why, can often help us locate the real issues, and this is the first step toward a reasonable position.

Of course, this still does not tell us *where* to draw the line. A separate argument is needed to show that the line should be drawn at one point, or in one area, rather than another. In the law, such arguments often appeal to value judgments about the effects of drawing the line at one place rather than another. For example, it is more efficient to draw a line where it is easy to detect, and drawing the line at one place will provide greater protection for some values or some people than will drawing it at another place. Different values often favor drawing different lines, and sometimes such arguments are not available at all. Thus, in the end, it will be difficult to solve many of these profound and important problems.

CAUSAL SLIPPERY-SLOPE ARGUMENTS

One more kind of slippery slope argument is also common. In these arguments, the claim is made that, once a certain kind of event occurs, other similar events will also occur, and this will lead eventually to disaster. The most famous, or infamous, argument of this kind was used by the United States government to justify its intervention in Vietnam in the 1960s. It was claimed that, if the Communists took over Vietnam, they would then take over Cambodia, the rest of Asia, and other continents, until they ruled the whole world. This was called the domino theory, since the fall of one country would make neighboring countries fall as well; arguments of this kind are sometimes called *domino arguments.* Such arguments claim that one event, which might not seem bad by itself, would lead to other, more-horrible events, so such arguments can also be called *parades of horrors.*

These arguments resemble other slippery-slope arguments in that they depend on a series of small changes regarding which it is hard to draw a line. The domino argument does not, however, claim that there is no difference between the first step and later steps—between Vietnam going Communist and the rest of Asia going Communist. Nor is there supposed to be anything unfair about letting Vietnam go Communist without letting other countries also go Communist. The point of a parade of horrors is that certain events will *cause* horrible effects because of their similarity or proximity to other events. Since the crucial claim is about causes and effects, these arguments will be called *causal slippery-slope arguments.*

We saw another example in Chapter 3. While arguing against an increase in the clerk hire allowance, Kyl says,

> The amount of increase does not appear large. I trust, however, there is no one among us who would suggest that the addition of a clerk would not entail allowances for another desk, another typewriter, more materials, and it is not beyond the realm of possibility that the next step would then be a request for additional office space, and ultimately new buildings.

Although this argument is heavily guarded, the basic claim is that increasing the clerk hire allowance is likely to lead to much larger expenditures that will break the budget. The argument can be represented more formally this way:

(1) If the clerk hire allowance is increased, other expenditures will also probably be increased.

(2) These other increases would be horrible.

∴ (3) The clerk hire allowance should not be increased.

Opponents can respond in several ways. One response is to deny that the supposedly horrible effects really are so horrible. One might argue, for example, that additional office space and new buildings would be useful. This response is often foreclosed by describing the effects in especially horrible terms.

A second possible response would be to deny that increasing the clerk hire allowance really would have the horrible effects that are claimed in the first premise. One might argue, for example, that the old offices already have adequate room for additional clerks.

Often the best response is a combination of these. One can admit that certain claimed effects would be horrible, but deny that these horrible effects really are likely. Then one can acknowledge that some more-minor problems will ensue, but argue that these costs are outweighed by the benefits of the program.

In order to determine which, if any, of these responses is adequate, one must look closely at each particular argument and ask the following questions:

(a) Are any of the claimed effects really very bad?

(b) Are any of these effects very likely?

(c) Do these dangers outweigh all the benefits of what is being criticized?

If the answers to all these questions are "Yes," then the causal slippery-slope argument is strong. But if any of these questions receives a negative answer, then the causal slippery-slope argument is questionable on that basis.

We have seen that conceptual, fairness, and causal slippery-slope arguments make different claims and are subject to different responses. Nonetheless, these kinds of arguments are not always distinguished in everyday life. Actual arguments will often combine these ideal types, for example, by claiming unfairness as well as horrible consequences. When this happens, the different arguments need to be separated and evaluated individually. This will not be easy, but it is necessary in order properly to appreciate the strengths and weaknesses of real slippery-slope arguments.

EXERCISE IV

Classify each of the following arguments as either (H) an argument from the heap, (C) a conceptual slippery-slope argument, (F) a fairness slippery-slope argument, or (S) a causal slippery-slope argument. Explain why you classify each example as you do.

(1) We have to take a stand against sex education in junior high schools. If we allow sex education in the eighth grade, then the seventh graders will want it, and then the sixth graders, and pretty soon we will be teaching sex education to our little kindergartners.

(2) It is not incest to touch your mother's big toe. If it is not incest to touch your mother's big toe, then it is not incest to touch her one millimeter up her foot. And one more millimeter can't turn it into incest. So nobody can commit incest.

(3) But, officer, you wouldn't arrest me if I drove only one inch left of the center of the lane. And if you wouldn't arrest me for driving at one place, it wouldn't be fair to arrest me for deviating just one inch further left. So you shouldn't arrest me for driving on the wrong side of the road.

(4) If you try to smoke one cigarette a day, you will end up smoking two and then three and four and five, and so on, until you smoke two packs every day. So don't try even one.

(5) People are found not guilty by reason of insanity when they cannot avoid breaking the law. But people who are brought up in certain deprived social circumstances are not much more able than the insane to avoid breaking the law. So it would be unjust to find them guilty.

(6) People are called mentally ill when they do very strange things, but many so-called eccentrics do things that are just as strange. So there is no real difference between insanity and eccentricity.

(7) If we let doctors kill dying patients who are in great pain, then they will kill other patients who are in less pain and patients who are only slightly disabled. Eventually, they will kill anyone who is not wanted by society.

(8) A human egg one minute after fertilization is not very different from what it is one minute later, or one minute after that, and so on. Thus, there is really no difference between just-fertilized eggs and adult humans.

(9) Since no moment in the continuum of development between an egg and a baby is especially significant, it is not fair to grant a right to life to a baby unless one grants the same right to every fertilized egg.

(10) A woman should be allowed to get an abortion to prevent a 100 percent chance of death. But if a 100 percent chance of death justifies abortion, then it would not be fair to forbid abortion in order to prevent a 99 percent chance of death. And 1 percent cannot make a difference anywhere down the line. So abortion should be allowed in order to prevent *any* chance of death to a mother.

(11) "If a man indulges himself in murder, very soon he comes to think little of robbing, and from robbing, he comes next to drinking, and Sabbath breaking, and from that to incivility and procrastination. Once begin upon this downward path, you never know where you are to stop. Many a man dated his ruin from some murder or other that perhaps he thought little of at the time."[2]

EXERCISE V

For fun, construct your own examples of an argument from the heap, a conceptual slippery-slope argument, a fairness slippery-slope argument, and a causal slippery-slope argument.

EXERCISE VI

Explain the reasons, if any, for drawing a definite line in each of the following cases. Then further explain how this line can be drawn, if at all, in a reasonable way.

(1) minimum (or maximum?) age to drive a car

---

[2] Thomas de Quincey, "Second Paper on Murder, Considered as One of the Fine Arts" in *Miscellaneous Essays* (Boston; Ticknor, Reed, and Fields, 1864), p. 63. Thanks to Julia Driver for sharing this example.

(2) minimum age to vote

(3) minimum age to enter (or be drafted into) the military

(4) minimum age to drink alcoholic beverages

(5) minimum age for election to the United States presidency

(6) maximum age before retirement becomes mandatory

EXERCISE VII

Determine whether each of the following arguments provides adequate support, or any support, for its conclusion. Explain why.

(1) We shouldn't require eye tests for bus drivers, because perfect eyesight and blindness differ only in degrees between 20/20 and 0/20.

(2) I shouldn't get a speeding ticket for going 56 miles per hour, because my driving did not all of a sudden get more dangerous when I passed the speed limit of 55.

(3) Someone who arrives a second after a party starts is not late, and one second cannot make the difference to whether someone is late, so nobody is ever late to a party.

(4) No student should ever be allowed to ask a question during a lecture, because once one student asks a question, then another one wants to ask a question, and pretty soon the teacher doesn't have any time left to lecture.

(5) Pornography shouldn't be illegal, because you can't draw a line between pornography and erotic art.

(6) Marijuana should be legal, because it is no more dangerous than alcohol or nicotine.

(7) Marijuana should be illegal, because people who try marijuana are likely to go on to try hashish, and then snorting cocaine, and then freebasing cocaine or shooting heroin.

(8) Humans do not have any special rights that other animals lack, because the theory of evolution shows us that the human species evolved from other species through a series of very minor changes.

(9) The concept of race makes no sense, because people fall at many points along a continuum between one race (such as the so-called Caucasian race) and another (such as the so-called Negro race).

(10) Governments should never bargain with any terrorist. Once you do, you will have to bargain with every other terrorist who comes along.

(11) The United States should oppose military aggression wherever it happens, no matter how minor, because letting any aggression go unpunished will just encourage even more and more horrible forms of aggression and will eventually lead to war throughout the world.

(12) When Kenneth Carr was chair of the Nuclear Regulatory Commission, he gave the following argument for extending the licenses of more nuclear power plants beyond the forty-year limit: "There's nothing that says that if they're safe when they're 39 years and 364 days old, then ipso facto they're unsafe the next day."[3]

(13) "That human life is a continuum from generation to generation seems irrefutably logical. Therefore, if it is wrong to take life at one point on the continuum, then it is wrong to take it at any point. If it is wrong to take life at the mid-point, it is wrong to take it at the beginning or the end."[4]

(14) If assault weapons are banned, Congress will ban handguns next, and then rifles. Eventually, hunters will not be able to hunt, and law-abiding citizens will have no way to defend themselves against criminals.

(15) "To conclude that the Government may permit designated symbols to be used to communicate only a limited set of messages would be to enter a territory having no discernible or defensible boundaries. Could the Government, on this theory, prohibit the burning of state flags? Of copies of the Presidential seal? Of the Constitution? In evaluating these choices under the First Amendment, how would we decide which symbols were sufficiently special to warrant this unique status? To do so, we would be forced to consult our own political preferences, and to impose them on the citizenry, in the very way the First Amendment forbids us to do."[5]

DISCUSSION QUESTIONS

(1) Explain and evaluate the following argument against restrictions on hate speech:

> To attempt to craft free speech exceptions only for racist speech would create a significant risk of a slide down the proverbial "slippery slope." . . . Censorial consequences could result from many proposed or adopted university policies, including the Stanford code, which sanctions speech intended to "insult or stigmatize" on the basis of race or other prohibited grounds. For example, certain feminists suggest that all heterosexual sex is rape because heterosexual men are aggressors who operate in a cultural climate

Continued on next page

---

[3] Quoted in the *New York Times*, June 24, 1991.

[4] From a letter written by then New Hampshire Senator Gordon Humphrey.

[5] From Justice Brennan's majority opinion in *Texas v. Johnson* 109 S. Ct. 2533 (1989), questioning the constitutionality of laws against burning the United States flag.

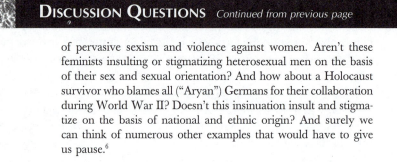

DISCUSSION QUESTIONS *Continued from previous page*

of pervasive sexism and violence against women. Aren't these feminists insulting or stigmatizing heterosexual men on the basis of their sex and sexual orientation? And how about a Holocaust survivor who blames all ("Aryan") Germans for their collaboration during World War II? Doesn't this insinuation insult and stigmatize on the basis of national and ethnic origin? And surely we can think of numerous other examples that would have to give us pause.[6]

(2) Explain and evaluate the following response to critics of college restrictions on hate speech:

[Defenders of such restrictions] will ask whether an educational institution does not have the power . . . to enact reasonable regulations aimed at assuring equal personhood on campus. If one characterizes the issue this way, . . . a different set of slopes will look slippery. If we do not intervene to protect equality here, what will the next outrage be?[7]

(3) What, if anything, is shown when slippery-slope arguments can be used on both sides of an issue?

AMBIGUITY

The idea of vagueness is based on a common feature of words in our language: Many of them leave open a range of borderline cases. The notion of ambiguity is also based on a common feature of our language: Words often have a number of different meanings. For example, the *New Merriam-Webster Pocket Dictionary* has the following entry under the word "cardinal":

cardinal adj. 1: of basic importance; chief, main, primary,
            2: of cardinal red color.
        n.   1: an ecclesiastical official of the Roman Catholic Church ranking next below the pope,
            2: a bright red,
            3: any of several American finches of which the male is bright red.

---

[6] Nadine Strossen, "Regulating Racist Speech on Campus: A Modest Proposal?" *Duke Law Journal* (1990): 537–538. When she wrote this, Strossen was on the National Board of Directors of the American Civil Liberties Union.

[7] Richard Delgado, "Campus Antiracism Rules: Constitutional Narratives in Collision," *Northwestern University Law Review* 85 (1991): 346.

In the plural, "the Cardinals" is the name of an athletic team that inhabits St. Louis; "cardinal" also describes the numbers used in simple counting.

It is not likely that people would get confused about these very different meanings of the word "cardinal," but we might imagine a priest, a bird-watcher, and a baseball fan all hearing the remark "The cardinals are in town." The priest would prepare for a solemn occasion, the bird-watcher would get out his binoculars, and the baseball fan would head for the stadium. In this context, the remark might be criticized as ambiguous. More precisely, we shall say that an expression in a given context is *ambiguous* or is used ambiguously if and only if it is misleading or potentially misleading because it is hard to tell which of a number of possible meanings is intended in that context.

Actually, the term "ambiguous" itself seems to be ambiguous. As defined above, an expression is used ambiguously only if it is obscure or unclear which meaning is intended. Using this definition, the word "bank" is *not* used ambiguously in the following sentence:

Joan deposited five hundred dollars in the bank and got a receipt.

Some writers, however, call an expression ambiguous simply if it admits of more than one interpretation, without adding that it is not possible to tell which meaning is intended. With this definition, the above sentence is ambiguous because it could mean that Joan placed five hundred dollars on a riverbank, and someone, for whatever reason, gave her a receipt for doing so. On this second definition of ambiguity, virtually every expression is ambiguous, since virtually every expression admits of more than one interpretation. On our first definition, only uses of expressions that are misleading or potentially misleading will be called ambiguous. In what follows, we will use the word "ambiguous" in accordance with the first definition. Ambiguity then depends on the context, because whether something is misleading also depends on context.

In everyday life, context usually settles which of a variety of meanings is appropriate. Yet sometimes genuine misunderstandings do arise. An American and a European discussing "football" may have different games in mind. The European is talking about what *we* call "soccer"; the American is talking about what *they* call "American football." It is characteristic of the ambiguous use of a term that when it comes to light we are likely to say something like "Oh, you mean that kind of cardinal!" or "Oh, you were talking about *American* football!" This kind of misunderstanding can cause trouble. When it does, if we want to criticize the expression that creates the problem, we call it ambiguous.

Thus, "ambiguous" is both dependent on context and a term of criticism in much the same ways as "vague." But these kinds of unclarity differ in other ways. In a context where the use of a word is ambiguous, we do not know which of two meanings to attach to a word. In a context where the use of a word is vague, we cannot attach *any* clear meaning to the use of a word.

So far we have talked about the ambiguity of individual terms or words. This is called *semantic ambiguity*. But sometimes we do not know which interpretation to give to a phrase or a sentence because its grammar or syntax admits of more than one interpretation. This is called *syntactic ambiguity* or *amphiboly*. Thus, if we talk about *the conquest of the Persians*, we might be referring either to the Persians' conquering someone or to someone's conquering the Persians. Sometimes the grammar of a sentence leaves open a great many possible interpretations. For example, consider the following sentence:

Only sons marry only daughters.

One thing this might mean is that a person who is a male only child will marry a person who is a female only child. Again, it might mean that sons are the only persons who marry daughters and do not marry anyone else. Other interpretations are possible as well.[8]

The process of rewriting a sentence so that one of its possible meanings becomes clear is called *disambiguating* the sentence. One way of disambiguating a sentence is to rewrite it as a whole, spelling things out in detail. That is how we disambiguated the sentence "Only sons marry only daughters." Another procedure is to continue the sentence in a way that supplies a context that forces one interpretation over others. Consider the sentence "Mary had a little lamb." Notice how the meaning changes completely under the following continuations:

(1) Mary had a little lamb; it followed her to school.

(2) Mary had a little lamb and then a little broccoli.

Just in passing, it is not altogether obvious how we should describe the ambiguity in the sentence "Mary had a little lamb." The most obvious suggestion is that the word "had" is ambiguous, meaning "owned" on the first reading and "ate" on the second reading. Notice, however, that this also forces alternative readings for the expression "a little lamb." Presumably, it was a small whole live lamb that followed Mary to school, whereas it would have been a small amount of cooked lamb that she ate. So if we try to locate the ambiguity in particular words, we must say that not only the word "had" but also the word "lamb" are being used ambiguously. This is a reasonable approach, but another is available. In everyday speech, we often leave things out. Thus, instead of saying "Mary had a little *portion of meat derived from a* lamb *to eat*," we simply say "Mary had a little lamb," dropping out the italicized words on the assumption that they will be understood. In most contexts, such deletions cause no misunderstanding. But sometimes deletions are misunderstood, and this can produce ambiguity.

EXERCISE VIII

Show that each of the following sentences admits of at least two interpretations by rewriting the sentence as a whole in two different ways and by expanding the sentence in two different ways in order to clarify the context:

---

[8] This example comes from Paul Benacerraf. Consider also that the word "only" can be inserted anywhere in the sentence "I hit him in the eye" to yield "Only I hit him in the eye," "I only hit him in the eye," "I hit only him in the eye," "I hit him only in the eye," "I hit him in only the eye," "I hit him in the only eye," and "I hit him in the eye only."

Example: Kenneth let us down.

Rewriting: Kenneth lowered us.
            Kenneth disappointed us.

Expanding: Kenneth let us down with a rope.
            Kenneth let us down just when we needed him.

(1) Reggie Jackson (the baseball player) was safe at home.

(2) I don't know what state Meredith is in.

(3) Where did you get bitten?

(4) The president sent her congratulations.

(5) Visiting professors can be boring.

(6) Wendy ran a marathon.

(7) The meaning of the term "altering" is changing.

(8) I don't want to get too close to him.

(9) I often have my friends for dinner.

(10) Slow Children Playing. (On a street sign.)

(11) Save Soap and Waste Paper. (On a sign during World War II.)

(12) In his will, he left $1,000 to his two sons, Jim and John.

(13) John married Pat and Chris.

(14) I'm not hungry or thirsty.

(15) There is some explanation for everything.

(16) She is an Asian historian.

(17) Nobody may be in the lounge this evening.

EXERCISE IX

Follow the same instructions for the following actual newspaper headlines:[9]

(1) Milk Drinkers Turn to Powder

(2) Anti-busing Rider Killed by Senate

(3) Mrs. Gandhi Stoned in Rally in India

(4) College Graduates Blind Senior Citizen

(5) Jumping Bean Prices Affect the Poor

(6) Tuna Biting off Washington Coast

(7) Time for Football and Meatball Stew

---

[9] Most of these examples come from Columbia Journalism Review Editors, *Squad Helps Dog Bite Victim and Other Flubs from the Nation's Press* (Garden City, N.Y.: Doubleday, 1980).

(8) Police Kill Man with Ax

(9) Squad Helps Dog Bite Victim

(10) Carter Plans Swell Budget

(11) Reverend Moon Marries 6200

(12) Child Teaching Expert to Speak

(13) Prostitutes Appeal to Pope

(14) Legalized Outhouses Aired by Legislature

(15) Survivor of Siamese Twins Joins Parents

(16) Judge Permits Club to Continue Sex Bar

(17) Kid Pajamas to Be Removed by Woolworth's

(18) Teenage Prostitution Problem Is Mounting

(19) Police Can't Stop Gambling

(20) Caribbean Islands Drift to the Left

(21) Greeks Fine Hookers

EXERCISE X

Poetry, songs, and jokes often intentionally exploit multiple meanings for effect. Find examples in poems, songs, and jokes that you like. Are these examples of ambiguity on the above definition? Why or why not?

FALLACIES OF AMBIGUITY

Ambiguity can cause a variety of problems for arguments. Often it produces hilarious or embarrassing side effects, and it is hard to get your arguments taken seriously if your listeners are giggling over an unintended double entendre in which one of the double meanings has risqué connotations.

Ambiguity can also generate bad arguments that involve the *fallacy of equivocation*. An argument is said to commit this fallacy when it uses the same expression in different senses in different parts of the argument, and this ruins the argument. Here is a silly example:[10]

> Six is an odd number of legs for a horse.
> Odd numbers cannot be divided by two.
> ———————————
> ∴ Six cannot be divided by two.

———————————

[10] We are indebted to Carl Wolf for this example.

Clearly, "odd" means "unusual" in the first premise, but it means "not even" in the second premise. Consequently, both premises are true, even though the conclusion is false, so the argument is not valid.

People rarely equivocate so blatantly in everyday life, except as a joke, but other fallacies of equivocation are more subtle and sometimes escape notice. Often it is not even clear whether a fallacy of equivocation is being committed. For example, suppose a newspaper is criticized as a scandalous rumormonger, and its editor responds by saying the following:

> It's not wrong for newspapers to pass on rumors about sex scandals. Newspapers have a duty to print stories that are in the public interest, and the public clearly has a great interest in rumors about sex scandals, since, when newspapers print such stories, their circulation increases, and they receive a large number of letters.[11]

The main argument in this passage seems to run this way:

> Newspapers should print stories that are in the public interest.
> Rumors about sex scandals are in the public interest.
> _____
> ∴ Newspapers should print rumors about sex scandals.

This argument might *seem* to be good, because it is grammatically similar to other arguments that are perfectly fine, such as this one:

> Parents should do what is in their children's interest.
> Reading to their children is in their children's interest.
> _____
> ∴ Parents should read to their children.

However, it is not clear that the previous argument about newspapers is a good one. The reason is that it is not clear what its premises mean.

It is natural to read the first premise as saying that papers should print stories that benefit the public. In contrast, the second premise is supported by claims about circulation and letters, so the second premise seems to use the phrase "in the public interest" to refer to things in which the public takes an interest. This is a separate issue, since people can be interested in things that it does not benefit them to know. Thus, the two premises seem to use the phrase "in the public interest" with different meanings; therefore the argument seems to commit the fallacy of equivocation.

However, this is not the only possible interpretation. The phrase "in the public interest" might be used with the same meaning in both premises, and then the argument does not equivocate. First, suppose that "are in the public interest" means "benefits the public" in both premises. The argument might then be valid, but its second premise is questionable, because it says that rumors about sex scandals benefit the public. This cannot be shown by increases in circulation and letters.

_____

[11] This is a paraphrase of an actual argument given by a newspaper editor and reported by Deni Elliot.

Moreover, the very opponents who deny the conclusion would also deny this second premise, so nobody should be convinced by the argument. (This is an example of the fallacy of begging the question, which will be discussed later in this chapter.)

The second premise is less dubious if the phrase "in the public interest" refers to what the public is interested in. The second premise then says that rumors about sex scandals are stories that the public takes an interest in, and this claim *is* supported by newspaper circulation and letters. However, the *first* premise is now questionable, since it claims that newspapers should print all stories that the public takes an interest in. Even if the public does take a great interest in battle plans during a war or in how to build nuclear bombs at home, printing stories about such topics might endanger military personnel or the public.

In response, defenders of the argument might insist that newspapers *should* print stories that the public is interested in, because the job of newspapers is not to do what is good for society but only to provide as much information as possible about what the public wants to know. However, this premise (that the only job of newspapers is to satisfy curiosity) is exactly what is denied by opponents who deny the conclusion (that newspapers should print rumors about sex scandals). Consequently, the argument makes no progress in resolving the issue.

Of course, the conclusion of the argument, along with its premises, still might be true. Even if so, the point here is just that we cannot properly evaluate such an argument without looking closely at the possible meanings of its components to determine whether or not it depends on an equivocation. To do this, we need to follow these steps:

(a) Distinguish the possible meanings of the potentially ambiguous expressions in the argument.

(b) For each possible meaning, restate the argument so that each expression clearly has the same meaning in all of the premises and the conclusion.

(c) Evaluate the resulting arguments separately.

EXERCISE XI

Each of the following arguments trades on an ambiguity. For each, locate the ambiguity by showing that one or more of the statements can be interpreted in different ways.

(1) We shouldn't hire Peter, because our company has a policy against hiring drug users, and I saw Peter take aspirin.

(2) Man is the only rational animal, and no woman is a man, so women are not rational.

(3) My doctor has been practicing medicine for thirty years, and practice makes perfect, so my doctor must be nearly perfect.

(4) "Our bread does have fiber, because it contains wood pulp." (The Federal Trade Commission actually ordered the Continental Baking Company to indicate in their advertising that this is the kind of fiber in their Fresh Horizons bread.)

(5) Our cereal is all natural, for there is obviously nothing supernatural about it.

(6) Ice cream is never all natural, since it never appears in nature without human intervention.

(7) The apostles were twelve. Matthew was an apostle. Hence, Matthew was twelve. (Attributed to Bertrand Russell.)

(8) I have a right to spend all my money on lottery tickets. Therefore, when I spend all my money on lottery tickets, I am doing the right thing.

(9) "All criminal actions ought to be punished. Prosecutions for theft are criminal actions. Therefore, prosecutions for theft ought to be punished."[12]

(10) Anyone who tries to violate a law should be punished, even if her attempt fails. People who try to fly are trying to violate the law of gravity. So they should be punished. (This argument is reported to have been used in an actual legal case during the nineteenth century.)

(11) The United States Supreme Court has recognized a right to privacy, so state governments should not interfere in private matters. But a private company is, by definition, a private matter, so my state government should not interfere with my private company by taxing it.

(12) You passed no one on the road; therefore, you walked faster than no one.

(13) Everything must have some cause; therefore, something must be the cause of everything.

(14) If I have only one friend, then I cannot say that I have any number of friends. So one is not any number.[13]

(15) "The only proof capable of being given that an object is visible is that people actually see it. The only proof that a sound is audible is that people hear it. In like manner the sole evidence it is possible to produce that anything is desirable is that people actually desire it."[14]

---

[12] Ruggero J. Aldisert, *Logic for Lawyers: A Guide to Clear Legal Thinking* (New York; Clark Boardman, 1989), 210.

[13] This example comes from Timothy Duggan.

[14] John Stuart Mill, *Utilitarianism* (Indianapolis; Hackett, 1979), Chapter 4, p. 34. First published in 1861.

DISCUSSION QUESTION

Many people argue that homosexuality is immoral because it is unnatural. In the following reading,[15] Burton Leiser criticizes this argument for equivocating on five meanings of the term "natural." Does the argument really equivocate? Why or why not?

Homosexuality and Natural Law
by Burton Leiser

When theologians and moralists speak of homosexuality, contraception, abortion, and other forms of human behavior as being unnatural and say that for that reason such behavior must be considered to be wrong, in what sense are they using the word *unnatural?* Are they saying that homosexual behavior and the use of contraceptives are [1] *contrary to the scientific laws of nature,* are they saying that they are [2] *artificial* forms of behavior, or are they using the terms *natural* and *unnatural* in some third sense?

They cannot mean that homosexual behavior (to stick to the subject presently under discussion) violates the laws of nature in the first sense [including, for example, Boyle's law that the volume of a gas varies inversely with the pressure that is applied to it], for . . . in *that* sense it is impossible to violate the laws of nature. Those laws, being merely descriptive of what actually does happen, would have to *include* homosexual behavior if such behavior does actually take place. . . .

If those who say that homosexual behavior is unnatural are using the term *unnatural* in the second sense as artificial, it is difficult to understand their objection. That which is artificial is often far better than what is natural. . . . [Moreover,] homosexual behavior can hardly be considered unnatural in this sense. There is nothing artificial about such behavior. On the contrary, it is quite natural, in this sense, to those who engage in it. And, even if it were not, this is not in itself a ground for condemning it.

It would seem, then, that those who condemn homosexuality as an unnatural form of behavior must mean something else by the word *unnatural,* something not covered by either of the preceding definitions. A third possibility is this:

3. *Anything uncommon or abnormal is unnatural.* If this is what is meant by those who condemn homosexuality on the ground that it is unnatural, it is quite obvious that their condemnation cannot be accepted without further argument. The fact that a given form of behavior is uncommon

---

[15] Burton Leiser, "Homosexuality and Natural Law," in Leiser, *Liberty, Justice, and Morals,* 3d ed. (New York: Macmillan, 1986), 52–57.

provides no justification for condemning it. . . . Great artists, poets, musicians, and scientists are uncommon in this sense; but clearly the world is better off for having them, and it would be absurd to condemn them or their activities for their failure to be common and normal. If homosexual behavior is wrong, then, it must be for some reason other than its unnaturalness in this sense of the word.

4. *Any use of an organ or an instrument that is contrary to its principal purpose or function is unnatural.* Every organ and every instrument—perhaps even every creature—has a function to perform, one for which it is particularly designed. Any use of those instruments and organs that is consonant with their purposes is natural and proper, but any use that is inconsistent with their principal functions is unnatural and improper, and to that extent evil or harmful. Human teeth, for example, are admirably designed for their principal functions—biting and chewing the kinds of food suitable for human consumption. But they are not particularly well suited for prying the caps from beer bottles. If they are used for that purpose, they are likely to crack or break under the strain. . . .

What are the sex organs peculiarly suited to do? Obviously, they are peculiarly suited to enable men and women to reproduce their own kind. No other organ in the body is capable of fulfilling that function. It follows, according to those who follow the natural-law line, that the proper or natural function of sex organs is reproduction, and that strictly speaking, any use of those organs for other purposes is unnatural, abusive, potentially harmful, and therefore wrong. . . .

But the problem is not so easily resolved. Is it really true that every organ has one and only one proper function? . . . A woman's eyes are well adapted to seeing, it is true. But they seem also to be well adapted to flirting. Is a woman's use of her eyes for the latter purpose sinful merely because she is not using them, at that moment, for their "primary" purpose of seeing? Our sexual organs are uniquely adapted for procreation, but that is obviously not the only function for which they are adapted. Human beings may—and do—use those organs for a great many other purposes, and it is difficult to see why any *one* use should be considered to be the only proper one. The sex organs seem to be particularly well adapted to give their owners and others intense sensations of pleasure. Unless one believes that pleasure itself is bad, there seems to be little reason to believe that the use of the sex organs for the production of pleasure in oneself or in others is evil. In view of the peculiar design of these organs, with their great concentration of nerve endings, it would seem that they were designed (if they *were* designed) with that very goal in mind, and that

Continued on next page

their use for such purposes would be no more unnatural than their use for the purpose of procreation.

Nor should we overlook the fact that human sex organs may be and are used to express, in the deepest and most intimate way open to man, the love of one person for another. Even the most ardent opponents of "unfruitful" intercourse admit that sex does serve this function. They have accordingly conceded that a man and his wife may have intercourse even though she is pregnant, or past the age of child bearing, or in the infertile period of her menstrual cycle. . . .

To sum up, then, the proposition that any use of an organ that is contrary to its principal purpose or function is unnatural assumes that organs *have* a principal purpose or function, but this may be denied on the ground that the purpose or function of a given organ may vary according to the needs or desires of its owner. It may be denied on the ground that a given organ may have more than one principal purpose or function, and any attempt to call one use or another the only natural one seems to be arbitrary, if not question-begging. Also, the proposition suggests that what is unnatural is evil or depraved. This goes beyond the pure description of things, and enters into the problem of the evaluation of human behavior, which leads us to the fifth meaning of *natural.*

5. *That which is natural is good, and whatever is unnatural is bad.* . . . Clearly, [people who say this] cannot have intended merely to reduce the word *natural* to a synonym of *good, right,* and *proper,* and *unnatural* to a synonym of *evil, wrong, improper, corrupt,* and *depraved.* If that were all they had intended to do, . . . it would follow inevitably that whatever is good must be natural, and vice versa, by definition. This is certainly not what the opponents of homosexuality have been saying when they claim that homosexuality, being unnatural, is evil. For if it were, their claim would be quite empty. They would be saying merely that homosexuality, being evil, is evil—a redundancy that could as easily be reduced to the simpler assertion that homosexuality is evil. This assertion, however, is not an argument. . . . "Unnaturalness" and "wrongfulness" are not synonyms, then, but different concepts.

The problem with which we are wrestling is that we are unable to find a meaning for *unnatural* that enables us to arrive at the conclusion that homosexuality is unnatural or that if homosexuality is unnatural, it is therefore wrongful behavior. We have examined [five] common meanings of *natural* and *unnatural,* and have seen that none of them performs the task that it must perform if the advocates of this argument are to prevail. Without some more satisfactory explanation of the connection between the wrongfulness of homosexuality and its alleged unnaturalness, the argument [that homosexuality is wrong because it is unnatural] must be rejected.

DEFINITIONS

It is sometimes suggested that a great many disputes could be avoided if people simply took the precaution of defining their terms. To some extent this is true: People do sometimes seem to disagree simply because they are using terms in different ways, even though they agree on the nonverbal issues.

Nonetheless, definitions will not solve all problems, and a mindless insistence on definitions can turn a serious discussion into a semantic quibble. If you insist on defining every term, you will never be satisfied, since every definition will introduce new terms to be defined. Furthermore, definitions themselves can be confusing or obfuscating, as, for example, when an economist tells us:

> I define inflation as too much money chasing too few goods.

Not only is this definition metaphorical and obscure, it also has a theory of the causes of inflation built into it.

To use definitions correctly, we must realize that they come in various forms and serve various purposes. There are at least five kinds of definitions that need to be distinguished.

1. *Lexical or dictionary definitions*: We consult a dictionary when we are ignorant about the meaning of a word in a particular language. A dictionary explains the meaning of a word primarily by using other words that, presumably, the reader already understands. If you do not happen to know what the words "jejune," "ketone," or "Kreis" mean, then you can look these words up in an English, a scientific, or a German dictionary, respectively. Lexical definitions supply us with factual information about the standard meanings of words in a particular language. They are the most common kind of definition.

2. *Disambiguating definitions* tells us in which sense a word is being used. ("When I said that the banks were collapsing, I meant the riverbanks, not the financial institutions.") Disambiguating definitions can tell us which lexical definition is intended in a particular context, or they can distinguish several meanings that might be intended. Thus, they can be used to respond to arguments that seem to commit the fallacy of equivocation.

3. *Stipulative definitions* are used to assign a meaning to a new (usually technical) term or to assign a new or special meaning to a familiar term. They have the following general form: "By such and such expression I (or we) will mean so and so." Thus mathematicians introduced the new term "googol" to stand for the number expressed by 1 followed by one hundred zeros. Physicists use such words as "charm," "color," and "strangeness" to stand for certain features of subatomic particles. Stipulative definitions do not report what a word means; they give a new word a meaning or an old word a new meaning.

Notice that if someone says "By 'plumpotion' I mean 'any drink made with grapes,'" it would be inappropriate to respond "No, you don't." Stipulative definitions differ in this way from dictionary definitions. If a dictionary defines a "plum" as a kind of grape or a kind of drink, this dictionary simply gets it wrong. But when someone *merely* stipulates a meaning for a term, he cannot be wrong in this way about the meaning of the term. Stipulative definitions can still be criticized in other ways. They can be vague or ambiguous. They can be useless or confusing. And someone who stipulates a meaning for a term might go on to use the term with a different meaning. But stipulative definitions cannot be false by virtue of failing to correspond to the real meaning of a word, because they in effect create that meaning for that word.[16]

4. *Precising definitions* are used to resolve problems of vagueness. They are used to draw a sharp (or sharper) boundary around the things to which a term refers, when this collection has a fuzzy or indeterminate boundary in ordinary usage. For example, for most purposes it is not important to decide how big a population center must be in order to count as a city rather than as a town. We can deal with the borderline cases by using such phrases as "very small city" or "quite a large town." On most occasions it will not make much difference which phrase we use. Yet it is not hard to imagine a situation in which it might make a difference whether a center of population is a city or not. As a city, it might be eligible for redevelopment funds that are not available to towns. Here a precising definition—a definition that draws a sharp boundary where none formerly existed—would be useful.

Precising definitions are, in effect, combinations of stipulative definitions and lexical definitions. Like stipulative definitions, they involve a choice. One could define a city as any population center with more than fifty thousand people, or one could decide to decrease the minimum to thirty thousand people. Precising definitions are not completely arbitrary, however, since they usually should conform to the generally accepted meaning of a term. It would be unreasonable to define a city as any population center with more than seventeen people.

Precising definitions are also not arbitrary for another reason: They often have important effects. If redevelopment funds are to be distributed only to cities, then to define cities as having more than fifty thousand people will deny those funds to smaller population centers with, say, thirty thousand people. Consequently, we need some reason to resolve the vagueness of the term "city" in one way rather than another. In this case, the choice might be based on the amount of funds available for redevelopment. However, a different kind of defense might be needed if someone uses a slippery-slope argument to show that it is unfair to provide redevelopment funds to one city with fifty thousand people but to deny such funds to its neighbor with forty-nine thousand people. In a more dramatic example, a precising definition of "death" might be used to resolve controversial issues about euthanasia—about what doctors may or must do to patients who are near death—and then our choices between possible precising definitions might be based on our deepest value commitments. In any case, we need some argument to show that one precising definition is better than other alternatives, and a precising definition can be criticized when it is not supported well enough.

5. *Systematic or theoretical definitions* are introduced to give a systematic order

---

[16] One explanation for this infallibility is that, if I say "I stipulate that such and such," I thereby stipulate that such and such, so such utterances are explicit performatives, and stipulation is a speech act. See Chapter 1.

or structure to a subject matter or a theory. For example, in mathematics, every term must be either a primitive (undefined) term or a term defined by means of these primitive terms. Thus, if we take points and distances as primitives, we can define a straight line as the shortest distance between two points. Then, assuming some more concepts, we can define a triangle as a closed figure with exactly three straight lines as sides. By a series of such definitions the terms in geometry are placed in systematic relationships with one another.

In a similar way, we might try to represent family relationships using only the primitive notions of parent, male, and female. We could then construct definitions of the following kind:

A is the brother of *B* = *A* and *B* have the same parents and *A* is male.

A is *B*'s grandmother = *A* is a parent of a parent of *B* and *A* is female.[17]

Things become more complicated when we try to define such notions as "second cousin once removed," yet by extending these definitions from simple to more-complicated cases, our system of family relationships can be given a systematic presentation.

Formulating systematic definitions for family relationships is relatively easy, but similar activities in science, mathematics, and other fields can demand genius. It often takes deep insight into a subject matter in order to see which concepts are genuinely fundamental and which are secondary and derivative. When Sir Isaac Newton defined force in terms of mass and acceleration, he was not simply stating how he proposed to use certain words; he was introducing a fundamental conceptual relationship for the understanding of the physical world. When water was defined as H_2O,[18] this made it possible to formulate more precise laws about how water interacted with other chemicals, with heat or pressure, and so on. Such theoretical definitions can then be evaluated on the basis of whether they really do help us formulate better theories and understand the world.

THE ROLE OF DEFINITIONS

In the middle of discussions people often ask for definitions or even state, usually with an air of triumph, that everything depends on the way you define your terms. We saw in the opening chapter that definitions are not always needed, and, in most cases, issues do not turn upon the way in which words are defined. When

---

[17] Notice that in these definitions an individual word is not defined in isolation; instead, a whole sentence containing the word is replaced by another whole sentence in which the defined word does not appear. Definitions of this kind are called "contextual definitions" because a context containing the word is the unit of definition. Lexical, disambiguating, stipulative, and precising definitions can also be presented in this contextual form.

[18] If one doubts that the identity "Water is H_2O" is used as a definition, just consider how you would react to someone who claims to have discovered some water that is *not* H_2O. We would dismiss this person as linguistically confused, since the discovered stuff cannot properly be called "water" it if is not H_2O.

asked for a definition, it is appropriate to reply "What sort of definition do you want, and why do you want it?" Of course, if you are using a word in a way that departs from customary usage, or using it in some special way of your own, or using a word that is too vague for the given context, or using a word in an ambiguous way, then the request for a definition is perfectly in order. In such cases the demand for a definition represents an important move within the argument rather than a distraction from it.

EXERCISE XII

Look up lexical or dictionary definitions for the following words. (For fun, you might try to guess the meanings of these words before you look them up, as in the game "Balderdash.")

(1) "jejune"

(2) "ketone"

(3) "fluvial"

(4) "xebec"

(5) "plangent"

EXERCISE XIII

(1) Give a stipulative definition for the word "klurg."

(2) Stipulate a word to stand for the chunks of ice that form under car fenders in winter.

(3) Describe something that does not have a common name, for which it would be useful to stipulate a name. Explain how the name would be useful.

EXERCISE XIV

Give precising definitions for the following words. In each case, supply a context that gives your precising definition a point.

(1) "book"

(2) "alcoholic beverage"

(3) "crime"

(4) "warm"

(5) "fast"

Give disambiguating definitions for the following words. In each case, supply a context in which your definition might be needed to avoid confusion.

(1) "run"

(2) "pen"

(3) "game"

(4) "painting"

(5) "fast"

Using the notions of parents, male, and female as basic, give systematic definitions of the following family relationships:

(1) *A* and *B* are sisters.

(2) *A* and *B* are siblings.

(3) *A* is *B*'s half-brother.

(4) *A* is *B*'s niece.

(5) *A* is *B*'s cousin.

FALLACIES OF RELEVANCE

In a good argument we present statements that are true in order to offer support for some conclusion. One way to depart from this ideal is to state things that are true themselves, but have no bearing on the truth of the conclusion.

We might wonder why irrelevant remarks can have any influence at all. The answer is that we generally assume that a person's remarks are relevant, for this is one of the conditions for smooth and successful conversation (as Grice pointed out in his rule of Relevance, discussed in Chapter 1). That it is possible to exploit people by violating this natural assumption is shown in the following passage from *The Catcher in the Rye*.

> The new elevator boy was sort of on the stupid side. I told him, in this very casual voice, to take me up the Dicksteins'. . . .
>
> He had the elevator doors all shut and all, and was all set to take me up, and then he turned around and said, "They ain't in. They're at a party on the fourteenth floor."
>
> "That's all right," I said. "I'm supposed to wait for them. I'm their nephew."

> He gave me this sort of stupid, suspicious look. "You better wait in the lobby, fella," he said.
>
> "I'd like to—I really would," I said. "But I have a bad leg. I have to hold it in a certain position. I think I'd better sit down in the chair outside their door."
>
> He didn't know what the hell I was talking about, so all he said was "oh" and took me up. Not bad, boy. It's funny. All you have to do is say something nobody understands and they'll do practically anything you want them to.[19]

It is clear what is going on here. When someone offers something as a reason, it is conversationally implied that there is some connection between it and the thing you are arguing for. In most cases, the connection is obvious, and there is no need to spell it out. In other cases, the connection is not obvious, but in the spirit of cooperation others are willing to assume that the connection exists. In the present case, there seems to be no connection between having a bad leg and sitting in one particular chair. Why, then, does the elevator operator not challenge this statement? Part of the reason is that it is not easy to challenge what people say; among other things, it is not polite. But politeness does not seem to hold the elevator operator back; instead, he does not want to appear stupid. The person who offers a reason conversationally implies a connection, and we do not like to admit that we fail to see this connection. This combination of generosity and fear of looking stupid leads us to accept all sorts of irrelevant statements as reasons.

Fallacies of relevance are surprisingly common in everyday life. The best strategy for dealing with them is simply to cross out all irrelevant claims and then see what is left. Sometimes nothing is left. On the other hand, we should not be heavy-handed in making charges of irrelevance. Sometimes the occurrence of irrelevance is innocent; good arguments often contain irrelevant asides. More importantly, relevance is often secured by way of a conversational implication, so we really have to know what is going on in a given context in order to decide whether a remark is relevant or not. We can illustrate this last point by examining two kinds of arguments that often involve fallacies of irrelevance: *arguments ad hominem* and *appeals to authority*.

ARGUMENTS AD HOMINEM

Literally, an argument ad hominem is an argument directed against a person who is arguing rather than against that person's claim or argument. On the face of it, this seems to involve irrelevance, for the character or social position or status of a person should have nothing to do with the truth of what that person says or with the soundness or strength of that person's arguments.

In some cases, however, it is appropriate to criticize a person for putting forward an argument. Consider the following exchange:

---

[19] J. D. Salinger, *The Catcher in the Rye* (New York: Bantam Books), 157–58.

A: The cold war is over, and bad relations between Cuba and the United States hurt both countries, so it is time for the United States to develop normal relations with Cuba.

B: Yeah, so you can make a bundle importing cigars from those Commies.

B's reply is an attack on the motives of *A* and not on the truth of what *A* said. Yet the remark is not without some relevance—it is not off the wall. In a conversational exchange, we rely on the integrity of the person who is speaking, and when we have reasons to believe that the person's integrity is questionable, we sometimes say so. This is the significance of *B*'s remark. *B* points to a fact that gives some reason for us not to trust *A*'s integrity in a discussion of the United States' relations with Cuba.

In another kind of case, the very *right* to present an argument might be questioned. Suppose Congress is debating relations with Cuba. During one session, *A* argues for normalization. *A* can be criticized if *A* is not a member of Congress, because then *A* lacks the status that confers the right to speak in this setting. In a more normal example, if a neighbor tells someone that she ought to take her children to a certain church, the mother might respond "You are in no position to tell me what to do, you busybody," or just "Mind your own business."

Such attacks on the character or person of a speaker, or on the person's right to perform certain speech acts, will be called *ad hominem attacks*. Some ad hominem attacks are justified, but others are not. In the exchange between *A* and *B*, if the only real reason *A* favors normal relations between the United States and Cuba is that this would enable *A* to make more money, then *B*'s ad hominem attack may be well founded. On the other hand, if *A*'s real reason for saying what she does is that normal relations would be good for the United States and for Cuba, then *A*'s position does not depend on any lack of integrity, and *B*'s ad hominem attack is not well founded, even if it so happens that *A* would profit from normal relations.

Although the conclusions of ad hominem attacks are about a speaker, ad hominem attacks are sometimes used *illicitly* to reach a further conclusion about the *truth* or *falsity* of what a speaker says or about the *soundness* or *unsoundness* of an argument. We then have an *ad hominem fallacy*. In an ad hominem fallacy, irrelevant (though perhaps true) statements about the arguer are improperly used to attack the argument itself. This is a fallacy because, in general, the truth of a statement and the soundness of an argument do not depend on the character or status of the person arguing.

To return to the previous example, suppose *A* actually produces a strong argument that the United States should develop more-normal relations with Cuba, and *B* again replies "Yeah, so you can make a bundle importing cigars from those Commies." This ad hominem attack on *A* might be justified, as we saw. Nonetheless, if this attack on *A*'s character is used as a reason for rejecting the argument itself or its conclusion, then we have an ad hominem fallacy. *A*'s lack of integrity is irrelevant to the strength of *A*'s argument and the truth of *A*'s conclusion. Even if *A* has no right to say anything, what *A* says still might be true and well-founded.

Once you get used to spotting ad hominem fallacies, they seem common and obvious. Many of them cite personal characteristics that have nothing to do with the matter at hand. A speaker's ethnic background, sex, physical appearance, bathing habits, or dress almost never give us a good reason to challenge the truth of what that person says or the soundness of that person's argument. Ad hominem fallacies often deal in such irrelevant matters.

In some unusual cases, however, a speaker's character or position *is* a reason to doubt the truth of what he says. Suppose Sheila is suspected of committing murder, but Louie testifies that he was with her all that day. Then the prosecution shows that Louie provided a similar alibi for an accused murderer at ten trials in the past year, and every time he was found to have lied in exchange for money. This background about Louie provides some reason to believe that what Louie said was false—that he was not with Sheila all that day.

Other cases are less clear. When people are known for passing on rumors without checking their truth, this might be a reason to doubt what they say when they pass on another, similar rumor (even if it is not a reason to believe that what they say is false). In assessing what they say, it would be best to look for additional evidence. If none is available, then we need to ask how often their testimony is true on matters of this kind. Only by careful inspection of individual cases can we determine the strength of such ad hominem arguments.

Overall, then, we have four kinds of ad hominem arguments:

	Justified	Not justified
Ad hominem attacks only against a speaker	E.g., *B*'s reply, if *A* holds the position for self-serving reasons	E.g., *B*'s reply, if *A* holds the position for impartial reasons
Ad hominem arguments against a speaker's claim or argument	E.g., Louie, the perjurer for hire	Ad hominem fallacies

When assessing an ad hominem argument, the first step is to determine whether it argues only against the speaker or also against what the speaker says, and the second step is to determine whether the argument provides adequate justification for its conclusion. This will allow you to place the argument in the above table, although these steps will not always be obvious or easy.

EXERCISE XVII

For each of the following arguments, indicate whether it involves (a) an ad hominem attack only against a person, or (b) an ad hominem argument against a speaker's claim or argument, or (c) neither. Explain your answer.

Example: Sure, Sara says she saw me cheat, but Sara's stupid, so you shouldn't pay any attention to her.

Answer: This is only an ad hominem attack against Sara. The speaker does not say that what Sara says is false.

(1) Sure, Sara says she saw me cheat, but it was very dark, and her vision is horrible, so she must have seen something else and thought it was me cheating.

(2) Sure, Sam says he saw me cheat, but the only reason he says it is that he wants to get the best grade in the class. He's a real jerk.

(3) Sure, Sybill says she saw me cheat, but I didn't even take the exam, so I couldn't have cheated on it.

(4) Red Motor Company claims to have documents showing that the president of Green Motors knew of a dangerous defect in Green Motors cars, and he did nothing to fix it, so he was reckless, immoral, and criminal.

(5) The president of Green Motors responds to the accusation in (4) by saying that the Red Motor Company lies all the time in its ads, so it is probably lying again now.

(6) The president of Green Motors responds to the accusation in (4) by arguing that the Red Motor Company is the main competitor of Green Motors, so the Red Motor Company is probably making this accusation in public just to get ahead.

(7) The president of Green Motors responds to the accusation in (4) by arguing that the documents were originally dated incorrectly, so the president did not know about the defects in time to prevent the danger.

EXERCISE XVIII

Explain the point of each of the following remarks. Indicate whether each remark involves an ad hominem attack, an ad hominem fallacy, both, or neither. Then say whether or not the argument provides an adequate justification for its conclusion, and why.

(1) I've heard all the reasons why you think smoking is bad, but you're still smoking yourself, so you're not being consistent. I can't believe what you say if you don't follow your own advice.

(2) The American Tobacco Company has argued for years that smoking is not really unhealthy, but what would you expect the company to say? It would take the same position regardless of any evidence, so I can't trust it.

(3) President Clinton is in no position to criticize human-rights violations in Guatemala when the United States is involved in so much injustice with regard to so many of its own citizens. He should keep quiet until his country has cleaned up its own act.

(4) The main opposition to tax reductions comes from people who depend on government programs funded by taxes, so we shouldn't pay any attention to them.

(5) The main support for tax reductions comes from people who pay taxes, so we shouldn't pay any attention to them.

(6) Very few citizens have studied the entire tax code, and nobody understands the effect of taxes on the economy, so we have little reason to believe them when they say that present tax policies will destroy the economy.

(7) The Joint Chiefs of Staff argue that the United States government needs to increase its military budget, but an opponent responds "Well, of course, *they* will want as much money as they can get for their departments, whether they really need it or not. So we should not attach much weight to what they say."

(8) After Congress passes a military draft during a war, an opponent says "If members of Congress were eligible for the draft, they would not vote for it. So we must not really need a draft."

(9) Of course, the party in power is opposed to term limits. That's just because they want to stay in power.

(10) An economist cites recent trends in sales of raw materials as evidence of an upturn in the economy, and then a critic, who doubts the economist's prediction, responds "If you're so smart, why ain't you rich?"

(11) As an argument against atheism, a theist says "There are no atheists in the foxholes."

(12) As a criticism of proabortionists, Ronald Reagan said "I've noticed that everybody who is for abortion has already been born."

(13) Attacking male opponents of abortion, a feminist claims "Most opponents of abortion are men."

(14) When a member of a fraternity argued for coed houses in place of fraternities, a critic responded "When he quits his fraternity in protest and joins a coed house, then his words will hold more weight."

(15) When George argues at a fraternity meeting that his house should not admit women, Fred responds "Don't you like women?"

(16) When Fred argues at a fraternity meeting that his house should admit women, another member announces "Let me remind you all that Fred held exactly the opposite position last year."

(17) Almost everyone who thinks that drugs are harmless has taken drugs, so we can't trust their views.

(18) Let he who is without sin among you cast the first stone. (John 8:7)

DISCUSSION QUESTIONS

(1) In the biblical story of Job, Job is described as a person who "was blameless and upright, one who feared God and turned away from evil" (Job 1:1). Satan challenges God to allow him to subject Job to the worst calamities to see if Job's faith will remain unchanged. After the most extreme misfortunes, Job finally cries out and asks why he should be made to suffer so (Job 38:1–4):

> Then the Lord answered Job out of the whirlwind:
> Who is this that darkens counsel by words without knowledge?
> Gird up your loins like a man.
> I will question you, and you shall declare to me.
> Where were you when I laid the foundation of the earth?
> Tell me, if you have understanding.

Does God's response to Job involve an ad hominem attack? An ad hominem fallacy? Why or why not?

(2) At the Republican convention in 1992, Patrick Buchanan gave the following argument for the Republican incumbent, President George Bush, and against the Democratic challenger, Bill Clinton (*Vital Speeches of the Day*, vol. 58 [September 15, 1992], pp. 712–715 at 713):

> A president of the United States is also America's commander-in-chief. He's the man we authorize to send fathers and sons and brothers and friends into battle. George Bush was 17 years old when they bombed Pearl Harbor. He left his high school graduation, he walked down to the recruiting office, and he signed up to become the youngest fighter pilot in the Pacific war. And Mr. Clinton? . . . I'll tell you where he was. When Bill Clinton's time came in Vietnam, he sat up in a dormitory in Oxford, England, and figured out how to dodge the draft. Let me ask the question of this convention. Which of these two men has won the moral authority to send young Americans into battle? I suggest, respectfully, it is the American patriot and war hero, Navy Lieutenant J. G. George Herbert Walker Bush.

Is this an ad hominem attack? An ad hominem fallacy? Is it a good argument? Why or why not?

(3) In a heated discussion people will sometimes ask an opponent "Why are you being so defensive?" This is obviously a rhetorical question. What is the point of this question? Does it implicitly involve an ad hominem fallacy?

APPEALS TO AUTHORITY

Often in the midst of an argument, we cite an authority to back up what we say. As we saw in Chapter 2, this is a standard way of offering assurances. In citing an authority, instead of giving reasons for what we say, we indicate that someone (the authority cited) could give them.

Although logicians sometimes speak of the *fallacy* of appealing to authorities, we should notice in the first place that there is often nothing wrong with citing authorities or experts to support what we say. An authority is a person or institution with a privileged position concerning certain information. Through training, a doctor is an expert on certain diseases. A person who works in the Department of Agriculture can be an expert on America's soybean production. Someone who grew up in the swamps might be an expert on trapping muskrats. Since some people stand in a better position to know things than others, there is nothing wrong with citing them as authorities. In fact, an appeal to experts and authorities is essential if we are to make up our minds on subjects outside our own range of competence.

At the same time, appeals to authority can be abused, and there are some obvious questions we should ask whenever such an appeal is made. Most obviously, we should always ask whether the person cited is, in fact, an authority in the area under discussion. If the answer to this question is "No," then we are dealing with a fallacy of *relevance*. For example, being a movie star does not qualify a person to speak on the merits of a particular brand of toothpaste. Endorsements by athletes of hair creams, deodorants, beer, and automobiles are in the same boat. Of course, we have to be careful in making this charge. It is possible that certain athletes make systematic studies of deodorants before giving one deodorant their endorsement. But it is not likely.

Most people realize that athletes, movie stars, and the like are featured in advertisements primarily to attract attention and not because they are experts concerning the products they are endorsing. It is more surprising how often the wrong authorities are brought in to judge serious matters. To cite one example, Uri Geller had little difficulty in convincing a group of distinguished British scientists that he possessed psychic powers. In particular, he was able to convince them that he could bend spoons by mental powers alone. In contrast, James Randi, a professional magician, had little difficulty in detecting and duplicating the tricks that bamboozled the scientific observers. The remarkable feature of this case was not that a group of scientists could be fooled by a magician, but rather that these scientists assumed that they had the expertise necessary to decide whether a paranormal phenomenon had taken place or not. After all, the most obvious explanation of Geller's feats was that he had somehow cheated. To test this possibility, what was needed was not a scientist with impeccable scholarly credentials, but a magician who could do the same tricks himself and therefore knew what to look for.[20]

---

[20] For an entertaining and instructive account of this case, see James Randi, *The Magic of Uri Geller* (New York: Ballantine Books, 1975).

It is, of course, difficult to decide whether someone is an expert in a field when you yourself are not. There are, however, certain clues that will help you make this decision. If the supposed authority claims to have knowledge of things that he or she could not possibly possess (for example, about private conversations the person could not have heard), then you have little reason to trust other things that person has to say. You know that he or she has no qualms about making things up. Furthermore, it is often possible to spot-check certain claims in order to make sure that they are correct. It may take one expert to tell another, but it often takes little more than good common sense and an unwillingness to be fooled to detect a fraud.

Even in those cases in which it is clear that the person cited is an expert in the field, we can still ask whether the question is of the kind that can now be settled by an appeal to experts. It is important to raise this question, because sometimes the best experts simply get things wrong. For example, in 1932 Albert Einstein, who was surely an expert in the field, declared that "there is not the slightest indication that [nuclear] energy will ever be obtainable. It would mean that the atom would have to be shattered at will." Just a year later, the atom was, in fact, split. Even so, a leading British physicist, Ernest, Lord Rutherford, insisted that the splitting of the atom would not lead to the development of nuclear power, saying "The energy produced by the atom is a very poor kind of thing. Anyone who expects a source of power from the transformation of these atoms is talking moonshine." Given the knowledge available at the time, both Einstein and Rutherford may have been justified in their claims, but their assertions were, after all, more speculations than scientifically supported statements of fact. The lesson to be learned from this is that the best experts are sometimes fallible, and become more fallible when they go beyond established facts in their discipline to speculate about the future.[21]

Although this may seem obvious, we often forget to ask whether the authority has been cited correctly. When a person cites an authority, he or she is making a factual claim that so-and-so holds some particular view. Sometimes the claim is false. Here is an example:

According to medical authorities, poison ivy is contagious when it is oozing.

It someone told you this, you would probably believe it. In fact, the citation is incorrect. According to medical authorities, poison ivy is never contagious. Yet many people hold that it is contagious, and they think that they have medical opinion on their side. It is hard to deal with people who cite authorities incorrectly, for we do not carry an almanac or encyclopedia around with us. Yet, again, it is

---

[21] Both quotations are from Christopher Cerf and Victor Navasky, *The Experts Speak* (New York: Pantheon Books, 1984), 215. This work contains a marvelous collection of false and sometimes just plain stupid things that have been claimed by experts. One notable example is the remark made by the Union general John B. Sedgwick just before being fatally shot in the head by a Confederate marksman: "They couldn't hit an elephant at this dist——" (135).

a good idea to spot-check appeals to authority, for, short of lying, people often twist authorities to support their own opinions.

It is also worth asking whether the authority cited can be trusted to tell the truth. To put this more bluntly, we should ask whether a particular authority has any good reason to lie or misrepresent facts. Presumably, the officials who know most about Chinese food production will be the heads of the various agricultural bureaus. But it would be utterly naive to take their reports at face value. Inadequate agricultural production has been a standing embarrassment of the Chinese economy. As a consequence, there is pressure at every level to make things look as good as possible. Even if the state officials were inclined to tell the truth, which is a charitable assumption, the information they receive is probably not very accurate.

Experts also lie because it can bring fame and professional advancement. Science, sometimes at the highest level, has been embarrassed by problems of the falsification and misrepresentation of data. Consider the case of Sir Cyril Burt. Burt's research concerned the inheritance of intelligence. More specifically, he wanted to show that there is a significant correlation between the IQs of parents and their children. The difficulty was to find a way to screen out other influences—for example, that of home environment. To overcome this, Burt undertook a systematic study of identical twins who had been separated at birth and raised in various social settings. His study revealed a very high correlation between the IQs of these twins, and that gave strong reason to believe that IQ, to some significant extent, depends on heredity rather than environment. Unfortunately, Burt's data, or at least a significantly large portion of it, were cooked—that is, made up.

It is interesting that Burt's bogus research could go unchallenged for so long. It is also interesting how he was finally unmasked. First, to many his results seemed too good to be true. He claimed to have found more than fifty identical twins who had been separated at birth and raised in contrasting environments. Given the rarity of such creatures, that is a very large number to have found. Second, the correlations he claimed to find were extremely high—indeed, much higher than those usually found in research in this area. Both these facts raised suspicions. Stephen Jay Gould describes Burt's final undoing as follows:

> Princeton psychologist Leon Kamin first noted that, while Burt had increased his sample of twins from fewer than twenty to more than fifty in a series of publications, the average correlation between pairs for IQ remained unchanged to the third decimal place—a statistical situation so unlikely that it matches the vernacular definition of impossible. Then, in 1976, Oliver Gillie, medical correspondent of the London *Sunday Times*, elevated the charge from inexcusable carelessness to conscious fakery. Gillie discovered, among many other things, that Burt's two "collaborators" . . . the women who supposedly collected and processed his data, either never existed at all, or at least could not have been in contact with Burt while he wrote the papers bearing their names.[22]

Outright fraud of this kind, especially by someone so highly placed, is, admittedly, uncommon. Yet it does occur, and it provides a good reason for being suspicious

---

[22] Stephen Jay Gould, *The Mismeasure of Man* (New York: W. W. Norton, 1981), 235.

of authorities, especially when their results have not been given independent confirmation.

One last question we can ask is why the appeal to authority is being made at all. To cite an authority is to give assurances and, as we noticed earlier, people usually give assurances to strengthen the weak points in their arguments. It is surprising how often we can see what is wrong with an argument just by noticing where it is backed by appeals to authority. Beyond this, we should be suspicious of arguments that rely on too many authorities. (We might call this the fallacy of excessive footnotes.) Good arguments tend to stand on their own.

To go back to the beginning, in our complicated and specialized world, reliance on experts and authorities is unavoidable. Yet we can still be critical of appeals to authority by asking these questions:

(1) Is the authority cited in fact an authority in the area under discussion?

(2) Is this the kind of question that can now be settled by expert opinion?

(3) Has the authority been cited correctly?

(4) Can the authority cited be trusted to tell the truth?

(5) Why is an appeal to authority being made at all?

If the answers to (1) through (4) are "Yes," then the appeal to authority is probably justified. Still, even the best appeal to authority is an inductive argument, and even the best authorities make mistakes, so the conclusion of any appeal to authority might turn out to be false. We can reduce errors by appealing to better authorities, but no authority can guarantee the truth.

EXERCISE XIX

Answer the five questions in the text about each of the following appeals to authority, and then decide whether each appeal to authority is legitimate or fallacious:

(1) The surgeon general says that smoking is hazardous to your health, so it is.

(2) The surgeon general says that abortion is immoral, so it is.

(3) Michael Jordan says that Air Jordan sneakers are springier, so they must be springier.

(4) This must be a great movie, because the billboard says that *Time* magazine called it "terrific."

(5) My friend Joe says that this new movie is hilarious, so it must be worth watching.

(6) Ben and Jerry's ice cream must be the best, because Fat Fred eats more ice cream than anyone else I know, and he says that Ben and Jerry's is the best.

(7) But Dad, I *did* leave the party by midnight, just like you told me to. Just

ask Anna or Lars or Katie or Greg or Sara or Carol or Ann. Even the parking attendant, Jeff, saw me leave. And I also saw Nick and Hannah and Andrew and Linnea in the parking lot, so they will also tell you that I am telling the truth. Please, Dad, believe me!

(8) There must be life on other planets, because many great scientists are looking for it, so they must think it is there.

(9) "The U.S. Geological Survey has told me that the proven potential for oil in Alaska alone is greater than the proven reserves in Saudi Arabia." (Ronald Reagan, *Detroit Free Press,* March 23, 1980)

(10) Lefty Lopez must be the best pitcher of the year, because he won the Cy Young Award (awarded by the Baseball Writers Association to the best pitcher of the year).

(11) Vanna must be the most beautiful woman in America, because she won the Miss America contest.

(12) Amnesty International has documented a tremendous number of serious human rights abuses in Guatemala, so that country's government must be horrible.

(13) There were 250,000 protesters at the rally, because organizers gave that figure.

(14) True Christians ought to give away all their money, because the Bible says "Blessed are the poor."

MORE FALLACIES OF RELEVANCE

Questions like those used to evaluate appeals to authority can also be used to assess some other common styles of reasoning that are often accused of being fallacious. Here is one example:

> The American people are convinced that, if we get involved in Bosnia, we will be stuck there for a long time. So we shouldn't get involved in the first place.

This argument, of course, depends on suppressed premises. On one reconstruction, the argument is that, because Americans fear getting stuck in Bosnia, they oppose American involvement, and a democratic government should not do what the people oppose, so we should not get involved in Bosnia. However, the argument also seems to suggest another reason why America should not get involved—namely, that if we do, our troops will be stuck in Bosnia. The only reason that is given for believing this is that lots of American people believe it. So the argument seems to be that, since so many Americans believe it, it must be true.

Such an argument is not an appeal to authority, since no person is claimed to be an authority or an expert. Instead, the argument is an *appeal to popular opinion.* When the popular opinion is supposed to have been shared for a long time, the argument can be called an *appeal to tradition.*

Such arguments assume that, when many people agree on some issue, they are likely to be right. This assumption is often wrong. An opinion might be shared by so many people just because they all learned it from a common source, such as television or some prominent politicians, and then the shared opinion is not reliable unless its source is reliable. Of course, the shared opinion might be true; America might get stuck in Bosnia if it does get involved. But the argument for this conclusion is still fallacious, because the mere fact that an opinion is widely held is not enough to show that the opinion is true.

Although such appeals to popular opinion are often fallacious, there are also some areas where popular opinion is evidence of truth. If most people think that a book is entertaining and easy to understand, then it is entertaining and easy to understand. If most people think that the sky looks blue, this is evidence that the sky does look blue. Thus, not all appeals to popular opinion are defective or fallacious.

In order to determine whether or not a particular appeal to popular opinion is fallacious, we need to ask questions that are much like the questions we asked about appeals to authority. These include:

(1) Is this opinion really widely held?

(2) Is this the kind of area where popular opinion is likely to be right?

(3) Why is an appeal to popular opinion being made at all?

Even when superficial examination reveals that an appeal to popular opinion is fallacious, such arguments still seem to convince many people. This might be because many people want to agree with others so that they will be popular and will not have to think for themselves.

Yet another argument in this family is an *appeal to ignorance*. For example, a jealous husband might argue this way:

My wife must be having an affair, because I can't prove that she isn't.

Of course, the conclusion does not follow. Indeed, the husband's inability to prove that his wife is *not* having an affair does not have any tendency to prove that his wife *is* having an affair. Why not? Because he would not be able to prove this even if she were not having an affair, unless he followed her all day long for weeks or months. This point also applies to the reverse argument:

My wife must not be having an affair, because I can't prove that she is.

Again, this premise does not adequately support the conclusion, because the husband might not be able to *prove* that his wife is having an affair even if she is.

But contrast these arguments with another that seems grammatically similar:

My wife does not keep a Winnebago in our garage, because I have never seen one there.

This argument is perfectly fine, and the reason is clear: If my wife did keep a Winnebago in our garage, then I would see it there. Thus, to determine whether an appeal to ignorance is fallacious, we need to ask (1) whether this is the kind of fact that I would know or see or be aware of or be able to prove, if it were true. We also should ask (2) whether the person really is ignorant on this matter, and (3) why an appeal to ignorance is being made at all. Questions such as these are useful whenever an argument might involve a fallacy of relevance.

One final caution is necessary. Appeals to authority, popular opinion, tradition, and ignorance are often combined within a single argument. This is sometimes done to confuse the issue. Moreover, everyday arguments are often stated so vaguely that it is not clear whether the appeal is to authority, popular opinion, tradition, or ignorance. The best strategy in responding to such arguments is usually to restate the arguments in clearer terms and then separate the different appeals that are being made. Each one can then be assessed on its own terms.

EXERCISE XX

For each of the following arguments, indicate whether it is an appeal to popular opinion, an appeal to tradition, or an appeal to ignorance. (The argument might fit into more than one of these categories. If so, explain why.) Then determine whether it is fallacious, and why.

(1) For centuries throughout Europe, women were burned for being witches, so there must have been a lot of witches.

(2) "Polls show an overwhelming majority of the American people want a lot less immigration or even an immigration moratorium. . . . These are persistent results over time. Most of the people cannot be wrong all of the time!"[23]

(3) Acupuncturists have no scientific basis for what they do, because nobody has ever been able to find one.

(4) Respected scientific journals never publish articles about flying saucers, so there must not be any real evidence for flying saucers.

(5) There must be life on other planets, because most people think there is. Just read a few tabloids.

(6) There is no life on other planets, because nobody has found any definite signs of it, even though very many scientists have been looking for very many years.

(7) Seth didn't leave his room all night. I know this because I didn't see him leave, and I stayed just outside the door to his room all night.

(8) Most people who live in the United States think that it is the greatest country ever, so it must be.

---

[23] From an advertisement placed by FAIR (Federation for American Immigration Reform), *Atlantic Monthly* (June 1995): 67.

(9) Nobody has ever found the causes of human behavior, so we must be free.

(10) Everything else is determined, and nobody can prove that human actions are any different, so human actions must also be determined.

(11) There are more Buddhists than followers of any other religion, so there must be more truth in Buddhism.

(12) Incest must be immoral, because people all over the world for many centuries have seen it as immoral.

(13) The Golden Rule is accepted in almost every system of ethics both in the past and in the present, so there is probably something to it.

(14) Chris must not be guilty, because twelve jurors, who saw all the evidence, agreed on a verdict of not guilty.

(15) The jury must find Pat not guilty, for the prosecution has not proven Pat's guilt beyond a reasonable doubt.

FALLACIES OF VACUITY

CIRCULAR REASONING

One purpose of arguments is to establish the truth of a claim to someone who doubts it. In a typical situation, one person, *A*, makes a claim; another person, *B*, raises objections to it; then *A* tries to find arguments that respond to the objections and justify the original statement. Schematically:

A asserts that *p* is true.

B raises objections *x, y,* and *z* against it.

A then offers reasons to overcome these objections.

What must *A*'s responses be like in order to meet *B*'s objections? To start with the simplest case, *A* cannot meet *B*'s challenge simply by repeating the original assertion. If someone is maintaining that arms races inevitably lead to war, it will not help to offer as a justification for this the very claim that is in dispute—that arms races inevitably lead to war. The argument would look like this:

Arms races inevitably lead to war.

∴ Arms races inevitably lead to war.

This argument is, of course, *valid*, since the premise cannot be true without the conclusion being true as well. Furthermore, if the premise is true, then the argument is also *sound*. All the same, the argument has no force in this conversational setting because any objection that *B* has to the conclusion is straight off an objection to the premise, since they are identical.

In fact, people usually do not make it so easy to tell when they reason in a circle. Often circular reasoning is disguised by restating the conclusion in different words. Someone might argue that arms races inevitably lead to war, since countries always eventually start fighting each other after they have built up their supplies of weapons in an attempt to gain more firepower than their adversaries. This premise means the same as the conclusion, since an arms race just is a competition in which countries build up their supplies of weapons to get more than their adversaries; so this reasoning is still circular. Another way to hide circular reasoning is to put forward a statement first as a conclusion to be proved, and then only much later—after several subarguments or tangents—use the same statement as a premise in its own behalf. Although this trick is often hard to detect in a long and complex argument, such reasoning is still indirectly circular if any premise in a chain of arguments repeats or restates the eventual conclusion. Thus, we have *circular reasoning* if and only if one of the premises that is used directly or indirectly to support a conclusion is equivalent to the conclusion itself.

BEGGING THE QUESTION

Reasoning in a circle is *often* bad reasoning, but is it *always* bad? It seems not.

The clearest examples occur when circular reasoning is used in the middle of larger stretches of theoretical reasoning. Suppose a scientist labels a chemical as bihydrogenic if its molecules contain exactly two atoms of hydrogen. The scientist goes on to show that certain properties $x, y,$ and z must be shared by all bihydrogenic compounds. Then the scientist argues: "There are two atoms of hydrogen in each water molecule, so water is bihydrogenic. Thus, water must also have properties $x, y,$ and z." The first sentence involves circular reasoning, but this circular reasoning is still useful, because it simplifies inferences or predictions about water from the theory.

Circular reasoning can even sometimes be useful when the purpose of an argument is not to simplify but is instead to justify or convince or persuade. Suppose Susie says to Joe "You have H_2O on your shirt." Joe responds "No. It's water." Then Susie might argue this way:

> You have water on your shirt.
> Water is H_2O.
> _____
> ∴ You have H_2O on your shirt.

The first premise is equivalent to the conclusion, because water is H_2O by definition. Thus, Susie's reasoning is circular. But the argument is still informative and should be persuasive, at least for Joe, who does not know that water is H_2O.

What these cases show is that not every circular argument is useless or bad. Yet the earlier examples show that many circular arguments are defective. What is the difference? What makes some circles fallacious and others not? This is controversial, but the answer seems to lie in the conversational context. Susie's argument does not seem fallacious, so it does not beg the question if Joe admits that he has water on his shirt and he simply has never heard water described as

H_2O. But contrast this with a different conversational context, in which Susie says "You have H_2O on your shirt," and Joe responds instead "No. That's water. Alcohol is H_2O; water is not." Suppose Susie gives the same argument: You have water on your shirt. Water is H_2O. Therefore, you have H_2O on your shirt. If this is all Susie says, then Susie's argument does not give Joe any reason to change his opinion or to believe Susie, even though Susie is right.

Of course, arguments do not fail *every* time an opponent would deny a premise. If they did, arguments would rarely succeed. Nonetheless, if Joe has just finished denying that water is H_2O, and if Susie asserts exactly what Joe denied, then Susie has done nothing to overcome Joe's objections, because any objection that Joe has to the conclusion will also be an objection to the premise. To get beyond this impasse, Susie owes Joe some new evidence for what she says. If Susie were to give some independent evidence that water is H_2O—even if only by citing a chemistry book—then this would give Joe a good reason to believe that water is H_2O. But the bare assertion of what Joe denies accomplishes nothing in the absence of any further evidence to help resolve their dispute.

In general, then, we can say that an argument *begs the question* in a context if and only if any objection in the context to its conclusion is also an objection to one of its premises, and that premise is not supported by any independent evidence. This is a fallacy because, when a premise is in dispute or subject to objection, it *needs* to be supported by some independent evidence, at least in a context in which the arguer's goal is to give an opponent reason to accept the premise and, on that basis, to accept the conclusion. When such a need for evidence is not satisfied, the argument commits the fallacy of begging the question.

This fallacy is often hard to detect, so people often use it to convince their opponents when they have nothing better to say, especially on a controversial issue. It is common, for example, to hear an argument something like the following:

> It's always wrong to murder human beings.
> Capital punishment involves murdering human beings.
> _____
> ∴ Capital punishment is wrong.

Here the first premise is definitionally true, since to call something murder is to call it wrongful killing. The second premise is, however, question begging, for in calling capital punishment murder, the point at issue has been assumed—that is, that capital punishment is something wrong. As a result, anyone who objects to the conclusion would or should raise exactly the same objections to the second premise, but one could not give any evidence for the premise without first arguing for the conclusion.

More subtly than this, opponents of abortion typically refer to the human fetus as an unborn baby, or simply as a baby. It may seem a matter of indifference how the fetus is referred to, but this is not true. One of the central points in the debate over abortion is whether the fetus has the status of a person and thus has the rights a person has. It is generally acknowledged in our society that babies are persons and therefore have the rights of persons. By referring to the fetus as an unborn baby (or simply as a baby), a point that demands argument is taken for granted without argument, and that counts as begging the question. Of course, many opponents of abortion argue for the claim that a human fetus has the moral status of a person and thus do not beg this central question in the debate. But if they give no such independent argument, then they do beg the question.

Similarly, if someone argues the pro-choice position simply on the grounds that a woman has a right to control the destiny of her own body, this also begs an important question, because it takes for granted the claim that the fetus is part of a woman's body and not an independent being with rights of its own. Of course, defenders of the pro-choice position need not beg the question in this way, but they often do.

Although the notion of circular reasoning can be defined quite precisely—the conclusion (or its equivalent) is used as a premise in its own behalf—the idea of begging the question is more elusive. Whether a particular argument or premise is question begging will depend on the context in which it appears. An argument is question begging if it relies, either explicitly or implicitly, on things that, in the argumentative context, are matters of dispute. Thus, referring to a human fetus as a baby will be question begging in contexts in which the moral status of the fetus is at issue, but it may not be question begging when this is not an issue.

EXERCISE XXIII

For each of the following arguments, does it involve circular reasoning? Does it beg the question in any context? If so, in which contexts? Explain your answers.

(1) Bush lost the election, because he got fewer electoral votes than his opponent.

(2) Intoxicating beverages should be banned, because they can make people drunk.

(3) Capitalism is the only correct economic system, because without it free enterprise would be impossible.

(4) Free trade is good for the country, because it brings all the advantages of an unimpeded flow of goods between countries.

(5) Gun-control laws are wrong, because they violate the citizen's right to bear arms.

(6) When *B* applies for a job from *A*:
   A: How can we know that you are trustworthy?
   B: Mr. Davidson will write me a recommendation.
   A: But why should we trust him?
   B: I assure you that he is honest.

(7) The Bible is the inerrant word of God, because God speaks only the truth, and because repeatedly in the Bible God tells us that the Bible consists of his words.

(8) We have to accept change, because without change there is no progress.

(9) College athletes should be paid to play sports, because they are professionals anyway.

(10) Premarital sex is wrong, because premarital sex is fornication, and fornication is a sin.

(11) I know this act is wrong, because my conscience tells me so. My conscience tells me so because it is wrong.

(12) The drinking age should be lowered to eighteen, because eighteen-year-olds are mature enough to drink.

(13) We should never give security clearances to homosexuals, because they can be blackmailed into revealing classified information. They are subject to blackmail, because we will revoke their security clearances if we find out they are gay.

(14) Contract killers should not be found guilty of murder, because, if they kill many people just for money, that alone shows they are insane.

(15) People with suicidal tendencies are insane, because they want to kill themselves.

(16) Jeffrey can't really be insane, because he says he is.

DISCUSSION QUESTIONS (ADVANCED)

(1) Explanations are often presented in the form of arguments, and sometimes these arguments seem circular. Here is one example:

> TOM: Why are so many people moving out of Claremont this year?
> SUE: Because its economy is going down so fast.
> TOM: But why is its economy going down so fast?
> SUE: Because so many people are moving out of town.

Does Sue really reason in a circle? If so, does this show that her explanations are defective or beg the question?

Next consider a second dialogue:

> AMY: Why is Jarred going down on the seesaw right now?
> JOHN: Because Jeremiah is going up on the other side of the seesaw.
> AMY: But why is Jeremiah going up right now?
> JOHN: Because Jarred is going down.

Does John reason in a circle? If so, does this make his explanations defective or question begging? More generally, when, if ever, can circular arguments provide good explanations?

Continued on next page

DISCUSSION QUESTIONS *Continued from previous page*

(2) John Stuart Mill wrote:

It must be granted that in every syllogism, considered as an argument to prove the conclusion, there is a *petitio principii* [a begging of the question]. When we say,

All men are mortal,
Socrates is a man,

∴ Socrates is mortal;

is unanswerably urged by the adversaries of the syllogistic theory that the proposition, "Socrates is mortal," is presupposed in the more general assumption, "All men are mortal"; that we cannot be assured of the mortality of all men unless we are already certain of the mortality of every individual man. . . . That, in short, no reasoning from generals to particulars can, as such, prove anything, since from a general principle we cannot infer any particulars but those which the principle itself assumes as known.[24]

Do you agree? Why or why not?

(3) In response to some philosophers who denied the existence of objects in the external world, G. E. Moore held up his hands and argued roughly like this: "Here is one hand. Here is another. Therefore, there are (at least two) objects in the external world."[25] Does this argument beg the question? Why or why not?

(4) Is the following argument circular? Does it beg the question in any contexts? If so, in which contexts?

Sue lives in the Buckeye State.
Ohio is the Buckeye State.

∴ Sue lives in Ohio.

(5) Does the following argument beg the question in any contexts? If so, in which contexts?

There is a fallacy of begging the question.

∴ There is a fallacy of begging the question.[26]

---

[24] John Stuart Mill, *A System of Logic* (London; 1843), Book 2, Chapter 3, Section 2.

[25] G. E. Moore, "Proof of an External World," in Moore, *Philosophical Papers* (London: Allen and Unwin, 1959), 127–50.

[26] This example comes from Roy Sorenson, "Unbeggable Questions," *Analysis* 56 (January 1996), pp. 51–55 at p. 51.

SELF-SEALERS

It is characteristic of certain positions that no evidence can *possibly* refute them. This may seem to be a wonderful feature for a position to have. In fact, however, it *usually* makes the position useless. We can start with a silly example. A Perfect Sage claims to be able to predict the future in detail. The Perfect Sage's predictions take the following form:

> Two weeks from today at 4:37 you are going to be doing *exactly* what you will be doing.

Of course, whatever you are doing at that time will be exactly what you are doing, so this prediction cannot possibly be wrong. But this is only because it does not tell us anything in particular about the future. *Whatever* happens, the prediction is going to be true, and this is just what is wrong with it. The prediction is *empty* or *vacuous*.

People do not, of course, go around making predictions of the kind just noticed, but they do sometimes hold positions that are empty or vacuous in much the same way. A clairvoyant claims to be able to predict the future, but every time a prediction fails, he says that this just proves that someone set up bad vibrations that interfered with his visions. So if the prediction turns out to be true, he claims that this shows his clairvoyance; if it turns out to be false, he cites this as evidence of interference. No matter what happens, then, the clairvoyant's claim to be clairvoyant cannot be refuted. His claim to clairvoyance is as empty and vacuous as the Perfect Sage's prediction.

Positions that are set up in this way so that nothing can possibly refute them will be called *self-sealers*.[27] A self-sealing position is one that is so constructed that no evidence can possibly be brought against it no matter what happens. This shows its vacuity, and it is precisely for this reason that we reject it.

People do not usually hold self-sealing positions in a blatant way; they tend to back into them. A person who holds that the American economy is controlled by an international Jewish conspiracy will point out people of Jewish extraction (or with Jewish names) who occupy important positions in financial institutions. This at least counts as evidence, though very weak evidence. And there seems to be much stronger evidence on the other side: There are a great many people in these institutions who are not Jews. To counter this claim, the person now argues that many of these other people are secretly Jews or are tools of the Jewish conspiracy. The Jews have allowed some non-Jews to hold important positions in order to conceal their conspiracy. What evidence is there for this? Well, really none, but that only helps prove how clever the Jewish conspiracy is. At this point, the position has become self-sealing, for all evidence cited against the existence of the conspiracy will be converted into evidence for its cleverness.

Self-sealing arguments are hard to deal with, because people who use them will often shift their ground. A person will begin by holding a significant position

---

[27] We owe this phrase to Ted Honderich. He owes it, directly or indirectly, to Leon Lipson.

that implies that facts are one way rather than another, but under the pressure of criticism will self-seal the position so that no evidence can possibly count against it. That is, the person will slide back and forth between two positions—one that is not self-sealed, and so is significant but subject to refutation, and another that is self-sealed, and so is not subject to criticism but is also not significant. The charge that is leveled against a theory that vacillates in this way is that it is either *vacuous* or *false*. It is vacuous if self-sealing, false if not.

One way of challenging a self-sealing position is to ask what possible fact could prove it wrong. This is a good question to ask, but it can be misunderstood and met with the triumphant reply: "Nothing can prove my position wrong, because it is right." A better way to show the insignificance of a self-sealing theory is to put the challenge in a different form: "If your position has any significance, it should tell us that certain things will occur whereas certain other things will not occur. If it cannot do this, it really tells us nothing at all; so please make some specific predictions, and we will see how they come out."

Ideologies and worldviews tend to be self-sealing. The Marxist ideology some-times has this quality. If you fail to see the truth of the Marxist ideology, that just shows that your social consciousness has not been raised. The very fact that you reject the Marxist ideology shows that you are not yet capable of understanding it and that you are in need of reeducation. This is perfect self-sealing. Sometimes psychoanalytic theory gets involved in this same kind of self-sealing. People who vigorously disagree with certain psychoanalytic claims can be accused of repressing these facts. If a boy denies that he wants to murder his father and sleep with his mother, this itself can be taken as evidence of the strength of these desires and of his unwillingness to acknowledge them. If this kind of reasoning gets out of hand, then psychoanalytic theory also becomes self-sealing and empty. Freud was aware of this danger and warned against it.

So far, we have seen two ways in which an argument can be self-sealing: (1) It can invent an ad hoc or arbitrary way of dismissing every possible criticism. The clairvoyant can always point to interfering conditions without going to the trouble of saying what they are. The anti-Semite can always cite Jewish cleverness to explain away counterevidence. We might call this self-sealing *by universal discount-ing*. (2) A theory can also counter criticism by attacking its critics. The critic of Marxism is charged with having a decadent bourgeois consciousness that blinds her to the facts of class conflict. The critic's response to psychoanalytic theory is analyzed (and then dismissed) as repression, a reaction formation, or something similar. Here self-sealing is achieved through an ad hominem fallacy. We might call this self-sealing *by going upstairs*, because the theorist is looking down on the critic.

Yet another form of self-sealing is this: (3) Words are used in such a way that a position becomes true *by definition*. For example, a person makes the strong claim that all human actions are selfish. This is an interesting remark, but it seems to be false, for it is easy to think of cases in which people have acted in self-sacrificing ways. To counter these obvious objections, the argument takes the following turn: When a person acts in a self-sacrificing way, what that person *wants* to do is help another even at his own expense. This is his desire or his motive, and that is what he acts to fulfill. So the action is selfish after all, since the person is acting in order to achieve what he wants. This is a self-sealing move, for it will not help to cite any behavior—even heroic self-destructive behavior—as counterevidence. If a person desires to do something even if it involves the sacrifice of his life, then he acts to fulfill his desire, and the act is again called selfish.

It is not hard to see what has happened in this case. The arguer has chosen to use the word "selfish" in a new and peculiar way: a person is said to act selfishly if he acts to do what he desires to do. This is not what we usually mean by this word. We ordinarily say that a person acts selfishly if he is too much concerned with his own interests at the expense of the interests of others. On this standard use of the word "selfish," there are any number of counterexamples to the claim that all human actions are selfish. But these counterexamples do not apply when the word "selfish" is used in a new way, where "acting selfishly" comes close to meaning just "acting." The point is that under this new meaning of "selfish" it becomes empty (or almost empty) to say that all human actions are selfish. We are thus back to a familiar situation. Under one interpretation (the ordinary interpretation), the claim that all human actions are selfish is interesting but false. Under another interpretation (an extraordinary interpretation), the claim is true but vacuous. The position gets all its *apparent* interest and plausibility from a rapid two-step back and forth between these positions.

Self-sealing arguments are not easy to handle, for they change their form under pressure. The best strategy is to begin by charging a person who uses such an argument with saying something trivial, vacuous, or boring. If, to meet this charge, he or she says something quite specific and important, then argument can proceed along normal lines. But it is not always easy to get down to brass tacks in this way. This becomes clear if you examine an argument between a Marxist and an anti-Marxist, between a psychoanalyst and a critic of psychoanalysis, or between individuals with different religious views. Their positions are often sealed against objections from each other, and then their arguments are almost always at cross-purposes.

Although we have emphasized how large-scale ideologies can become self-sealing, small-scale claims in everyday life are also often sealed against any possible refutation. In fact, a number of common words are used to this end. If someone says "All true conservatives support school prayer," and a critic points out a conservative who opposes school prayer, then the original claim might be defended by saying, "He is not *truly* (or *really*) a conservative." If this response is trotted out in every case, it turns out that the original claim does not exclude anything. Similarly, the claim that "some students need to work harder than others, but if any student works hard enough, he or she will get good grades" can be protected simply by declaring that any student who works hard but does not get good grades does not work hard *enough*. Finally, someone who says "If you think it over thoroughly, you will agree with me" can dismiss anyone who disagrees simply by denying that he thought it over *thoroughly*. Of course, these terms—"true," "real," "thorough(ly)," and "enough"—do not always make positions self-sealing. Nonetheless, these and other common terms are often used to seal positions against any possible criticism. When these terms are used in these ways, the resulting positions are empty and can be criticized in the same ways as self-sealing ideologies.

DISCUSSION QUESTIONS

(1) Antony Flew wrote:

> Someone tells us that God loves us as a father loves his children. We are reassured. But then we see a child dying of inoperable cancer of the throat. His earthly father is driven frantic in his efforts to help, but his Heavenly Father shows no obvious sign of concern. Some qualification is made—God's love is "not merely human love" or it is "an inscrutable love," perhaps—and we realize that such offerings are quite compatible with the truth of the assertion that "God loves us as a father (but, of course . . .)." We are reassured again. But then perhaps we ask: what is this assurance of God's (appropriately qualified) love worth, what is this apparent guarantee really a guarantee against? Just what would have to happen not merely (morally and wrongly) to tempt us but also (logically and rightly) to entitle us to say "God does not love us" or even "God does not exist"?[28]

How would you answer Flew's question? If the answer to Flew's question were that nothing could entitle us to say this, as Flew suggests, would this show that religious positions like this are self-sealing and empty?

(2) During the nineteenth century, evidence mounted that apparently showed that the earth had existed for millions, perhaps hundreds of millions, of years. This seemed to contradict the account given in Genesis that holds that the earth was created less than ten thousand years ago. In response to this challenge, Philip Henry Gosse replied roughly as follows: In creating Adam and Eve, God would endow them with navels, and thus it would seem that they had been born in the normal way, and thus also seem that they had existed for a number of years before they were created by God. Beyond this, their hair, fingernails, bones, and so on would all show evidence of growth, again giving evidence of previous existence. The same would be true of the trees that surrounded them in the Garden of Eden, which would have rings. Furthermore, the sediment in the rivers should suggest that they had flowed for very many years in the past. In sum,

---

[28] Antony Flew, "Theology and Falsification," in *New Essays in Philosophical Theology*, ed. A. Flew and A. MacIntyre (New York: Macmillan, 1955), 98–99.

although the earth was created fairly recently, God would have created it in a way that would make it appear that it had existed for many more years, perhaps millions of years in the past. Thus, the actual creation of the earth less than ten thousand years ago is compatible with scientific evidence that suggests that it is much older than this. Evaluate this line of reasoning.

(3) Some creationist critics of Darwin's theory of natural selection argue as follows:

> Natural selection is a tautologous concept (circular reasoning) because it simply requires the fittest organisms to leave the most offspring and at the same time it identifies the fittest organisms as those that leave the most offspring. Thus natural selection seemingly does not provide a testable explanation of how mutation would produce more fit organisms.[29]

Does this argument show that Darwin's theory is self-sealing? How could defenders of natural selection best respond?

(4) Freud claims that, no matter how much they deny it, all women at least unconsciously want to have penises. Could there be any evidence that this claim is false? Is so, what kind of evidence, and how could Freud best respond? If not, what does this show about Freud's claim?

(5) Christina Hoff Sommers wrote:

> The women currently manning—womanning—the feminist ramparts do not take well to criticism. How could they? As they see it, they are dealing with a massive epidemic of male atrocity and a constituency of benighted women who have yet to comprehend the seriousness of their predicament. Hence, male critics must be "sexist" and "reactionary," and female critics "traitors," "collaborators," or "backlashers." This kind of reaction has had a powerful inhibiting effect. It has alienated and silenced women and men alike.[30]

Do you agree? Why or why not? If feminists are guilty of what Sommers claims, does this make their positions self-sealing? ∎

---

[29] Duane T. Gish, Richard B. Bliss, and Wendell R. Bird, "Summary of Scientific Evidence for Creation," *Impact* nos. 95–96 (May/June 1981).

[30] Christina Hoff Sommers, *Who Stole Feminism? How Women Have Betrayed Women* (New York: Simon and Schuster, 1994), p. 18.

Chapter Eleven

OTHER USES OF ARGUMENTS

In earlier chapters, we have often spoken about arguments as if their only function was to justify claims. This chapter will attempt to correct this one-sided view by exploring some uses of arguments other than justification. In many cases, the primary purpose of an argument is not to establish some truth but is instead to *refute* another argument or claim. Another important use of arguments is to *systematize* and *simplify* a theory by revealing interconnections among its terms and claims. Arguments are also used to formulate *explanations*. In seeking an explanation, we are not trying to prove that something is true; we are trying to understand *why* it is true. Finally, the chapter considers arguments used to offer *excuses*, treating them as a special kind of explanation—namely, as an explanation of conduct intended to put it in a better light. As we shall see, these different uses of argument have distinctive criteria of adequacy, since arguments can be evaluated according to how well they serve the purpose for which they are used.

REFUTATIONS

To *refute* an argument is to show that it is no good. Some writers, however, have incorrectly used the term "refute" to mean something much weaker. They say such things as that Supreme Court Justice Clarence Thomas refuted the charges brought against him by Anita Hill, meaning nothing more by this than that he rejected them or replied to them. This, however, is not what the word "refute" means. To refute the charges brought against him, Thomas would have to *prove* that these charges were erroneous. Refuting a charge requires giving an adequate argument against it. This takes a lot more work than simply rejecting it.

Nonetheless, it is also important to remember that we can refute an *argument* without proving that its conclusion is false. A refutation of an argument is sufficient if it raises objections that cannot be answered. Consequently, the patterns of successful refutations mirror the criteria for a good argument, since the point of a refutation is to show that one of these criteria has not been met. Refutations then take three main forms: (1) we can show that the conclusion does not follow from the premises;[1] (2) we can argue that some of the premises are dubious or even false; and (3) we can show that the argument begs the question. This last charge was discussed in the preceding chapter, so here we will focus on the first two methods of refutation.

THAT'S JUST LIKE ARGUING . . .

We know that an argument is not valid if it starts from true premises and leads to a false conclusion. Often, however, we cannot point this out to refute an argument, because the truth or falsity of the conclusion is the very thing at issue. When this problem arises, a typical device is to point out that by arguing in the same way, or a similar way, we can reach a conclusion that is unsatisfactory.

Here is a simple example:

MATTHEW: If I had a higher salary, I could buy more things; so, if everyone had higher salaries, everyone could buy more things.

KIRSTY: That's just like arguing that, if one person stands up at a ball game, he will get a better view; so, if everyone stands up, everyone will get a better view.

At first sight, it may not be obvious whether Matthew's style of reasoning is valid or not. Kirsty's response shows that Matthew's argument is invalid by providing an instance in which the same style of reasoning takes us from something true to something that is obviously false, because, if everyone stands up at a ball game, only the tallest people will be able to see better. Kirsty's response also shows *why*

---

[1] To refute an inductive argument, it is not enough to show that the conclusion does not follow or that the argument is not valid, because inductive arguments are not intended to be valid. Instead, you need to show that the argument is weak by inductive standards. We discussed inductive arguments and their standards in Chapter 8. We will focus on deductive arguments in this chapter.

Matthew's argument is invalid: Just as one person's ability to see can be affected by other people standing up, because this raises the height that is necessary in order to see, so one person's ability to buy can be affected by other people having more money, if this raises prices and thereby raises the amount of money that is necessary in order to buy things.

Refuting an argument by showing that it is *just like another* argument that is obviously no good is a common device in everyday discussions. Here is another example:

> CARY: Most of the people in this class are college students. Most college students study hard. Therefore, most of the people in this class study hard.
>
> DAVID: That's just like arguing that most whales live in the sea, and most animals that live in the sea are fish, so most whales are fish.

At first sight, it might not be clear how the second argument could show anything about the first argument. What do whales have to do with students? However, the point is simply that the two arguments share a basic form. Thus, if the second argument is not valid by virtue of that form, then the first is also not valid by virtue of that same form. And the second argument is obviously not valid, since its premises are true but its conclusion is false. This shows that the first argument is not valid, at least by virtue of the shared form.[2]

----

[2] The first argument still might be valid on some other basis, as in the degenerate cases mentioned in Chapters 5 through 7. However, a defender of the first argument at least owes an alternative account of its validity.

Of course, not every refutation of this kind is so simple or so successful. To understand the criteria that must be met for such a refutation to work, it will be useful to consider a more complex example that reveals some of the ways to respond to a charge of "That's just like arguing. . . ." The example concerns proposed legal restrictions on gun ownership. The National Rifle Association (NRA) feared that these restrictions would lead to a total ban on guns, which they opposed, so they widely distributed a bumper sticker that read:

(1) If guns are outlawed, only outlaws will have guns.

The point, presumably, was that most people would add the suppressed premise

(2) It would be bad if only outlaws had guns,

and reach the conclusion

(3) Therefore, guns should not be outlawed.

This argument is not very clear, partly because it is not clear who counts as an "outlaw." Some critics poke fun at this bumper sticker because (1) seems true by definition if outlaws include anyone who breaks any law, since anyone with a gun breaks a law if guns are outlawed. However, what the NRA probably means by "outlaws" are people who commit violent crimes such as robbery, rape, and murder. It is not strictly true that these will be the only people with guns if guns are outlawed, since police and some present gun owners would keep their guns. Nonetheless, these exceptions do not touch the NRA's main claim, which is that law-abiding people who would give up their guns if guns were outlawed would then not have guns to defend themselves against violent criminals.

How can an opponent try to refute this argument? There are several possibilities, but what defenders of gun control in fact did was distribute other bumper stickers. One of them read:

(1′) If gum is outlawed, only outlaws will have gum.

The main point might be just to parody the NRA bumper sticker, but, if we take it more seriously, (1′) also suggests an application of the method of "That's just like arguing. . . ." The parallel suppressed premise would then be

(2′) It would be bad if only outlaws had gum,

and the parallel conclusion would be

(3′) Therefore, gum should not be outlawed.

This conclusion, however, is not obviously false. Indeed, it seems true: People should be allowed to chew gum. Moreover, (2′) seems false, since nothing particularly bad would happen if only outlaws chewed gum. For these reasons, this bumper sticker cannot be used to refute the original argument. This failure illustrates two general tests: The technique of "That's just like arguing . . ." works only if the conclusion of the parallel argument really is unacceptable and only if the premises of the parallel argument really are true.

But opponents of the NRA did not stop there. They distributed a third bumper sticker:

(1″) If guns are outlawed, only outlaws will shoot their children by mistake.

The argument behind this new bumper sticker is not at all clear. If it is a straightforward instance of "That's just like arguing . . . ," then the parallel argument would add "It would be bad if only outlaws shot their children by mistake" and conclude "Guns should not be outlawed." However, that is the very conclusion the NRA wants to reach; so this newest argument could not refute the original one. Nonetheless, a different argument might lie behind this third bumper sticker. The point seems to be that gun owners sometimes shoot their children by mistake, and we can minimize such tragedies by reducing the number of gun owners through laws against guns. The argument then runs something like this:

(1″) If guns are outlawed, only outlaws will shoot their children by mistake.

(2″) It would be good if outlaws were the only ones who shot their children by mistake.

(3″) Therefore, guns should be outlawed.

This conclusion would seem false to the NRA, and this argument might also seem to suggest that the same form of reasoning could lead to opposite conclusions: (3) and (3″). Moreover, (2″) seems true. This premise does not, of course, say that it is good for outlaws to shoot their children by mistake. Instead, it says that it would be good if nobody else shot their children by mistake. So far, so good. However, this latest argument, (1″)–(3″), does not really have the same form as the original argument, (1)–(3), since (2″) and (3″) are about what is good and what ought to be law, whereas (2) and (3) are about what is bad and what ought not to be law. The next question is whether this disanalogy is *important*. If not, the latest bumper sticker still might refute the original one. However, the NRA might argue that this difference *is* important, because the fact that a law has bad effects overall *does* show that the law should not be passed, whereas the fact that a law would have good effects overall is *not* enough to show that the law should be passed, since the law still might violate individual rights that cannot be overridden by good effects on others. This claim is controversial, but, if it can be defended, then this parallel argument, (1″)–(3″), fails to show that the original argument, (1)–(3), is invalid. More generally, then, the technique of "That's just like arguing . . ." works only if the two arguments really do have relevantly similar structures—that is, only if one argument really is *just like* the other in relevant respects.

In sum, the method of "That's just like arguing . . ." can be used to show that an argument is invalid by giving another argument with essentially the same form in which the inference takes us from an obvious truth to an obvious falsehood. In response to such an attack, a defender of the original argument has three main options. The defender might (1) deny that the conclusion of the parallel argument is false, or (2) deny that the premises of the parallel argument are true, or (3) deny that the supposedly parallel argument really has essentially the same form. If any of these responses is justified, then the charge of "That's just like arguing . . ." fails to refute the original argument.

Admittedly, this procedure is not precise. There will sometimes be disputes about whether the premises of the parallel argument really are true, or clearly true; and whether the conclusion of the parallel argument really is false, or clearly false. Moreover, we have given no general explanation of the notion that two arguments have the *same basic form*. The forms of argument that were discussed in Chapters 5–7 are only part of the story. Yet it remains a fact that people can often see that two arguments have the same basic form and, through seeing this, decide that an argument presented to them is invalid. This ability is the basis of sound logical judgment. It is also the basis of wit. It is at best mildly funny to say that if God had wanted us to fly, he would have given us wings. You have to be fairly clever to reply at once: "If God had wanted us to stay on the ground, he would have given us roots."

EXERCISE I

In each of the following examples, does the parallel argument succeed in refuting the original argument? Why or why not? Consider the three possible responses listed above. If the original argument is refuted, is there some simple way to fix it up so that it cannot be refuted in this way? If so, how? (You might try to add a premise whose analogue would be false in the parallel argument.)

(1) CHRIS: The United States is wealthy, so its citizens are wealthy as well.

   PAT: That's just like arguing that a building is expensive, so the nails in its walls are expensive as well.

(2) CHAUVINIST: Since women are the only people who can bear children, they should bear children.

   FEMINIST: That's like arguing that, if I am the only person who can wiggle my own ears, then I should wiggle my own ears.

(3) GINGRICH: Orphanages are fine places, as the movie *Boys Town* shows.

   CRITIC: That's just like saying that Oz is a fine place, as *The Wizard of Oz* shows.

(4) SCIENTIST: My initial steps toward embryo cloning, no matter how controversial, are important because they bring the debate out into the public.

   CRITIC: That's just like arguing that we should start a fire in a house in order to bring the debate about getting a new fire engine out into the public.[3]

---

[3] Paraphrased from an interview on National Public Radio. Thanks to an anonymous reviewer for this example.

(5) A Young Child at 6:00 a.m.: It's morning. Morning is the time to wake up. So it's time to wake up.

The Child's Sleepy Parent: That's just like arguing that it's daytime, and daytime is the time to eat lunch, so it's time to eat lunch.

(6) Mark: You shouldn't walk on that grass, because, if everybody did that, the grass would die.

Bob: That's just like arguing that I shouldn't go to this movie right now, because if everybody did that, the theater would be packed like a can of sardines.

(7) Thomas: Everything in the world has a cause, so the world itself must have a cause.

Tony: That's just like arguing that everyone in this class has a mother, so the class itself must have a mother.

(8) Liberal: We ought to provide condoms for high school students, because they are going to have sex anyway.

Limbaugh: That's just like arguing that we should provide high school students with guns, because they are going to use them anyway.[4]

(9) Caspar: Nuclear deterrence must work, because we have never had a nuclear exchange as long as we have maintained nuclear deterrence.

George: That's just like arguing that hanging garlic by the front door must keep thieves away, because I put garlic there and my house has never been robbed.

(10) A: He owns a red car, so he owns a car.

B: That's just like arguing that he owns a toy duck, so he owns a duck.

(11) A: He is holding a baby girl, so he is holding a baby.

B: That's just like arguing that he sees a fire truck, so he sees a fire.

EXERCISE II

For each of the following arguments, find another argument with the same basic form in which the premise or premises are clearly true and the conclusion is clearly false.

(1) If tea is dangerous, so is coffee. Tea isn't dangerous. So coffee isn't either.

(2) If it were about to rain, it would be cloudy. It is cloudy. So it's about to rain.

---

[4] Paraphrased from Rush Limbaugh, *See, I Told You So* (New York: Pocket Books, 1993), 222.

(3) Fred had either ice cream or cake for dessert. He had cake. So he must not have had ice cream.

(4) You cannot pass laws against dangerous drugs, because there is no way of drawing a sharp line between dangerous and nondangerous drugs.

(5) If you have never written a novel, then you are in no position to make judgments about novels. So don't presume to criticize mine.

(6) Women are the natural persons to raise children, because they are the ones who give birth to them.

(7) There's nothing wrong with smoking, since the longer you smoke, the longer you live.

(8) If one has nothing to hide, one should not be afraid of being investigated. So nobody should object to being investigated.

(9) Radicals should not be granted freedom of speech, because they deny this freedom to others.

(10) In nature, a species is more likely to survive when its weak members die out, so we should let the weak in our society die out.

(11) Buses use more gas than cars, so the city cannot reduce gas consumption by providing more buses.

(12) Boxing can't be very bad, since so many people like it.

(13) This war is just, for to say otherwise in public would be to aid our enemies.

(14) If you don't buy the most expensive shoes, you buy cheap ones. You don't want cheap shoes. So you should buy the most expensive shoes.

(15) I'd rather be smart than strong, so I am going to quit exercising and spend all day in the library.

(16) You don't want to be this murderer's next victim, so you had better convict her and send her to prison where she can't hurt you.

(17) If it weren't for America, these refugees would have nowhere to go; so they should adopt the American way of life and give up their old culture.

(18) You can't be right, because, if the answer were that obvious, someone would have thought of it before.

COUNTEREXAMPLES

The second main way to attack an argument is to challenge one of its premises. We can argue that there is no good reason to accept a particular premise as true, asking, for example, "How do you know that?" If there is no way to justify a premise, then the argument usually fails to justify its conclusion. More strongly, we can argue that the premise is actually false. In this second case, we refute an argument by refuting one of its premises.

As an example of this second method of refutation, we can examine St. Augustine's attack on astrology. For centuries many people have believed in astrology. They have believed, that is, that all important aspects of their lives are determined by the configuration of the stars at the time of their birth, so those aspects can be predicted by the skillful reading of astrological charts. As evidence for this, astrologers often point out successful predictions they made in the past. St. Augustine presented a beautiful refutation of this argument in his *Confessions*. St. Augustine tells us that he was captivated by astrology until his conversion to Christianity. He then abandoned it, he says, for the following reason:

> I turned my attention to the case of twins, who are generally born within a short time of each other. Whatever significance in the natural order the astrologers may attribute to this interval of time, it is too short to be appreciated by human observation and no allowance can be made for it in the charts which an astrologer has to consult in order to cast a true horoscope. His predictions, then, will not be true, because he would have consulted the same charts for both Esau and Jacob and would have made the same predictions for each of them, whereas it is a fact that the same things did not happen to them both. Therefore, either he would have been wrong in his predictions or, if his forecast was correct, he would not have predicted the same future for each. And yet he would have consulted the same chart in each case. This proves that if he had foretold the truth, it would have been by luck, not by skill.[5]

The central move in Augustine's attack on astrology is to produce what is called a *counterexample* to the claim that everyone's life can be predicted by the skillful reading of astrological charts. By citing the very different lives that twins have led and our inability to detect the differences between the stars at the times of twins' births, Augustine shows that some people's lives *cannot* be predicted by even the most skillful reading of any astrological charts.

DISCUSSION QUESTION

Could twins also be used to show that IQ is not completely determined by genes? If so, how? If not, why not?

Counterexamples are typically aimed at universal claims. This is true because a *single* contrary instance will show that a universal claim is false. If someone claims that *all* snakes lay eggs, then pointing out that rattlesnakes bear their young alive is sufficient to refute this universal claim. If the person retreats to the somewhat

---

[5] St. Augustine, *Confessions*, trans. R. S. Pine-Coffin (Harmondsworth, England: Penguin Books, 1961), 142.

weaker claim that *most* snakes lay eggs, the guarding term makes it much harder to refute the claim. A single example of a snake that bears its young alive is not enough to refute this claim; we would have to show that a majority of snakes do not lay eggs. Here, instead of trying to refute his statement, we may ask him to produce his *argument* in behalf of it. We can then attack this argument. Finally, if the person retreats to the very weak claim that at least *some* snakes lay eggs, then his statement becomes very difficult to refute. Even if it were false (which it is not), to show this we would have to check every fool snake and establish that it does not lay eggs. So, as a rough-and-ready rule, we can say that the stronger a statement is, the more subject it is to refutation; the weaker it is, the less subject it is to refutation.

When a universal claim is refuted by a single case, that case is a *counterexample*. The pattern of reasoning is perfectly simple: To refute a claim that *everything* of a certain kind has a certain feature, we need find only *one* thing of that kind lacking that feature. In response to a counterexample, many people just repeat the misleading saying, "That's the exception that proves the rule." What most people do not realize is that "proves" originally meant "tests," so all this saying means is that an apparent exception can be used to test a rule or a universal claim. When the exception is a true counterexample, the universal claim fails the test.

There are only two ways to defend a universal claim against a purported counterexample. Since the universal claim says that all things of a certain kind have a certain feature, (1) one can deny that the apparent counterexample really is a thing of that kind; or (2) one can deny that the supposed counterexample really lacks that feature. For example, a defender of the claim that all snakes lay eggs might deny (1) that rattlesnakes are snakes or (2) that rattlesnakes bear their young alive. Neither of these responses is plausible in this case. That is what makes this counterexample *decisive*.

Other counterexamples are not so decisive. Indeed, some purported counterexamples seem to miss their targets entirely. If a person claims that all snakes except rattlesnakes lay eggs, someone might respond with another counterexample: male snakes. This counterexample does not really refute the intended claim, since that claim was meant to be about the methods by which female snakes of various species give birth when they do give birth. Similarly, if you claim that stealing is always wrong, and a smart aleck responds that it is not wrong to steal bases in a baseball game, this counterexample would seem like a joke, since the intended claim was about stealing property, not stealing bases.

When a counterexample can be answered with a simple clarification or modification that does not affect the basic force of the original claim, it is a *shallow* counterexample. A *deep* counterexample is one that requires the original claim to be modified in more-important or interesting ways. Shallow counterexamples can sometimes be fun as jokes, but they are usually not much help in refuting arguments, since basically the same argument can be resurrected in a slightly different form. Indeed, people who give too many shallow counterexamples can be annoying. If you really want to understand a subject matter, you should look for counterexamples that are deep.

Deep and decisive counterexamples are not always easy to think up. Some people are much better at it than others. Socrates was a genius in this respect. He wandered through the streets of ancient Athens questioning various people, often important political figures, challenging them to explain what they meant by various terms such as *justice, knowledge, courage, friendship,* and *piety.* As narrated by Plato, these exchanges fall into a standard pattern: Socrates asks for a definition of some important notion; after some skirmishing, a definition is offered; Socrates immediately finds a counterexample to this definition; the definition is then changed or replaced by another; once more Socrates produces a counterexample; and so on. With effortless ease, Socrates seemed able to produce counterexamples to any definition or any principle that others offered. There is no better introduction to the art of giving counterexamples than a specimen of the Socratic method.

Theaetetus was a brilliant young man, gifted in mathematics. In the dialogue that bears his name, Theaetetus and Socrates try (unsuccessfully) to arrive at a correct definition of *knowledge.* They notice an important difference between knowledge and mere belief: It is possible for someone to *believe* something that is false, but it is not possible for someone to *know* something that is false. This leads Theaetetus to suggest a simple definition of knowledge: Knowledge equals true belief. This proposed definition is refuted in the following exchange:

SOCRATES: [There is] a whole profession to prove that true belief is not knowledge.

THEAETETUS: How so? What profession?

SOCRATES: The profession of those paragons of intellect known as orators and lawyers. There you have men who use their skill to produce conviction, not by instruction, but by making people believe whatever they want them to believe. You can hardly imagine teachers so clever as to be able, in the short time allowed by the clock, to instruct their hearers thoroughly in the true facts of a case of robbery or other violence which those hearers had not witnessed.

THEAETETUS: No, I cannot imagine that; but they can convince them.

SOCRATES: And by convincing you mean making them believe something.

THEAETETUS: Of course.

SOCRATES: And when a jury is rightly convinced of facts which can be known only by an eye-witness, then, judging by hearsay and accepting a true belief, they are judging without knowledge, although, if they find the right verdict, their conviction is correct?

THEAETETUS: Certainly.

SOCRATES: But if true belief and knowledge were the same thing, the best of jurymen could never have a correct belief without knowledge. It now appears that they must be different things.[6]

One thing to notice about this discussion is that Theaetetus does not dig in his heels and insist that the ignorant members of the jury do know that the person is innocent provided only that they believe it and it is true. Faced with the counterexample, he retreats at once. Why is this? Why not stay with the definition and reject the counterexample as false? The answer is that for many concepts there is general agreement about their application to particular cases, even if there is no general agreement about a correct definition. To take an extreme example, everyone agrees that Hitler was a dictator (even Hitler), and no one supposes that Thomas Jefferson was a dictator (even his enemies). So any definition of "dictator" must be wrong if it implies that Hitler was not a dictator or that Thomas Jefferson was a dictator. Of course, there are also borderline cases about which people disagree, so there might be no perfectly exact definition of a dictator. Nonetheless, any definition that does not square with the clear cases can be refuted by citing one of these clear cases as a counterexample.

Ethics is an area where arguments often turn upon counterexamples. Although various forms of relativity remain fashionable, in our day-to-day life there is a surprisingly wide range of agreement concerning which actions are right and which actions are wrong. That is, whichever theory we might hold, we usually agree

---

[6] Plato, *Theaetetus*, trans. Francis M. Cornford, in Cornford's *Plato's Theory of Knowledge* (New York: Liberal Arts Press, 1957), 141.

about a wide range of particular cases. We tend not to notice this agreement because disagreement is interesting and exciting, whereas agreement is not. The task of an ethical theory is to discover principles that tell us which actions are right and which actions are wrong. One important test of an ethical theory is whether it squares with these clear cases where agreement exists.

Consider the utilitarian principle. According to that principle, an action is right if it is the action that will produce the greatest possible total happiness. Admittedly, the idea of happiness is vague and stands in need of explanation. For this discussion, however, we can ignore this complication. At first sight, this principle has much to recommend it. How, we might ask, could it ever be better to act in a way that produces less happiness than would be produced by acting in another way? Furthermore, the world would be a much better place if people uniformly followed this principle. All the same, the utilitarian principle is subject to a counterexample that has led most—though not all—philosophers to reject it as the *single* basic principle of ethics. One version of this counterexample goes as follows: It is certainly possible for a society to exist in which a small slave population leading a wretched life allows the rest of the population to lead a blissfully happy life. In such a society, any other arrangement would, in fact, lower the total happiness. For example, any attempt to improve the lives of the slaves would be overbalanced by a loss of happiness in the slaveholding class. This may seem like a far-fetched situation, but if it were to occur, the utilitarian would have to approve of this society and argue against any changes in it. To most people this is unacceptable, for it offends our sense of fairness. "Why," we want to ask, "should one segment of society be assigned wretched lives so that others can be happy? How can the society be morally sound when human rights are infringed in this way?" Considerations of this kind have led *most* philosophers to abandon strict utilitarianism as the single principle of morality. Some philosophers have modified the principle to meet objections; some have supplemented it with other principles; some have simply rejected it in favor of another theory.

Sometimes counterexamples force clarification. Consider the traditional moral precept "Do unto others as you would have them do unto you." Like utilitarianism, this principle captures an important moral insight, but, if taken quite literally, it is also subject to counterexamples. Jones, a sadomasochist, enjoys beating other people. When asked whether he would like to be treated in that way, he replies "Yes." It is obvious that the Golden Rule was not intended to approve of Jones's behavior. The task, then, is to reformulate this rule to avoid this counterexample. That is not as easy as it might seem.

No discussion of counterexamples is complete without a mention of the Morgenbesser retort. Though the exact story is now shrouded in the mists of time, it has come down to us from the 1950s in the following form. In a lecture, a British philosopher remarked that he knew of many languages in which a double negative means an affirmative, but not one language in which a double affirmative means a negative. From the back of the room came Morgenbesser's retort: "Yeah, yeah."

EXERCISE III

Find a counterexample to each of the following claims, if possible.

Example: *Claim*: "Sugar" is the only word in which an *s* is pronounced *sh*.
Counterexample: Oh, sure.

(1) No prime number is even.

(2) Three points always determine a plane.

(3) Balloons that are filled with helium always rise in the air.

(4) All mammals bear their young live.

(5) You can never get too much of a good thing.

(6) What you don't know can't hurt you.

(7) You can't be too careful.

(8) You should never look a gift horse in the mouth.

(9) It is always wrong to tell a lie.

(10) You should never ask someone else to do something that you are not willing to do yourself.

(11) If lots of people do something, then it must not be wrong for me to do it.

(12) If it would be horrible for everyone to do something, then it would be morally wrong for anyone to do it.

(13) If it would not be horrible for everyone to do something, then it would not be morally wrong for anyone to do it.

(14) Wherever you use the word "nearly," you could use the word "almost" instead, without affecting the truth or the good sense of what you have said.

EXERCISE IV

There *cannot possibly* be any counterexamples to the following claims. Explain why.

(1) There is life on the moon.

(2) Killing is usually wrong.

(3) Any short person is a person.

(4) Every horse is an animal.

(5) Nothing is both red all over and green all over at the same time.

(6) $2 + 2 = 4$.

DISCUSSION QUESTIONS

(1) How can the Golden Rule best be reformulated so as to avoid the above counterexample of the sadomasochist? Can you think of any counterexamples to this reformulation of the Golden Rule?

(2) Is the Morgenbesser retort a shallow counterexample or a deep counterexample? Why?

(3) When theologians claim that God can do anything, atheists sometimes respond that God cannot make a stone that is so large that it cannot be lifted, or that God cannot make a circle with four sides. Are these really counterexamples to the theologians' claim? Why or why not?

(4) Suppose there are only two balls in a bag, and someone claims "Most of the balls in the bag are red." Does a single black ball in the bag refute this claim? Is it a counterexample to this claim? Does this show that counterexamples can refute some claims that are not universal?

(5) When people today respond to counterexamples by saying "That's the exception that proves the rule," they usually do not mean "That's the exception that tests the rule." What do they mean? Does this response with this meaning make the rule self-sealing in the sense discussed at the end of the previous chapter?

REDUCTIO AD ABSURDUM

Particular counterexamples can normally be used to refute only universal claims, so how can we refute claims that are not universal? One method is to show that the claim to be refuted implies something that is ridiculous or absurd in ways that are independent of any particular counterexample. This mode of refutation is called a *reductio ad absurdum*—which means a reduction to absurdity. Reductios, as they are called for short, can refute many different kinds of propositions. They are sometimes directed at a premise in an argument, but they are more often used to refute a conclusion. This will not show exactly *what* is wrong with the argument for that conclusion, but it will show that *something* is wrong with the argument, because it cannot be sound if its conclusion is false. That might be enough in some situations.

For example, suppose someone argues that, since there is a tallest mountain and a heaviest human, there must also be a largest integer. We might respond by arguing as follows. Suppose there is a largest integer. Call it N. Since N is an integer, $N + 1$ is also an integer. Moreover, $N + 1$ is larger than N. But it is absurd to think that any integer is larger than the largest integer. Therefore, our supposition—that there is a largest integer—must be false.

In this mathematical example a contradiction is derived, but absurdity also comes in other forms. Suppose a neighbor tells a parent "The local public schools are so bad that you ought to send your kids to private school," and the parent responds "Do you think I'm rich?" The point of this rhetorical question is that it is absurd to think that the parent is rich, presumably because of her lifestyle or house, which the neighbor can easily see. Without being rich, the parent cannot afford a private school, so the neighbor's advice is useless.

Often the absurdity is derived indirectly. A wonderful example occurred in the English parliamentary debate on capital punishment. One member of Parliament was defending the death penalty on the grounds that the alternative—life in prison—was much more cruel than death. This claim was met with the following reply: On this view, those found guilty of first-degree murder ought to be given life in prison, and the death penalty should be given to those who commit some lesser offense. The first speaker could respond in several ways, because this reductio depends on background assumptions that the first speaker could question. First, he might deny that the most severe crime should receive the most severe penalty possible. If the first speaker sees life in prison as too cruel to be inflicted on anyone, then he might call for the abolition of life imprisonment and keep the death penalty as the most severe punishment. Alternatively, the first speaker could claim that, even though the death penalty is less severe than life in prison, it is still fitting in some other way for the most severe crime, first-degree murder. Finally, of course, the first speaker could simply *accept* the supposedly absurd result and apply life imprisonment to first-degree murder, while using the death penalty for lesser crimes. In point of fact, however, the first speaker was unwilling to accept any of these alternatives. He simply tried a rhetorical trick and got caught.

These reductios are fairly good, but other reductios fail for a variety of reasons. In order for a reductio ad absurdum argument to succeed in refuting a claim, two main requirements must be met. First, the result must really be *absurd*. Often opponents try to reduce a view to absurdity but really only draw out implications of the view that are not absurd at all. For example, in a famous debate in which Thomas Huxley defended a theory of evolution, Bishop Wilberforce asked Huxley whether he had descended from apes on his mother's side or on his father's side of the family. This question was intended to draw laughter from the crowd, and it did, partly because they and Wilberforce thought that any answer to the question would be absurd. Nonetheless, Huxley could respond that he had descended from apes on both sides of his family. Since that response was not really absurd— regardless of how absurd it seemed to Wilberforce—the bishop's attempt did not really refute Huxley's claim.

In other cases, one cannot deny that a certain result really would be absurd, but the reductio still fails because the claim to be refuted does not really *imply* that absurdity. For example, opponents sometimes say that the theory of evolution implies that animals are constantly evolving, so they cannot be divided into separate species. This would be absurd, because it is easy to observe distinct species. However, the theory of evolution does not really imply this absurdity, so this reductio fails to refute that theory. It fails to meet the second requirement for successful reductios, which is that the claim to be refuted must actually imply the absurdity.

Finally, it is important to notice that reductios can be deep or shallow in much the same way as counterexamples. Sometimes a claim really does imply a result that is absurd, but it can be modified in some minor way so as to avoid the absurd result. For example, if a fan says "Nicklaus is better than any golfer ever," someone might respond that Nicklaus is himself a golfer, so this claim implies that Nicklaus is better than himself, which is absurd. However, the fan meant to say, "Nicklaus is better than any *other* golfer ever," so this reductio is shallow. The reductio does refute the original form of the claim, but the main force of the claim is restored by the minor modification. A reductio ad absurdum is deep only if it reveals that a claim implies an absurd result that cannot be avoided without modifying the claim in essential respects or giving it up entirely.

In sum, then, a reductio ad absurdum argument tries to show that one claim, *X*, is false because it implies another claim, *Y*, that is absurd. To evaluate such an argument, the following questions should be asked:

(1) Does *X* really imply *Y*?

(2) Is *Y* really absurd?

(3) Can *X* be modified in some minor way so that it no longer implies *Y*?

If either of the first two questions is answered in the negative, then the reductio fails; if the third question receives an affirmative answer, then the reductio is shallow. Otherwise, the reductio ad absurdum argument is both successful and deep.

EXERCISE V

Evaluate the following reductio ad absurdum arguments by asking the above three questions:

(1) CLAIM TO BE REFUTED: Even the worst enemies can become friends.

REDUCTIO: If people are enemies, they are not friends. If they do become friends, then they are not enemies. So it's absurd to think that enemies can be friends.

(2) CLAIM TO BE REFUTED: This ball is both red and green all over.

REDUCTIO: If it is red, it reflects light within a certain range of wavelengths. If it is green, it reflects light within a different range of wavelengths. These ranges do not overlap, so it is absurd to think that anything can reflect both kinds of light. Thus, a ball cannot be both red and green.

(3) CLAIM TO BE REFUTED: Most children in Lake Wobegon are above average (in intelligence).

REDUCTIO: If so, the average (intelligence) would really be higher than it is; and then it would not be true that most children in Lake Wobegon are above the real average (intelligence).

(4) ARGUMENT TO BE REFUTED: Your brain is mostly empty space, because the subatomic particles in it are very far apart.

REDUCTIO: That's absurd, because my brain is solid, and it works pretty well.

(5) ARGUMENT TO BE REFUTED: 2 divided by 2 is 1, and 1 divided by 1 is 1, so 0 divided by 0 is 1.

REDUCTIO: Let $x = 1$. Then $x^2 = 1$. So $x^2 - 1 = x - 1$. Now divide both sides by $x - 1$. The result is that $x + 1 = 1$. But then $x = 0$. Since we began by letting $x = 1$, we end up with $1 = 0$. That is absurd. How did this absurdity arise? The answer is that, when we divided both sides by $x - 1$, we divided both sides by 0, since we let $x = 1$, so $x - 1 = 0$. Thus, if we allow division by 0, we end up with the absurdity that $1 = 0$. To avoid this absurdity, we must forbid division by 0. So it is not true that 0 divided by 0 is 1.

(6) CLAIM TO BE REFUTED: Some things are inconceivable.

REDUCTIO: Consider something that is inconceivable. Since you are considering it, you are conceiving it. But then it is conceivable as well as inconceivable. That is absurd. So nothing is inconceivable.

EXERCISE VI

Spell out a reductio ad absurdum argument to refute each of the following claims. If no such reductio is possible, explain why.

(1) Some sisters are nephews.

(2) Some fathers were never children.

(3) Most students scored better than the mean grade on the last test.

(4) Almost everyone in this class is exceptional.

(5) There is an exception to every rule (that is, to every universal claim).

(6) I know that I do not know anything.

(7) Some morally wrong actions are morally permitted.

(8) There is a male barber in this town who shaves all and only the men in this town who do not shave themselves. (Hint: does he shave himself?)

(9) God exists outside time, and we will meet him someday.

(10) Most of the sentences in this exercise are true.

DISCUSSION QUESTIONS

(1) The legal case of *Plessy v. Ferguson* 163 U.S. 537 (1896), excerpted in Chapter 12, questioned a law requiring racial segregation in railroad cars. Opponents of the law gave the following reductio argument:

> The same argument that will justify the state legislature in requiring railways to provide separate accommodations for the two races will also authorize them to require separate cars to be provided for people whose hair is of a certain color, or who are aliens, or who belong to certain nationalities, or to enact laws requiring colored people to walk upon one side of the street, and white people upon the other, or requiring white men's houses to be painted white, and colored men's black, or their vehicles or business signs to be of different colors, upon the theory that one side of the street is as good as the other, or that a house or vehicle of one color is as good as one of another color.

How do defenders of segregation respond to this argument? Is their response adequate? Is any response adequate? Is this a slippery-slope argument? Are other slippery-slope arguments also reductio arguments?

(2) Many atheists use the following reductio ad absurdum argument against the existence of God: Suppose there is a God who is all-powerful, all-knowing, and all-good. Such a God would make this world as good as it could be. But it is absurd to think that this world is as good as possible, since this world contains much suffering and evil, including wars and birth defects. Therefore, there is no such God. Evaluate this reductio argument.

ATTACKING STRAW MEN

We have already seen some of the ways in which refutations can fail, but the most common mistake in refutation is worth discussing explicitly. The general rule is this: Before trying to refute someone's claim, it is important to make sure that you understand his or her position. If you misunderstand what your opponent is claiming, but you go ahead and attack a specific claim anyway, then the claim you attack will not be the claim that your opponent made, and your refutation might fail to refute any position that anyone ever really held. This is called the fallacy of *attacking a straw man*.

This mistake is so obvious that it is surprising how often people do attack straw men. We already saw one example in Exercise IV in Chapter 3. The R. J. Reynolds Tobacco Company placed an advertisement in the *New York Times* arguing against increases in cigarette taxes and restrictions on smoking in public places. In the course of its argument, it says "The Government . . . is attempting to prohibit smoking in America" and "They're pursuing a new era of prohibition." This simply distorts the government's position. Nobody in the government actually called for laws that would completely prohibit smoking, as prohibition did for alcohol. Thus, this advertisement attacks a straw man.

Another example comes from Rush Limbaugh, who wrote:

> Liberals tell kids in schools all over America that the best way to protect themselves from AIDS is to wear condoms while engaging in sexual intercourse. It's a lie. They are imposing a death sentence on kids. The failure rate for condoms is around 17 percent. They're teaching kids to play Russian roulette.[7]

This argument is aimed at a position that almost no liberals hold. Everyone who works in this area recognizes that abstinence is more effective than condom use, and teachers—no matter how liberal—usually tell this to students and believe that this should be told to students, even if condoms are also discussed. Moreover, most liberals do not advocate that school-age kids engage in sexual intercourse, even if they do advocate that kids use condoms *if* they engage in sexual intercourse. Thus, it mischaracterizes liberals to say that they are "teaching kids to play Russian Roulette."

Sometimes people attack a straw man intentionally. They mischaracterize their opponents' position on purpose in order to make their opponents look silly by associating their opponents with a position that is silly. In other cases, however, this fallacy is an honest mistake. Some people get so wrapped up in their own arguments that they forget the view against which they are arguing. The opponent can also be partly to blame. If someone states her position obscurely, it might not be clear whether the speaker would go so far as to make a certain claim. Then someone might attack that further claim, honestly believing that the speaker had adopted it. Alternatively, a critic might refute that further claim simply in order to make the speaker clarify her position by explicitly saying that that is not what she meant to say. In such ways, it might be useful to refute a position that the speaker does not really hold, even though, of course, doing so does not refute any position that the speaker actually does hold.

EXERCISE VII

Do the following arguments attack a straw man? Why or why not?

(1) Anyone who does not want to send United States troops to Bosnia must think that the dying Bosnians don't matter much.

(2) Anyone who does not want to send United States troops to Bosnia must think that some other action would be better.

---

[7] Limbaugh, *See, I Told You So*, 222. There are also problems with Limbaugh's claim that condoms have a 17 percent failure rate (whatever that means), and his analogy to Russian roulette (since people die every time they lose Russian roulette, but they do not get AIDS every time a condom fails during sexual intercourse).

(3) Humans could not have been created in the image of God, because God is not a physical being, and only physical beings can have images.

(4) Atheists think that God does not exist, so everything is permitted. But even atheists must admit that I would not be permitted to kill them! So atheism is nonsense.

(5) The theory of evolution says that humans are not different from apes, but humans are clearly smarter than apes, so the theory of evolution must be wrong.

DISCUSSION QUESTION

Find three more examples of attacking a straw man in your local newspaper or in the passages in the exercises in Chapter 3.

SYSTEM AND SIMPLICITY

We often use arguments to justify our claims and refute other claims when we disagree with other people about what is true, or when we are not sure ourselves about whether a claim is true. Nonetheless, arguments can also be useful in other ways even when everyone is sure that a certain claim is true. Nobody denies the Pythagorean theorem in Euclidean geometry, which says that the square of the hypotenuse of a right triangle is equal to the sum of the squares of the other two sides. Despite this agreement, however, geometry students are taught how to prove this theorem again. Even when one proof is accepted, geometers might look for another proof that is simpler in that it uses fewer steps or depends on fewer assumptions. Why? If everyone already accepts the theorem as proved, what is accomplished by proving it again, even if in a new way? The answer is not completely clear, but at least one purpose is to display or discover connections among various claims within geometry. When the Pythagorean theorem is proved from axioms, the proof shows that those axioms are sufficient conditions for the truth of the theorem. When a larger group of theorems is proved from the axioms, the overall theory becomes more systematic in that more of its parts are connected.

Why do geometers want the simplest proof? One reason is that simpler proofs are usually easier to follow, so a simpler proof will increase our understanding of the theorem and of why it is true. Moreover, a simpler proof reveals what is necessary to make the theorem true. If theorem T can be derived only by assuming axioms A, B, and C, then all three axioms seem to be part of what makes the theorem true, and it seems that the theorem would not be true if any of these axioms were not true. However, if someone comes up with a proof that uses only axioms *A* and *B*, but not axiom *C*, then this new proof or argument shows that axiom *C* is not needed to make theorem *T* true, and that *T* would still be a theorem even if axiom *C* had to be given up. In such ways, a geometric proof can increase our understanding of a theorem and of a whole theory, even if there never was any doubt about the truth of the theorem.

This use of arguments is best known in mathematics, but it is also common in other areas. Some biologists, for example, have tried to derive the theory of evolution from a small set of axioms, and economists sometimes do the same for their theories. Moral philosophers also often try to derive their moral beliefs from a small set of basic principles. One example is Immanuel Kant. Kant recognized that most people believe that killing, hurting, lying, and breaking promises are morally wrong except in unusual circumstances. In his moral theory, Kant tried to derive these common moral beliefs from his categorical imperative, which (in one version) says: Do not treat people as means only. What did Kant hope to gain by this derivation? Kant held that common people who had never heard of his categorical imperative could be fully justified in believing that it is usually morally wrong to lie. Thus, the argument from the categorical imperative was not intended to justify this common moral belief. Instead, it was supposed to show how this claim is related to other common moral beliefs and to other areas of ethics. It does so by revealing a feature that is shared by all of the acts that are morally wrong—namely, they all involve using other people as means only. Kant's derivation was also supposed to help us understand what makes these acts morally wrong. Of course, the categorical imperative is controversial, so it is not clear that it really does increase our understanding of morality. Nonetheless, the point here is simply that arguments deriving common moral beliefs from the categorical imperative or some other basic ethical principle aim at increasing our understanding of morality. This use of arguments is distinct from both justification and refutation.

EXPLANATIONS

A closely related use of arguments is to provide explanations. We already discussed explanations in Chapter 8, where the point was that some claims can be justified by showing that they are needed for the best explanation of something else. Here, however, we will focus on explanations that are used not to justify but solely to explain.

Explanations answer questions about *how* or *why* something happened. We explain how a mongoose got out of his cage by pointing to a hole he dug under the fence. We explain why Smith was acquitted by saying that he got off on a technicality. The purpose of explanations is to make sense of things.

Sometimes simply filling in the details of a story provides an explanation. For example, we can explain how a two-year-old girl foiled a bank robbery by saying that the robber tripped over her while fleeing from the bank. Here we have made sense out of an unusual event by putting it in the context of a plausible *narrative*.

It is unusual for a two-year-old girl to foil a bank robbery, but there is nothing unusual about a person tripping over a child when running recklessly at full speed.

Although the narrative is probably the most common form of explanation in everyday life, we also often use *arguments* to give explanations. We can explain a certain event by deriving it from established principles and accepted facts. This derivation has the following form:

> General principles or laws
> A statement of initial conditions
> _____
> ∴ A statement of the phenomenon to be explained

By "initial conditions" we mean those facts in the context that, together with the general principles and laws, allow us to derive the result that the event to be explained occurs.

This sounds quite abstract, which it is, but one example should clarify the basic idea. Suppose we put an ice cube into a glass and then fill the glass with water to the brim. The ice will stick out above the surface of the water. What will happen when the ice cube melts? Will the water overflow? Will it remain at the same level? Will it actually go down? Here we are asking for a *prediction*; and it will, of course, make sense to ask a person to *justify* whatever prediction he or she makes.

Stumped by this question, we let the ice cube melt to see what happens. In fact, the water level remains unchanged. After a few experiments, we convince ourselves that this result always occurs. We now have a new question: *Why* does this occur? We want an explanation of this phenomenon.

The explanation turns upon the law of buoyancy, which says:

> An object in water is buoyed up by a force equal to the weight of the water it displaces.

This law implies that, if we put an object in water, it will continue to sink until it displaces a volume of water whose weight is equal to its own weight (or else the object hits the bottom of the container). With this in mind, go back to the original problem. An ice cube is itself simply water in a solid state. Thus, when it melts, it will exactly fill in the volume of water it displaced, so the water level will remain unchanged.

We can now see how this explanation conforms to the argumentative pattern mentioned above:

> General principles or laws   (Primarily the law of buoyancy)
> Initial conditions   (An ice cube floating in a glass of water
>   filled to the brim)
> _____
> ∴ Phenomenon explained   (The level of the water remaining
>   unchanged after the ice cube melts)

Notice some things about this explanation. First of all, it is a fairly good explanation. People with only a slight understanding of science can follow it and see why the water level remains unchanged. We should also notice that it is not a *complete* explanation, since certain things are simply taken for granted—for example, that things do not change weight when they pass from a solid to a liquid state. To put the explanation into perfect argumentative form, this assumption and many others would have to be stated explicitly. This is never done in everyday life, and is only rarely done in the most exact sciences.

Here is an example of an explanation that is less technical.[8] Houses in Indonesia sometimes have their electrical outlets in the middle of the wall rather than at floor level. Why? A beginning of an explanation is that flooding is a danger in the Netherlands. Citing this fact does not help much, however, unless one remembers that Indonesia was formerly a Dutch colony. Even remembering this leaves gaps in the explanation. We can understand why the Dutch might put their electrical outlets above floor level in the Netherlands. It is safer in a country where flooding is a danger. Is flooding, then, a similar danger in Indonesia? Apparently not. So why did the Dutch continue this practice in Indonesia? To answer this question we must cite another broad principle: Colonial settlers tend to preserve their home customs, practices, and styles. In this particular case, the Dutch continued to build Dutch-style houses with the electrical outlets where (for them) they are normally placed—that is, in the middle of the wall rather than at floor level.

Even though this is not a scientific explanation, it shares many features of the scientific explanation examined previously. First, we have a curious fact: the location of electrical outlets in some houses in Indonesia. By way of explanation, certain important facts are cited:

> Indonesia was a Dutch colony.
>
> Flooding is a danger in the Netherlands.
>
> (And so on.)

These facts are then woven together by certain general principles:

> Where flooding is a danger, it is safer to put electrical outlets above floor level.
>
> People tend to do what is safer.
>
> Colonial settlers tend to preserve their home practices even when the practical significance of those practices is diminished.
>
> (And so on.)

Taken together, these facts and principles make sense of an anomalous fact—that is, they explain it.

Is this explanation any good? Explanations are satisfactory for *practical* purposes if they remove bewilderment or surprise. An explanation is satisfactory if it tells us *how* or *why* something happened in a way that is relevant to the concerns of a particular context. Our examples of explanations do seem to accomplish that much. Still, some explanations are better than others. In Chapter 8, we saw some criteria

---

[8] This example comes from Alan Ross Anderson.

for evaluating explanations, but it might seem that even the best explanations are not very useful, because they take so much for granted. In explaining why the water level remains the same when the ice cube melts, we cited the law of buoyancy. Now, why should that law be true? What explains *it*? To explain the law of buoyancy, we would have to derive it from other laws that are more general and, perhaps, more intelligible. In fact, this has been done. Archimedes simultaneously proved and explained the law of buoyancy by deriving it from the laws of the lever. How about the laws of the lever? Can they be proved and explained by deriving them from still higher and more-comprehensive laws? Perhaps. Yet reasons give out, and sooner or later explanation (like justification) comes to an end. It is the task of science and all rational inquiry to move that boundary further and further back. But even when there is more to explain, that does not show that a partial explanation is totally useless. As we have seen, explanations can be useful even when they are incomplete, and even though they are not used to justify any disputed claim. Explanation is, thus, a separate use of arguments.

EXERCISE VIII

Write a brief argument to explain each of the following. Indicate what facts and what general principles are employed in your explanations. (Do not forget those principles that may seem too obvious to mention.)

(1) Why a lighter-than-air balloon rises.

(2) Why there is an infield fly rule in baseball.

(3) Why there is an international date line.

(4) Why there are more psychoanalysts in New York City than in any other city or, for that matter, in most countries in the world.

(5) Why average temperatures tend to be higher closer to the equator.

(6) Why there are usually more college freshmen who plan to go to medical school than there are seniors who still plan to go to medical school.

(7) Why there are more seniors who major in philosophy than freshmen who plan to major in philosophy.

(8) Why almost no textbooks are more than eighteen inches high.

(9) Why most cars have four tires (instead of more or fewer).

(10) Why the cost of food tends to be higher in city slums than in wealthy suburbs.

(11) Why paintings by van Gogh cost so much.

(12) Why wages go up when unemployment goes down.[9]

---

[9] This claim is often disputed, but see D. Blanchflower and Andrew Oswald, *The Wage Curve* (Cambridge: MIT Press, 1994).

EXCUSES

Sometimes we are charged with acting in an improper or particularly stupid way. There are various ways in which we can defend ourselves against such a charge. (1) We can deny that we performed the action in question. Such a disclaimer might offer what is called an *alibi* intended to show that we were not in a position to perform the action with which we are charged. If we admit performing the action, we still have two more options. (2) We can try to *justify* the action—that is, show that it was not improper or stupid but was the right thing to do. (3) We can admit that we performed the action and also admit that it was improper or stupid, and then offer an *excuse* intended to show that we were not fully responsible for what we did.

The following exchanges between *A* and *B* illustrate these different kinds of defense.

> A: Why did you shove Harold into the gulch?
>
> B: I didn't shove him into the gulch. I was on the other side of town, as Gina will testify.

Here Gina provides an *alibi*, and *B* disclaims or denies performing the action.

> A: Why did you shove Harold into the gulch?
>
> B: He was about to be shot by an assassin.

Here *B* admits that he did shove Harold into the gulch. His response is supposed to explain why *B* did what he did, and it is also supposed to *justify* *B*'s action by showing that it was the right thing to do. To accomplish this, all *B* does is cite the single fact that an assassin was about to shoot Harold, but this justification also depends on some general principles that are so obvious that we simply take them for granted. For example, we assume that saving a person's life is, in general, a good thing; that a person in a gulch is less likely to be struck by a bullet than a person standing in plain view; that the amount of harm that might come from falling into a gulch is much less than the harm that would be caused by being struck by a bullet. Against the background of these principles and others, *B*'s remark explains his otherwise inexplicable conduct by showing that it was *justified*.

Notice what happens when we change the example in the following way:

> A: Why did you shove Harold into the gulch?
>
> B: I mistakenly thought that he was about to be shot.

B's remark still explains why he acted as he did; it still helps us understand his behavior. But this remark no longer justifies (or at least no longer fully justifies) his conduct, since he does not claim that what he did was the right thing to do. He thought it was the right thing to do at the time, but now he admits that he was mistaken. Here we would say that *B* is offering an *excuse* for what he did. Broadly speaking, an excuse is an explanation of human behavior intended to put it in a better light by reducing the agent's responsibility. It will often happen that even the best possible light will involve the admission of some wrongdoing. In the third dialogue, *B* admits to having made a mistake. In some contexts this might be a serious admission, but in the present context *B* does better by admitting that he was stupid, rather than acknowledging that he shoved poor Harold into the gulch as an act of sheer malice.

Even if *B* admits that he maliciously pushed Harold into the gulch, he may offer a weaker kind of excuse that cites *mitigating circumstances*:

A: Why did you shove Harold into the gulch?

B: He had been bugging me all afternoon, so I lost my temper.

You are not supposed to push people into gulches just because they have been bugging you, so *B*'s response does not justify his conduct. Yet it does provide a *partial* excuse, and thus makes it seem less vicious than if *B* had pushed Harold into the gulch with no provocation whatsoever.

We evaluate excuses in much the same way that we evaluate other explanations. An excuse will involve statements of fact, and these may be either true or false. We can also challenge the background principles employed in the excuse. We will not be impressed by someone who tells us that he ran seven stoplights so that he would not be late for a movie. The desire to see the start of a movie does not excuse such dangerous behavior, both because the danger to others is far greater than the expected gain for the driver and also because the driver should have left earlier. Finally, as with other explanations, the facts together with the background principles should make sense of the excused behavior and help us understand why it occurred.

To evaluate an excuse, we can ask the following questions:

(1) Broadly speaking, what are the facts?

(2) With what is the person being charged?

(3) What lesser wrong will the person settle for instead?

(4) How does the excuse answer the more serious charge?

In our third dialogue, (1) *B* shoved Harold into a gulch. (2) On the face of it, this looks like an attempt to injure Harold. (3) *B* is willing to admit that he made a mistake of fact. (4) Given this admission, his action was not malicious because it can be seen as a laudable, if flawed, attempt to save Harold from death or serious injury. These answers show that this excuse works fairly well, but other excuses will be found to be much more dubious when we look at them carefully in light of these questions.

EXERCISE IX

Determine whether each of the following is being offered as an alibi, a justification, or an excuse. Is each adequate for its intended use?

(1) People with an IQ of 40 should not be given the death penalty, because they are not capable of understanding the consequences of their actions.

(2) I had a very good reason to steal the drug: my wife would have died without it.

(3) Alice shouldn't be kept after school with the rest of the class. She can't be the one who threw the eraser, because she was in the bathroom.

(4) I had to give him the money. He would have killed me if I didn't.

(5) I just couldn't stop myself. When I saw the money lying on the ground, I had to take it. Then I just couldn't bring myself to turn it in. You would have done the same thing.

(6) I lied to you in order to keep the party a surprise. Surprise parties are lots of fun. Besides, I had promised not to tell.

(7) I dropped the baby because I was startled by a lightning flash nearby.

(8) I didn't know it was a closed-book exam. That's the only reason why I used my notes. I never would have looked at them if I had known.

EXERCISE X

Imagine that you are writing a letter home asking for money. In the closing paragraph, you feel called upon to offer some excuse for not having written for two months. Write such an excuse (not just an apology) in a perfectly natural way, and then analyze it, using the questions given above.

EXERCISE XI

In William Shakespeare's *Much Ado about Nothing*, Benedick, after previously denouncing women and marriage in the strongest terms, is trapped into falling in love with Beatrice. In the following passage (2.3. 231–40), he attempts to explain his sudden turnabout. Using the four questions given above, analyze this passage.

> I may chance have some odd quirks and remnants of wit broken on me because I have railed so long against marriage. But doth not the appetite alter? A man loves the meat in his youth that he cannot endure in his age. Shall quips and sentences and these paper bullets of the brain awe a man from the career of his humor? No, the world must be peopled. When I said I would die a bachelor, I did not think I should live till I were married.

EXERCISE XII

Find an example of a public official offering an excuse for something he or she has done. Analyze its structure using the above four questions.

DISCUSSION QUESTIONS

(1) Refuting an argument does not always require showing its conclusion to be false. Why not?

(2) It is sometimes said that science tells us *how* things happen but does not tell us *why* they happen. In what ways is this contention right, and in what ways is it wrong?

(3) When a claim is made that someone's conduct is *inexcusable*, what precisely is being asserted? How does it differ from calling the conduct simply bad or even very bad?

(4) Taken literally, "Excuse me" is a request. For what?

PART TWO

AREAS OF ARGUMENTATION

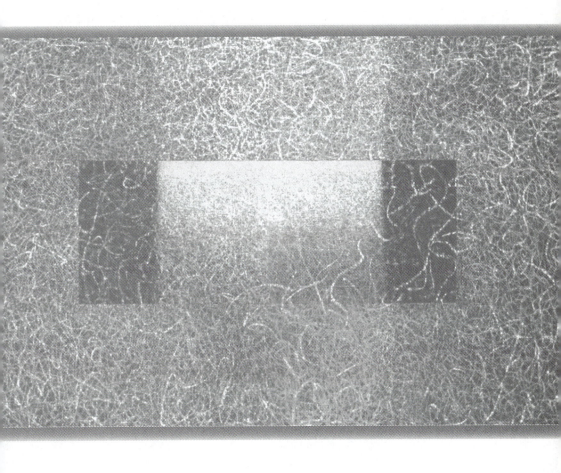

Chapter Twelve

LEGAL ARGUMENTS

One area where arguments are very important is the law. Legal decisions have concrete effects on people's lives. In criminal cases, judges can deprive people of their freedom or even their lives. In civil cases, judges often take away large sums of money, the custody of children, and so on. Constitutional decisions can affect the basic rights of all citizens, even those who have never been in a courtroom. These decisions are made because certain legal arguments are accepted and others are rejected. Consequently, in order to understand the law and its role in our lives, we need to understand legal arguments and the criteria for evaluating them.

Unfortunately, it is sometimes difficult to find any good reason for a legal decision. Important facts may not be known, and the law is sometimes unclear or inconsistent. Some cases "fall between the cracks," so no law seems to apply. Human beings have a remarkable ability to produce weird cases that would tax even the wisdom of Solomon.

Even in the toughest cases, judges must reach *some* decision. Outside the law, we can often just let matters ride—we can postpone a decision until further facts are established, or even declare that the issues are too vague to admit of any decision. This is rarely an option in a legal case. If *A* sues *B*, either *A* or *B* must win. The judge cannot say "This case is too tough for me. I'm not going to rule on it." Throwing the case out of court amounts to ruling in favor of the defendant. A decision must be made, usually in a relatively short period of time.

These pressures have led lawyers and judges to develop many ingenious ways in which to argue. Lawyers cite statutes, precedents, and their historical contexts. They claim the authority of common sense and science, and they cite scholarly articles, even some by philosophers. They deploy metaphors and rhetorical devices—almost anything to convince the judge or jury to decide in favor of their clients. The variety of these arguments makes legal reasoning complex and also fascinating.

Despite this variety, some rough generalizations can be made. A decision in a legal case usually depends on two kinds of questions: (1) questions of fact and (2) questions of law. These questions are handled differently in different kinds of cases.

COMPONENTS OF LEGAL REASONING

QUESTIONS OF FACT

A *criminal law* prohibits a certain kind of behavior and assigns a punishment to those who violate it. When a person is accused of violating this law, a trial is held to determine whether *in fact* he or she has done so. The judge instructs the jury on the law bearing on the case. If the members of the jury then decide that the accused has violated the law, they find him or her guilty, and the judge usually hands down the punishment stated in the statute.

In a *civil* suit, one party sues another, say, for breach of contract. Because states have laws governing contracts, once more a trial is held to decide whether *in fact* there was a contract (instead of some other speech act) and whether *in fact* it was breached. If a breach of contract is found, the judge or jury awards damages as the law specifies.

Although questions of fact arise in all cases, criminal and civil cases do differ in *the burden of proof*—in who is required to establish the facts and to what degree of certainty. In a criminal procedure, the prosecution must establish its case *beyond a reasonable doubt* (an inherently vague expression). In a civil case, the burden of proof is less. Generally, the case is won by the party who shows that the *preponderance* of evidence favors his or her side of the case. Although this is a bit too simple, it is sometimes said that if the scales tip ever so slightly in favor of *A* rather than *B*, then *A* wins the case. The complicated rules that govern civil procedure are supposed to give each party a fair chance to show that the preponderance of evidence falls on his or her side of the case.

The only way to carry the burden of proof is to present *evidence*. This evidence can contain conflicts and unclarities, which make it hard to prove the facts. Sleazy Sam is accused of murder. The prosecution presents eyewitnesses who saw Sam enter the victim's hotel room just before the body was found and expert witnesses who identify the fingerprints on the murder weapon as Sam's. And, of course, Sam had a fight in public with the victim on the day before the murder. Perry Mason defends Sam by arguing that the victim could have been killed hours earlier, and Sam's fingerprints got on the weapon when he found the body. In the movies, the next step is for the real murderer to confess in the courtroom. But real life is rarely that easy, so juries often have a hard job.

Sometimes the facts are so complex that they simply cannot be proved one way or the other, and sometimes the distinction between facts and law is not so clear. These problems arise often in cases that raise larger social issues. For example, in the case of *Brown v. Board of Education* (excerpted below), the Supreme Court answered the question of law by saying "the opportunity of an education . . . is a right which must be available to all on equal terms." The Court next asked: "Does segregation of children in public schools solely on the basis of race . . . deprive the children of the minority group of equal educational opportunities?" This question was presented as a question of fact. The Court answered in the affirmative and tried to justify its answer by citing various psychological studies of the performance of minority children from segregated schools. This answer would be accepted by most people today, but the studies used as proof were controversial and inconclusive, so the Court had to decide whether studies of this kind were reliable enough to serve as evidence in this case. Moreover, the answer to the above question also depends on what counts as "equal educational opportunities" for the purposes of the law. For example, the studies cited by the Court found that segregated schools "affect the motivation of a child to learn," but these factual studies could not determine whether lowered *motivation* to learn counts as lowered *opportunity* to learn. The Court had to decide this issue because it in effect determines what the law is—what it prohibits and what it allows. Thus, what was presented as a question of fact turned out to be at least partly a question of law. In such cases, it is not clear where law ends and facts begin.

QUESTIONS OF LAW

Even after the facts are determined, no decision can be reached without determining what the law is. The law varies from place to place and from time to time, so we have to know what the law is at the right time and place. This is determined mainly by looking at the legal institutions that actually exist. In our legal system, there are three main sources of the law: statutes, the Constitution, and precedents.

STATUTES

Roughly, statutes are general rules of law passed by legislatures. Statutes are made at various levels (federal, state, and local), and they cover various subjects, including crimes as well as property, contracts, and other areas of civil law. There are also statutes governing the procedures and kinds of evidence that can be presented in court.

When a general statute is applied to a particular case, the legal argument is often primarily deductive. For example, Sally drove 95 miles per hour in front of Hanover High School at 4:00 P.M. on a school day. It is illegal to drive over 15 m.p.h. in front of any school at 4:00 P.M. on a school day. Therefore, Sally's driving was illegal. Of course, there are lots of suppressed premises, such as that 95 m.p.h. is over 15 m.p.h. Even in this simple case, other assumptions are much trickier. Sally might not be found guilty if she had an excuse or justification, such as that a terrorist held a gun to her head. It is very difficult to give a complete and precise list of all possible excuses and justifications. It is at least as hard to say exactly when an excuse or justification is adequate. Nonetheless, it might be obvious that Sally had no excuse or justification. If we add this claim as a premise, then the legal argument against Sally is deductively sound. She might as well plead guilty.

Such simple cases are common, but they are also boring. Things get much more difficult and interesting when a statute is *vague*, so that it is not clear whether the statute applies to the case at issue. Then the statute must be *interpreted*. We need some way to tell more exactly what the law prohibits and what it allows. There is much disagreement about how to interpret statutes and about how to show that one interpretation is correct, but we can say which factors are commonly used in these arguments.

The first step in interpreting a statute is to look carefully at the *words* in the statute and their literal *meanings*. But the courts must often look beyond the mere words of the statute. This need arises when the words are unclear and when they lead to absurd results. For example, suppose a city council passes an ordinance requiring zoos to provide clean, dry cages for all mammals. This works fine until one zoo puts a whale in its aquarium. The whale would be in trouble if the courts stuck to the words of the ordinance. Fortunately, the courts can also consider the *intentions* of the legislators, which can be gleaned from their debates about the law. Of course, the city council might not have thought at all about whales, or they might have thought that whales are fish instead of mammals. Thus, if their intentions are what the legislators consciously had in mind, then we also need to consider the deeper, more general *purpose* of the legislators—the goal they were trying to reach or the moral outlook they were trying to express. This purpose is revealed by the wider historical context and by other laws made by the same legislature. In our example, the purpose of the statute was obviously to provide a healthy environment for mammals in zoos. This purpose is best served by interpreting the ordinance so that it does not require dry cages for whales.

In addition to words, intentions, and purposes, *moral beliefs* are often used to interpret statutes. Judges often argue that a statute should be interpreted one way by claiming that any other interpretation would lead to some kind of practical difficulty or moral unfairness. Such arguments are effective when everyone agrees about what is immoral or unfair, but judges often depend on more controversial moral beliefs. Critics claim that judges should not use their own moral views in this way, but there is no doubt that judges do in fact reason from such moral premises.

It should be clear that none of these methods of interpretation is mechanical, and none guarantees a single best interpretation of every statute. Part of the legal controversy is often over which factors can or should be used to argue for an interpretation. When all is said and done, legal reasoning from statutes is often far from the straightforward deduction that it appears to be in simple cases.

THE CONSTITUTION

Even when a statute has been interpreted, it is sometimes not clear whether the statute is *valid*–whether it has any legal force. This is determined by the Constitution. The Constitution occupies a special place in the legal system of the United States. If any statute conflicts with the Constitution, including its amendments, that statute has no legal force. Generally it is not the role of courts to enact laws, but the courts do have the power to strike down laws if they conflict with provisions in our Constitution.

It is easy to imagine clear cases of laws that violate constitutional provisions. If the State of Rhode Island began printing its own money, that would plainly violate the constitutional provision that reserves this right to the federal government. But, typically, those constitutional questions that reach the courts are not clear-cut. Even more so than statutes, provisions in the Constitution are very general and sometimes vague. This vagueness serves a purpose. The framers of the Constitution recognized that they could not foresee every eventuality, so they wanted to allow future courts to interpret the Constitution as cases arose. But the vagueness of the Constitution also creates problems. Interpretations can often conflict and become the source of controversy. As with statutes, arguments for and against interpretations of the Constitution usually refer to the words of the Constitution, the intentions and purposes of the framers of the Constitution, the effects of adopting an interpretation, moral beliefs, and so on. Such arguments are often inconclusive. The Supreme Court is then the final arbiter on questions of constitutionality.

PRECEDENTS

Our legal system is not only a constitutional system; it is also partly a system of common law. This means that lawyers and judges often cite precedents as arguments for present decisions. A *precedent* is simply a past case or decision that is supposed to be similar to the present case.

The practice of citing precedents might seem strange at first sight. Why should one case provide any reason for a decision in a different case? The answer is that the cases resemble each other in important respects. Of course, when there is an important enough difference between the cases, they should be *distinguished* and then the precedent provides no argument in the present case. But, when there is no important enough difference, like cases should be treated alike. If similar precedents were not followed, the legal system would lack continuity, and this would make it unfair and ineffective. Of course, past decisions that were mistaken or immoral should not be continued. That is why precedents can be *overturned*. Nonetheless, our legal system assumes that, if there is no adequate reason to overturn a precedent or to distinguish the precedent from the present case, then the precedent provides some reason to decide the present case in the same way as the precedent. This general doctrine of precedent is often called *stare decisis*–to adhere to previous decisions.

Precedents are used for many different purposes. When a statute is vague, precedents are often used to argue for one interpretation over another. When no statute applies directly, precedents are often used to argue about what the law is. Precedents can also be used in arguments for general questions of fact, or simply as sources of persuasive rhetoric.

The form of arguments from precedents also varies. Often a judge or lawyer merely quotes part of the opinion in the precedent and treats that quotation as an authoritative pronouncement of the law. Arguments from precedents are then similar to arguments from legislative statutes, and there often arises a similar need to interpret the judicial pronouncement in the precedent. In other precedents, the judge chooses to make the decision without explicitly formulating any general rule of law. The precedent can still be used to argue for future decisions by emphasizing analogies and discounting differences between the precedent and the present case.

One relatively simple example occurs in the case of *Plessy v. Ferguson* (1896) (excerpted below). Louisiana passed a statute that required blacks and whites to use "separate but equal" cars in trains. Plessy refused to comply, and he claimed that the Louisiana law violated the Fourteenth Amendment to the Constitution, which forbids states to deprive anyone of "the equal protection of the laws."

In his argument for this claim, Plessy cited the precedent of *Yick Wo v. Hopkins* 118 U.S. 356 (1886). That case was about an ordinance in San Francisco that required a permit from the Board of Supervisors for any public laundry not operated in a brick or stone building. On its face, this ordinance was supposed simply to prevent fires. In practice, however, the Board of Supervisors granted permits to all but one of the non-Chinese applicants and denied permits to all the Chinese applicants. Because of this practice, Yick Wo claimed that the ordinance violated the equal protection clause. The Supreme Court agreed and declared the ordinance unconstitutional, at least insofar as it gave the city power to grant and refuse permits "without regard to the competency of the persons applying, or the propriety of the places selected for the carrying on of business."

The argument from a precedent to a decision in a present case is often presented as an argument from *analogy*.[1] In this form, the argument emphasizes similarities

---

[1] For an elegant discussion of the role of analogical reasoning in the law, see Edward Levi, *An Introduction to Legal Reasoning* (Chicago: University of Chicago Press, 1963).

between the cases, and then concludes that the decision in the present case should be the same as in the precedent. Plessy's argument then appears to run something like this:

(1) The ordinance in *Yick Wo* was declared unconstitutional.

(2) The ordinance in *Yick Wo* is similar to the statute in *Plessy* in several respects.

(Conclusion) The statute in *Plessy* also ought to be declared unconstitutional.

This argument is not very good as it stands, so we need to add some suppressed premises.

The first step is to construct a list of the respects in which the cases are similar. That is not always so easy. When we are evaluating someone else's argument, we can focus on the similarities that he or she mentions. But when we are constructing our own legal arguments, we have to be more creative; we have to formulate the respects in which the cases are supposed to be similar.

The crucial point to realize is that it is not enough to list just any similarities. Some similarities do not matter. It is clearly irrelevant that the laws in *Yick Wo* and *Plessy* both contain more than ten words or that both apply to large cities. This much is assumed by both sides in the case, and legal reasoning would be impossible without assuming that many such similarities are irrelevant.

It is also obvious that there are always some differences between the precedent and the present case. This might seem to suggest that no precedent can give any reason for a similar decision in the present case. However, not all differences matter. It is not important, even if true, that Yick Wo was married and over fifty years old, but Plessy was not. To discount or distinguish the precedent, one must show that some difference between *Yick Wo* and *Plessy* is important enough to justify reaching different decisions in these cases.

The central question, then, asks which factors (similarities and differences) *do* matter. The point of the argument in our example is that the factor that justified the decision in *Yick Wo* also justifies a similar decision in *Plessy*. Consequently, the only similarities and differences that matter concern the factors that were needed to justify the decision in the precedent, *Yick Wo*. These are often called the *ratio decidendi*—the reason for the decision.

Using the doctrine of precedents as a suppressed premise, the argument can be reconstructed as follows:

(1) The ordinance in *Yick Wo* was declared unconstitutional.

(2) The ordinance in *Yick Wo* is similar to the statute in *Plessy* in several respects (*A, B, C, D,* and so on).

(3) These are the features that justified declaring the ordinance in *Yick Wo* unconstitutional.

(4) There are no important enough differences between *Yick Wo* and *Plessy* to justify distinguishing the precedent.

(5) *Yick Wo* ought not to be overturned.

(6) If a precedent is similar to a present case in the respects that justified the

> decision in the precedent, and if the precedent ought not to be either overturned or distinguished, then the present case ought to be decided in the same way as the precedent.

(Conclusion) The statute in *Plessy* ought to be declared unconstitutional.

This argument is now valid, but this does not get us very far. We still need to know whether its premises are true.

Clearly, the crucial question is this: How do we determine which features of the precedent are needed to justify that decision? What we need to do is to extract a general rule of law that provides the best justification for the precedent decision. There is no simple way to extract this rule of law, but some rough guidelines can be given.

The most obvious way to argue that a certain feature is important is to look at the written opinion in the precedent and see what the Court said—more specifically, what reasons it gave for its decision. In *Yick Wo*, the Court wrote:

> whatever may have been the intent of the ordinances as adopted, . . . though the law itself be fair on its face and impartial in appearance, yet, if it is applied and administered by public authority with an evil eye and an unequal hand, so as practically to make unjust and illegal discriminations between persons in similar circumstances, material to their rights, the denial of equal justice is still within the prohibition of the Constitution.

Here the Court explicitly announces that the intent of the ordinance and its appearance (for example, whether the ordinance explicitly mentions race or ethnic background) did *not* matter to their decision. The Court also declares that it *did* matter that the ordinance in practice creates inequalities in rights. Such official pronouncements by a court have considerable force for future courts in legal arguments.

Another way to determine which factors matter is to use the necessary-condition test or the sufficient-condition test from Chapter 8. These tests had to be passed by each side in the *Plessy* case. Plessy claimed that a sufficient condition of unconstitutionality is that a law has a discriminatory *effect* on the rights of a particular racial or ethnic group. This claim would fail the sufficient-condition test if there were any precedent still in force in which a law was found to have a discriminatory effect but the law was not found unconstitutional. Since there was no such precedent, the sufficient-condition test does not exclude Plessy's claim that discriminatory effect is sufficient by itself to make a law unconstitutional.

On the other side, the Court claimed that discriminatory effect is not sufficient, because discriminatory *motive* is a necessary condition for a law to be unconstitutional under the equal protection clause. For this claim to pass the necessary-condition test, there must have been no precedent still in force in which a law was held unconstitutional under the equal protection clause but the Court did not find any discriminatory motive. Plessy claimed that *Yick Wo* was such a case, but the Court responded that, even if those who passed the ordinance had no discriminatory motive, the administration of the ordinance in *Yick Wo* "was held to be a covert attempt on the part of the municipality to make an arbitrary and unjust discrimination against the Chinese race." If so, the necessary-condition test does not rule out the Court's claim that discriminatory motive is necessary for unconstitutionality in this case.

This disagreement reveals the limits on the tests of necessary conditions and sufficient conditions. These tests are useful when there is a rich body of coherent precedents. But when there are not enough precedents of the right kinds, and when the precedents are not coherent, the necessary-condition test and the sufficient-condition test cannot be used to rule out conflicting interpretations of the precedents.

When the actual precedents are not enough, judges sometimes refer to *hypothetical cases*. In *Plessy*, a judge might imagine a law with discriminatory effect but no discriminatory motive. If the judge can show why this law should be found unconstitutional, this would suggest that a discriminatory motive is not really necessary for a violation of the equal protection clause. This takes some imagination, and it also requires judges to apply their moral beliefs about which laws should be allowed. Some critics deny that moral arguments should have any legal force, because they are so controversial. Nonetheless, there is no doubt that judges often do in fact assume such moral beliefs in arguments from precedents.

A final point to remember is that arguments from precedents are usually inconclusive, like other inductive arguments. (See Chapter 8.) One reason is that more precedents might be found, and these new precedents might conflict with the precedents in the original argument. Another reason is that any precedent can be overturned. Precedents are not supposed to be overturned unless they are very badly mistaken or immoral, but this is always a possibility. Nonetheless, even though arguments from precedents always might be refuted in such ways, precedents can still provide some reasons for legal decisions.

So far we have looked at arguments from precedents as ways to determine what is necessary or sufficient to violate the law. Even after this is determined, the law still must be applied to the facts in the present case. In *Plessy*, the Court held that there was no intent to discriminate, because the statute in *Plessy* was "reasonable" and "enacted in good faith for the promotion of the public good and not for the annoyance or oppression of a particular class." This claim is highly questionable. In his famous dissent, Justice Harlan denies it when he writes:

> Everyone knows that the statute in question had its origin in the purpose, not so much to exclude white persons from railroad cars occupied by blacks, as to exclude colored people from coaches occupied by or assigned to white persons. . . . No one would be so wanting in candor as to assert the contrary.

If Harlan is right, the Court's argument has a false premise, so the statute in *Plessy* should have been found unconstitutional even if the Court was right about what was necessary to find a law unconstitutional.

We can summarize this discussion by listing various ways in which arguments from precedents can fail:

(1) The precedent and the present case might not *truly* resemble each other in the ways that the argument claims.

(2) The respects in which the cases resemble each other might not be *important* enough to justify the same decision in the present case.

(3) The precedent and the present case might also *differ* from each other in important respects that justify distinguishing the precedent.

(4) The precedent might be mistaken or immoral enough to be *overturned*.

(5) There might be other, stronger precedents that *conflict* with the precedent in the argument.

Whenever you evaluate or present any argument from a precedent, you need to ask whether the argument fails in any of these ways.

DISCUSSION QUESTION

Analyze and evaluate the legal reasoning from precedents and statutes in the following opinion. If you were a justice on the Court, how much in damages would you award to the Peevyhouses:

(a) Twenty-nine thousand dollars (the cost of fulfilling the contract)?

(b) Twenty-five thousand dollars (the amount sued for)?

(c) Five thousand dollars (the amount awarded by the trial jury)?

(b) Three hundred dollars (the diminution in the value of the property due to the failure to fulfill the contract)?

■ PEEVYHOUSE V. GARLAND COAL & MINING CO.
(Supreme Court of Oklahoma, 1962, 382 P.2d 109)

Justice JACKSON [with whom Justices WELCH, DAVISON, HALLEY, and JOHNSON concur]:

. . . Briefly stated, the facts are as follows: plaintiffs [Willie and Lucille Peevyhouse] owned a farm containing coal deposits, and in November, 1954, leased the premises to defendant [Garland Coal & Mining Company] for a period of five years for coal mining purposes. A "strip-mining" operation was contemplated in which the coal would be taken from pits on the surface of the ground, instead of from underground mine shafts. In addition to the usual covenants found in a coal mining lease, defendant specifically agreed to perform certain restorative and remedial work at the end of the lease period. It is unnecessary to set out the details of the work to be done, other than to say that it would involve the moving of many thousands of cubic yards of dirt, at a cost estimated by expert witnesses at about $29,000.00. However, plaintiffs sued for only $25,000.00.

During the trial, it was stipulated that all covenants and agreements in the contract had been fully carried out by both parties, except the remedial work above; defendant conceded that this work had not been done. . . . [The jury] returned a verdict for plaintiffs for $5,000.00—only a fraction of the "cost of performance," *but more than the total value of the farm even after the remedial work is done.*

On appeal, the issue is sharply drawn. Plaintiffs contend that the true measure of damages in this case is what it will cost plaintiffs to obtain performance of the work that was not done because of defendant's default. Defendant argues that the measure of damages is the cost of performance "limited, however, to the total difference in the market value before and after the work was performed."

Plaintiffs rely on *Groves v. John Wunder Co.* . . . In that case, the Minnesota court, in a substantially similar situation, adopted the "cost of performance" rule as opposed to the "value" rule. The result was to authorize a jury to give plaintiff damages in the amount of $60,000, where the real estate concerned would have been worth only $12,160, even if the work contracted for had been done.

It may be observed that *Groves v. John Wunder Co.* . . . is the only case which has come to our attention in which the cost of performance rule has been followed under circumstances where the cost of performance greatly exceeded the diminution in value resulting from the breach of contract. Incidentally, it appears that this case was decided by a plurality rather than a majority of the members of the court.

Defendant relies principally upon *Sandy Valley & E. R. Co. v. Hughes* . . . ; *Bigham v. Wabash-Pittsburg Terminal Ry. Co.* . . . ; and *Sweeney v. Lewis Const. Co.* . . . These were all cases in which, under similar circumstances, the appellate courts followed the "value" rule instead of the "cost of performance" rule.

The explanation may be found in the fact that the situations presented are artificial ones. It is highly unlikely that the ordinary property owner would agree to pay $29,000 (or its equivalent) for the construction of "improvements" upon his property that would increase its value only about ($300) three hundred dollars. The result is that we are called upon to apply principles of law theoretically based upon reason and reality to a situation which is basically unreasonable and unrealistic.

In *Groves v. John Wunder Co.* . . . , the Minnesota court apparently considered the contract involved to be analogous to a building and construction contract, and cited authority for the proposition that the cost of performance or completion of the building as contracted is ordinarily the measure of damages in actions for damages for the breach of such a contract.

In an annotation following the Minnesota case . . . , the annotator places the three cases relied on by defendant (*Sandy Valley, Bigham* and *Sweeney*) under the classification of cases involving "grading and excavation contracts."

Continued on next page

We do not think either analogy is strictly applicable to the case now before us. The primary purpose of the lease contract between plaintiffs and defendant was neither "building and construction" nor "grading and excavation." It was merely to accomplish the economical recovery and marketing of coal from the premises, to the profit of all parties. The special provisions of the lease contract pertaining to remedial work were incidental to the main object involved.

Even in the case of contracts that are unquestionably building and construction contracts, the authorities are not in agreement as to the factors to be considered in determining whether the cost of performance rule or the value rule should be applied. The American Law Institute's Restatement of the Law, Contracts, . . . submits the proposition that the cost of performance is the proper measure of damages "if this is possible and does not involve *unreasonable economic waste*"; and that the diminution in value caused by the breach is the proper measure "if construction and completion in accordance with the contract would involve *unreasonable economic waste*" [emphasis supplied]. In an explanatory comment immediately following the text, the Restatement makes it clear that the "economic waste" referred to consists of the destruction of a substantially completed building or other structure. Of course no such destruction is involved in the case now before us.

. . . 23 O.S. [Oklahoma statutes] 1961 §§ 96 and 97 provide as follows:

> § 96 . . . Notwithstanding the provisions of this chapter, no person can recover a greater amount in damages for the breach of an obligation, than he would have gained by the full performance thereof on both sides. . . .

> § 97 . . . Damages must, in all cases, be reasonable, and where an obligation of any kind appears to create a right to unconscionable and grossly oppressive damages, contrary to substantial justice no more than reasonable damages can be recovered.

Although it is true that the above sections of the statute are applied most often in tort cases [involving a private or civil wrong or injury other than the breach of a contract], they are by their own terms, and the decisions of this court, also applicable in actions for damages for breach of contract. It would seem that they are peculiarly applicable here where, under the "cost of performance" rule, plaintiffs might recover an amount about nine times the total value of their farm. Such would seem to be "unconscionable and grossly oppressive damages, contrary to substantial justice" within the meaning of the statute. Also, it can hardly be denied that if plaintiffs here are permitted to recover under the "cost of performance" rule, they will receive a greater benefit from the breach than could be gained from full performance, contrary to the provisions of Sec. 96.

An analogy may be drawn between the cited sections and the provisions of 15 O.S. 1961 §§ 214 and 215. These sections tend to render void any provisions of a contract which attempt to fix the amount of stipulated damages to be paid in case of a breach, except where it is impracticable or extremely difficult to determine the actual damages. This results in spite of the agreement of the parties, and the obvious and well known rationale is that insofar as they exceed the actual damages suffered, the stipulated damages amount to a penalty or forfeiture which the law does not favor.

23 O.S. 1961 §§ 96 and 97 have the same effect in the case now before us. *In spite of the agreement of the parties* , these sections limit the damages recoverable to a reasonable amount not "contrary to substantial justice"; they prevent plaintiffs from recovering a "greater amount in damages for the breach of an obligation" than they would have "gained by the full performance thereof."

We therefore hold that where, in a coal mining lease, lessee agrees to perform certain remedial work on the premises concerned at the end of the lease period, and thereafter the contract is fully performed by both parties except that the remedial work is not done, the measure of damages in an action by lessor against lessee for damages for breach of contract is ordinarily the reasonable cost of performance of the work; however, where the contract provision breached was merely incidental to the main purpose in view, and where the economic benefit which would result to lessor by full performance of the work is grossly disproportionate to the cost of performance, the damages which lessor may recover are limited to the diminution in value resulting to the premises because of the non-performance.

We believe the above holding is in conformity with the intention of the Legislature as expressed in the statutes mentioned, and in harmony with the better-reasoned cases from the other jurisdictions where analogous fact situations have been considered. It should be noted that the rule as stated does not interfere with the property owner's right to "do what he will with his own" . . . , or his right, if he chooses, to contract for "improvements" which will actually have the effect of reducing his property's value. Where such result is in fact contemplated by the parties, and is a main or principal purpose of those contracting, it would seem that the measure of damages for breach would ordinarily be the cost of performance.

We are of the opinion that the judgment of the trial court for plaintiffs should be, and it is hereby, modified and reduced to the sum of $300.00, and as so modified it is affirmed.

Justice IRWIN (dissenting) [along with Chief Justice WILLIAMS, Vice Chief Justice BLACKBIRD, and Justice BERRY]:

Continued on next page

In the instant action defendant has made no attempt to even substantially perform. The contract in question is not immoral, is not tainted with fraud, and was not entered into through mistake or accident and is not contrary to public policy. It is clear and unambiguous and the parties understood the terms thereof, and the approximate cost of fulfilling the obligations could have been approximately ascertained. There are no conditions existing now which could not have been reasonably anticipated when the contract was negotiated and executed. The defendant could have performed the contract if it desired. It has accepted and reaped the benefits of its contract and now urges that plaintiffs' benefits under the contract be denied. If plaintiffs' benefits are denied, such benefits would inure to the direct benefit of the defendant.

Therefore, in my opinion, the plaintiffs were entitled to specific performance of the contract and since defendant has failed to perform, the proper measure of damages should be the cost of performance. Any other measure of damage would be holding for naught the express provisions of the contract; would be taking from the plaintiffs the benefits of the contract and placing those benefits in defendant which has failed to perform its obligations; would be granting benefits to defendant without a resulting obligation; and would be completely rescinding the solemn obligation of the contract for the benefit of the defendant to the detriment of the plaintiffs by making an entirely new contract for the parties.

I therefore respectfully dissent to the opinion promulgated by a majority of my associates. ∎

THE LAW OF DISCRIMINATION

These general methods of legal reasoning can be seen at work in a particular area of constitutional law—the law of discrimination. To understand the cases in this area, some background will be helpful.

The provision of the Constitution that governs discrimination is the equal protection clause of the Fourteenth Amendment. It provides as follows:

> No state shall make or enforce any law which shall . . . deny to any person within its jurisdiction the equal protection of the laws.

The clearest thing about this clause is that it is not clear. Whatever it means, it cannot mean that laws cannot ever treat people unequally. Criminal laws treat those who commit crimes quite differently from those who do not. The general idea behind the clause seems to be that like cases should be treated in like ways. Put negatively, the clause prohibits unequal treatment when there is no significant difference. This, however, is still both general and vague, for we need principles that determine what sorts of likenesses matter and what kinds of differences are significant.

Going back to the historical context in which the Fourteenth Amendment was adopted, we know that it was *intended* to prohibit unequal treatment on the basis of "race, color, or previous condition of servitude" (a phrase that occurs in the companion Fifteenth Amendment on voting rights). More specifically, it was one of those constitutional provisions intended to protect the newly emancipated slaves. This was the primary *purpose* of these provisions, but the *language* is more general, giving like protection to all citizens of the United States.

After the Fourteenth Amendment was adopted, many questions arose concerning its interpretation and application. The amendment explicitly refers only to state laws, but the state does many things besides pass laws, so the courts had to determine what counts as a *state action*. In a series of cases, the amendment was interpreted to mean that only positive actions of the state fell under the amendment. Thus, when thugs broke up a black political rally, with the police standing by doing nothing to protect the demonstrators, the Supreme Court ruled that this was not a violation of the equal protection clause because the state itself had not participated in the action (*U.S. v. Cruikshank*). On this view, the state was forbidden to aid discrimination, but it was not required to protect anyone against it.

Another issue that arose concerned what the state has to do to justify treating people differently. Here the courts decided that it was not their business to examine the details of legislation to make sure that the laws were as equitable as possible. The task of making laws, they held, falls to legislatures, and the courts gave legislatures wide latitude in formulating these laws. Flagrant violations of the equal protection clause could lead to the decision that the law was unconstitutional, but only if the law failed what became known as the *rational-relation test*. This test required only that the unequal treatment of individuals be reasonably likely to achieve some legitimate end.

A final issue was whether the Fourteenth Amendment protected only the civil rights of citizens or also rights of other kinds. In *Strauder v. West Virginia* (1880), a law that made blacks ineligible for jury duty was struck down on the grounds that the equal protection clause prohibits discrimination in areas of civil rights. In *Yick Wo v. Hopkins* (1886), the Court applied the equal protection clause to discrimination in areas of economic rights. *Yick Wo* also established that the equal protection clause protects not only blacks but also other groups (such as Chinese), and that laws that do not explicitly mention racial or ethnic groups can violate the equal protection clause if they are applied unequally in practice.

In 1896, the Supreme Court decided the case of *Plessy v. Ferguson*, about a Louisiana statute enforcing racial segregation in public transportation. This was clearly a state action, and the Court continued to apply the rational-relation test; the main issues were whether the equal protection clause extends to social rights, whether the segregation law served any reasonable purpose, and whether the separate facilities were truly equal. The Court held that the segregation statute did not violate the equal protection clause so long as the facilities were equal. This became known as the *separate-but-equal doctrine*.

■ PLESSY V. FERGUSON
(163 U.S. 537, 1896)

Mr. Justice Brown delivered the opinion of the Court.

This case turns upon the constitutionality of an act of the general assembly of the State of Louisiana, passed in 1890, providing for separate railway carriages for the white and colored races.

The first section of the statute enacts "that all railway companies carrying passengers in their coaches in this state shall provide equal but separate accommodations for the white and colored races, by providing two or more passenger coaches for each passenger train, or by dividing the passenger coaches by a partition so as to secure separate accommodations: *Provided*, That this section shall not be construed to apply to street railroads. No person or persons shall be permitted to occupy seats in coaches other than the ones assigned to them, on account of the race they belong to."

By the second section it was enacted "that the officers of such passenger trains shall have power and are hereby required to assign each passenger to the coach or compartment used for the race to which such passenger belongs; any passenger insisting on going into a coach or compartment to which by race he does not belong, shall be liable to a fine of $25 or in lieu thereof to imprisonment for a period of not more than twenty days in the parish prison, and any officer of any railroad insisting on assigning a passenger to a coach or compartment other than the one set aside for the race to which said passenger belongs, shall be liable to a fine of $24, or in lieu thereof to imprisonment for a period of not more than twenty days in the parish prison; and should any passenger refuse to occupy the coach or compartment to which he or she is assigned by the officer of such railway, said officer shall have power to refuse to carry such passenger on his train, and for such refusal neither he nor the railway company which he represents shall be liable for damages in any of the courts of this state." . . .

The information filed in the criminal district court charged in substance that Plessy, being a passenger between two stations within the state of Louisiana, was assigned by officers of the company to the coach used for the race to which he belonged, but he insisted upon going into a coach used by the race to which he did not belong. Neither in the information nor plea was his particular race or color averred.

The petition for the writ of prohibition averred that the petitioner was seven-eights Caucasian and one-eighth African blood; that the mixture of colored blood was not discernible in him, and that he was entitled to every right, privilege, and immunity secured to citizens of the United States of the white race; and that, upon such theory, he took possession of a vacant seat in a coach where passengers of the white race were accommodated, and was ordered by the conductor to vacate said coach and take a seat in another assigned to persons of the colored race, and having refused to comply with such demand he was forcibly ejected with the aid of a police officer, and imprisoned in the parish jail to answer a charge of having violated the above act.

The constitutionality of this act is attacked upon the ground that it conflicts both with the 13th Amendment of the Constitution, abolishing slavery, and the 14th Amendment, which prohibits certain restrictive legislation on the part of the states.

1. That it does not conflict with the 13th Amendment, which abolished slavery and involuntary servitude, except as a punishment for crime, is too clear for argument. . . . Indeed, we do not understand that the 13th Amendment is strenuously relied upon by the plaintiff in error in this connection.

2. By the 14th Amendment, all persons born or naturalized in the United States, and subject to the jurisdiction thereof, are made citizens of the United States and of the state wherein they reside; and the states are forbidden from making or enforcing any law which shall abridge the privileges or immunities of citizens of the United States, or shall deprive any person within their jurisdiction the equal protection of the laws. . . .

The object of the amendment was undoubtedly to enforce the absolute equality of the two races before the law, but in the nature of things it could not have been intended to abolish distinctions based upon color, or to enforce social, as distinguished from political, equality, or a commingling of the two races upon terms unsatisfactory to either. Laws permitting, and even requiring, their separation in places where they are liable to be brought into contact do not necessarily imply the inferiority of either race to the other, and have been generally, if not universally, recognized as within the competency of the state legislatures in the exercise of their police power. The most common instance of this is connected with the establishment of separate schools for white and colored children, which have been held to be a valid exercise of the legislative power even by courts of states where the political rights of the colored race have been longest and most earnestly enforced. . . .

[Justice Brown next reviews a whole series of cases in which statutes similar to the one in question have been upheld as constitutional.]

It is . . . suggested by the learned counsel for the plaintiff in error that the same argument that will justify the state legislature in requiring railways to provide separate accommodations for the two races will also authorize them to require separate cars to be provided for people whose hair is of a certain color, or who are aliens, or who belong to certain nationalities, or to enact laws requiring colored people to walk upon one side of the street, and white people upon the other, or requiring white men's houses to be painted white, and colored men's black, or their vehicles or business signs to be of different colors, upon the theory that one side of the street is as good as the other, or that a house or vehicle of one color is as good as one of another color. The reply to all this is that every exercise of the police power must be reasonable, and extend only to such laws as are enacted in good faith for the promotion of the public good, and not for the annoyance or oppression of a particular class. Thus in *Yick Wo v. Hopkins* it was held by this court that a municipal ordinance of the city of San Francisco to regulate the carrying on of public laundries within the limits of the municipality violated the provisions of the Constitution of the United States if it conferred upon the municipal authorities arbitrary power, at their own will, and without regard to discretion, in the legal sense of the term, to give or withhold consent as to persons or places, without regard to the competency of the persons applying, or the propriety of the places selected for the carrying on of the business. It was held to be a covert attempt on the part of the municipality to make an arbitrary and unjust discrimination against the Chinese race. While this was the case of a municipal ordinance a like principle has been held to apply to acts of a state legislature passed in the exercise of the police power.

So far, then, as a conflict with the 14th Amendment is concerned, the case reduces itself to the question whether the statute of Louisiana is a reasonable regulation, and with respect to this there must necessarily be a large discretion on the part of the legislature. In determining the question of reasonableness it is at liberty to act with reference to the established usages, customs, and traditions of the people, and with a view to the promotion of their comfort, and the preservation of the public peace and good order. Gauged by this standard, we cannot say that a law which authorizes or even requires the separation of the two races in public conveyances is unreasonable or more obnoxious to the 14th Amendment than the acts of Congress requiring separate schools for colored children in the District of Columbia, the constitutionality of which does not seem to have been questioned, or the corresponding acts of state legislatures.

We consider the underlying fallacy of the plaintiff's argument to consist in the assumption that the enforced separation of the two races stamps the colored race with a badge of inferiority. If this be so, it is not by reason of anything found in the act, but solely because the colored race chooses to put that construction upon it. The argument necessarily assumes that if, as has been more than once the case, and is not unlikely to be so again, the colored race should become the dominant power in the state legislature, and should enact a law in precisely similar terms, it would thereby relegate the white race to an inferior position. We imagine that the white race, at least, would not acquiesce in this assumption. The argument also assumes that social prejudices may be overcome by legislation, and that equal rights cannot be secured to the Negro except by an enforced commingling of the two races. We cannot accept this proposition. If the two races are to meet on terms of social equality, it must be the result of natural affinity, a mutual appreciation of each other's merits and a voluntary consent of individuals. As was said by the court of appeals of New York in *People v. Gallagher*, "this end can neither be accomplished nor promoted by laws which conflict with the general sentiment of the community upon whom they are designed to operate. When the government, therefore, has secured to each of its citizens equal rights before the law and equal opportunities for improvement and progress, it has accomplished the end for which it is organized and performed all of the functions respecting social advantages with which it is endowed." Legislation is powerless to eradicate racial instincts or to abolish distinctions based upon physical differences, and the attempt to do so can only result in accentuating the difficulties of the present situation. If the civil and political rights of both races be equal, one cannot be inferior to the other civilly or politically. If one race be inferior to the other socially, the Constitution of the United States cannot put them upon the same plane. . . .

The judgement of the Court below is, therefore, affirmed.

FROM *PLESSY* TO *BROWN*

As soon as *Plessy* was decided, southern and some border states rapidly passed a whole series of segregation laws. These were subsequently upheld by the courts on the precedent of *Plessy* and its separate-but-equal doctrine. The result was the introduction of a system of racial segregation throughout much of the country.

The doctrine of the rational-relation test remained basically unchanged until the 1940s. During World War II, the Supreme Court had to decide whether it was constitutional to relocate Japanese Americans away from Pacific ports. In *Korematsu v. United States* 323 U.S. 214 at 216 (1944), the Court announced that

> all legal restrictions which curtail the rights of a single racial group are immediately suspect. That is not to say that all such restrictions are unconstitutional. It is to say that the courts must subject them to the most rigid scrutiny.

It is ironic that the Court did not strike down the Japanese relocation orders, but these cases established a new interpretation of equal protection that eventually greatly increased the power of the courts to strike down discriminatory laws.

On this new interpretation of the equal protection clause, most laws still need to pass only the rational-relation test, but there are two features of a law that serve as *triggers* of strict scrutiny. A law must pass *strict scrutiny* if the law either restricts a *fundamental right* or employs a *suspect classification.* Fundamental rights concern such things as the right to vote or the right to procreate. A classification is suspect if it concerns race, religion, national origin, and so on. Under the new interpretation of the equal protection clause, states could still pass laws restricting fundamental rights, and these laws could still employ suspect classifications, but, when they did so, a heavy burden of proof fell on them. To justify such a law, the state had to show that (1) the legislation serves a *legitimate* and *compelling* state interest, and also that (2) it does so in the *least intrusive* way possible. This is the strict-scrutiny test.

It should be clear that the rational-relation test is easy to meet, whereas the test of strict scrutiny is nearly impossible to satisfy. It is not hard to show that a piece of legislation has some chance of serving some legitimate goal—that is the rational-relation test. It is difficult to show that the purpose of a law is compelling—that is, of overwhelming importance; and it is even more difficult to show that the stated purpose cannot be achieved by any less-intrusive means. Thus, in adopting this new test, the Court no longer showed great deference to state legislatures, as it did in *Plessy*, when it applied the rational-relation test. Instead, the heaviest burden was shifted to the states in areas that involved what the Court declared to be suspect classifications or fundamental rights.

This new test is implicit in the decision of *Brown v. Board of Education* (1954), which declares segregation in public schools unconstitutional. The *Brown* opinion does not directly mention strict scrutiny, but this test looms in the background. Segregation clearly involves a suspect classification, but the Court emphasizes that "the opportunity of an education . . . is a *right* which must be available to all on equal terms" (emphasis added). The next step is to argue that segregated schools violate this right by their very nature, even if all "tangible" factors are equal. This violation of a fundamental right triggers strict scrutiny, and the *Brown* opinion then simply assumes that segregation in education will fail this test. Separate but equal is thus found unconstitutional, at least in education, and *Plessy* is in effect overturned.

■ BROWN V. BOARD OF EDUCATION
(347 U.S. 483, 1954)

Mr. Chief Justice Warren delivered the opinion of the Court.

These cases come to us from the States of Kansas, South Carolina, Virginia, and Delaware. They are premised on different facts and different local conditions, but a common legal question justifies their consideration together in this consolidated opinion.

In each of the cases, minors of the Negro race, through their legal representatives, seek the aid of the courts in obtaining admission to the public schools of their community on a nonsegregated basis. In each instance, they had been denied admission to schools attended by white children under laws requiring or permitting segregation according to race. This segregation was alleged to deprive the plaintiffs of the equal protection of the laws under the Fourteenth Amendment. In each of the cases other than the Delaware case, a three-judge federal district court denied relief to the plaintiffs on the so-called "separate but equal" doctrine announced by this Court in *Plessy v. Ferguson.* Under that doctrine, equality of treatment is accorded when the races are provided substantially equal facilities, even though these facilities be separate. In the Delaware case, the Supreme Court of Delaware adhered to that doctrine, but ordered that the plaintiffs be admitted to the white schools because of their superiority to the Negro schools.

The plaintiffs contend that segregated public schools are not "equal" and cannot be made "equal," and that hence they are deprived of the equal protection of the laws. Because of the obvious importance of the question presented, the Court took jurisdiction. Argument was heard in the 1952 Term, and reargument was heard this Term on certain questions propounded by the Court.

Reargument was largely devoted to the circumstances surrounding the adoption of the Fourteenth Amendment in 1868. It covered exhaustively consideration of the Amendment in Congress, ratification by the states, then existing practices in racial segregation, and the views of proponents and opponents of the Amendment. This discussion and our own investigation convince us that, although these sources cast some light, it is not enough to resolve the problem with which we are faced. At best, they are inconclusive. The most avid proponents of the post-War Amendments undoubtedly intended them to remove all legal distinctions among "all persons born or naturalized in the United States." Their opponents, just as certainly, were antagonistic to both the letter and the spirit of the Amendments and wished them to have the most limited effect. What others in Congress and the state legislatures had in mind cannot be determined with any degree of certainty.

An additional reason for the inconclusive nature of the Amendment's history, with respect to segregated schools, is the status of public education at that time. In the South, the movement toward free common schools, supported by general taxation, had not yet taken hold. Education of white children was largely in the hands of private groups. Education of Negroes was almost nonexistent, and practically all of the race were illiterate. In fact, any education of Negroes was forbidden by law in some states. Today, in contrast, many Negroes have achieved outstanding success in the arts and sciences as well as in the business and professional world. It is true that public school education at the time of the Amendment had advanced further in the North, but the effect of the Amendment on northern states was generally ignored in the congressional debates. Even in the North, the conditions of public education did not approximate those existing today. The curriculum was usually rudimentary; ungraded schools were common in rural areas; the school term was but three months a year in many states; and compulsory school attendance was virtually unknown. As a consequence, it is not surprising that there should be so little in the history of the Fourteenth Amendment relating to its intended effect on public education.

In the first cases in this Court construing the Fourteenth Amendment, decided shortly after its adoption, the Court interpreted it as proscribing all state-imposed discriminations against the Negro race. The doctrine of "separate but equal" did not make its appearance in this Court until 1896 in the case of *Plessy v. Ferguson* involving not education but transportation. American courts have since labored with the doctrine for over half a century. In this Court, there have been six cases involving the "separate but equal" doctrine in the field of public education. In *Cumming v. County Board of Education* and *Gong Lum v. Rice* the validity of the doctrine itself was not challenged. In more recent cases, all on the graduate school level, inequality was found in that specific benefits enjoyed by white students were denied to Negro students of the same educational qualifications. In none of these cases was it necessary to re-examine the doctrine to grant relief to the Negro plaintiff. And in *Sweatt v. Painter* the Court expressly reserved decision on the question whether *Plessy v. Ferguson* should be held inapplicable to public education.

In the instant cases, that question is directly presented. Here, unlike *Sweatt v. Painter*, there are findings below that the Negro and white schools involved have been equalized, or are being equalized, with respect to buildings, curricula, qualifications and salaries of teachers, and other "tangible" factors. Our decision, therefore, cannot turn on merely a comparison of these tangible factors in the Negro and white schools involved in each of the cases. We must look instead to the effect of segregation itself on public education.

In approaching this problem, we cannot turn the clock back to 1868 when the Amendment was adopted, or even to 1896 when *Plessy v. Ferguson* was written. We must consider public education in the light of its full development and its present place in American life throughout the Nation. Only in this way can it be determined if segregation in public school deprives these plaintiffs of the equal protection of the laws.

Today, education is perhaps the most important function of state and local governments. Compulsory school attendance laws and the great expenditures for education both demonstrate our recognition of the importance of education to our democratic society. It is required in the performance of our most basic public responsibilities, even service in the armed forces. It is the very foundation of good citizenship. Today it is a principal instrument in awakening the child to cultural values, in preparing him for later professional training, and in helping him to adjust normally to his environment. In these days, it is doubtful that any child may reasonably be expected to succeed in life if he is denied the opportunity of an education. Such an opportunity, where the state has undertaken to provide it, is a right which must be made available to all on equal terms.

We come then to the question presented: Does segregation of children in public schools solely on the basis of race, even though the physical facilities and other "tangible" factors may be equal, deprive the children of the minority group of equal educational opportunities? We believe that it does.

In *Sweatt v. Painter*, in finding that a segregated law school for Negroes could not provide them equal educational opportunities, this Court relied in large part on "those qualities which are incapable of objective measurement but which make for greatness in a law school." In *McLaurin v. Oklahoma State Regents* the Court, in requiring that a Negro admitted to a white graduate school be treated like all other students, again resorted to intangible considerations: ". . . his ability to study, to engage in discussions and exchange views with other students, and, in general, to learn his profession." Such considerations apply with added force to children in grade and high schools. To separate them from others of similar age and qualifications solely because of their race generates a feeling of inferiority as to their status in the community that may affect their hearts and minds in a way unlikely ever to be undone. The effect of this separation on their educational opportunities was well stated by a finding in the Kansas case by a court which nevertheless felt compelled to rule against the Negro plaintiffs:

> Segregation of white and colored children in public schools has a detrimental effect upon the colored children. The impact is greater when it has the sanction of the law; for the policy of separating the races is usually interpreted as denoting the inferiority of the Negro group. A sense of inferiority affects the motivation of a child to learn. Segregation with the sanction of law, therefore, has a tendency to [retard] the education and mental development of Negro children and to deprive them of some of the benefits they would receive in a racial[ly] integrated school system.

Whatever may have been the extent of psychological knowledge at the time of *Plessy v. Ferguson*, this finding is amply supported by modern authority. Any language in *Plessy v. Ferguson* contrary to this finding is rejected.

We conclude that in the field of public education the doctrine of "separate but equal" has no place. Separate educational facilities are inherently unequal. Therefore, we hold that the plaintiffs and others similarly situated for whom the actions have been brought are, by reason of the segregation complained of, deprived of the equal protection of the laws guaranteed by the Fourteenth Amendment. . . .

DISCUSSION QUESTIONS

(1) Can *Brown* be used as a precedent to argue against the constitutionality of racial segregation in *public transportation?* Why or why not? Be sure to consider the similarities and differences between education and transportation.

(2) Can *Brown* be used as a precedent to argue against the constitutionality of segregation by *gender* in public schools (for example, in sports)? Why or why not? Be sure to consider the similarities and differences between gender and race, and whether gender should be a suspect classification for the purposes of the strict scrutiny test.

(3) What should count as a *state action?* Apply your views to the case of *Moose Lodge v. Irvis* (407 U.S. 163, 1972), where Pennsylvania granted a liquor license to a private club that refused to serve blacks, but some blacks complained that they were deprived because only a limited number of liquor licenses were available.

FROM *BROWN* TO *BAKKE*

After *Brown*, the Supreme Court struck down segregation in many other areas—transportation, parks, libraries, and so on—as well as laws against racial intermarriage (in 1967). Another string of decisions required states to use busing as a means to end segregation in school systems. The Court also required some employers to hire or promote minimum percentages of minorities to overcome the effects of illegal discrimination in employment.

In response to these court decisions, some schools and companies voluntarily took steps to overcome what they saw as the effects of past discrimination. These steps required them to use racial classifications, and that raised the issue of reverse discrimination.

Part of the issue was about what to call such programs. Their opponents describe them as "reverse discrimination," but their defenders refer to them as "affirmative action." Both descriptions involve evaluation, so neither should be used without an argument. A more neutral description is "preferential treatment," so we will use this label.

The most important case in this area is *Regents of the University of California v. Bakke* (1978) (hereafter, *Bakke*). The basic situation was that the medical school of the University of California at Davis had very few minority students, so they created a special-admissions program that gave preferential treatment to minorities who were disadvantaged. Bakke applied to the school but was rejected even though he had higher scores on admissions tests than some minority members who were admitted under the special-admissions program.

Bakke claimed that Davis's special-admissions program violated the equal protection clause of the United States Constitution, the California Constitution, and Title VI of the Civil Rights Act of 1964, which provides: "No person in the

United States shall, on the ground of race, color, or national origin, be excluded from participation in, be denied the benefits of, or be subjected to discrimination under any program or activity receiving Federal financial assistance." The Supreme Court was thus asked to rule on four main issues:

(1) Did the Davis special-admissions program violate the equal protection clause of the Constitution?

(2) Does reference to race without judicial findings of particular past discrimination violate this constitutional guarantee?

(3) Did the Davis special-admissions program violate Title VI of the Civil Rights Act?

(4) Should Davis be required to admit Bakke into its medical school?

The decision of the Supreme Court on these issues is so complicated that it takes a scorecard to follow it:

	Brennan, Marshall, Blackmun, and White	Powell	Burger, Stewart, Stevens, and Rehnquist	The majority
(1)	No	Yes	No decision	No decision
(2)	No	No	No decision	No
(3)	No	Yes	Yes	Yes
(4)	No	Yes	Yes	Yes

Since the justices split into two groups of four, the remaining justice, Powell, determined the majority on most issues. However, Powell was the only justice who argued that the Davis program was unconstitutional. Four others (Brennan, Marshall, Blackmun, and White) dissented. The remaining four (Burger, Stevens, Stewart, and Rehnquist) chose not to address this constitutional issue, because they had already ruled out the Davis program under Title VI. Since a majority did not join Powell in his opinion, the Court did *not* explicitly declare the Davis program *unconstitutional*. But the Davis program was held to violate Title VI and Davis was ordered to admit Bakke, because Burger, Stevens, Stewart, and Rehnquist did join Powell on these issues. Despite Davis's loss, the Court took the opposite position on the second issue. Powell argued that it was not always unconstitutional for the state to refer to race, and he created a majority when he was joined by Brennan, Marshall, Blackmun, and White. Thus, each group of justices got part of what it wanted.

The constitutional issues are raised most directly in the opinions of Powell and Brennan (excerpted below). These opinions differ not only in their conclusions but also in their interpretations of the equal protection clause. Powell argued that the Davis program and any consideration of race must be subjected to the test of strict scrutiny. He held that the Davis program did not meet the high standards of this test, but some other consideration of race might.

In contrast, Brennan argued for a new interpretation of the equal protection clause. On this new interpretation, strict scrutiny would still be applied to most racial classifications, but, when certain conditions were met, the courts would apply a less exacting test—often called *middle-level scrutiny*. The test of middle-level scrutiny requires the state to show that (1) the state action serves a *legitimate, articulated,* and *important* state interest, (2) it does not *stigmatize* or inflict any pervasive injury on those who are excluded, and (3) it bears a *substantial* relation to the purpose, and there is no *significantly* less intrusive means to serve the purpose. Brennan argued that this more lenient test should be applied when the state uses a racial classification to serve a *benign, remedial purpose*. The purpose of a racial classification is benign when it was not adopted out of any discriminatory motive, and it is remedial if the state used the racial classification because the state found that, without the racial classification, an underprivileged group would suffer harm or differential impact because of past discrimination in society at large.

The conditions under which to apply middle-level scrutiny are the heart of the controversy. Powell criticized Brennan's conditions on the grounds that the notion of stigma is too vague and that it is not groups but individuals who are protected by the equal protection clause. Brennan responded by distinguishing stigma from other harms and by emphasizing the importance of groups. Powell also argued that some kinds of preferential treatment (which use *goals*, as in the Harvard admissions program) are less intrusive than other kinds of preferential treatment (which use *quotas*, as in the Davis program). Brennan responded that this difference is not significant, because both kinds of preferential treatment produce the same result for those who are excluded. These and many other disputes were not settled by this case. They are still alive today.

▪ REGENTS OF THE UNIVERSITY OF CALIFORNIA V. BAKKE
(438 U.S. 268, 1978)

Summary by the Reporter of Decisions:

[The Medical School of the University of California at Davis (hereinafter Davis) had two admissions programs for the entering class of 100 students—the regular admissions program and the special admissions program. Under the regular procedure, candidates whose overall undergraduate grade point average fell below 2.5 on a scale of 4.0 were summarily rejected. About one out of six applicants was then given an interview, following which he was rated on a scale of 1 to 100 by each of the committee members (five in 1973 and six in 1974), his rating being based on the interviewers' summaries, his overall grade point average, his science courses grade point average, and his Medical College Admissions Test (MCAT) scores, letters of recommendation, extracurricular activities, and other biographical data, all of which resulted in a total "benchmark score." The full admissions committee then made offers of admission on the basis of their review of the applicant's file and his score, considering and acting upon applications as they were received. The committee chairman was responsible for placing names on the waiting list and had discretion to include persons with "special skills." A separate committee, a majority of whom were members of minority groups, operated the special admissions program. The 1973 and 1974 application forms, respectively, asked candidates whether they wished to be considered as "economically and/or educationally disadvantaged" applicants and members of a "minority group" (blacks, Chicanos, Asians, American Indians). If an applicant of a minority group was found to be "disadvantaged," he would be rated in a manner similar to the one employed by the general admissions committee. Special candidates, however, did not have to meet the 2.5 grade point cut-off and were not ranked against candidates in the general admissions process. About one-fifth of the special applicants were invited for interviews in 1973 and 1974, following which they were given benchmark scores, and the top choices were then given to the general admissions committee, which could reject special candidates for failure to meet course requirements or other specific deficiencies. The special committee continued to recommend candidates until 16 special admission selections had been made. During a four-year period 63 minority students were admitted to Davis under the special program and 44 under the general program. No disadvantaged whites were admitted under the special program, though many applied.

Respondent, a white male, applied to Davis in 1973 and 1974, in both years being considered only under the general admissions program. Though he had a 468 out of 500 score in 1973, he was rejected since no general applicants with scores less than 470 were being accepted after respondent's application, which was filed late in the year, had been processed and completed. At that time four special admission slots were still unfilled. In 1974 respondent applied early, and though he had a total score of 549 out of 600, he was again rejected. In neither year was his name placed on the discretionary waiting list. In both years special applicants were admitted with significantly lower scores than respondent's. After his second rejection, respondent filed this action in state court for mandatory injunctive and declaratory relief to compel his admission to Davis, alleging that the special admissions program operated to exclude him on the basis of his race in violation of the Equal Protection Clause of the Fourteenth Amendment, a provision of the California Constitution, and §601 of Title VI of the Civil Rights Act of 1964. . . .

Excerpts from Justice Powell's Opinion:

III

Racial and ethnic classifications . . . are subject to stringent examination without regard to . . . additional characteristics. We declared as much in the first cases explicitly to recognize racial distinctions as suspect:

". . . [A]ll legal restrictions which curtail the rights of a single racial group are immediately suspect. That is not to say that all such restrictions are unconstitutional. It is to say that courts must subject them to the most rigid scrutiny" (*Korematsu*, 323 U.S. 214 at 216 [1944]).

The Court has never questioned the validity of those pronouncements. Racial and ethnic distinctions of any sort are inherently suspect and thus call for the most exacting judicial examination. . . .

Petitioner urges us to adopt for the first time a more restrictive view of the Equal Protection Clause and hold that discrimination against members of the white "majority" cannot be suspect if its purpose can be characterized as "benign." The clock of our liberties, however, cannot be turned back to 1868. It is far too late to argue that the guarantee of equal protection to *all* persons permits the recognition of special wards entitled to a degree of protection greater than that accorded others.

Moreover, there are serious problems of justice connected with the idea of preference itself. First, it may not always be clear that a so-called preference is in fact benign. Courts may be asked to validate burdens imposed upon individual members of particular groups in order to advance the group's general interest. . . . Nothing in the Constitution supports the notion that individuals may be asked to suffer otherwise impermissible burdens in order to enhance the societal standing of their ethnic groups. Second, preferential programs may only reinforce common stereotypes holding that certain groups are unable to achieve success without special protection based on a factor having no relationship to individual worth. . . . Third, there is a measure of inequity in forcing innocent persons in respondent's position to bear the burdens of redressing grievances not of their making.

Petitioner contends that on several occasions this Court has approved preferential classifications without applying the most exacting scrutiny. Most of the cases upon which petitioner relies are drawn from three areas: school desegregation, employment discrimination, and sex discrimination. Each of the cases cited presented a situation materially different from the facts of this case. . . . [W]e have never approved preferential classifications in the absence of proven constitutional or statutory violations. . . . When a classification denies an individual opportunities or benefits enjoyed by others solely because of his race or ethnic background, it must be regarded as suspect. . . .

IV

We have held that in "order to justify the use of a suspect classification, a State must show that its purpose or interest is both constitutionally permissible and substantial, and that its use of the classification is 'necessary . . . to the accomplishment' of its purpose or the safeguarding of its interest." The special admissions program purports to serve the purposes of: (i) "reducing the historic deficit of traditionally disfavored minorities in medical schools and the medical profession"; (ii) countering the effects of societal discrimination; (iii) increasing the number of physicians who will practice in communities currently underserved; and (iv) obtaining the educational benefits that flow from an ethnically diverse student body. It is necessary to decide which, if any, of these purposes is substantial enough to support the use of a suspect classification. . . .

If petitioner's purpose is to assure within its student body some specified percentage of a particular group merely because of its race or ethnic origin, such a preferential purpose must be rejected not as insubstantial but as facially invalid. Preferring members of any one group for no reason other than race or ethnic origin is discrimination for its own sake. This the Constitution forbids. . . .

The State certainly has a legitimate and substantial interest in ameliorating, or eliminating where feasible, the disabling effects of identified discrimination. The line of school desegregation cases, commencing with *Brown*, attests to the importance of this state goal and the commitment of the judiciary to affirm all lawful means toward its attainment. In the school cases, the States were required by court order to redress the wrongs worked by specific instances of racial discrimination. That goal was far more focused than the remedying of the effects of "societal discrimination," an amorphous concept of injury that may be ageless in its reach into the past.

We have never approved a classification that aids persons perceived as members of relatively victimized groups at the expense of other innocent individuals in the absence of judicial, legislative or administrative findings of constitutional or statutory violations. . . . After such findings have been made, the governmental interest in preferring members of the injured groups at the expense of others is substantial, since the legal rights of the victims must be vindicated. . . . Without such findings of constitutional or statutory violations, it cannot be said that the government has any greater interest in helping one individual than in refraining from harming another. Thus, the government has no compelling justification for inflicting such harm.

Petitioner does not purport to have made, and is in no position to make, such findings. Its broad mission is education, not the formulation of any legislative policy or the adjudication of particular claims of illegality. . . .

Hence, the purpose of helping certain groups whom the faculty of the Davis Medical School perceived as victims of "societal discrimination" does not justify a classification that imposes disadvantages upon persons like respondent, who bear no responsibility for whatever harm the beneficiaries of the special admissions program are thought to have suffered.

Petitioner identifies, as another purpose of its program, improving the delivery of health care services to communities currently underserved. It may be assumed that in some situations a State's interest in facilitating the health care of its citizens is sufficiently compelling to support the use of a suspect classification. But there is virtually no evidence in the record indicating that petitioner's special admissions program is either needed or geared to promote that goal. The court below addressed this failure of proof: "The University concedes it cannot assure that minority doctors who entered under the program, all of whom express an 'interest' in participating in a disadvantaged community, will actually do so. . . ."

[Thus the petitioner] simply has not carried its burden of demonstrating that it must prefer members of particular ethnic groups over all other individuals in order to promote better health care delivery to deprived citizens. Indeed, petitioner has not shown that its preferential classification is likely to have any significant effect on the problem. . . .

The fourth goal asserted by petitioner is the attainment of a diverse student body. This clearly is a constitutionally permissible goal for an institution of higher education. Academic freedom, though not a specifically enumerated constitutional right, long has been viewed as a special concern of the First Amendment. The freedom of a university to make its own judgments as to education includes the selection of its student body. . . . Thus, in arguing that its universities must be accorded the right to select those students who will contribute the most to the "robust exchange of ideas," petitioner invokes a countervailing constitutional interest, that of the First Amendment. In this light, petitioner must be viewed as seeking to achieve a goal that is of paramount importance in the fulfillment of its mission. . . .

It may be assumed that the reservation of a specified number of seats in each class for individuals from the preferred ethnic groups would contribute to the attainment of considerable ethnic diversity in the student body. But petitioner's argument that this is the only effective means of serving the interest of diversity is seriously flawed. In a most fundamental sense the argument misconceives the nature of the state interest that would justify consideration of race or ethnic background. It is not an interest in simple ethnic diversity, in which a specific percentage of the student body is in effect guaranteed to be members of selected ethnic groups, with the remaining percentage an undifferentiated aggregation of students. The diversity that furthers a compelling state interest encompasses a far broader array of qualifications and characteristics of which racial or ethnic origin is but a single though important element. Petitioner's special admissions program, focused *solely* on ethnic diversity, would hinder rather than further attainment of genuine diversity.

The experience of other university admissions programs, which take race into account in achieving the educational diversity valued by the First Amendment, demonstrates that the assignment of a fixed number of places to a minority group is not a necessary means toward that end. An illuminating example is found in the Harvard College program:

> In recent years Harvard College has expanded the concept of diversity to include students from disadvantaged economic, racial and ethnic groups. Harvard College now recruits not only Californians or Louisianans but also blacks and Chicanos and other minority students.
>
> In practice, this new definition of diversity has meant that race has been a factor in some admission decisions. When the Committee on Admissions reviews the large middle group of applicants who are 'admissible' and deemed capable of doing good work in their courses, the race of an applicant may tip the balance in his favor just as geographic origin or a life spent on a farm may tip the balance in other candidates' cases. A farm boy from Idaho can bring something to Harvard College that a Bostonian cannot offer. Similarly, a black student can usually bring something that a white person cannot offer. . . .
>
> In Harvard College admissions the Committee has not set target-quotas for the number of blacks, or of musicians, football players, physicists or Californians to be admitted in a given year. . . . But that awareness [of the necessity of including more than a token number of black students] does not mean that the Committee

sets the minimum number of blacks or of people from west of the Mississippi who are to be admitted. It means only that in choosing among thousands of applicants who are not only 'admissible' academically but have other strong qualities, the Committee, with a number of criteria in mind, pays some attention to distribution among many types and categories of students. (Brief for Columbia University, Harvard University, Stanford University, and the University of Pennsylvania, as *Amici Curiae*, App. 2, 3.)

In such an admissions program, race or ethnic background may be deemed a "plus" in a particular applicant's file, yet it does not insulate the individual from comparison with all other candidates for the available seats. The file of a particular black applicant may be examined for his potential contribution to diversity without the factor of race being decisive when compared, for example, with that of an applicant identified as an Italian-American if the latter is thought to exhibit qualities more likely to promote beneficial educational pluralism. Such qualities could include exceptional personal talents, unique work or service experience, leadership potential, maturity, demonstrated compassion, a history of overcoming disadvantage, ability to communicate with the poor, or other qualifications deemed important. In short, an admissions program operated in this way is flexible enough to consider all pertinent elements of diversity in light of the particular qualifications of each applicant, and to place them on the same footing for consideration, although not necessarily according them the same weight. Indeed, the weight attributed to a particular quality may vary from year to year depending upon the "mix" both of the student body and the applicants for the incoming class.

This kind of program treats each applicant as an individual in the admissions process. The applicant who loses out on the last available seat to another candidate receiving a "plus" on the basis of ethnic background will not have been foreclosed from all consideration for that seat simply because he was not the right color or had the wrong surname. It would mean only that his combined qualifications, which may have included similar nonobjective factors, did not outweigh those of the other applicant. His qualifications would have been weighed fairly and competitively, and he would have no basis to complain of unequal treatment under the Fourteenth Amendment.

It has been suggested that an admissions program which considers race only as one factor is simply a subtle and more sophisticated—but no less effective—means of according racial preference than the Davis program. A facial intent to discriminate, however, is evident in petitioner's preference program and not denied in this case. No such facial infirmity exists in an admissions program where race or ethnic background is simply one element—to be weighed fairly against other elements—in the selections process. "A boundary line," as Mr. Justice Frankfurter remarked in another connection, "is none the worse for being narrow." And a Court would not assume that a university, professing to employ a facially nondiscriminatory admissions policy, would operate it as a cover for the functional equivalent of a quota system. In short, good faith would be presumed in the absence of a showing to the contrary in the manner permitted by our cases.

In summary, it is evident that the Davis special admissions program involves the use of an explicit racial classification never before countenanced by this Court. It tells applicants who are not Negro, Asian, or "Chicano" that they are totally excluded from a specific percentage of the seats in an entering class. No matter how strong their qualifications, quantitative and extracurricular, including their own potential for contribution to educational diversity, they are never afforded the chance to compete with applicants from the preferred groups for the special admission seats. At the same time, the preferred applicants have the opportunity to compete for every seat in the class.

The fatal flaw in petitioner's preferential program is its disregard of individual rights as guaranteed by the Fourteenth Amendment. Such rights are not absolute. But when a State's distribution of benefits or imposition of burdens hinges on the color of a person's skin or ancestry, that individual is entitled to a demonstration that the challenged classification is necessary to promote a substantial state interest. Petitioner has failed to carry this burden. For this reason, that portion of the California court's judgment holding petitioner's special admissions program invalid under the Fourteenth Amendment must be affirmed.

Excerpts from Justice Brennan's Opinion:

The assertion of human equality is closely associated with the proposition that differences in color or creed, birth or status, are neither significant nor relevant to the way in which persons should be treated. Nonetheless, the position that such factors must be "[c]onstitutionally an irrelevance," summed up by the shorthand phrase "[o]ur Constitution is color-blind," has never been adopted by this Court as the proper meaning of the Equal Protection Clause. Indeed, we have expressly rejected this proposition on a number of occasions.

We conclude, therefore, that racial classifications are not per se invalid under the Fourteenth Amendment. Accordingly, we turn to the problem of articulating what our role should be in reviewing state action that expressly classifies by race. . . .

Respondent argues that racial classifications are always suspect and, consequently, that this Court should weigh the importance of the objectives served by Davis' special admissions program to see if they are compelling. In addition, he asserts that this Court must inquire whether, in its judgment, there are alternatives to racial classifications which would suit Davis' purposes. Petitioner, on the other hand, states that our proper role is simply to accept petitioner's determination that the racial classifications used by its program are reasonably related to what it tells us are its benign purposes. We reject petitioner's view, but, because our prior cases are in many respects inapposite to that before us now, we find it necessary to define with precision the meaning of that inexact term, "strict scrutiny." . . .

Unquestionably we have held that a government practice or statute which restricts "fundamental rights" or which contains "suspect classifications" is to be subjected to "strict scrutiny" and can be justified only if it furthers a compelling government purpose and, even then, only if no less restrictive alternative is available. . . . But no fundamental right is involved here. . . . Nor do whites as a class have any of the "traditional indicia of suspectness: the class is not saddled with such disabilities, or subjected to such a history of purposeful unequal treatment, or relegated to such a position of political powerlessness as to command extraordinary protection from the majoritarian political process."

[The] fact that this case does not fit neatly into our prior analytic framework for race cases does not mean that it should be analyzed by applying the very loose rational-basis standard of review that is the very least that is always applied in equal protection cases. " '[T]he mere recitation of a benign, compensatory purpose is not an automatic shield which protects against any inquiry into the actual purposes underlying a statutory scheme.' " Instead, a number of considerations— developed in gender discrimination cases but which carry even more force when applied to racial classifications—lead us to conclude that racial classifications de-signed to further remedial purposes " 'must serve important governmental objec-tives and must be substantially related to achievement of those objectives.' "

First, race, like "gender-based classifications too often [has] been inexcusably utilized to stereotype and stigmatize politically powerless segments of society." While a carefully tailored statute designed to remedy past discrimination could avoid these vices, we nonetheless have recognized that the line between honest and thoughtful appraisal of the effects of past discrimination and paternalistic stereotyping is not so clear and that a statute based on the latter is patently capable of stigmatizing all women with a badge of inferiority. State programs designed ostensibly to ameliorate the effects of past racial discrimination obviously create the same hazard of stigma, since they may promote racial separatism and reinforce the views of those who believe that members of racial minorities are inherently incapable of succeeding on their own.

Second, race, like gender and illegitimacy, is an immutable characteristic which its possessors are powerless to escape or set aside. While a classification is not per se invalid because it divides classes on the basis of an immutable characteristic, it is nevertheless true that such divisions are contrary to our deep belief that "legal burdens should bear some relationship to individual responsibility or wrongdoing," and that advancement sanctioned, sponsored, or approved by the State should ideally be based on individual merit or achievement, or at the least on factors within the control of an individual. . . .

In sum, because of the significant risk that racial classifications established for ostensibly benign purposes can be misused, causing effects not unlike those created by invidious classifications, it is inappropriate to inquire only whether there is any conceivable basis that might sustain such a classification. Instead, to justify such a classification an important and articulated purpose for its use must be shown. In addition, any statute must be stricken that stigmatizes any group or that singles out those least well represented in the political process to bear the brunt of a benign program. Thus our review under the Fourteenth Amendment should be strict—not " 'strict' in theory and fatal in fact," because it is stigma that causes fatality—but strict and searching nonetheless. . . .

Davis' articulated purpose of remedying the effects of past societal discrimina-tion is, under our cases, sufficiently important to justify the use of race-conscious admissions programs where there is a sound basis for concluding that minority underrepresentation is substantial and chronic, and that the handicap of past discrimination is impeding access of minorities to the medical school. . . .

Certainly, on the basis of the undisputed factual submissions before this Court, Davis had a sound basis for believing that the problem of underrepresentation of minorities was substantial and chronic and that the problem was attributable to handicaps imposed on minority applicants by past and present racial discrimination. Until at least 1973, the practice of medicine in this country was, in fact, if not in law, largely the prerogative of whites. In 1950, for example, while Negroes comprised 10% of the total population, Negro physicians constituted only 2.2% of the total number of physicians. The overwhelming majority of these, moreover, were educated in two predominantly Negro medical schools, Howard and Meharry. By 1970, the gap between the proportion of Negroes in medicine and their proportion in the population had widened: The number of Negroes employed in medicine remained frozen at 2.2% while the Negro population had increased to 11.1%. The number of Negro admittees to predominantly white medical schools, moreover, had declined in absolute numbers during the years 1955 to 1964.

Moreover, Davis had a very good reason to believe that the national pattern of underrepresentation of minorities in medicine would be perpetuated if it retained a single admissions standard. For example, the entering classes in 1968 and 1969, the years in which such a standard was used, included only one Chicano and two Negroes out of 100 admittees. Nor is there any relief from this pattern of underrepresentation in the statistics for the regular admissions program in later years.

Davis clearly could conclude that the serious and persistent underrepresentation of minorities in medicine depicted by these statistics is the result of handicaps under which minority applicants labor as a consequence of a background of deliberate, purposeful discrimination against minorities in education and in society generally, as well as in the medical profession. . . .

The second prong of our test—whether the Davis program stigmatizes any discrete group or individual and whether race is reasonably used in light of the program's objectives—is clearly satisfied by the Davis program.

It is not even claimed that Davis' program in any way operates to stigmatize or single out any discrete and insular, or even any identifiable, nonminority group. Nor will harm comparable to that imposed upon racial minorities by exclusion or separation on grounds of race be the likely result of the program. It does not, for example, establish an exclusive preserve for minority students apart from and exclusive of whites. Rather, its purpose is to overcome the effects of segregation by bringing the races together. True, whites are excluded from participation in the special admissions program, but this fact only operates to reduce the number of whites to be admitted in the regular admissions program in order to permit admission of a reasonable percentage—less than their proportion of the California population—of otherwise underrepresented qualified minority applicants.

Nor was Bakke in any sense stamped as inferior by the Medical School's rejection of him. . . . Unlike discrimination against racial minorities, the use of racial preferences for remedial purposes does not inflict a pervasive injury upon individual whites in the sense that wherever they go or whatever they do there is a significant likelihood that they will be treated as second-class citizens because of their color. This distinction does not mean that the exclusion of a white resulting from the preferential use of race is not sufficiently serious to require justification; but it does mean that the injury inflicted by such a policy is not distinguishable from disadvantages caused by a wide range of government actions, none of which has ever been thought impermissible for that reason alone.

In addition, there is simply no evidence that the Davis program discriminates intentionally or unintentionally against any minority group which it purports to benefit. The program does not establish a quota in the invidious sense of a ceiling on the number of minority applicants to be admitted. Nor can the program reasonably be regarded as stigmatizing the program's beneficiaries or their race as inferior. The Davis program does not simply advance less qualified applicants; rather, it compensates applicants, whom it is uncontested are fully qualified to study medicine, for educational disadvantage which it was reasonable to conclude was a product of state-fostered discrimination. Once admitted, these students must satisfy the same degree requirements as regularly admitted students; they are taught by the same faculty in the same classes; and their performance is evaluated by the same standards by which regularly admitted students are judged. Under these circumstances, their performance and degrees must be regarded equally with the regularly admitted students with whom they compete for standing. Since minority graduates cannot justifiably be regarded as less well qualified than non-minority graduates by virtue of the special admissions program, there is no reasonable basis to conclude that minority graduates at schools using such programs would be stigmatized as inferior by the existence of such programs. . . .

Finally, Davis' special admissions program cannot be said to violate the Constitution simply because it has set aside a predetermined number of places for qualified minority applicants rather than using minority status as a positive factor to be considered in evaluating the applications of disadvantaged minority applicants. For purposes of constitutional adjudication, there is no difference between the two approaches. In any admissions program which accords special consideration to disadvantaged racial minorities, a determination of the degree of preference to be given is unavoidable, and any given preference that results in the exclusion of a white candidate is no more or less constitutionally acceptable than a program such as that at Davis. Furthermore, the extent of the preference inevitably depends on how many minority applicants the particular school is seeking to admit in any particular year so long as the number of qualified minority applicants exceeds that number. There is no sensible, and certainly no constitutional, distinction between, for example, adding a set number of points to the admissions rating of disadvantaged minority applicants as an expression of the preference with the expectation that this will result in the admission of an approximately determined number of qualified minority applicants and setting a fixed number of places for such applicants as was done here.

Accordingly, we would reverse the judgment of the Supreme Court of California holding the Medical School's special admissions program unconstitutional and directing respondent's admission, as well as that portion of the judgment enjoining the Medical School from according any consideration to race in the admissions process.

SUMMARY

We have now seen the three main interpretations of the equal protection clause. They are summarized in the following chart:

	Segregation	Antidiscrimination	Affirmative Action
State Action	Only (1) the state is forbidden to perform positive acts of discrimination	(1) and also (2) the state is required to protect its citizens against future discrimination	(1), (2), & (3), the state is allowed or required to remedy the effects of past societal discrimination
Separation	Separation is not inherently unequal	Separation is inherently unequal	Same as Antidiscrimination
Levels of Scrutiny	Single-tier: (1) the rational-relation test	Two-tier: (1) except (2) strict scrutiny when suspect classification or fundamental right	Three-tier: (1) & (2) except (3) middle-level scrutiny when a benign, remedial purpose
Bearers of Rights	Individuals only	Individuals only	Individuals and groups
Found in	*Plessy v. Ferguson* (majority opinion)	*Brown* (court opinion) *Bakke* (Powell opinion)	*Bakke* (Brennan opinion)

BURDEN OF PROOF

A remarkable feature of the line of cases from *Plessy* through *Bakke* is the extent to which these interpretations of equal protection turn on the matter of *burden of proof*. Under the rational-relation test that governed *Plessy*, the state bears a light burden when it is asked to show that its actions do not conflict with the equal protection clause. In contrast, the strict-scrutiny test that governed *Brown*, and that Powell applied in *Bakke*, places a very heavy burden on the state to justify any use of suspect classification or any interference with fundamental rights. The middle-level test advocated by Brennan in *Bakke* is an effort to lighten the burden of strict scrutiny so as to permit legislation that explicitly tries to aid those who have been disadvantaged by past discrimination.

It may seem peculiar that an important legal decision can turn on such a technical and procedural matter as burden of proof. But the question of burden of proof often plays a decisive role in a legal decision, so it is worth knowing something about it.

The two basic questions concerning burden of proof are (1) *who* bears this burden and (2) how *heavy* is the burden. In our system of criminal justice, the rules governing burden of proof are fairly straightforward. The state has the burden of establishing the guilt of the accused. The defendant has no obligation to establish his or her innocence. That is what is meant by saying that the defendant is *innocent until proven guilty*. The burden of proof is also very heavy on the state in criminal procedures, for it must show *beyond a reasonable doubt* that the accused is guilty. If the prosecution shows only that it is more likely than not that the accused has committed a crime, then the jury should vote for acquittal.

Turning to civil law, there is no simple way of explaining burden of proof. Very roughly, the plaintiff (the one who brings the suit) has an initial burden to establish a *prima facie* case—that is, a case that is strong enough that it needs to be rebutted—on behalf of his or her complaint. The burden then shifts to the respondent (the one against whom the suit is being brought) to answer these claims. The burden may then shift back and forth depending on the nature of the procedure. Provided that both sides have met their legally required burdens of proof, the case is then decided on the basis of the *preponderance of evidence*; that is, the judge or jury decides which side has made the stronger case.

Burden of proof is primarily a legal notion, but it is sometimes used, often loosely, outside the law. The notion of burden of proof is needed within the law because law cases are adversarial and the Court has to come to a decision. Outside the law, people have a general burden to *have* good reasons for what they say. That is the second part of Grice's rule of Quality. More specifically, people have a burden to be able to *present* some reasons when they make accusations or statements that run counter to common opinion.

The important thing to see is that you cannot establish the truth of something through an appeal to the burden of proof. The following argument is perfectly weird:

> There is life in other parts of the universe, because you can't prove otherwise.

Of course, no one can prove that there is *not* life elsewhere in the universe, but this has no tendency to show that there *is*. Attempts to prove the truth of something through appeals to burden of proof—often called arguments from ignorance—are another example of a fallacy of *relevance*, which was discussed in Chapter 10.

Nonetheless, the importance of burden of proof in the law does give force to another kind of argument. In a criminal case, the following argument would be perfectly fine:

> The defendant ought to be found not guilty, because the prosecution has not proven beyond a reasonable doubt that she is guilty.

This argument would also be a fallacy of relevance if the burden of proof were not so important. But the relevant burden of proof makes this argument strong in a court of law.

Who bears the burden of proof and how heavy the burden is determine which legal arguments work. Consider the following argument:

> This law uses a suspect classification, and the state has not shown that it serves any compelling purpose, so the law is unconstitutional.

This argument is strong if the strict-scrutiny interpretation is accepted (assuming the premises are true). However, this argument fails if a weaker burden of proof is required, as in the middle-level-scrutiny interpretation. When one chooses between interpretations of equal protection and between different burdens of proof, one also chooses which arguments will have force in courts of law. This is another example of a general phenomenon that has been stressed throughout this book— that background assumptions can determine whether an argument is any good.

DISCUSSION QUESTIONS

(1) Some of the more technical arguments in *Bakke* concern precedents. Justice Powell cites precedents to argue for his crucial claim that strict scrutiny must be applied to all state actions that are like Davis's admissions program. Consequently, he needs to argue that *Bakke* is significantly different from all the precedents in which strict scrutiny was not applied, including:

   (a) school desegregation cases,
   (b) employment discrimination cases,
   (c) gender discrimination cases,
   (d) *Lau v. Nichols*, and
   (e) *United Jewish Organizations v. Carey*.

Specify exactly which feature distinguishes each of these cases from *Bakke*, according to Powell. Is each of these differences significant in your opinion? Why or why not?

The school desegregation cases are inapposite. Each involved remedies for clearly determined constitutional violations. . . . Racial classifications thus were designed as remedies for the vindication of constitutional entitlement. Here [in *Bakke*], there was no judicial determination of constitutional violation as a predicate for the formulation of a remedial classification.

The employment discrimination cases also do not advance petitioner's [Davis's] cause. For example, in *Franks v. Bowman Transportation Co.*, 424 U.S. 747 (1975), we approved a retroactive award of seniority to a class of Negro truck drivers who had been the victims of discrimination—not just by society at large, but by the respondent in that case. . . . The courts of appeals have fashioned various types of racial preferences as remedies for constitutional or statutory violations resulting in identified, race-based injuries to individuals held entitled to the preference.

Continued on next page

. . . Such preferences also have been upheld where a legislative or administrative body charged with the responsibility made determinations of past discrimination by the industries affected, and fashioned remedies deemed appropriate to rectify the discrimination. But we have never approved preferential classifications in the absence of proven constitutional or statutory violations.

Nor is a petitioner's view as to the applicable standard supported by the fact that gender-based classifications are not subjected to this level of scrutiny. E.g. *Califano v. Webster* 430 U.S. 313, 316–7 (1977); e.g. *Craig v. Boren* 429 U.S. 190, 211 n. (1976). . . . Gender-based distinctions are less likely to create the analytical and practical problems present in preferential programs premised on racial or ethnic criteria. With respect to gender there are only two possible classifications. The incidence of the burdens imposed by preferential classifications is clear. There are no rival groups who can claim that they, too, are entitled to preferential treatment. Classwide questions as to the group suffering previous injury and groups which fairly can be burdened are relatively manageable for reviewing courts. . . . The resolution of these same questions in the context of racial and ethnic preferences presents far more complex and intractable problems than gender-based classifications. More importantly, the perception of racial classifications as inherently odious stems from a lengthy and tragic history that gender-based classifications do not share. In sum, the Court has never viewed such classification as inherently suspect or as comparable to racial or ethnic classifications for the purpose of equal-protection analysis.

Petitioner also cites *Lau v. Nichols*, 414 U.S. 563 (1974), in support of the proposition that discrimination favoring racial or ethnic minorities has received judicial approval without the exacting inquiry ordinarily accorded "suspect" classifications. In *Lau*, we held that the failure of the San Francisco school system to provide remedial English instruction for some 1,800 students of oriental ancestry who spoke no English amounted to a violation of Title VI of the Civil Rights Act of 1964, 42 U.S.C. § 2000d, and the regulations promulgated thereunder. Those regulations required remedial instruction where inability to understand English excluded children of foreign ancestry from participation in educational programs. . . . Because we found that the students in *Lau* were denied "a meaningful opportunity to participate in the educational program," . . . we remanded for the fashioning of a remedial order.

Lau provides little support for petitioner's argument. The decision rested solely on the statute, which had been construed by the responsible administrative agency to reach educational practices "which have the effect of subjecting individuals to discrimination." We stated: "Under these state-imposed standards there is no equality of treatment merely by providing students with the same facilities, textbooks, teachers and curriculum; for students who do not understand English are effectively foreclosed from any meaningful education." . . . Moreover, the "preference" approved did not result in the denial of the relevant benefit—"meaningful participation in the educational program"—to anyone else. No other student was deprived by that preference of the ability to participate in San Francisco's school system, and the applicable regulations required similar assistance for all students who suffered similar linguistic deficiencies. . . .

In a similar vein, petitioner contends that our recent decision in *United Jewish Organizations v. Carey*, 430 U.S. 144 (1977), indicates a willingness to approve racial classifications designed to benefit certain minorities, without denominating the classifications as "suspect." The State of New York had redrawn its reapportionment plan to meet objections of the Department of Justice under § 5 of the Voting Rights Act of 1965, 42 U.S.C. § 1973c. Specifically, voting districts were redrawn to enhance the electoral power of certain "nonwhite" voters found to have been the victims of unlawful "dilution" under the original reapportionment plan. *United Jewish Organizations*, like *Lau*, properly is viewed as a case in which the remedy for an administrative finding of discrimination encompassed measures to improve the previously disadvantaged group's ability to participate, without excluding individuals belonging to any other group from enjoyment of the relevant opportunity—meaningful participation in the electoral process.

In this case [*Bakke*], unlike *Lau* and *United Jewish Organizations*, there has been no determination by the legislature or a responsible administrative agency that the University engaged in a discriminatory practice requiring remedial efforts. Moreover, the operation of petitioner's special admissions program is quite different from the remedial measures approved in those cases. It prefers the designated minority groups at the expense of other individuals who are totally foreclosed from competition for the 16 special admissions seats in every medical school class. Because of that foreclosure, some individuals are excluded from enjoyment of a state-provided benefit—admission to the medical school—they otherwise would receive. When a classification denies an individual opportunities or benefits enjoyed by others solely because of his race or ethnic background, it must be regarded as suspect. . . .

(2) In the following additional passage from his opinion in *Bakke*, Justice Brennan argues that strict scrutiny was not applied in some precedents that do not differ from *Bakke* in any essential respect, so strict scrutiny need not be applied to *Bakke* either. Reconstruct and evaluate Brennan's argument from precedents. Who wins this debate about the precedents, Powell or Brennan? Why?

Continued on next page

[In the school desegregation cases, the Court] held both that courts could enter desegregation orders which assigned students and faculty by reference to race, *Swann v. Charlotte-Mecklenburg Board of Ed.*, 402 U.S. 1 (1971), and that local school boards could *voluntarily* adopt desegregation plans which made express reference to race if this was necessary to remedy the effects of past discrimination. *McDaniel v. Barresi* [402 U.S. 39 (1971)]. Moreover, we stated that school boards, even in the absence of a judicial finding of past discrimination, could voluntarily adopt plans which assigned students with the end of creating racial pluralism by establishing fixed ratios of black and white students in each school. *Charlotte-Mecklenburg*, supra, at 16. In each instance, the creation of unitary school systems, in which the effects of past discrimination had been "eliminated root and branch," . . . was recognized as a compelling social goal justifying the overt use of race.

These cases cannot be distinguished simply by the presence of judicial findings of discrimination, for race-conscious remedies have been approved where such findings have not been made. *McDaniel v. Barresi*, supra; *UJO*, supra; see *Califano v. Webster*, supra; *Kahn v. Shevin*, 416 U.S. 351 (1974). See also *Katzenbach v. Morgan*, 384 U.S. 641 (1967). Indeed, the requirement of a judicial determination of a constitutional or statutory violation as a predicate for race-conscious remedial actions would be self-defeating. Such a requirement would severely undermine efforts to achieve voluntary compliance with the requirements of law. And, our society and jurisprudence have always stressed the value of voluntary efforts to further the objectives of the law. Judicial intervention is a last resort to achieve cessation of illegal conduct or the remedying of its effects rather than a prerequisite to action. . . .

Moreover, the presence or absence of past discrimination by universities or employers is largely irrelevant to resolving respondent's constitutional claims. The claims of those burdened by the race-conscious actions of a university or employer who has never been adjudged in violation of an antidiscrimination law are not any more or less entitled to deference than the claims of the burdened nonminority workers in *Franks v. Bowman*, 424 U.S. 747 (1976), in which the employer had violated Title VII, for in each case the employees are innocent of past discrimination.

Properly construed, therefore, our prior cases unequivocally show that a state government may adopt race-conscious programs if the purpose of such programs is to remove the disparate racial impact its actions might otherwise have and if there is reason to believe that the disparate impact is itself the product of past discrimination, whether its own or that of society at large. There is no question that Davis' program is valid under this test.

(3) Assume the *Bakke* case as a precedent and argue for or against the constitutionality of the laws in the following cases:

(a) *Fullilove v. Klutznik*, 448 U.S. 448 (1980), concerned a congressional spending program that required at least 10 percent of the federal funds granted for local public-works projects be used to procure services or supplies from businesses owned and controlled by members of minority groups. (Be sure to consider any significant differences between employment and education.)

(b) *California Federal Savings and Loan Association et al. v. Guerra, Director, Department of Fair Employment and Housing et al.*, 479 U.S. 272 (1987), concerned a California law requiring employers to provide unpaid leave and reinstatement to employees who are pregnant. (Compare other conditions that create similar temporary disabilities in men.)

(c) *Morton v. Mancari*, 417 U.S. 535 (1974), concerned a federal statute that gave members of federally recognized tribes a preference for employment in the Bureau of Indian Affairs. (Does the purpose of the bureau justify this statute?)

(d) The Clinton administration's policy that military service members will not be asked or required to reveal their sexual orientation, but will be separated from the military for homosexual conduct.

(4) Find out what kinds of preferential treatment programs exist in your own school or town, and then argue either that these programs are constitutional or that they are not. ■

Chapter Thirteen

MORAL ARGUMENTS

Many acts—such as lying to a friend—are not illegal, but they still seem to be immoral. Thus, even if such an act is *legally* permitted, this does not show that it is *morally* permitted. That is a separate issue, and it is one that many people care deeply about, because they want to do what is moral and avoid doing what is immoral.

So how can we show that an act is moral or immoral? One kind of argument will *not* do. We can often show that an act is illegal by citing official pronouncements by judges and legislators, such as precedents and statutes. In contrast, morality is not decided by any official. There are no authoritative books in which we can look up whether a certain act is immoral without asking whether that book is correct. This affects the nature of moral arguments and the criteria for evaluating them. We cannot appeal to any documents or officials to justify our moral beliefs, so moral beliefs must be based on something else. The kinds of arguments that *can* be used to justify moral beliefs will be the topic of this chapter.

People often disagree on moral questions. When these disagreements arise, it is often difficult—and sometimes impossible—to resolve them. At times these disagreements turn on questions of fact. If one person thinks an action will have a particular consequence, and another thinks it will not, they might well disagree on the moral worth of that action. For example, those who have defended the United States' decision to drop atomic bombs on Japan have often claimed that it was the only way to end the war quickly without creating a great number of casualties on both sides. Many critics of this decision have denied these factual claims.

Moral disagreements can also arise from disagreements about moral principles. To many people, it is immoral to have sex outside marriage. To others, it is immoral to interfere with such acts. Despite such disagreements, it is surprising how much agreement there is on general moral principles. In our society, most people accept a great many moral principles as a matter of course. If a policy has no other consequence but to produce widespread misery, it is rejected out of hand. We share a conception of justice that includes, among other things, equality of opportunity and equality before the law. Most people also have a conception of human dignity: a human being is not a thing to be used and disposed of for personal advantage.

With all this agreement, how does moral disagreement arise at all? The answer is that in certain circumstances, our moral principles *conflict* with one another, and people are inclined to resolve these conflicts in different ways. People often agree on principles about welfare, justice, and human dignity, and yet, by weighing these principles differently or seeing the situation in a different light, they arrive at opposing moral conclusions.

Another kind of moral disagreement concerns the *range* or *scope* of moral principles. Even if everyone agrees that death and suffering are bad, they often disagree about *whose* death and suffering counts. With few exceptions, it is thought to be wrong to inflict death and suffering on human beings. Most people have a similar attitude toward their pet dogs or cats. Some, however, go further and claim that it is also immoral to kill any animals—including cows, chickens, and fish—just to produce tasty food for humans.

The hardest problems combine issues of *range* with *conflicts of principles*. It is a disagreement of this complex kind that we will focus on in this chapter. The problem is abortion. The main issues are (i) whether fetuses lie within the range of a standard moral principle against killing, and (ii) how to resolve conflicts between the principles that protect the fetus and other principles concerning, for example, human welfare and a woman's control over her body.

THE PROBLEM OF ABORTION

WHAT IS THE PROBLEM?

When faced with a moral problem, it often seems clear what the problem is, but this assumption can be mistaken. Sometimes a problem is formulated so vaguely that there is no way even to begin to solve it. People can argue for hours or even years without realizing that they are really talking about different things.

To clarify a moral problem, the first step is to specify precisely what is being judged—which action or kind of action is at issue. In the problem of abortion, the first step is to specify exactly what counts as an abortion. It is common to define abortion as the termination of a pregnancy. This includes spontaneous abortions or miscarriages, but these raise no moral problems because they are not the result of human action. Furthermore, the moral problem of abortion arises only when the death of the fetus is an expected consequence of terminating the pregnancy. To focus on these problematic cases, from now on we will take "abortion" to mean the intentional termination of a pregnancy with the expected consequence that the fetus will die as a result.

After the class of actions is picked out, we need to determine what is being asked about this class of actions—what kind of moral judgment is at stake. It is one thing to ask whether abortion is *morally wrong*, and another thing to ask whether abortion *should be illegal*. These are both moral questions (since the second asks what the law should be and not what it is), but they can be answered differently. It is not uncommon for people to claim that abortion is morally wrong but should not be made illegal, because it is a matter of personal, not public, morality. (See the passage by Mario Cuomo in exercise III of Chapter 3.) It is also important to distinguish the question of whether abortion is or is not morally *wrong* from the separate question of whether abortion is or is not *good*. People who deny that abortion is morally wrong do not hold that abortion is a positive good. They do not, for example, recommend that people get pregnant so that they can have abortions. So, from now on, we will focus on the issue of the moral wrongness of abortion.

THE CONSERVATIVE ARGUMENT

We can begin to understand this problem if we reconstruct the main argument against abortion, using the method discussed in Chapter 4. Most opponents of abortion call themselves "pro-life" and base their position on an appeal to a moral principle involving the "right to life." Of course, most opponents of abortion are not opposed to killing weeds, germs, or even fish. What they have in mind, then, is probably a principle such as this:

It is always wrong to kill a human being.

This principle by itself does not rule out abortion. To reach this conclusion, we need further premises of the following kind:

Abortion involves killing a human fetus.

A human fetus is a human being.

With these premises, the antiabortion argument will have the following form:

(1) Abortion involves killing a human fetus.

(2) A human fetus is a human being.

(3) It is always wrong to kill a human being.

(4) Therefore, abortion is wrong.

This argument is valid and reasonably charitable, so we have completed the first stage of reconstruction.

We next ask if the premises of this argument are true. The first premise is not controversial, given our definition of abortion above. However, the second premise raises many problems. Much of the debate concerning abortion turns on the question of whether a fetus is a human being, and we will examine this question later on. For now, we will assume for the sake of argument that a fetus is a human being.

Some people—for example, strong pacifists—accept the third premise, but most people who adopt strong antiabortion positions do not. This comes out in the following way. Many of those who oppose abortion are in favor of the death penalty for certain crimes. Therefore, they do not accept the general principle that it is always wrong to take a human life. What they need, then, is a principle that allows taking a human life in some instances but not in others. In an effort to achieve this, those who oppose abortion could reformulate the third premise in these words.

It is always wrong to kill an innocent human being.

Here the word "innocent" allows an exception for the death penalty being imposed on those who are found guilty of certain crimes. Even stated this way, however, the principle seems to admit of counterexamples. If someone's life is threatened by a madman, it is generally thought that the person has the right to use whatever means are necessary against the madman to prevent being killed. This may include killing the madman, even though the insane are usually thought to be morally innocent of their deeds. If so, the principle must be modified again, and then we get something like this:

It is always wrong to kill an innocent human being except in certain cases of self-defense.

It is still possible to find difficulties with this principle that will lead some to add further modifications or clarifications. Children, for example, are often the innocent victims of bombing raids, yet the raids are often thought to be justified, because these deaths are not intended, even though they are foreseeable. At this point it is common to modify the principle again by including a reference to intentions. We shall not, however, pursue this complex line of reasoning here.[1]

---

[1] For a discussion of this approach, and for a model of how to argue about a moral principle, see Philippa Foot, "The Problem of Abortion and the Doctrine of Double Effect," in Foot, *Virtues and Vices and Other Essays in Moral Philosophy* (Berkeley and Los Angeles: University of California Press, 1978), 19–32.

We have arrived, then, at a principle that seems to make sense out of a position that is against abortion but in favor of the death penalty and self-defense. With these modifications included, the argument now looks like this:

(1*) Abortion involves killing a human fetus.

(2*) A human fetus is a human being.

(3*) A human fetus is innocent.

(4*) It is always wrong to kill an innocent human being except in certain cases of self-defense.

(5) Therefore, abortion is always wrong.

But, having made the premises more plausible, we confront a new problem: the argument is invalid as it stands, since the qualification "except in certain cases of self-defense" has been dropped from the conclusion. The proper conclusion of the argument should be:

(5*) Abortion is always wrong except in certain cases of self-defense.

Rewriting the conclusion in this way has an important consequence: the argument no longer leads to a conclusion that abortion is *always* wrong. This qualified conclusion could permit abortion in those cases in which it is needed to defend the life of the pregnant woman who bears the fetus. In fact, this is the position that many people who are generally opposed to abortion adopt: abortion is wrong except in those cases in which it is necessary to save the life of the mother. Although this does not lay down an absolute prohibition, it is a strong antiabortion position, since it would condone abortion in only a few exceptional cases.

LIBERAL RESPONSES

We can now examine the way in which those who adopt the liberal or "pro-choice" position will respond to the conservative argument as it has just been spelled out. The first premise should not be a subject for controversy. Nor does it seem likely that the third premise will be attacked on the ground that the fetus is not innocent. How could a fetus be guilty of anything?

This leaves three strategies for the liberal: (i) Further modify the moral principle in the fourth premise to allow more exceptions. (ii) Deny the second premise—that the fetus is a human being. (iii) Oppose this conservative argument with a different argument based on a different moral principle.

(i) Further modifications.   Even if it is agreed that abortion is justified when it saves the mother's life, we still need to ask whether this is the only exception or whether abortion is justified in other cases as well. Many conservatives admit that abortion is also justified when the pregnancy results from rape or incest. It is not easy to see how to modify the moral principle against killing to allow an exception in cases of rape and incest, so this exception is controversial. We will return to this issue later in this discussion. But even if exceptions are made both for life-threatening pregnancies and for pregnancies due to rape and incest, the range of morally permissible abortions will still be very small.

Liberals can, however, argue for a wider range of morally permissible abortions by extending the self-defense exception. It can be argued that a woman has a right to defend not only her life but also her physical and psychological well-being. Liberals can also argue that the exception of rape shows that abortion is allowed when the woman is not responsible for her pregnancy, and this might include cases in which the woman tried to prevent pregnancy by using contraceptives. Granting exceptions of this kind does not provide the basis for an absolute right to an abortion, but it does move things away from a conservative "pro-life" position in the direction of a liberal "pro-choice" position.

(ii) The status of the fetus.   So far we have assumed for the sake of argument that a human fetus is a human being. However, liberals often deny this premise. It may seem hard to deny that a human fetus is human. After all, it is not an aardvark. However, liberals claim that the real issue is not about biological species. The real issue is whether a human fetus is covered by the moral principle against killing, and whether it is protected to the same extent as an adult human. Anything that is protected to this extent is said to have a "right to life" and will be called a "person." The issue, then, is whether a human fetus is a person. If a fetus *is* a person, the burden of proof is on those who maintain the liberal position to show why the moral principle against killing should be set aside or modified. If a fetus is *not* a person, this moral principle cannot show that there is anything wrong with abortion for any reason—with what is called "abortion on demand."

Any argument that a fetus either is a person or is not a person must proceed from some idea of which properties make something a person—which properties warrant the protection of moral principles. To argue that a fetus is not a person, liberals need to find some feature that fetuses lack and that is necessary for personhood. In response, conservatives need to find some feature that fetuses have and that is sufficient for personhood.

Many conditions of personhood have been suggested. This list is not complete:

(a) genetic code (which determines biological species)

(b) ensoulment (when a soul enters the body)

(c) brain activity (first detected around eight weeks)

(d) capacity to feel pain and pleasure

(e) viability (when the fetus can survive outside the womb)

(f) rationality (and other related capacities)

Conservatives usually emphasize tests such as genetic code, which is formed at conception, or ensoulment, which is supposed to occur at or shortly after conception. In contrast, liberals usually employ tests such as viability, which is reached during the second trimester, or rationality, which comes sometime after birth (depending on what counts as rationality—ability to choose and plan, self-consciousness, and so on). Thus, the personhood of fetuses during the first trimester is usually asserted by conservatives and denied by liberals on this issue.

How can we determine whether a feature is necessary or sufficient for personhood? We can start by rejecting any test of personhood that leads to *implausible* results. Many conservatives argue that rationality is not necessary for personhood, because, whatever rationality is, newborn babies and severely retarded adults are not rational, but it is still morally wrong to kill them. Other tests of personhood are ruled out because they do not seem *important* enough. Many liberals argue that a certain genetic code is not sufficient to make something a person, because there is no reason to favor one genetic code over another except that it later produces other important features, such as rationality. It is also common to rule out a test of personhood if we cannot *know* when the test is passed. For example, some people reject ensoulment as a criterion of personhood, because they see no way to tell when, if ever, a fetus has a soul. And tests of personhood are also often rejected if they depend on factors that are *extraneous*. Conservatives often argue that viability cannot be a test of personhood because the point when a fetus can survive outside the womb depends on what technology happens to be available to doctors at the time.

In addition to features that fetuses have when they are fetuses, they also seem to have the *potential* to develop many more, including rationality. Conservatives often use this premise to argue that fetuses are persons and have a right to life. The first problem with this argument is that it seems to assume that something has a right if it has the potential to come to have that right. But this is clearly too strong. A three-year-old child does not have the right to vote even though it has the potential to develop into someone who will have the right to vote. Furthermore, the notion of potential is not clear. If the fetus has the potential, why do the egg and sperm not have it? This does not refute potentiality as a test of personhood, but much more must be done to show what potentiality is and why it is sufficient to make something a person even before the potential is realized.

All these positions on personhood are controversial, and many people feel uncertain about which is the correct one. A major issue in many moral problems is how to deal with uncertainties such as this.

One reaction is a position called "gradualism."[2] We have assumed so far that the fetus either has or does not have a right to life, but rights sometimes come in varying strengths. Gradualists claim that a fetus slowly develops a right to life which is at first very weak. As pregnancy progresses, this right gets stronger, so it takes more to justify abortion. Late abortions still might be permitted, but only in extreme circumstances. This position is still vague, but it is attractive to some people who want to avoid placing too much emphasis on any single point in fetal development.

Uncertainty is also exploited in many other ways. We discussed slippery-

---

[2] Gradualism is discussed in more detail in Joel Feinberg, "Abortion," in *Matters of Life and Death*, 2d ed., ed. Tom Regan (New York: Random House, 1986), 256–93.

slope arguments already in Chapter 10. Another way to exploit uncertainty is to put the burden on the other side to produce a reason for drawing a line at some point. For example, Ronald Reagan says, "anyone who doesn't feel sure whether we are talking about a second human life should clearly give life the benefit of the doubt." However, the same kind of argument is also available to liberals: Since we are not sure whether the fetus is a person, but we are sure that the pregnant woman has rights over her body, we should give the benefit of the doubt to the pregnant woman. We should always suspect that there is something wrong with an argument that can be used equally well in opposing directions.

(iii) Conflicting principles. A third kind of liberal response is to invoke another principle, which conflicts with the conservative principle against killing. Liberals often emphasize two such principles: one about the rights of the pregnant woman to control her own body and another about overall human welfare. We will focus here on human welfare.

Those who adopt a liberal position on abortion often argue that abortion can sometimes be justified in terms of the welfare of the woman who bears the fetus, or in terms of the welfare of the family into which it will be born, or even in terms of the welfare of the child itself, if it were to be born with a severe disability or into an impoverished situation. This argument, when spelled out, looks like this:

(1) An action that best increases overall human welfare is not morally wrong.

(2) Abortion is sometimes the best way of increasing overall human welfare.

(3) Therefore, abortion is sometimes not morally wrong.

What are we to say about this argument? It seems valid in form, so we can turn to the premises themselves and ask whether they are acceptable. The first (and leading) premise of the argument is subject to two immediate criticisms. First, it is vague. Probably what a person who uses this kind of argument has in mind by speaking of human welfare is a certain level of material and psychological well-being. Of course, this is still vague, but it is clear enough to make the premise a target of the second, more important, criticism. Although maximizing human welfare may, in general, be a good thing, it is not the only relevant consideration in deciding how to act. To cite a previous example (from Chapter 11), it might be true that our society would be much more prosperous on the whole if 10 percent of the population were designated slaves who would do all the menial work. Yet even if a society could be made generally happy in this way, most people would reject such a system on the grounds that it is unfair to the slave class. For reasons of this kind, most people would modify the first premise of the argument we are now examining in the following way:

(1*) An action that best increases human welfare is not morally wrong, provided that it is fairly applied.

But if the first premise is modified in this way, then the entire argument must be restated to reflect this revision. It will now look like this:

(1*) An action that best increases human welfare is not morally wrong, provided that it is fairly applied.

(2*) Abortion is sometimes an action that best increases human welfare.

(3*) Therefore, abortion is sometimes not morally wrong, provided that it is fairly applied.

It should be obvious how conservatives on abortion will reply to this argument. They will maintain that abortion almost always involves unfairness—namely, to the fetus—so abortion is still wrong in almost all cases, as the conservative argument claimed. Once more we have encountered a standard situation: given a strong premise (premise 1), it is possible to derive a particular conclusion, but this strong premise is subject to criticism and therefore must be modified. When the premise is modified, it no longer supports the original conclusion that the person presenting the argument wishes to establish.

The argument does not stop here. A person who holds a liberal position on abortion might reply in a number of ways. Some theory of fairness might be developed to argue that many abortions are not unfair to the fetus, since the fetus has no right to use the pregnant woman's body. The burden of the argument may shift to the question of whether or not a human fetus is a human being and therefore possessed of a right to fair treatment. It might also be argued that questions of human welfare are sometimes more important than issues of equal or even fair treatment. During war and some emergencies, for example, members of a certain segment of the population are called upon to risk their lives for the good of the whole in ways that might seem unfair to them.

When the argument is put on this new basis, the question then becomes this: Are there circumstances in which matters of welfare become so urgent that the rights of the fetus (here assuming that the fetus has rights) are overridden? The obvious case in which this might happen is when the life of the bearer of the fetus is plainly threatened. For many conservatives on abortion, this does count as a case in which abortion is permitted. Some who hold a liberal position will maintain that severe psychological, financial, or personal losses to the pregnant woman may also take precedence over the life of the fetus. Furthermore, if not aborted, many fetuses would live in very deprived circumstances, and some would not develop very far or live very long, because they have deadly diseases, such as Tay-Sachs. How severe must these losses, deprivations, and diseases be? From our previous discussion of slippery-slope arguments, we know that we should not expect any sharp lines here, and, indeed, people will tend to be spread out in their opinions along a continuum ranging from a belief in complete prohibition to no prohibition.

ANALOGICAL REASONING IN ETHICS

Using the method for reconstructing arguments, we now have a fairly clear idea of the main options on the abortion issue. But understanding the structure of the debate—though essential for dealing with it intelligently—does not settle it. If the reasons on all sides are fully spelled out and disagreement remains, what is to be done?

At this stage, those who do not simply turn to abuse often appeal to *analogical arguments*. The point of an analogical argument is to reach a conclusion in a controversial case by comparing it to a similar situation in which it is clearer what is right or wrong. In fact, a great deal of ethical reasoning uses such analogies. We have already seen one simple analogy between an abortion to save the life of the mother and self-defense against an insane person. To get a better idea of how analogical reasoning works in ethics, we will concentrate on a more complex analogy, which raises the issue of whether abortion is morally permissible in cases of pregnancy due to rape.

A classic analogical argument is given by Judith Jarvis Thomson in "A Defense of Abortion" (reprinted below), in which she tells the following story:

> You wake up in the morning and find yourself back to back in bed with an unconscious violinist. A famous unconscious violinist. He has been found to have a fatal kidney ailment, and the Society of Music Lovers has canvassed all the available medical records and found that you alone have the right blood type to help. They have therefore kidnapped you, and last night the violinist's circulatory system was plugged into yours, so that your kidneys can be used to extract poisons from his blood as well as your own. The director of the hospital now tells you, "Look, we're sorry the Society of Music Lovers did this to you—we would never have permitted it if we had known. But still, they did it, and the violinist now is plugged into you. To unplug you would be to kill him. But never mind, it's only for nine months. By then he will have recovered from his ailment, and can safely be unplugged from you."

Thomson claims that it is not wrong for you to unplug yourself from the violinist in this situation, and most people seem to agree with her judgment in this case. By analogy, abortion after rape is not wrong either.

The basic assumption of this analogical argument is that we should not make different moral judgments in cases that do not differ. More positively:

(1) If two actions are similar in all morally relevant respects, and if one of the acts is not morally wrong, then the other act is also not morally wrong.

Now we can apply this principle to Thomson's story:

(2) It is not morally wrong for you to unplug the violinist in Thomson's example.

(3) To unplug the violinist and to abort a pregnancy due to rape are similar in all morally relevant respects.

(4) Therefore, it is not morally wrong for a woman to abort a pregnancy due to rape.

This argument is valid, so, following the normal procedure, we can ask whether the premises are true. The first premise seems plausible, and it is accepted in most moral theories. Most people also accept the second premise. Consequently, the discussion usually focuses on the third premise—on the similarities and differences between Thomson's story and abortion in a pregnancy due to rape.

First consider these similarities between Thomson's story and abortion after rape:

(a) Both the fetus and the violinist are on or near the surface of the earth.

(b) Kidnapping is immoral and illegal, like rape.

(c) The hospital stay lasts nine months, like pregnancy.

(d) The violinist is innocent and a human being, like the fetus (given our present assumption).

(e) Unplugging the violinist is supposed to be killing, like an abortion.

Now here are some differences between the situations:

(f) The fetus cannot play the violin, but the violinist can.

(g) The person who is plugged into the violinist might not be female.

(h) The person who is plugged into the violinist cannot leave the hospital room, but pregnant women can still move around, even if they have some difficulty.

(i) Abortion involves killing, but unplugging the violinist is merely refusing to save.

It is obvious that some of the similarities and differences are not relevant. It does not matter whether killing occurs near the earth. Killing is usually wrong even on the Starship Enterprise. It is also accepted that differences in musical talent and in sex cannot justify killing. The other similarities and differences on our list do seem important. They each concern harm and responsibility, matters that must be considered in reaching a moral judgment about these actions. The force of Thomson's analogical argument is that the very features that lead us to conclude that it would not be wrong to unplug the violinist are also found in the case of pregnancy due to rape. Furthermore, there are no relevant differences that are important enough to override the significance of these similarities. These considerations, if correct, provide a reason for treating the two cases in the same way. If we then agree, as Thomson thinks we will, that it is not wrong to unplug the violinist, we have a reason to conclude that abortion after rape is not wrong either.

Responses to Thomson's argument have largely turned on emphasizing the differences between the two situations. Many critics claim that Thomson's argument fails because abortion involves *killing*, whereas unplugging does not. If you stay plugged to the violinist, this will save the violinist, so to unplug yourself is to *fail to save* the violinist. But critics deny that to unplug yourself from the violinist is the same as to *kill* the violinist, or to take the violinist's life. They argue that there is a crucial difference between killing and failing to save, because a negative duty not to kill is much stronger than any positive duty to save another person's life.

To determine whether unplugging the violinist is more like acts of killing or more like other acts of refusing to save, we might consider more analogies. Thomson also introduces additional analogies that seem more like abortions in which the pregnancy is not due to rape. In the end, our sense of which features seem most important will determine how we evaluate all such analogical arguments. The analogies bring certain features to our attention, but we have to decide which features are important, and how important they are.

WEIGHING FACTORS

Our discussion has brought us to the following point: disagreements concerning abortion in general cannot be reduced to a yes-no dispute. Most conservatives on abortion acknowledge that it is permissible in some (though very few) cases. Most liberals on abortion admit that there are some (though not restrictively many) limitations on its use. Where people place themselves on this continuum does not depend on any simple acceptance of one argument over another, but instead on the *weight* they give certain factors. To what extent does a fetus have rights? The conservative position we examined earlier grants the fetus a full (or close to full) right to life. The liberal position usually grants few or no rights to the fetus. In what areas do questions of welfare override certain individual rights? The conservative in this matter usually restricts this to those cases in which the very life of the mother is plainly threatened. As the position on abortion becomes more liberal, the more extensive becomes the range of cases in which the rights, if any, of the fetus are set aside in favor of the rights of the bearer of the fetus. Where a particular person strikes this balance is not only a function of basic moral beliefs but also a function of different weights assigned to them.

How can one deal with such bedrock disagreements? The first thing to see is that logic alone will not settle them. Starting from a certain conception of persons, it is possible to argue coherently for a liberal view on abortion; starting from another point of view, it is possible to argue coherently for a conservative view on abortion. The next important thing to see is that it is possible to *understand* an opposing view—that is, get a genuine feeling for its inner workings—even if you disagree with it completely. Logical analysis might show that particular arguments are unsound or have unnoticed and unwanted implications. This might force clarification and modification. But the most important service that logical analysis can perform is to lay bare the fundamental principles that lie beneath surface disagreements. Analysis will sometimes show that these disagreements are fundamental and perhaps irreconcilable. Dealing with such irreconcilable differences in a humane way is one of the fundamental tasks of a society dedicated to freedom and a wide range of civil liberties.

■ **A DEFENSE OF ABORTION***†
by Judith Jarvis Thomson

Most opposition to abortion relies on the premise that the fetus is a human being, a person, from the moment of conception. The premise is argued for, but, as I think, not well. Take, for example, the most common argument. We are asked to notice that the development of a human being from conception through birth into childhood is continuous; then it is said that to draw a line, to choose a point in this development and say "before this point the thing is not a person, after this point it is a person" is to make an arbitrary choice, a choice for which in the nature of things no good reason can be given. It is concluded that the fetus is, or anyway that we had better say it is, a person from the moment of conception. But this conclusion does not follow. Similar things might be said about the development of an acorn into an oak tree, and it does not follow that acorns are oak trees, or that we had better say they are. Arguments of this form are sometimes called "slippery slope arguments"—the phrase is perhaps self-explanatory—and it is dismaying that opponents of abortion rely on them so heavily and uncritically.

I am inclined to agree, however, that the prospects for "drawing a line" in the development of the fetus look dim. I am inclined to think also that we shall probably have to agree that the fetus has already become a human person well before birth. Indeed, it comes as a surprise when one first learns how early in its life it begins to acquire human characteristics. By the tenth week, for example, it already has a face, arms and legs, fingers and toes; it has internal organs, and brain activity is detectable.‡ On the other hand, I think that the premise is false, that the fetus is not a person from the moment of conception. A newly fertilized ovum, a newly implanted clump of cells, is no more a person than an acorn is an oak tree. But I shall not discuss any of this. For it seems to me to be of great interest to ask what happens if, for the sake of argument, we allow the premise. How, precisely, are we supposed to get from there to the conclusion that abortion is morally impermissible? Opponents of abortion commonly spend most of their time establishing that the fetus is a person, and hardly any time explaining the step from there to the impermissibility of abortion. Perhaps they think the step too simple and obvious to require much comment. Or perhaps instead they are simply being economical in argument. Many of those who defend abortion rely on the premise that the fetus is not a person, but only a bit of tissue that will become a person at birth; and why pay out more arguments than you have to? Whatever the explanation, I suggest that the step they take is neither easy nor

---

* *Philosophy and Public Affairs* 1, no. 1 (Fall 1971): 47–66.

† I am very much indebted to James Thomson for discussion, criticism, and many helpful suggestions.

‡ Daniel Callahan, *Abortion: Law, Choice and Morality* (New York, 1970), p. 373. This book gives a fascinating survey of the available information on abortion. The Jewish tradition is surveyed in David M. Feldman, *Birth Control in Jewish Law* (New York, 1968), Part 5; the Catholic tradition in John T. Noonan, Jr., "An Almost Absolute Value in History," in *The Morality of Abortion*, ed. John T. Noonan, Jr. (Cambridge, Mass., 1970).

obvious, that it calls for closer examination than it is commonly given, and that when we do give it this closer examination we shall feel inclined to reject it.

I propose, then, that we grant that the fetus is a person from the moment of conception. How does the argument go from here? Something like this, I take it. Every person has a right to life. So the fetus has a right to life. No doubt the mother has a right to decide what shall happen in and to her body; everyone would grant that. But surely a person's right to life is stronger and more stringent than the mother's right to decide what happens in and to her body, and so outweighs it. So the fetus may not be killed; an abortion may not be performed.

It sounds plausible. But now let me ask you to imagine this. You wake up in the morning and find yourself back to back in bed with an unconscious violinist. A famous unconscious violinist. He has been found to have a fatal kidney ailment, and the Society of Music Lovers has canvassed all the available medical records and found that you alone have the right blood type to help. They have therefore kidnapped you, and last night the violinist's circulatory system was plugged into yours, so that your kidneys can be used to extract poisons from his blood as well as your own. The director of the hospital now tells you, "Look, we're sorry the Society of Music Lovers did this to you—we would never have permitted it if we had known. But still, they did it, and the violinist now is plugged into you. To unplug you would be to kill him. But never mind, it's only for nine months. By then he will have recovered from his ailment, and can safely be unplugged from you." Is it morally incumbent on you to accede to this situation? No doubt it would be very nice of you if you did, a great kindness. But do you *have* to accede to it? What if it were not nine months, but nine years? Or longer still? What if the director of the hospital says, "Tough luck, I agree, but you've now got to stay in bed, with the violinist plugged into you, for the rest of your life. Because remember this. All persons have a right to life, and violinists are persons. Granted you have a right to decide what happens in and to your body, but a person's right to life outweighs your right to decide what happens in and to your body. So you cannot ever be unplugged from him." I imagine you would regard this as outrageous, which suggests that something really is wrong with that plausible-sounding argument I mentioned a moment ago.

In this case, of course, you were kidnapped; you didn't volunteer for the operation that plugged the violinist into your kidneys. Can those who oppose abortion on the ground I mentioned make an exception for a pregnancy due to rape? Certainly. They can say that persons have a right to life only if they didn't come into existence because of rape; or they can say that all persons have a right to life, but that some have less of a right to life than others, in particular, that those who came into existence because of rape have less. But these statements have a rather unpleasant sound. Surely the question of whether you have a right to life at all, or how much of it you have, shouldn't turn on the question of whether or not you are the product of a rape. And in fact the people who oppose abortion on the ground I mentioned do not make this distinction, and hence do not make an exception in the case of rape.

Nor do they make an exception for a case in which the mother had to spend the nine months of her pregnancy in bed. They would agree that would be a great pity, and hard on the mother; but all the same all persons have a right to life, the fetus is a person, and so on. I suspect, in fact, that they would not make an exception for a case in which, miraculously enough, the pregnancy went on for nine years or even the rest of the mother's life.

Some won't even make an exception for a case in which continuation of the pregnancy is likely to shorten the mother's life; they regard abortion as impermissible even to save the mother's life. Such cases are nowadays very rare, and many opponents of abortion do not accept this extreme view. All the same, it is a good place to begin: a number of points of interest come out in respect to it.

1. Let us call the view that abortion is impermissible even to save the mother's life "the extreme view." I want to suggest first that it does not issue from the argument I mentioned earlier without the addition of some fairly powerful premises. Suppose a woman has become pregnant, and now learns that she has a cardiac condition such that she will die if she carries the baby to term. What may be done for her? The fetus, being a person, has a right to life, but as the mother is a person too, so has she a right to life. Presumably they have an equal right to life. How is it supposed to come out that an abortion may not be performed? If mother and child have an equal right to life, shouldn't we perhaps flip a coin? Or should we add to the mother's right to life her right to decide what happens in and to her body which everybody seems to be ready to grant—the sum of her rights now outweighing the fetus's right to life?

The most familiar argument here is the following. We are told that performing the abortion would be directly killing* the child, whereas doing nothing would not be killing the mother, but only letting her die. Moreover, in killing the child, one would be killing an innocent person, for the child has committed no crime, and is not aiming at his mother's death. And then there are a variety of ways in which this might be continued. (1) But as directly killing an innocent person is always and absolutely impermissible, an abortion may not be performed. Or, (2) as directly killing an innocent person is murder, and murder is always and absolutely impermissible, an abortion may not be performed.† Or, (3) as one's duty to refrain from directly killing an innocent person is more stringent than one's duty to keep a person from dying, an abortion may not be performed. Or, (4) if one's only options are directly killing an innocent person or letting

---

* The term "direct" in the arguments I refer to is a technical one. Roughly what is meant by "direct killing" is either killing as an end by itself, or killing as a means to some end, for example, the end of saving someone else's life. See note † on page 448, for an example of its use.

† Cf. *Encyclical Letter of Pope Pius XI on Christian Marriage*, St. Paul Editions (Boston, n.d.), p. 32: "however much we may pity the mother whose health and even life is gravely imperiled in the performance of the duty allotted to her by nature, nevertheless what could ever be a sufficient reason for excusing in any way the direct murder of the innocent? This is precisely what we are dealing with here." Noonan (*The Morality of Abortion*, p. 43) reads this as follows: "What cause can ever avail to excuse in any way the direct killing of the innocent? For it is a question of that."

a person die, one must prefer letting the person die, and thus an abortion may not be performed.*

Some people seem to have thought that these are not further premises which must be added if the conclusion is to be reached; but that they follow from the very fact that an innocent person has a right to life.† But this seems to me to be a mistake, and perhaps the simplest way to show this is to bring out that while we must certainly grant that innocent persons have a right to life, the theses in (1) through (4) are all false. Take (2), for example. If directly killing an innocent person is murder, and thus is impermissible, then the mother's directly killing the innocent person inside her is murder, and thus is impermissible. But it cannot seriously be thought to be murder if the mother performs an abortion on herself to save her life. It cannot seriously be said that she *must* refrain, that she *must* sit passively by and wait for her death. Let us look again at the case of you and the violinist. There you are, in bed with the violinist, and the director of the hospital says to you, "It's all most distressing, and I deeply sympathize, but you see this is putting an additional strain on your kidneys, and you'll be dead within the month. But you *have* to stay where you are all the same. Because unplugging you would be directly killing an innocent violinist, and that's murder, and that's impermissible." If anything in the world is true, it is that you do not commit murder, you do not do what is impermissible, if you reach around to your back and unplug yourself from that violinist to save your life.

The main focus of attention in writings on abortion has been on what a third party may or may not do in answer to a request from a woman for an abortion. This is in a way understandable. Things being as they are, there isn't much a woman can safely do to abort herself. So the question asked is what a third party may do, and what the mother may do, if it is mentioned at all, is deduced, almost as an afterthought, from what it is concluded that third parties may do. But it seems to me that to treat the matter in this way is to refuse to grant to the mother that very status of person which is so firmly insisted on for the fetus. For we cannot simply read off what a person may do from what a third party may do. Suppose you find yourself trapped in a tiny house with a growing child. I mean a very tiny house, and a rapidly growing child—you are already up against the wall of the house and in a few minutes you'll be crushed to death. The child on the other hand won't be crushed to death; if nothing is done to stop him from

---

* The thesis in (4) is in an interesting way weaker than those in (1), (2), and (3): they rule out abortion even in cases in which both mother *and* child will die if the abortion is not performed. By contrast, one who held the view expressed in (4) could consistently say that one needn't prefer letting two persons die to killing one.

† Cf. the following passage from Pius XII, *Address to the Italian Catholic Society of Midwives*: "The baby in the maternal breast has the right to life immediately from God—Hence there is no man, no human authority, no science, no medical, eugenic, social, economic or moral 'indication' which can establish or grant a valid juridical ground for a direct deliberate disposition of an innocent human life, that is a disposition which looks to its destruction either as an end or as a means to another end perhaps in itself not illicit. The baby, still not born, is a man in the same degree and for the same reason as the mother" (quoted in Noonan, *The Morality of Abortion*, p. 45).

growing he'll be hurt, but in the end he'll simply burst open the house and walk out a free man. Now I could well understand it if a bystander were to say, "There's nothing we can do for you. We cannot choose between your life and his, we cannot be the ones to decide who is to live, we cannot intervene." But it cannot be concluded that you too can do nothing, that you cannot attack it to save your life. However innocent the child may be, you do not have to wait passively while it crushes you to death. Perhaps a pregnant woman is vaguely felt to have the status of house, to which we don't allow the right of self-defense. But if the woman houses the child, it should be remembered that she is a person who houses it.

I should perhaps stop to say explicitly that I am not claiming that people have a right to do anything whatever to save their lives. I think, rather, that there are drastic limits to the right of self-defense. If someone threatens you with death unless you torture someone else to death, I think you have not the right, even to save your life, to do so. But the case under consideration here is very different. In our case there are only two people involved, one whose life is threatened, and one who threatens it. Both are innocent: the one who is threatened is not threatened because of any fault, the one who threatens does not threaten because of any fault. For this reason we may feel that we bystanders cannot intervene. But the person threatened can.

In sum, a woman surely can defend her life against the threat to it posed by the unborn child, even if doing so involves its death. And this shows not merely that the theses in (1) through (4) are false; it shows also that the extreme view of abortion is false, and so we need not canvass any other possible ways of arriving at it from the argument I mentioned at the outset.

2. The extreme view could of course be weakened to say that while abortion is permissible to save the mother's life, it may not be performed by a third party, but only by the mother herself. But this cannot be right either. For what we have to keep in mind is that the mother and the unborn child are not like two tenants in a small house which has, by an unfortunate mistake, been rented to both: the mother *owns* the house. The fact that she does adds to the offensiveness of deducing that the mother can do nothing from the supposition that third parties can do nothing. But it does more than this: it casts a bright light on the supposition that third parties can do nothing. Certainly it lets us see that a third party who says "I cannot choose between you" is fooling himself if he thinks this is impartiality. If Jones has found and fastened on a certain coat, which he needs to keep him from freezing, but which Smith also needs to keep him from freezing, then it is not impartiality that says "I cannot choose between you" when Smith owns the coat. Women have said again and again "This is *my* body!" and they have reason to feel angry, reason to feel that it has been like shouting into the wind. Smith, after all, is hardly likely to bless us if we say to him, "Of course it's your coat; anybody would grant that it is. But no one may choose between you and Jones who is to have it."

We should really ask what it is that says "no one may choose" in the face of the fact that the body that houses the child is the mother's body. It may be simply a failure to appreciate this fact. But it may be something more interesting, namely the sense that one has a right to refuse to lay hands on people, even where it would be just and fair to do so, even where justice seems to require that somebody do so. Thus justice might call for somebody to get Smith's coat back from Jones, and yet you have a right to refuse to be the one to lay hands on Jones, a right to refuse to do physical violence to him. This, I think, must be granted. But then what should be said is not "no one may choose," but only "*I* cannot choose," and indeed not even this, but "*I* will not *act*," leaving it open that somebody else can or should, and in particular that anyone in a position of authority, with the job of securing people's rights, both can and should. So this is no difficulty. I have not been arguing that any given third party must accede to the mother's request that he perform an abortion to save her life, but only that he may.

I suppose that in some views of human life the mother's body is only on loan to her, the loan not being one which gives her any prior claim to it. One who held this view might well think it impartiality to say "I cannot choose." But I shall simply ignore this possibility. My own view is that if a human being has any just, prior claim to anything at all, he has a just, prior claim to his own body. And perhaps this needn't be argued for here anyway, since, as I mentioned, the arguments against abortion we are looking at do grant that the woman has a right to decide what happens in and to her body.

But although they do grant it, I have tried to show that they do not take seriously what is done in granting it. I suggest the same thing will reappear even more clearly when we turn away from cases in which the mother's life is at stake, and attend, as I propose we now do, to the vastly more common cases in which a woman wants an abortion for some less weighty reason than preserving her own life.

3. Where the mother's life is not at stake, the argument I mentioned at the outset seems to have a much stronger pull. "Everyone has a right to life, so the unborn person has a right to life." And isn't the child's right to life weightier than anything other than the mother's own right to life, which she might put forward as grounds for an abortion?

This argument treats the right to life as if it were unproblematic. It is not, and this seems to me to be precisely the source of the mistake.

For we should now, at long last, ask what it comes to, to have a right to life. In some views having a right to life includes having a right to be given at least the bare minimum one needs for continued life. But suppose that what in fact *is* the bare minimum a man needs for continued life is something he has no right at all to be given? If I am sick unto death, and the only thing that will save my life is the touch of Henry Fonda's cool hand on my fevered brow, then all the same, I have no right to be given the touch of Henry Fonda's cool hand on my fevered brow. It would be frightfully nice of him to fly in from the West Coast to provide it. It would be less nice, though no doubt well meant, if my friends flew out to the West Coast and carried Henry Fonda back with them. But I have no right at all against anybody that he should do this for me. Or again, to return to the story I told earlier, the fact that for continued life that violinist needs the continued use of your kidneys does not establish that he has a right to be given the continued use of your kidneys. He certainly has no right against you that *you* should give him continued use of your kidneys. For nobody has any right to use your kidneys unless you give him such a right; and nobody has the right against you that you shall give him this right—if you do allow him to go on using your kidneys, this is a kindness on your part, and not something he can claim from you as his due. Nor has he any right against anybody else that *they* should give him continued use of your kidneys. Certainly he had no right against the Society of Music Lovers that they should plug him into you in the first place. And if you now start to unplug yourself, having learned that you will otherwise have to spend nine years in bed with him, there is nobody in the world who must try to prevent you, in order to see to it that he is given something he has a right to be given.

Some people are rather stricter about the right to life. In their view, it does not include the right to be given anything, but amounts to, and only to, the right not to be killed by anybody. But here a related difficulty arises. If everybody is to refrain from killing that violinist, then everybody must refrain from doing a great many different sorts of things. Everybody must refrain from slitting his throat, everybody must refrain from shooting him—and everybody must refrain from unplugging you from him. But does he have a right against everybody that they shall refrain from unplugging you from him? To refrain from doing this is to allow him to continue to use your kidneys. It could be argued that he has a right against us that *we* should allow him to continue to use your kidneys. That is, while he had no right against us that we should give him the use of your kidneys, it might be argued that he anyway has a right against us that we shall not now intervene and deprive him of the use of your kidneys. I shall come back to third-party interventions later. But certainly the violinist has no right against you that *you* shall allow him to continue to use your kidneys. As I said, if you do allow him to use them, it is a kindness on your part, and not something you owe him.

The difficulty I point to here is not peculiar to the right to life. It reappears in connection with all the other natural rights; and it is something which an adequate account of rights must deal with. For present purposes it is enough just to draw attention to it. But I would stress that I am not arguing that people do not have a right to life—quite to the contrary, it seems to me that the primary control we must place on the acceptability of an account of rights is that it should turn out in that account to be a truth that all persons have a right to life. I am arguing only that having a right to life does not guarantee having either a right to be given the use of or a right to be allowed continued use of another person's body—even if one needs it for life itself. So the right to life will not serve the opponents of abortion in the very simple and clear way in which they seem to have thought it would.

4. There is another way to bring out the difficulty. In the most ordinary sort of case, to deprive someone of what he has a right to is to treat him unjustly. Suppose a boy and his small brother are jointly given a box of chocolates for Christmas. If the older boy takes the box and refuses to give his brother any of the chocolates, he is unjust to him, for the brother has been given a right to half of them. But suppose that, having learned that otherwise it means nine years in

bed with that violinist, you unplug yourself from him. You surely are not being unjust to him, for you gave him no right to use your kidneys, and no one else can have given him any such right. But we have to notice that in unplugging yourself, you are killing him; and violinists, like everybody else, have a right to life, and thus in the view we were considering just now, the right not to be killed. So here you do what he supposedly has a right you shall not do, but you do not act unjustly to him in doing it.

The emendation which may be made at this point is this: the right to life consists not in the right not to be killed, but rather in the right not to be killed unjustly. This runs a risk of circularity, but never mind: it would enable us to square the fact that the violinist has a right to life with the fact that you do not act unjustly toward him in unplugging yourself, thereby killing him. For if you do not kill him unjustly, you do not violate his right to life, and so it is no wonder you do him no injustice.

But if this emendation is accepted, the gap in the argument against abortion stares us plainly in the face: it is by no means enough to show that the fetus is a person, and to remind us that all persons have a right to life—we need to be shown also that killing the fetus violates its right to life, i.e., that abortion is unjust killing. And is it?

I suppose we may take it as a datum that in a case of pregnancy due to rape the mother has not given the unborn person a right to the use of her body for food and shelter. Indeed, in what pregnancy could it be supposed that the mother has given the unborn person such a right? It is not as if there were unborn persons drifting about the world, to whom a woman who wants a child says, "I invite you in."

But it might be argued that there are other ways one can have acquired a right to the use of another person's body than by having been invited to use it by that person. Suppose a woman voluntarily indulges in intercourse, knowing of the chance it will issue in pregnancy, and then she does become pregnant; is she not in part responsible for the presence, in fact the very existence of the unborn person inside her? No doubt she did not invite it in. But doesn't her partial responsibility for its being there itself give it a right to the use of her body?* If so, then her aborting it would be more like the boy's taking away the chocolates, and less like your unplugging yourself from the violinist—doing so would be depriving it of what it does have a right to, and thus would be doing it an injustice.

And then, too, it might be asked whether or not she can kill it even to save her own life: If she voluntarily called it into existence, how can she now kill it, even in self-defense?

The first thing to be said about this is that it is something new. Opponents of abortion have been so concerned to make out the independence of the fetus, in order to establish that it has a right to life, just as the mother does, that they

---

* The need for a discussion of this argument was brought home to me by members of the Society for Ethical and Legal Philosophy, to whom this paper was originally presented.

have tended to overlook the possible support they might gain from making out that the fetus is *dependent* on the mother, in order to establish that she has a special kind of responsibility for it, a responsibility that gives it rights against her which are not possessed by an independent person—such as an ailing violinist who is a stranger to her.

On the other hand, this argument would give the unborn person a right to its mother's body only if her pregnancy resulted from a voluntary act, undertaken in full knowledge of the chance a pregnancy might result from it. It would leave out entirely the unborn person whose existence is due to rape. Pending the availability of some further argument, then, we would be left with the conclusion that unborn persons whose existence is due to rape have no right to the use of their mothers' bodies, and thus that aborting them is not depriving them of anything they have a right to and hence is not unjust killing.

And we should also notice that it is not at all plain that this argument really does go even as far as it purports to. For there are cases and cases, and the details make a difference. If the room is stuffy, and I therefore open a window to air it, and a burglar climbs in, it would be absurd to say, "Ah, now he can stay, she's given him a right to the use of her house—for she is partially responsible for his presence there, having voluntarily done what enabled him to get in, in full knowledge that there are such things as burglars, and that burglars burgle." It would be still more absurd to say this if I had had bars installed outside my windows, precisely to prevent burglars from getting in, and a burglar got in only because of a defect in the bars. It remains equally absurd if we imagine it is not a burglar who climbs in, but an innocent person who blunders or falls in. Again, suppose it were like this: people-seeds drift about in the air like pollen, and if you open your windows, one may drift in and take root in your carpets or upholstery. You don't want children, so you fix up your windows with fine mesh screens, the very best you can buy. As can happen, however, and on very, very rare occasions does happen, one of the screens is defective; and a seed drifts in and takes root. Does the person-plant who now develops have a right to the use of your house? Surely not—despite the fact that you voluntarily opened your windows, you knowingly kept carpets and upholstered furniture, and you knew that screens were sometimes defective. Someone may argue that you are responsible for its rooting, that it does have a right to your house, because after all you *could* have lived out your life with bare floors and furniture, or with sealed windows and doors. But this won't do—for by the same token anyone can avoid a pregnancy due to rape by having a hysterectomy, or anyway by never leaving home without a (reliable!) army.

It seems to me that the argument we are looking at can establish at most that there are *some* cases in which the unborn person has a right to the use of its mother's body, and therefore *some* cases in which abortion is unjust killing. There is room for much discussion and argument as to precisely which, if any. But I think we should side-step this issue and leave it open, for at any rate the argument certainly does not establish that all abortion is unjust killing.

5. There is room for yet another argument here, however. We surely must all grant that there may be cases in which it would be morally indecent to detach

a person from your body at the cost of his life. Suppose you learn that what the violinist needs is not nine years of your life, but only one hour: all you need do to save his life is to spend one hour in that bed with him. Suppose also that letting him use your kidneys for that one hour would not affect your health in the slightest. Admittedly you were kidnapped. Admittedly you did not give anyone permission to plug him into you. Nevertheless it seems to me plain you *ought* to allow him to use your kidneys for that hour—it would be indecent to refuse.

Again, suppose pregnancy lasted only an hour, and constituted no threat to life or health. And suppose that a woman becomes pregnant as a result of rape. Admittedly she did not voluntarily do anything to bring about the existence of a child. Admittedly she did nothing at all which would give the unborn person a right to the use of her body. All the same it might well be said, as in the newly emended violinist story, that she *ought* to allow it to remain for that hour—that it would be indecent in her to refuse.

Now some people are inclined to use the term "right" in such a way that it follows from the fact that you ought to allow a person to use your body for the hour he needs, that he has a right to use your body for the hour he needs, even though he has not been given that right by any person or act. They may say that it follows also that if you refuse, you act unjustly toward him. This use of the term is perhaps so common that it cannot be called wrong; nevertheless it seems to me to be an unfortunate loosening of what we would do better to keep a tight rein on. Suppose that box of chocolates I mentioned earlier had not been given to both boys jointly, but was given only to the older boy. There he sits, stolidly eating his way through the box, his small brother watching enviously. Here we are likely to say "You ought not to be so mean. You ought to give your brother some of those chocolates." My own view is that it just does not follow from the truth of this that the brother has any right to any of the chocolates. If the boy refuses to give his brother any, he is greedy, stingy, callous—but not unjust. I suppose that the people I have in mind will say it does follow that the brother has a right to some of the chocolates, and thus that the boy does act unjustly if he refuses to give his brother any. But the effect of saying this is to obscure what we should keep distinct, namely the difference between the boy's refusal in this case and the boy's refusal in the earlier case, in which the box was given to both boys jointly, and in which the small brother thus had what was from any point of view clear title to half.

A further objection to so using the term "right" that from the fact that A ought to do a thing for B, it follows that B has a right against A that A do it for him, is that it is going to make the question of whether or not a man has a right to a thing turn on how easy it is to provide him with it; and this seems not merely unfortunate, but morally unacceptable. Take the case of Henry Fonda again. I said earlier that I had no right to the touch of his cool hand on my fevered brow, even though I needed it to save my life. I said it would be frightfully nice of him to fly in from the West Coast to provide me with it, but that I had no right against him that he should do so. But suppose he isn't on the West Coast. Suppose he has only to walk across the room, place a hand briefly on my brow—and lo, my life is saved. Then surely he ought to do it, it would be indecent to refuse. Is it to be said "Ah, well, it follows that in this case she has a right to the touch of his hand on her brow, and so it would be an injustice in him to refuse"? So that I have a right to it when it is easy for him to provide it, though no right when it's hard? It's rather a shocking idea that anyone's rights should fade away· and disappear as it gets harder and harder to accord them to him.

So my own view is that even though you ought to let the violinist use your kidneys for the one hour he needs, we should not conclude that he has a right to do so—we should say that if you refuse, you are, like the boy who owns all the chocolates and will give none away, self-centered and callous, indecent in fact, but not unjust. And similarly, that even supposing a case in which a woman pregnant due to rape ought to allow the unborn person to use her body for the hour he needs, we should not conclude that he has a right to do so; we should conclude that she is self-centered, callous, indecent, but not unjust, if she refuses. The complaints are no less grave; they are just different. However, there is no need to insist on this point. If anyone does wish to deduce "he has a right" from "you ought," then all the same he must surely grant that there are cases in which it is not morally required of you that you allow that violinist to use your kidneys, and in which he does not have a right to use them, and in which you do not do him an injustice if you refuse. And so also for mother and unborn child. Except in such cases as the unborn person has a right to demand it—and we were leaving open the possibility that there may be such cases—nobody is morally *required* to make large sacrifices, of health, of all other interests and concerns, of all other duties and commitments, for nine years, or even for nine months, in order to keep another person alive.

6. We have in fact to distinguish between two kinds of Samaritan: the Good Samaritan and what we might call the Minimally Decent Samaritan. The story of the Good Samaritan, you will remember, goes like this:

> A certain man went down from Jerusalem to Jericho, and fell among thieves, which stripped him of his raiment, and wounded him, and departed, leaving him half dead.
>
> And by chance there came down a certain priest that way; and when he saw him, he passed by on the other side.
>
> And likewise a Levite, when he was at the place, came and looked on him, and passed by on the other side.
>
> But a certain Samaritan, as he journeyed, came where he was and when he saw him he had compassion on him.
>
> And went to him, and bound up his wounds, pouring in oil and wine, and set him on his own beast, and brought him to an inn, and took care of him.
>
> And on the morrow, when he departed, he took out two pence, and gave them to the host, and said unto him, "Take care of him: and whatsoever thou spendest more, when I come again, I will repay thee."
>
> (Luke 10:30–35)

The Good Samaritan went out of his way, at some cost to himself, to help one in need of it. We are not told what the options were, that is, whether or not the priest and the Levite could have helped by doing less than the Good Samaritan did, but assuming they could have, then the fact they did nothing at all shows they were not even Minimally Decent Samaritans, not because they were not Samaritans, but because they were not even minimally decent.

These things are a matter of degree, of course, but there is a difference, and it comes out perhaps most clearly in the story of Kitty Genovese, who, as you will remember, was murdered while thirty-eight people watched or listened, and did nothing at all to help her. A Good Samaritan would have rushed out to give direct assistance against the murderer. Or perhaps we had better allow that it would have been a Splendid Samaritan who did this, on the ground that it would have involved a risk of death for himself. But the thirty-eight not only did not do this, they did not even trouble to pick up a phone to call the police. Minimally Decent Samaritanism would call for doing at least that, and their not having done it was monstrous.

After telling the story of the Good Samaritan, Jesus said "Go, and do thou likewise." Perhaps he meant that we are morally required to act as the Good Samaritan did. Perhaps he was urging people to do more than is morally required of them. At all events it seems plain that it was not morally required of any of the thirty-eight that he rush out to give direct assistance at the risk of his own life, and that it is not morally required of anyone that he give long stretches of his life—nine years or nine months—to sustaining the life of a person who has no special right (we were leaving open the possibility of this) to demand it.

Indeed, with one rather striking class of exceptions, no one in any country in the world is *legally* required to do anywhere near as much as this for anyone else. The class of exceptions is obvious. My main concern here is not the state of the law in respect to abortion, but it is worth drawing attention to the fact that in no state in this country is any man compelled by law to be even a Minimally Decent Samaritan to any person; there is no law under which charges could be brought against the thirty-eight who stood by while Kitty Genovese died. By contrast, in most states in this country women are compelled by law to be not merely Minimally Decent Samaritans, but Good Samaritans to unborn persons inside them. This doesn't by itself settle anything one way or the other, because it may well be argued that there should be laws in this country—as there are in many European countries—compelling at least Minimally Decent Samaritanism.* But it does show that there is a gross injustice in the existing state of the law. And it shows also that the groups currently working against liberalization of abortion laws, in fact working toward having it declared unconstitutional for a state to permit abortion, had better start working for the adoption of Good Samaritan laws generally, or earn the charge that they are acting in bad faith.

I should think, myself, that Minimally Decent Samaritan laws would be one thing, Good Samaritan laws quite another, and in fact highly improper. But we are not here concerned with the law. What we should ask is not whether anybody should be compelled by law to be a Good Samaritan, but whether we must accede to a situation in which somebody is being compelled—by nature, perhaps—to be

---

* For a discussion of the difficulties involved, and a survey of the European experience with such laws, see *The Good Samaritan and the Law*, ed. James M. Ratcliffe (New York, 1966).

a Good Samaritan. We have, in other words, to look now at third-party interventions. I have been arguing that no person is morally required to make large sacrifices to sustain the life of another who has no right to demand them, and this even where the sacrifices do not include life itself; we are not morally required to be Good Samaritans or anyway Very Good Samaritans to one another. But what if a man cannot extricate himself from such a situation? What if he appeals to us to extricate him? It seems to me plain that there are cases in which we can, cases in which a Good Samaritan would extricate him. There you are, you were kidnapped, and nine years in bed with that violinist lie ahead of you. You have your own life to lead. You are sorry, but you simply cannot see giving up so much of your life to the sustaining of his. You cannot extricate yourself, and ask us to do so. I should have thought that—in light of his having no right to the use of your body—it was obvious that we do not have to accede to your being forced to give up so much. We can do what you ask. There is no injustice to the violinist in our doing so.

7. Following the lead of the opponents of abortion, I have throughout been speaking of the fetus merely as a person, and what I have been asking is whether or not the argument we began with, which proceeds only from the fetus being a person, really does establish its conclusion. I have argued that it does not.

But of course there are arguments and arguments, and it may be said that I have simply fastened on the wrong one. It may be said that what is important is not merely the fact that the fetus is a person, but that it is a person for whom the woman has a special kind of responsibility issuing from the fact that she is its mother. And it might be argued that all my analogies are therefore irrelevant—for you do not have that special kind of responsibility for that violinist, Henry Fonda does not have that special kind of responsibility for me. And our attention might be drawn to the fact that men and women both *are* compelled by law to provide support for their children.

I have in effect dealt (briefly) with this argument in section 4 above; but a (still briefer) recapitulation now may be in order. Surely we do not have any such "special responsibility" for a person unless we have assumed it, explicitly or implicitly. If a set of parents do not try to prevent pregnancy, do not obtain an abortion, and then at the time of birth of the child do not put it out for adoption, but rather take it home with them, then they have assumed responsibility for it, they have given it rights, and they cannot *now* withdraw support from it at the cost of its life because they now find it difficult to go on providing for it. But if they have taken all reasonable precautions against having a child, they do not simply by virtue of their biological relationship to the child who comes into existence have a special responsibility for it. They may wish to assume responsibility for it, or they may not wish to. And I am suggesting that if assuming responsibility for it would require large sacrifices, then they may refuse. A Good Samaritan would not refuse—or anyway, a Splendid Samaritan, if the sacrifices that had to be made were enormous. But then so would a Good Samaritan assume responsibility for that violinist; so would Henry Fonda, if he is a Good Samaritan, fly in from the West Coast and assume responsibility for me.

8. My argument will be found unsatisfactory on two counts by many of those who want to regard abortion as morally permissible. First, while I do argue that

abortion is not impermissible, I do not argue that it is always permissible. There may well be cases in which carrying the child to term requires only Minimally Decent Samaritanism of the mother, and this is a standard we must not fall below. I am inclined to think it a merit of my account precisely that it does *not* give a general yes or a general no. It allows for and supports our sense that, for example, a sick and desperately frightened fourteen-year-old schoolgirl, pregnant due to rape, may *of course* choose abortion, and that any law which rules this out is an insane law. And it also allows for and supports our sense that in other cases resort to abortion is even positively indecent. It would be indecent in the woman to request an abortion, and indecent in a doctor to perform it, if she is in her seventh month, and wants the abortion just to avoid the nuisance of postponing a trip abroad. The very fact that the arguments I have been drawing attention to treat all cases of abortion, or even all cases of abortion in which the mother's life is not at stake, as morally on a par ought to have made them suspect at the outset.

Secondly, while I am arguing for the permissibility of abortion in some cases, I am not arguing for the right to secure the death of the unborn child. It is easy to confuse these two things in that up to a certain point in the life of the fetus it is not able to survive outside the mother's body; hence removing it from her body guarantees its death. But they are importantly different. I have argued that you are not morally required to spend nine months in bed, sustaining the life of that violinist; but to say this is by no means to say that if, when you unplug yourself, there is a miracle and he survives, you then have a right to turn around and slit his throat. You may detach yourself even if this costs him his life; you have no right to be guaranteed his death by some other means, if unplugging yourself does not kill him. There are some people who will feel dissatisfied by this feature of my argument. A woman may be utterly devastated by the thought of a child, a bit of herself, put out for adoption and never seen or heard of again. She may therefore want not merely that the child be detached from her, but more, that it die. Some opponents of abortion are inclined to regard this as beneath contempt—thereby showing insensitivity to what is surely a powerful source of despair. All the same, I agree that the desire for the child's death is not one which anybody may gratify, should it turn out to be possible to detach the child alive.

At this place, however, it should be remembered that we have only been pretending throughout that the fetus is a human being from the moment of conception. A very early abortion is surely not the killing of a person, and so is not dealt with by anything I have said here.

▓ WHY ABORTION IS IMMORAL*
by Don Marquis

The view that abortion is, with rare exceptions, seriously immoral has received little support in the recent philosophical literature. No doubt most philosophers

---

* *The Journal of Philosophy,* vol. 86, no. 4 (April 1989), pp. 183–202.

affiliated with secular institutions of higher education believe that the anti-abortion position is either a symptom of irrational religious dogma or a conclusion generated by seriously confused philosophical argument. The purpose of this essay is to undermine this general belief. This essay sets out an argument that purports to show, as well as any argument in ethics can show, that abortion is, except possibly in rare cases, seriously immoral, that it is in the same moral category as killing an innocent adult human being.

The argument is based on a major assumption. Many of the most insightful and careful writers on the ethics of abortion—such as Joel Feinberg, Michael Tooley, Mary Anne Warren, H. Tristram Engelhardt, Jr., L. W. Sumner, John T. Noonan, Jr., and Philip Devine*—believe that whether or not abortion is morally permissible stands or falls on whether or not a fetus is the sort of being whose life it is seriously wrong to end. The argument of this essay will assume, but not argue, that they are correct.

Also, this essay will neglect issues of great importance to a complete ethics of abortion. Some anti-abortionists will allow that certain abortions, such as abortion before implantation or abortion when the life of a woman is threatened by a pregnancy or abortion after rape, may be morally permissible. This essay will not explore the casuistry of these hard cases. The purpose of this essay is to develop a general argument for the claim that the overwhelming majority of deliberate abortions are seriously immoral.

I.

A sketch of standard anti-abortion and pro-choice arguments exhibits how those arguments possess certain symmetries that explain why partisans of those positions are so convinced of the correctness of their own positions, why they are not successful in convincing their opponents, and why, to others, this issue seems to be unresolvable. An analysis of the nature of this standoff suggests a strategy for surmounting it.

Consider the way a typical anti-abortionist argues. She will argue or assert that life is present from the moment of conception or that fetuses look like babies or that fetuses possess a characteristic such as a genetic code that is both necessary and sufficient for being human. Anti-abortionists seem to believe that (1) the truth of all of these claims is quite obvious, and (2) establishing any of these claims is sufficient to show that abortion is morally akin to murder.

A standard pro-choice strategy exhibits similarities. The pro-choicer will argue

---

* Feinberg, "Abortion," in *Matters of Life and Death: New Introductory Essays in Moral Philosophy*, Tom Regan, ed. (New York: Random House, 1986), pp. 256–293; Tooley, "Abortion and Infanticide," *Philosophy and Public Affairs*, II, 1 (1972):37–65, Tooley, *Abortion and Infanticide* (New York: Oxford, 1984); Warren, "On the Moral and Legal Status of Abortion," *The Monist*, LVII, 1 (1973):43–61; Engelhardt, "The Ontology of Abortion," *Ethics*, LXXXIV, 3 (1974):217–234; Sumner, *Abortion and Moral Theory* (Princeton: University Press, 1981); Noonan, "An Almost Absolute Value in History," in *The Morality of Abortion: Legal and Historical Perspectives*, Noonan, ed. (Cambridge: Harvard, 1970); and Devine, *The Ethics of Homicide* (Ithaca: Cornell, 1978).

or assert that fetuses are not persons or that fetuses are not rational agents or that fetuses are not social beings. Pro-choicers seem to believe that (1) the truth of any of these claims is quite obvious, and (2) establishing any of these claims is sufficient to show that an abortion is not a wrongful killing.

In fact, both the pro-choice and the anti-abortion claims do seem to be true, although the "it looks like a baby" claim is more difficult to establish the earlier the pregnancy. We seem to have a standoff. How can it be resolved?

As everyone who has taken a bit of logic knows, if any of these arguments concerning abortion is a good argument, it requires not only some claim characterizing fetuses, but also some general moral principle that ties a characteristic of fetuses to having or not having the right to life or to some other moral characteristic that will generate the obligation or the lack of obligation not to end the life of a fetus. Accordingly, the arguments of the anti-abortionist and the pro-choicer need a bit of filling in to be regarded as adequate.

Note what each partisan will say. The anti-abortionist will claim that her position is supported by such generally accepted moral principles as "It is always prima facie seriously wrong to take a human life" or "It is always prima facie seriously wrong to end the life of a baby." Since these are generally accepted moral principles, her position is certainly not obviously wrong. The pro-choicer will claim that her position is supported by such plausible moral principles as "Being a person is what gives an individual intrinsic moral worth" or "It is only seriously prima facie wrong to take the life of a member of the human community." Since these are generally accepted moral principles, the pro-choice position is certainly not obviously wrong. Unfortunately, we have again arrived at a standoff.

Now, how might one deal with this standoff? The standard approach is to try to show how the moral principles of one's opponent lose their plausibility under analysis. It is easy to see how this is possible. On the one hand, the anti-abortionist will defend a moral principle concerning the wrongness of killing which tends to be broad in scope in order that even fetuses at an early stage of pregnancy will fall under it. The problem with broad principles is that they often embrace too much. In this particular instance, the principle "It is always prima facie wrong to take a human life" seems to entail that it is wrong to end the existence of a living human cancer-cell culture, on the grounds that the culture is both living and human. Therefore, it seems that the anti-abortionist's favored principle is too broad.

On the other hand, the pro-choicer wants to find a moral principle concerning the wrongness of killing which tends to be narrow in scope in order that fetuses will *not* fall under it. The problem with narrow principles is that they often do not embrace enough. Hence, the needed principles such as "It is prima facie wrong to kill only persons" or "It is prima facie wrong to kill only rational agents" do not explain why it is wrong to kill infants or young children or the severely retarded or even perhaps the severely mentally ill. Therefore, we seem again to have a standoff. The anti-abortionist charges, not unreasonably, that pro-choice principles concerning killing are too narrow to be acceptable; the pro-choicer charges, not unreasonably, that anti-abortionist principles concerning killing are too broad to be acceptable.

Attempts by both sides to patch up the difficulties in their positions run into further difficulties. The anti-abortionist will try to remove the problem in her position by reformulating her principle concerning killing in terms of human beings. Now we end up with: "It is always prima facie seriously wrong to end the life of a human being." This principle has the advantage of avoiding the problem of the human cancer-cell culture counterexample. But this advantage is purchased at a high price. For although it is clear that a fetus is both human and alive, it is not at all clear that a fetus is a human *being*. There is at least something to be said for the view that something becomes a human being only after a process of development, and that therefore first trimester fetuses and perhaps all fetuses are not yet human beings. Hence, the anti-abortionist, by this move, has merely exchanged one problem for another.*

The pro-choicer fares no better. She may attempt to find reasons why killing infants, young children, and the severely retarded is wrong which are independent of her major principle that is supposed to explain the wrongness of taking human life, but which will not also make abortion immoral. This is no easy task. Appeals to social utility will seem satisfactory only to those who resolve not to think of the enormous difficulties with a utilitarian account of the wrongness of killing and the significant social costs of preserving the lives of the unproductive.† A pro-choice strategy that extends the definition of "person" to infants or even to young children seems just as arbitrary as an anti-abortion strategy that extends the definition of "human being" to fetuses. Again, we find symmetries in the two positions and we arrive at a standoff.

There are even further problems that reflect symmetries in the two positions. In addition to counterexample problems, or the arbitrary application problems that can be exchanged for them, the standard anti-abortionist principle "It is prima facie seriously wrong to kill a human being," or one of its variants, can be objected to on the grounds of ambiguity. If "human being" is taken to be a *biological* category, then the anti-abortionist is left with the problem of explaining why a merely biological category should make a moral difference. Why, it is asked, is it any more reasonable to base a moral conclusion on the number of chromosomes in one's cells than on the color of one's skin?‡ If "human being," on the other hand, is taken to be a *moral* category, then the claim that a fetus is a human being cannot be taken to be a premise in the anti-abortion argument, for it is precisely what needs to be established. Hence, either the anti-abortionist's main category is a morally irrelevant, merely biological category, or it is of no use to the anti-abortionist in establishing (noncircularly, of course) that abortion is wrong.

---

* For interesting discussions of this issue, see Warren Quinn, "Abortion: Identity and Loss," *Philosophy and Public Affairs*, XIII, 1 (1984):24–54; and Lawrence C. Becker, "Human Being: The Boundaries of the Concept," *Philosophy and Public Affairs*, IV, 4 (1975):334–359.

† For example, see my "Ethics and The Elderly: Some Problems," in Stuart Spicker, Kathleen Woodward, and David Van Tassel, eds., *Aging and the Elderly: Humanistic Perspectives in Gerontology* (Atlantic Highlands, NJ: Humanities 1978), pp. 341–355.

‡ See Warren, *op. cit.*, and Tooley, "Abortion and Infanticide."

Although this problem with the anti-abortionist position is often noticed, it is less often noticed that the pro-choice position suffers from an analogous problem. The principle "Only persons have the right to life" also suffers from an ambiguity. The term "person" is typically defined in terms of psychological characteristics, although there will certainly be disagreement concerning which characteristics are most important. Supposing that this matter can be settled, the pro-choicer is left with the problem of explaining why *psychological* characteristics should make a *moral* difference. If the pro-choicer should attempt to deal with this problem by claiming that an explanation is not necessary, that in fact we do treat such a cluster of psychological properties as having moral significance, the sharp-witted anti-abortionist should have a ready response. We do treat being both living and human as having moral significance. If it is legitimate for the pro-choicer to demand that the anti-abortionist provide an explanation of the connection between the biological character of being a human being and the wrongness of being killed (even though people accept this connection), then it is legitimate for the anti-abortionist to demand that the pro-choicer provide an explanation of the connection between psychological criteria for being a person and the wrongness of being killed (even though that connection is accepted).*

Feinberg has attempted to meet this objection (he calls psychological personhood "commonsense personhood"):

> The characteristics that confer commonsense personhood are not arbitrary bases for rights and duties, such as race, sex or species membership; rather they are traits that make sense out of rights and duties and without which those moral attributes would have no point or function. It is because people are conscious; have a sense of their personal identities; have plans, goals, and projects; experience emotions; are liable to pains, anxieties, and frustrations; can reason and bargain, and so on—it is because of these attributes that people have values and interests, desires and expectations of their own, including a stake in their own futures, and a personal well-being of a sort we cannot ascribe to unconscious or nonrational beings. Because of their developed capacities they can assume duties and responsibilities and can have and make claims on one another. Only because of their sense of self, their life plans, their value hierarchies, and their stakes in their own futures can they be ascribed fundamental rights. There is nothing arbitrary about these linkages. (*op. cit.*, p. 270)

The plausible aspects of this attempt should not be taken to obscure its implausible features. There is a great deal to be said for the view that being a psychological person under some description is a necessary condition for having duties. One cannot have a duty unless one is capable of behaving morally, and a being's capability of behaving morally will require having a certain psychology. It is far from obvious, however, that having rights entails consciousness or rationality, as Feinberg suggests. We speak of the rights of the severely retarded or the severely mentally ill, yet some of these persons are not rational. We speak of the rights of

---

* This seems to be the fatal flaw in Warren's treatment of this issue.

the temporarily unconscious. The New Jersey Supreme Court based their decision in the Quinlan case on Karen Ann Quinlan's right to privacy, and she was known to be permanently unconscious at that time. Hence, Feinberg's claim that having rights entails being conscious is, on its face, obviously false.

Of course, it might not make sense to attribute rights to a being that would never in its natural history have certain psychological traits. This modest connection between psychological personhood and moral personhood will create a place for Karen Ann Quinlan and the temporarily unconscious. But then it makes a place for fetuses also. Hence, it does not serve Feinberg's pro-choice purposes. Accordingly, it seems that the pro-choicer will have as much difficulty bridging the gap between psychological personhood and personhood in the moral sense as the anti-abortionist has bridging the gap between being a biological human being and being a human being in the moral sense.

Furthermore, the pro-choicer cannot any more escape her problem by making person a purely moral category than the anti-abortionist could escape by the analogous move. For if person is a moral category, then the pro-choicer is left without the resources for establishing (noncircularly, of course) the claim that a fetus is not a person, which is an essential premise in her argument. Again, we have both a symmetry and a standoff between pro-choice and anti-abortion views.

Passions in the abortion debate run high. There are both plausibilities and difficulties with the standard positions. Accordingly, it is hardly surprising that partisans of either side embrace with fervor the moral generalizations that support the conclusions they preanalytically favor, and reject with disdain the moral generalizations of their opponents as being subject to inescapable difficulties. It is easy to believe that the counterexamples to one's own moral principles are merely temporary difficulties that will dissolve in the wake of further philosophical research, and that the counterexamples to the principles of one's opponents are as straightforward as the contradiction between *A* and *O* propositions in traditional logic. This might suggest to an impartial observer (if there are any) that the abortion issue is unresolvable.

There is a way out of this apparent dialectical quandary. The moral generalizations of both sides are not quite correct. The generalizations hold for the most part, for the usual cases. This suggests that they are all *accidental* generalizations, that the moral claims made by those on both sides of the dispute do not touch on the *essence* of the matter.

This use of the distinction between essence and accident is not meant to invoke obscure metaphysical categories. Rather, it is intended to reflect the rather atheoretical nature of the abortion discussion. If the generalization a partisan in the abortion dispute adopts were derived from the reason why ending the life of a human being is wrong, then there could not be exceptions to that generalization unless some special case obtains in which there are even more powerful countervailing reasons. Such generalizations would not be merely accidental generalizations; they would point to, or be based upon, the essence of the wrongness of killing, what it is that makes killing wrong. All this suggests that a necessary condition of resolving the abortion controversy is a more theoretical account of the wrongness of killing. After all, if we merely believe, but do not understand, why killing adult human beings such as ourselves is wrong, how could we conceivably show that abortion is either immoral or permissible?

II.

In order to develop such an account, we can start from the following unproblematic assumption concerning our own case: it is wrong to kill *us*. Why is it wrong? Some answers can be easily eliminated. It might be said that what makes killing us wrong is that a killing brutalizes the one who kills. But the brutalization consists of being inured to the performance of an act that is hideously immoral; hence, the brutalization does not explain the immorality. It might be said that what makes killing us wrong is the great loss others would experience due to our absence. Although such hubris is understandable, such an explanation does not account for the wrongness of killing hermits, or those whose lives are relatively independent and whose friends find it easy to make new friends.

A more obvious answer is better. What primarily makes killing wrong is neither its effect on the murdered nor its effect on the victim's friends and relatives, but its effect on the victim. The loss of one's life is one of the greatest losses one can suffer. The loss of one's life deprives one of all the experiences, activities, projects, and enjoyments that would otherwise have constituted one's future. Therefore, killing someone is wrong, primarily because the killing inflicts (one of) the greatest possible losses on the victim. To describe this as the loss of life can be misleading, however. The change in my biological state does not by itself make killing me wrong. The effect of the loss of my biological life is the loss to me of all those activities, projects, experiences, and enjoyments which would otherwise have constituted my future personal life. These activities, projects, experiences, and enjoyments are either valuable for their own sakes or are means to something else that is valuable for its own sake. Some parts of my future are not valued by me now, but will come to be valued by me as I grow older and as my values and capacities change. When I am killed, I am deprived both of what I now value which would have been part of my future personal life, but also what I would come to value. Therefore, when I die, I am deprived of all of the value of my future. Inflicting this loss on me is ultimately what makes killing me wrong. This being the case, it would seem that what makes killing *any* adult human being prima facie seriously wrong is the loss of his or her future.*

How should this rudimentary theory of the wrongness of killing be evaluated? It cannot be faulted for deriving an 'ought' from an 'is', for it does not. The analysis assumes that killing me (or you, reader) is prima facie seriously wrong. The point of the analysis is to establish which natural property ultimately explains the wrongness of the killing, given that it is wrong. A natural property will ultimately

---

* I have been most influenced on this matter by Jonathan Glover, *Causing Death and Saving Lives* (New York: Penguin, 1977), ch. 3; and Robert Young, "What Is So Wrong with Killing People?" *Philosophy*, LIV, 210 (1979):515–528.

explain the wrongness of killing, only if (1) the explanation fits with our intuitions about the matter and (2) there is no other natural property that provides the basis for a better explanation of the wrongness of killing. This analysis rests on the intuition that what makes killing a particular human or animal wrong is what it does to that particular human or animal. What makes killing wrong is some natural effect or other of the killing. Some would deny this. For instance, a divine-command theorist in ethics would deny it. Surely this denial is, however, one of those features of divine-command theory which renders it so implausible.

The claim that what makes killing wrong is the loss of the victim's future is directly supported by two considerations. In the first place, this theory explains why we regard killing as one of the worst of crimes. Killing is especially wrong, because it deprives the victim of more than perhaps any other crime. In the second place, people with AIDS or cancer who know they are dying believe, of course, that dying is a very bad thing for them. They believe that the loss of a future to them that they would otherwise have experienced is what makes their premature death a very bad thing for them. A better theory of the wrongness of killing would require a different natural property associated with killing which better fits with the attitudes of the dying. What could it be?

The view that what makes killing wrong is the loss to the victim of the value of the victim's future gains additional support when some of its implications are examined. In the first place, it is incompatible with the view that it is wrong to kill only beings who are biologically human. It is possible that there exists a different species from another planet whose members have a future like ours. Since having a future like that is what makes killing someone wrong, this theory entails that it would be wrong to kill members of such a species. Hence, this theory is opposed to the claim that only life that is biologically human has great moral worth, a claim which many anti-abortionists have seemed to adopt. This opposition, which this theory has in common with personhood theories, seems to be a merit of the theory.

In the second place, the claim that the loss of one's future is the wrong-making feature of one's being killed entails the possibility that the futures of some actual nonhuman mammals on our own planet are sufficiently like ours that it is seriously wrong to kill them also. Whether some animals do have the same right to life as human beings depends on adding to the account of the wrongness of killing some additional account of just what it is about my future or the futures of other adult human beings which makes it wrong to kill us. No such additional account will be offered in this essay. Undoubtedly, the provision of such an account would be a very difficult matter. Undoubtedly, any such account would be quite controversial. Hence, it surely should not reflect badly on this sketch of an elementary theory of the wrongness of killing that it is indeterminate with respect to some very difficult issues regarding animal rights.

In the third place, the claim that the loss of one's future is the wrong-making feature of one's being killed does not entail, as sanctity of human life theories do, that active euthanasia is wrong. Persons who are severely and incurably ill, who face a future of pain and despair, and who wish to die will not have suffered a loss if they are killed. It is, strictly speaking, the value of a human's future which makes killing wrong in this theory. This being so, killing does not necessarily wrong some persons who are sick and dying. Of course, there may be other reasons for a prohibition of active euthanasia, but that is another matter. Sanctity-of-human-life theories seem to hold that active euthanasia is seriously wrong even in an individual case where there seems to be good reason for it independently of public policy considerations. This consequence is more implausible, and it is a plus for the claim that the loss of a future of value is what makes killing wrong that it does not share this consequence.

In the fourth place, the account of the wrongness of killing defended in this essay does straightforwardly entail that it is prima facie seriously wrong to kill children and infants, for we do presume that they have futures of value. Since we do believe that it is wrong to kill defenseless little babies, it is important that a theory of the wrongness of killing easily account for this. Personhood theories of the wrongness of killing, on the other hand, cannot straightforwardly account for the wrongness of killing infants and young children.* Hence, such theories must add special ad hoc accounts of the wrongness of killing the young. The plausibility of such ad hoc theories seems to be a function of how desperately one wants such theories to work. The claim that the primary wrong-making feature of a killing is the loss to the victim of the value of its future accounts for the wrongness of killing young children and infants directly; it makes the wrongness of such acts as obvious as we actually think it is. This is a further merit of this theory. Accordingly, it seems that this value of a future-like-ours theory of the wrongness of killing shares strengths of both sanctity-of-life and personhood accounts while avoiding weaknesses of both. In addition, it meshes with a central intuition concerning what makes killing wrong.

The claim that the primary wrong-making feature of a killing is the loss to the victim of the value of its future has obvious consequences for the ethics of abortion. The future of a standard fetus includes a set of experiences, projects, activities, and such which are identical with the futures of adult human beings and are identical with the futures of young children. Since the reason that is sufficient to explain why it is wrong to kill human beings after the time of birth is a reason that also applies to fetuses, it follows that abortion is prima facie seriously morally wrong.

This argument does not rely on the invalid inference that, since it is wrong to kill persons, it is wrong to kill potential persons also. The category that is morally central to this analysis is the category of having a valuable future like ours; it is not the category of personhood. The argument to the conclusion that abortion is prima facie seriously morally wrong proceeded independently of the notion of person or potential person or any equivalent. Someone may wish to start with this analysis in terms of the value of a human future, conclude that abortion is, except perhaps in rare circumstances, seriously morally wrong, infer

---

* Feinberg, Tooley, Warren, and Engelhardt have all dealt with this problem.

that fetuses have the right to life, and then call fetuses "persons" as a result of their having the right to life. Clearly, in this case, the category of person is being used to state the *conclusion* of the analysis rather than to generate the *argument* of the analysis.

The structure of this anti-abortion argument can be both illuminated and defended by comparing it to what appears to be the best argument for the wrongness of the wanton infliction of pain on animals. This latter argument is based on the assumption that it is prima facie wrong to inflict pain on me (or you, reader). What is the natural property associated with the infliction of pain which makes such infliction wrong? The obvious answer seems to be that the infliction of pain causes suffering and that suffering is a misfortune. The suffering caused by the infliction of pain is what makes the wanton infliction of pain on me wrong. The wanton infliction of pain on other adult humans causes suffering. The wanton infliction of pain on animals causes suffering. Since causing suffering is what makes the wanton infliction of pain wrong and since the wanton infliction of pain on animals causes suffering, it follows that the wanton infliction of pain on animals is wrong.

This argument for the wrongness of the wanton infliction of pain on animals shares a number of structural features with the argument for the serious prima facie wrongness of abortion. Both arguments start with an obvious assumption concerning what it is wrong to do to me (or you, reader). Both then look for the characteristic or the consequence of the wrong action which makes the action wrong. Both recognize that the wrong-making feature of these immoral actions is a property of actions sometimes directed at individuals other than postnatal human beings. If the structure of the argument for the wrongness of the wanton infliction of pain on animals is sound, then the structure of the argument for the prima facie serious wrongness of abortion is also sound, for the structure of the two arguments is the same. The structure common to both is the key to the explanation of how the wrongness of abortion can be demonstrated without recourse to the category of person. In neither argument is that category crucial.

This defense of an argument for the wrongness of abortion in terms of a structurally similar argument for the wrongness of the wanton infliction of pain on animals succeeds only if the account regarding animals is the correct account. Is it? In the first place, it seems plausible. In the second place, its major competition is Kant's account. Kant believed that we do not have direct duties to animals at all, because they are not persons. Hence, Kant had to explain and justify the wrongness of inflicting pain on animals on the grounds that "he who is hard in his dealings with animals becomes hard also in his dealing with men."* The problem with Kant's account is that there seems to be no reason for accepting this latter claim unless Kant's account is rejected. If the alternative to Kant's account is accepted, then it is easy to understand why someone who is indifferent to

---

* "Duties to Animals and Spirits," in *Lectures on Ethics*, Louis Infeld, trans. (New York: Harper, 1963), p. 239.

inflicting pain on animals is also indifferent to inflicting pain on humans, for one is indifferent to what makes inflicting pain wrong in both cases. But, if Kant's account is accepted, there is no intelligible reason why one who is hard in his dealings with animals (or crabgrass or stones) should also be hard in his dealings with men. After all, men are persons: animals are no more persons than crabgrass or stones. Persons are Kant's crucial moral category. Why, in short, should a Kantian accept the basic claim in Kant's argument?

Hence, Kant's argument for the wrongness of inflicting pain on animals rests on a claim that, in a world of Kantian moral agents, is demonstrably false. Therefore, the alternative analysis, being more plausible anyway, should be accepted. Since this alternative analysis has the same structure as the anti-abortion argument being defended here, we have further support for the argument for the immorality of abortion being defended in this essay.

Of course, this value of a future-like-ours argument, if sound, shows only that abortion is prima facie wrong, not that it is wrong in any and all circumstances. Since the loss of the future to a standard fetus, if killed, is, however, at least as great a loss as the loss of the future to a standard adult human being who is killed, abortion, like ordinary killing, could be justified only by the most compelling reasons. The loss of one's life is almost the greatest misfortune that can happen to one. Presumably abortion could be justified in some circumstances, only if the loss consequent on failing to abort would be at least as great. Accordingly, morally permissible abortions will be rare indeed unless, perhaps, they occur so early in pregnancy that a fetus is not yet definitely an individual. Hence, this argument should be taken as showing that abortion is presumptively very seriously wrong, where the presumption is very strong—as strong as the presumption that killing another adult human being is wrong.

III.

How complete an account of the wrongness of killing does the value of a future-like-ours account have to be in order that the wrongness of abortion is a consequence? This account does not have to be an account of the necessary conditions for the wrongness of killing. Some persons in nursing homes may lack valuable human futures, yet it may be wrong to kill them for other reasons. Furthermore, this account does not obviously have to be the sole reason killing is wrong where the victim did have a valuable future. This analysis claims only that, for any killing where the victim did have a valuable future like ours, having that future by itself is sufficient to create the strong presumption that the killing is seriously wrong.

One way to overturn the value of a future-like-ours argument would be to find some account of the wrongness of killing which is at least as intelligible and which has different implications for the ethics of abortion. Two rival accounts possess at least some degree of plausibility. One account is based on the obvious fact that people value the experience of living and wish for that valuable experience to continue. Therefore, it might be said, what makes killing wrong is the discontinu-

ation of that experience for the victim. Let us call this the *discontinuation account.**
Another rival account is based upon the obvious fact that people strongly desire
to continue to live. This suggests that what makes killing us so wrong is that it
interferes with the fulfillment of a strong and fundamental desire, the fulfillment
of which is necessary for the fulfillment of any other desires we might have. Let
us call this the *desire account.*†

Consider first the desire account as a rival account of the ethics of killing
which would provide the basis for rejecting the anti-abortion position. Such an
account will have to be stronger than the value of a future-like-ours account of
the wrongness of abortion if it is to do the job expected of it. To entail the
wrongness of abortion, the value of a future-like-ours account has only to provide
a sufficient, but not a necessary, condition for the wrongness of killing. The desire
account, on the other hand, must provide us also with a necessary condition for
the wrongness of killing in order to generate a pro-choice conclusion on abortion.
The reason for this is that presumably the argument from the desire account
moves from the claim that what makes killing wrong is interference with a very
strong desire to the claim that abortion is not wrong because the fetus lacks a
strong desire to live. Obviously, this inference fails if someone's having the desire
to live is not a necessary condition of its being wrong to kill that individual.

One problem with the desire account is that we do regard it as seriously
wrong to kill persons who have little desire to live or who have no desire to live
or, indeed, have a desire not to live. We believe it is seriously wrong to kill the
unconscious, the sleeping, those who are tired of life, and those who are suicidal.
The value-of-a-human-future account renders standard morality intelligible in these
cases; these cases appear to be incompatible with the desire account.

The desire account is subject to a deeper difficulty. We desire life, because
we value the goods of this life. The goodness of life is not secondary to our desire
for it. If this were not so, the pain of one's own premature death could be done
away with merely by an appropriate alteration in the configuration of one's desires.
This is absurd. Hence, it would seem that it is the loss of the goods of one's future,
not the interference with the fulfillment of a strong desire to live, which accounts
ultimately for the wrongness of killing.

It is worth noting that, if the desire account is modified so that it does not
provide a necessary, but only a sufficient, condition for the wrongness of killing,
the desire account is compatible with the value of a future-like-ours account. The
combined accounts will yield an anti-abortion ethic. This suggests that one can
retain what is intuitively plausible about the desire account without a challenge to
the basic argument of this paper.

It is also worth noting that, if future desires have moral force in a modified
desire account of the wrongness of killing, one can find support for an anti-abortion

---

* I am indebted to Jack Bricke for raising this objection.

† Presumably a preference utilitarian would press such an objection. Tooley once suggested that his
account has such a theoretical underpinning. See his "Abortion and Infanticide," pp. 44–5.

ethic even in the absence of a value of a future-like-ours account. If one decides that a morally relevant property, the possession of which is sufficient to make it wrong to kill some individual, is the desire at some future time to live—one might decide to justify one's refusal to kill suicidal teenagers on these grounds, for example—then, since typical fetuses will have the desire in the future to live, it is wrong to kill typical fetuses. Accordingly, it does not seem that a desire account of the wrongness of killing can provide a justification of a pro-choice ethic of abortion which is nearly as adequate as the value of a human-future justification of an anti-abortion ethic.

The discontinuation account looks more promising as an account of the wrongness of killing. It seems just as intelligible as the value of a future-like-ours account, but it does not justify an anti-abortion position. Obviously, if it is the continuation of one's activities, experiences, and projects, the loss of which makes killing wrong, then it is not wrong to kill fetuses for that reason, for fetuses do not have experiences, activities, and projects to be continued or discontinued. Accordingly, the discontinuation account does not have the anti-abortion consequences that the value of a future-like-ours account has. Yet, it seems as intelligible as the value of a future-like-ours account, for when we think of what would be wrong with our being killed, it does seem as if it is the discontinuation of what makes our lives worthwhile which makes killing us wrong.

Is the discontinuation account just as good an account as the value of a future-like-ours account? The discontinuation account will not be adequate at all, if it does not refer to the *value* of the experience that may be discontinued. One does not want the discontinuation account to make it wrong to kill a patient who begs for death and who is in severe pain that cannot be relieved short of killing. (I leave open the question of whether it is wrong for other reasons.) Accordingly, the discontinuation account must be more than a bare discontinuation account. It must make some reference to the positive value of the patient's experiences. But, by the same token, the value of a future-like-ours account cannot be a bare future account either. Just having a future surely does not itself rule out killing the above patient. This account must make some reference to the value of the patient's future experiences and projects also. Hence, both accounts involve the value of experiences, projects, and activities. So far we still have symmetry between the accounts.

The symmetry fades, however, when we focus on the time period of the value of the experiences, etc., which has moral consequences. Although both accounts leave open the possibility that the patient in our example may be killed, this possibility is left open only in virtue of the utterly bleak future for the patient. It makes no difference whether the patient's immediate past contains intolerable pain, or consists in being in a coma (which we can imagine is a situation of indifference), or consists in a life of value. If the patient's future is a future of value, we want our account to make it wrong to kill the patient. If the patient's future is intolerable, whatever his or her immediate past, we want our account to allow killing the patient. Obviously, then, it is the value of that patient's future which is doing the work in rendering the morality of killing the patient intelligible.

This being the case, it seems clear that whether one has immediate past experiences or not does no work in the explanation of what makes killing wrong. The addition the discontinuation account makes to the value of a human future account is otiose. Its addition to the value-of-a-future account plays no role at all in rendering intelligible the wrongness of killing. Therefore, it can be discarded with the discontinuation account of which it is a part.

IV.

The analysis of the previous section suggests that alternative general accounts of the wrongness of killing are either inadequate or unsuccessful in getting around the anti-abortion consequences of the value of a future-like-ours argument. A different strategy for avoiding these anti-abortion consequences involves limiting the scope of the value of a future argument. More precisely, the strategy involves arguing that fetuses lack a property that is essential for the value-of-a-future argument (or for any anti-abortion argument) to apply to them.

One move of this sort is based upon the claim that a necessary condition of one's future being valuable is that one values it. Value implies a valuer. Given this one might argue that, since fetuses cannot value their futures, their futures are not valuable to them. Hence, it does not seriously wrong them deliberately to end their lives.

This move fails, however, because of some ambiguities. Let us assume that something cannot be of value unless it is valued by someone. This does not entail that my life is of no value unless it is valued by me. I may think, in a period of despair, that my future is of no worth whatsoever, but I may be wrong because others rightly see value—even great value—in it. Furthermore, my future can be valuable to me even if I do not value it. This is the case when a young person attempts suicide, but is rescued and goes on to significant human achievements. Such young people's futures are ultimately valuable to them, even though such futures do not seem to be valuable to them at the moment of attempted suicide. A fetus's future can be valuable to it in the same way. Accordingly, this attempt to limit the anti-abortion argument fails.

Another similar attempt to reject the anti-abortion position is based on Tooley's claim that an entity cannot possess the right to life unless it has the capacity to desire its continued existence. It follows that, since fetuses lack the conceptual capacity to desire to continue to live, they lack the right to life. Accordingly, Tooley concludes that abortion cannot be seriously prima facie wrong (*op. cit.*, pp. 46–7).

What could be the evidence for Tooley's basic claim? Tooley once argued that individuals have a prima facie right to what they desire and that the lack of the capacity to desire something undercuts the basis of one's right to it (*op. cit.*, pp. 44–5). This argument plainly will not succeed in the context of the analysis of this essay, however, since the point here is to establish the fetus's right to life on other grounds. Tooley's argument assumes that the right to life cannot be established in general on some basis other than the desire for life. This position was considered and rejected in the preceding section of this paper.

One might attempt to defend Tooley's basic claim on the grounds that, because a fetus cannot apprehend continued life as a benefit, its continued life cannot be a benefit or cannot be something it has a right to or cannot be something that is in its interest. This might be defended in terms of the general proposition that, if an individual is literally incapable of caring about or taking an interest in some *X*, then one does not have a right to *X* or *X* is not a benefit or *X* is not something that is in one's interest.*

Each member of this family of claims seems to be open to objections. As John C. Stevens[†] has pointed out, one may have a right to be treated with a certain medical procedure (because of a health insurance policy one has purchased), even though one cannot conceive of the nature of the procedure. And, as Tooley himself has pointed out, persons who have been indoctrinated, or drugged, or rendered temporarily unconscious may be literally incapable of caring about or taking an interest in something that is in their interest or is something to which they have a right, or is something that benefits them. Hence, the Tooley claim that would restrict the scope of the value of a future-like-ours argument is undermined by counterexamples.[‡]

Finally, Paul Bassen[§] has argued that, even though the prospects of an embryo might seem to be a basis for the wrongness of abortion, an embryo cannot be a victim and therefore cannot be wronged. An embryo cannot be a victim, he says, because it lacks sentience. His central argument for this seems to be that, even though plants and the permanently unconscious are alive, they clearly cannot be victims. What is the explanation of this? Bassen claims that the explanation is that their lives consist of mere metabolism and mere metabolism is not enough to ground victimizability. Mentation is required.

The problem with this attempt to establish the absence of victimizability is that both plants and the permanently unconscious clearly lack what Bassen calls "prospects" or what I have called "a future life like ours." Hence, it is surely open to one to argue that the real reason we believe plants and the permanently unconscious cannot be victims is that killing them cannot deprive them of a future life like ours; the real reason is not their absence of present mentation.

Bassen recognizes that his view is subject to this difficulty, and he recognizes that the case of children seems to support this difficulty, for "much of what we do for children is based on prospects." He argues, however, that, in the case of children and in other such cases, "potentiality comes into play only where victimizability has been secured on other grounds" (*ibid.*, p. 333).

Bassen's defense of his view is patently question-begging, since what is adequate

---

* Donald VanDeVeer seems to think this is self-evident. See his "Whither Baby Doe?" in *Matters of Life and Death*, p. 233.

[†] "Must the Bearer of a Right Have the Concept of That to Which He Has a Right?" *Ethics*, xcv, 1 (1984):68–74.

[‡] See Tooley again in "Abortion and Infanticide," pp. 47–49.

§ "Present Sakes and Future Prospects: The Status of Early Abortion," *Philosophy and Public Affairs*, xi, 4 (1982):322–326.

to secure victimizability is exactly what is at issue. His examples do not support his own view against the thesis of this essay. Of course, embryos can be victims: when their lives are deliberately terminated, they are deprived of their futures of value, their prospects. This makes them victims, for it directly wrongs them.

The seeming plausibility of Bassen's view stems from the fact that paradigmatic cases of imagining someone as a victim involve empathy, and empathy requires mentation of the victim. The victims of flood, famine, rape, or child abuse are all persons with whom we can empathize. That empathy seems to be part of seeing them as victims.*

In spite of the strength of these examples, the attractive intuition that a situation in which there is victimization requires the possibility of empathy is subject to counterexamples. Consider a case that Bassen himself offers: "Posthumous obliteration of an author's work constitutes a misfortune for him only if he had wished his work to endure" (*op. cit.*, p. 318). The conditions Bassen wishes to impose upon the possibility of being victimized here seem far too strong. Perhaps this author, due to his unrealistic standards of excellence and his low self-esteem, regarded his work as unworthy of survival, even though it possessed genuine literary merit. Destruction of such work would surely victimize its author. In such a case, empathy with the victim concerning the loss is clearly impossible.

Of course, Bassen does not make the possibility of empathy a necessary condition of victimizability: he requires only mentation. Hence, on Bassen's actual view, this author, as I have described him, can be a victim. The problem is that the basic intuition that renders Bassen's view plausible is missing in the author's case. In order to attempt to avoid counterexamples, Bassen has made his thesis too weak to be supported by the intuitions that suggested it.

Even so, the mentation requirement on victimizability is still subject to counterexamples. Suppose a severe accident renders me totally unconscious for a month, after which I recover. Surely killing me while I am unconscious victimizes me, even though I am incapable of mentation during that time. It follows that Bassen's thesis fails. Apparently, attempts to restrict the value of a future-like-ours argument so that fetuses do not fall within its scope do not succeed.

V.

In this essay, it has been argued that the correct ethic of the wrongness of killing can be extended to fetal life and used to show that there is a strong presumption that any abortion is morally impermissible. If the ethic of killing adopted here entails, however, that contraception is also seriously immoral, then there would appear to be a difficulty with the analysis of this essay.

But this analysis does not entail that contraception is wrong. Of course, contraception prevents the actualization of a possible future of value. Hence, it follows from the claim that futures of value should be maximized that contraception

---

* Note carefully the reasons he gives on the bottom of p. 316.

is prima facie immoral. This obligation to maximize does not exist, however; furthermore, nothing in the ethics of killing in this paper entails that it does. The ethics of killing in this essay would entail that contraception is wrong only if something were denied a human future of value by contraception. Nothing at all is denied such a future by contraception, however.

Candidates for a subject of harm by contraception fall into four categories: (1) some sperm or other, (2) some ovum or other, (3) a sperm and an ovum separately, and (4) a sperm and an ovum together. Assigning the harm to some sperm is utterly arbitrary, for no reason can be given for making a sperm the subject of harm rather than an ovum. Assigning the harm to some ovum is utterly arbitrary, for no reason can be given for making an ovum the subject of harm rather than a sperm. One might attempt to avoid these problems by insisting that contraception deprives both the sperm and the ovum separately of a valuable future like ours. On this alternative, too many futures are lost. Contraception was supposed to be wrong, because it deprived us of one future of value, not two. One might attempt to avoid this problem by holding that contraception deprives the combination of sperm and ovum of a valuable future like ours. But here the definite article misleads. At the time of contraception, there are hundreds of millions of sperm, one (released) ovum and millions of possible combinations of all of these. There is no actual combination at all. Is the subject of the loss to be a merely possible combination? Which one? This alternative does not yield an actual subject of harm either. Accordingly, the immorality of contraception is not entailed by the loss of a future-like-ours argument simply because there is no nonarbitrarily identifiable subject of the loss in the case of contraception.

VI.

The purpose of this essay has been to set out an argument for the serious presumptive wrongness of abortion subject to the assumption that the moral permissibility of abortion stands or falls on the moral status of the fetus. Since a fetus possesses a property, the possession of which in adult human beings is sufficient to make killing an adult human being wrong, abortion is wrong. This way of dealing with the problem of abortion seems superior to other approaches to the ethics of abortion, because it rests on an ethics of killing which is close to self-evident, because the crucial morally relevant property clearly applies to fetuses, and because the argument avoids the usual equivocations on "human life," "human being," or "person." The argument rests neither on religious claims nor on Papal dogma. It is not subject to the objection of "speciesism." Its soundness is compatible with the moral permissibility of euthanasia and contraception. It deals with our intuitions concerning young children.

Finally, this analysis can be viewed as resolving a standard problem—indeed, *the* standard problem—concerning the ethics of abortion. Clearly, it is wrong to kill adult human beings. Clearly, it is not wrong to end the life of some arbitrarily chosen single human cell. Fetuses seem to be like arbitrarily chosen human cells in some respects and like adult humans in other respects. The problem of the ethics of abortion is the problem of determining the fetal property that settles this moral controversy. The thesis of this essay is that the problem of the ethics of abortion, so understood, is solvable.

DISCUSSION QUESTIONS

(1) Exactly what is Thomson trying to show with her examples of the burglar and the people-seeds? Reconstruct and evaluate these arguments from analogy. Remember to say which similarities and differences are important, and why.

(2) Thomson distinguishes what is morally indecent from what is morally wrong. Explain her distinction. Are any acts morally indecent but not morally wrong? If so, give examples. If not, why not? Does Thomson deny that abortion is morally indecent? If so, does she argue for this denial?

(3) In the first part of his article, does Marquis show that the issue of whether a fetus is a person is unresolvable. Why or why not?

(4) Marquis's argument against abortion can be seen as an inference to the best explanation of why it is morally wrong to kill normal adult human beings. What does Marquis take to be the best explanation of this? Why does he think it is better than the alternatives? Can you give an even better explanation that accounts for all the cases that Marquis discusses?

(5) Is Marquis's argument different in important ways from the traditional argument based on the premise that a fetus is a person? Why or why not?

(6) Reconstruct and evaluate the arguments against abortion that are stated or suggested in the following passages from Ronald Reagan, *Abortion and the Conscience of the Nation* (Thomas Nelson; New York, 1984). Be sure to specify the exact conclusion and spell out important suppressed premises. How would an opponent best respond to each argument?

   (a) "We cannot diminish the value of one category of human life—the unborn—without diminishing the value of all human life." (18)

   (b) "I have often said that when we talk about abortion, we are talking about two lives—the life of the mother and the life of the unborn child. Why else do we call a pregnant woman a mother?" (21)

   (c) "I have also said that anyone who doesn't feel sure whether we are talking about a second human life should surely give life the benefit of the doubt. If you don't know whether a body is alive

Continued on next page

or dead, you would never bury it. I think this consideration itself should be enough for all of us to insist on protecting the unborn." (21)

(d) "Medical practice confirms at every step the correctness of these moral sensibilities. Modern medicine treats the unborn child as a patient. Medical pioneers have made great breakthroughs in treating the unborn—for genetic problems, vitamin deficiencies, irregular heart rhythms, and other medical conditions." (21–22)

(e) "I am convinced that Americans do not want to play God with the value of human life. It is not for us to decide who is worthy to live and who is not." (30)

(f) "Malcolm Muggeridge, the English writer, goes right to the heart of the matter: 'Either life is always and in all circumstances sacred, or intrinsically of no account; it is inconceivable that it should be in some cases the one and in some the other.'" (34)

(7) Reconstruct and evaluate the arguments in defense of abortion that are stated or suggested in the following passages from Mary Gordon, "A Moral Choice," *Atlantic Monthly*, April 1990, 78–84. Be sure to specify the exact conclusion and spell out important suppressed premises. How would an opponent best respond to each argument?

(a) "Common sense, experience, and linguistic usage point clearly to the fact that we habitually consider, for example, a seven-week-old fetus to be different from a seven-month-old one. . . . We have different language for the experience of the involuntary expulsion of the fetus from the womb depending upon the point of gestation at which the expulsion occurs. If it occurs early in the pregnancy, we call it a miscarriage; if late, we call it a stillbirth." (80)

(b) "Our ritual and religious practices underscore the fact that we make distinctions among fetuses. If a woman took the bloody matter—indistinguishable from a heavy period—of an early miscarriage and insisted upon putting it in a tiny coffin and marking its grave, we would have serious concerns about her mental health. By the same token, we would feel squeamish about flushing a seven-month-old fetus down the toilet—something we would normally do with an early miscarriage. There are no prayers for the matter of a miscarriage, nor do we feel there should be. Even a Catholic priest would not baptize the issue of an early miscarriage." (80)

(c) "We must make decisions on abortion based on an understanding of how people really do live. We must be able to say that poverty is worse than not being poor, that having dignified and meaningful work is better than working in conditions of degradation, that raising a child one loves and has desired is better than raising a child in resentment and rage, that it is better for a twelve-year-old not to endure the trauma of having a child when she is herself a child." (81–82)

(d) "It is possible for a woman to have a sexual life unriddled by fear only if she can be confident that she need not pay for a failure of technology or judgment (and who among us has never once been swept away in the heat of a sexual moment?) by taking upon herself the crushing burden of unchosen motherhood." (82)

(e) "There are some undeniable bad consequences of a woman's being forced to bear a child against her will. First is the trauma of going through a pregnancy and giving birth to a child who is not desired, a trauma more long-lasting than that experienced by some (only some) women who experience an early abortion. The grief of giving up a child at its birth—and at nine months it is a child one has felt move inside one's body—is underestimated both by anti-choice partisans and by those for whom access to adoptable children is important. This grief should not be forced on any woman—or, indeed, encouraged by public policy." (84)

(f) "We must be realistic about the impact on society of millions of unwanted children in an overpopulated world." (84)

(g) "Making abortion illegal will result in the deaths of women, as it has always done. Is our historical memory so short that none of us remember aunts, sisters, friends, or mothers who were killed or rendered sterile by septic abortions? . . . Can anyone genuinely say that it would be a moral good for us as a society to return to those conditions?" (84)

(8) Determine whether you think abortion is morally wrong in the following cases:

(a) where the mother is in danger of dying if she does not have an abortion,

(b) where the pregnancy is due to rape,

(c) where contraception was used, but it failed,

(d) where the fetus has a disease that usually causes death within a year or two,

Continued on next page

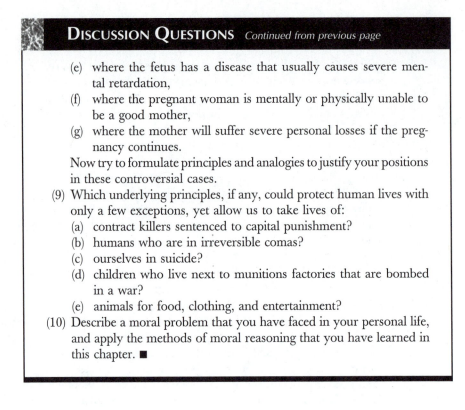

DISCUSSION QUESTIONS   *Continued from previous page*

(e)   where the fetus has a disease that usually causes severe mental retardation,

(f)   where the pregnant woman is mentally or physically unable to be a good mother,

(g)   where the mother will suffer severe personal losses if the pregnancy continues.

Now try to formulate principles and analogies to justify your positions in these controversial cases.

(9)   Which underlying principles, if any, could protect human lives with only a few exceptions, yet allow us to take lives of:

(a)   contract killers sentenced to capital punishment?

(b)   humans who are in irreversible comas?

(c)   ourselves in suicide?

(d)   children who live next to munitions factories that are bombed in a war?

(e)   animals for food, clothing, and entertainment?

(10)   Describe a moral problem that you have faced in your personal life, and apply the methods of moral reasoning that you have learned in this chapter. ■

Chapter Fourteen

SCIENTIFIC REASONING

The products of science are all around us. We depend on science when we drive cars, listen to compact discs, and cook food in a microwave. Still, few people understand how science operates. To some, the scientific enterprise seems to consist of nothing more than amassing huge quantities of data to prove or disprove some hypothesis. Of course, careful observation and experimental data are the final court of appeal in much scientific research, but there is more to science than just collecting and organizing data. One way to see this is to look closely at the ways in which scientists talk. When scientists praise each other's work, they sometimes say that the analysis of some phenomenon is profound and far-reaching, or even elegant, beautiful, and tasteful. This kind of praise would be out of place if the point of science were simply to amass data and test hypotheses. Such praise is appropriate because one important point of scientific theory is to make sense of nature, to explain it, to make it more intelligible. To choose among conflicting scientific theories, we have to decide which theory makes the most sense and provides the best explanations. It is in its explanatory power that a scientific theory can be elegant, beautiful, or even tasteful.

STANDARD SCIENCE

The beginning of science lies in observation. When we look at the world around us, we see that many things happen. Apples fall off trees, the leaves of some trees change color in the autumn, the tides come in and go out, chickens lay eggs, and so on. One job of scientists is to describe and classify what happens and what exists. But scientists also wonder *why* some things happen rather than others. Maple trees change color in the fall, and spruce trees do not, but why? Chickens lay eggs, and monkeys do not, but why? A sphere of wood floats in water, and a gold sphere does not, but why? And why does gold float when pressed into the shape of a boat? These questions ask for *explanations*.

To provide an explanation, scientists often give arguments of the kind discussed in Chapter 11. The event to be explained is derived from a general principle plus a statement of initial conditions or particular facts. For example, given the general principle that a solid sphere floats in water if and only if it is less dense than water, and also given the particular facts that wood is less dense than water, whereas gold is more dense than water, we can explain why a wooden sphere floats in water and a gold sphere does not.

Scientists often seek *deeper* explanations by asking why certain general principles themselves are true. The principle that a sphere floats in water only when it is less dense than water can be explained as an instance of the more general principle that *anything* floats only when it displaces more than its own weight in water. This broader principle not only explains why a wooden sphere floats in water but also why a piece of gold will float when molded into the form of a boat. This broader principle is in turn explained by deriving it from even more basic principles about gravity and the mutual repulsion of molecules. A larger scientific theory is thus used to explain not only why particular things happen but also why certain general principles hold.

Of course, scientists often put forward conflicting theories, so we need some way to test which theory is correct. One simple method is to use the theory to make *predictions*. Since an explanation depends on principles that are general, these principles have implications beyond the particular phenomenon that they were originally intended to explain. The theory thus predicts what will happen in circumstances that the scientist has not yet observed. We can then test the theory by seeing whether these predictions hold true. For example, we can make spheres out of a wide variety of materials, calculate their densities, and then see which ones float. If any sphere floats that is denser than water, then we have to give up our principle that a sphere floats in water *only if* it is less dense than water. (This is an application of the necessary-condition test discussed in Chapter 8.) If we find a sphere that is less dense than water but does not float, then we have to give up the principle that a sphere floats *if* it is less dense than water. (This is an application of the sufficient-condition test discussed in Chapter 8.) These methods help us rule out certain scientific principles, but the fact that a principle implies true predictions does not, by itself, prove that the principle is true. That argument would commit something like the fallacy of affirming the consequent. (See Chapter 5.) Nonetheless, we can still say that a theory is *confirmed* if it yields true predictions, and it is confirmed more strongly if it yields more, more-varied, and more-unexpected true predictions.

Scientific method is actually much more complex than this simple example suggests. This becomes apparent when we encounter *anomalies*. Suppose we have confirmed and explained the principle that a sphere floats in water if and only if it is less dense than water. Suppose also that another principle is well confirmed: a substance gets smaller and more dense as it gets colder. Taken together, these principles predict that a sphere of ice should sink in water. Ice is colder than water, so, according to the second principle, ice should be more dense than water, and that, given the first principle, means that it should not float in water. Of course, our prediction is wrong, since spheres of ice do float in water. What do we do now? The obvious solution is to modify the principle that a substance gets smaller and more dense as it gets colder. This holds for most substances, but not for water. Water expands and thus gets less dense as it freezes.

We could have tried another solution. We could have denied the other principle: that a sphere floats in water if and only if it is less dense than water. Why do scientists not do this? One reason is that we have independent evidence that water expands when it freezes. That is why jars of water burst when they are left in a freezer. Another reason is that we could not give up this principle alone, since it follows from more-basic principles about gravity and the mutual repulsion of molecules. Thus, many other areas of science would be affected if we gave up the principle that a sphere floats in water if and only if it is less dense than water. That all these other scientific theories are not only well confirmed but useful is what makes scientists give up one principle rather than another when an anomaly arises.

At this point we might seek an even deeper explanation and ask why water expands when it freezes. In fact, to this day, nobody seems to have a fully adequate explanation of this common phenomenon. There are various theories but no agreement about how to explain the expansion of water. Does this show that certain phenomena are beyond scientific understanding? Probably not. But it does suggest that science may never be complete. More questions arise as science progresses, and there may always be questions that remain unanswered. As scientists discover and explain more and more phenomena and see connections among principles in different areas, every new step gives rise to more questions that need to be answered. That is one way in which science makes progress.

CONFLICTING SCIENTIFIC INTERPRETATIONS

Another type of scientific development is more radical—knowledge is not simply extended, but instead one scientific framework is replaced (or largely replaced) by another. In biology, the germ theory of disease and the theory of evolution through natural selection are examples of such revolutionary developments. Einstein's theory of relativity and the rise of quantum mechanics were also revolutionary developments. Indeed, every branch of science has undergone at least one such revolutionary change during the pasts few centuries.

There are some important differences between scientific progress within a framework and the replacement of one framework by another.[1] In the first place, such changes in framework usually meet with strong resistance. A new conceptual framework will be unfamiliar and hard to understand, and may even seem absurd or unintelligible. Even today, for example, the thought that the earth is spinning on its axis and revolving around the sun seems completely counter to our common-sense view of the world. Also, arguments on behalf of a new framework will be very different from arguments that occur *within* a framework. Disputes over conceptual frameworks cannot be settled by a straightforward appeal to facts. The long debate between Albert Einstein and Niels Bohr concerning quantum theory did not turn upon matters of fact, but upon their interpretation. Einstein could not accept the indeterminacy involved in the quantum theory's interpretation of the world, and he worked until the end of his life to find some alternative to it. At present, almost no scientist shares Einstein's reservations.

The selection given below illustrates a clash between two such scientific frameworks. It is taken from Galileo's *Dialogue Concerning the Two World Systems—Ptolemaic and Copernican.* The interlocutors are Salviati, Sagredo, and Simplicio. Salviati represents the Copernican system; Simplicio, the Ptolemaic system; Sagredo acts as a moderator, forcing the other two participants in the dialogue to clarify and defend their positions. In attacking the Copernican system, Simplicio lists various arguments from Aristotle that are supposed to show that the earth does not move. Some of these arguments are taken, he says,

> from experiments with heavy bodies which, falling from a height, go perpendicularly to the surface of the earth. Similarly, projectiles thrown vertically upward come down again perpendicularly by the same line, even though they have been thrown to immense height. These arguments are necessary proofs that their motion is toward the center of the earth, which, without moving in the least, awaits and receives them.[2]

Salviati replies that these phenomena do not show that the Ptolemaic system is correct and the Copernican system incorrect, since they can be explained in either world system. More generally, Salviati argues that no terrestrial phenomenon—that is, no phenomenon observable on the earth—can be cited to show that one of these systems is true and the other false. For that matter, no celestial phenomena will settle this issue either, since both world systems provide interpretations of the motions of heavenly bodies. That proponents of each of these systems can agree

---

[1] Thomas Kuhn gives prominence to this difference in his important work, *The Structure of Scientific Revolutions,* 2d ed. (Chicago: University of Chicago Press, 1970).

[2] Galileo Galilei, *Dialogue Concerning the Two World Systems—Ptolemaic and Copernican,* trans. Stillman Drake (Berkeley and Los Angeles: University of California Press, 1953), 125. The extract below is from 139–49.

on particular facts, yet disagree profoundly on their correct interpretation, shows that we are dealing with a conflict between general frameworks, or general world systems. Arguments of this kind are quite different from those that take place within a given scientific framework.

■ DIALOGUE CONCERNING THE TWO WORLD SYSTEMS— PTOLEMAIC AND COPERNICAN
by Galileo Galilei

SALVIATI: Aristotle says, then, that a most certain proof of the earth's being motionless is that things projected perpendicularly upward are seen to return by the same line to the same place from which they were thrown, even though the movement is extremely high. This, he argues, could not happen if the earth moved, since in the time during which the projectile is moving upward and then downward it is separated from the earth, and the place from which the projectile began its motion would go a long way toward the east, thanks to the revolving of the earth, and the falling projectile would strike the earth that distance away from the place in question. Thus we can accommodate here the argument of the cannon ball as well as the other argument, used by Aristotle and Ptolemy, of seeing heavy bodies falling from great heights along a straight line perpendicular to the surface of the earth. Now, in order to begin to untie these knots, I ask Simplicio by what means he would prove that freely falling bodies go along straight and perpendicular lines directed toward the center, should anyone refuse to grant this to Aristotle and Ptolemy.

SIMPLICIO: By means of the senses, which assure us that the tower is straight and perpendicular, and which show us that a falling stone goes along grazing it, without deviating a hairsbreadth to one side or the other, and strikes at the foot of the tower exactly under the place from which it was dropped.

SALV: But if it happened that the earth rotated, and consequently carried along the tower, and if the falling stone were seen to graze the side of the tower just the same, what would its motion then have to be?

SIMP: In that case one would have to say "its motions," for there would be one with which it went from top to bottom, and another one needed for following the path of the tower.

SALV: The motion would then be a compound of two motions: the one with which it measures the tower, and the other with which it follows it. From this compounding it would follow that the rock would no longer describe that simple straight perpendicular line, but a slanting one, and perhaps not straight.

SIMP: I don't know about its not being straight, but I understand well enough that it would have to be slanting, and different from the straight perpendicular line it would describe with the earth motionless.

SALV: Hence just from seeing the falling stone graze the tower, you could not say for sure that it described a straight and perpendicular line, unless you first assumed the earth to stand still.

SIMP: Exactly so; for if the earth were moving, the motion of the stone would be slanting and not perpendicular.

SALV: Then here, clear and evident, is the paralogism of Aristotle and of Ptolemy, discovered by you yourself. They take as known that which is intended to be proved.

SIMP: In what way? It looks to me like a syllogism in proper form, and not a *petitio principii*.

SALV: In this way: Does he not, in his proof, take the conclusion as unknown?

SIMP: Unknown, for otherwise it would be superfluous to prove it.

SALV: And the middle term; does he not require that to be known?

SIMP: Of course; [otherwise it would be an attempt to prove *ignotum per aeque ignotum*.]

SALV: Our conclusion, which is unknown and is to be proved; is this not the motionlessness of the earth?

SIMP: That is what it is.

SALV: Is not the middle term, which must be known, the straight and perpendicular fall of the stone?

SIMP: That is the middle term.

SALV: But wasn't it concluded a little while ago that we could not have any knowledge of this fall being straight and perpendicular unless it was first known that the earth stood still? Therefore in your syllogism, the certainty of the middle term is drawn from the uncertainty of the conclusion. Thus you see how, and how badly, it is a paralogism.

SAGREDO: On behalf of Simplicio I should like, if possible, to defend Aristotle, or at least to be better persuaded as to the force of your deduction. You say that seeing the stone graze the tower is not enough to assure us that the motion of the rock is perpendicular (and this is the middle term of the syllogism) unless one assumes the earth to stand still (which is the conclusion to be proved). For if the tower moved along with the earth and the rock grazed it, the motion of the rock would be slanting, and not perpendicular. But I reply that if the tower were moving, it would be impossible for the rock to fall grazing it; therefore, from the scraping fall is inferred the stability of the earth.

SIMP: So it is. For to expect the rock to go grazing the tower if that were carried along by the earth would be requiring the rock to have two natural motions; that is, a straight one toward the center, and a circular one about the center, which is impossible.

SALV: So Aristotle's defense consists in its being impossible, or at least in his having considered it impossible, that the rock might move with a motion mixed of straight and circular. For if he had not held it to be impossible that the stone might move both toward and around the center at the same time, he would have understood how it could happen that the falling rock might go grazing the tower whether that was moving or was standing still, and consequently he would have been able to perceive that this grazing could imply nothing as to the motion or rest of the earth.

Nevertheless this does not excuse Aristotle, not only because if he did have this idea he ought to have said so, it being such an important point in the argument, but also, and more so, because it cannot be said either that such an effect is impossible or that Aristotle considered it impossible. The former cannot be said because, as I shall shortly prove to you, this is not only possible but necessary; and the latter cannot be said either, because Aristotle himself admits that fire moves naturally upward in a straight line and also turns in the diurnal motion which is imparted by the sky to all the element of fire and to the greater part of the air. Therefore if he saw no impossibility in the mixing of straight-upward with circular motion, as communicated to fire and to the air up as far as the moon's orbit, no more should he deem this impossible with regard to the rock's straight-downward motion and the circular motion natural to the entire globe of the earth, of which the rock is a part.

SIMP: It does not look that way to me at all. If the element of fire goes around together with the air, this is a very easy and even a necessary thing for a particle of fire, which, rising high from the earth, receives that very motion in passing through the moving air, being so tenuous and light a body and so easily moved. But it is quite incredible that a very heavy rock or a cannon ball which is dropped without restraint should let itself be budged by the air or by anything else. Besides which, there is the very appropriate experiment of the stone dropped from the top of the mast of a ship, which falls to the foot of the mast when the ship is standing still, but falls as far from that same point when the ship is sailing as the ship is perceived to have advanced during the time of the fall, this being several yards when the ship's course is rapid. . . .

SALV: Tell me, Simplicio: Do you feel convinced that the experiment on the ship squares so well with our purpose that one may reasonably believe that whatever is seen to occur there must also take place on the terrestrial globe?

SIMP: So far, yes; . . .

SALV: Rather, I hope that you will stick to it, and firmly insist that the result on the earth must correspond to that on the ship, so that when the latter is perceived to be prejudicial to your case you will not be tempted to change your mind.

You say, then, that since when the ship stands still the rock falls to the foot of the mast, and when the ship is in motion it falls apart from there, then conversely, from the falling of the rock at the foot it is inferred that the ship stands still, and from its falling away it may be deduced that the ship is moving. And since what happens on the ship must likewise happen on the land, from the falling of the rock at the foot of the tower one necessarily infers the immobility of the terrestrial globe. Is that your argument?

SIMP: That is exactly it, briefly stated, which makes it easy to understand.

SALV: Now tell me: If the stone dropped from the top of the mast when the ship was sailing rapidly fell in exactly the same place on the ship to which it fell when the ship was standing still, what use could you make of this falling with regard to determining whether the vessel stood still or moved?

SIMP: Absolutely none; just as by the beating of the pulse, for instance, you cannot know whether a person is asleep or awake, since the pulse beats in the same manner in sleeping as in waking.

SALV: Very good. Now, have you ever made this experiment of the ship?

SIMP: I have never made it, but I certainly believe that the authorities who adduced it had carefully observed it. Besides, the cause of the difference is so exactly known that there is no room for doubt.

SALV: You yourself are sufficient evidence that those authorities may have offered it without having performed it, for you take it as certain without having done it, and commit yourself to the good faith of their dictum. Similarly it not only may be, but must be that they did the same thing too—I mean, put faith in their predecessors, right on back without ever arriving at anyone who had performed it. For anyone who does will find that the experiment shows exactly the opposite of what is written: that is, it will show that the stone always falls in the same place on the ship: whether the ship is standing still or moving with any speed you please. Therefore, the same cause holding good on the earth as on the ship, nothing can be inferred about the earth's motion or rest from the stone falling always perpendicularly to the foot of the tower.

SIMP: If you had referred me to any other agency than experiment, I think that our dispute would not soon come to an end; for this appears to me to be a thing so remote from human reason that there is no place in it for credulity or probability.

SALV: For me there is, just the same.

SIMP: So you have not made a hundred tests, or even one? And yet you so freely declare it to be certain? I shall retain my incredulity, and my own confidence that the experiment has been made by the most important authors who make use of it, and that it shows what they say it does.

SALV: Without experiment, I am sure that the effect will happen as I tell you, because it must happen that way; and I might add that you yourself also know that it cannot happen otherwise, no matter how you may pretend not to know it—or give that impression. But I am so handy at picking people's brains that I shall make you confess this in spite of yourself. . . .

Now tell me: Suppose you have a plane surface as smooth as a mirror and made of some hard material like steel. This is not parallel to the horizon, but somewhat inclined, and upon it you have placed a ball which is perfectly spherical and of some hard and heavy material like bronze. What do you believe this will do when released? Do you think, as I do, that it will remain still?

SIMP: If that surface is tilted?

SALV: Yes, that is what was assumed.

SIMP: I do not believe that it would stay still at all; rather, I am sure that it would spontaneously roll down. . . .

SALV: Now how long would the ball continue to roll, and how fast? Remember that I said a perfectly round ball and a highly polished surface, in order to remove all external and accidental impediments. Similarly I want you to take away any impediment of the air caused by its resistance to separation, and all other accidental obstacles, if there are any.

SIMP: I completely understood you, and to your question I reply that the ball would continue to move indefinitely, as far as the slope of the surface extended, and with a continually accelerated motion. For such is the nature of heavy bodies, which *vires acquirunt eundo*; and the greater the slope, the greater would be the velocity.

SALV: But if one wanted the ball to move upward on this same surface, do you think it would go?

SIMP: Not spontaneously, no; but drawn or thrown forcibly, it would.

SALV: And if it were thrust along with some impetus impressed forcibly upon it, what would its motion be, and how great?

SIMP: The motion would constantly slow down and be retarded, being contrary to nature, and would be of longer or shorter duration according to the greater or lesser impulse and the lesser or greater slope upward.

SALV: Very well: up to this point you have explained to me the events of motion upon two different planes. On the downward inclined plane, the heavy moving body spontaneously descends and continually accelerates, and to keep it at rest requires the use of force. On the upward slope, force is needed to thrust it along or even to hold it still, and motion which is impressed upon it continually diminishes until it is entirely annihilated. You say also that a difference in the two instances arises from the greater or lesser upward or downward slope of the plane, so that from a greater slope downward there follows a greater speed, while on the contrary upon the upward slope a given movable body thrown with a given force moves farther according as the slope is less.

Now tell me what would happen to the same movable body placed upon a surface with no slope upward or downward.

SIMP: Here I must think a moment about my reply. There being no downward slope, there can be no natural tendency toward motion; and there being no upward slope, there can be no resistance to being moved, so there would be an indifference between the propensity and the resistance to motion. Therefore it seems to me that it ought naturally to remain stable. But I forgot; it was not so very long ago that Sagredo gave me to understand that this is what would happen.

SALV: I believe it would do so if one set the ball down firmly. But what would happen if it were given an impetus in any direction?

SIMP: It must follow that it would move in that direction.

SALV: But with what sort of movement? One continually accelerated, as on the downward plane, or increasingly retarded as on the upward one?

SIMP: I cannot see any cause for acceleration or deceleration, there being no slope upward or downward.

SALV: Exactly so. But if there is no cause for the ball's retardation, there ought to be still less for its coming to rest; so how far would you have the ball continue to move?

SIMP: As far as the extension of the surface continued without rising or falling.

SALV: Then if such a space were unbounded, the motion on it would likewise be boundless? That is, perpetual?

SIMP: It seems so to me, if the movable body were of durable material.

SALV: That is of course assumed, since we said that all external and accidental impediments were to be removed, and any fragility on the part of the moving body would in this case be one of the accidental impediments.

Now tell me, what do you consider to be the cause of the ball moving spontaneously on the downward inclined plane, but only by force on the one tilted upward?

SIMP: That the tendency of heavy bodies is to move toward the center of the earth, and to move upward from its circumference only with force; now the downward surface is that which gets closer to the center, while the upward one gets farther away.

SALV: Then in order for a surface to be neither downward nor upward, all its parts must be equally distant from the center. Are there any such surfaces in the world?

SIMP: Plenty of them; such would be the surface of our terrestrial globe· if it were smooth, and not rough and mountainous as it is. But there is that of the water, when it is placid and tranquil.

SALV: Then a ship, when it moves over a calm sea, is one of these movables which courses over a surface that is tilted neither up nor down, and if all external and accidental obstacles were removed, it would thus be disposed to move incessantly and uniformly from an impulse once received?

SIMP: It seems that it ought to be.

SALV: Now as to that stone which is on top of the mast: does it not move, carried by the ship, both of them going along the circumference of a circle about its center? And consequently is there not in it an ineradicable motion, all external impediments being removed? And is not this motion as fast as that of the ship?

SIMP: All this is true, but what next?

SALV: Go on and draw the final consequence by yourself, if by yourself you have known all the premises.

SIMP: By the final conclusion you mean that the stone, moving with an indelibly impressed motion, is not going to leave the ship, but will follow it, and finally will fall at the same place where it fell when the ship remained motionless. And I, too, say that this would follow if there were no external impediments to disturb the motion of the stone after it was set free. But there are two such impediments; one is the inability of the movable body to split the air with its own impetus alone, once it has lost the force from the oars which it shared as part of the ship while it was on the mast; the other is the new motion of falling downward, which must impede its other, forward, motion.

SALV: As for the impediment of the air, I do not deny that to you, and if the falling body were of very light material, like a feather or a tuft of wool, the retardation would be quite considerable. But in a heavy stone it is insignificant, and if, as you yourself just said a little while ago, the force of the wildest wind is not enough to move a large stone from its place, just imagine how much the quiet air could accomplish upon meeting a rock which moved no faster than the ship! All the same, as I said, I concede to you the small effect which may depend upon such an impediment, just as I know you will concede to me that if the air were moving at the same speed as the ship and the rock, this impediment would be absolutely nil.

As for the other, the supervening motion downward, in the first place it is obvious that these two motions (I mean the circular around the center and the straight motion toward the center) are not contraries, nor are they destructive of one another, nor incompatible. As to the moving body, it has no resistance whatever to such a motion, for you yourself have already granted the resistance to be against motion which increases the distance from the center, and the tendency to be toward motion which approaches the center. From this it follows necessarily that the moving body has neither a resistance nor a propensity to motion which does not approach toward or depart from the center, and in consequence no cause for diminution in the property impressed upon it. Hence the cause of motion is not a single one which must be weakened by the new action, but there exist two distinct causes. Of these, heaviness attends only to the drawing of the movable body toward the center, and impressed force only to its being led around the center, so no occasion remains for any impediment.

WHAT KILLED THE DINOSAURS?

Although the Copernican worldview has come to dominate contemporary astronomy, many other scientific disputes, of course, remain unsettled. As an example of a live scientific problem, we have chosen the question of what caused the mass extinction during which the dinosaurs died out. This issue is not about overall scientific frameworks or paradigms, as was the debate started by Copernicus. Nonetheless, scientific views about what killed the dinosaurs are important both because of their relation to the origin of human life and because of their implications for the methodology of geology and related sciences, which usually try to explain the world in terms of gradual evolution rather than sudden catastrophes. Besides, the dinosaurs are simply fascinating in themselves.

The following articles, from *Scientific American*, October 1990, 78–92, present complex and yet clear arguments for opposing positions on the death of the dinosaurs. Although more information might be needed to resolve this debate fully, these articles include wonderful illustrations of the kinds of arguments scientists use to support their positions, and that is our main concern here.

■ **AN EXTRATERRESTRIAL IMPACT**
by Walter Alvarez and Frank Asaro

About 65 million years ago something killed half of all the life on the earth. This sensational crime wiped out the dinosaurs, until then undisputed masters of the animal kingdom, and left the humble mammals to inherit their estate. Human beings, descended from those survivors, cannot avoid asking who or what committed the mass murder and what permitted our distant ancestors to survive.

For the past dozen years researchers from around the world, in disciplines ranging from paleontology to astrophysics, have mustered their observational skills, experimental ingenuity and theoretical imagination in an effort to answer these questions. Those of us involved in it have lived through long months of painstaking measurement, periods of bewilderment, flashes of insight and episodes of great excitement when parts of the puzzle finally fell into place.

We now believe that we have solved the mystery. Some 65 million years ago a giant asteroid or comet plunged out of the sky, striking the earth at a velocity of more than 10 kilometers per second. The enormous energy liberated by that impact touched off a nightmare of environmental disasters, including storms, tsunamis, cold and darkness, greenhouse warming, acid rains and global fires. When quiet returned at last, half the flora and fauna had become extinct. The history of the earth had taken a new and unexpected path.

Other suspects in the dinosaur murder mystery, such as sea level changes, climatic shifts and volcanic eruptions, have alibis that appear to rule them out. Some issues, however, are still unclear: Where was the impact site? Was it a single or multiple impact? Have such impacts occurred on a regular, periodic timetable? What is the role of such catastrophes in evolution?

The puzzle presented by a mass extinction is both like and unlike that of a more recent murder. There is evidence—chemical anomalies, mineral grains and isotopic ratios instead of blood or fingerprints or torn matchbooks—scattered throughout the world. No witnesses remain, however, and no chance exists of obtaining a confession. The passage of millions of years has destroyed or degraded most of the evidence in the case, leaving only the subtlest clues.

Indeed, it is difficult even to be sure which of the individual fossils that survive are those of victims killed by the impact. But paleontologists know there must have been victims because fossil-bearing sedimentary rocks show a great discontinuity 65 million years ago. Creatures such as dinosaurs and ammonites, abundant for tens of millions of years, suddenly disappeared forever. Many other groups of animals and plants were decimated.

This discontinuity defines the boundary between the Cretaceous period, during which dinosaurs reigned supreme, and the Tertiary, which saw the rise of the mammals. (It is known as the KT boundary after *Kreide*, the German word for "Cretaceous.")

When we began to study the KT boundary, we wanted to find out just how long the extinction had taken to occur. Was it sudden—a few years or centuries— or was it a gradual event that took place over millions of years? Most geologists and paleontologists had always assumed that the extinction had been slow. (These fields have a long tradition of gradualism and are uncomfortable with invoking catastrophes.) Because dinosaur fossils are relatively rare, their age provides little detailed information on the duration of the extinction. It was possible to view the extinction of dinosaurs as gradual.

When paleontologists looked at the fossils of pollen or single-celled marine animals called foraminifera, however, they found the extinction to be very abrupt. In general, smaller organisms produce more abundant fossils and so yield a sharper temporal picture.

The extinction also appears more sudden as paleontologists study closely the fossil record for medium-size animals such as marine invertebrates. Among these are the ammonites (relatives of the modern chambered nautilus), which died out at the end of the Cretaceous period. The best record of their extinction is found in the coastal outcrops of the Bay of Biscay on the border between Spain and France.

In 1986 Peter L. Ward and his colleagues at the University of Washington made detailed studies of these outcrops at Zumaya in Spain. Ward found that the ammonites appeared to die out gradually—one species disappearing after another over an interval of about 170 meters, representing about five million years. But in 1988 Ward studied two nearby sections in France and found evidence that these ammonite species actually survived right up to the KT boundary. The apparent gradual extinction at Zumaya was merely the artifact of an incomplete fossil record. If organisms whose fossils are well preserved died out abruptly, then it is likely that others that perished about the same time, such as dinosaurs, whose remains are more sparsely preserved, did so as well.

This establishes that the extinction was abrupt in geologic terms, but it does not establish how many years this extinction took, because it is a major accomplishment to date a rock to an accuracy of a million years. Intervals in the geologic records can be determined with precision only to within 10,000 years (.01 Myr), a period longer than the entire span of human civilization.

The duration of the mass extinction that marks the KT boundary can be estimated more precisely than this. In the deep-water limestones at Gubbio in Italy, a thin layer of clay separates Cretaceous and Tertiary sediments. The layer, discovered by Isabella Premoli Silva of the University of Milan, is typically about one centimeter thick. In the 1970s one of us (Alvarez) was part of a group that found the clay falls within a six-meter thickness of limestone deposited during the .5-Myr period of reversed geomagnetic polarity designated 29R. On the face of it, this suggests that the clay layer, and the mass extinction it marks, represents a span of no more than .001 Myr, about 1,000 years.

Jan Smit of the University of Amsterdam did a similar study of sediments at Caravaca in southern Spain, where the stratigraphic record is even more precise, and estimated the extinction lasted no more than 50 years. By geologic standards this is blindingly fast!

Our work on the KT boundary began in the late 1970s when we and our Berkeley colleagues Luis W. Alvarez and Helen V. Michel tried to develop a more accurate way to determine how long the Gubbio KT clay layer took to be deposited. Our efforts failed, but they did provide a crucial first clue to the identity of the mass killer. (That is what detectives and scientists need: a lot of hard work and an occasional lucky break.)

The method depended on the rarity of iridium in the earth's crust—about .03 part per billion as compared with 500 parts per billion, for example, in the primitive stony meteorites knows as carbonaceous chondrites. Iridium is rare in the earth's crust because most of the planet's allotment is alloyed with iron in the core.

We suspected that iridium would enter deep-sea sediments, such as those at Gubbio, predominantly through the continual rain of micrometeorites, sometimes called cosmic dust. This constant infall would provide a clock: the more iridium in a sedimentary layer, the longer it must have taken to lay down. Moreover, iridium could be measured at very low concentrations by means of neutron-activation analysis, a technique in which neutron bombardment converts the metal into a radioactive and hence detectable form.

One scenario we considered was that the KT boundary clay layer formed over a period of about 10,000 years when organisms that secrete calcareous shells died out, and so no calcium carbonate (which makes up most of the limestone) was deposited. Most layers at Gubbio contain about 95 percent calcium carbonate and 5 percent clay; the boundary layer contains 50 percent clay. If this scenario was correct, the ratio of iridium to clay would be the same in the boundary clay as in higher and lower layers. If clay deposition had slowed at the same time as calcium carbonate deposition, the ratio would be higher than that in adjacent rocks.

In June of 1978 our first Gubbio iridium analyses were ready. Imagine our astonishment and confusion when we saw that the boundary clay and the immediately adjacent limestone contained far more iridium than any of our scenarios predicted—an amount comparable to that in all the rest of the rock deposited during the 500,000 years of interval 29R.

Clearly, this concentration could not have come from the usual sprinkling of cosmic dust. For a year we debated possible sources, testing and rejecting one idea after another. Then in 1979 we proposed the one solution that had survived our testing: a large comet or asteroid about 10 kilometers in diameter had struck the earth and dumped an enormous quantity of iridium into the atmosphere.

Since we first proposed the impact hypothesis, so much confirming evidence has come to light that most scientists working in the field are persuaded that a great impact occurred. More than 100 scientists in 21 laboratories in 13 countries have found anomalously high levels of iridium at the KT boundary at about 95 sites throughout the world. The anomaly has been found in marine and nonmarine sediments, at outcrops on land and in oceanic sediment cores. Further, we have analyzed enough other sediments to know that iridium anomalies are very rare. As far as we know, the one at the KT boundary is unique.

The iridium anomaly is well explained by impact because the ratio of iridium to elements with similar chemical behavior, such as platinum, osmium, ruthenium, rhodium and gold, is the same in the boundary layer as it is in meteorites. Miriam Kastner of the Scripps Institution of Oceanography, working with our group, has determined that the gold-iridium ratio in the carefully studied KT boundary at Stevns Klint in Denmark agrees to within 5 percent with the ratio in the most primitive meteorites (type 1 carbonaceous chondrites).

Indeed, the ratios of all the platinum-group elements found in the KT boundary give evidence of extraterrestrial origin. George Bekov of the Institute of Spectroscopy in Moscow and one of us (Asaro) have found that the relative abundances of ruthenium, rhodium and iridium can distinguish stony meteorites from terrestrial samples. Analysis of KT boundary samples from Stevns Klint, Turkmenia in the Soviet Union and elsewhere support the impact hypothesis.

So do ratios of isotopes. Jean-Marc Luck, then at the Institute of Physics of the Earth in Paris, and Karl K. Turekian of Yale University found that most of the osmium in KT boundary samples from Denmark and New Mexico could not have come from a continental source, because the abundance of osmium 187 is too low. The ratio of osmium 187 to osmium 186 is higher in continental rocks than in meteorites or in the earth's mantle because those rocks are relatively enriched in rhenium, whose radioactive isotope, rhenium 187, decays to osmium 187. The osmium in KT samples must be extraterrestrial or from the earth's mantle.

Not only does the composition of rocks at the KT boundary suggest impact, but so does their mineralogy. In 1981 Smit discovered another telltale clue: mineral spherules as large as a millimeter in diameter in the Caravaca KT clay. (Alessandro Montanari of Berkeley confirmed their presence in Italy as well.) The spherules originated as droplets of basaltic rock, shock-melted by impact and rapidly cooled during ballistic flight outside the atmosphere, then chemically altered in the boundary clay. They are the basaltic equivalent of the more silica-rich glassy tektites and microtektites that are the known result of smaller impacts. The basaltic chemistry suggests that the impact took place on oceanic crust.

In addition to the spherules, shocked grains of quartz have been discovered by Bruce F. Bohor of the U.S. Geological Survey in Denver and Donald M. Triplehorn of the University of Alaska. Painstaking studies by E. E. Foord, Peter J. Modreski and Glen A. Izett of the USGS show that the grains carry the multiple intersecting planar "lamellae"—bands of deformation—symptomatic of hypervelocity shock. Such grains are found only in known impact craters, at nuclear test sites, in materials subjected to extreme shock in the laboratory—and in the KT boundary.

There is in fact a candidate crater beneath the glacial drift at Manson, Iowa; it lies in a quartz-rich bedrock, and its location is suitable to explain the size and abundance distribution of the shocked quartz grains. At 32 kilometers in diameter, the crater is too small to have been formed by the single body posited as having caused the extinction. Nevertheless, detailed studies of the crater show it to have an age indistinguishable from that of the KT boundary, and so it probably played a part in the mystery.

How would an impact disperse shocked and molten materials around the globe? A 10-kilometer asteroid moving at more than 10 kilometers per second would ram a huge hole in the atmosphere. When it hit the ground, its kinetic energy would be converted to heat in a nonnuclear explosion 10,000 times as strong as the total world arsenal of nuclear weapons. Some vaporized remains of the asteroid and rock from the ground near the impact point would then be ejected through the hole before the air had time to rush back in.

The fireball of incandescent gas created by the explosion would also propel material out of the atmosphere. The fireball of an atmospheric nuclear explosion expands until it reaches the same pressure as the surrounding atmosphere, then rises to an altitude where its density matches that of the surrounding air. At that point, usually around 10 kilometers high, the gas spreads laterally to form the head of the familiar mushroom cloud.

Computer models of explosions with energies of 1,000 megatons—about 20 times the energy of the largest nuclear bombs but only 1/100,000 the energy of the KT impact—have shown that the fireball never reaches pressure equilibrium with the surrounding atmosphere. Instead, as the fireball expands to altitudes where the density of the atmosphere declines significantly, its rise accelerates and the gas leaves the atmosphere at velocities fast enough to escape the earth's gravitational field. The fireball from an even greater asteroid impact would simply burst out the top of the atmosphere, carrying any entrained ejecta with it, sending the material into orbits that could carry it anywhere on the earth.

The impact of a comet-size body on the earth, creating a crater 150 kilometers in diameter would clearly kill everything within sight of the fireball. Researchers are refining their understanding of the means by which an impact would also trigger extinction worldwide. Mechanisms proposed include darkness, cold, fire, acid rain and greenhouse heat.

In our original paper, we proposed that impact-generated dust caused global darkness that resulted in extinctions. According to computer simulations made in 1980 by Richard P. Turco of R&D Associates, O. Brian Toon of the National Aeronautics and Space Administration and their colleagues, dust lofted into the atmosphere by the impact of a 10-kilometer object would block so much light that for months you would literally be unable to see your hand in front of your face.

Without sunlight, plant photosynthesis would stop. Food chains everywhere would collapse. The darkness would also produce extremely cold temperatures, a condition termed impact winter. (After considering the effects of the impact, Turco, Toon and their colleagues went on to study nuclear winter, a related phenomenon as capable of producing mass extinctions today as impact winter was 65 million years ago.)

In 1981 Cesare Emilliani of the University of Miami, Eric Krause of the University of Colorado and Eugene M. Shoemaker of the USGS pointed out that an oceanic impact would loft not only rock dust but also water vapor into the atmosphere. The vapor, trapping the earth's heat, would stay aloft much longer than the dust, and so the impact winter would be followed by greenhouse warming. More recently John D. O'Keefe and Thomas J. Ahrens of the California Institute of Technology have suggested that the impact might have occurred in a limestone area, releasing large volumes of carbon dioxide, another greenhouse gas. Many plants and animals that survived the extreme cold of impact winter could well have been killed by a subsequent period of extreme heat.

Meanwhile John S. Lewis, G. Hampton Watkins, Hyman Hartman and Ronald G. Prinn of the Massachusetts Institute of Technology have calculated that shock heating of the atmosphere during impact would raise temperatures high enough for the oxygen and nitrogen in the air to combine. The resulting nitrous oxide would eventually rain out of the air as nitric acid—an acid rain with a vengeance. This mechanism may well explain the widespread extinction of marine invertebrate plants and animals, whose calcium carbonate shells are soluble in acidic water.

Another killing mechanism came to light when Wendy Wolbach, Ian Gilmore and Edward Anders of the University of Chicago discovered large amounts of soot in the KT boundary clay. If the clay had been laid down in a few years or less, the amount of soot in the boundary would indicate a sudden burning of vegetation equivalent to half of the world's current forests. Jay Meos of the University of Arizona and his colleagues have calculated that infrared radiation from ejecta heated to incandescence while reentering the atmosphere could have ignited fires around the globe.

Detailed studies of the KT boundary sediments may eventually provide evidence supporting a particular killing mechanism. For example, dissolution patterns in the Italian limestone show that bottom waters were acidic immediately after the extinction. And work we have done with William Lowrie of ETH-Zurich shows that those waters also changed briefly from their normal oxidizing state to a reducing condition, possibly because of the massive death of marine organisms.

It has always been a major disappointment that no one has found the 150-kilometer crater a 10-kilometer impacting object should have produced. The crater might be hidden under the Antarctic ice sheet, or it might have been on the 20 percent of the earth's surface that has subsequently been consumed in subduction zones at the edges of oceanic plates. The evidence regarding the location is contradictory: the basaltic spherules in the boundary clay point to an impact on the ocean floor, but the shocked quartz grains argue for a continental hit.

A newly emerging point of view suggests, unlikely as it may seem, that the KT extinction may have been caused by two or more nearly simultaneous impacts. Shoemaker and Piet Hut of the Institute for Advanced Study in Princeton, N.J., have identified a number of mechanisms that could yield multiple impacts, either on the same day or over the course of many years. Double or multiple craters have been found on the earth, the moon and other planets, suggesting that some asteroids may consist of two or more objects mutually orbiting one another. Alternatively, the earth may have been struck by two or more large fragments of a comet nucleus in the process of breaking up.

Multiple impacts over longer periods could have occurred if a dispersing comet nucleus left several large fragments in an earth-crossing orbit. Such impacts could also occur randomly if some other factor increased the average number of comets in the inner solar system. Although not one scenario has won out, collectively they indicate that multiple impacts are not as improbable as might be thought.

The comet theory gains credibility from the discovery of apparently extraterrestrial materials near the KT boundary. Meixun Zhao and Jeffrey L. Bada of the University of California at San Diego analyzed chalk layers just above and below the KT boundary in Denmark. They found amino acids that are not used by life on the earth but do occur in carbonaceous chondrite meteorites. It seems unlikely that amino acids could survive the heat of a large impact, and they in fact do not appear in the KT boundary itself.

Kevin Zahnle and David Grinspoon of NASA have proposed that dust from a disintegrating comet entered the earth's atmosphere over an extended period and carried these extraterrestrial amino acids with it. During that interval the impact of a large fragment of the comet would have caused the KT extinction.

An apparently unrelated line of inquiry, based on statistical rather than chemical analyses, has yielded a hypothesis explaining how comets could hit the earth periodically. In 1984 David M. Raup and John J. Sepkoski, Jr., of the University of Chicago published an analysis of the fossil record, which seemed to indicate that mass extinctions have occurred at 32-million-year intervals. Like most scientists working with the KT boundary, we were very skeptical of their results. But astrophysicist Richard A. Muller of the University of California at Berkeley reexamined Raup and Sepkoski's data and convinced himself that the periodicity was real.

Muller, Marc Davis of Berkeley and Hut hypothesized that a dim, unrecognized companion star orbiting the sun every 32 million years (which they provisionally dubbed Nemesis) might regularly disturb the orbits of comets on the outer fringe of the solar system. The disturbance should send a million-year storm of comets into the inner solar system, greatly increasing the chance of a large impact (or multiple impacts) on the earth. Daniel Whitmire of the University of Southwestern Louisiana and Albert Jackson of Computer Sciences Corporation independently proposed the same hypothesis.

When Muller showed one of us (Alvarez) the paper proposing Nemesis, I was very skeptical. I remember telling him that I thought it was "an ingenious solution to a nonproblem" because I was not convinced of Raup and Sepkoski's evidence for periodic mass extinctions. If the hypothesis was correct, I pointed out, terrestrial impact craters should show the same periodicity in their ages. Muller and I found, to his delight and to my surprise, that crater ages do show essentially the same periodicity as mass extinctions. Since then I have felt that the hypothesis must at least be taken seriously.

It turns out, however, that it is very difficult to find a dim red star close to the sun when one has no idea where to look. Muller and Saul Perlmutter of Berkeley are now about halfway through a computerized telescopic search for a star with the characteristics of Nemesis; they expect to finish in a couple of years. Meanwhile new analysis of crater ages and extinction dates has raised questions about whether they actually are periodic. The small number of events and the sketchy information available make the question difficult to answer unequivocally.

Murder suspects typically must have means, motive and opportunity. An impact certainly had the means to cause the Cretaceous extinction, and the evidence that an impact occurred at exactly the right time points to opportunity. The impact hypothesis provides, if not motive, then at least a mechanism behind the crime. How do other suspects in the killing of dinosaurs fare?

Some have an air-tight alibi: they could not have killed all the different organisms that died at the KT boundary. The venerable notion that mammals ate the dinosaurs' eggs, for example, does not explain the simultaneous extinction of marine foraminifera and ammonites.

Stefan Gartner of Texas A&M University once suggested that marine life was killed by a sudden huge flood of fresh water from the Arctic Ocean, which apparently was isolated from other oceans during the late Cretaceous and filled with fresh water. Yet this ingenious mechanism cannot account for the extinction of the dinosaurs or the loss of many species of land plants.

Other suspects might have had the ability to kill, but they have alibis based on timing. Some scientific detectives have tried to pin the blame for mass extinction on changes in climate or sea level, for example. Such changes, however, take much longer to occur than did the extinction; moreover, they do not seem to have coincided with the extinction, and they have occurred repeatedly throughout the earth's history without accompanying extinctions.

Others consider volcanism a prime suspect. The strongest evidence implicating volcanoes is the Deccan Traps, an enormous outpouring of basaltic lava in India that occurred approximately 65 million years ago. Recent paleomagnetic work by Vincent E. Courtillot [see "A Volcanic Eruption," on page 500] and his colleagues in Paris confirms previous studies. They show that most of the Deccan Traps erupted during a single period of reversed geomagnetic polarity, with slight overlaps into the preceding and succeeding periods of normal polarity. The Paris team has found that the interval in question is probably 29R, during which the KT extinction occurred, although it might be the reversed-polarity interval immediately before or after 29R as well.

Because the outpouring of the Deccan Traps began in one normal interval and ended in the next, the eruptions that gave rise to them must have taken place over at least .5 Myr. Most workers interested in mass extinction therefore have not considered volcanism a serious suspect in a killing that evidently took place over .001 Myr or less.

Some researchers have argued that, contrary to the fossil record, the KT extinctions took place over many thousands of years and that volcanism can account for quartz grains, spherules and the iridium anomaly.

In 1983 William H. Zoller and his colleagues at the University of Maryland at College Park discovered high concentrations of iridium in aerosols from Kilauea volcano in Hawaii collected on filters 50 kilometers away; however, the ratio between iridium and other rare elements in the volcanic aerosols does not match the ratio found at the KT boundary. The ratio of gold to iridium in the Kilauea aerosols is more than 35 times that in the KT boundary at Stevns Klint.

There has also been debate as to whether an explosive volcanic eruption might produce shocked quartz. It now seems agreed, however, that volcanic explosions can produce some deformation but that the distinctive multiple lamellae seen in the KT boundary quartz can only be formed by impact shocks. In addition, John

McHone of Arizona State University has found that they contain stishovite, a form of quartz produced only at pressures far greater than those of volcanic eruptions. And Mark H. Anders of Columbia University and Michael R. Owen of St. Lawrence University have used a technique known as cathode luminescence, in which an electric field causes quartz to glow, to determine the origin of the KT grains. The colors produced by the grains are not volcanic; they argue instead for impact on an ordinary sedimentary sandstone.

Moreover, basaltic spherules in the KT boundary argue against explosive volcanism in any case; spherules might be generated by quieter forms of volcanism, but then they could not be transported worldwide.

The apparent global distribution of the iridium anomaly, shocked quartz and basaltic spherules is strong evidence exonerating volcanism and pointing to impact. Eruptions take place at the bottom of the atmosphere; they send material into the high stratosphere at best. Spherules and quartz grains, if they came from an eruption, would quickly be slowed by atmospheric drag and fall to the ground.

Nevertheless, the enormous eruptions that created the Deccan Traps did occur during a period spanning the KT extinction. Further, they represent the greatest outpouring of lava on land in the past quarter of a billion years (although greater volumes flow continually out of mid-ocean ridges). No investigator can afford to ignore that kind of coincidence.

It seems possible that impact triggered the Deccan Traps volcanism. A few minutes after a large body hit the earth the initial crater would be 40 kilometers deep, and the release of pressure might cause the hot rock of the underlying mantle to melt. Authorities on the origin of volcanic provinces, however, find it very difficult to explain in detail how an impact could trigger large-scale basaltic volcanism.

In the past few years the debate between supporters of each scenario has become polarized: impact proponents have tended to ignore the Deccan Traps as irrelevant, while volcano backers have tried to explain away evidence for impact by suggesting that it is also compatible with volcanism. Our sense is that the argument is a Hegelian one, with an impact thesis and a volcanic antithesis in search of a synthesis whose outlines are as yet unclear.

Even in its present incompletely solved form, the mystery of the KT mass killing carries a number of lessons. The late 18th and early 19th centuries, when the study of the earth was first becoming a science, was a period marked by a long battle between catastrophists—who though that sudden great events were crucial to the evolution of the planet—and uniformitarians—who explained all history in terms of gradual change.

Steven J. Gould of Harvard University has shown how the uniformitarians so thoroughly won this battle that generations of geology students have been taught catastrophism is unscientific. The universe, however, is a violent place, as astronomy has shown, and it is now becoming clear that the earth has also had its violent episodes.

Evidence that a giant impact was responsible for the extinctions at the end of the Cretaceous has finally rendered the catastrophic viewpoint respectable. Future geologists, with the intellectual freedom to think in both uniformitarian and catastrophic terms, have a better chance of truly understanding the processes and history of the planet than did their predecessors.

Catastrophes have an important role to play in evolutionary thinking as well. If a chance impact 65 million years ago wiped out half the life on the earth, then survival of the fittest is not the only factor that drives evolution. Species must not only be well adapted, they must also be lucky.

If chance disaster occasionally wipes out whole arrays of well-adapted organisms, then the history of life is not preordained. There is no inevitable progress leading inexorably to intelligent life—to human beings. Indeed, Norman Sleep of Stanford University and his colleagues have suggested that in the very early history of the earth, when impacts were more frequent, incipient life may have been extinguished more than once.

Impact catastrophes may also prevent evolution from bogging down. The fossil record indicates that in normal times each species becomes increasingly well adapted to its particular ecological niche. Thus, it becomes ever more difficult for another species to evolve into that niche.

As a result, the rate of evolution slows. Wholesale removal of species by impact, however, provides a great opportunity for the survivors to evolve into newly vacant niches. (We have heard graduate students compare this situation with the excellent job prospects they would face if half of all tenured professors were suddenly fired.) Indeed, the fossil record shows that the rate of evolution accelerated immediately after the end of the Cretaceous.

Among the happy survivors of the KT extinction were the early Tertiary mammals, our ancestors. When dinosaurs dominated the earth, mammals seem always to have been small and insignificant. Warm-blooded metabolism, small size, large number of other traits may have suited them to endure the harsh conditions imposed by impact—or they may just have been lucky. And with the removal of the huge reptiles from the scene, mammals began an explosive phase of evolution that eventually produced human intelligence. As detectives attempting to unravel this 65-million-year-old mystery, we find ourselves pausing from time to time and reflecting that we owe our very existence as thinking beings to the impact that destroyed the dinosaurs.

■ A VOLCANIC ERUPTION
by Vincent E. Courtillot

The mysterious mass extinction that took place 65 million years ago has been attributed to either the impact of a large asteroid or a massive volcanic eruption. Both hypotheses presume that clouds of dust and chemical changes in the atmosphere and oceans created an ecological domino effect that eradicated large numbers of animal and plant families. The geologic record generally is consistent with either scenario; the central issue has been how rapid the event was. New evidence implies that the mass extinction occurred over tens or even hundreds of thousands of years. Such a duration closely corresponds to an episode of violent volcanic eruptions in

India that occurred at the time of the mass extinction. Moreover, other extinction events also appear to be roughly simultaneous with periods of major volcanic activity.

The conventional divisions of geologic history reflect times of significant geologic and biological change. The mass extinction 65 million years ago defined the end of the Mesozoic era, when reptiles enjoyed great evolutionary success, and the beginning of the Cenozoic era, when mammals became extremely prevalent. Because the last period of the Mesozoic is the Cretaceous and the first period of the Cenozoic the Tertiary, the time of the most recent mass extinction is called the Cretaceous-Tertiary, or KT, boundary.

At this boundary the dinosaurs met their demise and, even more remarkable, 90 percent of all genera of protozoans and algae disappeared. John J. Sepkoski, Jr., and David M. Raup of the University of Chicago conclude that from 60 to 75 percent of all species vanished then. Equally important, many species, among them the ancestors of human beings, survived.

In 1980 Luis W. and Walter Alvarez (father and son) of the University of California at Berkeley, along with their colleagues Frank Asaro and Helen V. Michel, discovered unusually high concentrations of the metal iridium—from 10 to 100 times the normal levels—in rocks dating from the KT boundary in Italy, Denmark and New Zealand. Iridium is rare in the earth's crust but can be relatively abundant in other parts of the solar system. The Berkeley group therefore concluded that the iridium came from outer space, and thus the asteroid hypothesis was born.

A large asteroid impact would have cloaked the earth with a cloud of dust, resulting in darkness, suppression of photosynthesis, the collapse of food chains and, ultimately, mass extinction. The iridium is contained in a thin layer of clay whose chemical composition differs from that of the layers both above and below the boundary. Alvarez's group interpreted the clay as being the altered remains of the dust thrown up by the impact. In this view the boundary layer was laid down in less than one year, a flickering instant in geologic time. Other unusual findings at the KT boundary, most notably quartz crystals that appear to have been subjected to extremely powerful physical shocks, also could be explained by an asteroid impact.

An alternative to the asteroid hypothesis had already been brewing for some time. As early as 1972 Peter R. Vogt of the Naval Research Laboratory in Washington, D.C., pointed out that extensive volcanism had taken place at roughly the time of the KT boundary, principally in India. The volcanism produced extensive lava flows, known as the Deccan Traps (*deccan* means "southern" in Sanskrit, and *trap* means "staircase" in Dutch). Vogt suggested that the traps might be connected to the many changes that took place at the end of the Cretaceous period.

In the mid-1970s Dewey M. McLean of the Virginia Polytechnic Institute proposed that volcanoes could produce mass extinctions by injecting vast amounts of carbon dioxide into the atmosphere that would trigger abrupt climate changes and alter ocean chemistry. Charles B. Officer and Charles L. Drake of Dartmouth College analyzed sediments from KT boundary sections and concluded that the iridium enrichment and other chemical anomalies at the boundary were not deposited instantaneously but rather over a period of 10,000 to 100,000 years. They also argued that the anomalies were more consistent with a volcanic rather than meteoritic origin.

The amount of time represented by the clay layer at the KT boundary emerged as a major point of contention. Dating a 100-million-year-old rock with a precision of one part in 1,000 (that is, to within 100,000 years) is not yet possible. Yet much of the debate focuses on whether the boundary clay was deposited in less than one year (as would be expected from an impact) or in 10,000 (from an extended period of volcanism).

The sheer size of the Deccan Traps suggests that their formation must have been an important event in the earth's history. Individual lava flows extend well over 10,000 square kilometers and have a volume exceeding 10,000 cubic kilometers. The thickness of the flows averages from 10 to 50 meters and sometimes reaches 150 meters. In western India the accumulation of lava flows is 2,400 meters thick (more than a quarter the height of Mount Everest). The flows may have originally covered more than two million square kilometers, and the total volume may have exceeded two million cubic kilometers.

An important, unresolved question was whether the date and duration of Deccan volcanism are compatible with the age and thickness of the KT boundary. Until recently the lava samples from the Deccan Traps were thought to range in age from 80 to 30 million years (estimated by measuring the decay of the radioactive isotope potassium 40 in rocks). Whether this range was real or just reflected an error in measurement was unknown. So in 1985 I joined forces with a number of colleagues to try to clarify the picture.

One important clue emerged from the fact that the Deccan rocks are basalts, volcanic rocks rich in magnesium, titanium and iron that are rather strongly magnetic. When basaltic lava cools, the magnetization of tiny crystals of iron-titanium oxides in the rock becomes frozen, aligned with the earth's magnetic field. The polarity of the field occasionally reverses, so that the magnetic north pole becomes south and vice versa. These brief reversals—about 10,000 years long—occur in random fashion at a rate that has varied from about one reversal every million years at the end of the Cretaceous to roughly four every million years in recent times.

Jean Besse and Didier Vandamme at the Institute of Physics of the Earth in Paris and I found that more than 80 percent of the rock samples from the Deccan Traps had the same, reversed polarity. Had the volcanism truly continued from 80 to 30 million years ago, we would have expected to find approximately equal numbers of normal- and reverse-magnetized samples, because tens of reversals took place during that 50-million-year stretch.

In fact, the thickest (1,000-meter-thick) exposed sections of the traps record only one or two reversals. We therefore concluded in 1986 that Deccan volcanism began during an interval of normal magnetic activity, climaxed in the next, reversed interval, then waned in a final, normal interval. Judging from the usual frequency of reversals, our results implied that the volcanism could not have lasted much more than one million years.

If so, the spread of ages found by potassium 40 dating must have been wrong. My colleagues Henri Maluski of the University of Montpellier and Gilbert Féraud of the University of Nice and other researchers used a newer, more reliable technique—argon-argon dating—to determine how much potassium 40 had decayed during the lifetime of the rock samples. Their results confirmed that the Deccan flows were laid down over a relatively brief period. Age estimates for the Deccan lavas now cluster between 64 and 68 million years, and much of the remaining scatter in ages may result from alteration of the samples or differing laboratory standards.

Although accurate dating of sedimentary rock is difficult, recent findings by Ashok Sahni of the University of Chandigarh, J. J. Jaeger of the University of Montpellier and their colleagues further narrow estimates of the age of the Deccan Traps. Sediments immediately below the Deccan flows contain dinosaur fossil fragments that seem to date from the Maastrichtian stage, the last eight million years of the Cretaceous. Dinosaur and mammalian teeth and dinosaur egg fragments that appear to be of Maastrichtian age have also been found in layers of sediment between the flows. This implies that Deccan volcanism began during the very last stage of the Cretaceous.

More precise data come from oil-exploration wells on the east coast of India, which crossed three thin trap flows, each separated by a layer of sedimentary rock. The lowest level of lava rests on sedimentary layers that contain fossils of a plankton called *Abatomphalus mayaroensis*, which thrived during the last one million years of the Cretaceous and became extinct shortly thereafter. The sedimentary rock layers between the lava flows also contain fossils from the exact same time, but the layers above the flows do not.

A. mayaroensis fossils appear in strata with normal magnetic polarity that lie below (before) the KT boundary and disappear at the boundary itself, which is located in the next, magnetically reversed set of strata.

The most reasonable conclusion from the various evidence is that Deccan volcanism began during the last normal magnetic interval of the Cretaceous, climaxed during the following reversed interval (at or very near the Cretaceous-Tertiary boundary) and ended in the first normal magnetic interval of the Cenozoic era.

Magnetic and fossil studies together reduce the estimated duration of Deccan volcanism to about 500,000 years, the best time resolution that can be obtained using present techniques. The fact that Deccan volcanism—one of the largest and fastest episodes of lava flow of the past 250 million years—coincided with the KT boundary to within the best time accuracy now attainable made it hard for us to escape the conclusion that a link existed between the Deccan Traps and the mass extinction.

Having established that the Deccan Traps erupted roughly simultaneously with the extinction at the end of the Cretaceous period, we next sought to determine whether a volcanic eruption could explain the observed features of the KT boundary layers. In general, either a huge volcanic eruption or an asteroid impact could plausibly have produced these features.

The unusual iridium-rich deposit that appears to have been laid down simultaneously around the earth need not have come from outer space. William H. Zoller, Ilhan Olmez and their colleagues at the University of Maryland at College Park discovered unusual iridium enhancements in particles emitted by the Kilauea volcano in Hawaii. J. P. Toutain and G. Meyer of the Institute of Physics of the Earth found iridium in particles emitted by another volcano, the Piton de la Fournaise on the island of Réunion, which (as discussed below) is related to the Deccan volcanism. Iridium-rich volcanic dust has been found embedded in the Antarctic ice sheet, thousands of kilometers from the source volcanoes.

The composition of the clay at the boundary layer differs from that of the clays above and below the layer. The usual mineral in clay, illite, is replaced by smectite, which can be created when basaltic rock is altered. Recent studies of the mineralogy of the KT boundary clay at Stevns Klint in Denmark led W. Crawford Elliott of Case Western Reserve University and his co-workers and Birger Schmitz of the University of Göteborg to conclude that the clay consists of a distinctive kind of smectite that in fact is altered volcanic ash.

The KT boundary clay can be simulated by mixing 10 parts of material from the earth's crust with one part of material from common stony meteorites. The earth's mantle (the layer below the crust), however, has a composition similar to that of stony meteorites and so could generate the same chemical anomalies. Karl K. Turekian of Yale University and Jean-Marc Luck, then at the Institute of Physics of the Earth, found that the relative abundance of the elements rhenium and osmium in the clay resembles the ratio in both meteorites and in the earth's mantle.

Peculiar physical features in material from the KT boundary also can be explained by either hypothesis. Boundary layers contain large numbers of tiny spherules. Some spherules consist of clay minerals that appear to be altered remains of molten basaltic droplets, but it is impossible to say whether they originated as volcanic ejecta or from oceanic crust melted by an asteroid impact. Matters are somewhat confused by the fact that at least some of the spheres turned out to be round fossil algae or even recent insect eggs that contaminated the material.

The discovery of shocked, deformed grains of quartz crystal in KT boundary layers, first made by Bruce F. Bohor and Glen A. Izett of the U.S. Geological Survey in Denver, is often considered the strongest evidence in favor of the impact hypothesis. Such shocked grains had been found previously only from known impact craters (such as Meteor Crater in Arizona) or from sites of underground nuclear explosions. They are produced by dynamic shock stress at more than 100,000 times atmospheric pressure, but shocked structures can be produced at much lower pressures if the rock is heated before the shock occurs, as would be the case in a volcanic eruption.

As magma rises to the earth's surface, it decompresses and releases dissolved gases. At the same time, the magma often cools and thickens. If it cools particularly quickly, it becomes so stiff that the gases cannot escape. Pressure therefore builds up, possibly leading to an explosion and powerful shock waves. Such stresses might be sufficient to shock quartz crystals if the temperatures and duration were great enough.

Magma that is rich in silicate material is viscous and especially prone to provoke explosive eruptions; examples of silicic volcanism include Vesuvius and Mount St. Helens. In 1986 Neville L. Carter of Texas A&M University and his associates discovered evidence of shock features similar to those at the KT boundary in rocks from some geologically recent silicic volcanic explosions, such as the large Toba, Sumatra, eruption of 75,000 years ago. Using transmission electron microscopy, Jean-Claude Doukhan of the University of Lille recently found that shock features produced by laboratory impact, meteorite impact and those observed in samples from the KT boundary are all different from one another in some respects and that the similarity between laboratory and meteorite features has been overstated. Shock features from KT samples are decorated with microscopic bubbles that are not observed in samples from meteorite impacts and that seem to indicate a higher formation temperature, compatible with a volcanic origin.

Explosive silicic volcanism commonly precedes periods of relatively quiet, Deccan-type (flood basaltic) volcanism, during which basaltic lava flows freely and copiously. Ten to 15 percent of the volume of lava from known Deccan-type flows erupts in episodes of explosive silicic volcanism. A rising plume of hot magma would melt its way through the continental crust, producing the viscous silicic (acidic) magmas that lead to explosive volcanism.

The unusual chemical and physical features in the KT boundary layers are present worldwide. An asteroid impact could have propelled material into the stratosphere, where it would have been transported around the globe. On the other hand, Richard B. Stothers and his co-workers at the National Aeronautics and Space Administration's Goddard Space Flight Center in Greenbelt, Md., modeled the manner in which fountains of lava, such as those from Kilauea in Hawaii, expel dust and ejecta. When scaled up to the dimensions of the Deccan volcanism, their models predict that large amounts of material should also be lofted into the stratosphere. Atmospheric circulation would distribute material rather evenly between the two hemispheres, no matter where it was originally emitted.

The appalling consequences of an asteroid impact and a massive volcanism would be quite similar. The first effect would have been darkness resulting from large amounts of dust (either impact ejecta or volcanic ash) into the atmosphere. The darkness would have halted photosynthesis, causing food chains to collapse. Such environmental trauma appears to be reflected in the fossil record. Freshwater creatures were much less affected than land- or sea-based ones, perhaps because freshwater animals did not feed on vascular plants (as do many land-dwelling animals) or on photosynthetic plankton (an important food source for marine vertebrates that was devastated at the end of the Cretaceous).

Life would also have been confronted by large-scale toxic acid rain. The heat of a large impact would have triggered chemical reactions in the atmosphere that would in turn produce nitric acid. Alternatively, volcanic eruptions would have emitted sulfur that would form sulfuric acid in the air. The environmental effects of sulfur-rich volcanism can be significant even in the case of fairly moderate eruptions. The 1783 eruption at Laki, Iceland, killed 75 percent of all livestock and eventually 24 percent of the country's population, even though it released only 12 cubic kilometers of basaltic lava. The event was followed by strange dry fogs and an unusually cold winter in the Northern Hemisphere.

Using the Kilauea eruption as a model, Terrence M. Gerlach of Sandia National Laboratory in Albuquerque estimated that the Deccan Traps injected up to 30 trillion tons of carbon dioxide, six trillion tons of sulfur and 60 billion tons of halogens (reactive elements such as chlorine and fluorine) into the lower atmosphere over a few hundred years. The emissions from the Laki eruption seem to have been far greater than would be expected from simply scaling up the figures for Kilauea, so the estimates may represent a lower limit. Airborne sulfur and dust from a 1,000-cubic-kilometer lava flow could decrease average global temperatures by three to five degrees Celsius (five to nine degrees Fahrenheit).

Other factors could contribute to an opposite effect, however. Marc Javoy and Gil Michard, both of the Institute of Physics of the Earth and the University of Paris, propose that sulfur dioxide from Deccan volcanoes turned the ocean surface acidic, killing the algae that normally extract carbon dioxide from the atmosphere and then carry it to the ocean bottom when they die. Acidic ocean waters also would have dissolved carbonate sediments at the bottom, releasing trapped carbon dioxide. Altogether atmospheric carbon dioxide levels would shoot up to about eight times the present concentration, producing a rise in temperature of five degrees C (nine degrees F). The interaction between cooling from dust and warming from carbon dioxide which may occur on widely different time scales) is unclear, but the resulting climate gyrations probably would have been especially traumatic for the global ecosystem. Both the asteroid and volcanic hypotheses predict overlapping cooling and warming effects.

So far the evidence discussed has been equally consistent with both hypotheses. But many details suggest that the mass extinction and odd physical processes that occurred at the end of the Cretaceous took place over hundreds of thousands of years. This period is comparable to the duration of Deccan volcanism but incompatible with a sudden asteroid impact.

A number of paleontologists have pointed out that the extinction at the end of the Cretaceous was not a single, instantaneous event. Extinction rates appear to have started to increase up to a million years before the KT boundary. Even near the boundary, the pattern is not uniform: for instance, planktonic foraminifera and nanoplankton (microscopic calcareous algae) species exhibit different patterns of extinction and recovery. This ragged sequence is known as stepwise mass extinction.

One of the most thorough recent studies of the pattern of extinctions was conducted by Gerta Keller of Princeton University. When she analyzed the well-preserved sections of the KT boundary in Tunisia and Texas, Keller found evidence for a first phase of extinction (also seen in the macrofossil record) that began 300,000 years before the KT iridium event and for another extinction event that took place 50,000 years after the boundary. Keller attributes the first event to falling sea levels and global cooling.

Other evidence confirms that the earth experienced not one but many disruptions at the end of the Cretaceous. Abrupt change occurred, for example, in the abundance of carbon 13 and oxygen 18 (respectively, light and heavy versions of these elements, whose concentrations vary according to the ocean temperature and acidity and to the number of living creatures present). Extinctions and carbon 13 fluctuations observed in strata in Spain occur in magnetic intervals that fit the same normal-reversed-normal polarity pattern found in the Deccan Traps.

Even the iridium appears to display a number of fine fluctuations near the KT boundary. Robert Rocchia and his colleagues at the Atomic Energy Commission and National Center for Scientific Research in Gif-sur-Yvette and Saclay, France, found secondary iridium peaks above and below the primary iridium layer (corresponding to time intervals of about 10,000 years) in KT boundary clay in Spain and Denmark. Rocchia, I and our colleagues found that the layer of iridium enrichment in Gubbio, Italy, seems spread over about 500,000 years. The much discussed shocked quartz crystals exhibit a similar pattern of distribution. Officer and Carter discovered that shocked minerals extend through four meters of the Gubbio section, again corresponding to a time span of about 500,000 years.

James C. Zachos of the University of Rhode Island and his co-workers measured the chemical composition of microscopic fossils from the North Pacific seafloor and found that the productivity of open-sea marine life was suppressed at the time of the KT boundary and for about 500,000 years thereafter. They also concluded that significant environmental changes, including cooling, began at least 200,000 years before the boundary.

Some proponents of the impact theory, most prominently Piet Hut of the Institute for Advanced Study in Princeton, N.J., and his colleagues, quickly substituted a series of comet impacts for the single asteroid impact to explain these findings. The search for an all-encompassing answer also led to the suggestion that the Deccan Traps might mark the site of the asteroid impact, but there are many difficulties with that idea. No traces of an impact have been found in India. Robert S. White of the University of Cambridge has shown that large impacts cannot trigger massive volcanism, because the section of the mantle just below the lithosphere (the relatively rigid crust and upper mantle) does not normally contain large reserves of molten rock. Moreover, Deccan volcanism started during a normal geomagnetic interval, a few hundred thousand years before the reversed magnetic interval containing the KT iridium anomaly and the clay layer.

During the Cretaceous period, volcanism increased, the sea level rose and fell drastically and the global mantle shifted significantly. The Cretaceous period and the one that preceded it, the Jurassic, were also times of major continental breakups. Between 120 and 85 million years ago, the earth's magnetic field did not undergo a single magnetic reversal, but 15 to 20 million years before the KT boundary, the field started reversing again. Reversal frequency, which indicates activity in the earth's core and at the core-mantle boundary, has increased regularly since then to about once every 250,000 years at present.

All these features can be related to an episode of energetic mantle convection that began tens of millions of years before the KT boundary. To me, the existence of overlapping short- and long-term geodynamic, geologic and paleontological anomalies points to a common internal cause.

What might that cause be? A likely answer comes from the theory of mantle hot spots, developed most prominently by W. Jason Morgan of Princeton University and others. Peter L. Olson and Harvey Singer of Johns Hopkins University developed a model that may explain these regions of persistent volcanic activity. A plume of hot, low-density and low-viscosity material rises from the lowermost parts of the mantle, forming a quasi-spherical head as it pushes its way through cooler, thicker mantle. The head keeps growing as long as it is fed by a conduit of molten rock rising from below.

White and Dan P. McKenzie, also of Cambridge, along with Mark Richards and Robert A. Duncan of Oregon State University and myself, think that as a hot mantle plume rises, the crust above the plume lifts and stretches, leading to continental rifting [see "Volcanism at Rifts," by Robert S. White and Dan P. McKenzie; SCIENTIFIC AMERICAN, July, 1989]. The plume material decompresses as it reaches the surface and so melts rapidly (in less than one million years). The head of the plume would elevate a large area of crust, so that when the magma finally breaks through to the surface, it runs rapidly downhill, producing extensive flows.

The Deccan eruptions could have followed the arrival of such a head at the base of the lithosphere. Volcanism from a hot plume would be rapid and highly episodic. Individual flows would be extruded in days or weeks; the next flow would follow years to thousands of years later. The far-reaching ecological consequences of each flow could explain the stepwise mass extinctions.

The giant mantle plume that produced the Deccan Traps should have left structural and dynamic relics. In 1987 the Ocean Drilling Program, led by Duncan, explored and dated an undersea chain of volcanoes that extends from southwest India, near the Deccan Traps, to Réunion, the active volcano east of Madagascar. Réunion is a hot spot volcano—one powered by a deep, rising flow of hot magma from the mantle—that burned its way through the Indian and African continents as they drifted over it. The ages of the Réunion seamounts increase steadily from zero to two million years around Réunion itself to 55 to 60 million years just south of the Deccan Traps.

Richards, Duncan and I believe that the Réunion hot spot may represent the tail of hot magna that would be expected to follow in the wake of the plume that produced the traps. Besse, Vandamme and I verified that the mantle hot spot now beneath Réunion was located precisely under the Deccan Traps at the end of the Cretaceous. There is no trace of the hot spot from before the KT boundary; the episode of violent Deccan volcanism appears to mark the appearance of the hot spot at the surface of the earth.

The internal geologic activity associated with a rising mantle plume fits the behavior of the earth's magnetic field at the time of the KT boundary. Slow convection of the molten iron in the earth's outer core—10 kilometers per year—is thought to produce the earth's magnetic field. Instabilities at the boundary between the core and the mantle above it may cause magnetic reversals.

Heat escaping from the core raises the temperature and so lowers the density of material in the deepest layer of the mantle (called the D″), which grows thicker until it becomes unstable and forms rising plumes of magma. Long durations with few or no magnetic reversals, such as the span from 120 to 85 million years ago, indicate a lack of outer core activity and the growth of the D″ layer.

About 80 million years ago the layer broke up, sending enormous hot magma plumes upward. At this point, flow of heat from the core to the mantle would have increased, and magnetic reversals would have resumed. At typical mantle velocities of about one meter a year, the plumes would have traveled a few million years before reaching the surface, where their sudden decompression of the plumes would have led to explosive volcanism followed by large lava flows. Smaller, secondary plumes would not have reached the surface but could have accelerated mantle convection, seafloor spreading, sea level changes and other geologic disruptions that took place during the Cretaceous.

This kind of geologic upheaval may be a natural consequence of the fact that the earth is an active, complex heat engine composed of layers that have vastly different physical and chemical properties. Smooth, well-regulated mantle convection and brutal, plumelike instabilities are perhaps just two extremes of the ways in which the earth's internal heat escapes to the outside.

If this is indeed the way the earth functions, similar catastrophes should have taken place. In fact, most major, relatively recent extinction events (those since the Mesozoic era began 250 million years ago) seem to correlate in time with a large flood basalt eruption. Interestingly, the longest known period during which the earth's magnetic field did not reverse also ended with the largest mass extinction, the one that marked the dawn of the Mesozoic era. More than 95 percent of marine species disappeared at that time. The 250-million-year-old Siberian Traps are a prime candidate for having caused this extinction.

Both the asteroid impact and volcanic hypotheses imply that short-term catastrophes are of great importance in shaping the evolution of life. This view would seem to contradict the concept of uniformitarianism, a guiding principle of geology that holds that the present state of the world can be explained by invoking currently occurring geologic processes over long intervals. On a qualitative level, volcanic eruptions and meteorite impacts happen all the time and are not unusual. On a quantitative level, however, the event witnessed by the dinosaurs is unlike any other of at least the past 250 million years.

Magnetic reversals in the earth's core and eruptions of large plumes in the mantle may be manifestations of the fact that the earth is a chaotic system. Variations in the frequency of magnetic reversals and breakup of continents over the past few hundred million years hint that the system may be quasi-periodic: catastrophic volcanic episodes seem to occur at intervals of 200 million years, with lesser events spaced some 30 million years apart.

It is tempting to speculate that the dawn of the Paleozoic era 570 million years ago, when multicellular life first appeared, might have coincided with one such episode. Large extinctions abruptly open broad swaths of ecological space that permit new organisms to develop. Events that at first seem to have been disasters may in fact have been agents essential in the evolution of complex life.

DISCUSSION QUESTIONS

(1) Alvarez and Asaro cite a layer of clay found by Isabella Premoli Silva as evidence that the mass extinction took no more than a thousand years. Reconstruct this argument. Be sure to spell out any important suppressed premises.

(2) Alvarez and Asaro argue that the ratio of iridium to other elements in the boundary layer is the same as in meteorites, so the elements in the boundary layer probably also came from meteorites. Reconstruct this as an argument from analogy, and evaluate it using the standards for arguments from analogy discussed in Chapter 8.

(3) Alvarez and Asaro argue that the mass extinction could not have been caused by volcanism in the Deccan Traps because:
  (a) the extinction occurred more quickly than the series of volcanic eruptions,
  (b) the ratio of gold to iridium in volcanic outputs is much higher than in the KT boundary,
  (c) the KT boundary quartz could be formed only at pressures higher than those of volcanic eruptions, and
  (d) the KT boundary iridium, shocked quartz, and basaltic spherules are distributed more widely than they would be if they came from volcanic eruptions.
Reconstruct each of these arguments. How does (or could) Courtillot respond to each of these arguments?

(4) Courtillot cites evidence for
  (a) stepwise mass extinction,
  (b) secondary iridium peaks, and
  (c) a four-meter-thick distribution of shocked quartz crystals
in support of his volcanism hypothesis. Reconstruct his argument from these phenomena to his hypothesis as an inference to the best explanation. How could Alvarez and Asaro best respond?

(5) Courtillot mentions magnetic reversals at several points in his article. In what ways, if at all, does he use this phenomenon to support his hypothesis?

(6) Overall, do you think that the arguments of Alvarez and Asaro or those of Courtillot are stronger? Why? Is either argument strong enough to show that one hypothesis is true? Why or why not?

(7) What more evidence could you look for to support or refute one hypothesis or the other in this debate?

Chapter Fifteen

PHILOSOPHICAL ARGUMENTS

It is not easy to explain the character of philosophical reasoning. Indeed, the nature of philosophical reasoning is itself a philosophical problem. We can, however, acquire some sense of it by comparing philosophical reasoning with reasoning as it occurs in daily life. In the opening chapters of this book we noticed that, in everyday discussions, much is taken for granted and left unsaid. In general, there is no need to state points that are already a matter of agreement. In contrast, philosophers usually try to make underlying assumptions explicit and then subject them to critical examination. But, even for the philosopher, something must trigger an interest in underlying assumptions—and this usually arises when the advance of knowledge creates fundamental conflicts within the system of hitherto accepted assumptions. Thus, much that counts as modern philosophy is an attempt to come to terms with the relationship between modern science and the traditional conception of man's place in the universe.

In recent years, a striking example of such a conflict has been generated by the rise of computer theory and computer technology. Traditionally, humans have cited the capacity to think as the feature that sets them apart from and, of course, above all other creatures. Humans have been defined as rational animals. But we now live in an age in which computers seem able to perform tasks that, had a human being performed them, would certainly count as thinking. Not only can computers perform complex calculations very rapidly, they can also play an excellent game of chess. Do machines think? The question seems forced upon us, and it is more than a semantic quibble. In deciding it, we are also reevaluating the status of an aspect of humanity that has long been considered its unique or distinctive feature. Once we decide whether machines can think, the next question is whether human beings are not themselves merely thinking machines.

The two essays presented in this chapter address such questions. The writer of the first essay, A. M. Turing, is one of the geniuses of this century. He not only developed much of the mathematics that underlies modern computer theory but helped give computers their first remarkable application: the cracking of the German secret codes during World War II. In this essay, Turing considers whether machines can or cannot think. The brilliance of the essay does not depend on the answer he gives to the question, but rather on his attempt to formulate it in a way that would allow reasonable debate to take place concerning it. For this reason, Turing's essay has been considered a classic work on the subject for more than forty years. In the second essay, John Searle presents and defends an analogy intended to refute not only Turing's argument but also any other claim that machines could ever think solely by virtue of having the right formal program.

■ COMPUTING MACHINERY AND INTELLIGENCE*
by A. M. Turing

1. The Imitation Game

I propose to consider the question "Can machines think?" This should begin with definitions of the meaning of the terms "machine" and "think." The definitions might be framed so as to reflect so far as possible the normal use of the words, but this attitude is dangerous. If the meaning of the words "machine" and "think" are to be found by examining how they are commonly used, it is difficult to escape the conclusion that the meaning and the answer to the question, "Can machines think?" is to be sought in a statistical survey such as a Gallup poll. But this is absurd. Instead of attempting such a definition I shall replace the question by another, which is closely related to it and is expressed in relatively unambiguous words.

The new form of the problem can be described in terms of a game which we call the "imitation game." It is played with three people, a man (A), a woman (B),

---

* *Mind*, vol. LIX, No. 236 (1950).

and an interrogator (C) who may be of either sex. The interrogator stays in a room apart from the other two. The object of the game for the interrogator is to determine which of the other two is the man and which is the woman. He knows them by labels X and Y, and at the end of the game he says either "X is A and Y is B" or "X is B and Y is A." The interrogator is allowed to put questions to A and B thus:

C: Will X please tell me the length of his or her hair?

Now suppose X is actually A, then A must answer. It is A's object in the game to try to cause C to make the wrong identification. His answer might therefore be

"My hair is shingled, and the longest strands are about nine inches long."

In order that tones of voice may not help the interrogator the answers should be written, or better still, typewritten. The ideal arrangement is to have a teleprinter communicating between the two rooms. Alternatively the question and answers can be repeated by an intermediary. The object of the game for the third player (B) is to help the interrogator. The best strategy for her is probably to give truthful answers. She can add such things as "I am the woman, don't listen to him!" to her answers, but it will avail nothing as the man can make similar remarks.

We now ask the question, "What will happen when a machine takes the part of A in this game?" Will the interrogator decide wrongly as often when the game is played like this as he does when the game is played between a man and a woman? These questions replace our original, "Can machines think?"

2. Critique of the New Problem

As well as asking, "What is the answer to this new form of the question," one may ask, "Is this new question a worthy one to investigate?" This latter question we investigate without further ado, thereby cutting short an infinite regress.

The new problem has the advantage of drawing a fairly sharp line between the physical and the intellectual capacities of a man. No engineer or chemist claims to be able to produce a material which is indistinguishable from the human skin. It is possible that at some time this might be done, but even supposing this invention available we should feel there was little point in trying to make a "thinking machine" more human by dressing it up in such artificial flesh. The form in which we have set the problem reflects this fact in the condition which prevents the interrogator from seeing or touching the other competitors, or hearing their voices. Some other advantages of the proposed criterion may be shown up by specimen questions and answers. Thus:

Q: Please write me a sonnet on the subject of the Forth Bridge.

A: Count me out on this one. I never could write poetry.

Q: Add 34957 to 70764.

A: (Pause about 30 seconds and then give as answer) 105621.

Q: Do you play chess?

A: Yes.

Q: I have K at my K1, and no other pieces. You have only K at K6 and R
      at R1. It is your move. What do you play?

A: (After a pause of 15 seconds) R-R8 mate.

The question and answer method seems to be suitable for introducing almost
any one of the fields of human endeavor that we wish to include. We do not wish
to penalize the machine for its inability to shine in beauty competitions, nor to
penalize a man for losing in a race against an airplane. The conditions of our game
make these disabilities irrelevant. The "witnesses" can brag, if they consider it
advisable, as much as they please about their charms, strength or heroism, but
the interrogator cannot demand practical demonstrations.

The game may perhaps be criticized on the ground that the odds are weighted
too heavily against the machine. If the man were to try and pretend to be the
machine, he would clearly make a very poor showing. He would be given away
at once by slowness and inaccuracy in arithmetic. May not machines carry out
something which ought to be described as thinking but which is very different
from what a man does? This objection is a very strong one, but at least we can
say that if, nevertheless, a machine can be constructed to play the imitation game
satisfactorily, we need not be troubled by this objection.

It might be urged that when playing the "imitation game" the best strategy
for the machine may possibly be something other than imitation of the behavior
of a man. This may be, but I think it is unlikely that there is any great effect of
this kind. In any case there is no intention to investigate here the theory of the
game, and it will be assumed that the best strategy is to try to provide answers
that would naturally be given by a man.

3. The Machines Concerned in the Game

The question which we put in §1 will not be quite definite until we have specified
what we mean by the word "machine." It is natural that we should wish to permit
every kind of engineering technique to be used in our machines. We also wish to
allow the possibility that an engineer or team of engineers may construct a machine
which works, but whose manner of operation cannot be satisfactorily described by
its constructors because they have applied a method which is largely experimental.
Finally, we wish to exclude from the machines men born in the usual manner. It
is difficult to frame the definitions so as to satisfy these three conditions. One
might for instance insist that the team of engineers should be all of one sex, but
this would not really be satisfactory, for it is probably possible to rear a complete
individual from a single cell of the skin (say) of a man. To do so would be a feat
of biological technique deserving of the very highest praise, but we would not be
inclined to regard it as a case of "constructing a thinking machine." This prompts
us to abandon the requirement that every kind of technique should be permitted.
We are the more ready to do so in view of the fact that the present interest in
"thinking machines" has been aroused by a particular kind of machine, usually
called an "electronic computer" or "digital computer." Following this suggestion
we only permit digital computers to take part in our game.

This restriction appears at first sight to be a very drastic one. I shall attempt to show that it is not so in reality. . . . The digital computers considered [here] are classified among the "discrete state machines." These are the machines which move by sudden jumps or clicks from one quite definite state to another. . . . [A] special property of digital computers [is] that they can mimic any discrete state machine. [This property] is described by saying that they are *universal* machines. The existence of machines with this property has the important consequence that, considerations of speed apart, it is unnecessary to design various new machines to do various computing processes. They can all be done with one digital computer, suitably programed for each case. It will be seen that as a consequence of this all digital computers are in a sense equivalent. . . .

It was suggested tentatively that the question, "Can machines think?" should be replaced by "Are there imaginable digital computers which would do well in the imitation game?" If we wish we can make this superficially more general and ask "Are there discrete state machines which would do well?" But in view of the universality property we see that either of these questions is equivalent to this, "Let us fix our attention on one particular digital computer C. Is it true that by modifying this computer to have an adequate storage, suitably increasing its speed of action, and providing it with an appropriate program, C can be made to play satisfactorily the part of A in the imitation game, the part of B being taken by a man?"

6. Contrary Views on the Main Question

We may now consider the ground to have been cleared and we are ready to proceed to the debate on our question, "Can machines think?" and the variant of it quoted at the end of the last section. We cannot altogether abandon the original form of the problem, for opinions will differ as to the appropriateness of the substitution and we must at least listen to what has to be said in this connection.

It will simplify matters for the reader if I explain first my own beliefs in the matter. Consider first the more accurate form of the question. I believe that in about fifty years' time it will be possible to program computers, with a storage capacity of about 10^9, to make them play the imitation game so well that an average interrogator will not have more than 70 per cent chance of making the right identification after five minutes of questioning. The original question, "Can machines think?" I believe to be too meaningless to deserve discussion. Nevertheless I believe that at the end of the century the use of words and general educated opinion will have altered so much that one will be able to speak of machines thinking without expecting to be contradicted. I believe further that no useful purpose is served by concealing these beliefs. The popular view that scientists proceed inexorably from well-established fact to well-established fact, never being influenced by any unproved conjecture, is quite mistaken. Provided it is made clear which are proved facts and which are conjectures, no harm can result. Conjectures are of great importance since they suggest useful lines of research.

I now proceed to consider opinions opposed to my own.

(1) *The Theological Objection.* Thinking is a function of man's immortal soul.

God has given an immortal soul to every man and woman, but not to any other animal or to machines. Hence no animal or machine can think.

I am unable to accept any part of this, but will attempt to reply in theological terms. I should find the argument more convincing if animals were classed with men, for there is a greater difference, to my mind, between the typical animate and the inanimate than there is between man and the other animals. The arbitrary character of the orthodox view becomes clearer if we consider how it might appear to a member of some other religious community. How do Christians regard the Moslem view that women have no souls? But let us leave this point aside and return to the main argument. It appears to me that the argument quoted above implies a serious restriction of the omnipotence of the Almighty. It is admitted that there are certain things that He cannot do such as making one equal to two, but should we not believe that He has freedom to confer a soul on an elephant if He sees fit? We might expect that He would only exercise this power in conjunction with a mutation which provided the elephant with an appropriately improved brain to minister to the needs of this soul. An argument of exactly similar form may be made for the case of machines. It may seem different because it is more difficult to "swallow." But this really only means that we think it would be less likely that He would consider the circumstances suitable for conferring a soul. The circumstances in question are discussed in the rest of this paper. In attempting to construct such machines we should not be irreverently usurping His power of creating souls, any more than we are in the procreation of children: rather we are, in either case, instruments of His will providing mansions for the souls that He creates.

However, this is mere speculation. I am not very impressed with theological arguments whatever they may be used to support. Such arguments have often been found unsatisfactory in the past. In the time of Galileo it was argued that the texts, "And the sun stood still . . . and hasted not to go down about a whole day" (Joshua x. 13) and "He laid the foundations of the earth, that it should not move at any time" (Psalm cv. 5) were an adequate refutation of the Copernican theory. With our present knowledge such an argument appears futile. When that knowledge was not available it made a quite different impression.

(2) *The "Heads in the Sand" Objection.* "The consequences of machines thinking would be too dreadful. Let us hope and believe that they cannot do so."

This argument is seldom expressed quite so openly as in the form above. But it affects most of us who think about it at all. We like to believe that Man is in some subtle way superior to the rest of creation. It is best if he can be shown to be *necessarily* superior, for then there is no danger of him losing his commanding position. The popularity of the theological argument is clearly connected with this feeling. It is likely to be quite strong in intellectual people, since they value the power of thinking more highly than others, and are more inclined to base their belief in the superiority of Man on this power.

I do not think that this argument is sufficiently substantial to require refutation. Consolation would be more appropriate: perhaps this should be sought in the transmigration of souls.

(3) *The Mathematical Objection.* There are a number of results of mathematical

logic which can be used to show that there are limitations to the powers of discrete state machines. The best known of these results is known as Gödel's theorem, and shows that in any sufficiently powerful logical system statements can be formulated which can neither be proved nor disproved within the system, unless possibly the system itself is inconsistent. There are other, in some respects similar, results due to *Church, Kleene, Rosser,* and *Turing.* The latter result is the most convenient to consider, since it refers directly to machines, whereas the others can only be used in a comparatively indirect argument: for instance if Gödel's theorem is to be used we need in addition to have some means of describing logical systems in terms of machines, and machines in terms of logical systems. The result in question refers to a type of machine which is essentially a digital computer with an infinite capacity. It states that there are certain things that such a machine cannot do. If it is rigged up to give answers to questions as in the imitation game, there will be some questions to which it will either give a wrong answer, or fail to give an answer at all however much time is allowed for a reply. There may, of course, be many such questions, and questions which cannot be answered by one machine may be satisfactorily answered by another. We are of course supposing for the present that the questions are of the kind to which an answer "Yes" or "No" is appropriate, rather than questions such as "What do you think of Picasso?" The questions that we know the machines must fail on are of this type, "Consider the machine specified as follows. ... Will this machine ever answer 'Yes' to any question?" The dots are to be replaced by a description of some machine in a standard form. ... When the machine described bears a certain comparatively simple relation to the machine which is under interrogation, it can be shown that the answer is either wrong or not forthcoming. This is the mathematical result: it is argued that it proves a disability of machines to which the human intellect is not subject.

The short answer to this argument is that although it is established that there are limitations to the powers of any particular machine, it has only been stated, without any sort of proof, that no such limitations apply to the human intellect. But I do not think this view can be dismissed quite so lightly. Whenever one of these machines is asked the appropriate critical question, and gives a definite answer, we know that this answer must be wrong, and this gives us a certain feeling of superiority. Is this feeling illusory? It is no doubt quite genuine, but I do not think too much importance should be attached to it. We too often give wrong answers to questions ourselves to be justified in being very pleased at such evidence of fallibility on the part of the machines. Further, our superiority can only be felt on such an occasion in relation to the one machine over which we have scored our petty triumph. There would be no question of triumphing simultaneously over *all* machines. In short, then, there might be men cleverer than any given machine, but then again there might be other machines cleverer again, and so on.

Those who hold to the mathematical argument would, I think, mostly be willing to accept the imitation game as a basis for discussion. Those who believe in the two previous objections would probably not be interested in any criteria.

(4) *The Argument from Consciousness.* This argument is very well expressed in

Professor Jefferson's Lister Oration for 1949, from which I quote, "Not until a machine can write a sonnet or compose a concerto because of thoughts and emotions felt, and not by the chance fall of symbols, could we agree that machine equals brain—that is, not only write it but know that it had written it. No mechanism could feel (and not merely artificially signal, an easy contrivance) pleasure at its successes, grief when its values fuse, be warmed by flattery, be made miserable by its mistakes, be charmed by sex, be angry or depressed when it cannot get what it wants."

This argument appears to be a denial of the validity of our test. According to the most extreme form of this view the only way by which one could be sure that a machine thinks is to *be* the machine and to feel oneself thinking. One could then describe these feelings to the world, but of course no one would be justified in taking any notice. Likewise according to this view the only way to know that a *man* thinks is to be that particular man. It is in fact the solipsist point of view [which claims that only oneself exists]. It may be the most logical view to hold but it makes communication of ideas difficult. A is liable to believe "A thinks but B does not" while B believes "B thinks but A does not." Instead of arguing continually over this point it is usual to have the polite convention that everyone thinks.

I am sure that Professor Jefferson does not wish to adopt the extreme and solipsist point of view. Probably he would be quite willing to accept the imitation game as a test. The game (with the player B omitted) is frequently used in practice under the name of *viva voce* to discover whether someone really understands something or has "learned it parrot fashion." Let us listen in to a part of such a *viva voce*:

INTERROGATOR: In the first line of your sonnet which reads "Shall I compare thee to a summer's day," would not "a spring day" do as well or better?

WITNESS: It wouldn't scan.

INTERROGATOR: How about "a winter's day." That would scan all right.

WITNESS: Yes, but nobody wants to be compared to a winter's day.

INTERROGATOR: Would you say Mr. Pickwick reminded you of Christmas?

WITNESS : In a way.

INTERROGATOR: Yet Christmas is a winter's day, and I do not think Mr. Pickwick would mind the comparison.

WITNESS: I don't think you're serious. By a winter's day one means a typical winter's day, rather than a special one like Christmas.

And so on. What would Professor Jefferson say if the sonnet-writing machine was able to answer like this in the *viva voce*? I do not know whether he would regard the machine as "merely artificially signaling" these answers, but if the answers were as satisfactory and sustained as in the above passage I do not think he would describe it as "an easy contrivance." This phrase is, I think, intended to cover such devices as the inclusion in the machine of a record of someone reading a sonnet, with appropriate switching to turn it on from time to time.

In short then, I think that most of those who support the argument from consciousness could be persuaded to abandon it rather than be forced into the solipsist position. They will then probably be willing to accept our test.

I do not wish to give the impression that I think there is no mystery about consciousness. There is, for instance, something of a paradox connected with any attempt to localize it. But I do not think these mysteries necessarily need to be solved before we can answer the question with which we are concerned in this paper.

(5) *Arguments from Various Disabilities.* These arguments take the form, "I grant you that you can make machines do all the things you have mentioned but you will never be able to make one to do X." Numerous features X are suggested in this connection. I offer a selection:

> Be kind, resourceful, beautiful, friendly, have initiative, have a sense of humor, tell right from wrong, make mistakes, fall in love, enjoy strawberries and cream, make someone fall in love with it, learn from experience, use words properly, be the subject of its own thought, have as much diversity of behavior as a man, do something really new.

No support is usually offered for these statements. I believe they are mostly founded on the principle of scientific induction. A man has seen thousands of machines in his lifetime. From what he sees of them he draws a number of general conclusions. They are ugly, each is designed for a very limited purpose, when required for a minutely different purpose they are useless, the variety of behavior of any one of them is very small, etc., etc. Naturally he concludes that these are necessary properties of machines in general. Many of these limitations are associated with the very small storage capacity of most machines. (I am assuming that the idea of storage capacity is extended in some way to cover machines other than discrete state machines. The exact definition does not matter as no mathematical accuracy is claimed in the present discussion.) A few years ago, when very little had been heard of digital computers, it was possible to elicit much incredulity concerning them, if one mentioned their properties without describing their construction. That was presumably due to a similar application of the principle of scientific induction. These applications of the principle are of course largely unconscious. When a burned child fears the fire and shows that he fears it by avoiding it, I should say that he was applying scientific induction. (I could of course also describe his behavior in many other ways.) The works and customs of mankind do not seem to be very suitable material to which to apply scientific induction. A very large part of space-time must be investigated if reliable results are to be obtained. Otherwise we may (as most English children do) decide that everybody speaks English, and that it is silly to learn French.

There are, however, special remarks to be made about many of the disabilities that have been mentioned. The inability to enjoy strawberries and cream may have struck the reader as frivolous. Possibly a machine might be made to enjoy this delicious dish, but any attempt to make one do so would be idiotic. What is important about this disability is that it contributes to some of the other disabilities, e.g., to the difficulty of the same kind of friendliness occurring between man and machine as between white man and white man, or between black man and black man.

The claim that "machines cannot make mistakes" seems a curious one. One is tempted to retort, "Are they any the worse for that?" But let us adopt a more sympathetic attitude, and try to see what is really meant. I think this criticism can be explained in terms of the imitation game. It is claimed that the interrogator could distinguish the machine from the man simply by setting them a number of problems in arithmetic. The machine would be unmasked because of its deadly accuracy. The reply to this is simple. The machine (programed for playing the game) would not attempt to give the *right* answers to the arithmetic problems. It would deliberately introduce mistakes in a manner calculated to confuse the interrogator. A mechanical fault would probably show itself through an unsuitable decision as to what sort of a mistake to make in the arithmetic. Even this interpretation of the criticism is not sufficiently sympathetic. But we cannot afford the space to go into it much further. It seems to me that this criticism depends on a confusion between two kinds of mistakes. We may call them "errors of functioning" and "errors of conclusion." Errors of functioning are due to some mechanical or electrical fault which causes the machine to behave otherwise than it was designed to do. In philosophical discussions one likes to ignore the possibility of such errors; one is therefore discussing "abstract machines." These abstract machines are mathematical fictions rather than physical objects. By definition they are incapable of errors of functioning. In this sense we can truly say that "machines can never make mistakes." Errors of conclusion can only arise when some meaning is attached to the output signals from the machine. The machine might, for instance, type out mathematical equations, or sentences in English. When a false proposition is typed we say that the machine has committed an error of conclusion. There is clearly no reason at all for saying that a machine cannot make this kind of mistake. It might do nothing but type out repeatedly "$0 = 1$." To take a less perverse example, it might have some method for drawing conclusions by scientific induction. We must expect such a method to lead occasionally to erroneous results.

The claim that a machine cannot be the subject of its own thought can of course only be answered if it can be shown that the machine has *some* thought with *some* subject matter. Nevertheless, "the subject matter of a machine's operations" does seem to mean something, at least to the people who deal with it. If, for instance, the machine was trying to find a solution of the equation $x^2 - 40x - 11 = 0$ one would be tempted to describe this equation as part of the machine's subject matter at that moment. In this sort of sense a machine undoubtedly can be its own subject matter. It may be used to help in making up its own programs, or to predict the effect of alterations in its own structure. By observing the results of its own behavior it can modify its own programs so as to achieve some purpose more effectively. These are possibilities of the near future, rather than Utopian dreams.

The criticism that a machine cannot have much diversity of behavior is just a way of saying that it cannot have much storage capacity. Until fairly recently a storage capacity of even a thousand digits was very rare.

The criticisms that we are considering here are often disguised forms of the argument from consciousness. Usually if one maintains that a machine *can* do one of these things, and describes the kind of method that the machine could use, one will not make much of an impression. It is thought that the method (whatever it may be, for it must be mechanical) is really rather base. Compare the parenthesis in Jefferson's statement quoted above.

(6) *Lady Lovelace's Objection.* Our most detailed information of Babbage's Analytical Engine [a digital computer planned in the 1830s] comes from a memoir by Lady Lovelace. In it she states, "The Analytical Engine has no pretensions to *originate* anything. It can do *whatever we know how to order it* to perform" (her italics). This statement is quoted by Hartree who adds: "This does not imply that it may not be possible to construct electronic equipment which will 'think for itself,' or in which, in biological terms, one could set up a conditioned reflex, which would serve as a basis for 'learning.' Whether this is possible in principle or not is a stimulating and exciting question, suggested by some of these recent developments. But it did not seem that the machines constructed or projected at the time had this property."

I am in thorough agreement with Hartree over this. It will be noticed that he does not assert that the machines in question had not got the property, but rather that the evidence available to Lady Lovelace did not encourage her to believe that they had it. It is quite possible that the machines in question had in a sense got this property. For suppose that some discrete state machine has the property. The Analytical Engine was a universal digital computer, so that, if its storage capacity and speed were adequate, it could by suitable programing be made to mimic the machine in question. Probably this argument did not occur to the Countess or to Babbage. In any case there was no obligation on them to claim all that could be claimed. . . .

A variant of Lady Lovelace's objection states that a machine can "never do anything really new." This may be parried for a moment with the saw, "There is nothing new under the sun." Who can be certain that "original work" that he has done was not simply the growth of the seed planted in him by teaching, or the effect of following well-known general principles. A better variant of the objection says that a machine can never "take us by surprise." This statement is a more direct challenge and can be met directly. Machines take me by surprise with great frequency. This is largely because I do not do sufficient calculation to decide what to expect them to do, or rather because, although I do a calculation, I do it in a hurried, slipshod fashion, taking risks. Perhaps I say to myself, "I suppose the voltage here ought to be the same as there: anyway let's assume it is." Naturally I am often wrong, and the result is a surprise for me, for by the time the experiment is done these assumptions have been forgotten. These admissions lay me open to lectures on the subject of my vicious ways, but do not throw any doubt on my credibility when I testify to the surprises I experience.

I do not expect this reply to silence my critic. He will probably say that such surprises are due to some creative mental act on my part, and reflect no credit on the machine. This leads us back to the argument from consciousness, and far from the idea of surprise. It is a line of argument we must consider closed, but it is perhaps worth remarking that the appreciation of something as surprising requires as much of a "creative mental act" whether the surprising event originates from a man, a book, a machine or anything else.

The view that machines cannot give rise to surprises is due, I believe, to a fallacy to which philosophers and mathematicians are particularly subject. This is the assumption that as soon as a fact is presented to a mind all consequences of that fact spring into the mind simultaneously with it. It is a very useful assumption under many circumstances, but one too easily forgets that it is false. A natural consequence of doing so is that one then assumes that there is no virtue in the mere working out of consequences from data and general principles.

(7) *Argument from Continuity in the Nervous System.* The nervous system is certainly not a discrete state machine. A small error in the information about the size of a nervous impulse impinging on a neuron, may make a large difference to the size of the outgoing impulse. It may be argued that, this being so, one cannot expect to be able to mimic the behavior of the nervous system with a discrete state system.

It is true that a discrete state machine must be different from a continuous machine. But if we adhere to the conditions of the imitation game, the interrogator will not be able to take any advantage of this difference. The situation can be made clearer if we consider some other simpler continuous machine. A differential analyzer will do very well. (A differential analyzer is a certain kind of machine not of the discrete state type used for some kinds of calculation.) Some of these provide their answers in a typed form, and so are suitable for taking part in the game. It would not be possible for a digital computer to predict exactly what answers the differential analyzer would give to a problem, but it would be quite capable of giving the right sort of answer. For instance, if asked to give the value of π (actually about 3·1416) it would be reasonable to choose at random between the values 3·12, 3·13, 3·14, 3·15, 3·16 with the probabilities of 0·05, 0·15, 0·55, 0·19, 0·06 (say). Under these circumstances it would be very difficult for the interrogator to distinguish the differential analyzer from the digital computer.

(8) *The Argument from Informality of Behavior.* It is not possible to produce a set of rules purporting to describe what a man should do in every conceivable set of circumstances. One might for instance have a rule that one is to stop when one sees a red traffic light, and to go if one sees a green one, but what if by some fault both appear together? One may perhaps decide that it is safest to stop. But some further difficulty may well arise from this decision later. To attempt to provide rules of conduct to cover every eventuality, even those arising from traffic lights, appears to be impossible. With all this I agree.

From this it is argued that we cannot be machines. I shall try to reproduce the argument, but I fear I shall hardly do it justice. It seems to run something like this. "If each man had a definite set of rules of conduct by which he regulated his life he would be no better than a machine. But there are no such rules, so men cannot be machines." The undistributed middle is glaring. I do not think the argument is ever put quite like this, but I believe this is the argument used nevertheless. There may however be a certain confusion between "rules of conduct" and "laws of behavior" to cloud the issue. By "rules of conduct" I mean precepts such as "Stop if you see red lights," on which one can act, and of which one can be conscious. By "laws of behavior" I mean laws of nature as applied to a man's body such as "if you pinch him he will squeak." If we substitute "laws of behavior which regulate his life" for "laws of conduct by which he regulates his life" in the argument quoted the undistributed middle is no longer insuperable. For we believe that it is not only true that being regulated by laws of behavior implies being some sort of machine (though not necessarily a discrete state machine), but that conversely being such a machine implies being regulated by such laws. However, we cannot so easily convince ourselves of the absence of complete laws of behavior as of complete rules of conduct. The only way we know of for finding such laws is scientific observation, and we certainly know of no circumstances under which we could say, "We have searched enough. There are no such laws."

We can demonstrate more forcibly that any such statement would be unjustified. For suppose we could be sure of finding such laws if they existed. Then given a discrete state machine it should certainly be possible to discover by observation sufficient about it to predict its future behavior, and this within a reasonable time, say a thousand years. But this does not seem to be the case. I have set up on the Manchester computer a small program using only 1000 units of storage, whereby the machine supplied with one sixteen figure number replies with another within two seconds. I would defy anyone to learn from these replies sufficient about the program to be able to predict any replies to untried values. . . .

▦ MINDS, BRAINS, AND PROGRAMS*
by John R. Searle

What psychological and philosophical significance should we attach to recent efforts at computer simulations of human cognitive capacities? In answering this question, I find it useful to distinguish what I will call "strong" AI from "weak" or "cautious" AI (artificial intelligence). According to weak AI, the principal value of the computer in the study of the mind is that it gives us a very powerful tool. For example, it enables us to formulate and test hypotheses in a more rigorous and precise fashion. But according to strong AI, the computer is not merely a tool in the study of the mind; rather, the appropriately programmed computer really *is* a mind, in the sense that computers given the right programs can be literally said to *understand* and have other cognitive states. In strong AI, because the programmed computer has cognitive states, the programs are not mere tools that enable us to test psychological explanations; rather, the programs are themselves the explanations.

I have no objection to the claims of weak AI, at least as far as this article is concerned. My discussion here will be directed at the claims I have defined as

* *The Behavioral and Brain Sciences,* vol. 3 (1980).

those of strong AI, specifically the claim that the appropriately programmed computer literally has cognitive states and that the programs thereby explain human cognition. When I hereafter refer to AI, I have in mind the strong version, as expressed by these two claims.

I will consider the work of Roger Schank and his colleagues at Yale (Schank and Abelson 1977), because I am more familiar with it than I am with any other similar claims, and because it provides a very clear example of the sort of work I wish to examine. But nothing that follows depends upon the details of Schank's programs. The same arguments would apply to Winograd's SHRDLU (Winograd 1973), Weizenbaum's ELIZA (Weizenbaum 1965), and indeed any Turing machine simulation of human mental phenomena.

Very briefly, and leaving out the various details, one can describe Schank's program as follows: The aim of the program is to simulate the human ability to understand stories. It is characteristic of human beings' story-understanding capacity that they can answer questions about the story even though the information that they give was never explicitly stated in the story. Thus, for example, suppose you are given the following story: "A man went into a restaurant and ordered a hamburger. When the hamburger arrived it was burned to a crisp, and the man stormed out of the restaurant angrily, without paying for the hamburger or leaving a tip." Now, if you are asked "Did the man eat the hamburger?" you will presumably answer, "No, he did not." Similarly, if you are given the following story: "A man went into a restaurant and ordered a hamburger; when the hamburger came he was very pleased with it; and as he left the restaurant he gave the waitress a large tip before paying his bill," and you are asked the question, "Did the man eat the hamburger?" you will presumably answer, "Yes, he ate the hamburger." Now Schank's machines can similarly answer questions about restaurants in this fashion. To do this, they have a "representation" of the sort of information that human beings have about restaurants, which enables them to answer such questions as those above, given these sorts of stories. When the machine is given the story and then asked the question, the machine will print out answers of the sort that we would expect human beings to give if told similar stories. Partisans of strong AI claim that in this question and answer sequence the machine is not only simulating a human ability but also (1) that the machine can literally be said to *understand* the story and provide the answers to questions, and (2) that what the machine and its program do *explains* the human ability to understand the story and answer questions about it.

Both claims seem to me to be totally unsupported by Schank's* work, as I will attempt to show in what follows.

One way to test any theory of the mind is to ask oneself what it would be like if my mind actually worked on the principles that the theory says all minds work on. Let us apply this test to the Schank program with the following *Gedankenexperiment.* Suppose that I'm locked in a room and given a large batch of Chinese writing. Suppose furthermore (as is indeed the case) that I know no Chinese, either

---

* I am not, of course, saying that Schank himself is committed to these claims.

written or spoken, and that I'm not even confident that I could recognize Chinese writing as Chinese writing distinct from, say, Japanese writing or meaningless squiggles. To me, Chinese writing is just so many meaningless squiggles. Now suppose further that after this first batch of Chinese writing I am given a second batch of Chinese script together with a set of rules for correlating the second batch with the first batch. The rules are in English, and I understand these rules as well as any other native speaker of English. They enable me to correlate one set of formal symbols with another set of formal symbols, and all that "formal" means here is that I can identify the symbols entirely by their shapes. Now suppose also that I am given a third batch of Chinese symbols together with some instructions, again in English, that enable me to correlate elements of this third batch with the first two batches, and these rules instruct me how to give back certain Chinese symbols with certain sorts of shapes in response to certain sorts of shapes given me in the third batch. Unknown to me, the people who are giving me all of these symbols call the first batch a "script," they call the second batch a "story," and they call the third batch "questions." Furthermore, they call the symbols I give them back in response to the third batch "answers to the questions," and the set of rules in English that they gave me, they call the "program." Now just to complicate the story a little, imagine that these people also give me stories in English, which I understand, and they then ask me questions in English about these stories, and I give them back answers in English. Suppose also that after a while I get so good at following the instructions for manipulating the Chinese symbols and the programmers get so good at writing the programs that from the external point of view—that is, from the point of view of somebody outside the room in which I am locked—my answers to the questions are absolutely indistinguishable from those of native Chinese speakers. Nobody just looking at my answers can tell that I don't speak a word of Chinese. Let us also suppose that my answers to the English questions are, as they no doubt would be, indistinguishable from those of other native English speakers, for the simple reason that I am a native English speaker. From the external point of view—from the point of view of someone reading my "answers"—the answers to the Chinese questions and the English questions are equally good. But in the Chinese case, unlike the English case, I produce the answers by manipulating uninterpreted formal symbols. As far as the Chinese is concerned, I simply behave like a computer; I perform computational operations on formally specified elements. For the purposes of the Chinese, I am simply an instantiation of the computer program.

Now the claims made by strong AI are that the programmed computer understands the stories and that the program in some sense explains human understanding. But we are now in a position to examine these claims in light of our thought experiment.

1. As regards the first claim, it seems to me quite obvious in the example that I do not understand a word of the Chinese stories. I have inputs and outputs that are indistinguishable from those of the native Chinese speaker, and I can have any formal program you like, but I still understand nothing. For the same reasons, Schank's computer understands nothing of any stories, whether in Chinese, English, or whatever, since in the Chinese case the computer is me, and in cases

where the computer is not me, the computer has nothing more than I have in the case where I understand nothing.

2. As regards the second claim, that the program explains human understanding, we can see that the computer and its program do not provide sufficient conditions of understanding since the computer and the program are functioning, and there is no understanding. But does it even provide a necessary condition or a significant contribution to understanding? One of the claims made by the supporters of strong AI is that when I understand a story in English, what I am doing is exactly the same—or perhaps more of the same—as what I was doing in manipulating the Chinese symbols. It is simply more formal symbol manipulation that distinguishes the case in English, where I do understand, from the case in Chinese, where I don't. I have not demonstrated that this claim is false, but it would certainly appear an incredible claim in the example. Such plausibility as the claim has derives from the supposition that we can construct a program that will have the same inputs and outputs as native speakers, and in addition we assume that speakers have some level of description where they are also instantiations of a program. On the basis of these two assumptions we assume that even if Schank's program isn't the whole story about understanding, it may be part of the story. Well, I suppose that is an empirical possibility, but not the slightest reason has so far been given to believe that it is true, since what is suggested—though certainly not demonstrated—by the example is that the computer program is simply irrelevant to my understanding of the story. In the Chinese case I have everything that artificial intelligence can put into me by way of a program, and I understand nothing; in the English case I understand everything, and there is so far no reason at all to suppose that my understanding has anything to do with computer programs, that is, with computational operations on purely formally specified elements. As long as the program is defined in terms of computational operations on purely formally defined elements, what the example suggests is that these by themselves have no interesting connection with understanding. They are certainly not sufficient conditions, and not the slightest reason has been given to suppose that they are necessary conditions or even that they make a significant contribution to understanding. Notice that the force of the argument is not simply that different machines can have the same input and output while operating on different formal principles—that is not the point at all. Rather, whatever purely formal principles you put into the computer, they will not be sufficient for understanding, since a human will be able to follow other formal principles without understanding anything. No reason whatever has been offered to suppose that such principles are necessary or even contributory, since no reason has been given to suppose that when I understand English I am operating with any formal program at all.

Well, then, what is it that I have in the case of the English sentences that I do not have in the case of the Chinese sentences? The obvious answer is that I know what the former mean, while I haven't the faintest idea what the latter mean. But in what does this consist and why couldn't we give it to a machine, whatever it is? I will return to this question later, but first I want to continue with the example.

I have had the occasions to present this example to several workers in artificial intelligence, and, interestingly, they do not seem to agree on what the proper reply to it is. I get a surprising variety of replies, and in what follows I will consider the most common of these (specified along with their geographic origins).

But first I want to block some common misunderstandings about "understanding": In many of these discussions one finds a lot of fancy footwork about the word "understanding." My critics point out that there are many different degrees of understanding; that "understanding" is not a simple two-place predicate; that there are even different kinds and levels of understanding, and often the law of excluded middle doesn't even apply in a straightforward way to statements of the form "*x* understands *y*"; that in many cases it is a matter for decision and not a simple matter of fact whether *x* understands *y*; and so on. To all of these points I want to say: of course, of course. But they have nothing to do with the points at issue. There are clear cases in which "understanding" literally applies and clear cases in which it does not apply; and these two sorts of cases are all I need for this argument.* I understand stories in English; to a lesser degree I can understand stories in French; to a still lesser degree, stories in German; and in Chinese, not at all. My car and my adding machine, on the other hand, understand nothing: they are not in that line of business. We often attribute "understanding" and other cognitive predicates by metaphor and analogy to cars, adding machines, and other artifacts, but nothing is proved by such attributions. We say, "The door *knows* when to open because of its photoelectric cell," "The adding machine *knows how (understands how, is able)* to do addition and subtraction but not division," and "The thermostat *perceives* changes in the temperature." The reason we make these attributions is quite interesting, and it has to do with the fact that in artifacts we extend our own intentionality;† our tools are extensions of our purposes, and so we find it natural to make metaphorical attributions of intentionality to them; but I take it no philosophical ice is cut by such examples. The sense in which an automatic door "understands instructions" from its photoelectric cell is not at all the sense in which I understand English. If the sense in which Schank's programmed computers understand stories is supposed to be the metaphorical sense in which the door understands, and not the sense in which I understand English, the issue would not be worth discussing. But Newell and Simon (1963) write that the kind of cognition they claim for computers is exactly the same as for human beings. I like the straightforwardness of this claim, and it is the sort of claim I will be considering. I will argue that in the literal sense the programmed computer understands what the car and the adding machine understand, namely, exactly nothing. The computer understanding is not just (like my understanding of German) partial or incomplete; it is zero.

---

* Also, "understanding" implies both the possession of mental (intentional) states and the truth (validity, success) of these states. For the purposes of this discussion we are concerned only with the possession of the states.

† Intentionality is by definition that feature of certain mental states by which they are directed at or about objects and states of affairs in the world. Thus, beliefs, desires, and intentions are intentional states; undirected forms of anxiety and depression are not.

Now to the replies:

1. The Systems Reply (Berkeley). "While it is true that the individual person who is locked in the room does not understand the story, the fact is that he is merely part of a whole system, and the system does understand the story. The person has a large ledger in front of him in which are written the rules, he has a lot of scratch paper and pencils for doing calculations, he has 'data banks' of sets of Chinese symbols. Now, understanding is not being ascribed to the mere individual; rather it is being ascribed to this whole system of which he is a part."

My response to the systems theory is quite simple: Let the individual internalize all of these elements of the system. He memorizes the rules in the ledger and the data banks of Chinese symbols, and he does all the calculations in his head. The individual then incorporates the entire system. There isn't anything at all to the system that he does not encompass. We can even get rid of the room and suppose he works outdoors. All the same, he understands nothing of the Chinese, and a fortiori neither does the system, because there isn't anything in the system that isn't in him. If he doesn't understand, then there is no way the system could understand because the system is just a part of him.

Actually I feel somewhat embarrassed to give even this answer to the systems theory because the theory seems to me so implausible to start with. The idea is that while a person doesn't understand Chinese, somehow the *conjunction* of that person and bits of paper might understand Chinese. It is not easy for me to imagine how someone who was not in the grip of an ideology would find the idea at all plausible. Still, I think many people who are committed to the ideology of strong AI will in the end be inclined to say something very much like this; so let us pursue it a bit further. According to one version of this view, while the man in the internalized systems example doesn't understand Chinese in the sense that a native Chinese speaker does (because, for example, he doesn't know that the story refers to restaurants and hamburgers, etc.), still "the man as a formal symbol manipulation system" *really does understand Chinese.* The subsystem of the man that is the formal symbol manipulation system for Chinese should not be confused with the subsystem for English.

So there are really two subsystems in the man; one understands English, the other Chinese, and "it's just that the two systems have little to do with each other." But, I want to reply, not only do they have little to do with each other, they are not even remotely alike. The subsystem that understands English (assuming we allow ourselves to talk in this jargon of "subsystems" for a moment) knows that the stories are about restaurants and eating hamburgers, he knows that he is being asked questions about restaurants and that he is answering questions as best he can by making various inferences from the content of the story, and so on. But the Chinese system knows none of this. Whereas the English subsystem knows that "hamburgers" refers to hamburgers, the Chinese subsystem knows only that "squiggle squiggle" is followed by "squoggle squoggle." All he knows is that various formal symbols are being introduced at one end and manipulated according to rules written in English, and other symbols are going out at the other end. The whole point of the original example was to argue that such symbol manipulation by itself couldn't be sufficient for understanding Chinese in any literal sense because the man could write "squoggle squoggle" after "squiggle squiggle" without understanding anything in Chinese. And it doesn't meet that argument to postulate subsystems within the man, because the subsystems are no better off than the man was in the first place; they still don't have anything even remotely like what the English-speaking man (or subsystem) has. Indeed, in the case as described, the Chinese subsystem is simply a part of the English subsystem, a part that engages in meaningless symbol manipulation according to rules in English.

Let us ask ourselves what is supposed to motivate the systems reply in the first place; that is, what *independent* grounds are there supposed to be for saying that the agent must have a subsystem within him that literally understands stories in Chinese? As far as I can tell the only grounds are that in the example I have the same input and output as native Chinese speakers and a program that goes from one to the other. But the whole point of the examples has been to try to show that that couldn't be sufficient for understanding, in the sense in which I understand stories in English, because a person, and hence the set of systems that go to make up a person, could have the right combination of input, output, and program and still not understand anything in the relevant literal sense in which I understand English. The only motivation for saying there *must* be a subsystem in me that understands Chinese is that I have a program and I can pass the Turing test; I can fool native Chinese speakers. But precisely one of the points at issue is the adequacy of the Turing test. The example shows that there could be two "systems," both of which pass the Turing test, but only one of which understands; and it is no argument against this point to say that since they both pass the Turing test they must both understand, since this claim fails to meet the argument that the system in me that understands English has a great deal more than the system that merely processes Chinese. In short, the systems reply simply begs the question by insisting without argument that the system must understand Chinese.

Furthermore, the systems reply would appear to lead to consequences that are independently absurd. If we are to conclude that there must be cognition in me on the grounds that I have a certain sort of input and output and a program in between, then it looks like all sorts of noncognitive subsystems are going to turn out to be cognitive. For example, there is a level of description at which my stomach does information processing, and it instantiates any number of computer programs, but I take it we do not want to say that it has any understanding (cf. Pylyshyn 1980). But if we accept the systems reply, then it is hard to see how we avoid saying that stomach, heart, liver, and so on are all understanding subsystems, since there is no principled way to distinguish the motivation for saying the Chinese subsystem understands from saying that the stomach understands. It is, by the way, not an answer to this point to say that the Chinese system has information as input and output and the stomach has food and food products as input and output, since from the point of view of the agent, from my point of view, there is no information in either the food or the Chinese—the Chinese is just so many meaningless squiggles. The information in the Chinese case is solely in the eyes of the programmers and the interpreters, and there is nothing to prevent them from treating the input and output of my digestive organs as information if they so desire.

This last point bears on some independent problems in strong AI, and it is worth digressing for a moment to explain it. If strong AI is to be a branch of psychology, then it must be able to distinguish those systems that are genuinely mental from those that are not. It must be able to distinguish the principles on which the mind works from those on which nonmental systems work; otherwise it will offer us no explanations of what is specifically mental about the mental. And the mental-nonmental distinction cannot be just in the eye of the beholder but it must be intrinsic to the systems; otherwise it would be up to any beholder to treat people as nonmental and, for example, hurricanes as mental if he likes. But quite often in the AI literature the distinction is blurred in ways that would in the long run prove disastrous to the claim that AI is a cognitive inquiry. McCarthy, for example, writes, "Machines as simple as thermostats can be said to have beliefs, and having beliefs seems to be a characteristic of most machines capable of problem solving performance" (McCarthy 1979). Anyone who thinks strong AI has a chance as a theory of the mind ought to ponder the implications of that remark. We are asked to accept it as a discovery of strong AI that the hunk of metal on the wall that we use to regulate the temperature has beliefs in exactly the same sense that we, our spouses, and our children have beliefs, and furthermore that "most" of the other machines in the room—telephone, tape recorder, adding machine, electric light switch—also have beliefs in this literal sense. It is not the aim of this article to argue against McCarthy's point, so I will simply assert the following without argument. The study of the mind starts with such facts as that humans have beliefs, while thermostats, telephones, and adding machines don't. If you get a theory that denies this point you have produced a counterexample to the theory and the theory is false. One gets the impression that people in AI who write this sort of thing think they can get away with it because they don't really take it seriously, and they don't think anyone else will either. I propose, for a moment at least, to take it seriously. Think hard for one minute about what would be necessary to establish that that hunk of metal on the wall over there had real beliefs, beliefs with direction of fit, propositional content, and conditions of satisfaction; beliefs that had the possibility of being strong beliefs or weak beliefs; nervous, anxious, or secure beliefs; dogmatic, rational, or superstitious beliefs; blind faiths or hesitant cogitations, any kind of beliefs. The thermostat is not a candidate. Neither is stomach, liver, adding machine, or telephone. However, since we are taking the idea seriously, notice that its truth would be fatal to strong AI's claim to be a science of the mind. For now the mind is everywhere. What we wanted to know is what distinguishes the mind from thermostats and livers. And if McCarthy were right, strong AI wouldn't have a hope of telling us that.

2. **The Robot Reply (Yale).** "Suppose we wrote a different kind of program from Schank's program. Suppose we put a computer inside a robot, and this

computer would not just take in formal symbols as input and give out formal symbols as output, but rather would actually operate the robot in such a way that the robot does something very much like perceiving, walking, moving about, hammering nails, eating, drinking—anything you like. The robot would, for example, have a television camera attached to it that enabled it to see, it would have arms and legs that enabled it to 'act,' and all of this would be controlled by its computer 'brain.' Such a robot would, unlike Schank's computer, have genuine understanding and other mental states."

The first thing to notice about the robot reply is that it tacitly concedes that cognition is not solely a matter of formal symbol manipulation, since this reply adds a set of causal relations with the outside world (cf. Fodor 1980). But the answer to the robot reply is that the addition of such "perceptual" and "motor" capacities adds nothing by way of understanding, in particular, or intentionality, in general, to Schank's original program. To see this, notice that the same thought experiment applies to the robot case. Suppose that instead of the computer inside the robot, you put me inside the room and, as in the original Chinese case, you give me more Chinese symbols with more instructions in English for matching Chinese symbols to Chinese symbols and feeding back Chinese symbols to the outside. Suppose, unknown to me, some of the Chinese symbols that come to me come from a television camera attached to the robot and other Chinese symbols that I am giving out serve to make the motors inside the robot move the robot's legs or arms. It is important to emphasize that all I am doing is manipulating formal symbols: I know none of these other facts. I am receiving "information" from the robot's "perceptual" apparatus, and I am giving out "instructions" to its motor apparatus without knowing either of these facts. I am the robot's homunculus, but unlike the traditional homunculus, I don't know what's going on. I don't understand anything except the rules for symbol manipulation. Now in this case I want to say that the robot has no intentional states at all; it is simply moving about as a result of its electrical wiring and its program. And furthermore, by instantiating the program I have no intentional states of the relevant type. All I do is follow formal instructions about manipulating formal symbols.

3. The Brain Simulator Reply (Berkeley and M.I.T.). "Suppose we design a program that doesn't represent information that we have about the world, such as the information in Schank's scripts, but simulates the actual sequence of neuron firings at the synapses of the brain of a native Chinese speaker when he understands stories in Chinese and gives answers to them. The machine takes in Chinese stories and questions about them as input, it simulates the formal structure of actual Chinese brains in processing these stories, and it gives out Chinese answers as outputs. We can even imagine that the machine operates, not with a single serial program, but with a whole set of programs operating in parallel, in the manner that actual human brains presumably operate when they process natural language. Now surely in such a case we would have to say that the machine understood the stories; and if we refuse to say that, wouldn't we also have to deny that native Chinese speakers understood the stories? At the level of the synapses, what would or could be different about the program of the computer and the program of the Chinese brain?"

Before countering this reply I want to digress to note that it is an odd reply for any partisan of artificial intelligence (or functionalism, etc.) to make: I thought the whole idea of strong AI is that we don't need to know how the brain works to know how the mind works. The basic hypothesis, or so I had supposed, was that there is a level of mental operations consisting of computational processes over formal elements that constitute the essence of the mental and can be realized in all sorts of different brain processes, in the same way that any computer program can be realized in different computer hardwares: On the assumptions of strong AI, the mind is to the brain as the program is to the hardware, and thus we can understand the mind without doing neurophysiology. If we had to know how the brain worked to do AI, we wouldn't bother with AI. However, even getting this close to the operation of the brain is still not sufficient to produce understanding. To see this, imagine that instead of a monolingual man in a room shuffling symbols we have the man operate an elaborate set of water pipes with valves connecting them. When the man receives the Chinese symbols, he looks up in the program, written in English, which valves he has to turn on and off. Each water connection corresponds to a synapse in the Chinese brain, and the whole system is rigged up so that after doing all the right firings, that is after turning on all the right faucets, the Chinese answers pop out at the output end of the series of pipes.

Now where is the understanding in this system? It takes Chinese as input, it simulates the formal structure of the synapses of the Chinese brain, and it gives Chinese as output. But the man certainly doesn't understand Chinese, and neither do the water pipes, and if we are tempted to adopt what I think is the absurd view that somehow the *conjunction* of man *and* water pipes understands, remember that in principle the man can internalize the formal structure of the water pipes and do all the "neuron firings" in his imagination. The problem with the brain simulator is that it is simulating the wrong things about the brain. As long as it simulates only the formal structure of the sequence of neuron firings at the synapses, it won't have simulated what matters about the brain, namely its causal properties, its ability to produce intentional states. And that the formal properties are not sufficient for the causal properties is shown by the water pipe example: we can have all the formal properties carved off from the relevant neurobiological causal properties.

4. The Combination Reply (Berkeley and Stanford).   "While each of the previous three replies might not be completely convincing by itself as a refutation of the Chinese room counterexample, if you take all three together they are collectively much more convincing and even decisive. Imagine a robot with a brain-shaped computer lodged in its cranial cavity, imagine the computer programmed with all the synapses of a human brain, imagine the whole behavior of the robot is indistinguishable from human behavior, and now think of the whole thing as a unified system and not just as a computer with inputs and outputs. Surely in such a case we would have to ascribe intentionality to the system."

I entirely agree that in such a case we would find it rational and indeed irresistible to accept the hypothesis that the robot had intentionality, as long as we knew nothing more about it. Indeed, besides appearance and behavior, the other elements of the combination are really irrelevant. If we could build a robot whose behavior was indistinguishable over a large range from human behavior, we would attribute intentionality to it, pending some reason not to. We wouldn't need to know in advance that its computer brain was a formal analogue of the human brain.

But I really don't see that this is any help to the claims of strong AI, and here's why: According to strong AI, instantiating a formal program with the right input and output is a sufficient condition of, indeed is constitutive of, intentionality. As Newell (1979) puts it, the essence of the mental is the operation of a physical symbol system. But the attributions of intentionality that we make to the robot in this example have nothing to do with formal programs. They are simply based on the assumption that if the robot looks and behaves sufficiently like us, then we would suppose, until proven otherwise, that it must have mental states like ours that cause and are expressed by its behavior and it must have an inner mechanism capable of producing such mental states. If we knew independently how to account for its behavior without such assumptions we would not attribute intentionality to it, especially if we knew it had a formal program. And this is precisely the point of my earlier reply to objection II.

Suppose we knew that the robot's behavior was entirely accounted for by the fact that a man inside it was receiving uninterpreted formal symbols from the robot's sensory receptors and sending out uninterpreted formal symbols to its motor mechanisms, and the man was doing this symbol manipulation in accordance with a bunch of rules. Furthermore, suppose the man knows none of these facts about the robot, all he knows is which operations to perform on which meaningless symbols. In such a case we would regard the robot as an ingenious mechanical dummy. The hypothesis that the dummy has a mind would now be unwarranted and unnecessary, for there is now no longer any reason to ascribe intentionality to the robot or to the system of which it is a part (except of course for the man's intentionality in manipulating the symbols). The formal symbol manipulations go on, the input and output are correctly matched, but the only real locus of intentionality is the man, and he doesn't know any of the relevant intentional states; he doesn't, for example, *see* what comes into the robot's eyes, he doesn't *intend* to move the robot's arm, and he doesn't *understand* any of the remarks made to or by the robot. Nor, for the reasons stated earlier, does the system of which man and robot are a part.

To see this point, contrast this case with cases in which we find it completely natural to ascribe intentionality to members of certain other primate species such as apes and monkeys and to domestic animals such as dogs. The reasons we find it natural are, roughly, two: We can't make sense of the animal's behavior without the ascription of intentionality, and we can see that the beasts are made of similar stuff to ourselves—that is an eye, that a nose, this is its skin, and so on. Given the coherence of the animal's behavior and the assumption of the same causal stuff underlying it, we assume both that the animal must have mental states underlying its behavior, and that the mental states must be produced by mechanisms made out of the stuff that is like our stuff. We would certainly make similar assumptions about the robot unless we had some reason not to, but as soon as we knew that the behavior was the result of a formal program, and that the actual causal properties of the physical substance were irrelevant we would abandon the assumption of intentionality. (See [Multiple authors] 1978.)

There are two other responses to my example that come up frequently (and so are worth discussing) but really miss the point.

5. The Other Minds Reply (Yale).

"How do you know that other people understand Chinese or anything else? Only by their behavior. Now the computer can pass the behavioral tests as well as they can (in principle), so if you are going to attribute cognition to other people you must in principle also attribute it to computers."

This objection really is only worth a short reply. The problem in this discussion is not about how I know that other people have cognitive states, but rather what it is that I am attributing to them when I attribute cognitive states to them. The thrust of the argument is that it couldn't be just computational processes and their output because the computational processes and their output can exist without the cognitive state. It is no answer to this argument to feign anesthesia. In "cognitive sciences" one presupposes the reality and knowability of the mental in the same way that in physical sciences one has to presuppose the reality and knowability of physical objects.

6. The Many Mansions Reply (Berkeley).

"Your whole argument presupposes that AI is only about analog and digital computers. But that just happens to be the present state of technology. Whatever these causal processes are that you say are essential for intentionality (assuming you are right), eventually we will be able to build devices that have these causal processes, and that will be artificial intelligence. So your arguments are in no way directed at the ability of artificial intelligence to produce and explain cognition."

I really have no objection to this reply save to say that it in effect trivializes the project of strong AI by redefining it as whatever artificially produces and explains cognition. The interest of the original claim made on behalf of artificial intelligence is that it was a precise, well defined thesis: mental processes are computational processes over formally defined elements. I have been concerned to challenge that thesis. If the claim is redefined so that it is no longer that thesis, my objections no longer apply because there is no longer a testable hypothesis for them to apply to.

Let us now return to the question I promised I would try to answer: Granted that in my original example I understand the English and I do not understand the Chinese, and granted therefore that the machine doesn't understand either English or Chinese, still there must be something about me that makes it the case that I understand English and a corresponding something lacking in me that makes it the case that I fail to understand Chinese. Now why couldn't we give those somethings, whatever they are, to a machine?

I see no reason in principle why we couldn't give a machine the capacity to understand English or Chinese, since in an important sense our bodies with our brains are precisely such machines. But I do see very strong arguments for saying that we could not give such a thing to a machine where the operation of the machine is defined solely in terms of computational processes over formally defined elements; that is, where the operation of the machine is defined as an instantiation of a computer program. It is not because I am the instantiation of a computer program that I am able to understand English and have other forms of intentionality (I am, I suppose, the instantiation of any number of computer programs), but as far as we know it is because I am a certain sort of organism with a certain biological (i.e., chemical and physical) structure, and this structure, under certain conditions, is causally capable of producing perception, action, understanding, learning, and other intentional phenomena. And part of the point of the present argument is that only something that had those causal powers could have that intentionality. Perhaps other physical and chemical processes could produce exactly these effects; perhaps, for example, Martians also have intentionality but their brains are made of different stuff. That is an empirical question, rather like the question whether photosynthesis can be done by something with a chemistry different from that of chlorophyll.

But the main point of the present argument is that no purely formal model will ever be sufficient by itself for intentionality because the formal properties are not by themselves constitutive of intentionality, and they have by themselves no causal powers except the power, when instantiated, to produce the next stage of the formalism when the machine is running. And any other causal properties that particular realizations of the formal model have, are irrelevant to the formal model because we can always put the same formal model in a different realization where those causal properties are obviously absent. Even if, by some miracle, Chinese speakers exactly realize Schank's program, we can put the same program in English speakers, water pipes, or computers, none of which understand Chinese, the program notwithstanding.

What matters about brain operations is not the formal shadow cast by the sequence of synapses but rather the actual properties of the sequences. All the arguments for the strong version of artificial intelligence that I have seen insist on drawing an outline around the shadows cast by cognition and then claiming that the shadows are the real thing.

By way of concluding I want to try to state some of the general philosophical points implicit in the argument. For clarity I will try to do it in a question-and-answer fashion, and I begin with that old chestnut of a question:

"Could a machine think?"

The answer is, obviously, yes. We are precisely such machines.

"Yes, but could an artifact, a man-made machine, think?"

Assuming it is possible to produce artificially a machine with a nervous system, neurons with axons and dendrites, and all the rest of it, sufficiently like ours, again the answer to the question seems to be obviously, yes. If you can exactly duplicate the causes, you could duplicate the effects. And indeed it might be possible to produce consciousness, intentionality, and all the rest of it using some other sorts of chemical principles than those that human beings use. It is, as I said, an empirical question.

"OK, but could a digital computer think?"

If by "digital computer" we mean anything at all that has a level of description where it can correctly be described as the instantiation of a computer program, then again the answer is, of course, yes, since we are the instantiations of any number of computer programs, and we can think.

"But could something think, understand, and so on *solely* in virtue of being a computer with the right sort of program? Could instantiating a program, the right program of course, by itself be a sufficient condition of understanding?"

This I think is the right question to ask, though it is usually confused with one or more of the earlier questions, and the answer to it is no.

"Why not?"

Because the formal symbol manipulations by themselves don't have any intentionality; they are quite meaningless; they aren't even *symbol* manipulations, since the symbols don't symbolize anything. In the linguistic jargon, they have only a syntax but no semantics. Such intentionality as computers appear to have is solely in the minds of those who program them and those who use them, those who send in the input and those who interpret the output.

The aim of the Chinese room example was to try to show this by showing that as soon as we put something into the system that really does have intentionality (a man), and we program him with the formal program, you can see that the formal program carries no additional intentionality. It adds nothing, for example, to a man's ability to understand Chinese.

Precisely that feature of AI that seemed so appealing–the distinction between the program and the realization–proves fatal to the claim that simulation could be duplication. The distinction between the program and its realization in the hardware seems to be parallel to the distinction between the level of mental operations and the level of brain operations. And if we could describe the level of mental operations as a formal program, then it seems we could describe what was essential about the mind without doing either introspective psychology or neurophysiology of the brain. But the equation "mind is to brain as program is to hardware" breaks down at several points, among them the following three:

First, the distinction between program and realization has the consequence that the same program could have all sorts of crazy realizations that had no form of intentionality. Weizenbaum (1976, Ch. 2), for example, shows in detail how to construct a computer using a roll of toilet paper and a pile of small stones. Similarly, the Chinese story understanding program can be programmed into a sequence of water pipes, a set of wind machines, or a monolingual English speaker, none of which thereby acquires an understanding of Chinese. Stones, toilet paper, wind, and water pipes are the wrong kind of stuff to have intentionality in the first place–

only something that has the same causal powers as brains can have intentionality–and though the English speaker has the right kind of stuff for intentionality you can easily see that he doesn't get any extra intentionality by memorizing the program, since memorizing it won't teach him Chinese.

Second, the program is purely formal, but the intentional states are not in that way formal. They are defined in terms of their content, not their form. The belief that it is raining, for example, is not defined as a certain formal shape, but as a certain mental content with conditions of satisfaction, a direction of fit (see Searle 1979), and the like. Indeed the belief as such hasn't even got a formal shape in this syntactic sense, since one and the same belief can be given an indefinite number of different syntactic expressions in different linguistic systems.

Third, as I mentioned before, mental states and events are literally a product of the operation of the brain, but the program is not in that way a product of the computer. . . .

References

Fodor, J. A. (1980). "Methodological Solipsism Considered as a Research Strategy in Cognitive Psychology." *Behavioral and Brain Sciences* 3:63–110.

McCarthy, J. (1979). "Ascribing Mental Qualities to Machines." In M. Ringle (ed.), *Philosophical Perspectives in Artificial Intelligence*, pp. 161–95. Atlantic Highlands, NJ: Humanities Press.

[Multiple authors] (1978). "Cognition and Consciousness in Non-Human Species." *Behavioral and Brain Sciences* 1(4): entire issue.

Newell, A. (1979). "Physical Symbol Systems." Lecture at the La Jolla Conference on Cognitive Science. Later published in *Cognitive Science* 4 (1980): 135–83.

————, and Simon, H. A. (1963). "GPS–A Program That Simulates Human Thought." In E. A. Feigenbaum and J. A. Feldman (eds.), *Computers and Thought*, pp. 279–96. New York: McGraw-Hill.

Pylyshyn, Z. W. (1980). "Computation and Cognition: Issues in the Foundation of Cognitive Science." *Behavioral and Brain Sciences* 3: 111–32.

Schank, R. C. and Abelson, R. P. (1977). *Scripts, Plans, Goals, and Understanding*. Hillsdale, NJ: Erlbaum.

Searle, J. R. (1979a). "Intentionality and the Use of Language." In A. Margolit (ed.), *Meaning and Use*. Dordrecht: Reidel.

————, (1979b). "What is an Intentional State?" *Mind* 88: 74–92.

Weizenbaum, J. (1965). "ELIZA–A Computer Program for the Study of Natural Language Communication Between Man and Machine." *Commun. ACM* 9: 36–45.

————, (1976). *Computer Power and Human Reason*. San Francisco: W. H. Freeman.

Winograd, T. (1973). "A Procedural Model of Language Understanding." In R. C. Schank and K. M. Colby (eds.), *Computer Models of Thought and Language*. pp. 152–86. San Francisco: W. H. Freeman.

DISCUSSION QUESTIONS

(1) Why does Turing replace the question "Can machines think?" with the question "Can any machine ever win the imitation game?" Must anyone who answers "Yes" to the first question also answer "Yes" to the second question? Must anyone who answers "No" to the first question also answer "No" to the second question? Is Turing's replacement fair to his opponents? Why or why not?

(2) Turing predicts that by the year 2000, average interrogators will be fooled 70 percent of the time by machines after playing the imitation game for five minutes. It is almost 2000, but no machine is even close to this degree of success. Suppose Turing's prediction turns out to be false (and not even close to true). Would this show that Turing's main argument is fallacious? Would it support Searle's argument? Why or why not?

(3) Turing claims that Jefferson's argument from consciousness lands him in solipsism. Reconstruct and evaluate this reductio ad absurdum refutation. How could Jefferson best reply? (Compare Searle's response to the other minds reply.)

(4) One variant of Lady Lovelace's objection claims that machines are programmed, so they "never do anything really new." Turing responds by arguing that machines can "take us by surprise." Is this response adequate? Why or why not? What does it mean to do something "really new"? Is there any sense in which humans do things that are really new but machines cannot? How can you tell?

(5) Reconstruct and evaluate Searle's Chinese room argument in the form of an argument from analogy. Be sure to state his conclusion as precisely as you can.

(6) Searle argues that "the systems reply would appear to lead to consequences that are independently absurd." Does the systems reply really lead to these consequences? Are these consequences really absurd? Why or why not?

(7) Searle argues that "the problem with the brain simulator is that it is simulating the wrong things about the brain." What does it simulate? What does it not simulate? Why does Searle think that the latter things are the important ones to simulate? Do you agree? Why or why not?

(8) In his conclusion, Searle says that a digital computer could think. What exactly does he mean by this? Is this an admission that Turing was right? Why or why not?

Copyrights and Acknowledgments

INDEX